UNQUALIFIED RESERVATIONS
VOL.01
MENCIUS MOLDBUG

A FORMALIST MANIFESTO

AN OPEN LETTER TO OPEN-MINDED PROGRESSIVES

HOW DAWKINS GOT PWNED

FOREWORD BY CURTIS YARVIN

2023 Passage Publishing

Copyright © 2008 by Mencius Moldbug
A formalist manifesto
An Open Letter to Open-Minded Progressives
How Dawkins Got Pwned

Copyright © 2023 by Curtis Yarvin
Author's Foreword

Cover art by Wide Dog

This version of the text was originally published at Unqualified-Reservations.org, lightly edited for clarity from the original text at unqualified-reservations.blogspot.com, all with permission from the author.

The author retains copyright of the text with all rights reserved under International and American copyright conventions.

Produced by Gild House

Printed in Canada

ISBN: 978-1-959403-00-5

First edition, first printing

Passage.press

CONTENTS

Editors' Note V

Author's Foreword IX

A formalist manifesto 1

An Open Letter to Open-Minded Progressives 17
    Chapter 1: A Horizon Made of Canvas 19
    Chapter 2: The American Rebellion 41
    Chapter 3: The Jacobite History of The World 65
    Chapter 4: Dr. Johnson's Hypothesis 89
    Chapter 5: The Shortest Way to World Peace 105
    Chapter 6: The Lost Theory of Government 151
    Chapter 7: The Ugly Truth About Government 167
    Chapter 8: A Reset Is Not a Revolution 201
    Chapter 9: How to Uninstall a Cathedral 229
    Chapter X: A Simple Sovereign Bankruptcy Procedure 251
    Chapter XI: The Truth About Left and Right 279
    Chapter XII: What Is to Be Done? 297
    Chapter XIII: Tactics and Structures of Any Prospective Restoration 321
    Chapter XIV: Rules for Reactionaries 339

How Dawkins Got PWND 375
    Chapter 1: A Really Ugly Bug 377
    Chapter 2: M.41 and M.42 387
    Chapter 3: *Manitou* and the *Zeitgeist* 409
    Chapter 3: A Mystery Cult of Power 421
    Chapter 5: Planet 3.01 443
    Chapter 6: The Logic of Law and Power 461
    Chapter 7: The Age of Democide 469

Index 493

Recommended Books 499

EDITORS' NOTE

To our knowledge, there is nothing in the world of print media that approximates, in form or substance, the volume you now hold in your hands. The original *Unqualified Reservations* was a unique and curious work in its own right. Totalling over 350 posts, and nearly 1.5 million total words, the blog was a rich exhibition of stand-alone essays, musings, poetry, and several collections of serialized "chapters" resembling the breadth and scope of traditional books.

Bringing this all to print has presented a number of complex editorial challenges, including the selection of content, how to organize the material, and, most daunting of all, how to translate writing that was originally designed for the digital medium onto the physical page.

For the first of these challenges, we knew from the start that *Unqualified Reservations* would require multiple volumes. Rather than print everything, we determined we could provide added utility by curating the blog and selecting for publication the posts that best capture the full spirit of the entire corpus. After consulting with the author, we settled on three volumes to be organized in the following fashion: The first volume, which you are now reading, contains the first ever post, "A formalist manifesto," as well as the first two book-length series, *An Open Letter to Open-Minded Progressives*, and *How Dawkins Got Pwned*. The second volume will contain three more serialized books, *A Gentle Introduction to Unqualified Reservations*, *Moldbug on Carlyle*, and *Patchwork: A Political System for the 21st Century*. Finally, the third volume will contain a sampling of "essential" posts that fill out the remainder of the blog's central arguments, and best represent its humor, style, and intellectual ambition.

The second of these considerations, how to translate a natively online text into print, required us to reimagine the possibilities for how these two mediums could work alongside, rather than against one another. We attempted to balance two editorial objectives: on the one hand, preserving the experience of reading the original blog online, while on the other hand preserving the coherence of the full text for the reader who is not logged on.

We found these two objectives were often in direct conflict. *Unqualified Reservations* can never be fully disconnected from the internet. Its humor, references, and basic composition depend on links (as many as a dozen per written page) and other conventions of digital media that simply cannot be recreated in physical space. Yet we believe, or we would not have attempted this project at all, that we managed to resolve these tensions, and that the print version you are now reading has its own advantages that readers will appreciate, and even come to prefer.

To these ends, you will find in this book the following editorial features:

Firstly, we have decided it is important to allow the reader the option to read the book with the aid of the internet and make full use of the text's original links. Links as they appeared on the blog, now appear in the text in semibold grayscale font **like this**. All original links have been converted to QR codes and can be found in the End Notes at the back of every chapter and individual post. On the occasion that readers are asked to view a particular link before moving on, a relevant QR code can be found in the footnotes on the same page as the link.

We also had in mind a reader who does not want to be constantly pulling up links on his phone or computer (or doing so at all), and so we have also provided brief descriptions of links, and their context, where it has been determined such descriptions are necessary to make sense of the text. When a sentence or reference can only be understood with the aid of the link, this description has been provided in the footnotes. When the link provides additional color to the text's main argument, or might lead the reader down an interesting, though perhaps tangential sidepath, the descriptions have been provided in the End Notes. This has been done to avoid cluttering the main text with an excess of footnotes, and to help guide the reader toward the links that are most central to the author's rhetorical aims.

We have also archived a significant number of the original links to avoid the likely possibility that certain websites or individual pages will eventually be moved or *re*moved from the internet entirely. Likewise, we have provided traditional citations for all articles, books, films, and other referenced material so they can be located in the event that the archived links no longer work or are not otherwise available. Where possible, books and other longform texts have been linked to free online pdfs or scans, for example at Google Books or The Internet Archive. Original links to Amazon purchase pages, or to IMDB, or other sites that provide no additional context have been replaced by traditional citations. Redundant links have been

EDITORS' NOTE

removed or cross-referenced. Where relevant, links have been replaced using the Wayback Machine, backdated to the time of the blog's original publication.

Finally, the book also makes use of a sizable index to catalog the major themes, events, concepts, people, books, and ideas that are central to the blog. Because of its discursive nature, *Unqualified Reservations* does not easily lend itself to a traditional index. There would simply be too many index entries for it to be useful. So, rather than index every instance in which the blog uses the term "Cathedral" (over 100 times in this volume alone), the index instead directs the reader to those pages where the concept of the Cathedral is defined, explained, or otherwise the subject of analysis. More signal; less noise.

We encourage you to read this book with the aid of the internet, so that you can experience the full scope of its ideas and their presentation, and to indulge your intellectual curiosity, but each reader will make use of the internet to a different degree, and some not at all. In any case, enjoy. And cure your brain.

-Editors

AUTHOR'S FOREWORD
SEPTEMBER 5TH, 2022

My origin story

Why did I ever write all this stuff? Why did I even think it? Why did I even start? Let me try to set my creaky old time machine for twenty years ago.

I was childless. I had just met my late wife (Jennifer Kollmer, who made all possible). She had encouraged me to set out on the first of my two deranged decadal missions. This *technical* quest, which I will not dwell on here, was originally a relatively vague desire to do some independent system software research, with a bit of money I'd made in the dot-com bubble.

Some kind of "unsupervised thesis" had always been my plan when I dropped out of the **Berkeley CS program**. (I think I still have an open bet with **Raph Levien** on which of us wins the Turing Award first—probably neither, alas.) A lot of crazy had gone under the bridge in my Silicon Valley career between 1994 and 2002, but there I was, with enough self-funding (actually not enough lol) to do the job. And quite a bit of ugly-real experience at all layers of the systems stack as well.

But... it turns out that you can't really spend all day as an "architecture astronaut." It was a good time to reactivate my interest in things beyond engineering—which had more or less lapsed in a literary sense when I ragequit Usenet in '95 or so, and lapsed in a scholarly sense when my father (once a professor of philosophy) suggested wisely that he wouldn't pay for a history degree. (Actually Brown was super cool because it let me take *only* engineering classes, a privilege I am grateful for indeed.)

I needed a side quest. It would be literary, historical, economic, legal, political. It would keep the right end of my brain from going insane. It would involve the Internet.

In the later '90s, I had not really been on the Internet. I was too busy working 80 hours a week on pre-iPhone smartphone operating systems. Later, as the IPO high of 2000 began to tune down, I started reading ye early blogs. Though these barbaric kingdoms were crude compared to Usenet's fallen Athens, they had a certain rustic charm...

And where was I politically? In the 90s, I was a light-libertarian like everyone else like me. I didn't like "political correctness" and I didn't like the "religious right." I liked raves and free software and spontaneous order. I was, of course, an atheist. (I still am!) Cultural anthropologists refer to this state of early Internet man as "Basal Reddit."

The early bloggers who said what I wanted to hear were people like **Instapundit, Powerline, Eugene Volokh**. Smart lawyers, who thought like engineers. They were Republicans, of course, which didn't bother me—the fusty schoolmarm smell of progressivism, already palpable 30 years ago, had already driven me from the cult of my birth. Which was of course NPR, or overseas even the BBC—alas, I was a globalist. "This is John Hockenberry, for All Things Considered."

These bloggers were also neocons. Then 9/11 happened. (This was especially weird for me, since I was in Japan doing some smartphone thing, and got stuck. So I bought some buttons in Shibuya and went to the **Yasukuni Shrine**. It was a long time ago...)

Neoconservatives had a really good and logical explanation of 9/11. In a way, you see, 9/11 was just World War II all over again. Osama and Saddam were like Hitler and Stalin: both mass murderers, both bad, both needing to be stopped. Like all dictators. But once every country in the world had a McDonald's, not just the dead would know the end of war. Anyway, the Internet was going to make the world flat—a good thing.

Well. As this theory interacted with the world, as all history knows, at first it seemed to be going quite well. Then it seemed to be going not so well. What we thought: the world has changed America, now America must change herself and the world. What we got: failed nation-building and taking off our shoes at the airport.

This dissonance created a certain... *anomie*. A restlessness. A feeling that there was more out there than free markets and the fight against political correctness, etc.

And then, I had a bit of dot-com money to manage. I like to understand a thing at its fundamentals—to cut nature at its joints. What was this *money* thing? What is *economics*? Should I put it all in Krugerrands? (I should have put it all in Krugerrands.)

Since I was a libertarian, of sorts—what was libertarian economics? What were these beautiful spontaneous orders? Also, in these spontaneous orders—why did, like, the government have to set interest rates? Why is it so hard to define the money supply? Why business cycles? What?

I started going deeper into the Austrians... Hayek is for posers... I read all of Rothbard and Mises... in the end I got into the DMT of libertarianism, Hans-Hermann Hoppe. Hoppe used to teach in Vegas and there is something Vegas about his work, though I think the old fellow mostly hangs out in Turkey these days. And who can blame him. This "Vegas school" is not the end of the liberal world—but you can see it from there.

So, from my unpromising, Reddit-tier beginnings, I have three origin stories in a way—three directions of thinking that made me think history was not over or even close, but would have to be invented again for the 21st century. Each of these directions, each moment of scalding truth, was triggered by a specific stimulus that I can recall as if it had scattered radioactive shrapnel around my brain.

The first stimulus was John Kerry. The second was Hoppe's book, *Democracy: The God That Failed*. And the third was a crudely-made YouTube video I saw in like 2006. Let's go through these three interesting stimuli in order.

The black card

In 2004, Senator John Kerry ran for President. He lost. But one of the things that happened was that it turned out that this mad dude had *inflated his war record*.

Specifically, he had claimed to have driven his machine-gun riverboat, ideal for spraying Cong on the banks and cruising by before they get their RPG out of the bag, on secret missions into Cambodia—which his crew, his commanding officer, and that officer's commander, swore had never happened and was impossible. And there was certainly no *historical* evidence of any US naval missions into Cambodia. Soo...

Well, this is how *I* experienced the notorious Swiftboat Affair. My experience (which I believe to be accurate) taught me a lesson I could never forget about modern media and politics. Here is how I went through it.

Maybe embroidering your war record seems unremarkable in the Age of Trump, but even as late as 2004 this country still had some self-respect. Or so I thought. But...

Back then the news cycle was slower than these new "blogs." So the "blogosphere" (for so, I kid you not, it was called) could kick around information for days before the press picked it up. This was how Sen. Kerry's Cambodian fantasies were discovered.

So I heard about Cambodia from the blogs well before I read about it in the paper. And when I heard about it, I made a monumental misprediction. Since it seemed utterly clear to me (as it still does) that the Senator had been embroidering, I assumed that the truth first scented by the blogs would come out in the press. As usual.

Of course, there would be no way he could run. But it was after the convention—after Sen. Kerry stepped down, who would be the new candidate? Edwards? Surely there was some party rule for if he, like, died... this would be a new event in US history...

But of course... that's not what happened at all. No. What happened is that the press just *added a new word to the dictionary*. They called it *Swiftboating*: the denigration of an American hero for crass political advantage. And I was like...

Can I be at loss for words, in print? I was like... I was like... I'd been concerned by this *media bias* machine—by *political correctness*—I thought I'd seen some *pretty bad stuff*—but it was like... I'd seen the machine... I thought it was turned up to 10 sometimes... man, it was turned up to *two*. *Now* it was at 10. (Now I would put that one at like, 4.)

Later I came up with a sports metaphor with which to describe this awakening event. Suppose you are a soccer fan ("football supporter," for my English friends). You have been watching soccer for years. You are super into your team—the *red* team.

One day they are playing against their longtime rivals—the *blue* team. The red team is up 2-1. You are feeling good—as one does, when one's team is winning.

Then your striker scores. But there's a foul—you didn't see anything? The goal is called off. The referee comes over. Waves his hand wildly. In it is a card. But—

It's not a yellow card. It's not a red card. It's a card you've never seen. A *black* card.

What does it mean? Your striker seems to know what it means. He kneels down, slowly. He puts his head on the ground and his hands behind his back. The ref pulls out a Glock and shoots him in the back of the neck. The striker crumples. Way less blood than you'd expect.

Another player comes running up. He's not into it. *He* gets the black card. It's over in seconds—play resumes. With the bodies, there. 9 on 11. The final score is 5-2, *blue*.

Now: as a fan of the *red* team, how would you feel about that game? How would you feel after watching it? I don't know. It would obviously be an emotional experience. But I am pretty sure most fans would agree on one point. I am pretty sure they would all say: I don't know what I just saw. I just know what it *wasn't*: a soccer game.

Previously, as a good Instapundit reader, I had known that the "mainstream media" was "biased." Biased! When I hear that word, I feel like the professor at the end of a Lovecraft story, reflecting in his last moment before Cthulhu eats him alive, on that queer little Fijian statuette... *biased*.

The media was *biased*. The refs are *biased*. Sure. I mean... I don't know what I just saw. But... it was *biased*. I guess.

Anyway, that's exactly how Instapundit and Powerline and everyone else responded. I expected these very reasonable bloggers to be like: okay. We had this illusion of a fair and level playing field. But now... it's gone. It can't be sustained after this.

They were like: wow! Those biased refs, again! Well... let's hope for better luck in next week's game! Also the red team has grounds for a really big lawsuit! So we're winning! And I was like... it's gone. It can't be sustained after this.

Kerry loses the election. But it doesn't matter. Once you know the black card exists, how can you ever take a soccer game seriously again? You know that if you lose, you lose, and if you win, you also lose. Bush wins the election. He might as well be Kerry. What in this world would be different if Kerry had won, instead of Bush? Nothing matters, nothing counts, nothing is real. That was not a soccer game.

This is historically normal. When you challenge sovereignty, either you win absolutely, or lose absolutely. Are you winning, son? And if you do win, do you actually win? If not, the joke is always and forever on you. (Imagine how the fans of the *blue* team felt about watching that "soccer game.")

But what is... after this? What would come next? If... classical liberalism isn't enough to defeat modern liberalism... but what else is there? What is there that is good and right and true? A real mystery, man. I didn't see anything... I didn't see anything *safe*...

The god that failed

The Overton window is not a window. It is an electric fence. Everyone in every society has one of these fences around their minds—Orwell called it "crimestop." Inside this fence is sanity; outside the fence is insanity, heresy, misinformation and hate speech.

Sometimes power wraps you in a physical fence; always in you is some *emotional* fence. You are the jailer of your own mind. It is inevitable; we are a social species. Freedom, actual freedom, is for the leopard and the tiger—who meet only to mate. We are not cats. We must live together, we must think together. To bond, we must bind. As a massive sperg myself I think this is unfortunate, but it's how it has to be.

For me, the inside of that fence was the so-called Enlightenment and its revolutions. Of course I admitted that the French Revolution had gone wrong—that its vision of liberty was a leftist vision of chaotic license, not a rightist vision of spontaneous order. I could even see how anarchy led ineluctably to tyranny. But walk wherever I would, I was always within the fence.

Given that the revolutions had begun in a completely unaccountable tyranny, namely the old regime, wasn't even the progress from old dictator (king) to new dictator (general secretary) at worst an absence of progress? If the purpose of the state is to secure our freedoms, revolution against a dictator, who allows us no freedoms, is always right. Obviously, if I believed anything else, I would be, like, a *bad person*...

Professor Hoppe (in *Democracy: The God That Failed*) broke the window for me in the spergiest possible way: he made the connection between the *nation* and the *firm*. Even small children, just as they can see that the face of South America fits into the crotch of Africa, can see that CEOs are like kings and their companies like countries; and they even make "war" in the marketplace, not to mention in court.

What is neat about this framework is that if you squint at it from the right point of view, it almost looks *legitimate*. Can a nation be owned by one man? Or a family? That sounds awful, right? But is it?

When a country is entrusted to a politician elected to sit uneasily astride it for a few years at most, his interests are inherently short-term and cannot align with the long-term interests of the country.

When a nation is the *property* of one monarch who owns it for a lifetime—or even better, the property of a *family* who owns it *forever*—the long-term interests of the ownership are aligned with the long-term interests of the property. (I believe this is what "effective altruists" refer to as "longtermism.")

Once we see the superior alignment of the incentive structure, and especially once we see the resonance between the Darwinian competition of capitalism, the generative rivalry of corporations, and the equally Darwinian competition of sovereignty, the generative rivalry of nations—a door cracks open.

A door cracks open because we can see the nondemocratic world as *okay*. We can step outside our revolutionary thinking in which the prerevolutionary world—which is, of course, like, basically all of history—was fundamentally wrong and unacceptable. Note that this is exactly how the Islamic tradition regards pre-Islamic Arab history—the period of "jahiliyyah," meaning merely "ignorance."

Perhaps the millennium and a half in which the Western world was created was not—merely ignorant? The Roman Empire, a half millennium of ignorance? All antiquity, ignorant—except for certain short periods of Athens and Rome?

The era of Athenian democracy is well-attested—but not by writers who saw it as a success. There must have been some. Their work did not seem worth copying. As for the old Roman Republic, it was so racist and fascist (obviously *inventing* the fasces) it made Pretoria look like Berkeley, and the Caesars did not overthrow the Republic—they saved Rome itself from the Republic's burning wreck. Etc.

And while Voltaire was cool and everything, the last 250 years in Europe are hardly something to write home about. Every experiment must be judged by standards set out at at its start. Consider how Europeans of 1772 would judge the Europe of 2022—including all historical events between those dates—and you are correctly judging the whole democratic experiment. Suppose your witness was Hume or Gibbon, both Enlightenment scholars, both of whom saw stable monarchy as the best government? What news would make Hume and Gibbon contradict their prerevolutionary priors?

It would feel obvious to them that democracy was the ultimate cause of the Holocaust, for instance. Didn't Hitler come to power as a politician—even a populist politician? Why do you think populism is the opposite of democracy? And wasn't anti-Semitism an obscure peasant prejudice until Hitler discovered he could use it to win elections? Hume and Gibbon would be surprised that you are confused by these obvious points.

What about our modern, peaceful, prosperous democratic era? Defining "democracy" simply as good or legitimate government (the formal name of North Korea is the DPRK—that's one place name, three synonyms for democracy) has let us "No True Scotsman" it right through.

If democracy is defined as peace and prosperity, democracy is always peaceful and prosperous. Also, if anything that isn't *true* democracy (in some mysterious sense) is at war with *true* democracy, it can't be peaceful or prosperous. Since it also loses, it was obviously bad.

So we forget about Robespierre, Stalin, Mao, Pol Pot and Idi Amin as products of the democratic era. They were illegitimate *dictators*—they should be grouped with kings, bad people, like Louis XVI or Nicholas II or Charles II. Maybe Lenin was bad but he wasn't bad like Nicholas II, whose Cossacks whipped serfs and Jews with the knout. And there is certainly nothing democratic about Hitler, who wasn't the elected leader of a political party or anything like that... Autocrats, autocrats, autocrats all. True!

But pull back the camera, and we see that the democratic era of Europe is the chaotic era of Europe. Visible societal decline is easy to observe. Any independent observer 250 years ago, asked whether in the light of hindsight any of the revolutions was a good idea, would have to say no. If the rule is that power belongs to the people, and that rule brought us to *this*, of what use is the rule?

But what about the technical achievements of the democratic era? Science is not the product of democracy but of European civilization. The modern scientific tradition traces its lineage to the 17th-century Royal Society—chartered under Charles II. Yes, there was a scientific and industrial revolution. Who knows what that Europe would have created, had it not been repeatedly torn by democratic wars and rebellions?

All this I got through Professor Hoppe's little book. I wanted to get out of the present, but I couldn't see how. He broke the glass of the Overton Window, and I climbed out—into the rest of human history. Which suddenly actually made sense to me.

Hate and social media

Do you know the moment in *Apocalypse Now*, when Marlon Brando as Colonel Kurtz tells the story of how the Viet Cong cut off the immunized children's arms? Brando feels a *revelation of power*—in an instant he discovers a force he could never have previously imagined, like a great spiritual awakening. But... not a *nice* awakening.

I don't even know how I was linked to this video. Or even when, but it was like 2006. It wasn't even a video, really. It was just stills, animated with a gentle, slow zoom effect—a *calm* zoom—over a slow, sad piano track.

There were two classes of still, alternating. There was no voice and no captions. The music set the tone and the screen spoke for itself.

The *odd* stills were high-res color images of contemporary human decay. Tents in the streets, heaps of trash, flagrant public lewdness, everything no one wants to look at. At the time I lived in San Francisco, so I saw this stuff all the time anyway. But...

The *even* stills were formal dress photographs, in sepia, of *young German officers*. They seemed to have been picked for faces that showed not sneering martial pride, but dignity and resolution. Needless to say... they were from the... mid-century period.

I thought: there is *something* here. I don't know what it is. But it's *something*.

With Faulkner I thought: The past isn't dead. It isn't even past. Whatever this is, it is not within the philosophy of John McCain. And it has the power to move the heart. It is useless to deny this power—it would move the average Berkeley Bowl shopper. Heck, it would move the average drag queen.

And obviously it can move our hearts in many different directions, not all good. To say this force is dangerous... goes unsaid. To say that it can be *abolished* is plain wrong.

To say that it can be mastered, controlled, used for good... it is and it must be. And it has never not been. You don't need a time machine. You don't need to go to Germany. Wherever you live, your life is defended by a uniformed paramilitary hierarchy with special powers of violence: the police. If they go on strike—*fear*.

We, as a society, might not be ready to "defund the police." Yet the whole institution is clearly a heritage from another time. We might not defund the police—but if the police did not exist, would we invent them? Could we? If we could not, the institution is clinging on by its fingertips.

And—while not all policemen may be Nazis—can't we say objectively, regardless of how we feel about the Third Reich, that there *is* something *more Nazi* about being a cop, than a member of most professions? If we have zero tolerance for Nazism, don't we need to get rid of the police? If we *do* need some trace dose of Nazism, *why*? Also, if we *do* need this raw and toxic drug, can we separate the medicine from the poison?

We allow these inherited exceptions to survive, since without them we would perish. We hate them so much that someday we will cancel them, and perish. But there are no random exceptions. The exceptions are part of nature. We live in nature; we must, for our lives, study her. We must live up to her challenges.

What I learned from this silly little video is the same as Solzhenitsyn's lesson: that the line between good and evil runs through every human heart. Nothing is out of bounds—"nothing human is alien to me."

The dissident is not trying to reshape the Overton window, or even to break out of it. The dissident is trying to banish it. He may prudently pretend to believe in it, like a Christian forced to sacrifice to the emperor—he will certainly obey it when he has to. But he does not believe in it.

He does not believe history is a Marvel movie, ever. Clean lines between good and bad guys can never be drawn. To draw them is to write cartoon history, children's history, comicbook history. No one would think of writing a history of the Wars of the Roses in which the Yorkists were the good guys and the Lancastrians were the bad guys.

This sort of garbage is not history, but a nutrient-free replacement made to displace it. Unlike actual history, it is utterly infertile, inert and powerless. The real past isn't dead—it isn't even past.

These three old texts

I have a crippling allergy to reading not only anything about myself, but even anything by myself. I can barely edit my own drafts—a proper post is a kind of fresco painting. This makes it hard to do certain things, but it keeps me from sucking my own fumes. It lets me change my mind through the long, slow growth and withering of neurons.

Therefore, I will do what Nicholson Baker did in his great U and I (where he wrote an appreciation of John Updike without reading any John Updike), and review my old own work, from 15 years ago or so, without reading it again. Sorry if this is, like, weird.

A formalist manifesto

The other day someone asked me where I found James Burnham's *The Machiavellians*. It was in a '60s paperback edition in one of four grocery bags I filled at a closeout sale at a used bookstore on Clement St. in SF, probably in 2005 or 2006. They pointed out how lucky this was—I managed to drive the price of the book up to like $500, until someone reprinted it. I probably would have run into it some other way. Who knows.

In any case, Burnham's rigorous insistence on distinguishing between symbolic forms of power and actual practices of power, as the essential north star of disenchantment, the jaws-of-life of any attempt to rip ourselves free from our burning crashed illusion, and his summary of the Italian School's merciless and unsympathetic study of reality, not as it should be but merely as it is, is the 20th century's only essential reading in political science. I should probably insist that you read it before you read this.

I immediately saw that Burnham's vision of disenchantment converged perfectly with the Confucian ideal of the rectification of names. Confucius said: "If names be not correct, language is not in accordance with the truth of things. If language be not in accordance with the truth of things, affairs cannot be carried on to success."

In case the application of this principle is not clear, let me apply it to present things. You can apply it yourself. Go to DC and talk to anyone in the Beltway business, and tell them: "the agencies aren't actually an executive branch. They're a legislative branch." Half of your interlocutors will get it immediately.

The other half, who are not idiots but just have their microscope zoomed in too close, need to be reminded that every arm of the so-called executive branch has its authority delegated from the Congress, which both in theory and practice controls the budget, policy and personnel of the agencies. Whose staff are never seen testifying before the President lol. The President can issue "executive orders"—which from a hostile White House are glorified tweets, and from a friendly White House are permission slips for the agency to do something that it already wants to do.

The so-called "deep state" is permanent because the Congress is the airlock between democracy and oligarchy. The Congress is the roof of the regime. While in theory it is democratic, 98% incumbency rates in the House and 90% in the Senate, plus seniority rules that make old Venice look like a startup, protect its important, delicate business. And—is that business "carried on to success?"

The business of the Congress is to sell its power, generally at ridiculously low prices, to keep itself in office. America is ruled by this self-licking ice-cream cone. It passes 2000-page bills because it has a lot of mouths to feed.

Fortunately, the items in these bills are usually tiny course corrections which have been fought over by many power buyers, Most compromises are not that dangerous or harmful. But they are also too small to be useful. Most of the worst things the US Government does are just a matter of this ship having been pointed in a certain direction when it was launched 80 years ago. Often, only historians can accurately explain this direction today, yet its divergence from reality is far too great to change. Oligarchy means no one is at the helm—in fact, there is no helm at all.

There are two kinds of power buyers: activists and lobbyists. Activist groups buy power to generate a sense of importance for their donors, who are buying vanity. Lobbyist groups buy power for corporations to help them make money. Populist groups, like the NRA, are technically nonprofits, but are always called "lobbyists" anyway, because they are acting on behalf of their donors, not their donors' clients.

This system, which is the way the Beltway works, is almost completely invisible to the average American voter. How? Language.

Washington is *described* to the voter in a false language which sounds *sort of* as if the President is an elected king—a dictator—a national CEO. And when they read the Constitution, they see this confirmed—chief executive of the executive branch.

He does this... he does that... he "does" so many things, how can he sleep? In fact he spends half his day on photo-ops. This is one way to tell he doesn't have a real job—or at least, not the job it says he has on paper.

Unfortunately, filling this largely ceremonial office, which nominally is in charge of all of Washington, is all the voters care about. If they could replace all of Congress at the same time, and all the replacements obeyed a central staff (like UK MPs), the voters could actually take control of the country! Sounds like democracy to me.

But when they vote for Congress they vote randomly on the basis of lawn signs. So the incumbent, who can afford more lawn signs, generally wins. And the public loses. The public, in this century at least, is a loser. It's hard out there for a loser.

And when the public is a loser, democracy is *literally* impossible—just as, when the king is a 3-year-old, absolute monarchy is *literally* impossible. No constitution—no piece of paper, nor parchment, nor nanowoven molecular graphene—can put the weak in charge of the strong. Political science, like physics, knows its limitations.

So in this "democracy," the wires between the voter and real power are effectively cut. And no one notices—because the legislative branch is called the "executive branch." And any pressure against this system is "populism," which is bad for our "democracy." Good luck trying to think amidst this maze of mirrors.

When we imagine a *formalist* state, we imagine one whose righteousness is so plain that it has no need for this kind of Orwellian fortification. Alas, for every term or label I've invented, I've come up with 20 that suck. I've long since stopped trying to make "formalism" happen—but there is nothing wrong with the idea, dammit.

When apparent and real power structures diverge, the real power structure is typically dumping accountability onto the apparent power structure. If it has any to dump—it is operating in the shadows, its real role unacknowledged.

Justice Sotomayor, almost 20 years ago, once let one of these cats out of the bag—she was like: "Appeals courts are where policy is made." How many people, walking the streets of San Francisco, relate the condition of those streets to the decisions of the Ninth Circuit? Also: which is more accountable—to the people, or to anyone—the Ninth Circuit, or Louis XIV?

Oligarchic autocracy is what you get when you try to avoid monarchical autocracy. Even if the monarch is accountable only to God—who never seems to actually, like, *do* anything—he concentrates all accountability in his person. Oligarchic autocracy pours it away on the ground everywhere. Nothing at all could be less accountable.

The open-minded progressive

This is one of the most frequently assigned of my texts, which makes it unfortunate that I remember it the least. The Open Letter was a pretty good piece of propaganda in its day, but I do I think I have improved on the technology.

I have always considered it most important to speak to the ruling class. If leftism was true, regime change would happen because the ruled overthrow the rulers. Actually this pretty much never happens. So haranguing the ruled to overthrow the rulers is not a winning strategy, unless it is the surface appearance of a very different strategy.

What happens is: regime change happens because the rulers get tired of ruling. A well-honeyed voice can encourage this lassitude and enervation. Note that almost all purported rebellious tactics are almost perfectly designed to energize the ruling class—to rouse them into fear and anger. So they are actually reinforcing their enemies.

A strategic dissident voice should aim to either soothe the libs, or depress them, or seduce them—in order of desirability. While any of these three outcomes corresponds to "owning the libs" in a strategic sense, each expands the scope of the victory.

When addressing readers brought up, like myself, on a diet of NPR, I addressed myself to what they think are their most important character qualities. Liberals are generous, logical, and open-minded. Or at least this is how they see themselves.

And if you want to speak to someone, it's often good to speak to the person they think they are. So I appealed to the charity of liberals, their reason and their open minds. Or at least that's how I remember it. I do think the results were pretty good.

But you can sometimes do even better. You can speak to who they actually are. Since *no one* speaks directly to who they actually are, this note, when hit, becomes *electric*. Their ears have actually *never been fucked like this*.

These days I go straight for "seduce." I define *monarchy*—literally the rule of one—, then ask them to replace their image of a monarch (generally a blend of Hitler, Henry VIII, or Elizabeth II) with their favorite modern monarch—FDR. (Or, for Cenk Uygur, Atatürk.) Then I tell them that the New Deal was awesome because it was essentially a sovereign startup whose business plan was to rule the world—and it succeeded.

This is speaking to who they are, because who the libs are is *ambitious*. Underneath all the concern for others, etc., is the fundamental desire of all aristocrats—to be *special*.

If we offer the libs a new regime which is their mortal enemy, whose program is to line them up, shoot them, dump them in a ditch, soak them with gas and burn them, they will fight fanatically with the last drop of blood in their bodies. And they will fight even harder if we threaten any such fate for the client bodies they protect!

But if we offer them a new, better way to be special, which has the same general goal as their existing mission—ruling all the peoples for their own good—but actually is not 90 years old—but feels fresh, and exciting, and slightly dangerous, and totally new—but is also gloriously retro—but will help *them*, the elves, live their own best lives—but has no less love for all its hobbits, dwarves, orcs and zombies—you may even get them to sit up, and listen. This is way better than either soothing or depressing them.

Do you want to *win?* Or do you want to be a *dick?* The fate of the world depends on your answer. Personally, I want to win—and I will defend that to the last drop.

Pwning Dawkins

I have a very clear memory of when I wrote the Dawkins piece. It was in the early fall of 2008, which I know because my wife was pregnant and we took one last road trip, in the old black Cougar, up to Vancouver. The border guards did *not* like that we had crossed and returned in one day. But I mean, hey, Canada. Anyway, I did a lot of the work on Dawkins on that trip. Also, the title is kind of tacky.

Nowadays the dogs in the street know that "wokeness" aka "political correctness" aka "progressivism" aka "social justice" is a religion. In 2008 it was an Archimedes-tier insight. That flash of genius was so bomb-intense it gave me, like, genius Tourette's, and I wanted to run naked out of the bathtub screaming Eureka and the N-word.

It was like discovering that birds are actually dinosaurs, or South America actually used to be connected to Africa, or Shakespeare was Edward de Vere. When I found the Archeopteryx of this connection—the **"American Malvern" article in Time**, which shows the prewar mainline Protestant missionary-industrial complex in the process of morphing into the postwar secular aid-industrial complex—it felt like Howard Carter shooting up in King Tut's tomb. Like schlepping around the Wyoming Badlands till you run into two Tyrannosaurs, fucking. When a single page of primary source unequivocally demonstrates a historical hypothesis—that doesn't happen often, kids.

In a way I was still a Reddit-tier atheist libertarian. Having shown that our supposedly secular technocracy was in fact a *theocracy*—and not only that, a theocracy tied to what had been the most powerful English-speaking religious movement for *400 years*—felt to me like a complete and sufficient disproof of the state.

After all, the fundamental principle of modern government is the separation of church and state. Nothing could be more important! And yet, simply by evolving away its belief in God—the way a cancer cell evolves away its MHC complex, which tags it for the immune system—this religion has become basically as powerful as Islam in Iran. Certainly, if you replace all instances of "social justice" etc. with a reference to Allah, etc., you are looking at a pretty darned Muslim country.

Unfortunately, this perspective—while valid—was only a small step on the way out of Plato's Overton cave. Yes: "woke" is a religion. Cladistically—according to the vertical descent and branching that characterizes DNA, language, and tradition—this culture has a historical name—while almost all its tenets have mutated, it is a form of English Calvinism. Tracing it to the 16th century is easy. Across time, its devotees have been called Calvinists, Brownists, Independents, Dissenters, Puritans, Unitarians, and so on. It was the founding religion of Harvard. It remains the ruling religion of Harvard. Nothing ever happens, nothing ever changes. Nobody can get rid of these fuckers.

The truth is that every stable government is a theocracy—a marriage of church and state. The problem with modern Puritanism is not that it is too integrated with the regime. It is *not integrated enough*. It is superior to the state; it should be subordinate.

The "woke religion" holds unaccountable power over the regime—whereas it (and all other religions) should actually be *subject* to the secular authorities. (Historically, this is the *Erastian*[1] viewpoint.)

Dawkins may have been pwned by a god-free religion—but this ultra-integralist neo-Erastian stance would *blow his tiny mind*. (Even the modern tradcath integralist agrees with his liberal opponents that the church should be supreme over the state. Wrong.) Even at the time I wrote this essay, I am not sure I was quite ready for this reality.

A neo-Erastian stance—a system of multiple churches, each of which is a state church—is proper in the modern world because it reflects the temporal weakness of religion. Innocent III is not in the building. The day of churches that had the power to resist the state is long gone—except for the one dominant church, which is not "religion" but "education."

But it's still a church. The church of education—the cathedral of press and university—is powerful enough to steer the government. But not to *resist* the government—not a government that plays its cards right.

Could that new regime build a church strong enough to resist itself? Yes. Should it? Yes. But that will probably take two or three generations, as the moral order and Roman virtue of the population is restored. At this point, democracy will become an issue again as well. There is no winning forever—not if the nation needs to blossom.

The only church that can come close to resisting the state is the church of education. Nothing must be left of this church—from Yale to a one-room schoolhouse in Alaska, from the New York Times to the Anderson Valley Advertiser.

Cry havoc, and let slip the dogs of war! Every door can be locked—every file can be impounded—every endowment can be seized—every building can be torn down. Your sons will curse you if you do too little—yet merely mutter if you do too much. Without harming a single hair on a human head, the entire cathedral can be

---

1 From 16th c. Swiss theologian Thomas Erastus, "the idea that the State should have supremacy in ecclesiastical matters."

both demolished, and made impossible to resurrect, in three months or at most six. And if you have a choice between doing it quickly and doing it slowly—for God's sake, do it quickly!

Be aware, however, that there is no marketplace of ideas. A church is not dispensable. At the very least, you will need a ministry of truth—and the truer its truth, the longer your new regime will last. Truth does not install itself; it needs a legion of teachers; and so on. As the old church is broken to its foundation, the new church is already pouring its own new foundation. Do not expect a foundation to pour itself!

To nothing, and beyond

So, all well and good! You believe all this. You've read all the holy texts. (I can't wait to be the Marx of some really awful 22nd-century despotism). But what should you do?

Do? My child—do? There is nothing to do. I have done nothing at all. I have no cult, no staff, no organization, no nothing. I am a guy in a little room looking out at some trees. In the summer they all have leaves. In the winter, only some; and through the branches I see the skyline of the city. It is what it is. It will become what it becomes. I try to look at it as coldly as I can. If I think of something interesting, I write it down. Sometimes I have a party. That's what I do—maybe, like, do *that?*

As Robinson Jeffers wrote:

> It is better to be silent than make a noise.
> It is better to strike dead than strike often.
> It is better not to strike.

Here is my big plan for the future: nothing. Be silent. Do not strike. Do not make a noise. Do nothing. When you are ready to make a noise, say nothing. When you are ready to strike, do nothing. When you are ready to strike dead, do not strike. When destiny asks you to strike dead, say no. When destiny *tells* you to strike dead, say no. When destiny is down on her knees, *begging*... then, strike dead.

If you are doing it right, it will be almost instant—and instantly irreversible—and perfectly bloodless. Until you can even imagine that (and you *definitely* can't)—by all means, I pray you: do nothing. For between you and empire is nothing but patience.

-Curtis Yarvin
September 5th, 2022

XXIV   LINKS & NOTES

 IX Berkeley CS program Link to an academic paper lead-authored by Yarvin from 1993. Curtis Yarvin, Richard Bukowski, and Thomas Anderson. "Anonymous RPC: low-latency protection in a 64-bit address space." *In Proceedings of the USENIX Summer 1993 Technical Conference - Volume 1* (Usenix-stc'93). USENIX Association, USA, Article 13, 1–12.

 IX Raph Levien

 X Instapundit Conservative blog of law professor Glenn Reynolds, started in 2001. Instapundit was likely the most influential political blog of its time, and Reynolds among the most prominent Iraq-War boosters after 9/11.The archived link here is from around the time period referenced in the Foreword. This will provide some flavor of what reading the blog was like in the early to mid-aughts. (Archived links from this period are also provided for the two sites listed directly below.)

 X Powerline Popular early conservative blog run by John Hinderaker.

 X Eugene Volokh Lead contributor of the libertarian legal blog, *The Volokh Conspiracy*, now hosted at Reason.com, previously at the Washington Post. The blog often featured other libertarian-leaning academics like Tyler Cowen, Orin Kerr, and Randy Barnett.

 X Yasukuni Shrine

 XV Royal Society

 XVII U and I: A True Story by Nicholson Baker (Random House, 1991).

 XVIII rectification of names

 XIX she was like Robert Yoon. "Sotomayor: 'Policy is made' at Appeals Court." *CNN*, Politicalticker. 26 May, 2009.

 XXI "American Malvern" article in Time See Chapter 5 of *Open Letter* and Chapter 2 of *Dawkins* for a detailed account of this episode. "American Malvern." *Time Magazine*, Religion, Vol. XXXIX No.11, p. 16 Mar. 1942, now permanently archived at Unqualified-Reservations.org.

AUTHOR'S FOREWORD XXV

XXII Erastian

A FORMALIST MANIFESTO

A FORMALIST MANIFESTO
APRIL 23, 2007

The other day I was tinkering around in my garage and I decided to build a new ideology.

What? I mean, am I crazy or something? First of all, you can't just build an ideology. They're handed down across the centuries, like lasagna recipes. They need to age, like bourbon. You can't just drink it straight out of the radiator.

And look what happens if you try. What causes all the problems of the world? Ideology, that's what. What do Bush and Osama have in common? They're both ideological nutcases. We're supposed to need more of this?

Furthermore, it's simply not possible to build a new ideology. People have been talking about ideology since Jesus was a little boy. At least! And I'm supposedly going to improve on this? Some random person on the Internet, who flunked out of grad school, who doesn't know Greek *or* Latin? Who do I think I am, Wallace Shawn?[1]

All excellent objections. Let's answer them and then we'll talk about formalism.

First, of course, there are a couple of beautifully aged traditional ideologies which the Internet now brings us in glorious detail. They go by lots of names, but let's call them **progressivism** and **conservatism**.

My beef with progressivism is that for at least the last 100 years, the vast majority of writers and thinkers and smart people in general have been progressives. Therefore, any intellectual in 2007, which unless there has been some kind of Inter-

---

1 Reference to Wallace Shawn's character Vizzini in the *The Princess Bride* (1987).

net space warp and my words are being carried live on Fox News, is anyone reading this, is basically marinated in progressive ideology.

Perhaps this might slightly impair one's ability to see any problems that may exist in the progressive worldview.

As for conservatism, not all Muslims are terrorists, but most terrorists are Muslims. Similarly, not all conservatives are cretins, but most cretins are conservatives. The modern American conservative movement—which is paradoxically much younger than the progressive movement, if only because it had to be reinvented after the Roosevelt dictatorship—has been distinctly affected by this audience. It also suffers from the electoral coincidence that it has to despise everything that progressivism adores, a bizarre birth defect which does not appear to be treatable.

Most people who don't consider themselves "progressives" or "conservatives" are one of two things. Either they're "moderates," or they're "libertarians."

In my experience, most sensible people consider themselves "moderate," "centrist," "independent," "unideological," "pragmatic," "apolitical," etc. Considering the vast tragedies wrought by 20th-century politics, this attitude is quite understandable. It is also, in my opinion, responsible for most of the death and destruction in the world today.

Moderation is not an ideology. It is not an opinion. It is not a thought. It is an absence of thought. If you believe the status quo of 2007 is basically righteous, then you should believe the same thing if a time machine transported you to Vienna in 1907. But if you went around Vienna in 1907 saying that there should be a European Union, that Africans and Arabs should rule their own countries and even colonize Europe, that any form of government except parliamentary democracy is evil, that paper money is good for business, that all doctors should work for the State, etc., etc.—well, you could probably find people who agreed with you. They wouldn't call themselves "moderates," and nor would anyone else.

No, if you were a moderate in Vienna in 1907, you thought Franz Josef I was the greatest thing since sliced bread. So which is it? Hapsburgs, or Eurocrats? Pretty hard to split the difference on that one.

In other words, the problem with moderation is that the "center" is not fixed. It moves. And since it moves, and people being people, people will try to move it. This creates an incentive for violence—something we formalists try to avoid. More on this in a bit.

That leaves libertarians. Now, I love libertarians to death. My CPU practically has a permanent open socket to the Mises Institute. In my opinion, anyone who has intentionally chosen to remain ignorant of libertarian (and, in particular, Misesian-Rothbardian) thought, in an era when a couple of mouse clicks will feed you enough high-test libertarianism to drown a moose, is not an intellectually serious person. Furthermore, I am a computer programmer who has read far too much science fiction—two major risk factors for libertarianism. So I could just say, "read Rothbard," and call it a day.

On the other hand, it is hard to avoid noticing two basic facts about the universe. One is that libertarianism is an extremely obvious idea. The other is that it has never been successfully implemented.

This does not prove anything. But what it suggests is that libertarianism is, as its detractors are always quick to claim, an essentially impractical ideology. I would love to live in a libertarian society. The question is: is there a path from here to there? And if we get there, will we stay there? If your answer to both questions is obviously "yes," perhaps your definition of "obvious" is not the same as mine.

So this is why I decided to build my own ideology—"formalism."

Of course, there is nothing new in formalism. Progressives, conservatives, moderates, and libertarians will all recognize large chunks of their own undigested realities. Even the word "formalism" is borrowed from **legal formalism**, which is basically the same idea in more modest attire.

I am not **Vizzini**. I am just some dude who buys a lot of obscure used books, and is not afraid to grind them down, add flavor, and rebrand the result as a kind of political **surimi**. Most everything I have to say is available, with better writing, more detail and much more erudition, in **Jouvenel, Kuehnelt-Leddihn, Leoni, Burnham, Nock**, etc., etc.

If you've never heard of any of these people, neither had I until I started the procedure. If that scares you, it should. Replacing your own ideology is a lot like do-it-yourself brain surgery. It requires patience, tolerance, a high pain threshold, and very steady hands. Whoever you are, you already have an ideology in there, and if it wanted to come out it would have done so on its own.

There is no point in starting this messy experiment only to install some other ideology that's the way it is just because someone said so. Formalism, as we'll see, is an ideology designed by geeks for other geeks. It's not a kit. It doesn't come with batteries. You can't just pop it in. At best, it's a rough starting point to help you build your own DIY ideology. If you're not comfortable working with a table saw, an oscilloscope and an autoclave, formalism is not for you.

That said:

The basic idea of formalism is just that the main problem in human affairs is violence. The goal is to design a way for humans to interact, on a planet of remarkably limited size, without violence.

Especially organized violence. Next to organized human-on-human violence, a good formalist believes, all other problems—Poverty, Global Warming, Moral Decay, etc., etc., etc.—are basically insignificant. Perhaps once we get rid of violence we can worry a little about Moral Decay, but given that organized violence killed a couple of hundred million people in the last century, whereas Moral Decay gave us "American Idol," I think the priorities are pretty clear.

The key is to look at this not as a moral problem, but as an engineering problem. Any solution that solves the problem is acceptable. Any solution that does not solve the problem is not acceptable.

For example, there is an existing idea called pacifism, part of the general progressive suite, which claims to be a solution for violence. As I understand it, the idea of pacifism is that if you and I can not be violent, everyone else will not be violent, too.

There's no doubt in my mind that pacifism is effective in some cases. In Northern Ireland, for example, it seems to be just the thing. But there is a kind of "hundredth-monkey" logic to it that consistently eludes my linear, Western mind. It strikes me that if everyone is a pacifist and then one person decides not to be a pacifist, he will wind up ruling the world. Hm.

A further difficulty is that the definition of "violence" isn't so obvious. If I gently relieve you of your wallet, and you chase after me with your Glock and make me beg to be allowed to give it back, which of us is being violent? Suppose I say, well, it was your wallet—but it's my wallet now?

This suggests, at the very least, that we need a rule that tells us whose wallet is whose. Violence, then, is anything that breaks the rule, or replaces it with a different rule. If the rule is clear and everyone follows it, there is no violence.

In other words, violence equals *conflict plus uncertainty*. While there are wallets in the world, conflict will exist. But if we can eliminate uncertainty—if there is an unambiguous, unbreakable rule that tells us, in advance, who gets the wallet—I have no reason to sneak my hand into your pocket, and you have no reason to run after me shooting wildly into the air. Neither of our actions, by definition, can affect the outcome of the conflict.

Violence of any size makes no sense without uncertainty. Consider a war. If one army knows it will lose the war, perhaps on the advice of some infallible oracle, it has no reason to fight. Why not surrender and get it over with?

But this has only multiplied our difficulties. Where do all these rules come from? Who makes them unbreakable? Who gets to be the oracle? Why is the wallet "yours," rather than "mine"? What happens if we disagree on this? If there's one rule for every wallet, how can everyone remember them all? And suppose it's not you, but me, who's got the Glock?

Fortunately, great philosophers have spent many long hours pondering these details. The answers I give you are theirs, not mine.

First, one sensible way to make rules is that you're bound by a rule if, and only if, you agree to it. We don't have rules that are made by the gods somewhere. What we have is actually not rules at all, but agreements. Surely, agreeing to something and then, at your own convenience, un-agreeing to it, is the act of a cad. In fact, when you make an agreement, the agreement itself may well include the consequences of this kind of irresponsible behavior.

If you're a wild man and you agree to nothing—not even that you won't just kill people randomly on the street—this is fine. Go and live in the jungle, or something. Don't expect anyone to let you walk around on their street, any more than they would tolerate, say, a polar bear. There is no absolute moral principle that says that polar bears are evil, but their presence is just not compatible with modern urban living.

We are starting to see two kinds of agreements here. There are agreements made with other specific individuals—I agree to paint your house, you agree to pay me. And there are agreements like, "I won't kill anyone on the street." But are these agreements really different? I don't think so. I think the second kind of agreement is just your agreement with *whoever owns the street*.

If wallets have owners, why shouldn't streets have owners? Wallets have to have owners, obviously, because ultimately someone has to decide what happens with the wallet. Does it ride off in your pocket, or mine? Streets stay put, but there are still a lot of decisions that have to be taken—who paves the street? When and why? Are people allowed to kill people on the street, or is it one of those special no-killing streets? What about street vendors? And so on.

Obviously, if I own 44th Street and you own 45th and 43rd, the possibility of a complex relationship between us becomes nontrivial. And complexity is next to ambiguity, which is next to uncertainty, and the Glocks come out again. So, realistically, we are probably talking more about owning not streets, but larger, more clearly-defined units—blocks, maybe, or even cities.

Owning a city! Now that would be pretty cool. But it gets us back to an issue that we've completely skipped, which is who owns what. How do we decide? Do I deserve to own a city? Am I so meritorious? I think I am. Maybe you could keep your wallet, and I could get, say, Baltimore.

There is this idea called social justice that a lot of people believe in. The notion is, in fact, fairly universal as of this writing. What it tells us is that Earth is small and has a limited set of resources, such as cities, which we all want as much of as possible. But we can't all have a city, or even a street, so we should share equally. Because all of us people are equal and no one is more equal than anyone else.

Social justice sounds very nice. But there are three problems with it.

One is that many of these nice things are not directly comparable. If I get an apple and you get an orange, are we equal? One could debate the subject—with Glocks, perhaps.

Two is that even if everyone starts with equal everything, people being different, having different needs and skills and so on, and the concept of ownership implying that if you own something you can give it to someone else, all is not likely to stay equal. In fact, it's basically impossible to combine a system in which agreements stay agreed with one in which equality stays equal.

This tells us that if we try to enforce permanent equality, we can probably expect permanent violence. I am not a big fan of "empirical evidence," but I think this prediction corresponds pretty well to reality.

But three, which is the real killer—so to speak—is that we are not, in fact, designing an abstract utopia here. We are trying to fix the real world, which in case you hadn't noticed, is extremely screwed up. In many cases, there is no clear agreement on who owns what (Palestine, anyone?), but most of the good things in the world do seem to have a rather definite chain of control.

If we have to start by equalizing the distribution of goods, or in fact by changing this distribution at all, we are putting ourselves quite unnecessarily behind the 8-ball. We are saying, we come in peace, we believe all should be free and equal, let us embrace. Put your arms around me. Feel that lump in my back pocket? Yup, that's what you think it is. And it's loaded. Now hand over your city/wallet/apple/orange, because I know someone who needs it more than you.

The goal of formalism is to avoid this unpleasant little detour. Formalism says: let's figure out exactly who has what, *now*, and give them a fancy little certificate. Let's not get into who *should* have what. Because, like it or not, this is simply a recipe for more violence. It is very hard to come up with a rule that explains why the Palestinians should get Haifa back, and doesn't explain why the Welsh should get London back.

So far this probably sounds a lot like libertarianism. But there's a big difference.

Libertarians may think the Welsh should get London back. Or not. I am still not sure I can interpret Rothbard on this one—which is, as we've seen, in itself a problem.

But if there is one thing all libertarians do believe, it's that *the Americans should get America back*. In other words, libertarians (at least, real libertarians) believe the US is basically an illegitimate and usurping authority, that taxation is theft, that they are essentially being treated as fur-bearing animals by this weird, officious armed mafia, which has somehow convinced everyone else in the country to worship it like it was the Church of God or something, not just a bunch of guys with fancy badges and big guns.

A good formalist will have none of this.

Because to a formalist, the fact that the US can determine what happens on the North American continent between the 49th parallel and the Rio Grande, AK and HI, etc., means that it is the entity which owns that territory. And the fact that the US extracts regular payments from the aforementioned fur-bearing critters means no more than that it owns that right. The various maneuvers and pseudo-legalities by which it acquired these properties are all just history. What matters is that it has them now and it doesn't want to give them over, any more than you want to give me your wallet.

So if the responsibility to fork over some cut of your paycheck makes you a serf (a reasonable reuse of the word, surely, for our less agricultural age), that's what Americans are—serfs.

Corporate serfs, to be exact, because the US is nothing but a corporation. That is, it is a formal structure by which a group of individuals agree to act collectively to achieve some result.

So what? So I'm a corporate serf. Is this so horrible? I seem to be pretty used to it. Two days out of the week I work for Lord Snooty-Snoot. Or Faceless Global Products. Or whoever. Does it matter who the check is written to?

The modern distinction between "private" corporations and "governments" is actually a rather recent development. The US is certainly different from, say, Microsoft, in that the US handles its own security. On the other hand, just as Microsoft depends on the US for most of its security, the US depends on Microsoft for most of its software. It's not clear why this should make one of these corporations special, and the other not-special.

Of course, the purpose of Microsoft is not to write software, but to make money for its shareholders. The American Cancer Society is a corporation, too, and it has a purpose as well—to cure cancer. I have lost a lot of work on account of Microsoft's so-called "software," and its stock, frankly, is going nowhere. And cancer still seems to be around.

In case the CEO of either MSFT or the ACS is reading this, though, I don't really have a message for you guys. You know what you're trying to do and your people are probably doing as good a job of it as they can. And if not, fire the bastards.

But I have no idea what the purpose of the US is.

I have heard that it's supposedly run by George W. Bush. But he doesn't appear to even be able to fire his own employees,[2] which is probably good, because I hear he's not exactly Jack Welch, if you know what I mean.[3] In fact, if anyone can identify one significant event that has occurred in North America because Bush and not Kerry was elected in 2004, I'd be delighted to hear of it. Because my impression is that basically the President has about as much effect on the actions of the US as the Heavenly Sovereign Emperor, the Divine Mikado, has on the actions of Japan. Which is pretty much none.

Obviously, the US exists. Obviously, it does stuff. But the way in which it decides what stuff it's going to do is so opaque that, as far as anyone outside the Beltway is concerned, it might as well be consulting ox entrails.

So this is the formalist manifesto: that the US is just a corporation. It is not a mystic trust consigned to us by the generations. It is not the repository of our hopes and fears, the voice of conscience and the avenging sword of justice. It is just a big old company that holds a huge pile of assets, has no clear idea of what it's trying to do with them, and is thrashing around like a ten-gallon shark in a five-gallon bucket, red ink spouting from each of its bazillion gills.

To a formalist, the way to fix the US is to dispense with the ancient mystical horseradish, the corporate prayers and war chants, figure out who owns this monstrosity, and let them decide what in the heck they are going to do with it. I don't think it's too crazy to say that all options—including restructuring and liquidation—should be on the table.

---

2 In 2007, the Whitehouse was put under investigation by the Inspector General after seven US attorneys were fired in the wake of the midterm elections. Nine senior staff at the Department of Justice resigned as a result of the investigations.
3 A reference to Arbusto Energy, an oil and gas company founded by George W. Bush in 1984.

Whether we're talking about the US, Baltimore, or your wallet, a formalist is only happy when ownership and control are one and the same. To reformalize, therefore, we need to figure out who has actual power in the US, and assign shares in such a way as to reproduce this distribution as closely as possible.

Of course, if you believe in the mystical horseradish, you'll probably say that every citizen should get one share. But this is a rather starry-eyed view of the US's actual power structure. Remember, our goal is not to figure out who *should* have what, but to figure out who *does* have what.

For example, if the New York Times was to endorse our reformalization plan, it would be much more likely to happen. This suggests that the New York Times has quite a bit of power, and therefore that it should get quite a few shares.

But wait. We haven't answered the question. What is the purpose of the US? Suppose, solely for illustration, we give *all* the shares to the New York Times. What will **"Punch" Sulzberger** do with his shiny new country?

Many people, probably including Mr. Sulzberger, seem to think of the US as a charitable venture. Like the American Cancer Society, just with a broader mission. Perhaps the purpose of the US is simply to do good in the world.

This is a very understandable perspective. Surely, if anything ungood remains in the world, it can be vanquished by a gigantic, heavily armed mega-charity, with H-bombs, a flag, and 250 million serfs. In fact, it's actually rather astounding that, considering the prodigious endowments of this great philanthropic institution, it seems to do so little good.

Perhaps this has something to do with the fact that it's run so efficiently that it hasn't balanced its budget since the 1830s. Perhaps, if you reformalized the US, ran it like an actual business, and distributed its shares among a large set of separate charities, each presumably with some specific charter for some actual specific purpose, more good might occur.

Of course, the US doesn't just have assets. Sadly, it also has debts. Some of these debts, such as T-bills, are already very well-formalized. Others, such as Social Security and Medicare, are informal and subject to political uncertainties. If these obligations were reformalized, their recipients could only benefit. Of course, they would thus become negotiable instruments and could be, for example, sold. Perhaps in exchange for crack. Reformalization thus requires us to distinguish between property and charity, a hard problem but an important one.

All this fails to answer the question: are nation-states, such as the US, even useful? If you reformalized the US, the question would be left to its shareholders. Perhaps cities work the best when they're independently owned and operated. If so, they should probably be spun off as separate corporations.

The existence of successful city-states such as Singapore, Hong Kong and Dubai certainly suggests an answer to this question. Whatever we call them, these places are remarkable for their prosperity and their relative absence of politics. In fact, perhaps the only way to make them more stable and secure would be to transform them from effectively family-owned (Singapore and Dubai) or subsidiary

(Hong Kong) corporations, to anonymous public ownership, thus eliminating the long-term risk that political violence might develop.

Certainly, the absence of democracy in these city-states has not made them comparable in any way to Nazi Germany or the Soviet Union. Any restrictions on personal freedom that they do maintain seem primarily aimed at preventing the development of democracy—an understandable concern given the history of rule by the People. In fact, both the **Third Reich** and the **Communist world** often claimed to represent the true spirit of democracy.

As **Dubai** in particular shows, a government (like any corporation) can deliver excellent customer service without either owning or being owned by its customers. Most of Dubai's residents are not even citizens. If **Sheik Al Maktoum** has a cunning plan to seize them all, chain them and make them work in the salt mines, he's doing it in a very devious way.

Dubai, as a place, has almost nothing to recommend it. The weather is horrible, the sights are nonexistent, and the neighborhood is atrocious. It's tiny, in the middle of nowhere, and surrounded by Allah-crazed maniacs with a suspicious affinity for high-speed centrifuges. Nonetheless it has a quarter of the world's cranes and is growing like a weed. If we let the Maktoums run, say, Baltimore, what would happen?

One conclusion of formalism is that democracy is—as most writers before the 19th century agreed—an ineffective and destructive system of government. The concept of democracy without politics makes no sense at all, and as we've seen, politics and war are a continuum. Democratic politics is best understood as a sort of symbolic violence, like deciding who wins the battle by how many troops they brought.

Formalists attribute the success of Europe, Japan and the US after World War II not to democracy, but to its absence. While retaining the symbolic structures of democracy, much as the Roman Principate retained the Senate, the postwar Western system has assigned almost all actual decision-making power to its civil servants and judges, who are "apolitical" and "nonpartisan," i.e., nondemocratic.

Because in the absence of effective external control, these civil services more or less manage themselves, like any unmanaged enterprise they often seem to exist and expand for the sake of existing and expanding. But they avoid the **spoils system** which invariably develops when the tribunes of the people have actual power. And they do a reasonable, if hardly stellar, job of maintaining some semblance of law.

In other words, "democracy" appears to work because it is not in fact democracy, but a mediocre implementation of formalism. This relationship between symbolism and reality has received an educational if depressing test in the form of Iraq, where there is no law at all, but which we have endowed with the purest and most elegant form of democracy (proportional representation), and ministers who actually seem to run their ministries. While history does no controlled experiments, surely the comparison of Iraq to Dubai makes a fine case for formalism over democracy.

3 *Wallace Shawn*

 3 *progressivism*

 3 *conservatism*

4 *Roosevelt dictatorship* The significance of the FDR presidency—i.e., "dictatorship"—becomes a major theme throughout UR, including the posts "The case against democracy: ten red pills," "The Democrats: party of lies" and Chapters 7 & 8 of *An Open Letter to Open-Minded Progressives*

 4 *Mises Institute*

 4 *Misesian* Biography and detailed profile of Ludwig von Mises hosted at mises.org

 4 *Rothbardian* Ibid. Murray Rothbard, written by David Gordon.

 4 *read Rothbard* Llewellyn H. Rockwell Jr. "Read Rothbard." *Mises Institute*, Mises Daily Articles, 29 Jul. 2013.

 5 *legal formalism*: Legal scholar Brian Tamanaha, on his blog *Balkinization*, provides a definition of "legal formalism" from his colleague, Lawrence B. Solum: "The core idea of formalism is that the law (constitutions, statutes, regulations, and precedent) provides rules and that these rules can, do, and should provide a public standard for what is lawful (or not)." "Fellow Liberals: Be a 'Legal Formalist,' Join the Recovering Realists Club (Small Meetings Likely)." 29 Dec. 2006.

 5 *Vizzini* YouTube clip from Princess Bride of Vizzini comparing himself to the "morons" Plato, Aristotle and Socrates. See "Wallace Shawn" above.

 5 *surimi*

5 *Jouvenel*, Bertrand de. *On Power: The Natural History of Its Growth*. Liberty Fund, 2019.

5 *Kuehnelt-Leddihn*, Erik von. *Liberty or Equality: The Challenge of Our Time*. Mises Institute, 2014.

 5 *Leoni*, Bruno, and Arthur Kemp. *Freedom and the Law*. Liberty Fund, Incorporated, 2014.

 5 *Burnham*, James. *The Machiavellians: Defenders of Freedom*. Lume Books, 2020.

 5 *Nock*, Albert Jay. *Memoirs of a Superfluous Man*. Ludwig Von Mises Institute, 2016.

 6 *pacifism*

 6 *hundredth-monkey* A discredited sociology concept to account for seemingly spontaneous cultural transmission, but which nonetheless has become a popular feature of "New Age" epistemology.

 7 *social justice*

 8 *serf*

 9 *rather recent development* Nick Szabo, on his blog *Unenumerated*, makes the case that a limited legal distinction between public and private corporations has been the predominant view from medieval Royal law onward, and is necessary for understanding the formation of the United States government and the language and substance of its Constitution. Ultimately this builds toward a far more expansive view of the powers of the Executive, and creates a clear precedent for the corporate model of governance expounded upon by Moldbug in subsequent posts, notably in *Patchwork: A Political System for the 21st Century*.

 9 *employees* "Dismissal of U.S. attorneys controversy"

 9 *Jack Welch*

 9 *mean* "Arbusto Energy"

LINKS & NOTES

 9 ox entrails "Haruspex"

 9 corporate prayers "Bellamy salute"

 9 war chants "Battle Hymn of the Republic"

 10 "Pinch" Sulzberger

 10 debts The US federal debt was roughly $8.5 trillion at the time of this post. David M. Walker, Comptroller General. "Bureau of the Public Debt's Fiscal Years 2007 and 2006 Schedules of Federal Debt." *U.S. Government Accountability Office,* Nov. 2007.

 11 Third Reich Link to a Google search for "nazi plebiscites"

 11 Communist world Link to a Google search for "people's democracy"

 11 Dubai Anthony Shadid. "The Towering Dream of Dubai." *Washington Post,* 30 Apr. 2006.

 11 Sheik Al Maktoum

 11 spoils system

AN OPEN LETTER TO OPEN-MINDED PROGRESSIVES

CHAPTER 1:
A HORIZON MADE OF CANVAS
APRIL 17, 2008

Are you an open-minded progressive? Maybe not, but you probably have friends who are. This is for them. Perhaps it can serve as a sort of introduction to this strange blog, **Unqualified Reservations**.

If you are an open-minded progressive, you are probably not a Catholic. (If you are, you probably don't take the Pope too seriously.) Imagine writing an open letter to Catholics, suggesting ways for them to free their minds from the insidious grip of Rome. That sort of thing is quite out of style these days—and in any case, how would you start? But here at UR, we are never afraid of being out of style. And as for starting, we already have.

Is being a progressive like being a Catholic? Why shouldn't it be? Each is a way of understanding the world through a set of beliefs. These beliefs may be true, they may be false, they may be **nonsense**[1] which does not even make enough sense to be false. As an open-minded progressive (or an open-minded Catholic), you would like to think all the beliefs you hold are true, but you are willing to reevaluate them—perhaps with a little gentle assistance.

There is one big difference between Catholicism and progressivism: Catholicism is what we call a "religion." Its core beliefs are claims about the spirit world, which no Catholic (except of course the Pope) has experienced firsthand. Whereas progressive beliefs tend to be claims about the real world—about government and

1

history and economics and society. These are phenomena which, unlike the Holy Trinity, we all experience firsthand.

Or do we? Most of us have never worked for a government, and those who have have seen only some tiny corner of one. History is something out of a book. It isn't the Bible, but it might as well be. What is our personal experience of economics? Gasoline prices? And so on. Unless your life has been both long and quite unusual, I suspect your memories shed very little light on the great questions of government, history, etc. Mine certainly don't.

Of course, much of progressive thought claims to be a product of pure reason. Is it? Thomas Aquinas derived Catholicism from pure reason. John Rawls derived progressivism from pure reason. At least one of them must have made a mistake. Maybe they both did. Have you checked their work? One bad variable will bust your whole proof.

And is this really how it happened? Are you a progressive because you started by believing in nothing at all ("We are nihilists! We believe in nothing!"), thought it through, and wound up a progressive? Of course I can't speak for your own experience, but I suspect that either you are a progressive because your parents were progressives, or you were converted by some book, teacher, or other intellectual experience. Note that this is exactly how one becomes a Catholic.

There is one difference, though. To be a Catholic, you have to have *faith*, because no one has ever seen the Holy Ghost. To be a progressive, you have to have *trust*, because you believe that your worldview accurately reflects the real world—as experienced not just by your own small eyes, but by humanity as a whole.

But you have not shared humanity's experience. You have only read, heard and seen a corpus of text, audio and video compiled from it. And compiled by whom? Which is where the trust comes in. More on this in a little bit.

I am not a progressive, but I was raised as one. I live in San Francisco, I grew up as a Foreign Service brat, I went to Brown, I've been brushing my teeth with Tom's of Maine since the mid-80s. What happened to me is that I lost my trust.

David Mamet lost his trust, too. His Village Voice essay[2] is worth reading, if just for the shock value of the world's most famous playwright declaring that he's no longer a "brain-dead liberal." There are about five hundred comments on the article. Perhaps I missed one, but I didn't notice any in which the commenter claimed that Mamet had opened his eyes.

Of course, Mamet is Mamet. He's out to shock, not convert. Even the word "liberal," at least as it refers to a present-day political persuasion, borders on hate speech. It's like an ex-Catholic explaining "why I am no longer a brain-dead Papist." John Stuart Mill was a liberal. Barack Obama is a progressive, and so are you. Basic rule of politeness: don't call people names they don't call themselves.

2

AN OPEN LETTER TO OPEN-MINDED PROGRESSIVES

Worse, Mamet doesn't just reject progressivism. He endorses conservatism. Dear God! Talk about making your problem harder. Imagine you live in a country in which everyone is one of two things: a Catholic or a Hindu. Isn't it hard enough to free a man's mind from the insidious grip of Rome? Must he accept Kali, Krishna and Ganesha at the same time?

For example, Mamet endorses the conservative writer **Thomas Sowell**, who he claims is "our greatest contemporary philosopher." Well. I like Thomas Sowell, his work is certainly not without value, but really. And if you Google him, you will see that his columns frequently appear on a conservative website called **townhall.com**.[3]

Click that link. Observe the *atrocious* graphic design. (Have you noticed how far above the rest Obama's graphic design is? Some font designers **have**.) Observe the general horribleness, so reminiscent of Fox News. Then hit "back." Or, I don't know, read an Ann Coulter column, or something. Dear Lord.

I am not a progressive, but I'm not a conservative either. (If you must know, I'm a **Jacobite**.) Over time, I have acquired the ability to process American conservative thought—if generally somewhat upmarket from Fox News or townhall.com. This is an extremely acquired taste, if "taste" is even the word. It is probably very similar to the way Barack Obama handled the **Rev. Wright's more colorful sermons**.[4] When David Mamet points his readers in the general direction of townhall.com, it's sort of like explaining to your uncle who's a little bit phobic that he can understand the value of gay rights by watching this great movie—it's called *120 Days of Sodom*. It's not actual communication. It's a fuck-you. It's Mamet.

But many people will think exactly this: if you stop being a progressive, you have to become a conservative. I suspect that the primary emotional motivation for most progressives is that they're progressives because they think something needs to be done about conservatives. Game over. Gutterball. Right back to the insidious grip.

Where does this idea that, if NPR is wrong, Fox News must be right, come from? They can't both be right, because they contradict each other. But couldn't they both be wrong? I don't mean slightly wrong, I don't mean each is half right and each is half wrong, I don't mean the truth is somewhere between them, I mean *neither* of them *has any consistent relationship to reality*.

Let's think about this for a second. As a progressive, you believe—you must believe—that conservatism is a mass delusion. What an extraordinary thing! A hundred-plus million people, many quite dull but some remarkably intelligent, all acting under a kind of mass hypnosis. We take this for granted. We are used to it. But we have to admit that it's really, really weird.

---

[3]  townhall.com archived link from April 17, 2008.

[4] Days after 9/11, Wright delivered a sermon, "The Day of Jerusalem's Fall," declaring that "America's chickens are coming home to roost."

What you have to believe is that conservatives have been *systematically misinformed*. They are not stupid—at least not all of them. Nor are they evil. You can spend all the time you want on townhall.com, and you will not find anyone cackling like Gollum over their evil plan to enslave and destroy the world. They all think, just like you, that by being conservatives they are standing up for what's sweet and good and true.

Conservatism is a theory of government held by a large number of people who have no personal experience of government. They hold this theory because their chosen information sources, such as Fox News, townhall.com, and their local megachurch, feed them a steady diet of facts (and possibly a few non-facts) which tend to support, reinforce, and confirm the theory.

And why does this strange pattern exist? Because conservatism is not just an ordinary opinion. Suppose instead of a theory of government, conservatism was a theory of basketball. "Conservatism" would be a system of views about the pick-and-roll, the outside game, the triangle defense and other issues of great importance to basketball players and coaches.

The obvious difference is that, unless you are a basketball coach, your opinions on basketball matter not at all—because basketball is not a democracy. The players don't even get a vote, let alone the fans. But conservatism can maintain a systematic pattern of delusion, because its fans are not just fans: they are supporters of a political machine. This machine will disappear if it cannot keep its believers, so it has an incentive to keep them. And it does. Funny how that works.

So, as a progressive, here is how you see American democracy: as a contest in which truth and reason are pitted against a quasicriminal political machine built on propaganda, ignorance and misinformation. Perhaps a cynical view of the world, but if you believe that progressivism is right, you must believe that conservatism is wrong, and you have no other option.

But there is an even more pessimistic view. Suppose American democracy is not a contest between truth and reason and a quasicriminal political machine, but a contest between *two* quasicriminal political machines? Suppose progressivism is just like conservatism? If it was, who would tell you?

Think of conservatism as a sort of mental disease. Virus X, transmitted by Fox News much as mosquitoes transmit malaria, has infected the brains of half the American population—causing them to believe that George W. Bush is a "regular guy," global warming isn't happening, and the US Army can bring democracy to Sadr City. Fortunately, the other half of America is protected by its progressive antibodies, which it imbibes every day in the healthy mother's milk of the Times and NPR, allowing it to bask securely in the sweet light of truth.

Or is it? Note that we've just postulated two classes of entity: viruses and antibodies, mosquitoes and mother's milk. **William of Ockham** wouldn't be happy. Isn't it simpler to imagine that we're dealing with a virus Y? Rather than one set of people being infected and the other being immune, everyone is infected—just with different strains.

AN OPEN LETTER TO OPEN-MINDED PROGRESSIVES

What makes virus X a virus is that, like the shark in *Jaws*, its only goals in life are to eat, swim around, and make baby viruses. In other words, its features are best explained adaptively. If it can succeed by accurately representing reality, it will do so. For example, you and I and virus X agree on the subject of the international Jewish conspiracy: there is no such thing. We disagree with the evil virus N, which fortunately is scarce these days. This can be explained in many ways, but one of the simplest is that if Fox News stuck a swastika in its logo and told Bill O'Reilly to start raving about the Elders of Zion, its ratings would probably go down.

This is what I mean by "no consistent relationship to reality." If, for whatever reason, an error is better at replicating within the conservative mind than the truth, conservatives will come to believe the error. If the truth is more adaptive, they will come to believe the truth. It's fairly easy to see how an error could make a better story than the truth on Fox News, which is why one would be ill-advised to get one's truth from that source.

So our first small step toward doubt is easy: we simply allow ourselves to suspect that the institutions which progressives trust are fallible in the same way. If NPR can replicate errors just as Fox News does, we are indeed looking at a virus Y. Virus Y may be right when virus X is wrong, wrong when virus X is right, right when virus X is wrong, or wrong when virus X is wrong. Since the two have no consistent relationship to reality, they have no consistent relationship to each other.

There's a seductive symmetry to this theory: it solves the problem of how one half of a society, which (by global and historical standards) doesn't seem *that* different from the other, can be systematically deluded while the other half is quite sane. The answer: it isn't.

Moreover, it explains a bizarre contradiction which emerges beautifully in Mamet's piece. At one point he writes, in his new conservative persona:

What about the role of government? Well, in the abstract, coming from my time and background, I thought it was a rather good thing, but tallying up the ledger in those things which affect me and in those things I observe, I am hard-pressed to see an instance where the intervention of the government led to much beyond sorrow.

But earlier, he told us:

As a child of the '60s, I accepted as an article of faith that government is corrupt, that business is exploitative, and that people are generally good at heart.

Okay, Dave. As a child of the '60s, you accepted as an article of faith that government is bad, but now you believe that... government is bad? Who's doin' donuts on the road to Damascus?

One of the fascinating facts of American politics today is that *both* progressives and conservatives hate their government. They just hate different parts of it, and they love and cherish the others. In foreign policy, for example, progressives hate the Pentagon, and love and cherish the State Department. Conservatives hate the State Department, and love and cherish the Pentagon.

CHAPTER 1

Look at how nicely this fits in with our virus X–Y theory. Washington contains many mansions, some of which are part of the virus X machine, others of which are perma-infected with virus Y. Outside the Beltway is our herd of drooling, virus-ridden zombie voters. The X zombies hate the Y agencies, the Y zombies hate the X agencies.

But *none* of them hates Washington as a whole. So they can never unite to destroy it, and the whole machine is stable. See how beautiful this is? By separating voters into two competing but cooperating parties, neither of which can destroy the other, the two-party system creates a government which will survive indefinitely, no matter how much happier its citizens might be without it.

This is the prize at the end of our mystery. If you can find a way to stop being a progressive without becoming a conservative, you might even find a way to *actually oppose the government*. At the very least, you can decide that none of these politicians, movements or institutions is *even remotely* worthy of your support. Trust me—it's a very liberating feeling.

But we are nowhere near there yet. We have not actually found a genuine reason to doubt progressivism. Minor errors—some little fact-checking mistake at the Times or whatever—don't count, because they don't do anything about your conviction that progressivism is basically right and conservatism is basically wrong. Even with a few small eccentricities, progressivism as a cure for conservatism is worth keeping. It may not be an antibody, but perhaps virus Y is at least a vaccine.

Moreover, we've overlooked some major asymmetries between the progressive and conservative movements. They are not each others' evil twins. They are very different things. It is quite plausible that one would be credible and the other wouldn't, and the advantages all seem to be on the progressive side.

First of all, let's look at the *people* who are progressives. As the expressions "blue-state" and "red-state" indicate, progressives and conservatives in America today are different tribes. They are not randomly distributed opinions. They follow clear patterns.

My wife and I had a daughter a few weeks ago, and right before she was due to be discharged the doctors found a minor (and probably harmless) heart problem which required a brief visit from UCSF's head of pediatric cardiology. A very pleasant person. And one of the first things he said, part of his bedside manner, a way of putting us at ease, was a remark about George W. Bush. Somehow I suspect that if he had diagnosed us as hicks from Stockton, he would not have emitted this noise.

Rather, the good doctor had identified us as members of the **Stuff White People Like**[5] tribe. This little satirical site has attracted roughly 100 times UR's traffic in a tenth the time, which is a pretty sure sign that it's on to something. The author, Chris Lander, really only has one joke: he's describing a group that doesn't like to be described, and he's assigned them the last name they'd choose for themselves.

5

AN OPEN LETTER TO OPEN-MINDED PROGRESSIVES   25

Lander's "white people" are indeed overwhelmingly white, as anyone who has been to **Burning Man** can testify. But there are plenty of "white people" who are Asian, or even black or Latino. In fact, as **Lander points out**, "white people" are the opposite of racist—they are desperate to have minorities around. Thus the humor of calling them "white." In fact, as anyone who went to an integrated high school can testify, Lander's use of the word "white" is almost exactly the black American usage—as in, "that's so white." Add the word "bread" and you have it down.

Who are these strange people? Briefly, they are America's ruling class. Here at UR we call them *Brahmins*. The Brahmin tribe is adoptive rather than hereditary. Anyone can be a Brahmin, and in fact the less "white" your background the better, because it means your achievements are all your own. As with the Hindu original, your status as a Brahmin is not a function of money, but of your success as a scholar, scientist, artist, or public servant. Brahmins are people who work with their minds.

Brahmins are the ruling class because they are literally the people who govern. Public policies in the modern democratic system are generally formulated by Brahmins, typically at the **NGOs** where these "white people" like to congregate. And while not every progressive is a Brahmin and not every Brahmin is a progressive, the equation generally follows.

Most important, the Brahmin identity is inextricably bound up with the American university system. If you are a Brahmin, your status is either conferred by academic success, or by some quasi-academic achievement, like writing a book, saving the Earth, etc. Thus it's unsurprising that most Brahmins are quite intelligent and sophisticated. They have to be. If they can't at least fake it, they're not Brahmins.

The natural enemy of the Brahmin is, of course, the red-state American. I used to use another Hindu caste name for this tribe—*Vaisyas*—but I think it's more evocative to call them *Townies*. As a progressive you are probably a Brahmin, you know these people, and you don't like them. They are fat, they are *exclusively* white, they live in the suburbs or worse, they are into oak and crochet and minivans, and of course they tend to be Republicans. If they went to college at all, they gritted their teeth through the freshman diversity requirement. And their work may be white-collar, but it has no real intellectual content.

(It's interesting how much simpler American politics becomes once you look at it through this tribal lens. You often see this in Third World countries—there will be, say, the Angolan People's Movement and the Democratic Angolan Front. Each will swear up and down that they work for the future of the entire Angolan people. But you notice that everyone in the APM is an Ovambo, and everyone in the DAF is a Bakongo.)

The status relationship between Brahmins and Townies is clear: Brahmins are higher, Townies are lower. When Brahmins hate Townies, the attitude is contempt. When Townies hate Brahmins, the attitude is resentment. The two are impossible to confuse. If Brahmins and Townies shared a **stratified dialect**, the Brahmins would speak acrolect and the Townies mesolect.

In other words, Brahmins are *more fashionable* than Townies. Brahmin tastes, which are basically better tastes, flow downward toward Townies. Twenty years ago, "health food" was a niche ultra-Brahmin quirk. Now it's everywhere. Suburbanites drink espresso, shop at Whole Foods, listen to alternative rock, you name it.

Thus we see why progressivism is more fashionable than conservatism. Progressive celebrities, for example, are everywhere. Conservative ones are exceptions. Although many progressive celebrities appear to be quite sincere in their beliefs, cold calculation would suffice: Bono's PR people are happy that he's speaking out against AIDS. Mel Gibson's PR people are not happy that he's speaking out against the Jews.[6]

So when we question conservatism, we are thinking in a way that is natural and sensible for people of our tribe: we are attacking the enemy. And the enemy is, indeed, a pushover. In fact the enemy is suspiciously easy to push over.

Look at the entire lifecycle of conservatism. The whole thing stinks. Virus X replicates in the minds of uneducated, generally less intelligent people. Townies are, in fact, the same basic tribe that gave us Hitler and Mussolini. Its intellectual institutions, such as they are, are subsidized fringe newspapers, TV channels, and weirdo think-tanks supported by eccentric tycoons. In government, the bastions of conservatism are the military, whose purpose is to kill people, and any agency in which corporate lobbyists can make a buck, e.g., by raping the environment.

Whereas virus Y, if "virus" is indeed the name for it, replicates in the most distinguished circles in America, indeed the world: the top universities, the great newspapers, the old foundations such as Rockefeller and Carnegie and Ford. Its drooling zombies are the smartest and most successful people in the country, indeed the world. In government it builds world peace, protects the environment, looks after the poor, and educates children.

The truth of the matter is that progressivism *is* the mainstream American tradition. This is not to say it hasn't changed in the last 200 years, or even the last 50: it has. However, if we look at the ideas and ideals taught and studied at Harvard during the life of the country, we see a smooth progression up to now, we do not see any violent reversals or even inflection points, and we end up with good old modern-day progressivism. Of course, by "American tradition" we mean the New England tradition—if the Civil War had turned out differently, things might have gone otherwise. But when you realize that Nathaniel Hawthorne wrote *The Blithedale Romance* about a hippie commune 150 years ago, you realize that nothing is new under the sun.

As Machiavelli put it: if you strike at a king, strike to kill. Conservatism, which is barely 50 years old, and which has numerous shabby roots, can be mocked and belittled and scorned. The difference between criticizing conservatism and criticizing progressivism is the difference between criticizing Mormonism and criticizing

---

6 Reference to Gibson's DUI arrest in 2006 when he told the arresting officer, "Fucking Jews...the Jews are responsible for all the wars in the world. Are you a Jew?" Gibson's comments were met with broad public opprobrium.

Christianity. You can't doubt progressivism just a little. You have to doubt it on a grand scale.

To say that conservatism is a corrupt and delusional tradition, no more than some "virus X," is to say that it's a tick on the side of America, an aberration, an abortion, an error to be corrected. A failure of education, of leadership, of progress. A small thing, really.

To doubt progressivism is to doubt the American idea itself—because progressivism is where that idea has ended up. If progressivism is "virus Y," America itself is infected. What is the cure for that? It is a strange and terrible thought, a promise of apocalypse.

And yet it makes an awful kind of sense. For one thing, if you were a mental virus, which tradition would you choose to infect? The central current of American thought, or some benighted backwater? The Brahmins, or the Townies? The fashionable people, or the unfashionable ones?

Copy your DNA into the New York Times, and it will trickle down to Fox News in twenty or thirty years. Copy yourself into Fox News, and you might influence the next election. Or two. But how lasting is that? How many people are intellectually moved by George W. Bush? (Repulsion doesn't count.)

As a Brahmin (I'll assume you're a Brahmin), you live inside virus Y. You are one of the zombies. Your entire worldview has been formed by Harvard, the Times, and the rest of what, back in David Mamet's day, they used to call the Establishment. Everything you know about government and history and science and society has been filtered by these institutions. Obviously, this narrative does not contradict itself. But is it true?

Well, it mostly doesn't contradict itself. It's very well put together. In some places, though, if you look really closely, I think you can see a stitch or two. You don't need to sail to the edge of the world, like Jim Carrey in *The Truman Show*. All you need, for starters, just to tickle your doubt muscle and get it twitching a little, is a few details that don't quite fit.

Let's start off with three questions. We'll play a little game: you try coming up with a progressive answer, I'll try coming up with a non-progressive answer. We'll see which one makes more sense.

I don't mean these questions don't have progressive answers, because they do. Everything has a progressive answer, just as it has a conservative answer. There is no shortage of progressives to compose answers. But I don't think these questions have *satisfying* progressive answers. Of course, you will have to judge this yourself with your own good taste.

One: what's up with the Third World?

Here, for example, is a Times story[7] on the fight against malaria. Often, as with politicians, journalists speak the truth in a fit of absent-mindedness, when

---

7

their real concern is something else. If you read the story, you might notice the same astounding graf that I did:

> And the world changed. Before the 1960s, colonial governments and companies fought malaria because their officials often lived in remote outposts like Nigeria's hill stations and Vietnam's Marble Mountains. Independence movements led to freedom, but also often to civil war, poverty, corrupt government and the collapse of medical care.

Let's focus on that last sentence. *Independence movements led to freedom, but also often to civil war, poverty, corrupt government and the collapse of medical care.*

I often find it useful to imagine that I'm an alien from the planet Jupiter. If I read this sentence, I would ask: what is this word *freedom*? What, exactly, does this writer mean by *freedom*? Especially in the context of *civil war, poverty, and corrupt government*?

What we see here is that *independence movements*—which the writer clearly believes are a good thing—led to some very concrete and very, very awful results, in addition to this curious abstraction—*freedom*. Clearly, whatever *freedom* means in this particular context, it's such a great positive that even when you add it to *civil war, poverty, corrupt government and the collapse of medical care,* the result still exceeds zero.

Isn't that strange? Might we not be tempted to revisit this particular piece of arithmetic? But we can't—because if we postulate that *colonial governments and companies* (whatever these were), with their absence of *freedom,* were somehow preferable to *independence movements,* which created this same *freedom* (the words *freedom* and *independence* appear to be synonyms in this context), we are off the progressive reservation.

In fact, not only are we off the progressive reservation, we're off the *conservative* reservation. No one believes this. You will not find anyone on Fox News or townhall.com or any but the fringiest of fringe publications claiming that colonialism, with its intrinsic absence of *freedom* and its strangely effective malaria control (note how the writer implies, without actually saying, that this was only delivered for the selfish purposes of the evil colonial overlords), was in any way superior to postcolonialism, with its *freedom,* its malaria, its civil war, etc.

And what, exactly, is this word *independence*? It seems to mean the same thing as *freedom*, and yet, it is strange. For example, consider this Post op-ed,[8] by Michelle Gavin of the Council on Foreign Relations, which starts with the following intriguing lines:

8

AN OPEN LETTER TO OPEN-MINDED PROGRESSIVES

When Zimbabwe became an independent country in 1980, it was a focal point for international optimism about Africa's future. Today, Zimbabwe is a basket case of a country.

Let's put our alien-from-Jupiter hat back on, and consider the phrase: *When Zimbabwe became an independent country in 1980...*

In English as she is normally spoke, the word *independent* is composed of the prefix *in*, meaning "not," and the suffix *dependent*, meaning "dependent." So, for example, when the United States became *independent*, it meant that no external party was funding or controlling her government. If my daughter were to become *independent*, it would mean that she was making her own decisions in the world, and I didn't need to give her a bottle every three hours.

In the case of Zimbabwe, however, this word seems to have changed strangely and taken on an almost opposite meaning. From **La Wik**:

> The Unilateral Declaration of Independence (UDI) of Rhodesia from the United Kingdom was signed on November 11, 1965 by the administration of Ian Smith, whose Rhodesian Front party opposed black majority rule in the then British colony. Although it declared independence from the United Kingdom it maintained allegiance to Queen Elizabeth II. The British government, the Commonwealth, and the United Nations condemned the move as illegal. Rhodesia reverted to de facto and de jure British control as "the British Dependency of Southern Rhodesia" for a brief period in 1979 to 1980, before regaining its independence as Zimbabwe in 1980.

So, strangely enough, the country now known as Zimbabwe declared *independence* in 1965, much as the US declared *independence* in 1776. The former, however, was not *genuine* independence, but rather *illegal* independence. In order to gain genuine, *legal* independence, the country now known as Zimbabwe had to first revert to British control, i.e., surrender its *illegal* independence. Are you feeling confused yet? It gets better:

> When Zimbabwe became an independent country in 1980, it was a focal point for international optimism about Africa's future. Today, Zimbabwe is a basket case of a country. Over the past decade, the refusal of President Robert Mugabe and his ruling party to tolerate challenges to their power has led them to systematically dismantle the most effective workings of Zimbabwe's economic and political systems, replacing these with structures of corruption, blatant patronage and repression.

So: the *independent* rulers of the new, *free* Zimbabwe have *refused to tolerate challenges to their power*. Thus, the *international optimism* held by Ms. Gavin (who perhaps needed a bottle or two herself in 1980) and her ilk, has given way to pessimism, and the place is now a *basket case*. And who might have been challenging good President Mugabe's power? Presumably someone who did not intend to dismantle *the most effective workings of Zimbabwe's economic and political systems*—thus earning the friendship of Ms. Gavin and her not-uninfluential ilk. This *independence*, as you can see, is a very curious thing.

In the sense of doing its own thing and never, ever needing a bottle, there is actually one remarkably independent country in the world. It's called **Somaliland**, and it is not *recognized* by anyone in the *international community*. The Wikipedia page for Somaliland's capital, **Hargeisa**, achieves a glorious level of unintentional high comedy:

> Aid from foreign governments was non-existent, making it unusual in Africa for its low level of dependence in foreign aid. While Somaliland is de-facto as an independent country it is not de-jure (legally) recognized internationally. Hence, the government of Somaliland can not access IMF and World Bank assistance.

Isn't all of this quite curious? Doesn't it remind you even a little bit of the scene in which Jim Carrey rams his yacht into the matte painting at the edge of the world?

Two: what is nationalism? And is it good, or bad?

This question is rather similar to question one. I thought of it when a **progressive blogger**[9] for whom I have great respect made the offhand comment that "Ho Chi Minh was a nationalist." "Sure," I found myself thinking. "And so is Pat Buchanan." It wasn't the time, but I saved this little *mot d'escalier* and can't resist bringing it back up now, like bad fish.

Unlike *independence*, I think everyone pretty much agrees on the definition of *nationalism*. Nationalism (from the Latin *natus*, birth) is when people of a common linguistic, ethnic, or racial heritage feel the need to act collectively as a single political entity. German nationalism is when Germans do it, Vietnamese nationalism is when Vietnamese do it, black nationalism is when African-Americans do it, American nationalism is when Pat Buchanan does it.

And this is where the agreement ends. La Wik's **opening paragraph** on Nationalism is a masterpiece of obfuscation:

> Nationalism is a term referring to a doctrine or political movement that holds that a nation, usually defined in terms of eth-

---

9  Cassandra of *Cassandra Does Tokyo*.

nicity or culture, has the right to constitute an independent or autonomous political community based on a shared history and common destiny. Most nationalists believe the borders of the state should be congruent with the borders of the nation. However, recently nationalists have rejected the concept of "congruency" for sake of its reciprocal value. Contemporary nationalists would argue that the nation should be administered by a single state, not that a state should be governed by a single nation. Occasionally, nationalist efforts can be plagued by chauvinism or imperialism. These ex-nationalist efforts such as those propagated by fascist movements in the twentieth century, still hold the nationalist concept that nationality is the most important aspect of one's identity, while some of them have attempted to define the nation, inaccurately, in terms of race or genetics. Fortunately, contemporary nationalists reject the racist chauvinism of these groups, and remain confident that national identity supersedes biological attachment to an ethnic group.

Everything between them is pure nonsense as far as I can tell, but note the direct contradiction of the first and the last sentences. How can you be a *nationalist*, even a *contemporary nationalist*, if you believe that *national identity supersedes biological attachment to an ethnic group*? If nationalism isn't *plagued* by *racist chauvinism*, in what sense is it nationalism at all?

And so: if I'm a Czech and I live in Austria-Hungary, do I have a right to my own country? Should I make violence and terror and bomb until I get it? What if I'm a German and I live in Czechoslovakia? Should I make violence and terror and bomb?

A number of Germans noticed this very odd thing in the '20s and '30s. They noticed that America and her friends were very much committed to *national self-determination*, that is, unless you happened to be German. Czech nationalism was good—very good. German nationalism was bad—very bad.

Once you start looking for this little stitch in the canvas, you find it everywhere. It is good, very good, to be a black nationalist. In *l'affaire Wright*[10] we have seen the intimacy between progressivism and black nationalism—so well illustrated in Tom Wolfe's **Radical Chic & Mau Mauing the Flak Catchers**. Indeed, every reputable university in America has a department in which students can essentially major in black nationalism.

On the other hand, it is bad, very bad, to be a Southern nationalist. Any connection to Southern nationalism instantly renders one a pariah.[11] Of course,

---

10 See footnote 4 above.
11 Reference to Trent Lott's resignation as Senate Republican leader in 2002 on the heels of a public statement in support of Strom Thurmond's 1948 Dixiecrat Presidential bid.

Southern nationalists have **sinned**.[12] But then again, so have black **nationalists**.[13] Are Americans, black or white, really better off for the activities of the Black Panthers, the Nation of Islam, or even the good Rev. Wright?

Similarly, it is good to be a Vietnamese nationalist. It is still bad to be a German nationalist, or a British nationalist, or even a French nationalist. Germans, Brits, and Frenchmen are supposed to believe in the common destiny of all humanity. Vietnamese, Mexicans, or Czechs are free to believe in the common destiny of Vietnamese, Mexicans, or Czechs. (Actually, I'm not sure about the Czechs. This one may have changed.)

Does this make sense? Does it make *any freakin' sense at all*?

Since this subject is so touchy, I will let my feelings on it slip: I don't believe in any kind of nationalism. Of course, being a Jacobite and all, I also believe in Strafford's **Thorough**, so you might not want to be getting your constitutional tips from me.

Three: why are the Nazis considered to be so much worse than other comparably murderous groups?

There's no question that the Nazis murdered ten million people or so. That's bad. There's really no defending the unprovoked massacre of millions of civilians.

On the other hand, I really really recommend *Human Smoke* by **Nicholson Baker**, which (according to the book blurb) gives "a wide-ranging, astonishingly fresh perspective on the political and social landscape that gave rise to World War II." Baker is a progressive and pacifist of immaculate credentials (his previous achievement was a novel which fantasized about assassinating President Bush), and what *Human Smoke* drums into you is not a specific message, but the same thing I keep saying: the pieces of the picture do not fit together. They almost fit, but they don't quite fit. The genius of Baker's book is that he simply shows you the picture not fitting, and leaves the analysis up to you.

For example: we are taught that the Nazis were bad because they committed mass murder, to wit, the Holocaust. On the other hand... (a): none of the parties fighting against the Nazis, including us, seems to have given much of a damn about the Jews or the Holocaust; (b): one of the parties on our side was the Soviet Union, whose record of mass murder was known at the time and was at least as awful as the Nazis'.

And, of course, (c): the Allies positively reveled in the aerial mass incineration of German and Japanese civilians. They didn't kill six million, but they killed one or two. There was a military excuse for this, but it was quite strained. It was better than the Nazis' excuse for murdering the Jews (who they saw, of course, as enemy civilians), but the death toll was still appalling.

And as Baker does not mention, our heroes, the Allies, also had no qualms about deporting **a million Russian refugees** to the gulag after the war, or about lending hundreds of thousands of German prisoners as **slave laborers** to the So-

---

12 Reference to the Klu Klux Klan.
13 Reference to the racially motivated anti-white "Zebra Murders" of the 1970's.

viets. The idea of World War II as a war for human rights is simply ahistorical. It doesn't fit. If Nazi human-rights violations were not the motivation for the war that created the world we live in now—what was?

Furthermore, Baker, who is of course a critic of American foreign policy today, sees nothing but confusion when he tries to apply the same standards to Iraq and to Germany. If **Abu Ghraib** is an unbridgeable obstacle to imposing democracy by force on Iraq, what about the bombing of **Dresden** or **Hamburg** and Germany? Surely it's worse to burn tens of thousands of people alive, than to make one **stand on a box**[14] wearing fake wires and a funny hat? Or is Iraq just different from Germany? But that would be racism, wouldn't it?

Beyond this is the peculiar asymmetry in the treatment of fascist mass murder, versus Marxist mass murder. Both ideologies clearly have a history of mass murder. If numbers count—and why wouldn't they?—Marxism is ahead by an **order of magnitude**.[15] Yet somehow, today, fascism or anything reminiscent of it is pure poison and untouchable, whereas Marxism is at best a kind of peccadillo. John Zmirak pulls off a lovely parody of this **here**,[16] and while I have yet to read **Roberto Bolaño** the **reviews**[17] are quite glowing.

Neither the Soviet Union nor the Third Reich is with us today, but the most recent historical examples are North Korea and South Africa. North Korea is clearly somewhat Stalinist, while apartheid South Africa had looser but still discernible links to Nazism. I welcome anyone who wants to claim that South Africa, whose border fences were designed to keep immigrants out, was a worse violator of human rights than North Korea, an entire country turned into a prison. And yet we see the same asymmetry—"**engagement**"[18] with North Korea, pure hostility against South Africa. If you can imagine the New York Philharmonic visiting Pretoria in an attempt to build trust between the two countries, you are firmly in Bolañoworld.

Again: this is just weird. As with nationalism, each individual case can be explained on its own terms. Put all the cases together, and double standards are everywhere. And yet the inconsistencies do not seem random. There seems to be a mysterious X factor which the Nazis have and the Soviets don't, or the South Africans have and the North Koreans don't. The treatment may not just be based on X, it

---

14 Famous Abu Ghraib prisoner photo, "The Hooded Man."

15 Reference to the 1997 book *The Black Book of Communism* edited by Stéphane Courtois.

16

17 NYT review of Bolaño's *Nazi Literature in the Americas* (2008).

18 Reference to 2008 New York Philharmonic concert in Pyongyang, North Korea.

may be X + human rights, but it is definitely not just human rights. And yet X does not appear in the explanation.

X seems to be related to the fact that the Nazis are "right-wing" and the Soviets "left-wing." As the French put it: *pas d'ennemis à gauche, pas d'amis à droite*.[19] But why? What do "right-wing" and "left-wing" even mean? Weren't the Soviet and Nazi systems both totalitarian dictatorships? If Communism is "too hot," fascism is "too cold," and liberal democracy is "just right," why not oppose Communism and fascism equally? In fact, the former is much more successful, at least since 1945, so you'd think people would be more worried about it.

Again, we are left with pure confusion. It is simply not possible that the horizon is made of canvas. And yet our boat has crashed into it, and left a big rip.

---

[19] "No enemies to the left, no friends to the right."

AN OPEN LETTER TO OPEN-MINDED PROGRESSIVES

 19 *Unqualified Reservations*

 19 *nonsense,* archived link to Chapter 7 of philosopher David Stove's *The Plato Cult and Other Philosophical Follies* (Blackwell, 1991) in which he discusses problems of philosophy inherent in the abuses of language.

 20 *nihilists* YouTube clip from *The Big Lebowski.*

 20 *Tom's of Maine*

 20 *David Mamet*

 20 *Village Voice essay,* David Mamet. "Why I Am No Longer a 'Brain-Dead Liberal'." *The Village Voice,* 11 Mar. 2008.

 21 *Thomas Sowell*

 21 *townhall.com* web archive from April 17, 2008.

 21 *have,* "Good Fonts, Bad Fonts and the Presidency." *Typography.com* (Hoefler & Co.), captured on 7 Jan. 2020.

 21 *Jacobite*

 21 *Rev. Wright*

21 more colorful sermons, Rev. Jeremiah Wright's most controversial sermon, "The Day of Jerusalem's Fall," was delivered a few days after 9/11, where he quoted Malcolm X, saying that "America's chickens are coming home to roost," among other inflammatory statements implying the US, at least in part, brought the attacks on itself. In a later sermon, "Confusing God and Government," delivered in 2003, Wright proclaimed "No, no, no. Not God Bless America. God damn America." These statements, and others like them, were interpreted by the media as generally anti-American and forced Obama to carefully distance himself from the reverend.

21 120 Days of Sodom A controversial 1975 Italian film loosely based on the Marquis de Sade novel of the same name, recontextualized to the setting of the fascist Republic of Salò at the end of World War II. Graphic. Depraved. The ur-text of "extreme cinema." Pier Paolo Pasolini director. 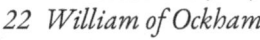 *Salò, Or, the 120 Days of Sodom*. 1975.

 22 William of Ockham

 24 Stuff White People Like The blog and the cultural signifiers it satirized became a metonym for a certain type of liberal yuppie of the early 2000's, a close cousin to the hipster, but distinctly upwardly mobile.

 25 Burning Man Link to an article from the Burning Man online journal lamenting the festival's "whiteness," retroactively added to Unqualified Reservations. Caveat Magister. "Is Burning Man a 'White People Thing?'" *The Burning Man Journal*, 4 Jan. 2012.

 25 Lander points out Christian Lander. "#14 Having Black Friends." *Stuff White People Like*, 21 Jan. 2008.

 25 NGOs Ibid.

 25 Townies Moldbug later coined an even better term for this group: Amerikaners, in analogy with the Afrikaners of South Africa. As he writes in "How to occupy and govern a foreign territory:" "Like their lexical analogues, the Amerikaners are a cultural group of European stock, but their present-day traditions cannot be easily connected with any group in modern Europe." (ed. UR).

 25 stratified dialect "Post-creole continuum"

26 against AIDS

AN OPEN LETTER TO OPEN-MINDED PROGRESSIVES

26 against the Jews In 2006 Gibson was arrested for a DUI and alledgedly said to the arresting officer, "Fucking Jews...the Jews are responsible for all the wars in the world. Are you a Jew?" After the incident became a point of public controversy, Gibson went on a media apology tour and committed himself to an alcohol recovery program.

26 he Blithedale Romance Nathaniel Hawthorne. (Ticknor and Fields, 1852.)

26 put it, This formulation is attributed to Ralph Waldo Emerson and was popularized by Oliver Wendell Holmes. The quote that inspired it appears in Machiavelli's The Prince: "Upon this, one has to remark that men ought either to be well treated or crushed, because they can avenge themselves of lighter injuries, of more serious ones they cannot; therefore the injury that is to be done to a man ought to be of such a kind that one does not stand in fear of revenge." (ed. UR).

27 Times story Donald G. McNeil. "Eradicate Malaria? Doubters Fuel Debate." *New York Times,* 4 Mar. 2008.

28 Post op-ed Michelle Gavin. "Looking Toward Zimbabwe's Future." *Washington Post,* Think Tank Town, 24 Nov. 2007.

28 Council on Foreign Relations

29 La Wik Rhodesia's "Unilateral Declaration of Independence"

30 Somaliland

30 Hargeisa

30 progressive blogger Cassandra. "Ho Chi Minh Sandals." *Cassandra Does Tokyo,* 1 Nov. 2007.

30 nationalism

30 opening paragraph The Wikipedia page for Nationalism has changed since the time of this writing. Provided here is a link to an archived version of the page closest to the date of this post.

LINKS & NOTES

 31 *Radical Chic & Mau Mauing the Flak Catchers* Tom Wolfe. (Farrar, Straus & Giroux, 1970).

 31 *department* Link to Harvard's "African and African American Studies Department" homepage.

 31 *pariah*

 32 *sinned*

 32 *black nationalists* "Zebra Murders"

 32 *Thorough*

32 *Human Smoke: the Beginnings of World War II, the End of Civilization.* Nicholson Baker. (Simon & Schuster, 2008).

 32 *Nicholson Baker*

 32 *a million Russian refugees*, Jacob G. Hornberger. "Repatriation-- The Dark Side of World War II, Part 3." *The Future of Freedom Foundation.* 1 Apr. 1995.

 32 *slave laborers* "Forced Labor of Germans in the Soviet Union"

 33 *Abu Ghraib*

 33 *Dresden*

 33 *Hamburg*

 33 *stand on a box* "The Hooded Man," taken by Staff Sgt. Ivan Frederick, later identified as Abdou Hussain Saad Faleh.

AN OPEN LETTER TO OPEN-MINDED PROGRESSIVES 39

 33 order of magnitude, ed. Stéphane Courtois, Andrzej Paczkowski, Nicolas Werth, Jean-Louis Margolin, et al. *The Black Book of Communism: Crimes, Terror, Repression.* (Harvard University Press, 1997).

 33 here, John Zmirak. "Saying NO to Tenured Fascists." *Taki's Magazine,* 25 Feb. 2008.

 33 Roberto Bolaño

 33 reviews Link to the New York Times review of Bolaño's posthumously published *Nazi Literature in the Americas.* Stacey D'erasmo. "The Sound and the Führer." *New York Times,* Sunday Book Review, 24 Feb. 2008.

 33 engagement

CHAPTER 2:
THE AMERICAN REBELLION
JANUARY 15, 2009

In Chapter 1, we looked at three anomalies in progressive political thought: a surprising definition of the word *independence*, an oscillatory ambivalence around the concept of *nationalism*, and a chiral gradient in sensitivity to *human rights violations*.

These particular anomalies are not just progressive. They are in fact modern. They are generally shared across the conservative–progressive spectrum. They are even shared by most libertarians—except maybe the Randians, who have epistemic troubles of their own. They are simply as close to universal as it comes.

Unless, of course, the past is allowed to dissent. Because when we look backward a little, we see that these ideas come along quite recently. They are fresh. Very fresh. To a progressive, of course, this is mere progress. But if you are also an evolutionary geneticist, you might also call it a *selective sweep*.[1] Obviously, our anomalies have some competitive advantage. But what might that advantage be?

Well, perhaps the anomalies have prevailed because—in some way that we maybe don't quite understand completely yet—they are *good and sweet and true*. After all, people would rather think thoughts that are good and sweet and true. They would also prefer to share such with their friends. Because it is so obvious, so elegant, and so widely believed, we'll label this the *null hypothesis*.

I'm going to interrupt the discussion for a moment and digress. Since this is after all the 21st century, perhaps we can enliven our proceedings with a little mixed media.

---

1 A mutation that "sweeps" through a population and becomes fixed.

Here's a YouTube clip[2] of a protester in the recent violence in Kenya. As far as I can tell, no one is harmed in this 80-second clip, but otherwise it's as dramatic as it gets: it has a talky start, a shocking climax, and a happy ending.

Well, it's sort of a happy ending. At least, the blue car gets away. BTW, I lied: the "protester" is hard to follow, but his corner seems to be at the intersection of Sahara Ave and S. Las Vegas Blvd, in Las Vegas, Nevada. "Metro" is slang for the Las Vegas Metro Police Department. If you were fooled (sorry), try watching it again with this perspective.

I think this clip is a good litmus test for whether you've sneaked into the auditorium without a permission slip, or whether you really are a progressive.

If you really are a progressive, when you try to connect the clip above (which might well have been staged) with the broad sweep of human history, you will think of Hitler or Mussolini or maybe even George W. Bush.

Why? Because our protagonist is behaving exactly like them. His actions are *tribal*, *territorial*, and *predatory*. As one of our great Vulcan thinkers, Jonah Goldberg once put it: "Every ten years or so, the United States needs to pick up some small crappy little country and throw it against the wall, just to show the world we mean business." I'm sure the people who decided to invade Iraq had many goals, all of which they imagined in entirely benevolent terms. But I really have trouble believing that this wasn't at least one of them.

If you sneaked in—who knows what you think? Something awful, I suspect. Kids, this presentation is not for you. Can't you just slink back to your slimy holes for once? (Note to all: in case you ever find your nice, clean, progressive discussion forums overrun with Nazis, you can drive them away by making the Jew-noise: "Joo! Joo!" It's better than the Mosquito.[3])

In any case, thanks for participating in our first experimental test of URTV. More videos are not coming soon. Let's get back to these anomalies.

We will continue by assuming two things about the null hypothesis. One is that it's basically true. Two is that any small ways in which it may be imperfect are (a) minor, (b) accidental, and (c) either self-correcting or at least correctable. Since this is basically what progressives (and most non-progressives) believe, it is only fair to start with it.

It's a pity, though, that it leaves us with these odd asymmetries. It is easy to note that progressives, as well as most non-progressives, express these mental adaptations. It is hard to understand *why*. This is especially true since progressive thought seems to lack any sort of theology, which can explain just about anything. (Why are people with red hair and blue eyes evil? Because that's how Baal made them.)

So our three anomalies have three things in common. One: progressives have explanations for all of them, but these explanations seem less than usually compel-

---

2 The famous "Corner Man" video.

3 A device that emits high-frequency buzzing to deter loiterers.

ling. Two: these strained explanations are generally shared not just by progressives, but also by their enemies, the "conservatives."

And three: there is a single anti-progressive hypothesis, which is obviously on its face wrong or at least incomplete, but can at least be explained in terms that do not require a gentleman to hurl his *Sartor Resartus* at his dinner companions, and seems to explain them all quite nicely with plenty of headroom left over.

The hypothesis is that the "international community"—a phrase we see used on a pretty regular basis, although perhaps we are not quite as clear as we might be as to what exactly it might mean—is, and always has been, a fundamentally predatory force.

The fact that falsifies the hypothesis—at least for me—is that my father was a US diplomat, and if the "international community" means anything it must mean **Foggy Bottom**.[4] And I can tell you that it is simply impossible to mistake a transnational bureaucrat (or **tranzi**[5]) for an SS officer, or vice versa. If the Third Reich is your image of an international predator—and why shouldn't it be? Can't we make Hitler work for us?—the adjective is clearly misapplied.

As anyone who has ever known any number of progressives knows, progressives are generally decent, intelligent and well-meaning people. Moreover, this fact does not stop at the edges of government. By definition, decent, intelligent and well-meaning people are not predatory. Since the "international community" is clearly progressive, the hypothesis is falsified. Whew!

But, not endorsing this false hypothesis, but simply using it as a tool of argument, it sure is interesting to look at how nicely it explains our little anomalies. It may or may not be productive to replace three poorly explained phenomena by one incorrect assumption. But at least it reduces the number of problems. Let's work through them one by one.

First: what happened to the Third World?

Well, that's pretty easy. It was conquered and devastated by the "international community." Admittedly, the "devastated" part kind of sucks. But when you're a predator, it's better to conquer and devastate than not to conquer at all, *n'est-ce pas*?

Let's take a look at this *independence* thing. What exactly is a *multilateral declaration of independence*? Since in the previous chapter we established it's not the Rhodesian Unilateral Declaration of Independence, then what is it?

Well, on the sweet and good and true side, a multilateral declaration of independence seems to involve a change in the ethnicity of government officials. Foreign officials are replaced by native-born officials. Clearly, for example, it would be an outrage for true-born Americans to be governed by a dirty no-good Mex—oh, wait. We're progressives. We're not racists. Ethnicity means nothing to us.

Well, the postcolonial regimes are no longer controlled from overseas. They can do whatever they want. They're free!

---

4 Metonym for the State Department.
5 "transnational progressive"

Sure they are. They're so free that they've received $2.6 trillion in aid since 1960. Does the phrase "who pays the piper calls the tune" ring any bells? Again, in English at least, the word "independence" is a compound of the prefix *in-*, meaning *not*, and *dependent*, meaning *dependent*.

And what does it mean for a government to be "free," anyway? Is the government of North Korea "free?" What about ExxonMobil? Or the Democratic Party? I have a fairly good understanding of what it means for a *human being* to be "free." When it comes to an organization, especially one which claims to be a "government," I'm quite without a clue.

One test we can apply for *independence*, which should be pretty conclusive, is that the structures of government in a genuinely independent country should tend to resemble the structures that existed before it was subjugated—rather than the structures of some other country on which it may happen to be, um, dependent. These structures should be especially unlikely to resemble structures in other newly independent countries, with which it presumably has nothing in common.

In other words: after 1960, did the Third World become more Westernized or less Westernized? Did it revert to its pre-Western political systems, rejecting the foreign tissue like a bad transplant? Or did it become a more and more slavish imitation of the West?

There is exactly one region in which the former happened: the Persian Gulf. Not that the Gulf states are utterly un-Westernized, but their political systems are clearly the least Western in the world. Oddly enough, the Gulf states also happen to be "independent" in the good old financial sense of the word. There are also two exceptions in Africa: **Somaliland**, which fell through the cracks, and **Botswana**, which has diamonds.

(You will sometimes hear Botswana described as a model of African democracy. How fortunate that the Botswanan people should be so wise as to elect, as their first President, none other than their hereditary monarch, **Seretse Khama**. In practice the place is more or less run by De Beers, on the good old **United Fruit** model.)

Across most of the Third World, however, we see a very simple transition: from the traditional forms of government and tribal leaders whom the British, French, Rhodesians, etc., supported at a local or even regional level in the policy of **indirect rule**, to a new elite selected and educated in Western missions, schools and universities. In Africa these men are called the **wa-Benzi**—"wa" is the Swahili prefix for "tribe," and I think "Benzi"[6] speaks for itself.

Moreover, the rhetoric of *tiers-mondisme*[7] is and was almost the same everywhere. If Algeria and Vietnam were truly growing up and following their own destinies, you might think the former would be ruled by a Dey and the latter by **emperors and mandarins**. You'd certainly be surprised to find that they both had an organization called the "National Liberation Front."

---

6 Reference to Mercedes-Benz.
7 *third-worldism*

AN OPEN LETTER TO OPEN-MINDED PROGRESSIVES 45

And finally, perhaps the subtlest aspect of dependency is power dependency. To whom did this rash of fresh presidents, congresses and liberation fronts owe its existence? Where, exactly, did Macmillan's **Wind of Change** blow from? For that matter, who cares about all these people now? Why does a vast river of cash still flow from European and American taxpayers to these weird, camo-bedecked, mirrorshaded thugs?

Well, one theory is that the brave liberation fronts seized power through their own military prowess. Or the unquenchable anger of the people at foreign domination, which could no longer be repressed. Or the fiery will of the workers, which blazed out once too often. Or the shining light of education, which brought the dream of democracy to our little brown brothers. Or... I'm afraid **Professor Frankfurt**[8] has taught us much on this subject.

In fact you'll see that in pretty much every case, including some that may surprise you[9] (here's a great **primary source**[10]) the liberation fronts achieved power because they had powerful friends. Sometimes the friends were in Paris, sometimes they were in London, sometimes they were even in Moscow. But for the most part they were in New York and Washington. (There's an excellent new film on this subject—from Barbet Schroeder, the man who gave us *General Idi Amin Dada*, reality's answer to Forest Whitaker. It's called *Terror's Advocate*, and you gotta see it.)

Once again: if this is "independence," I'm a three-eyed donkey. Note that the English language has a perfectly good word for a regime which appears to be independent, but in reality is dependent. It starts with "p" and rhymes with "muppet." In fact, perhaps "muppet" is a good term for the post-1945 postcolonial regimes.

A muppet state is not quite a puppet state. It delivers a far more lifelike impression of individual identity. It has not just an invisible hand supporting it from below, but invisible strings pulling it from above. In fact, muppet states often appear quite hostile to their masters. There are a variety of reasons for this—one is internal conflict within the master state, which we'll get to in a bit—but the simplest is just camouflage.

The classic story is de Gaulle's legendary obstreperousness during World War II. De Gaulle had to cause problems for the British and Americans, because his whole story was that he represented the true spirit of oppressed France—rather than being just some guy that Churchill set up in an office, which is of course exactly what he was. Furthermore, because a blatant display of puppetry would have been no use to the Allies, they had to tolerate his acting out.

The phenomenon of dependent rebellion is quite familiar to anyone who has ever been a teenager, an analogy that's a good guide to the sort of "independence"

---

8 Reference to philosopher Harry G. Frankfurt's 2005 book, *On Bullshit*.
9 Reference to Fidel Castro's rise to international celebrity based on the reportage of New York Times correspondent Herbert L. Matthews in 1957.
10

we see in the likes of a Mugabe, a Castro or even a Khomeini—each a member of the "I got my job through the New York Times" club.

It's easy to see what a network of postcolonial muppet states harnessed to the hegemonic will of an imperial alien overlord looks like. We have the perfect example: the Warsaw Pact, and its assorted flunkeys in Africa and Asia. (In fact, we have two evil muppet empires to look at, because the Maoists spun off their own.) The Marxist–Leninist muppet states all insisted fervently that they were liberated, independent, etc., and that their alliances were brotherly partnerships of equals, with their own Politburos and everything. And of course the whole enterprise was run by Comrade Brezhnev, from the white phone in his *petit salon*. Even Hitler's quislings in New Order Europe did not exhibit quite this level of gall—there was no pretence that Vichy France, for example, was an equal of the Third Reich.

And since the Soviet and Western blocs often competed for the same set of muppets—for example, Nasser, Tito, and even Ho Chi Minh, who never lost his popularity out in Langley—I'm afraid the pattern is really quite clear.

So from our counterfactual perspective, the story of the Third World is quite clear. In the second half of the 20th century, the Third World passed from its old colonial masters, the British, French and Portuguese, who were certainly no angels but who were perhaps at least a little less brazen, to a new set of ruthless and cynical overlords, the Cold War powers, whose propaganda skills were matched only by the devastation that their trained thugs unleashed. Under the mendacious pretext of "liberation" and "independence," most remnants of non-European governing traditions were destroyed. Major continents such as Africa were reduced to desolate slums ruled by **corrupt, well-connected fat cats**, much of whose loot went straight from Western taxpayers to Swiss banks.

What's especially interesting is that when we step back and consider the history of the non-Western world since 1500, we see a broad trend that does not reverse course at all the 20th century. If anything, the 20th century is more of the same, only more so.

We see four basic structures of government: native rule with private Western trade, native rule under the protection of chartered companies or other monopolies (like the **East India Company**, the **British South Africa Company**, **Anaconda Copper**, etc., etc.), classic nationalized colonialism with indirect rule, and the postcolonial muppet states.

Across all these stages, as time increases, we see the following trends. One, the non-European world becomes culturally and politically Westernized. Two, more and more Westerners are employed in the actual task of governing them. (I don't know the ratio of aid workers today to colonial administrators 50 years ago, but I'm sure it's tremendous.) And three, the profits accruing to the West from all of this activity dwindle away and are replaced by massive losses. ("Aid" is essentially a subsidy to the muppet states, which are to the old chartered companies as a **Lada** factory is to a Honda factory.)

AN OPEN LETTER TO OPEN-MINDED PROGRESSIVES

Who benefits from these trends? The "international community," i.e., the vast army of international administrators who labor diligently and ineffectively at healing the great wounds they have torn in the side of the world. Who loses? Everyone else—Western taxpayers in the usual slow, relentless dribble, Africans and Asians in the gigantic revolutionary hemorrhage of "civil war, poverty, corrupt government and the collapse of medical care."

If you read travel narratives of what is now the Third World from before World War II (I've just been enjoying Erna Fergusson's *Guatemala*, for example), you simply don't see anything like the misery, squalor and barbarism that is everywhere today. (Fergusson describes Guatemala City as "clean." I kid you not.) What you do see is social and political structures, whether native or colonial, that are clearly not American in origin, and that are unacceptable not only by modern American standards but even by 1930s American standards.

So, again, we have two theories of the "international community." One, its own, depicts it as the savior and liberator of the planet, and essentially global and universal in nature. Two, the one I've just developed, shows it as a ravenous predator, the dominant player in a second **Scramble for Africa** with Asia and South America added to the plate—essentially, a new version of the **Delian League**, with Washington in the part of Athens.

And neither quite makes sense. The first hypothesis is very hopeful and reassuring, and most people believe it, but it has these odd, Orwellian tics in the way it uses English. And the second is, once again, quite counterfactual. I know these people. They are not at all predatory. There is no denying that transnational bureaucrats have the world's best interests at heart, and they are certainly not in any way American nationalists. They simply do not remind me, in any way, shape or form, of Corner Man.[11]

So let's put this conundrum aside and move on to the second anomaly: nationalism. I hope it's not too much of a surprise that this turns out to be a special case of the first.

Nationalist regimes and movements are good when they're doing God's work, i.e., their goal is to become nice, multilateral members of the "international community." Nationalist regimes and movements are bad when they "defy international opinion" and turn against said community, which wants nothing other than to be able to love them as its beloved children. In other words: the enemy of my enemy is my friend. Typical Machiavellian predatory behavior.

It is always pleasant to depart from the bleak, mendacious twentieth century and return to its predecessor, whose leaders could be just as unscrupulous but who dressed much better. There was an "international community" in the nineteenth century as well, and at least in the Old World, it operated out of one place: London.

Quick association test! The unification of Italy—good or bad? I'll bet you said "good." Well, here's a little story.

---

11 See footnote 2.

CHAPTER 2

A couple of years ago Mrs. Moldbug and I spent three weeks in Italy. For the first week we split a villa in Cilento with some friends, which was lovely if a little buggy, and involved inhaling enormous quantities of limoncello. Next we thought we'd take our backpacks and bop around on the train a little. Our first stop: Naples.

I'm afraid it's not for nothing that northern Italians say "Garibaldi didn't unite Italy, he divided Africa." Obviously, this is a racist statement and I can't condone it. But even the Lonely Planet warns travellers that "you might think you're in Cairo or Tangier." I have never been to Cairo or Tangier, but if they are anything like Naples, God help them.

The 3000-year-old city of Naples is a reeking, garbage-ridden sewer. This year there was an actual **garbage strike**, but the problem is perennial—there was a giant, seemingly permanent mound of it right across the street from our LP-recommended albergo. At all times, almost everyone on the street appears to be a criminal, especially at night. The streets are ruinous, unlit, and patrolled by thieves on mopeds. We saw one pull up in front of an old lady carrying a bag of groceries, openly inspect her goods for anything worth stealing, then scoot away. Apparently they have a reputation for ripping earrings out of womens' ears.

From Naples you can take the Circumvesuviana to Pompeii. This train has a wonderful name, but its main purpose appears to be to transport criminals from the Stalinist banlieues in which they live, to the city in which they steal. Signs in every language known to humanity warn the tourist that pickpockets are everywhere. The trains are stripped to the metal and covered with graffiti, which is not in Latin. As the train stopped at one station, we saw a couple of *carabinieri* carrying a body-bag away from the platform.

The night after this we wandered the historic district of Naples, simply looking for one open-air cafe in which to sit and chat. Eventually we found one. We were pretty much the only people there. It was Saturday night. We moved on and discovered one clean thing in Naples—the new, EU-funded subway. Tried a couple of stops. Everything was the same.

Finally, I remembered a snarky little use of the word "bourgeois" in the Planet and marched Mrs. Moldbug over to the *funicula*, which goes up the hill to the Vomero, a sort of internal suburb. *Quelle différence!* You go three hundred feet up a cliff, and you have gone from Cairo to Milan. We immediately found a wine-bar with an English-speaking hostess and enjoyed several lovely glasses.

Suddenly we realized that it was late, and we didn't know when the subway stopped running, to get us back to our albergo, near the *Stazione Centrale*. So we asked. And no one knew. Not the waitress, not anyone in the bar. These hip young people had no idea of the subway hours in their own city. I believe the waitress actually said something like, "why do you want to go *there*?"

We hurried, and I think we got the last train. The next day, Mrs. Moldbug, who is far more tasteful than I and who would never repeat that nasty line about Garibaldi, expressed the desire to "just hop on the Eurostar and stay on it until we get to Stockholm." In fact we ended up in Perugia, which is, of course, lovely.

So: Naples. Obviously, Naples being this way, I assumed that Naples had always been this way. There was that old line, "see Naples and die," but presumably it referred to a knife in the ribs. That poor bastard on the Circumvesuviana had seen Naples, and died. Was it worth it?

So I was surprised to discover a different version of reality, from British historian Desmond Seward's *Naples: A Travellers' Companion*:

> 'In size and number of inhabitants she ranks as the third city of Europe, and from her situation and superb show may justly be considered the Queen of the Mediterranean,' wrote John Chetwode Eustace in 1813. Until 1860 Naples was the political and administrative centre of the Kingdom of The Two Sicilies, the most beautiful kingdom in the world. Consisting of Southern Italy and Sicily, it had a land mass equal to that of Portugal and was the richest state in Europe... For five generations—from 1734 till 1860—it was ruled by a branch of the French and Spanish royal family of Bourbon who filled the city with monuments to their reign...
>
> The 'Borboni' as their subjects called them, were complete Neapolitans, wholly assimilated, who spoke and thought in Neapolitan dialect (indeed the entire court spoke Neapolitan)... Until 1860, glittering Court balls and regal gala nights at the San Carlo which staggered foreigners by their opulence and splendour were a feature of Neapolitan life... In 1839 that ferocious Whig Lord Macaulay was staying in the city and wrote, 'I must say that the accounts I which I have heard of Naples are very incorrect. There is far less beggary than in Rome, and far more industry... At present, my impressions are very favourable to Naples. It is the only place in Italy that has seemed to me to have the same sort of vitality which you find in all the great English ports and cities. Rome and Pisa are dead and gone; Florence is not dead, but sleepeth; while Naples overflows with life.'
>
> The Borboni's memory have been systematically blackened by partisans of the regime which supplanted them, and by admirers of the Risorgimento. They have had a particularly bad press in the Anglo-Saxon world. Nineteenth-century English liberals loathed them for their absolutism, their clericalism and loyalty to the Papacy, and their opposition to the fashionable cause of Italian unity. Politicians from Lord William Bentinck to Lord Palmerston and Gladstone, writers such as Browning and George Eliot, united in detesting the 'tyrants'; Gladstone convinced himself that their regime was 'the negation of God.' Such critics, as prejudiced as they were ill informed, ignored the dynasty's eco-

nomic achievement, the kingdom's remarkable prosperity compared with other Italian states, the inhabitants' relative contentment, and the fact that only a mere handful of Southern Italians were opposed to their government. Till the end, The Two Sicilies was remarkable for the majority of its subjects' respect for, and knowledge of, its laws—so deep that even today probably most Italian judges, and especially successful advocates, still come from the south. Yet even now there is a mass of blind prejudice among historians. All too many guidebooks dismiss the Borboni as corrupt despots who misruled and neglected their capital. An entire curtain of slander conceals the old, pre-1860 Naples; with the passage of time calumny has been supplemented by ignorance, and it is easy to forget that history is always written by the victors. However Sir Harold Acton in his two splendid studies of the Borboni has to some extent redressed the balance, and his interpretation of past events is winning over increasing support—especially in Naples itself.

Undoubtedly the old monarchy had serious failings. Though economically and industrially creative, it was also absolutist and isolationist, disastrously out of touch with pan-Italian aspirations... Beyond question there was political repression under the Bourbons—the dynasty was fighting for its survival—but it has been magnified out of all proportion. On the whole prison conditions were probably no worse than in contemporary England, which still had its hulks; what really upset Gladstone was seeing his social equals being treated in the same way as working-class convicts, since opposition to the regime was restricted to a few liberal romantics among the aristocracy and bourgeoisie...

The Risorgimento was a disaster for Naples and for the south in general. Before 1860 the Mezzogiorno was the richest part of Italy outside the Austrian Empire; after it quickly became the poorest. The facts speak for themselves. In 1859 money circulating in The Two Sicilies amounted to more than that circulating in all other independent Italian states, while the Bank of Naples's gold reserve was 443 million gold lire, twice the combined reserves of the rest of Italy. This gold was immediately confiscated by Piedmont—whose own reserve had been a mere 27 million—and transferred to Turin. Neapolitan excise duties, levied to keep out the north's inferior goods and providing four-fifths of the city's revenue, were abolished. And then the northerners imposed crushing new taxes. Far from being liberators, the Piedmontese administrators who came in the wake of the Risorgimento behaved like Yankees in the post-bellum Southern States; they ruled

The Two Sicilies as an occupied country, systematically demolishing its institutions and industries. Ferdinand's new dockyard was dismantled to stop Naples competing with Genoa (it is now being restored by industrial archeologists). Vilification of the Borboni became part of the school curriculum. Shortly after the Two Sicilies' enforced incorporation into the new Kingdom of Italy, the Duke of Maddaloni protested in the 'national' Parliament: 'This is invasion, not annexation, not union. We are being plundered like an occupied territory.' For years after the 'liberation,' Neapolitans were governed by northern *padroni* and carpet-baggers. And today the Italians of the north can be as stupidly prejudiced about Naples as any Anglo-Saxon, affecting a superiority which verges on racism—'Africa begins South of Rome'—and lamenting the presence in the North of so many workers from the Mezzogiorno. (The ill-feeling is reciprocated, the Neapolitan translation of SPQR being *Sono porci, questi Romani*.) Throughout the 1860s 150,000 troops were needed to hold down the south.

Note the pattern. What made Italian unification happen? Why did Ferdinand of Naples, with his 443 million gold lire, just roll over for Charles Albert of Piedmont, with his mere 27? Two reasons: **Lord Palmerston** and **Napoleon III**. Where did exiles such as **Mazzini** and **Garibaldi** find their backers? Not in Pompeii, that's for sure.

The unification of Italy was an event in the 19th century's great struggle between liberalism and reaction. The international liberal movement of the 20th century, in which a figure such as **Carl Schurz** could go from German revolutionary in 1848 to Civil War general in 1861, was the clear precursor of today's "international community." And once again, we see it playing the same predatory role: conquering and destroying in the name of liberation and independence.

Unless you count the American Revolution, perhaps the first and clearest case of this strange phenomenon—multilateral independence—was the **Greek War of Independence**. As La Wik, without a trace of irony, puts it: "After a long and bloody struggle, and with the aid of the Great Powers, independence was finally granted by the Treaty of Constantinople in July 1832." Indeed.

And if we look at the citizens of said Great Powers—principally, of course, Great Britain—who gave us Greek "independence," we see the same type of people who were behind Mazzini, Schurz, and all the way down to today's "international community": liberals, radicals, thinkers, artists. Progressives. (**Lord Byron** is of course the archetype.) Again, these are the best and nicest people in the world, now or then. So why in the world do they always seem to turn up in the same breath as phrases like "long and bloody struggle?"

So we have not solved the anomaly of nationalism. But at least we have reduced it to the same problem as our first anomaly, which has to be something. What happened to the Third World? It was devoured by predatory, cynical, bogus nationalism. Why would educated, cosmopolitan, and civilized thinkers support predatory, cynical, bogus nationalism? Again we hit the wall.

Let's move on to our third problem: Hitler.

Of course I hold no brief for Hitler. "Joo! Joo!" The anomaly, to reprise, is that Hitler today is detested for his human-rights violations, i.e., the Holocaust. And the Allies are therefore revered for defeating Hitler, wrapping the whole problem up in a neat little bow. The only problem with this human-rights theory of World War II is that it has no resemblance to reality.

First, the Allies included Stalin, a fellow whose human-rights record was at least as bad as Hitler's. Second, Roosevelt and Churchill not only didn't seem to much mind the extermination of the Jews (whom they had **many opportunities**[12] to save)—if anything, they **covered it up.**[13] (Which makes neo-Nazi claims that the Holocaust was Allied war propaganda grimly comical, to say the least.) And third, the Allies didn't at all mind barbecuing as many enemy civilians as they could fit on the **grill**.

Put these facts together, and the human-rights theory of World War II makes about as much sense as the suggestion that Caesar invaded Britain because he wanted to see Manchester United play Chelsea. So why did it happen? The nominal cause of the European war was that Britain wanted to preserve a free Poland. You'd think that if this was their key goal, they would have found a way to come out of the war with a free Poland—especially having won, and all. Much the same can be said with respect to the **US and China**.[14]

Note that what we are interested in, here, is not the motives of Hitler and Mussolini and Tojo. These men are dead and so are their movements. The movements that defeated them, however, live on—I think it's pretty clear that the "international community" and the Allies are one and the same. Our question is why said community had such a harsh reaction to Nazi Germany. Especially since its response to Soviet Russia, which was just as aggressive and just as murderous, was so different.

One simple answer, continuing our counterfactual, was that the fascist movement was a competing predator. Perhaps the Allies destroyed the Nazis for the same reason that a lion will kill a leopard, if it gets the chance: not because leopards are all that good to eat, but because there are only so many antelope in the world.

Unfortunately, the waters here are freshly muddied by Jonah Goldberg's **half-educated bestseller** *Liberal Fascism* which argues that fascism was really a left-wing movement. **Erik von Kuehnelt-Leddihn**, a far better writer, made the case <u>far earlier and far more erudite</u><u>ly. He was still wrong.</u>

12 Reference to the invitation in 1938 from Rafael Trujilo to resettle European Jews to the Dominican Republic.
13 Reference to Laura Leff's book *Buried by the Times,* that claims The New York Times downplayed its reporting on the Holocaust.
14 Reference to the Hull Note, a final proposal sent eleven days before the attack on Pearl Harbor by the United States to Japan that included demands for Japanese withdrawal from Chinese territory.

AN OPEN LETTER TO OPEN-MINDED PROGRESSIVES

As a reactionary Jacobite myself, I feel it's especially important to face up to the basically reactionary nature of the fascist movement. Fascism (and Nazism) were certainly creatures of the democratic era—nothing like them could have been imagined in the 19th century. They certainly borrowed many techniques of government from both liberals and Bolsheviks. And the experience of living in a totalitarian state does not much depend on whether that state is Communist, Fascist, Buddhist or Scientologist. Nonetheless, Goldberg is wrong: there is a fundamental difference.

In the 1930s, there was no confusion at all as to whether the fascist movements were parties of the extreme Right or of the extreme Left. Everyone agreed. They were parties of the Right. Populist right-wingers to be sure, but right-wingers nonetheless. For once, the conventional wisdom is perfectly accurate.

For example, in 1930 Francesco Nitti (nephew of a **liberal Prime Minister** by the same name) published a book called *Escape*, about his escape from internal exile on an Italian island. (Let's just say that it wasn't exactly the Gulag.) In the preface, his uncle the PM explains Mussolini for the English-speaking reader:

> Mussolini represents a mediaeval adventure in Italy. Until some fifteen years ago, Communist and Anarchist, he defended regicide, anarchist crime, political assassination. He has written and predicted individual revolt. He has always considered all religions (these are his very words) like opium, to lull people to sleep. He has written and repeated for twenty years in his discourses that the abyss between Capitalism and the Proletariat should be filled with the heads of Capitalists. Again in the year 1920 he incited workmen to occupy factories and to pilfer. In 1914 he laughed at the Belgian occupation and urged the Italians to rebel against those who wanted to drag them into the war.

Which all sounds very well for Goldberg's thesis. But wait:

> Not having succeeded in making a red revolution, he attempted a white reaction, taking advantage of the discontent after the war. He succeeded with the help of a few generals and part of the army who wanted reaction... Becoming Dictator, Mussolini has not only forswore all his past, but has introduced the most terrible reaction. All form of liberty has been suppressed; press liberty, association liberty, reunion liberty. Members of Parliament are practically nominated by the government. All political associations have been dissolved...

For those not versed in the color symbolism of 19th-century Europe, white is the color of reaction, just as red is the color of revolution. Thus, Nitti is telling us, unlike the old socialist Mussolini, the new fascist Mussolini is a reactionary. Just like the Borboni.

As we've seen, if the "international community" is a predator, reactionaries are its prey. So, while the Soviets might be seen as a competing predator, fascism is something quite different. Fascism is a species of prey that (unlike the Borboni) decided to fight back. And it was not exactly averse to fighting dirty.

Here is my perception of fascism: it was a reactionary movement that combined the worst ideas of the *ancien régime*, the worst politics of the democrats, and the worst tyrannies of the Bolsheviks. And what was the result? It is every bit as vanished as the Borboni. For a reactionary, fascism is more or less a short course in what not to do.

Even a lifetime later, our emotional responses to fascism and Nazism make these concepts very difficult to handle. (Full disclosure: my grandfather, a Jewish communist, enlisted in the US Army to kill Nazis. And I'm pretty sure he bagged a few.) One way to step away from these associations is to look not at the Third Reich but at the Second—the strange regime of Kaiser Bill, and the war he made.

A less loaded name for fascism might be *neomilitarism*. The ideology of Wilhelmine Germany was generally described as *militarism*, a perfectly accurate description. It was certainly reactionary, and also quite populist—for a monarchy. (World War I was extremely popular in Germany, as in all countries.) Under the Kaiser, the highest social status available was conferred by military rank. You might be a distinguished professor of physics, but if your reserve rank as a military officer was low or (worse) nonexistent, no one would talk to you at parties. Even for Americans who know something of the military, it's almost impossible to imagine living in a true militaristic society.

Why did the last survivors of the *ancien régime* become so aggressive and militaristic? Why, for example, did the German military jump at the opportunity to start a war in 1914? Because they believed our counterfactual—that the "international community" was a killer with fangs.

The German theory in 1914 was that the British alliance with France and Russia was designed to "encircle" Germany—not exactly implausible, if one glances at a map. And we have already seen how the British dealt with reactionaries when they got the chance. The theory of the German General Staff in 1914 was that Germany, surrounded and besieged, had to attack or it would be gradually choked to death.

This **bit of Nazi propaganda**[15] from 1939 explains the German militarist theory of modern history quite well:

> The deepest roots of this war are in England's old claim to rule the world, and Europe in particular. Although its homeland is relatively small, England has understood how to cleverly exploit

---

15

others to expand its possessions. It controls the seas, the important points along major sea routes, and the richest parts of our planet. The contrast between England itself and its overseas territories is so grotesque that England has always has a certain inferiority complex with respect to the European continent. Whenever a continental power reached a certain strength, England believed itself and its empire to be threatened. Every continental flowering made England nervous, every attempt at growth by nations wanting their place in the sun led England to take on the policeman's role.

One must understand this to make sense of England's German policy from Bismarck to our own day. England was not happy with the results of the war of 1870–1871. British sympathies were already on France's side, since for the previous one hundred years it had never had the same fear of France as it had of Germany. France had secured its own colonial empire, and its shrinking biological strength left enough room for expansion within its own natural boundaries. Things were different in Germany. England knew that the German people were strong when they had good leadership, and that nature had given them limited, resource-poor territory with a limited coast. Great Britain kept an eye on Germany, all the more whenever Germany expressed its strength, even in the most natural ways. The Second Reich experienced England's "balance of power" policy. We know that England did not want a true balance of power. It wants a situation in which England is always in a position with the help of its allies to have its way with a minority of confident, forward-moving nations.

Obviously, this is propaganda. But one bit of real history that I can recommend to anyone is the viewpoint of the fellow on the other side of this "encirclement" business: **Lord Grey of Fallodon**. If you've ever wondered who said "the lights are going out all over Europe; we shall not see them lit again in our lifetime," Lord Grey is your man. His **memoirs** are extremely readable—indeed, reading them one sees just why we have not seen the lamps lit again. There is simply no individual of Grey's caliber, politician or civil servant, in the whole government racket these days.

Needless to say, to Lord Grey (writing after the war), no one would ever dream of trying to encircle Germany. Rather, the German militarists are paranoid and jingoistic, constantly trying to enhance their domestic political position by triggering European crises. And indeed the pot that boiled over at Sarajevo was by no means the first such crisis—**Agadir**[16] is a fine example. The British, on the other hand, are

---

16 Barely averted military crisis between Germany and France in 1911 over a territory dispute in Morocco.

simply doing their best to keep the peace. In the end they failed, Germany attacked Belgium without provocation, and British honor bound her to respond.

I find Grey completely credible. I have no reservations about his sincerity. He certainly strikes me as a far more trustworthy character than the slippery Palmerston, who really was a bit of a snake. And his summary of the causes of the war is peerless:

> After 1870 Germany had no reason to be afraid, but she fortified herself with armaments and the Triple Alliance in order that she might never have reason to be afraid in future. France naturally was afraid after 1870, and she made her military preparations and the Dual Alliance (with Russia). Britain, with a very small Army and a very large Empire, became first uncomfortable and then (particularly when Germany began a big-fleet program) afraid of isolation. She made the Anglo-Japanese Alliance, made up her quarrels with France and Russia, and entered into the Entente. Finally Germany became afraid that she would presently be afraid, and struck the blow, while she believed her power to be invincible. Heaven alone knows the whole truth about human affairs, but I believe the above sketch to be as near to a true statement of the causes of war as an ordinary intelligence can get in a few sentences.

And yet—did Germany, or more precisely the **Hohenzollern monarchy**, have no reason to be afraid? The Borboni were certainly caught napping. And note that, while Germany was challenging British naval hegemony, the overdog remained Britain and the underdog Germany. Who, exactly, had more reason to be afraid of whom? Grey is not exactly shy in waxing Palmerstonian about the contest between democracy and reaction:

> We had no thought ourselves of going to war in 1914 because we supposed that sooner or later we should have to fight. We just strove to prevent war happening at all. But when, in spite of our efforts, war came, it is well that we took our place in it and at the outset. The latent forces at work became apparent as the war proceeded, and the incidents in which the war originated were forgotten as these forces were revealed. It was a great struggle between the Kultur that stood for militarism and the free unmilitarist democratic ideal. It was the perception of this, whether consciously or unconsciously, that brought the United States into the war—the United States, which as a whole had cared little about the incidents that caused the war at the outset, and which did not as a whole then perceive it. But it was the perception of it, revealed to us as the war developed, that made us know that we

AN OPEN LETTER TO OPEN-MINDED PROGRESSIVES 57

> were fighting for the very life of what Britain and the self-governing Dominions cared for. We could not have escaped that struggle between militarism and democracy by turning our backs on the war in August 1914. The thing would have pursued us until we had to turn our backs and face it, and that would have been when it was even stronger and when we had become weak and isolated.

Who sounds a little paranoid here? The British Empire covered the globe. The forces of democracy and liberalism were clearly on the advance. Reactionary militarism was beleaguered. Did it absolutely have to be utterly crushed, right then and there, bang?

Note that for most of World War I, it was Germany who wanted peace on the basis of the status quo, and the Allies who insisted that Germany be defeated and militarism eradicated. Perhaps Hitler considered his war a crusade to stamp out democracy forever, but the Kaiser did not. His opponents, however, felt no such compunctions. Grey reproduces a memo from his ambassador in Washington that states the basic German perspective, as of September 1914:

> German Ambassador has stated in Press that Germany is anxious for peace on basis of *status quo*, and desires no new territory, but that England has declared intention of fighting to finish for her selfish purposes, and is consequently responsible for further bloodshed.

Grey responds:

> Germany has planned this war and chosen the time for forcing it upon Europe. No one but Germany was in the same state of preparation.
>
> We want in future to live free from the menace of this happening again.
>
> Treitschke and other writers of repute and popularity in Germany have openly declared that to crush Great Britain and destroy the British Empire must be the objective for Germany.
>
> We want to be sure that this idea is abandoned. A cruel wrong has been done to Belgium—an unprovoked attack aggravated by the wanton destruction of Louvain and other wholesale vandalism. What reparation is Germany to make to Belgium for this?

Is Grey's real concern reparations to Belgium (more or less a British client state)? Clearly, it is not. His concern is setting a condition that the German militarists cannot accept without losing face, because his objective is to crush Germany and destroy the German Empire. As he wrote in early 1916:

> Nothing but the defeat of Germany can make a satisfactory end to this war and secure future peace...
>
> We must, however, be careful in stating our determination to continue the war to make it clear that our object is not to force, but to support our Allies. Increasing mischief is being made between us and our Allies by German propaganda. This propaganda represents the war as one of rivalry between Great Britain and Germany; it insinuates that France, Russia and Belgium could have satisfactory terms of peace now, and that they are continuing the war in the interest of Great Britain to effect the ruin of Germany, which is not necessary for the safety of the Allies, but which alone will satisfy Great Britain.
>
> It is just possible that this insidious misrepresentation, false though it be, may create in France, Russia, Italy and Belgium a dangerous peace movement—a movement positively unfriendly to us.
>
> It would be well if we could all, Ministers and Press alike, strike one note, that of determination to help the Allies who have suffered the most grievous wrong, to secure the liberation of their territory, reparation for wrong done, and the advantages necessary for their future security. We should emphasize the impossibility and disgrace of thinking of peace till the Allies are secure, but should let it be understood that it is for them whose territory is occupied by the enemy, whose population has been, and is being, so grossly ill-treated, rather than for us, to say when it is opportune to speak of peace. Till that time comes, we use all our efforts and make every sacrifice to defeat the enemy in the common cause, and have no other thought but this.

Can you make this stuff up?

We're fighting for the sake of the Allies. If they would prefer peace, it is their place to speak of peace, not ours. But let's make sure we don't let them think it's okay to think of peace, because Germany must be defeated. It's especially important to counter the insidious German peace propaganda, which may lead our Allies to think we can only be satisfied by the defeat of Germany. Which is nonsense—we're only fighting to redress the wrongs to our Allies.

Again, I am not sure these excerpts really convey the flavor of Lord Grey's thinking. Obviously I am not presenting it at its best. I really do find Grey a congenial character, as I'm sure I would not find, say, **Erich Ludendorff**.[17] It is simply impossible to think of him as a predator.

And yet once again, it is difficult not to see the fangs. In any war, each side presents itself as the injured party, and the other side as the aggressor. Is Germa-

---

17 World War I German general and major figure in the rise of Nazism.

ny trying to crush Britain? Or is Britain trying to crush Germany? Or are they both aggressors?

Again, we are at an impasse. We have a very tempting theory that seems to explain all of these anomalies quite neatly, but the theory is obviously not true. Reject it, however, and the anomalies are back—and they seem to have friends. What to do?

41 selective sweep

 42 YouTube clip Link to the famous "Corner Man" video depicting a belligerent vagrant violently guarding his "turf" at the intersection of Sahara Ave. and S. Las Vegas Blvd., in Las Vegas, Nevada.

 42 put it Jonah Goldberg. "Baghdad Delenda Est, Part Two." *National Review Online*, 23 Apr. 2002.

 43 Sartor Resartus: The Life and Opinions of Herr Teufelsdröckh in Three Books. A satirical novel written by Thomas Carlyle, first published by Fraser's Magazine in 1831.

 43 Foggy Bottom

 43 tranzi Coined by David Carr at Samizdat.net.

 43 Rhodesian Unilateral Declaration of Independence Transcript of the declaration from the *Modern History Sourcebook*, hosted at Fordham University.

 44 $2.6 trillion Anup Shah. "Official global foreign aid shortfall: $5 trillion." *Global Issues*, archived 28 Sep. 2014.

 44 Somaliland

 44 Botswana

 44 Seretse Khama

 44 United Fruit

 44 indirect rule

 44 wa-Benzi Julian Champkin. "The WaBenzi." *New Internationalist*, archived 3 Jul. 2002.

AN OPEN LETTER TO OPEN-MINDED PROGRESSIVES

 44 *Benzi* "Mercedes-Benz"

 44 *Dey* "List of governors and rulers of the Regency of Algiers"

 44 *emperors and mandarins* "Gia Long"

 45 *Wind of Change* Speech delivered by British Prime Minister Harold Macmillan to the Parliament of South Africa, 1960.

45 *Professor Frankfurt* Harry G. Frankfurt. *On Bullshit.* (Princeton University Press, 2005).

 45 *surprise you* Heroic portrayals of Castro by New York Times correspondent Herbert L. Matthews in 1957 turned Castro into an international celebrity and helped influence the overthrow of the Batista regime. Original link to Anthony DePalma's book on the episode, *The Man Who Invented Fidel: Castro, Cuba, and Herbert L. Matthews of the New York Times.* (Public Affairs, 2007).

 45 *primary source* Testimony of Arthur Gardner and Earl E.T. Smith before the 86th cong. "Communist Threat to the United States Through the Caribbean" (1960).

 45 *General Idi Amin Dada* James Surowiecki. "Cult of Personalism: A remarkable documentary about Idi Amin gets to the heart of his politics." *Slate*, 21 Aug. 2003.

45 *Terror's Advocate*, Barbet Schroeder. (Magnolia Pictures, 2007).

 46 *corrupt, well-connected fat cats* Interview with Kenyan economist James Shikwati. "For God's Sake, Please Stop the Aid!" *Spiegel International*, 4 Jul. 2005.

 46 *East India Company*

 46 *British South Africa Company*

 46 *Anaconda Copper*

46 Lada

47 Guatemala, Erna Fergusson. *Guatemala*. (Alfred A. Knopf, 1944).

 47 Scramble for Africa

 47 Delian League

 48 garbage strike "Naples waste management crisis"

49 Naples: A Travellers' Companion, Desmond Seward. (Macmillan, 1986).

 49 Risorgimento "Unification of Italy"

 51 Lord Palmerston

 51 Napoleon III

 51 Mazzini

 51 Garibaldi

 51 Carl Schurz

 51 Greek War of Independence

 51 Lord Byron

52 many opportunities Lauren Levy. "Dominican Republic Provides Sosua as a Haven for Jewish Refugees." *Jewish Virtual Library*. Original source: *Jerusalem Post*, 1995.

52 covered it up Laura Leff. *Buried by the Times: The Holocaust and America's Most Important Newspaper* (Cambridge University Press, 2005).

52 grill "Bombing of Hamburg in World War II"

*52 US and China* "Hull note"

52 half-educated bestseller Jonah Goldberg. *Liberal Fascism*. (Crown Forum, 2009).

52 Erik von Kuehnelt-Leddihn

53 liberal Prime Minister "Francesco Saverio Nitti"

53 Escape

54 ancien régime

54 bit of Nazi propaganda "Warum und Wofür?" *Die Wehrmacht*, 3 (1939). Republished by the *Nazi Propaganda Archive* at Calvin University. Randy Bytwerk, 1998.

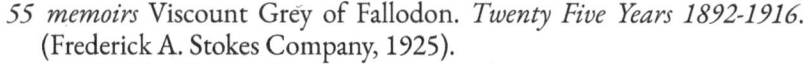*55 Lord Grey of Fallodon*

55 memoirs Viscount Grey of Fallodon. *Twenty Five Years 1892-1916*. (Frederick A. Stokes Company, 1925).

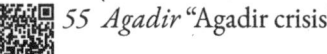*55 Agadir* "Agadir crisis"

56 Hohenzollern monarchy

58 Erich Ludendorff

CHAPTER 3:
THE JACOBITE HISTORY OF THE WORLD

MAY 1, 2008

Okay, open-minded progressives. You've read Chapter 1 and Chapter 2. Quite a bushel of prose. And has any of it changed your mind? Are you ready to stop being a progressive, and start being a reactionary?

Almost certainly not. We haven't really learned anything here. All we've done is plant a couple of little, tiny seeds of doubt. Now we're going to throw a little water on those seeds, and see if we can maybe get a leaf or two to poke its head out. Don't expect a full-grown redwood to fly up and hit you in the face. Even when they work, which isn't often, conversions don't work that way. Doubt is a slow flower. You have to give it time.

What we've seen is that the story of the world that you and I grew up with—a story that is the common heritage of progressives and conservatives alike, although progressives are certainly truer to it—is oddly complicated in spots. The great caravan of the past comes with quite a baggage wagon of paradoxes, each of which needs its own explanation.

So, for example, by one set of standards which seem essential to the progressive mind, the end of colonialism was a great victory for humanity. By another set of standards which it is equally difficult to imagine rejecting, it was a vast human tragedy. Could it be both? A tragic victory, perhaps? **Clio** was always both poet and historian, and the idea of a tragic victory has definite **Empsonian**[1] potential. On the other hand, however...

---

1 Reference to literary critic William Empson, and his 1947 book, *Seven Types of Ambiguity*.

History is big. We shouldn't expect it to be simple. But we'd like it to be as simple as possible. When we study the errors of others, we see that nonsense often conceals the obvious. And what is nonsense, to those who believe in it? To a Catholic, what is the Trinity? A mystery. Some things are truly mysterious. But others have simple explanations. The Trinity is a compromise designed by a standards committee.[2] History 1, mystery 0.

I hate to beat this colonialism thing to death, but there is an odd little op-ed[3] this morning by former Times foreign correspondent John Darnton. It's about Robert Mugabe and T. S. Eliot. It's short and worth a read.

I've seen a few similar reminiscences in the fishwrap recently—we'll let this one serve as an example:

> I first heard mention of Mr. Mugabe in May 1976 in the Quill Club of the Ambassador Hotel, a watering hole where Prime Minister Ian Smith's police, guerrilla sympathizers, reporters and agents from various factions suspended normal antipathies for the sake of gossip. We foreign correspondents used to toss around names of the ultimate leader of the emergent new country like miners testing gold nuggets: Would it be Joshua Nkomo? Ndabaningi Sithole? Jason Moyo?

What's fascinating about these pieces is how close they come to being apologies. And yet how far away they are.

Because why should John Darnton apologize? What could he possibly be sorry for? You apologize when you're responsible for something bad that has happened. President Mugabe is clearly a bad egg. But how could Mr. Darnton and his Quill Club friends be responsible for him? They are reporters, that's all. They report. You decide. And yet there is that phrase—"responsible journalism."

While we're on the fishwrap beat, another puzzle was inflicted on Americans this week by a man of the cloth. As one might expect, the smart people of the world have smart explanations,[4] whereas the dumb ones[5] scratch their heads and say "duh":

---

2 Reference to the First Council of Nicaea.

3

4

5

AN OPEN LETTER TO OPEN-MINDED PROGRESSIVES 67

> Chris Matthews said it best when he said if anything like the 9/11 remarks had been said in his church the weekend after he would certainly have know [*sic*]. I know that's true. In 20 years you have never heard anything inflamatory [*sic*]? It just isn't believable. He initally [*sic*] lied the when ABC first aired the tapes. The next night he was asked by three different news medias [sic] and he said he did not hear nor did he know of any of these remarks. Then the following Tuesday, he acknowledged he had heard about them before he announced his candidacy and that's why he asked him not to come out. Too wierd [*sic*]!

"Too weird." Indeed, weirdness is the mother of doubt. Is it not slightly weird that a twenty-year member of the **Church of Hate Whitey**[6] could become not only the leading candidate for the Presidency, but the candidate who stands for racial harmony? Is it more weird, or less weird, than the fact that Robert Mugabe had no interest in T. S. Eliot?

The thing is: these things *don't* seem weird to me. In the progressive story of the world, they are mysteries. They can be explained, but they need to be explained. In the reactionary story of the world, however, they are firmly in dog-bites-man territory.

I have yet to justify this assertion. But as a progressive, you can swallow it without fear. It is not the red pill that will turn you to an instant Jacobite, forcing you to abandon your life, your beliefs, your friends and lovers, and replace them with an ascetic and fanatical devotion to the doomed old cause of the **Royal Stuarts**. (Though at least you'd still "oppose Republicanism.")

Because even if we admit that the progressive story has these little lacunae, the reactionary story has giant, gaping holes. In fact, it's hard to even say there is a reactionary story. If there was, how would you know it? What would **Archbishop Laud** make of the iPhone? Of jazz? Of Harley-Davidson? The mind, she boggles.

Hopefully she will boggle slightly less after you read the following. Which will still not turn you into a Jacobite—but might at least help you understand the temptation.

Before we can tell the reactionary story, we have to define these weird words, *progressive* and *reactionary*. Vast tomes have been devoted to this purpose. But let's make it as simple: to be progressive is to be left-wing. To be reactionary is to be right-wing.

What is this weird political axis? As you may know, the terms *left* and *right* come from the seating arrangements in the French **Legislative Assembly**. A body no longer in existence. Yet somehow, the dimension remains relevant. It is easy to say that if Barack, Hillary and McCain were seated in the Legislative Assembly, Hillary would be sitting to the right of Barack, and McCain would be to the right of Hillary.

---

6 Reference to Trinity Unity Church.

Moreover, we can apply the axis to events even before 1791. For example, we can say that in the Reformation, Catholicism was right-wing and Protestantism left-wing. This gets a little confusing in the post-1945 era—most pre-20th c. Catholics would find the present-day Church quite, um, Protestant. (If you are unconvinced of this, you may enjoy **Novus Ordo Watch**.) But there is really no Catholic equivalent of the **Münster Republic**, the **Levellers**, etc., etc.

Of course, politics is not a quantitative science (or a science at all), and sometimes it can be a little tricky to decide who is to the left or right of whom. But it's really quite amazing that this linear criterion can be applied so effectively across five centuries of human history. (It even works pretty well on the Greeks and Romans.)

Imagine, for instance, that we wanted to classify *music* along a linear axis. Is Bach to the right of the Beatles? Okay, probably. Are the Stones to the left of the Beatles? Where does the Cure fit in? And John Coltrane? And the Dead Kennedys? What about Einstürzende Neubauten? Are they to the right of Tom Petty, or the left? Is Varg Vikernes between them? And how does he stack up next to 50 Cent?

Each of these musicians represents a way of thinking about music. None of them invented music, nor are any of them unique. They are members of movements. If we have trouble classifying the individual artists, we should at least be able to classify the movements. So is punk to the left of goth? Is baroque to the right of death metal, gangsta rap, ragtime, etc.? We remain completely lost. I'm sure you could arrange all these musical forms on a line, if you had to. And so could I. But I doubt our answers would be the same.

Yet strangely, in the political sphere, this works. Indeed we take it for granted. Why should philosophies of music be all over the map, but philosophies of government arrange themselves along one consistent dimension?

Feel free to come up with your own answer. Here is mine.

Let's start with the obvious. A reactionary—i.e., a right-winger—is someone who believes in *order*, *stability*, and *security*. All of which he treats as synonyms.

Think, as a progressive, about the simplicity of this proposition. It is so stupid as to be almost mindless. What is the purpose of government? Why do we have government, rather than nothing? Because the alternative is Corner Man.

Note that Corner Man has his own philosophy of government. He exercises **sovereignty**. That's *his* corner. ("Metro [the Las Vegas PD] can't even get me off this ---- corner.") Indeed, he has much the same relationship to the government that you and I know and love, that Henry VIII had to the Pope. And how did he acquire his corner? "I've been on this ---- corner for ten ---- years." In legal theory this is called **adverse possession**, which is more or less how the Tudors acquired *their* little island.

Of course, we reactionaries are not fans of Corner Man, largely because his claim to the corner is contested by a superior authority which will prevail in any serious conflict. Why does he attack the blue PT Cruiser? Is it because he's on crack? Perhaps, but perhaps it's also because the driver owes allegiance to the other side of the conflict—"Metro"—and neither has nor would acknowledge Corner Man's authority. For example, she has not paid him any taxes, fees, or rents for the privilege of positioning her vehicle on his (so-called) territory.

One synonym for *reactionary* is legitimist.[7] When the legitimist asks whether Corner Man really owns his corner, he is not asking whether Corner Man *should* own his corner. He asks whether Corner Man *does* own his corner. And his answer is "no." He prefers the claim of "Metro," not (or not just) because "Metro" is not in the habit of getting loaded and bashing the holy heck out of random peoples' cars, but because "Metro" and Corner Man have conflicting claims, and in the end, the former is almost certain to win.

And when he asks whether the Bourbons are the legitimate rulers of France or the Stuarts of England, he is not asking whether (a) the Bourbon or Stuart family has some hereditary biological property that makes their scions ideal for the job (midichlorians, perhaps), or (b) the Bourbon or Stuart will suffer intolerably as a result of being deprived of the throne, or even (c) the Bourbon or Stuart families obtained their original claims fairly and squarely. At least, not if he has any sense. None of these arguments is even close to viable.

Thus, the order that the rational reactionary seeks to preserve and/or restore is *arbitrary*. Perhaps it can be justified on some moral basis. But probably not. It is good simply because it is order, and the alternative to order is violence at worst and politics at best. If the Bourbons do not rule France, someone will—Robespierre, or Napoleon, or Corner Man.[8]

One of the difficulties in resurrecting classical reactionary thought is that when this idea was expressed in the 17th century, it came out in the form of theology. Who put the Stuarts in charge of England? God did. Obviously. And you don't want to argue with God. For a believer in Divine Providence, this is pretty much unanswerable. For a 21st-century reactionary, it won't do at all.

Perhaps the best and most succinct statement of the reactionary philosophy of government—especially considering the context—was that of King Charles in the moments before his execution:

> Truly I desire their liberty and freedom as much as anybody whomsoever; but I must tell you that their liberty and freedom consists of having of government, those laws by which their life and their goods may be most their own. It is not for having a share in government, sir, that is nothing pertaining to them. A subject and sovereign are clean different things.

While I'm not prepared to endorse the author on all matters whatsoever (and I feel that chartered companies are more likely to produce effective neoreactionary government than royal families, Stuart or otherwise), I agree with every word of

---

7 Reference to French royalists who supported traditional hereditary succession of the Bourbon dynasty after the 1830 July Revolution.
8 See Chapter 2.

the above. At least for me, it makes a fine endpoint to the axis: it is impossible to be more reactionary than **Charles I**.

So we know what a reactionary is: a believer in order. What is a progressive?

Here is the problem. We only have one dimension to work with. We know that a progressive is the polar opposite of a reactionary. So if a reactionary is a believer in order, a progressive is—a believer in disorder? A believer in mayhem? A believer in chaos?

Well, of course, this is exactly what a reactionary would say. (In fact, Dr. Johnson did say it.[9]) The only problem is that it's obviously not true. When you, dear progressive, watch the clip of Corner Man, do you revel in the crunch of smashing glass, the screams of the victims, the thrill of wanton destruction? Um, no. You're horrified, just like me.

Let's put aside this question of order for the moment. We know that reactionaries believe in order. We know that progressives do not believe in chaos. But we know that reactionaries are the opposite of progressives. Is this a paradox? It is, and we will resolve it. But not quite yet.

We can say quite easily that a progressive is someone who believes in *progress*. That is, he or she believes the world is moving toward—or at least should be moving toward—some state which is an improvement on the present condition of affairs.

This is what Barack Obama means when he talks about *change*. Why do he and his listeners assume so automatically that this *change* will be for the better? Isn't this word neutral? *Change* means a transition to something different. Different could be better. Or it could be worse. Surely the matter deserves some clarification.

The obvious explanation is that since Obama and his followers will be doing the changing, they will make sure that the result is desirable—at least, to them.

I find this answer inadequate. It implies that progressives are egocentric, humorless, and incapable of self-criticism. I'm sure this is true of some. I'm sure it is also true of some reactionaries—although these days you need a pretty solid sense of humor to even consider being a reactionary. But it is rude to apply a pejorative derivation to an entire belief system, and nor is it particularly accurate in my experience.

A better answer is that today's progressives see themselves as the modern heirs of a tradition of *change*, stretching back to the Enlightenment. They see change as inherently good because they see this history as a history of progress, i.e., improvement. In other words, they believe in **Whig history**.

Whether you are a progressive, a reactionary, or anything in between, I highly recommend the recent documentary *Your Mommy Kills Animals!*, about the animal-rights movement. In it there is a clip of **Ingrid Newkirk**[10] in which she makes the following proposition: animal rights is a social-justice movement. All social-justice movements in the past have been successful. Therefore, the animal-rights movement will inevitably succeed.

---

9 Reference to the Samuel Johnson quote, "The first Whig was the Devil."
10 President of PETA.

AN OPEN LETTER TO OPEN-MINDED PROGRESSIVES

This is pure Whig history. It postulates a mysterious force that animates the course of history, and operates inevitably in the progressive direction. Note the circular reasoning: social justice succeeds because social justice is good. How do we know that social justice is good? Because it succeeds, and good tends to triumph over evil. How do we know that good tends to triumph over evil? Well, just look at the record of social-justice movements.

Which is impressive indeed. If there is any constant phenomenon in the last few hundred years of Western history, it's that—with occasional reversals[11]—reactionaries tend to lose and progressives tend to win. Whether you call them progressives, **liberals, Radicals, Jacobins, republicans,** or even revolutionaries, socialists or communists, the left is your winning team.

What's interesting about this effect is the number of theories that have been proposed to explain it. **Richard Dawkins,** in his 2006 book *The God Delusion,* attributes it to a mysterious force which he calls the Zeitgeist. Dawkins, to his great credit, allows as how he has **no understanding** of the effect. It is just a variable without which his equations won't balance, like Einstein's **cosmological constant.**

Others of a more theological bent have attributed the effect to **Divine Providence.** (Note that the success of progressivism quite conclusively disproves the Providential theory of divine-right monarchy.) And then of course there is our old friend, **dialectical materialism.** Since all these theories are mutually inconsistent, let's reserve our judgment by calling this mysterious left-favoring force the W-force—W, for Whig.

What explains the W-force? One easy explanation is that it's just the interaction of hindsight and a random walk. Everything changes over time—including opinions. Since by definition we consider ourselves enlightened, history appears as a progress from darkness to light.

For example, Professor Dawkins, since he is a progressive, sees the modern tolerance of gays and lesbians as genuine progress (I happen to agree). And for the same reason, he sees the modern intolerance of slavery in just the same way.

However, if these changes are indeed arbitrary, a random walk could reverse them. Professor Dawkins' great-great-grandchildren could then explain to us, just as sincerely, the great moral advance of society, which early in the 21st century still turned a blind eye to rampant sodomy and had no conception of the proper relationship between man and servant.

While this theory is amusing, it is pretty clearly wrong. It depends on the fact that we don't yet have a good definition of what it means to be "progressive." But it clearly does mean *something.* We don't see these kinds of reversals. We see consistent movement in a single direction. Furthermore, we know that progress is the opposite of reaction, and we have a very good definition of reaction. And we know that reaction tends to lose. That isn't random.

---

11 Reference to the Austrian conservative Klemens von Metternich and his tenure at the center of European politics in the first half of the 19th century.

Another phenomenon that people often invoke implicitly is the advance of science and engineering, which indeed is very like the W-force. It is easy to assume, for example, that Charles I could not possibly have anything to say to us on the theory of government, because—to **paraphrase**[12] Hilaire Belloc—we have the iPhone, and he did not.

Of course, all the forms of government we know today were known not only to Charles I, but also to Aristotle. We know why science and engineering have advanced monotonically: it is much easier to create knowledge than destroy it. Since the American approach to government, which has now spread around the world, not only considerably predates iPhones but was in fact based on ancient Greek models, the analogy is quite spurious. It rests on little more than the double meaning of the word "progress."

Another way to evaluate this question is to imagine that the technology of the present suddenly became available to the societies of the past. Stuart iPhones simply break the brain, but we can imagine what the reactionary England of 1808, in which approximately twelve people had the vote and small children were hanged for inappropriate use of the word "God," would make of 21st-century technology. I suspect they would do pretty much what they did with 19th-century technology—use it to take over the world.

We should also seriously consider the possibility that the W-force is exactly what it claims to be, and that good really does have a tendency to triumph over evil. Unfortunately, when we examine political turmoil at the micro level, this is not the tendency we see—the classic case being the French Revolution.

Why did the French Revolution, the vast majority of whose initiators meant nothing but the best for their country, go so sour? A simple explanation is that good people are scrupulous, and evil ones are not. Thus, the latter have more freedom of action than the former. Thus, those who are amoral and simply wish to get ahead in life should choose the side of evil. Thus, good is outnumbered and evil is reinforced, producing the **Yeats effect**:

> The best lack all conviction, while the worst
> Are full of passionate intensity.

Anyone who has not seen this in practice has no experience of human affairs.

I'm afraid I have no rational progressive explanation for the W-force. If anyone else does, I'd be curious to hear it. (Professor Dawkins might be curious to hear it as well.) I do, however, have a reactionary explanation.

First, let's consider the famous first paragraph of Macaulay's *History of England*, which (as La Wik notes[13]) has long served as the case study of Whig history:

---

12 "Whatever happens, we have got the Maxim Gun, and they have not" from Belloc's *The Modern Traveler*.
13 See "Whig History" in the End Notes.

AN OPEN LETTER TO OPEN-MINDED PROGRESSIVES

I purpose to write the history of England from the accession of King James the Second down to a time which is within the memory of men still living. I shall recount the errors which, in a few months, alienated a loyal gentry and priesthood from the House of Stuart. I shall trace the course of that revolution which terminated the long struggle between our sovereigns and their parliaments, and bound up together the rights of the people and the title of the reigning dynasty. I shall relate how the new settlement was, during many troubled years, successfully defended against foreign and domestic enemies; how, under that settlement, the authority of law and the security of property were found to be compatible with a liberty of discussion and of individual action never before known; how, from the auspicious union of order and freedom, sprang a prosperity of which the annals of human affairs had furnished no example; how our country, from a state of ignominious vassalage, rapidly rose to the place of umpire among European powers; how her opulence and her martial glory grew together; how, by wise and resolute good faith, was gradually established a public credit fruitful of marvels which to the statesmen of any former age would have seemed incredible; how a gigantic commerce gave birth to a maritime power, compared with which every other maritime power, ancient or modern, sinks into insignificance; how Scotland, after ages of enmity, was at length united to England, not merely by legal bonds, but by indissoluble ties of interest and affection; how, in America, the British colonies rapidly became far mightier and wealthier than the realms which Cortes and Pizarro had added to the dominions of Charles the Fifth; how in Asia, British adventurers founded an empire not less splendid and more durable than that of Alexander.

Okay. Imagine you are the leader of a daring, futuristic, secret science project whose goal is to resurrect the mind of Macaulay, by digitizing scraps of rotten tissue from his cranium, applying a holographic reconstruction algorithm, and simulating the result in a giant supercomputer. After great effort, you succeed. Macaulay lives. You connect the computer to the Internet. Running at superhuman speed, it downloads gigabytes of information from La Wik and other reliable sources. It says nothing. It is merely processing. Macaulay is revising his great history of England. You wait, breathless, as he reacts to the last 150 years. Finally the screen flashes to life and produces a single sentence:

And then it all went to shit.

The trouble is that the people who run England now, while they are progressive to a T and consider themselves very much the heirs of the British liberal tradition, have different objective standards of success than Macaulay. By Tony Blair's standards, Great Britain is doing better than ever. By Macaulay's standards, it is a disaster area.

What happened? The W-force itself. With its customary glacial irresistibility, it has been driving the center of British politics steadily to the left for the last 150 years. Meanwhile, poor Macaulay has been stuck in his own cranium, just rotting. He has had no chance to adapt. So he still has the same opinions he held in 1859, which in the world of 2008 put him somewhere to the right of **John Tyndall**.[14] If I think of Gordon Brown's Labour as the left edge of my screen and David Cameron's Tories as the right, Macaulay is somewhere out on the fire escape.

Of course, if you are a progressive with a soft spot for Macaulay—despite some of his rather, um, Eurocentric **opinions**—you might assume that by reading the last 150 years of history, he would realize that New Labour is exactly where it's at. I suppose this is a matter of opinion. Perhaps Gordon Brown really is that convincing.

However, we also need to consider the possibility that Macaulay would be convinced in the *opposite direction*. Given the fact that the state of England today would horrify him, he might well be open to moving further out on the fire escape—a reaction not dissimilar to the response that 18th-century Whigs, such as **Edmund Burke** (yes, Burke was a Whig) had to the Reign of Terror.

The absolute shibboleth of the 18th-century and 19th-century British liberal movement, for example, was the proposition that a fundamentally aristocratic government could resist democratic pressures by conceding a mixed constitution. Contemporary commenters on the Reform Acts of **1832** and **1867** are constantly explaining that Tory or **Adullamite** right-wing resistance to these measures was not only futile, but actually dangerous—it could spark an actual, French-style revolution.

Indeed the entire constitution of post-1688 Britain was based on this proposition, because it was based on the concept of **constitutional monarchy**—as opposed to that dreaded Jacobite abomination, "absolute" monarchy. And how exactly did that one work out? As La Wik puts it:

> As originally conceived, a constitutional monarch was quite a powerful figure, head of the executive branch even though his or her power was limited by the constitution and the elected parliament... An evolution in political thinking would, however, eventually spawn such phenomena as universal suffrage and political parties. By the mid 20th century, the political culture in Europe had shifted to the point where most constitutional monarchs had been reduced to the status of figureheads, with no effective power at all. Instead, it was the democratically elected parliaments,

---

14 One-time chairman of the British National Front. Described as a "far-right activist."

and their leader, the prime minister who had become those who exercised power.

If, in 1688, you had insisted that the concept of a "constitutional monarchy" was a contradiction in terms, that "constitutional" simply meant "symbolic" and the upshot of the whole scheme would simply be a return to the rule of Parliament, you were a Jacobite. Plain and simple.

And you were also dead wrong—for about two centuries. Most of the royal powers died with George III, but even Queen Victoria exercised a surprising amount of authority over the operations of "her" government. No longer. If the W-force has made anything clear, it's that constitutional monarchy is not a stable form of government. Nor is restricted suffrage. There is simply no compromise with democracy—good or bad.

Moreover, 19th-century classical liberals promised over and over again that democracy, despite the obvious mathematics of the situation, need not lead to what we now call "socialism." Supposedly the English people, with their stern moral fibre, would never tolerate it. Etc.

The lesson of history is quite clear. Whether you love the W-force or hate it, surrendering to it is not an effective way to resist it. There is no stable point along the left–right axis at which the W-force, having exacted all the concessions to which justice entitles it, simply disappears. Oh, no. It always wants more. "I can has cheezburger?" The persistence of this delusion in Anglo-American thought is quite remarkable. For example, I was reading **Harold Temperley's** life of **George Canning**, from 1905, when I came across this amazing passage on the **Holy Alliance**:

> Despite the great revolution the despots of Europe had learnt nothing and forgotten nothing, except their one saving grace of benevolence. The paternal system of government has not succeeded where strong local institutions or feelings exist, and for this reason Austria has never conciliated or subdued Hungary. But the Holy Alliance proposed a sort of patriarchal system of government for all Europe, which could not really have applied to those nations where free constitutions or strong patriotic feeling still remained. These proved indeed to be to **Metternich** and **Alexander** what **Kossuth** and **Deak** have been to **Francis Joseph**. Metternich did not understand the changes created by the French Revolution in the ideas and hearts of men. He thought he could tear a page from the Book of History, and destroy both the memory and the hope of liberty. He believed that re-action could be permanent, that new ideals and opinions could be crushed, and the world again beguiled into the dreary inaction which characterized the home politics of all nations before 1789.

"Dreary inaction!" "Their one saving grace of benevolence!"

Friends, the world today is not such an awful place. Corner Man aside. But compared to what it would be if "dreary inaction" had prevailed in the world since 1905, it is a sewer and a slum and a dungheap.

Think of all the beautiful people who would have lived, all the beautiful cities that would not have been bombed, all the hideous ones that would not have been built. The Napoleonic Wars were a garden-party compared to the First and Second World Wars. The French Revolution was a garden-party compared to the Russian. And, as we've seen, the Whig foreign policy of exporting democracy as a universal remedy for all ills, as practiced by both Canning and Temperley, does not appear entirely unconnected with these tragedies.

Temperley is even wrong about the small stuff. The hot-blooded Hungarians? Snoring soundly in the arms of Brussels. And before that, Moscow. Which had far less trouble with Nagy than Franz Josef had with Kossuth. No constitutions conceded there! So much for the "Book of History."

Moreover, Temperley didn't even need the future to prove him wrong about Metternich—who, as Deogolwulf **points out**, if anything exaggerated the eventual futility of his efforts. Europe's era of pure reaction was short, but the years between 1815 and 1848 were great ones. (Don't miss the Wulf's rare sally into long form, wherein he **devastates the Enlightenment** in the shape of the distinguished **Professor Grayling**—who turns up in the comment barrel, and receives the brisk filleting his **name suggests**.)

This brings us to the failed project of conservatism, which puts its money in a slightly different place—the proposition that all the concessions made to the W-force in the past are good and necessary, but any further concessions are bad and unnecessary. The Confederate theologian **R. L. Dabney** dispensed with this **quite eloquently:**

> It may be inferred again that the present movement for women's rights will certainly prevail from the history of its only opponent, Northern conservatism. This is a party which never conserves anything. Its history has been that it demurs to each aggression of the progressive party, and aims to save its credit by a respectable amount of growling, but always acquiesces at last in the innovation. What was the resisted novelty of yesterday is today one of the accepted principles of conservatism; it is now conservative only in affecting to resist the next innovation, which will tomorrow be forced upon its timidity and will be succeeded by some third revolution, to be denounced and then adopted in its turn. American conservatism is merely the shadow that follows Radicalism as it moves forward towards perdition. It remains behind it, but never retards it, and always advances near its leader. This pretended salt bath utterly lost its savor: wherewith shall it be salted? Its impo-

tency is not hard, indeed, to explain. It is worthless because it is the conservatism of expediency only, and not of sturdy principle. It intends to risk nothing serious for the sake of the truth, and has no idea of being guilty of the folly of martyrdom. It always when about to enter a protest very blandly informs the wild beast whose path it essays to stop, that its "bark is worse than its bite," and that it only means to save its manners by enacting its decent role of resistance. The only practical purpose which it now subserves in American politics is to give enough exercise to Radicalism to keep it "in wind," and to prevent its becoming pursy and lazy, from having nothing to whip. No doubt, after a few years, when women's suffrage shall have become an accomplished fact, conservatism will tacitly admit it into its creed, and thenceforward plume itself upon its wise firmness in opposing with similar weapons the extreme of baby suffrage; and when that too shall have been won, it will be heard declaring that the integrity of the American Constitution requires at least the refusal of suffrage to donkeys. There it will assume, with great dignity, its final position.

I'm sure Rev. Dabney would have regarded the era of Ingrid Newkirk with great amusement.

However, note how thoroughly hoist by his own petard he is. The proposition that suffrage is a bad idea, period, may not be one you regard as defensible—but it is surely more defensible than the proposition that all men should be able to vote, but not all women. (Or white men and not black men, another proposition of which the Rev. Dabney was convinced. Note that this bastion also proved impractical to defend.)

So: we still do not understand the W-force. Nor do we understand why reaction is the polar opposite of progressivism. Nor do we have any theory which explains in which cases the latter is good, and in which cases it is bad.

But Dabney and Metternich suggest a very different way of dealing with it. Perhaps if you actually oppose the W-force, the most effective way to oppose it is simply to... oppose it.

After all, as a progressive, you oppose racism. Is the most effective way to oppose racism to give it a little air, to let it blow off steam—to be just a little bit racist, but not too much? It strikes me that the most effective way to oppose racism is simply to not tolerate it at all.

As a progressive, you support democracy. But if you set this aside, wouldn't your advice to a government that opposed democracy simply be the same? If you, with full hindsight, were advising Charles I, would you really advise him to let the Parliament execute **Strafford**,[15] on the grounds that it might sate their lust for necks?

What I'm suggesting is that the W-force actually behaves as an **inverted pendulum**,[16] perhaps with a bit of a delay loop. As an "absolute" monarch, the best strategy for maintaining your rule is to preserve your sovereignty entirely intact. Ripping off chunks of it and throwing them to the wolves only seems to encourage the critters.

Why was this not obvious to the kings and princes of old Europe? Perhaps it was obvious. The trouble was that absolute monarchy was always an ideal, never a reality. Every sovereign in history has been a creature of politics—not democratic politics, perhaps, but politics still. At the very least, a king who loses the support of the army is finished. So the pendulum is not quite vertical, and it's all too easy to let it do what it obviously wants to do.

The inverted-pendulum model suggests that, for a stable and coherent nondemocratic state, eliminating politics requires very little repressive energy. Singapore, Dubai and China, for example, all have their secret police—as did the 19th-century Hapsburgs. Each of these governments is very different from the others, but they are all terrified of the W-force. Yet they manage to restrain it, without either falling prey to democracy or opening death camps.

Residents of these countries can think whatever they like. They can even say whatever they like. It is only when they actually organize that they get in trouble. If you don't want the **Ministry of Public Security** to bother you, don't start or join an antigovernment movement. Certainly this is not ideal—I don't think this blog would be tolerated in China, and my image of the ideal state is one in which you can start all the antigovernment movements you want, as long as they don't involve guns or bombs. However, when we compare this level of infringement of personal freedom to the experience of daily life under Stalin or Hitler, we are comparing peanuts to pumpkins.

Why does China not tolerate peaceful antigovernment politics? Because "people power" can defeat the People's Liberation Army? No. Because China is not a perfectly stable state, and it knows that quite well. Within the Chinese Communist Party, there is politics galore. One move that is off-limits for contending figures within the Chinese regime, however, is imposing one's will on one's adversaries by means of mob politics. Almost everyone in any position of responsibility in the PRC today was personally scarred by the Cultural Revolution, in which China felt all the vices of democracy and none of its virtues. Only by outlawing politics can the Party hold itself together.

---

15 Thomas Wentworth, 1st Earl of Strafford, close adviser to Charles I and a strong ally of the monarch, but for whom Charles I nonetheless signed a death warrant when Parliament charged him with the crime of high treason.

16 An upside-down pendulum that is inherently unstable and depends on active controls to stay upright.

AN OPEN LETTER TO OPEN-MINDED PROGRESSIVES

Note that in 1989 the Chinese government broke the cardinal rule of Whig government: never fire on a mob. As John F. Kennedy put it, "Those who make peaceful revolution impossible will make violent revolution inevitable." Not only did the Chinese government make peaceful revolution impossible—they made peaceful revolution violent. And the result? Violent revolution? No—twenty years of peace, unparalleled prosperity, and personal if not political freedom. As philosophers say, one white raven refutes the assertion that all ravens are black.

The inverted-pendulum model of the W-force gives us a great way to understand Hitler. Yes: Hitler was a reactionary. I am a reactionary. Yikes! If I ever feel the need to grow a mustache, which I won't, I'll have to make sure it extends well past the nose on both sides. Perhaps waxing and curling the tips is just the only way.

Nazism, and fascism in general, was a reactionary movement. It was also the product of a very unusual set of circumstances in history. The fascisms emerged in countries in which the top level of the political system had been turned over to liberals, but many remnants of the *ancien régime* still existed—notably in the security forces and judiciary system—and retained considerable popular support among the petit-bourgeois or Townie caste.

So the pendulum was a long, long way from top dead center. But the system still had a crude mechanism by which it could be brutally yanked back: street violence. Hitler and Mussolini came to power partly by good old democratic politics, and partly by using their thugs to intimidate their political opponents. This would not have been possible without a security system which tolerated this sort of behavior. When the SA had street fights with the Communists, the SA men tended to get off and the Communists get long jail sentences.

Note how much effort post-1945 governments invest in making sure this particular horse does not escape from this particular barn. There is zero official tolerance for right-wing political violence in any Western country today. (There is a good bit of tolerance for left-wing violence, notably the European **antifas**, who are the real heirs of **Ernst Röhm**.) Classical fascism simply does not work without a hefty supply of judges who are willing to "let boys be boys."

The Western judicial systems today cannot be described as reactionary in any way, shape or form. Thus, if you are a progressive, you can cross fascism—at least, good old 1930s-style fascism—off your list of worries. And if you are a reactionary, you can cross it off your list of tricks to try. Considering the results of the 1930s, I have to regard this as a good thing.

Okay. Enough suspense. Enough digressions. Let's explain the W-force. Let's also explain why progressivism is the opposite of reaction. In fact, let's explain them both with the same theory.

Progressives do not, in general, believe in chaos. (Imagine breaking into the Obama website and replacing all uses of the word "change" with "chaos." Happy, chanting crowds, holding placards that just say "CHAOS..." Frankly, the whole thing is creepy enough as it is.) Nor do they believe in disorder, mayhem, destruction, or doing a massive pile of crack and smashing the crap out of some poor woman's car.

Rather, when you look at what progressives, Whigs, republicans, and other anti-reactionaries *actually believe in*—whether they are supporters of Obama, Lafayette, Herzen, or any other paladin of the people's cause—it is rarely (although not never) the simple, nihilistic liquidation of the present order. It is always the construction of some new order, which is at least intended as an improvement on the present one.

However, in order to construct this new order, two things need to happen. One: the builders of the new order need to gain power. Two: they need to destroy the old order, which by its insistence on continuing to exist obstructs the birth of the new.

In the progressive mind, these indispensable tasks are not objectives. They are methods. They may even be conceived as unpleasant, if necessary, duties.

One fascinating fact about the presidential campaign of 2008 is that both Democratic candidates are, or at least at one point were, disciples of **Saul Alinsky**. Clinton actually studied and corresponded with Alinsky. Obama was an Alinskyist "**community organizer.**" Next year, we may well have our first Alinskyist president.

Last year, the New Republic—not a reactionary publication—published an excellent article on Obama's Alinskyist roots. I'm afraid this piece is required reading for all progressives. If you are still a progressive after reading it, at least you know what you're involved with. Here's the bit that jumped out for me:

> Alinsky's contribution to community organizing was to create a set of rules, a clear-eyed and systemic approach that ordinary citizens can use to gain public power. The first and most fundamental lesson Obama learned was to reassess his understanding of power. Horwitt says that, when Alinsky would ask new students why they wanted to organize, they would invariably respond with selfless bromides about wanting to help others. Alinsky would then scream back at them that there was a one-word answer: "You want to organize for power!"
>
> Galluzzo shared with me the manual he uses to train new organizers, which is little different from the version he used to train Obama in the '80s. It is filled with workshops and chapter headings on understanding power: "power analysis," "elements of a power organization," "the path to power." Galluzzo told me that many new trainees have an aversion to Alinsky's gritty approach because they come to organizing as idealists rather than realists. But Galluzzo's manual instructs them to get over these hang-ups. "We are not virtuous by not wanting power," it says. "We are really cowards for not wanting power," because "power is good" and "powerlessness is evil."

AN OPEN LETTER TO OPEN-MINDED PROGRESSIVES

The other fundamental lesson Obama was taught is Alinsky's maxim that self-interest is the only principle around which to organize people. (Galluzzo's manual goes so far as to advise trainees in block letters: "get rid of do-gooders in your church and your organization.") Obama was a fan of Alinsky's realistic streak. "The key to creating successful organizations was making sure people's self-interest was met," he told me, "and not just basing it on pie-in-the-sky idealism. So there were some basic principles that remained powerful then, and in fact I still believe in."

[...]

Obama so mastered the workshops on power that he later taught them himself. On his campaign website, one can find a photo of Obama in a classroom teaching students Alinskian methods.[17] He stands in front of a blackboard on which he has written, "Power Analysis" and "Relationships Built on Self Interest," an idea illustrated by a diagram of the flow of money from corporations to the mayor.

Here is my theory about progressivism: it is a "Relationship Built on Self Interest." It is exactly what Alinsky says it is: a way for people who want power to organize. It brings them together around the oldest human pleasure other than sex: ganging up on your enemies. It lets them rationalize this ruthless, carnivorous activity as a philanthropic cause. But the real attraction is the thrill of power and victory—sometimes with a little money thrown in.

This is why the likes of a Temperley cannot imagine a world of "dreary inaction," with no politics at all for anyone. "That is nothing pertaining to them." Obama once tried to take a regular job at an ordinary company. He felt dead in it. It was like feeding a dog on turnips. Carnivores need meat.

What made Alinsky so effective was that he dispensed with the romantic euphemisms. He just described the thing as what it is. You have to admire him for that, I feel. A Lafayette, a Herzen, or almost any 19th-century republican outside the Marxist department, would have been absolutely appalled by Alinsky. But the fact is that they were basically in the same business.

So the progressive is, indeed, the polar opposite of the reactionary. Just as order and stability are essential to reaction, disorder and destruction are essential to progressivism.

The progressive never sees it this way. His goal is never to produce disorder and destruction. Unless he is Alinsky himself, he is very unlikely to think directly in terms of seizing power and smashing his enemies. Usually there is some end which is unequivocally desirable—often even from the reactionary perspective.

17

But if you could somehow design a progressive movement that could achieve its goal without seizing power or smashing its enemies, it would have little energy and find few supporters. What makes these movements so popular is the opportunity for action and the prospect of victory. To defeat them, ensure that they have no chance of success. No one loves a loser.

This theory also explains why progressive movements can produce results which are good. One: their goals have to be good, at least from their followers' perspective. Since these are not evil people we're talking about, their definition of good is often the same as yours or mine. And two: if progressivism is an essentially destructive force, some things still do need destroying.

Let's take homophobia, for example, because this is one area on which (despite my breeder tendencies) I am fully in agreement with the most advanced progressive thinking. And yet, the destruction of homophobia is an act of violent cultural hegemony. Americans and Europeans have considered homosexuality sick, evil and wrong since Jesus was a little boy. If you have the power to tell people they can't believe this anymore, you have the power to tell them just about anything. In this case, you are using your superpowers for good. Is this always so?

As for the W-force, while the inverted pendulum is a good physical analogy, there is another: entropy.

Progressivism is obviously entropic. Obviously, its enemy is order. Progressives instinctively despise formality, authority, and hierarchy. Reactionary political theorists such as Hobbes liked to conceive the state in terms of an ordered system, a sort of clockwork. Progressivism is sand in the gears of the clock.

More subtly, however, the real entropic effect is in the progressive method of capturing power not by seizing the entire state, but by biting off little chunks of it wherever it sticks out. The effect is a steady increase in the complexity of the state's decision-making process. And complexity, of course, is the same thing as entropy.

65 *Clio*

 65 *Empsonian*, William Empson. *Seven Types of Ambiguity*. (New Directions, 1947).

 66 *standards committee* "First Council of Nicaea"

 66 *little op-ed* John Darnton. "The Hollow Man." *New York Times*, 30 Apr. 2008.

 66 *Ian Smith*

 66 *Joshua Nkomo*

 66 *Ndabaningi Sithole*

 66 *Jason Moyo*

 66 *smart explanations* Originally linked to an article at the progresisve group blog Firedoglake. Later reposted to author Dave Neiwert's blog, Orcinus. Dave Neiwert. "Things Americans don't like to talk about." *Orcinus.* 29 Apr. 2008.

 66 *dumb ones* Andrew Malcolm. "Is Obama wrong or Wright? Vote here." *Los Angeles Times*, 30 Apr. 2008.

 67 *Church of Hate Whitey* "Trinity United Church of Christ"

 67 *Royal Stuarts* Link to the Royal Stuart society homepage.

 67 *Archbishop Laud*

 67 *Legislative Assembly*

LINKS & NOTES

 68 *Novus Ordo Watch* Website devoted to "educating the public" about the "illegitimate" occupation of the Vatican by adherents of the "Vatican II sect," or "Novus Ordo."

 68 *Münster Republic*

 68 *Levellers*

 68 *sovereignty*

 68 *adverse possession*

 69 *legitimist*

 69 *midichlorians* Microscopic bio-elements that constitutes "The Force" in Star Wars lore.

 69 *Divine Providence-1*

 69 *that of King Charls* King Charles. "His Speech, made upon the scaffold at Whitehall-Gate." London. 30 Jan. 1649.

 69 *chartered companies*

 70 *Charles I*

 70 *say it* "The first Whig was the Devil." Samuel Johnson, as quoted by James Boswell, 28 Apr. 1778, *Life of Johnson*, ed., R.W. Chapman (Oxford University Press, 1998).

 70 *Whig history*

70 *Your Mommy Kills Animals!* Curt Johnson. 2007.

AN OPEN LETTER TO OPEN-MINDED PROGRESSIVES

 70 Ingrid Newkirk

 71 occasional reversals "Klemens von Metternich"

 71 liberals

 71 Radicals

 71 Jacobins

 71 republicans

 71 Richard Dawkins. The God Delusion. (Bantam Books, 2006).

71 no understanding See section 3 of this volume, "How Dawkins Got Pwned" for a thorough elaboration on Dawkins' historical and conceptual oversights.

 71 cosmological constant

 71 dialectical materialism

72 paraphrase Hillaire Belloc. *The Modern Traveler.* (E. Arnold, 1898).

72 Yeats effect W.B. Yeats. "The Second Coming." *Michael Robartes and the Dancer.* 1920.

 72 History of England Lord Thomas Babington Macauley. *The History of England from the Accession of James the Second.* (London, 1848).

 74 John Tyndall

74 opinions

 74 Edmund Burke

 74 1832

 74 1867

 74 Adullamite

 74 constitutional monarchy

75 *Harold Temperley's* Harold Temperely. *Life of Canning.* (London, J. Finch & Co., 1905).

 75 George Canning

 75 Holy Alliance

 75 Alexander

 75 Kossuth

 75 Deak

 75 Francis Joseph

76 points out "I have had the misfortune to belong to the revolutionary epoch.... Fate has laid upon me in part the duty of restraining, so far as my powers permit, a generation whose destiny seems to be that of losing itself upon a slope which will surely lead to its ruin." So said Klemens von Metternich, yet events showed his prediction to be a little off the mark, at least as stated in Dearieme's Laws of Political Dynamics: — First Law: Conservatives are good at inferring the direction of change; Second Law: ... but are prone to overestimate the pace of change." Klemens von Metternich, letter dated 3 Sep. 1819, in Richard Metternich (ed.), *Mémoires, Ducuments et Écrits laissés par le Prince de Metternich*, 8 Vols (Paris, 1880-84), vol. III, p.307, quoted by Alan Palmer, Metternich: Councillor of Europe (London: Phoenix Giant, 1997), p.186. Original link and citation are from the blogger Deogolwulf's blog *The Joy of Curmudgeonry*.

 76 devastates the Enlightenment Deogolwulf. "Professor Grayling's Enlightenment Club." *The Joy of Curmudgeonry*. 23 Apr. 2008.

 76 Professor Grayling

 76 R. L. Dabney

 76 quite eloquently Robert L. Dabney. "Women's Rights Women." *The Southern Magazine*, Vol. 1, No. 3. March, 1871. Excerpt posted at *covenanter.org*.

 78 Strafford

 78 inverted pendulum

 78 Ministry of Public Security

 79 Ernst Röhm

 80 Saul Alinsky

 80 community organizer Serge Koaveleski. "Obama's Organizing Years, Guiding Others and Finding Himself." *New York Times*, 7 Jul. 2008.

80 excellent article Ryan Lizza. "The Agitator." *The New Republic*, 18 Mar. 2007.

 81 ordinary company Obama writes about this experience in his autobiography *Dreams From My Father* (1995), though his version of events is challenged by blogger, and former co-worker Dan Armstrong. Dan Armstrong. "Barack Obama Embellishes His Resume." *Analyze This*. 9 Jul. 2005.

CHAPTER 4: DR. JOHNSON'S HYPOTHESIS
MAY 8, 2008

In the first three chapters, dear open-minded progressive, we've tried to build up some tools that will help you evaluate the disturbing proposition we're about to present.

The proposition is neither new nor mysterious. We'll call it Dr. Johnson's hypothesis—from **this quip** by the great **Doctor:**[1]

> *And I have always said, the first Whig was the Devil.*

Of course this is not a hypothesis in the scientific sense of the word—we cannot prove it, nor will we try. It is just a phrase you can agree with, or not.

The great advantage of Dr. Johnson's formulation is that it has a pleasant boolean quality. You can agree or disagree. It is pretty hard to be indifferent. Let's take it for granted that, as a progressive, you disagree, and we'll try to figure out what might change your mind.

What does it mean that "the first Whig was the Devil?" What do you think of when you think of the Devil? I always think of Mick Jagger:

> Please allow me to introduce myself
> I'm a man of wealth and taste
> I've been around for a long, long year
> Stole many a man's soul to waste

---

1 Samuel Johnson

CHAPTER 4

> And I was 'round when Jesus Christ
> Had his moment of doubt and pain
> Made damn sure that Pilate
> Washed his hands and sealed his fate
> Pleased to meet you
> Hope you guess my name
> But what's puzzling you
> Is the nature of my game
> I stuck around St. Petersburg
> When I saw it was a time for a change
> Killed the czar and his ministers
> Anastasia screamed in vain
> I rode a tank
> Held a general's rank
> When the Blitzkrieg raged
> And the bodies stank

Surely we can agree that the Devil *rode a tank, held a general's rank, when the Blitzkrieg raged and the bodies stank.* What Dr. Johnson is proposing is that the **Adversary** clapped at the **Putney Debates**, that he smeared his face and shook his tomahawk on the **Dartmouth**, that he leered and cackled as he swore the **Tennis Court Oath**. Not that it's a short song, but I don't recall these bits.

Of course, there is that part about *St. Petersburg*, when it was *time for a change*... I actually have been holding out on you guys here. I have a little family secret to reveal.

I am not a progressive. But my father's parents were. **Great Neck** Jews of the Yiddish variety, *progressive* is the exact word they always used to describe their views. And they meant exactly the same thing by it that Barack Obama does. One of the last things my grandmother said to me, before she fell down the stairs and smashed her frontal lobe (kids, when your elderly relatives sign living wills, they generally mean it—make sure the doctors are reminded, often), was that **Frank Rich** is a really, really wonderful writer.

Only, you know what? For Gramps and Grandma, who were about the nicest people you could imagine, who certainly had no interest in the Devil or any of his works, not even Mick Jagger, *progressive* was a code word. A sort of dog-whistle. What they really were was Communists.

I don't mean just **pinkos** or **fellow travelers** of the "**Alger**—I mean, **Adlai**" variety. I mean actual, dues-paying members of the **CPUSA**.[2] From the '30s through at least the '70s. Did they have cards? Did they **carry them?** Did they ever pull out their Party cards by mistake at Safeway? "I'm sorry, ma'am, this may entitle you to free travel on the Moscow subway, but it does not provide access to our low-priced specials." I'm afraid these details are lost to history.

---

[2] Communist Party of the U.S.A.

But my brother has wartime letters from my grandfather in which he closes by asking his wife to "keep faith with the Party." My parents recall dinner-table conversations from the early '70s in which the phrase "party line" was used in a non-ironic context. And the story goes that the two of them actually met at a Party meeting, at which Gramps stood on a chair in someone's kitchen and made some kind of a rabble-rousing speech.

I am relying on family hearsay here. Because my grandmother would never admit any of it, *even to me*. Not that I outed myself as a Jacobite, but it must have been clear that I hadn't been reading quite enough Frank Rich. Once I screwed up my courage and asked her if the story about owing my existence to a Party cell was true. "Oh, no," she said. "It was a meeting of the **American League for Peace and Democracy**."[3] I'm afraid Grandma's conspiratorial reflexes were not made for a world with Wikipedia.

So, in 2008 terms, what we're saying when we say that *the first Whig was the Devil* is that this idea of "progress" might be kind of, well, *creepy and weird*. As you see, my family background predisposes me to this suspicion. There is no use in trying to convince me that there was never any such thing as an international Communist conspiracy.

As a modern progressive, of course, you are not a Communist but (like **Sartre**) an anti-anti-Communist. You think of Communism as a mistake, which of course is exactly what it was. The anti-Communism of a Joe McCarthy or a Robert Welch still shocks and appalls you. Its opposite does not. "McCarthyist" is a live insult in your mind. So is "fascist." "Communist," or any of its variants, is kind of dated and almost funny. "You Communist!"

At most you might say that Obama is a communist the same way Mitt Romney is a Mormon. Romney is not a Mormon because he, personally, read the Book of Mormon and felt the awe and mystery of Joseph Smith's golden plates. He is a Mormon because his parents were Mormons. Just as Obama's were **communists**. (I use the small 'c' to mean **sympathy**, not membership.) Even if you made Romney absolute king of the universe, I suspect that re-establishing the **State of Deseret** would not be high on his agenda. I'm sure the same goes for Obama and the Politburo.

The anti-anti-Communist theory of history has a special niche for Communism. It is not good, exactly, but it is also not good to attack it. So we won't. The truth is that Communism is only one small part of the progressive experience. The conclusion that progressivism must be bad because Stalin called himself "progressive" is just as facile and fallacious as the conclusion that reaction must be bad because Hitler (though he did not use the word) was a reactionary.

At best Communism is an example of how "progress" could be creepy and weird. But, because of these historical associations, it's not an effective example of "creepy and weird." Here's a better one: *Scientology*.

---

3 Malapropism of the "American League Against War and Fascism."

CHAPTER 4

Did you watch the Tom Cruise **Scientology video**?[4] I really think this is a necessity. If you go straight from this to the Obama **We Are The Ones**[5] video (not, I hasten to point out, an official campaign production), what is your gut response? Coincidence? Or, um, conspiracy?

What I'm suggesting is that progressivism, from Dr. Johnson's Whigs (and even well before) to "will.i.am," is a little like Scientology. Let me emphasize the word *little*. I'd say progressivism resembles Scientology in the same way that Scarlett Johansson resembles the *Caenorhabditis* nematode, a Porsche Cayenne resembles a wheelbarrow, or LSD resembles green tea. On the surface, they are totally different things. The similarities are all low-level.

Scientology is obviously creepy and weird. To make the case that progressivism is creepy and weird, we have one overwhelming challenge: the fact that progressives are not, in general, creepy and weird. Progressives are, in general, pleasant, well-educated and well-grounded. This cannot be said of **Scientologists**.

Then again, there's another thing that Scientologists don't have: friends in high places. At least as far as I'm aware. I would like to think that the penetration of Scientology in government and other prestigious institutions is fairly minor. Perhaps I am mistaken about this. I hope not. Because I really have no reason to think that if Scientologists take control of any institution—the CIA, Cirque du Soleil, the New York Times, Starbucks, the NBA, Yale, Apple, you name it—they will ever depart of their own free will. At least if you believe Mr. Cruise, they seem quite sincere about their desire to take over the world. For its own good, of course.

Again, does this ring a bell? Maybe. But there's only so much we can learn from this kind of innuendo. I'm afraid it's time for some heavy political theory.

Our concern is the relationship, past and present, between progressivism and American institutions. Clearly a tricky question. There is no plausible null answer, as for Scientology. There is *something* going on. But what is it? What is the big picture?

Let's play a fun little game. We'll separate civilized societies into three types—1, 2, and 3—according to their relationship between opinion and authority. To make the game fun, I'll describe the classes abstractly, without giving examples. Then we'll try to figure out which class we live in.

Type 3 is what Karl Popper called the **open society**.[6] In a type 3 society, thoughts compete on the basis of their resemblance to reality. Institutions which

---

4

5

6 In *The Open Society and Its Enemies* (1945) Popper broadly makes the case that the free flow of information in Western liberal democracies produces better political and moral outcomes than in "closed" societies.

AN OPEN LETTER TO OPEN-MINDED PROGRESSIVES

propagate thoughts compete on the basis of the quality of the thoughts they propagate. Is this rocket science? It is not.

Good ideas outcompete bad ideas in a type 3 society, because most of us would rather be clueful than deluded. While many individuals have cognitive biases—such as a natural preference for optimistic over pessimistic predictions, or the reverse—these average out and are dwarfed by the general ambition of intellectuals to see reality as it actually is. Intellectuals are brutally competitive by nature, and delight in exploding the delusions of others. Nonsense should not last long around them.

Thus, in a type 3 society, we cannot say that everyone will agree and they will all be right. But we can be quite confident that the best thoughts will be readily available to those who care to think them. In a type 3 society there will always be superstitions, because there will always be superstitious people, who may like everyone else think and speak as they please. There will always be differences of opinion, because many questions cannot be answered by precise and objective methods—whose performance is better, Humphrey Bogart's in *Casablanca* or Rutger Hauer's in *Split Second*? But since reality is one thing, and people are people, people who are smart and want to understand reality will generally cluster around the truth.

So when you live in a type 3 society, while you *can* think for yourself, you generally don't *have* to think for yourself. Why buy a cow, when milk is so cheap? The type 3 society makes an accurate perception of reality easily available to anyone who wants it. If you want an accurate understanding of history, just buy a history book. If you want a weird, creepy understanding of history, you can probably find that as well, but first you will need to find a group of historians who share your weird, creepy biases. The sane ones will almost certainly be in the majority.

I think you and I can agree that a type 3 society is where we want to live. The question is: *do* we live in one? Let's take a rain check on this baby.

Type 1 is basically the opposite of type 3. Let's call it the *loyal society*. In a type 1 society, your thoughts are *coordinated by the government*. Public opinion is a matter of state security.

Why is public opinion a matter of state security? Because people are freakin' dangerous. Anyone who has ever raised a male child has seen its instinctive affection for weapons. Heck, *chimpanzees* are **freakin' dangerous**. And you'll notice that most of the earth's surface is controlled by their hairless relatives, which is clearly not how it would be if our brother apes had their druthers.

In a type 1 society, the State establishes two categories of thoughts: good thoughts and bad thoughts. It penalizes people for expressing bad thoughts, or rewards them for expressing good thoughts, or ideally, of course, both.

A bad thought is any thought that, if a sufficient number of people were to think it, might be threatening to the safety of the State. A good thought is any thought that is useful to the State, even if just because it fits in the spot where a bad one might otherwise go.

To install its good thoughts in your brain, the State supports a set of *official information organs*, institutions which churn out good thinking on a cradle-to-grave basis. The organs install good thoughts in the young, and maintain them in the adult. Hominids are learning machines. They learn what's put in front of them. It's really not that hard.

To keep bad thoughts from spreading, the State uses its powers to discourage, prohibit or destroy unofficial or otherwise uncoordinated information organs. It constructs a legal environment in which direct, person-to-person transmission of bad thoughts is socially and professionally imprudent at best, actionable at worst. It may exempt dissenters from the protection of the law, or impose legal disabilities on them, or on those who tolerate them. Or, of course, it can imprison, banish or execute them.

In a successful type 1 society—there have been many—the range of good thoughts may be rich and broad. Many if not all of them can be quite sensible. It should be possible for an intelligent member of the governing classes to live a normal and successful life without once being tempted to venture off the reservation.

However, from the perspective of the security forces, it may be quite useful to have one or two questions for which the bad answer is true, and the good one is nonsense. Some people are just natural-born troublemakers. Others are naturally loyal. Separating the sheep from the goats gives the authorities a great way to focus on the latter.

Of course, not *everyone* in a type 1 society needs to be a believer. The more the better, however, especially among the governing classes. An ideal structure is one in which believers are concentrated among the most fashionable and successful social circles, and dissenters (if there are any) tend to be poorly educated, less intelligent, and nowhere near as wealthy. If this can be achieved, the believers will feel a natural and healthy contempt for the dissenters, who will be inclined to abandon any bad thoughts they may have been brought up with if they have any desire to succeed in life.

The *sine qua non* of a type 1 society is central coordination of information. Because the organs are the instruments which make state security a reality, they cannot be allowed to contradict each other. In a state which is secured purely by military force, can various units of the army and navy get into little catfights with each other? Um, no. Likewise, in a state secured by thought control (as well as probably some military force), any intellectual conflict is a menace of the first order. Even on trivial details, disagreement means instability.

In other words, the information organs of a type 1 society are *synoptic*. They see the world through one eye, one set of doctrines, one official story. Call it the *synopsis*.

How does a type 1 state maintain the coherence of its synopsis? One easy way is to have a single leader, who exercises unified executive supervision. Ideally the same leader manages both physical and intellectual security. If the type 1 state doesn't have a single leader, it should at least have a single authoritative institution. Since security depends on synoptic coherence, any divergence can quite literally lead to civil war.

There is no mystery around the historical identity of type 1 societies. This is an unambiguously right-wing pattern. It is also the default structure of human government: the god-king. The Greeks called it "oriental despotism." In Christian history it is known as **caesaropapism**. In Anglo-American history, it is the throne-and-altar state, as represented by the high-church Anglican or Catholic tradition. When Americans express an affection for separation of Church and State, they are expressing an antipathy to the type 1 design.

And, of course, in 20th-century history we see the type 1 state most clearly in National Socialism and Italian Fascism. The fascisms discarded most of the trappings of Christian theism, but reused the basic caesaropapist design. Under Hitler's supervision, of course, Goebbels was more or less the pope of Nazi Germany. His executive authority over all intellectual content in the Third Reich, from films to schools to universities, was easily the equal of any medieval pontiff's. (I highly recommend watching *The Goebbels Experiment*.)

The Nazi term *Gleichschaltung*, generally translated as "coordination," is more or less the modern epitome of the type 1 design. The Nazis also used the word *Aufklärung*, meaning "enlightenment" or literally "clearing-up," for the inculcation of useful thoughts in the German people. I think of this term every time I see a "public service message."

We also see the type 1 pattern, if not quite as distinctly, in the Communist states. It tends to be more institutional and less personal. It is easy to identify Communist Hitlers, but there is no clear Communist equivalent of Goebbels. Communist states over time experienced a decay of personal authority, which passed instead to institutions. But the Party in a modern one-party state is more or less equivalent to the Church in the old Christian dispensation, and an established church is an established church whether governed by pope or synod.

The type 1 state is certainly the most common form in history. It is not the end of the world. China today is a type 1 society. It also has the world's most successful economy, and is not such a bad place to live at all. Elizabethan England, which experienced perhaps the greatest artistic explosion in human history, was a type 1 society, with **secret police galore**.[7] On the other hand, North Korea is a type 1 society, and it's awful in almost every possible way. I can say generally that I would rather live in a type 3 society than in a type 1 society, but the details matter.

But here is the problem.

The problem is: modern, post-1945 Western society certainly does not match the description of a type 1 society. For example, there is no coordinating authority. Unless you can come up with some conspiracy theory (Joo! Joo!), it simply doesn't exist. There is no Goebbels who tells writers what to write, filmmakers what to film, journalists what to print, or professors what to profess. There is no Pope, there is no Church, there is no Party, there is nothing. And as we've seen, the type 1 design makes no sense without coordination.

---

7 Reference to Francis Walsingham, principal secretary and "spymaster" during the reign of Elizabeth I.

On the other hand, however...

One, while our society does not match the type 1 description in this essential sense, it seems to match it quite well in others. And two, while it matches the type 3 description in some ways, it does not seem to match it in others.

In a type 3 society, for example, we should see intellectual inhomogeneities between competing institutions. Harvard and Yale should *mostly* agree, because reality is one thing. So should the New York Times and the Washington Post. But there will always be sclerosis, stagnation, drift. Competition, not just among ideas but among institutions, is essential to the Popperian ideal. We should see these institutions drift away from reality. And we should see the marketplace of ideas punish them when they do, and reward those which do not.

Do you see this? Because I sure don't. What I see is a synopsis.

From my perspective, not just Harvard and Yale, but in fact all major American universities in the Western world, offer exactly the same intellectual product. Which institution is more to the left, for example? Harvard, or Yale? You can pick any two mainstream universities, and you will not be able to answer this question. It's a sort of intellectual **peloton**.

And it's not that we don't see drift. There is plenty of drift. If you ask which is more to the left, Harvard today or Harvard in 1958, the answer is easy. Yet somehow, the entire peloton is drifting in the same direction at the same speed. Does this scream "type 3" to you? And yet, if there is some Goebbels telling Harvard and Yale professors what to profess, the secret is awfully well-kept.

The same is true of newspapers. The so-called "mainstream media" is certainly a synopsis. Just as there is a bright line between mainstream and non-mainstream universities, there is a bright line between mainstream and non-mainstream media. The latter may be all over the map. The former constitute a synopsis. And the journalistic and academic synopses are clearly identical—mainstream journalists do not, as a rule, challenge mainstream academic authority.

These "mainstream" institutions look very, very like the set of information organs that we'd expect to see in a type 1 society. And their product is clearly a synopsis. Yet they are clearly not subject to any kind of central coordination.

I think the post-1945 mainstream synopsis is important enough to be a proper noun. Let's call it the Synopsis. Let's also give the set of institutions that produce and propagate the Synopsis—mainstream academia, journalism and education—a name. Let's call them the **Cathedral**. What explains these phenomena?

The Synopsis, of course, has an answer. The answer is that we live in a type 3 society, and the Synopsis is the set of all reasonable ideas. As for the Cathedral, it is simply the culmination of the great human quest for knowledge. It is just as permanent as the reality it exists within and elucidates, which is why there will still be a Harvard and a Yale in 2108, 2208, and 3008.

Here again is our null hypothesis. If you believe in the Synopsis and trust the Cathedral, you are either a progressive or an idiot. There is no way to receive a mainstream university education, read the Times every morning, trust both of them, and not be a progressive. Unless, of course, you're an idiot.

But there is another hypothesis, which is that we live in a type 2 society.

The type 2 society is the *consensus society*. Its hallmark is the phenomenon of *spontaneous coordination*. You might call it *Gleichschaltung* without Goebbels. Spontaneous coordination can produce an official information system which in all other respects resembles that of a type 1 society, but which is not responsible to any central authority or institution.

Basically, a type 1 society is a government in which the State controls the press and the universities. A type 2 society is one in which the press and the universities control the State. It is easy to tell the two forms apart, but the customer experience is pretty much the same.

Like a type 1 society, a type 2 society can be reasonably comfortable and pleasant to live in. The type 2 design is more stable in some ways, and less stable in others. It is not the end of the world. As one who would prefer a type 3 society, however, I consider it pernicious.

Type 2 societies tend to form from the breakdown of central authority in type 1 societies. Recall that in a type 1 society, public opinion is power. It is the power of the mob. A mob cannot defeat an army, but if the army is neutral, whoever has the biggest mob wins.

What happens in a type 1 society when the center fails? When censorship no longer operates, journalists no longer take orders, heretics are no longer burned at the stake, professors are no longer hired or fired for their political beliefs? You might think that the natural outcome would be a type 3 society, a marketplace of ideas in which only freedom rules and thoughts compete on their value alone.

But the connection between public opinion and political power still holds. Therefore, the information organs are still acting as power centers. If their views diverge, as without type 1 supervision they will, they can compete in two ways: on the basis of intellectual righteousness, or on the basis of political power. If they choose the former and abjure the latter, they will be at a disadvantage against those to whom all weapons are friends. Moreover, since political power is a deadlier weapon, successful competitors are likely to resolve any tradeoffs between power and righteousness in favor of the former.

We can describe the type 1 pathology as *coercive power distortion*. Political power distorts the landscape of ideas, rendering the playing field non-flat. Ideas that the State favors are artificially popularized. Ideas that it disfavors are artificially discouraged.

The type 2 equivalent is *attractive power distortion*. The coercive State does not exist, or at least does not coerce. But the connection between power and public opinion remains. Ideas, therefore, are selectively favored on the basis of their capacity to serve as standards around which to organize coalitions, which can struggle for power by whatever means are effective.

Again, from the type 3 perspective, attractive power distortion is pathological for the same reason as coercive power distortion. It is an alternative criterion which contributes to the success or failure of ideas, and has nothing to do with their validity.

For example, in many ways nonsense is a more effective organizing tool than the truth. Anyone can believe in the truth. To believe in nonsense is an unforgeable demonstration of loyalty. It serves as a political uniform. And if you have a uniform, you have an army. We saw this effect earlier in the cohesive type 1 state, but it works just as well for competing type 2 factions.

This does not explain, however, how the chaotic post-type-1 society congeals into the mature, spontaneously coordinated type 2 society. Why do we have one Synopsis and one Cathedral, rather than a whole host of competing synopses and cathedrals?

The answer, I think, is that even the type 2 society has only one government. It is impossible for two competing information system to capture a single government. And capturing a government gives an information system a considerable advantage over any competitors. It can subsidize itself. It can penalize its competitors. It can indulge in the entire sordid range of type 1 pathologies.

Without acquiring a central coordinator, the Cathedral can capture the resources and powers of the State. It can devise theories of government which it can incorporate into the Synopsis, and which the State must follow. These theories naturally involve lavish support for the Cathedral, which becomes responsible for the production of "public policy," i.e., government decisions. I.e., real power is held by the professors and journalists, i.e., the Cathedral, not through their purity and righteousness but through their self-sustaining control of public opinion. Lenin's great question, "Who? Whom?" is answered.

But why does the Cathedral not break into factions? What keeps Harvard aligned with Yale? Why doesn't one of the two realize that there is no need for a thousand synoptic progressive universities, and a vast unfilled demand for a single top-notch conservative university? Why, in short, is the Synopsis stable?

I think the answer is that the Synopsis includes only political propositions whose adoption tends to strengthen the Cathedral, and weaken its enemies. It rejects and opposes all other propositions. Inasmuch as these sets shift over time, the Synopsis will shift as well. It follows a sort of **hill-climbing strategy**[8]—not in the landscape of truth, but that of power. Thus, by definition, it cannot be opposed from within.

To be progressive is simply to support the Cathedral and the Synopsis. Today's Synopsis is the lineal descendant of the first type 2 movement in modern history, the Reformation. Through the Reformation we reach the Enlightenment, whose link to the Synopsis is obvious. The post-1945 Western regime, whose victory over all pre-Reformation or anti-Enlightenment forces appears final and irreversible, is the Whig millennium.

---

8 Iterative, incremental improvements

(I mean "millennium" only in the sense of "utopia." I don't actually expect it to last a thousand years. The terminal condition of our present system of government is that it satisfies the demand for power only by expanding. As it expands, its policymaking process includes more and more input, to the point at which it is completely ineffective. It can thus no longer expand. I don't think analogies to the stellar cycle are at all misplaced.)

This analysis, which is obviously broad and facile, still explains a few things. For example, let's consider the case of libertarianism.

Libertarians often call themselves "classical liberals," and indeed the word "libertarian" today means about what John Stuart Mill meant when he called himself a "liberal." In fact, in Europe today, "liberal" still means more or less "libertarian."

Why (in the US) did the term stay the same, and the meaning change? Because, in fact, the real meaning has not changed. In 1858 as in 2008, a "liberal" is a supporter of the Cathedral: i.e., a Whig, a progressive, a Radical, etc. It is the Synopsis that shifted, and it is today's libertarians who are not with the program.

Nineteenth-century liberal Whigs and Radicals supported economic freedom because economic freedom meant the destruction of Tory privileges, such as the Corn Laws (whose beneficiaries were landed aristocrats), which harmed their supporters and benefited their enemies. This position may have been explained on the basis of principle. But if it had not been politically advantageous, spontaneous coordination would have produced other principles. Either Mill would have embraced these other principles, in which case you still would know his name, or he would have been genuinely committed to economic freedom, in which case you wouldn't.

By the start of the 20th century, the old British aristocracy was in full flight, only scraps remained of the Throne-and-Altar system, and by the standard of a half-century earlier, basically everyone was a Radical. Therefore, the progressive movement could become socialist, and stand for economic centralization and official charity. These aims were not attainable in the era of Mill, because the Radicals were too weak and the Tories too strong. These tactical changes did not emerge from any secret cabal—spontaneous coordination is entirely to blame.

Libertarianism in the late 20th and early 21st centuries has gained little political traction. Why? One, it opposes the Cathedral, which controls most real power and does not deal kindly with its enemies. Two, by definition it has no mechanism for using any power it does gain to create jobs for its followers, because it does not believe in the expansion of government. Three, it either appeals to the anti-Cathedral Townies or "conservatives," making itself unfashionable, thus unpopular, and thus ineffective as an opposition, or it tries to ingratiate itself with the Cathedral, making itself thus ineffective as an opposition. It has nowhere to go. It cannot recreate the world of John Stuart Mill, with its target-rich environment of Tory landlordism.

Thus we see again Dr. Johnson's hypothesis: all the principles of Whigs, even those which seem austere and noble, are consistent with the objective of seizing power. Moreover, the Whig is concerned with his own power rather than with the state of society. He would much rather rule in Hell than serve in Heaven, and he will turn any heaven into a hell to get there. And yet he is quite sincere in all his Whiggery, which makes him all the more dangerous.

Of course, there is also the null hypothesis. Maybe we already do live in the open society, and the Synopsis is no more than sweet reason itself. It would certainly be nice.

But if Dr. Johnson was right, what is the answer? Having left the loyal society far behind, how can we proceed from the consensus society to the open society?

AN OPEN LETTER TO OPEN-MINDED PROGRESSIVES

 89 *this quip* Samuel Johnson, as quoted by James Boswell, 28 Apr. 1778, *Life of Johnson*, ed., R.W. Chapman (Oxford University Press, 1998).

 90 *Adversary* Satan

 90 *Putney Debates*

 90 *Dartmouth* The tea ship "Dartmouth" of the Boston Tea Party.

 90 *Tennis Court Oath*

 90 *time for a change* "Russian Revolution"

 90 *Great Neck*

 90 *Frank Rich*

 90 *pinkos*

 90 *fellow travelers*

 90 *Alger* "Alger Hiss"

 90 *Adlai* "Adlai Stevenson"

 90 *CPUSA*

 90 *carry them* "Card-carrying communist"

91 *American League for Peace and Democracy*

 91 *Sartre* Ian Birchall. "Sartre: Part Two." *International Socialism*, 1st Series, No. 46, Encyclopedia of Trotskyism OnLine, Feb.-Mar. 1971.

 91 *communists* Specifically, Obama's mother, Ann Dunham, dedicated herself to progressive, if not explicitly Communist political causes. Obama described his mother as "...a soldier for New Deal, Peace Corps, position-paper liberalism." Original link to Ann Dunham's Wikipedia page.

 91 *sympathy* As in, "Fellow traveler"

 91 *State of Deseret*

 92 *Scientology video* a 9-minute promotional video produced by the Church of Scientology from 2008 in which Cruise enthusiastically discusses the tenets of Scientology and their significance to him.

 92 *We Are The Ones* will.i.am. "We Are the Ones." *Change is Now: Renewing America's Promise*. 2008.

 92 *Caenorhabditis nematode*

 92 *Scientologists* Razib Khan. "Tom & Katie's Freak Is Here!!!!" *Unz Review*, 18 Apr. 2008.

 92 *open society* The reference in the main text is to Popper's *The Open Society and Its Enemies* (Rutledge, 1945) in which Popper argues on behalf of liberal democracy and its core tenets of humantiarianism and personal freedoms. The original link is to the "Open society" Wikipedia entry, which deals with the broader concept first coined by the philosopher Henri Bergson a decade earlier.

93 *Split Second* Gary Scott Thompson. 1992.

 93 *freakin' dangerous* Originally linked video was removed, and was subsequently replaced with a link to a YouTube search for "chimp attack" provided here.

 95 *caesaropapism*

AN OPEN LETTER TO OPEN-MINDED PROGRESSIVES

 95 *The Goebbels Experiment* Lutz Hachmeister. *The Goebbels Experiment.* 2005. Originally linked to a New York Times review of the film by Jeanette Catsoulis, archived here.

 95 *Gleichschaltung*

 95 *secret police galore* "Francis Walsingham"

 96 *peloton*

96 *Cathedral* This is the first enunciation of what is perhaps Moldbug's most prominent coinage.

 98 *hill-climbing strategy*

 99 *stellar cycle*

CHAPTER 5:
THE SHORTEST WAY TO WORLD PEACE
MAY 15, 2008

After four loping and windy installments, in this chapter I thought I'd vary the formula. Instead of an open letter to open-minded progressives at large, this is an open letter to just one: **Charles Stross**, the science-fiction writer.

My first excuse for this audacity is that I know Charlie—sort of. At least, we hung out on the same Usenet group in the early '90s, when he was an aspiring novelist and I was an annoying teenager. Frankly, anyone who could tolerate me even slightly in my **Rimbaud** period is too supine to protest at any atrocity I could possibly perpetrate now.

My second excuse is that last year on his **Christmas wish list**, Charlie included a goodie which I know a lot of you open-minded progressives have been wishing for as well—world peace.

Well, it just so happens I have a plan for world peace. Only one problem—it's not a progressive plan. Do ya wanna hear it? C'mon, I know you do.

My proposal is the most obvious one imaginable. Perhaps this is why I've never heard anyone propose it. It can be expressed in one sentence. Are you ready? Here we go. The US should recognize the independence and sovereignty of every government on earth, and respect it according to the principles of classical international law.

Perhaps this proposal sounds progressive to you. (It's meant to sound progressive.) As we'll see, it's about as progressive as William the Conqueror.

Perhaps you doubt its power to produce that fantastic desideratum, world peace. Reader, I will simply have to rely on your patience. All will be uncovered. But not immediately.

Why can't I just explain my peace plan directly? Why do you have to churn through another few thousand words? Because you are a progressive and I am a reactionary, and terms like independence, sovereignty, and international law don't mean the same things to us.

As Wittgenstein said: if a lion could talk, we would not understand him. As citizens of the progressive 20th century, we grew up with the progressive theory of government and history. All, or almost all, intelligent people today believe this theory. And if we accept it as reality, the concept of a reactionary plan for world peace makes no more sense than a talking lion.

There are two explanations of why everyone today (including "conservatives," whose deviations from Whiggery are negligible by historical standards) is a progressive. The first is that progressive values are universal, and progressive analysis is irrefutable. The second is that the progressive worldview has some property, other than truth and righteousness, which has enabled it to consistently defeat its enemies.

I say "defeat" because I mean "defeat." Imagine, for example, that the Axis had won the war. There are many easy ways to construct this counterfactual, but perhaps the easiest is to imagine that Heisenberg had done a better job with the **Nazi bomb**. If the Nazis have nukes in, say, 1943, the road to a Nazi 2008 is pretty straight.

The question is: in our Nazi 2008, what would Wikipedia look like? Let's assume there is a Nazi Wikipedia. Let's assume it has exactly the same **Neutral Point of View policy** it has today:

> All Wikipedia articles and other encyclopedic content must be written from a neutral point of view (NPOV), representing fairly, and as far as possible without bias, all significant views that have been published by reliable sources.

Of course, in the Nazi 2008, all "significant views" are Nazi views. All "reliable sources" are Nazi sources. All the Wikipedia editors, all the contributors, are—you get it. Of course, there will be diversity of opinion—there will be radical Nazis, conservative Nazis, and moderate Nazis. Nazipedia must reflect all the major currents of the great river of Nazi thought.

(If you really want to break your brain, imagine if the Nazi 2008 found a way to send a film crew into the real 2008, and made a propaganda documentary showing the world as it would be if the Jewish Bolshevik plutocrats had not been vanquished. The camera eye is, of course, selective. But what would it select? Hm.)

But in the real 2008, Nazipedia does not exist. Why? Because there are not enough Nazis to write it. There are actually no Nazis at all in 2008. There are neo-Nazis, but they are lowlife scum. Neo-Nazism attracts only weirdos and losers, because (a) it is idiotic, and (b) it has no chance of success. National Socialism proper, while no less idiotic, was successful. Even among the intellectual classes, not exactly its political base, it found supporters galore. There was never any shortage of talented and ambitious Nazis. Why would there be?

So there is no Nazi Wikipedia, but there could be. There is no Confederate Wikipedia, but there could be. And there is no Jacobite Wikipedia, but there could be. If you can imagine the first, can you imagine the second? I can't even imagine the third—and I'm a Jacobite myself.

On certain subjects, I'm sure Nazipedia would be quite reliable. Medicine, for example. Or physics—Nazi nukes would have spelled finis for *Deutsche Physik*. It's not at all improbable that in many technical areas, the Axis scientists and engineers of 2008 would have outperformed our own. It'd certainly be cool to see what, say, a Nazi CPU looks like.

But on the subjects of Jews, Judaism, Judaeology, etc., etc., do we care what Nazipedia has to say? We don't. We know that it is nonsense. Or to be more exact, some combination of truth and misinterpretation. Perhaps there will even be some factual errors. But why should there be? As Goebbels always said, the truth is the best propaganda. If the page for Jew links you to all the sinister deeds that have ever been performed by anyone who happened to be Jewish, it will certainly suffice. (Kevin MacDonald is a modern master of this game.)

So here is my claim about government: as a progressive, your theory of government—its history, its principles, even its present-day structure and operation—is nonsense.

Just as a misunderstanding of Jews is a fundamental element of the Nazi synopsis, a misunderstanding of government is a fundamental element of the Whig synopsis. It is simply beyond repair. If you are a progressive and you want to understand government, past and present, your best strategy is to forget everything you know and start from scratch. "Zen mind, beginner's mind."

A fun way to demonstrate this, I find, is the method of mysteries. Using my reactionary Jedi mind tricks, painstakingly sifted from the ashcan of history, I ask a question you can't answer. Then I answer it. And you are enlightened—whether or not you want to be.

Here is a question: what is the most successful Protestant denomination in the US today?

Given that North America was colonized largely by Protestant refugees, you'd think the answer would be pretty obvious. I think it's extremely obvious. It's almost a trick question. Is it obvious to you? If not, let's see if we can find some enlightenment.

Suppose you're poking through old books one day, and you find a strange little essay that was written 300 years ago. The author is certainly one of the ten most important writers in the history of your language. Perhaps even one of the top five.

The essay was originally printed as a pamphlet. It is a polemical pamphlet, written with great wit and sharpness, and its politics are extremely, well, extreme. It advocates policies that perhaps would have been approved by some figures of the time, but never publicly endorsed. Nothing like them was applied. In fact, the political winds shifted in the opposite direction.

Yet what's strange is that the arguments seem quite cogent. Not just from the perspective of 300 years ago—but from the perspective of now. Not that the extreme policies of 300 years ago are now mainstream—at least not these extreme policies. But the pamphlet warns that, if X is not done, Y will happen. X was not done. And Y happened.

What's even stranger is that the pamphlet was printed anonymously, as a sort of provocation or **black propaganda**. It was not a **Swiftian** satire. It was believable. Its readers took it quite seriously. But its actual author was quite opposed to X, and when his identity was disclosed the authorities were not amused.

The author was **Daniel Defoe**. The pamphlet was *The Shortest-Way with the Dissenters*.[1] I recommend reading *The Shortest-Way* in its entirety. It is, of course, short, and quite fun.

What's neat about The Shortest-Way is that it gives us a more or less complete Tory history of England in the 17th century, without any mealy-mouthed pandering or Whig double-talk. From the viewpoint of the narrator, who of course is an über-high Tory, the history of 17th-century England is the history of a nation beset by a kind of mental virus.

The virus is called Dissent. Its slavering zombies, who somehow manage to be both religious fanatics and Communist conspirators, are the Dissenters. The fruit of this tree is clear: war, poverty, revolution and tyranny. The only way to deal with the contagion is to root it out with a rod of iron. "Now, LET US CRUCIFY THE THIEVES!" If the 2008 election gets your blood flowing, woo baby. Politics in 1704 was certainly a contact sport.

And yet no historian would dispute the essential claim of the piece: that the Anglicans, when in power, were far more tolerant of the **Dissenters** than vice versa. (In case you're wondering, a Dissenter is more or less the same thing as a **Puritan**.)

And what's really fascinating is the arch-Tory prediction of what will happen if, despite all reason, these wretches are allowed to continue with their conspiring:

> How just will such reflections be, when our posterity shall fall under the merciless clutches of this uncharitable Generation! when our Church shall be swallowed up in Schism, Faction, Enthusiasm, and Confusion! when our Government shall be devolved upon Foreigners, and our Monarchy dwindled into a Republic!

Rowan Williams,[2] anyone? **Brussels**, anyone? Granted, England retains its symbolic monarchy, but I'd hate to imagine what any writer who could describe

---

1

2 The Archbishop of Canterbury at the time of original publication.

William of Orange as a Mock King would make of the present royals, who are as *machtlos*[3] as they are feckless.

Of course, to today's Whig, our modern progressive, all these changes are good. The English monarchy has not dwindled into a republic. It has grown into a republic. Its government has not devolved upon foreigners. It has joined with them in a great act of principled unity. Etc.

Yet I see no reason to think that even Defoe himself, let alone an old high Tory, would have seen it this way. "Republic" in 1704 meant Praise-God Barebone.[4] A republican in Queen Anne's England was about as hard to find as a Nazi in modern Germany. Okay, I exaggerate. Slightly.

But here is the conundrum: we have here a 300-year-old document whose proposals, even by the standards of 1704, were so right-wing that no one could utter them seriously. The only thing to the right is—literally—the Spanish Inquisition. And yet its analysis and its predictions are spot on. Don't you find that a little weird?

Does this answer the Protestant question? Is it the key to world peace? Neither. It is just a little clue—that's all.

You go back to poking through old books. And you find another one.

This one is a history book. It is only 100 years old—a spring chicken, really. I had never heard of the author and I can't find any biographical information on him. He is simply a historian. A rather good one, too, as far as I can tell, and quite reputable in his day.

But the book is a little stick of dynamite. It is a critical reevaluation of the foundation myth of the most important government on earth. It is deeply subversive.

According to the official story, the founders were prudent and principled men whose rights had been violated once too often by a tyrannical occupation regime, whose love of freedom finally overcame their love of peace, and who prevailed by their courage and force of arms after a desperate struggle. According to the historian, however...

But why spoil it? The book is Sydney George Fisher's *True History of the American Revolution*. (Here is the original New York Times review.) I believe Fisher was an American himself, which is remarkable considering his results. As he puts it in his first paragraph:

> The purpose of this history of the Revolution is to use the original authorities rather more frankly than has been the practice with our historians. They appear to have thought it advisable to omit from their narratives a great deal which, to me, seems essential to a true picture.

---

3 *powerless*
4 A Fifth Monarchist after whom Barebone's Parliament, the English governing body that immediately preceded Cromwell's takeover, was named.

To a revision junkie like me, a paragraph like this produces an almost physical excitement. Imagine you're a crackhead, just walking down the street looking for car windows to smash, when suddenly on the sidewalk you see an enormous rock the size of a softball. Whose is it? Who left it there? Will it fit in your pipe? Who cares? You're on it like a wolf on a baby.

What (if we are to believe Mr. Fisher) did the historians omit? Let's resort again to the method of mysteries. Here are some questions about the American Revolution for which you may find you have no good answer:

One: why do the American loyalists share a nickname with a British political party? Is this just a coincidence, or does it imply some kind of weird alliance? And what is on the other side of said alliance? If the loyalists are called Tories, why does no one call the Patriots Whigs?

Two: what on earth is the British strategy? Why do the redcoats seem to be spending so much time just hanging around in New York or Philadelphia? Valley Forge is literally twenty miles from Philly. Okay, I realize, it's winter. But come on, it's twenty miles. General Washington is starving in the snow out there. His troops are deserting by the score. And Lord Howe can't send a couple of guys with muskets to go bring him in? Heck, it sounds like a well-phrased dinner invitation would probably have done the trick.

Three: if the Stamp Act was such an intolerable abuse, how did the British Empire have all these other colonies—Canada, Australia, yadda yadda—where everyone was so meek? Surely we can understand the idea that taxation without representation was the first step toward tyranny. So where is the tyranny? Where are Her Majesty's concentration camps? Okay, there was the Boer War, I guess. But more generally, why is the history of America so different from that of the other colonies?

Four: why does no one outside America seem to resent these unfortunate events at all? I mean, the Revolution was a war. People got pretty violent on both sides. In some parts of the world, when people lose a war, they don't feel that it was just God's will. They feel that God would be much more satisfied if there was some payback. And they tend to transmit this belief to their offspring. In the American unpleasantness, a lot of people—loyalists—got kicked out of their homes. They had to leave with only a small travel bag. When this sort of thing happens in the Middle East, it's remembered for the life of the known universe.

There is actually a slight clue to two of these questions in the text we just left—The Shortest-Way. Defoe, or rather his hyper-Tory alter-ego, writes:

> The first execution of the Laws against Dissenters in England, was in the days of King James I; and what did it amount to? Truly, the worst they suffered was, at their own request, to let them go to New England, and erect a new colony; and give them great privileges, grants, and suitable powers; keep them under protection, and defend them against all invaders; and receive no taxes or revenue from them!

> This was the cruelty of the Church of England! Fatal lenity! It was the ruin of that excellent Prince, King Charles I. Had King James sent all the Puritans in England away to the West Indies; we had been a national unmixed Church! the Church of England had been kept undivided and entire!

(I think we can take it for granted that the difference between sending the Puritans to Massachusetts or Jamaica is not, at least in the narrator's mind, a matter of climate. Oh, no.)

We learn three things from this passage. One, the issues of the Revolution were already in play 70 years earlier. Two, since Whiggery is the political projection of Puritanism (elsewhere our narrator refers to Fanatical Whiggish Statesmen), this is indeed a conflict of Whig and Tory. And three, at least from the Tory perspective, New England—far from being subjected to unprecedented despotism—has enjoyed a unique set of privileges.

Indeed. As Fisher puts it:

> The British government, only too glad to be rid of rebellious Puritans, Quakers, and Roman Catholics, willingly gave them liberal charters. This explains that freedom in many of the old charters which has surprised so many students of our colonial history. Some of these liberal instruments were granted by the Stuart kings, with the approval of their officials and courtiers, all of whom showed by almost every other act of their lives that they were the determined enemies of free parliaments and free representation of the people.
>
> Connecticut, for example, obtained in 1662 from Charles II a charter which made the colony almost independent; and to-day there is no colony of the British empire that has so much freedom as Connecticut and Rhode Island always had, or as Massachusetts had down to 1685. Connecticut and Rhode Island elected their own legislatures and governors, and did not even have to send their laws to England for approval. No modern British colony elects its own governor; and, if it has a legislature elected by its people, the acts of that legislature can be vetoed by the home government. A community electing its own governor and enacting whatever laws it pleases is not a colony in the modern English meaning of the word. Connecticut and Rhode Island could not make treaties with foreign nations, but in other respects they were, as we would now say, semi-independent commonwealths under the protectorate or suzerainty of England.

One of the many neat things about Fisher's history is that it was written when the British Empire was actually a going concern, not a shadowy boogeyman from the past. From the British perspective, the condition of the "semi-independent commonwealths" was irregular at best, and corrupt at worst. Generally the latter. This space is too short to contain the vast tapestry of corruption and venality that Fisher presents—read the book.

Basically, both England and America were happy not to force the issue while there was a third party on the scene—France. But in 1763, this changed:

> Canada being conquered and England in possession of it, the colonies and England suddenly found themselves glaring at each other. Each began to pursue her real purpose more directly. England undertook to establish her sovereignty, abolish abuses, or, as she expressed it at that time, to remodel the colonies. The patriotic party among the colonists resisted the remodelling, sought to retain all their old privileges, and even to acquire new ones.

Again, I don't have the space to copy Fisher's encyclopedic evisceration of the bizarre jailhouse-lawyer barratry that the Americans, newly safe from Frenchification, put forth in their attempts to wriggle out of Britain's embrace. Read the book. And along with the barratry, there was another and more ominous development—mob violence:

> During that summer of 1765, while the assemblies of the different colonies were passing resolutions of protest, the mobs of the patriot party were protesting in another way. It certainly amazed Englishmen to read that the mob in Boston, not content with hanging in effigy the proposed stamp distributors, levelled the office of one of them to the ground and smashed the windows and furniture of his private house; that they destroyed the papers and records of the court of admiralty, sacked the house of the comptroller of customs, and drank themselves drunk with his wines; and, finally, actually proceeded to the house of Lieutenant-Governor Hutchnison, who was compelled to flee to save his life. They completely gutted his house, stamped upon the chairs and mahogany tables until they were wrecked, smashed the large, gilt-framed pictures, and tore up all the fruit-trees in his garden. Governor Hutchinson was a native of the province, was its historian, and with his library perished many invaluable historical manuscripts which he had been thirty years collecting. The mob cut open the beds and let the feathers out, which they scattered with his clothes, linen, smashed furniture, and pictures in the street.

> That this outrage had been incited the day before by the preaching of the Rev. Dr. Mayhew, a Puritan divine, did not lessen its atrocity in the eyes of Englishmen. He had held forth on the text, "I would they were even cut off which trouble you;" and the mob came very near obeying his instructions literally. A great many respectable citizens were shocked, or appeared to be shocked, at this violence and excess. They held town meetings of abhorrence, a guard was organized to prevent such outrages in the future, and rewards were offered for rioters. But it is quite significant that, although the rioters were well-known, as the historians assure us, no one was punished. Two or three were arrested, but were rescued by their friends, and it was found impossible to proceed against them.

I love that "appeared to be shocked." Does it not capture the essence of Dr. Johnson's hypothesis? As a more recent thinker[5] put it: "Guilty as sin, free as a bird, it's a great country."

But we now reach the heart of the problem, which is that not all Americans are Whigs, and not all Englishmen are Tories.

The history of the Whig-Tory conflict is best told as a series of three civil wars: one east of the pond in the 17th century, one across the pond in the 18th, and one west of the pond in the 19th. So the American Revolution: a civil war with an ocean in the middle. As Fisher describes:

> The whole question of the taxation of the colonies was raised again; witnesses, experts on trade, all sorts of persons familiar with the colonies, including Franklin, were called to the bar of the House, examined, and cross-examined. The agents of the different colonies were constantly in attendance in the lobbies. No source of information was left unexplored. The ablest men of the country were pitted against each other in continual debates, and colonial taxation was the leading topic of conversation among all classes. There were two main questions: Was the Stamp Act constitutional? and, If constitutional, was it expedient? It was the innings of a radical section of the Whigs, and, being favorable to liberalism and the colonies, they decided that the Stamp Act was not expedient. They accordingly repealed it within a year after its passage. But they felt quite sure, as did also the vast majority of Englishmen, that Parliament had a constitutional right to tax the colonies as it pleased, and so they passed what became known as the Declaratory Act, asserting the constitutional right of Parlia-

---

5 Bill Ayers

ment to bind the colonies "in all cases whatsoever;" and this is still the law of England.

The rejoicing over the repeal of the Stamp Act was displayed, we are told, in a most extraordinary manner, even in England. The ships in the Thames hoisted their colors and houses were illuminated. The colonists had apparently been able to hit a hard blow by the stoppage of trade. The rejoicing, however, as subsequent events showed, was not universal. It was the rejoicing of Whigs or of the particular ship-owners, merchants, and workingmen who expected relief from the restoration of the American trade. It was noisy and conspicuous. There must have been some exaggeration in the account of the sufferings from loss of trade. It is not improbable that Parliament had been stampeded by a worked-up excitement in its lobbies; for very soon it appeared that the great mass of Englishmen were unchanged in their opinion of proper colonial policy; and, as was discovered in later years, the stoppage of the American trade did not seriously injure the business or commercial interests of England.

But in America the rejoicing was, of course, universal. There were letters and addresses, thanksgivings in churches, the boycotting associations were instantly dissolved, trade resumed, homespun given to the poor, and the people felt proud of themselves and more independent than ever because they could compel England to repeal laws.

The colonists were certainly lucky in having chanced upon a Whig administration for their great appeal against taxation. It has often been said that both the Declaratory Act and the repeal of the Stamp Act were a combination of sound constitutional law and sound policy, and that if this same Whig line of conduct had been afterwards consistently followed, England would not have lost her American colonies. No doubt if such a Whig policy had been continued the colonies would have been retained in nominal dependence a few years longer. But such a policy would have left the colonies in their semi-independent condition without further remodelling or reform, with British sovereignty unestablished in them, and with a powerful party of the colonists elated by their victory over England. They would have gone on demanding more independence until they snapped the last string.

In fact, the Whig repeal of the Stamp Act advanced the colonies far on their road to independence. They had learned their power, learned what they could do by united action, and had beaten the British government in its chosen game. It was an impressive lesson. Consciously or unconsciously the rebel party among them was moved a step forward in that feeling for a distinct nationality which a naturally separated people can scarcely avoid.

Such a repeal, such a going backward and yielding to the rioting, threats, and compulsion of the colonists, was certainly not that "firm and consistent policy" which both then and now has been recommended as the true course in dealing with dependencies. The Tories condemned the repeal on this account, and in the course of the next ten or fifteen years ascribed to it the increasing coil of colonial entanglement.

This is the very nub of the issue. What's fascinating here is that we have two practical theories of how to deal with dependencies. One says that the most effective way to retain a dependency is to redress its grievances, tolerate its errors, and understand its complaints. The other says that the "true course" is a "firm and consistent policy."

This is not a moral disagreement. This is a case of "is," not of "ought." Both parties in England agree—or, at least, appear to agree—on the goal: American colonies that acknowledge the authority of Parliament. The Whigs think the most effective means to this end is to persuade America that England is really their friend, by making concessions when concessions are demanded. The Tories think the most effective means to this end is to use firm and consistent force, to show the Americans that they have no alternative.

After the war, the Whig theory became generally accepted in Britain. This answers question four: why the British have no hard feelings. They have no hard feelings because they believe the war resulted from a British mistake. In Chapter 3 we read the first paragraph in Macaulay's *History of England*, that famous archetype of Whig history. From the second:

> It will be seen how, in two important dependencies of the crown, wrong was followed by just retribution; how imprudence and obstinacy broke the ties which bound the North American colonies to the parent state; how Ireland, cursed by the domination of race over race, and of religion over religion, remained indeed a member of the empire, but a withered and distorted member, adding no strength to the body politic, and reproachfully pointed at by all who feared or envied the greatness of England.

Later, of course, England followed Macaulay's advice and made concessions in Ireland. As a result, the Irish have enjoyed many years of peace and have rewarded the British Empire with their eternal devotion and love. Not.

History is not science. Nor is government. Neither the American experiment nor the Irish is a general case with all variables controlled. They are more like parenting—every kid is different. Nonetheless, you'll find that most parenting experts—a few progressives excepted—indeed endorse the "firm and consistent" approach. And most parents consider it obvious.

From a purely intellectual standpoint, the Whig theory of government is attractive because it is not obvious. In fact, it's counterintuitive. If you want to keep your colonies, set them free. It's almost a Sting song. And there is a place in this theory for the intellectual. It demands explanation. Whereas the "firm and consistent policy" is, again, obvious. And who ever made a living by explaining the obvious?

On the other hand, the Whig theory has another attraction, of a more practical sort.

Suppose the Whig theory is right and the Tory theory is wrong. In that case, the Tories are working against their own interests. Unusual, certainly. But not unheard of.

Suppose the Whig theory is wrong and the Tory theory is right. In that case, the Tories are advancing their own interests. And the Whigs are...

See, here's the funny thing. There's a natural alliance between the American patriot party and the British Whigs. They are both, after all, Whigs. You'd expect some solidarity. Why don't the British Whigs just endorse the American rebels?

Because it's not 2008, is why. In the 21st century, encouraging an enemy in arms against your own government is normal politics. The word treason is almost funny. In the 18th, it was a different matter:

> The doctrine, exclusively American in its origin, that rebels were merely men in arms fighting for an idea, mistaken or otherwise, who, when once subdued, were to be allowed to go their way like paroled prisoners of war, had not yet gained ground. Rebellion was at that time a more serious thing than it has since become under the American doctrine of the right of revolution. Most of the colonists could remember the slaughter and beheading inflicted in England on the rebels under the Pretender of 1745. The frightful hanging, torturing, and transportation of men, women, and even children, for such rebellions as that of Monmouth, were by no means yet forgotten. There was not a colonist who had not heard descriptions of London after a rebellion, with the bloody arms and hindquarters of rebels hung about like butchers' meat, the ghastly heads rotting and stinking for months on the poles at Temple Bar and on London Bridge, with the hair gradually falling off the grinning skulls, as the people passed them day by day.

If the Whigs in Parliament had openly sided with the rebels, dreams of The Shortest-Way would have danced in the eyes of the Tories. The **pro-American stance** taken by the likes of **Edmund Burke** (who later redeemed himself with the *Reflections*, but was always a Whig) was in fact the most effective way for a British politician to support the rebels: not on the grounds that they deserve independence, but on the grounds that conciliation is the most effective way to prevent it, as military coercion cannot possibly work. (Does this sound at all familiar?)

We see here also why the American patriots never described themselves as Whigs, and nor did their friends in Britain. If we think of the revolutionaries as Whigs, we are tempted to ask who is in the driver's seat—the ragtag armies and mobs in America, or the British intellectuals who encouraged their rebellion. We are tempted to see the revolution as a continuation of British politics by other means—much as our Republicans and Democrats of today might find themselves backing opposing armies in some insignificant country halfway around the world. (Obviously, this could never happen, but it would be very disturbing.)

You'll note that the Whig theory of the American revolution cannot in any way be regarded as directly proven. America was not conciliated into a return to the fold. In the Whig mind, this of course is because Whig conciliation was not really tried. Or at least not tried enough. A higher dose, no doubt, would have cured the patient.

However, the Tory theory is disproved indirectly, because the Tories tried to fight a war and failed. One of the two must be right, so the Whig theory is proven—indirectly. A very typical piece of Whig logic.

There is only one problem. Suppose I am a civil engineer and I send a letter to Caltrans, warning them that serious design flaws in the new Bay Bridge will cause it to collapse. If they hire me, I will fix it for them. They ignore my letter. The bridge collapses. This makes me a prophet, or at least a "whistleblower."

On the other hand, suppose an acetylene torch with my fingerprints on it is found around the base of the bridge. This puts the matter in a different light, n'est-ce pas?

And so, for the failure of the Tories to suppress the American Revolution to be regarded as evidence for the Whig theory of conciliation, it sure would be nice to know that the reason that the Tories failed isn't that the Whigs prevented them from succeeding.

I am neither a specialist in the period, nor a historian at all. So I will simply point out one undisputed fact in the matter, which is that two of the leading British generals, **William Howe and Charles Cornwallis**, were Whigs—in fact, Whig MPs. For the rest, I will leave you in Fisher's hands. Perhaps he is right, and perhaps he isn't.

What's really interesting is that no one seems to care. After all, we live in a world which is more or less ruled by the US government—whether through its military power, or its "moral leadership." Washington is not without critics. And you'd think that anti-Americans everywhere would leap at an interpretation of history that presented the American project as more or less fraudulent from day one.

And perhaps they will. Perhaps Sydney George Fisher will "go viral." Perhaps by next week Ayman al-Zawahiri will have a printout in his cave. (Unfortunately, the True History has a lot of bad page scans, but you can also try his Struggle for

American Independence, a later two-volume expansion: I[6], II[7]. I'm afraid no Arabic translation is available.)

But I doubt it. Because the True History, as a loyalist or Tory history, is a reactionary history. It would afford rich amusement to any reactionary anti-Americans that might bump into it. However, since there are only about fifteen reactionary anti-Americans left in the world, none of whom is under the age of 60, I think Google can put off that server upgrade for a while.

What is reactionary anti-Americanism, anyway? Charles Francis Adams expresses it well in his essay "A National Change of Heart" (1902):

> I recalled my first experiences in England far back in the "sixties," — in the dark and trying days of our Civil War; and again, more recently, during the commercial depression, and contest over the free coinage of silver, in 1896. Then, especially in the earlier period, nothing was too opprobrious—nothing too bitter and stinging—for English lips to utter of America, and men and things American. We were, as the Times, echoing the utterances of the governing class, never wearied of telling us, a "dishonest" and a "degenerate" race,—our only worship was of the Almighty Dollar. A hearty dislike was openly expressed, in terms of contempt which a pretence of civility hardly feigned to veil. They openly exulted in our reverses; our civilization was, they declared, a thin veneer; democracy, a bursted bubble.

In the 1960s, too, nothing was too opprobrious for English lips to utter of America. But were we a degenerate race of barbarians, ruled by the mob? Au contraire. Now, America was not democratic enough. We had become reactionary fascist capitalist pigs. And in between, as Adams describes, there was a honeymoon:

> And now what a change!—and so very sudden! Nothing was too good or too complimentary to say of America. Our representatives were cheered to the echo. In the language of Lord Rosebery, at the King Alfred millenary celebration at Winchester, on the day following the McKinley [funeral], the branches of the great Anglo-Saxon stock were clasping hands across the centuries and across the sea; and the audience applauded him loudly as he spoke.

Ah, the "great Anglo-Saxon stock." As Hunter S. Thompson put it,[8] we've certainly learned a lot about race relations since then.

So in the course of a century, we see Britain passing from anti-Americanism, through pro-Americanism, back to anti-Americanism. Is this a reversal? Did the pendulum swing, then swing back? But when we look at the actual political motifs in the two kinds of anti-Americanism, we see very little in common—besides of course hatred of America.

Clearly it's this word anti-American that's confusing us. If we split it in half we can see the trend clearly. To be counter-American is to resist American political theory. To be ultra-American is to accept American political theory so completely that you become more American than America itself, and you feel America is not living up to her own principles.

Thus we have a monotonic trend: increasing acceptance of American political theory. Adams has an interesting explanation:

> The first was the outcome of our gigantic, prolonged Civil War. At one stage of that struggle, America—loyal America, I mean—touched its lowest estate in, the estimation of those called, and in Great Britain considered, the ruling class,—the aristocracy, the men of business and finance, the army and navy, the members of the learned professions. None the less, they then saw us accomplish what they had in every conceivable form of speech pronounced "impossible." We put down the Rebellion with a strong hand; and then, peacefully disbanding our victorious army, made good our every promise to pay. We accomplished our results in a way they could not understand,—a way for which experience yielded no precedent. None the less, the dislike, not unalloyed by contempt, was too deep-rooted to disappear at once, much more to be immediately transmuted into admiration and cordiality. They waited. Then several striking events occurred in rapid succession, — all within ten years.
>
> I am no admirer of President Cleveland's Venezuela diplomacy. I do not like brutality in public any more than in private dealings. Good manners and courtesy can always be observed, even when firmness of bearing is desirable. None the less, bad for us as the precedent then established was, and yet will prove, there can be no question that, so far as Great Britain was concerned, the tone and attitude on that occasion adopted were productive of results at once profound and, in some ways, beneficial. The average Englishman from the very bottom of his heart respects a

man who asserts himself,—provided always he has the will, as well as the power, to make the self-assertion good.

This, as a result of our Civil War, they felt we had. We had done what they had most confidently proclaimed we could not do, and what they, in their hearts, feel they have failed to do. Throughout our Rebellion they had insisted that, even if the conquest of the Confederacy was possible,—which they declared it manifestly was not,—the pacification of the Confederates was out of the question. They thought, also, they knew what they were talking about. Had they not for centuries had Ireland on their hands? Was it not there now? Were they not perpetually floundering in a bottomless bog of Hibernian discontent? Would not our experience be the same, except on a larger scale and in more aggravated form? The result worked out by us wholly belied their predictions. Not only was the rebellion suppressed, but the Confederates were quickly conciliated. The British could not understand it; in the case of the Transvaal they do not understand it now. They merely see that we actually did what they had been unable to do, and are still trying to do. The Spanish war showed that our work of domestic conciliation was as complete as had been that of conquest.

In other words, they love us because we're bad-asses. Quite a contrast to the present-day theory of anti-Americanism! But hardly refuted by it—quite a bit of bad-assery has flowed under the bridge since the Venezuela arbitration.[9] Supposedly Eisenhower used barnyard language on the phone to Anthony Eden in the Suez crisis. Eden was not an uncultured man, he was surely familiar with the old counter-American tradition, and I suspect he muttered once or twice to himself that if Palmerston and Russell had just bit the bullet and recognized the freakin' Confederacy, none of this would be happening.

Adams' point boils down to the truism that a rational actor, if forced to take sides in a conflict, should choose the side more likely to win. (Recently, another prominent statesman[10] expressed the same point in more equestrian terms.[11])

Thus we understand ultra-Americanism: in a world where all the real shots are called in Washington, ultra-Americanism is the most effective way to influence said calls.

---

9 Venezuelan Crisis of 1895, in which Britain tacitly conceded to the authority of the Monroe Doctrine.
10 Osama Bin Laden
11

AN OPEN LETTER TO OPEN-MINDED PROGRESSIVES 121

First, you ally yourself with the ultra-Americans in America proper, of which there has never been any shortage. (What is **Howard Zinn**? An Eskimo?) By definition, power in America is moving in the direction of these actors, so you are on the winning team. Second, you add your weight to the winning team, thus entitling yourself to some kind of payback, by expressing the following sentiment ad nauseam: America, we hate you, and if you don't start living up to American principles, we will continue to hate you.

Of course, none of this is a conscious strategy—it just happens to work. You might be surprised how many Americans ascribe their support for ultra-American politics to this phenomenon, which enables the likes of a Barack Obama to talk about "America's moral leadership." As a counter-American might put it, if America is a moral leader, you really have to wonder who the moral followers are. Has the planet really sunk so low? Yes, I'm afraid it has.

If you hate America but you're tired of being an ultra-American, especially now that everyone else is one, why not consider a switch to the counter-American persuasion? I have just the perfect book for you. It's called *Memoirs of Service Afloat* by Admiral **Raphael Semmes**, and it is the Great Confederate Novel, or would be if it was fiction. If you have ever felt yourself tempted to use the phrase "Universal Yankee Nation" in a disparaging sort of way, run, do not walk, to Admiral Semmes. Bear in mind, however, that many of your other opinions will need to change.

But we note something else in Adams' presentation—it is quite inconsistent with the Whig theory of the American Revolution. No wonder the British are impressed! Macaulay has just been telling them that Americans cannot be conquered and pacified by mere military force. Along comes the Universal Yankee Nation, and does just that. Perhaps it's just Yankees proper who are invulnerable, like the Lord's Resistance Army,[12] to bullets.

And we are reminded, once again, of The Shortest-Way:

> Sir Roger L'Estrange tells us a story in his collection of Fables, of the Cock and the Horses. The Cock was gotten to roost in the stable among the horses; and there being no racks or other conveniences for him, it seems, he was forced to roost upon the ground. The horses jostling about for room, and putting the Cock in danger of his life, he gives them this grave advice, "Pray, Gentlefolks! let us stand still! for fear we should tread upon one another!"

There are some people in the World, who, now they are unperched, and reduced to an equality with other people, and under strong and very just apprehensions of being further treated as they deserve, begin, with Aesop's Cock, to preach up Peace and Union and the Christian duty of Moderation; forgetting that, when they had the Power in their hands, those Graces were strangers in their gates!

---

12 Uganda-based rebel group led by Joseph Kony.

So we see that when Whigs rebel against Tories, Tories should "stand still! for fear we should tread upon each other." When the shoe is on the other foot, however, "those Graces were strangers in their gates."

This is not a matter of the merits of the rebel causes in the American Revolution and the Civil War. As a progressive, of course, you believe (not very strongly) that the first rebellion was just, and you believe (very strongly) that the second was unjust. These are matters of morality, over which we cannot argue.

The question is the physical efficacy of coercive suppression in both cases. Your theory of history, which of course you did not invent but have received, assures you that coercion could not have worked in the first case. No theory is required to know that it worked in the second. If you were truly a believer in the Calvinist Providence, like your Whig forebears of old, the problem would be solved: God, whose ways are mysterious but whose arms are invincible, is on the side of the just. Therefore it is futile to attempt to overcome a just cause, whereas an unjust one must be resisted with all our might—God helps those who help themselves.

You have long since given up this belief. But its corollary persists—out of sheer habit, I must assume. I can find no other explanation. And since the belief, true or false, is clearly central to any strategy for world peace—most of today's wars being insurgencies of one sort or another—we have to resolve it.

In our pursuit of the Whig theory of war, we have advanced from the early 17th century to the late 19th. Let's pull just a little way into the 20th, and pick an episode which everyone will recognize, but hopefully few have strong attachments to.

Joseph Tumulty, a New Jersey politician, was one of Woodrow Wilson's advisers—think **Colonel Edward M. House**, minus 20 IQ points. In 1921 he published an adoring political memoir, a genre somewhat new to history, called *Woodrow Wilson as I Know Him*.

It includes the following passage, which I'd like to think at this point is self-explanatory. If you get bored, you can skim, but don't be discouraged—there is a punchline.

> No one standing on the side-lines in the capital of the nation and witnessing the play of the ardent passions of the people of the Irish race, demanding that some affirmative action be taken by our government to bring about the realization of the right of self-determination for Ireland, it seemed as if the American President, Woodrow Wilson, who first gave utterance to the ideal of self-determination for all the oppressed peoples of the world, was woefully unmindful of the age-long struggle that Irishmen had been making to free their own beloved land from British domination. But to those, like myself, who were on the inside of affairs, it was evident that in every proper and legitimate way the American President was cautiously searching for efficient means to advance

AN OPEN LETTER TO OPEN-MINDED PROGRESSIVES

the cause of self-government in Ireland and to bring about a definite and satisfactory solution of this complicated problem.

[...]

Long before the European war the President and I had often discussed the Irish cause and how to make his influence felt in a way that would bring results without becoming involved in diplomatic snarls with Great Britain. He was of the opinion that the Irish problem could not be settled by force, for the spirit of Ireland, which for centuries had been demanding justice, was unconquerable. He pointed out to me on many occasions when we discussed this delicate matter, that the policy of force and reprisal which the English Government had for centuries practised in had but strengthened the tenacious purpose of the Irish people and had only succeeded in keeping under the surface the seething dissatisfaction of that indomitable race. I recall that at the conclusion of one of our talks after a Cabinet meeting, shaking his head as if he despaired of a settlement, the President said: "European statesmen can never learn that humanity can be welded together only by love, by sympathy, and by justice, and not by jealousy and hatred." He was certain that the failure of England to find an adjustment was intensifying feeling not only in our own country, but throughout the world, and that the agitation for a settlement would spread like a contagion and would inevitably result in a great national crisis.

[...]

In discussing the matter with me, he said: "The whole policy of Great Britain in its treatment of the Irish question has unfortunately been based upon a policy of fear and not a policy of trusting the Irish people. How magnificently the policy of trust and faith worked out in the case of the Boers. Unfortunately, the people of Ireland now believe that the basis of England's policy toward them is revenge, malice, and destruction. You remember, Tumulty, how the haters of the South in the days of reconstruction sought to poison Lincoln's mind by instilling into it everything that might lead him in his treatment of the South toward a policy of reprisal, but he contemptuously turned away from every suggestion as a base and ignoble thing. Faith on the part of Great Britain in the deep humanity and inherent generosity of the Irish people is the only force that will ever lead to a settlement of this question. English statesmen must realize that in the last analysis force never permanently settles anything. It only produces hatreds and resentments that make a solution of any question difficult and almost impossible. I have tried to impress upon the Englishmen with whom I have discussed this matter that there never can be a real comradeship between America and England until this issue is definitely settled and out of the way." Many times in informal discussions with British representatives that came to the White House the President sought to impress upon them the necessity for a solution, pointing out to them how their failure was embarrassing our relations with Great Britain at every point. I am sure that if he could with propriety have done so, Woodrow Wilson would long ago have directly suggested to Great Britain a settlement of the Irish question, but, unfortunately, serious diplomatic obstacles lay in the way of an open espousal of the Irish cause. He was sadly aware that under international law no nation has the right to interest itself in anything that directly concerns the affairs of another friendly nation, for by the traditions of diplomacy such "interference" puts in jeopardy the cordial relations of the nations involved in such controversy.

Long before he became president, Woodrow Wilson had eloquently declared his attitude with reference to self- government for Ireland and had openly espoused the cause of Irish freedom. In a speech delivered at New Brunswick, New Jersey, on October 26, 1910, he said:

> Have you read the papers recently attentively enough to notice the rumours that are coming across the waters? What are the rumours? The rumours are that the English programme includes, not only self-government for Ireland, but self-government for Scotland, and the drawing together in London or somewhere else of a parliament which will represent the British Empire in a great confederated state upon the model, no doubt, of the United States of America, and having its power to the end of the world. What is at the bottom of that programme? At the bottom of it is the idea that no little group of men like the English people have the right to govern men in all parts of the world without drawing them into real substantial partnership, where their voice will count with equal weight with the voice of other parts of the country. This voice that has been crying in Ireland, this voice for home rule, is a voice which is now supported by the opinion of the world; this impulse is a spirit which ought to be respected and recognized in the British Constitution. It means not mere vague talk of men's rights, men's emotions, and men's inveterate and traditional principles, but it means the embodiment of these things in something that is going to be done, that will look with hope to the programme that may

AN OPEN LETTER TO OPEN-MINDED PROGRESSIVES

> come out of these conferences. If those who conduct the Government of Great Britain are not careful the restlessness will spread with rapid agitation until the whole country is aflame, and then there will be revolution and a change of government.

In this speech he plainly indicated that his plan for the settlement of the Irish question was the establishment of some forum to which the cause of Ireland might be brought, where the full force of the public opinion of the world, including the United States, could be brought to play in a vigorous and whole-hearted insistence upon a solution of this world-disturbing question. As we read the daily papers, containing accounts of the disturbances in Ireland, what a prophetic vision underlay the declaration contained in the speech of Woodrow Wilson in 1910!

> If those who conduct the Government of Great Britain are not careful the restlessness will spread with rapid agitation until the whole country is aflame, and then there will be revolution and a change of government.

I recall his passionate resentment of the attitude and threats of Sir Edward Carson, leader of the Unionist forces in the British Parliament, when he read the following statement of Carson carried in the American Press, after the passage of Home Rule through the House of Lords: "In the event of this proposed parliament being thrust upon us, we solemnly and mutually pledge ourselves not to recognize its authority. I do not care two pence whether this is treason or not." Discussing Carson's utterance the President said: "I would like to be in Mr. Asquith's place. I would show this rebel whether he would recognize the authority of the Government or flaunt it. He ought to be hanged for treason. If Asquith does not call this gentleman's bluff, the contagion of unrest and rebellion in Ireland will spread until only a major operation will save the Empire. Dallying with gentlemen of this kind who openly advocate revolution will only add to the difficulties. If those in authority in England will only act firmly now, their difficulties will be lessened. A little of the firmness and courage of Andrew Jackson would force a settlement of the Irish question right now."

I swear to God, I have elided nothing except where indicated. Tumulty segues directly from the unconquerable spirit of the Irish to the "firmness and courage of Andrew Jackson." There is not even a segue. It's just bam, bam. Check it for yourself—page 397.[13]

Did you catch, also, that bit about "how magnificently the policy of trust and faith worked out with the Boers?" Yeah—trust, faith, and **concentration camps**. What Wilson means, as in his reference to the South, is that after the Boer war Britain devolved a large amount of local responsibility on the South African government. After, of course, delivering a thorough and comprehensive ass-whooping, with "the firmness and courage of Andrew Jackson."

Mr. Tumulty, of course, was an Irish ward-boss political hack. He was not writing for 2008. But he made the wonderful gaffe of emitting the Whig theory of revolution and the Whig theory of rebellion in a single breath, where we can see how oddly they fit together. The Whig theory of rebellion turns out to just be the Tory theory of revolution. They can coexist, but only with a distinction between (justified) revolution and (unjustified) rebellion that is implausible to say the least.

And yet, as a progressive, you believe them both, and you will never confuse the two. Imagine, for example, that some confused conservative intellectual had responded to the crimes of **Timothy McVeigh**, or **Eric Rudolph**, or **Byron de la Beckwith**, with Wilsonian rhetoric about deep-seated grievances, or age-old struggles, or what-not. These men were not revolutionaries. They were rebels. That is, they were right-wing political criminals, rather than left-wing ones. They deserved to be crushed. And somehow this did not prove hard at all. Nor did right-wing intellectuals experience any difficulty in choosing not to excuse their acts.

Here's a fact that may have escaped your attention. There has never been a successful right-wing insurgency. That is, there has never been any successful movement employing the tactics of guerrilla or "urban guerrilla" (or "terrorist") war, in which the guerrilla forces were to the political right of the government forces. To some extent you can classify Franco in Spain as a successful right-wing rebel, but his forces were more organized and disciplined than the government's—Franquismo was a coup that turned into a rebellion, and it succeeded in the end only because, for unusual reasons, England and the US declined to intervene against it.

For example, if oppression and injustice really are the cause of insurgent movements, why was there never anything even close to an insurgency in any of the Soviet-bloc states? Excepting, of course, Afghanistan—a rather suspicious exception. You may be a progressive, but you can't be such a progressive that you believe there was no such thing as Communist oppression. Yet it never spawned any kind of violent reaction. What up with that, dog?

The obvious answer is just Defoe's. "When they had the Power in their hands, those Graces were strangers in their gates." The cause of revolutionary violence is not oppression. The cause of revolutionary violence is weak government. If people avoid revolting against strong governments, it is because they are not stupid, and

13

they know they will lose. There is one and only one way to defeat an insurgency, which is the same way to defeat any movement—make it clear that it has no chance of winning, and no one involved in it will gain by continuing to fight.

I mean, think about it. You hear that in country X, the government is fighting against an insurgency. You know nothing else. Which side would you bet on? The government, of course. Because it is stronger by definition—it has more men and more guns. If it didn't, it wouldn't be the government.

So insurgency in the modern age is not what it appears to be. It is an illusion constructed for a political audience. If Fisher is right, it was not the Continental Army that prevailed in 1783, but the alliance of the Continental Army and the British Whigs. Together they produced a new Whig republic to replace the old one that had collapsed with Cromwell's death. Neither could conceivably have achieved this mission alone.

Insurgency, including what we now call "terrorism," is thus a kind of theater. Guerrilla theater, you might say. It exists as an adjunct to democratic politics, and could not exist without it. (I exclude partisan campaigns of the **Peninsular War**[14] type, in which the guerrillas are an adjunct to a war proper.)

The goal of an insurgency is simply to demonstrate that the violence will continue until the political demands of its supporters are met. The military arm produces the violence. The political arm explains, generally while deploring the violence, that the violence can be stopped by meeting the demands—and only by meeting the demands.

What's so beautiful about this design, at least from the Devil's perspective, is that it requires no coordination at all. It is completely distributed. There is no "command and control." It often arouses suspicion when politicians and terrorists are **good friends**.[15] With the insurgency design, both can benefit from each others' actions, without any incriminating connections. They do not even need to think of the effort as a cooperation.

Insurgents and politicians need not even share a value system. There is no reason at all, for example, to think that Ayman al-Zawahiri shares any values with American progressives. I have a fair idea of the kind of government that Sheikh al-Zawahiri would create if he had his druthers. I can certainly say the same for progressives. They have nothing at all to do with each other—regardless of anyone's **middle name**.[16]

Yet when Sheikh al-Zawahiri **attributed** the Democratic victory in the 2006 elections to the mujahedeen, he was objectively right. The Democrats won because their prediction that Iraq would become a quagmire for the US military (which everyone and his dog knows is a Republican outfit) turned out to be true. Without the mujahedeen, who would have turned Iraq into a quagmire? Space aliens?

---

14 Military conflict along the Iberian Peninsula, a spillover of the Napoleonic Wars engulfing Europe at the time.
15 Reference to Barack Obama's relationship to Weather Underground leader Bill Ayers.
16 Barack *Hussein* Obama

To make a proper feedback loop, the efforts of the politicians must assist the insurgents, and the efforts of the insurgents must assist the politicians. The al-Zawahiri effect—which is not exactly a unique case—is a good example of the latter. The former is provided by a tendency in Whig politics that we can call antimilitarism.

Antimilitarism assists the "armed struggle" in the most obvious way: by opposing its opponents. All things being equal, any professional military force will defeat its nonprofessional opponent, just as an NBA team will defeat the women's junior varsity. The effect of antimilitarism is to adjust the political and military playing field until the insurgents have an equal, or even greater, chance of victory.

Wars in which antimilitarism plays an important role are often described as "asymmetric." The term is a misnomer. A real "asymmetric" war would be a conflict in which one side was much stronger than the other. For obvious reasons, this is a rara avis. A modern asymmetric war is one in which one side's strength is primarily military, and the other's is primarily political. Of course this does not work unless the political and military sides are at least nominally parts of the same government, which means that all asymmetric wars are civil—although they may be fought by foreign soldiers on foreign territory.

How does antimilitarism do its thing? As always in war, in any way it can. In the case of Lord Howe we see what looks very much like deliberate military incompetence. Military mismanagement may occur at the level of military leadership, as in the case of Lord Howe, or in civil-military relations, as with McNamara. The military may win the war and its civilian masters may then simply surrender, as in the case of French Algeria.

The most popular approach today, however, is to alter the rules of war. War is brutal. If you were a space alien, you might expect a person opposed to this brutality to ameliorate it, or at least attempt to, by: (a) deciding to support whichever side is the least brutal; (b) promoting rules of war which minimize the incentive for brutal conduct; and (c) encouraging the war to end as quickly as possible with a decisive and final result.

Modern progressivism does not resemble any of these actions. In fact, it resembles their polar opposite. It is certainly motivated by opposition to brutality, but the actions are not calculated to achieve the effects. In a word, it is antimilitarism.

For example, the modern US military has by far the highest lawyer-to-soldier ratio in any military force in history. It requests legal opinions as a routine aspect of even minor attacks. It is by no means averse to trying its own soldiers for judgment calls made in the heat of battle, a practice that would strike Lord Howe as completely insane. (Here is a personal narrative[17] of the consequences.) Meanwhile, its

---

17 Archived link from May 21, 2008.

AN OPEN LETTER TO OPEN-MINDED PROGRESSIVES 129

enemies relish the most **barbaric tortures**.[18] And which side does the progressive prefer? Or rather, which side do his objective actions favor?

Adjusting the rules of war in this way is an excellent strategy for the 21st-century antimilitarist. He does not have to actually express support for the insurgents, as his crude predecessors of the 1960s did. (As Tom Hayden put it, "We are all Viet Cong now.") Today anyone who can click a mouse can learn that the **National Liberation Front** was the **People's Army of Vietnam (NVA)** and the NVA were cold-blooded killers,[19] but this knowledge was controversial and hard-to-obtain at the time. The people who knew it were not, in general, the smart ones. "We are all al-Qaeda now" simply does not compute, and you don't hear it. But nor do you need to.

An arbitrary level of antimilitarism can be achieved simply by converging military tactics with judicial and police procedure. Suppose, for example, Britain was invaded by the Bolivian army, in a stunning seaborne coup. Who would win? Probably not the Bolivians, which is why they don't try it.

But suppose that the Bolivian soldiers have the full protection of British law. The only way to detain them is to arrest them, and they must be charged with an actual crime on reasonable suspicion of having committed it. Being a Bolivian in Britain is not a crime. You cannot, of course, shoot them, at least not without a trial and a full appeal process. Any sort of indiscriminate massacre, as via artillery, airstrikes, etc., is of course out of the question. Etc.

So Britain becomes a province of Bolivia. War is always uncertain, but the Bolivians certainly ought to give it a shot. What do they have to lose? A few soldiers, who might have to spend a little time in a British jail. Not exactly the Black Hole of Calcutta. So why not?

And this is how antimilitarism produces war. War is horrible, and no one is willing to fight in it unless they have a chance of winning. Antimilitarism gives the insurgents that chance. And this is the other half of the feedback loop.

Now we're ready to answer the question that you've probably forgotten about: what is the most successful Protestant denomination in the United States?

"Successful" is a tricky word. Should we count it statistically, by mere numbers? But I am a reactionary—headcount and warm bodies mean nothing to me. Better to count it by influence and importance. Whose counsels are heard in the corridors of power? To what sect do the rich, famous and fashionable belong? Who controls the prestigious institutions?

But an even trickier word is "denomination." The problem is that denominations don't always seem to mean that much. In many cases, they seem to be meaningless labels inherited from the past. To define people as members of separate sects, you'd expect them to disagree about something important. When was the last time

---

18 [QR code]

19 Reference to the Massacre at Hue, Feb. 1968.

you saw, say, a Congregationalist having it out with an Episcopalian? Do Unitarians and Methodists castigate each other in furious theological catfights?

Um, no. I suspect the major reason for this is the ecumenical movement. It's unsurprising that this would result in a convergence of opinion. In practice today, in the US, there are two kinds of Protestant: mainline (i.e., ecumenical), and evangelical. (Confusingly, the people described as "evangelical" in the 19th century are the ancestors of today's mainliners—I prefer to say "traditionalist.") As one would expect from the history of the great Christian faith, these two sects hate each other like cats and dogs. Mystery resolved.

And as the name suggests, mainliners are more socially prestigious and far more likely to be found in positions of influence or authority. Does this answer our question? Not quite.

The thing about mainline Protestant beliefs is that they are not only shared by Protestants. You can find Catholics, Jews, Muslims, and quite a few atheists who hold essentially the same worldview as the mainline Protestants. What is a "moderate Muslim?" A Protestant Muslim, more or less.

For the last century and a half, one of the most influential American sects has been the Unitarians. The beliefs held by Unitarians have changed over time, but modern Unitarians (or Unitarian Universalists) believe that you can be a Unitarian while being any religion, or no religion at all. Of course, if you are a Muslim or a Catholic, you need to discard almost all the traditional beliefs of these sects, often retaining just the name. But since Unitarians have done more or less the same to their own beliefs, it's no sweat, man.

The neat thing about primary sources is that often, it takes only one to prove your point. If you find the theory of relativity mentioned in ancient Greek documents, and you know the documents are authentic, you know that the ancient Greeks discovered relativity. How? Why? It doesn't matter. Your understanding of ancient Greece needs to include Greek relativity.

One of the discoveries that impelled me to start this blog was an ancient document. Well, not that ancient, actually. It's from 1942. It is of unquestionable authenticity. In fact, it is still hosted by the same organization that wrote it. If you're an old UR reader you have seen this before. If you're an open-minded progressive, you may be surprised. The document is here:[20]

Religion: American Malvern
Monday, Mar. 16, 1942

> These are the high spots of organized U.S. Protestantism's super-protestant new program for a just and durable peace after World War II:

---

[20]

AN OPEN LETTER TO OPEN-MINDED PROGRESSIVES 131

- Ultimately, "a world government of delegated powers."
- Complete abandonment of U.S. isolationism.
- Strong immediate limitations on national sovereignty.
- International control of all armies & navies.
- "A universal system of money... so planned as to prevent inflation and deflation."
- Worldwide freedom of immigration.
- Progressive elimination of all tariff and quota restrictions on world trade.
- "Autonomy for all subject and colonial peoples" (with much better treatment for Negroes in the U.S.).
- "No punitive reparations, no humiliating decrees of war guilt, no arbitrary dismemberment of nations."
- A "democratically controlled" international bank "to make development capital available in all parts of the world without the predatory and imperialistic aftermath so characteristic of large-scale private and governmental loans."

This program was adopted last week by 375 appointed representatives of 30-odd denominations called together at Ohio Wesleyan University by the Federal Council of Churches. Every local Protestant church in the country will now be urged to get behind the program. "As Christian citizens," its sponsors affirmed, "we must seek to translate our beliefs into practical realities and to create a public opinion which will insure that the United States shall play its full and essential part in the creation of a moral way of international living."

Among the 375 delegates who drafted the program were 15 bishops of five denominations, seven seminary heads (including Yale, Chicago, Princeton, Colgate-Rochester), eight college and university presidents (including Princeton's Harold W. Dodds), practically all the ranking officials of the Federal Council and a group of well-known laymen, including John R. Mott, Irving Fisher and Harvey S. Firestone Jr. "Intellectually," said Methodist Bishop Ivan Lee Holt of Texas, "this is the most distinguished American church gathering I have seen in 30 years of conference-going."

The meeting showed its temper early by passing a set of 13 "requisite principles for peace" submitted by Chairman John Foster Dulles and his inter-church Commission to Study the Bases of a Just and Durable Peace. These principles, far from putting all the onus on Germany or Japan, bade the U.S. give thought to the short sighted selfishness of its own policies after World War I, declared that the U.S. would have to turn over a new leaf if the world is to enjoy lasting peace.

Excerpts:

> For at least a generation we have held preponderant economic power in the world, and with it the capacity to influence decisively the shaping of world events. It should be a matter of shame and humiliation to us that actually the influences shaping the world have largely been irresponsible forces. Our own positive influence has been impaired because of concentration on self and on our short-range material gains. ... If the future is to be other than a repetition of the past, the U.S. must accept the responsibility for constructive action commensurate with its power and opportunity.
>
> The natural wealth of the world is not evenly distributed. Accordingly the possession of such natural resources... is a trust to be discharged in the general interest. This calls for more than an offer to sell to all on equal terms. Such an offer may be a futile gesture unless those in need can, through the selling of their own goods and services, acquire the means of buying.

With these principles accepted, the conference split up into four groups to study, respectively, the social, economic and political problems of the post-war world and the problem of the church's own position in that world.* Discussion waxed hot & heavy, with one notable silence: in a week when the Japs were taking Java, discussion of the war itself was practically taboo. Reason: The Federal Council felt that, since five of its other commissions are directly connected with the war effort, the conference's concern should be with plans for peace. One war statement—the Christian Church as such is not at war—was proposed by Editor Charles Clayton Morrison, of the influential and isolationist-before-Pearl-Harbor Christian Century. This statement was actually inserted in a subcommittee report by a 64–58 vote after a sharp debate. In the plenary session, however, it was ruled out of order.

Some of the conference's economic opinions were almost as sensational as the extreme internationalism of its political program. It held that a new order of economic life is both imminent and imperative—a new order that is sure to come either through voluntary cooperation within the framework of democracy or through explosive political revolution. Without condemning the profit motive as such, it denounced various defects in the profit system for breeding war, demagogues and dictators, mass unemployment, widespread dispossession from homes and farms, destitution, lack of opportunity for youth and of security for old age. Instead, the church must demand economic arrangements measured by human welfare... must appeal to the Christian motive of human service as paramount to personal gain or governmental coercion.

"Collectivism is coming, whether we like it or not," the delegates were told by no less a churchman than England's Dr. William Paton, co-secretary of the World Council of Churches, but the conference did not veer as far to the left as its definitely pinko British counterpart, the now famous **Malvern Conference** (TIME, Jan. 20, 1941). It did, however, back up Labor's demand for an increasing share in industrial management. It echoed Labor's shibboleth that the denial of collective bargaining "reduces labor to a commodity." It urged taxation designed "to the end that our wealth may be more equitably distributed." It urged experimentation with government and cooperative ownership.

"Every individual," the conference declared, "has the right to full-time educational opportunities... to economic security in retirement... to adequate health service [and an] obligation to work in some socially necessary service."

The conference statement on the political bases of a just and durable peace proclaimed that the first post-war duty of the church "will be the achievement of a just peace settlement with due regard to the welfare of all the nations, the vanquished, the overrun and the victors alike." In contrast to the blockade of Germany after World War I, it called for immediate provision of food and other essentials after the war for every country needing them. "We must get back," explained Methodist Bishop Francis J. McConnell, "to a stable material prosperity not only to strengthen men's bodies but to strengthen their souls."

Politically, the conference's most important assertion was that many duties now performed by local and national governments "can now be effectively carried out only by international authority." Individual nations, it declared, must give up their armed forces "except for preservation of domestic order" and allow the world to be policed by an international army & navy. This League-of-Nations-with-teeth would also have "the power of final judgment in controversies between nations... the regulation of international trade and population movements among nations."

> The ultimate goal: "a duly constituted world government of delegated powers: an international legislative body, an international court with adequate jurisdiction, international-administrative bodies with necessary powers, and adequate international police forces and provision for enforcing its worldwide economic authority."
>
> *Despite their zeal for world political, social and economic unity, the churchmen were less drastic when it came to themselves. They were frank enough to admit that their own lack of unity was no shining example to the secular world, but did no more than call for "a new era of interdenominational cooperation in which the claims of cooperative effort should be placed, so far as possible, before denominational prestige."

The program of the Federal Council is immediately recognizable as the modern progressive agenda. But that adjective is not used (except in its dictionary sense). Nor is the other adjective that is generally associated with the same program, liberal. (I really hate using this word—it makes me sound like Rush Limbaugh.)

Instead, what is the adjective our reporter uses to describe this program? Super-protestant. In other words, we have a candidate for the most successful Protestant denomination in the US today. That denomination is progressivism itself.

Progressives, at least the majority of progressives, do not think of themselves as a religious movement. In fact, presumably for adaptive reasons, they have discarded almost every trace of theology, though there is still some lingering fondness for the Prince of Peace. But the line of descent from the English Dissenters to Bill Moyers is as clear as that from chimp to man.

After some failed experiments I coined the name Universalism, for progressivism understood as a Protestant sect, and have been using it here for a while. I am still not sure about this word, though it is appropriate for several reasons theological and mundane. It seems inoffensive, and progressives will often describe themselves as small-u universalists. But progressive is what its adherents call themselves, and it seems polite to respect this. I may just go back and forth.

Whatever you call it, progressivism is not just a religious movement. It is not just a matter of spiritual opinion. Like classical Islam, it is a complete way of life. And it comes with a political arm—Whiggery. Whether you believe the Dissenter–Whig complex is good or evil, you cannot avoid admitting that it is the most successful religious and political movement in the history of the known universe.

So that's one answer to our question. There is an even more disturbing answer, though.

Another way to measure success is by fidelity of transmission. While Universalism is most certainly descended from the 17th-century American Puritans (read *The Puritan Origins of American Patriotism* by George McKenna if you don't

AN OPEN LETTER TO OPEN-MINDED PROGRESSIVES

believe me), your average Puritan would be absolutely horrified by progressive beliefs. As would just about anyone in the 17th century. But who is the closest?

Actually, there is a 17th-century of extremist Dissenters whose beliefs closely track modern progressivism. They are not identical—that would be too much to expect—but you will have to work hard to find any point on which the two conflict, at least to the point where someone might get into an argument. Many superficial rituals and traditions have been discarded, but modern members of this sect are certainly progressives. And the sect, though young by Dissenter standards, has been quite influential ever since the writing of The Shortest-Way.

I refer, of course, to the **Quakers.** If the Time reporter had described the program of the Federal Council as super-Quaker, he might well have confused his audience, but his theology would have been if anything more accurate. The history of mainline Protestantism in America is more or less the history of its Quakerization. Basically, we are all Quakers now. Even I find Quaker writings remarkably sympathetic, and I'm a reactionary Jacobite.

> There is a reason, though, that they were expelled from England. Here, in this **fascinating 1917 discussion** of Quakers and World War I (which in the great Quaker style, both innocent and shameless, is hosted by... the Quaker Heritage Press), is an example of what creeps some people out about the Quakers:[21]
>
> It should be noted, in the first place, that in practice the Quaker attitude upon this issue [the war] is no more than that of Socialists, of whom some are ardent nationalists and some inveterate pacifists. The Friends have their patriotic and military heroes. Betsy Ross, who made our first flag, was a member of the society. Thomas Mifflin, a major general and Washington's first aide-de-camp, was a Quaker; so was Major General Nathaniel Greene; so was Jacob Brown, a Bucks county schoolmaster who rose to be commander-in-chief of the United States army. Robert Morris financed the Revolution largely by means of Quaker loans. John Bright, one of the foremost of English Quakers, justified the American war to exterminate slavery. Whittier's abolition poems were militant to the last degree. Even William Penn proposed an international "league to enforce peace," requiring compulsion by arms if necessary. The doctrine of pacifism, nevertheless, always has been vital in the principles of Quakerism, and one of the curious chapters in American history deals with the strange expedients which members of the society employed to make their genuine love of country harmonize with their beliefs

21

by supporting necessary projects of defense which they could not officially countenance. Franklin gives an illuminating account of "the embarrassment given them (in the Pennsylvania assembly) whenever application was made to grant aids for military purposes." Unwilling to offend the government, and averse to violating their principles, he says, they used "a variety of evasions," the commonest one being to grant money "for the king's use" and avoid all inquiry as to the disbursement. But once, when New England asked Pennsylvania for a grant to buy powder, this ingenious device would not serve:

> They could not grant money to buy powder, for that was an ingredient of war; but they voted an aid of 3000 Pounds, and appropriated it for the purchasing of bread, flour, wheat "and other grain." Some of the council, desirous of giving the House still further embarrassment, advised the governor not to accept the provision, as not being the thing he had demanded; but he reply'd, "I shall take the money, for I understand very well their meaning—other grain is gunpowder." Which he accordingly bought, and they never objected to it.

If this makes no sense to you, black powder of the time came in "corns," i.e., grains. The story of "other grain," which I would be prepared to accept as apocryphal (Franklin is hardly a trustworthy source), is rather famous among Quaker-haters. Note also William Penn's "league to enforce peace," of which I was entirely unaware until five minutes ago. Ya learn something new every day.

Even I find it hard to restructure my brain to think of progressivism as a religious movement. Frankly, the proposition that our society, far from advancing into a bright future of rationality and truth, is slipping inexorably into the iron grip of an ancient religious sect, is one I find almost impossible to contemplate. One thought-experiment for this purpose, however, is to imagine that—perhaps through the action of evil aliens—every progressive (whether or not he or she self-identifies as a "Christian") was converted automatically into a traditionalist, and vice versa. Except, of course, for you.

You'd suddenly realize that you lived in a world in which all the levers of power, prestige, and influence were held by dangerous religious maniacs. At least, people you consider dangerous religious maniacs. Being a progressive and all.

Well, exactly. I am not a progressive. But I am also not a traditionalist. I am not a Christian at all. I believe it is worth some effort to try to wake up from all this historical baggage.

We are now prepared to consider the subject we started with, world peace.

From a semiotic perspective (I didn't go to Brown for nothing, kids), the fascinating thing about world peace is that, while these two little words are remarkably precise and their compound is hardly less exact, the phrase is not without its Empsonian edge. It reminds us of two concepts which are not logically connected: a goal in which Planet Three is free from the state of human interaction known as war, and a strategy for achieving that goal.

This strategy is generally known as pacifism. In 19th-century and 20th-century history, pacifism is associated with a movement—i.e., a group of people acting collectively, if not within any fixed organizational structure—which might be called the internationalist movement. While this inevitably fuzzy category embraces an enormous set of individuals and projects across the last two hundred years, I think it's a fair summary to say that an internationalist believes that the best way to achieve world peace is to build global institutions which act in the interest of humanity as a whole. Tennyson's *Locksley Hall* is the classic expression:

> Till the war-drum throbb'd no longer, and the battle-flags were furl'd
> In the Parliament of man, the Federation of the world.
> There the common sense of most shall hold a fretful realm in awe,
> And the kindly earth shall slumber, lapt in universal law.

On an issue as important as world peace, there is certainly no point in confusing ourselves. So I object to the word pacifism. This sign, by joining two signifieds in one signifier—the goal of a world without war, and the strategy of Locksley Hall internationalism—sneaks in three assumptions which, while they may very well be true, strike me as quite nonobvious.

One: internationalism is the only strategy which can achieve the goal. Two: internationalism is an effective strategy with which to achieve the goal. Three: internationalism is not the principal obstacle to the achievement of the goal.

If you have actually read this far in the post, without skimming even a little, I'd like to think that you know Whiggery and Quakerism when you see it. So let me suggest an alternative to the Locksley Hall strategy for world peace: a return to classical international law.

Of course, our internationalists talk of nothing but international law. But what they mean is modern international law. They believe, good Whigs that they are, that the changes they have made in the last century are improvements. Quakerization is always an improvement, and international law has certainly been quite thoroughly Quakerized.

By "classical," I mean anything before World War I. But a century is a nice dividing line. Let's take as our text, therefore, *Elements of International Law,* 3rd edition, 1908, by George B. Davis. I know nothing about this book or its author, but it is obviously a standard text. There are little bits of proto-Universalism to be found in it, but they are easily identified and discarded. For the most part it contains all the wisdom on statecraft of the classical European world, and it is very good at citing its sources. It is certainly not a mere collection of the personal opinions of George B. Davis, whoever he was.

> Here, for example, is classical international law on guerrilla warfare:
> Guerillas. The term guerilla is applied to persons who, acting singly or joined in bands, carry on operations in the vicinity of an army in the field in violation of the laws of war. They wear no uniform, they act without the orders of their government, and their operations consist chiefly in the killing of picket guards and sentinels, in the assassination of isolated individuals or detachments, and in robbery and other predatory acts. As they are not controlled in their undertakings by the laws of war, they are not entitled to their protection. If captured, they are treated with great severity, the punishment in any case being proportioned to the offence committed. Their operations have no effect upon the general issue of the war, and only tend to aggravate its severity. Life taken by them is uselessly sacrificed, and with no corresponding advantage.

Quelle différence! Here, on the rightfulness of war:

> Rightfulness of War. With the inherent rightfulness of war international law has nothing to do. War exists as a fact of international relations, and, as such, it is accepted and discussed. In defining the law of war, at any time, the attempt is made to formulate its rules and practices, and to secure the general consent of nations to such modifications of its usages as will tend towards greater humanity, or will shorten its duration, restrict its operations, and hasten the return of peace and the restoration of the belligerent states to their normal relations.

Friends, this is the sweet music of reason, scanned, de-Quakerized and presented for your perusal by the good progressives behind Google Books—who do much better than they know.

I cannot quote this entire book. If you care about the subject—and who doesn't?—it is simply worth reading. You can skip the chapters on diplomatic protocol, treaties, etc. War and sovereignty are your main concerns.

Classical international law, while never perfect, was simply a beautiful piece of engineering. It solved, not perfectly but quite effectively, a problem that today strikes us as unsolvable: enforcing good behavior among sovereign nations, without a central enforcer. You might call it a peer-to-peer architecture for world peace.

I'm afraid what we have now is more a client–server approach. It works, sort of. It does not strike me as stable or scalable. International law was designed for a world of equals. It broke down when one nation—first Great Britain, and later the United States—took it upon itself, for motives that were superficially charitable and fundamentally Whiggish, to act as a global enforcer. At that point, it ceased to be an instrument of peace and independence, and became one of domination and war. "Other grain."

If the entire tradition of classical international law were condensed down to two words, they might well be the Latin words *uti possidetis*.[22] If there is a single phrase that is the key to world peace, it is this one. Amazingly enough, it even has a Wikipedia page, although the classical concept is confused with the modern, and quite oxymoronic, one of *uti possidetis juris*.[23]

The idea of uti possidetis is the principle that every government is legitimate and sovereign. All governments are de facto. Their borders are defined by the power of their military forces. If two states disagree on their borders, it is up to them to settle the dispute. Their settlement should be respected by all. As Davis puts it:

> Treaties of peace resemble ordinary treaties in form, in the detailed method of preparation, and in binding force. They differ from ordinary treaties, and from private contracts, in respect to the position of the contracting parties, who, from the necessities of the case, do not enter them upon equal terms. This in no respect detracts from their obligatory character, which cannot be too strongly insisted upon. "Agreements entered into by an individual while under duress are void, because it is for the welfare of society that they should be so. If they were binding, the timid would be constantly forced by threats or violence into a surrender of their rights, and even into secrecy as to the oppression under which they were suffering. The [knowledge] that such engagements are void makes the attempt to extort them one of the rarest of human crimes. On the other hand, the welfare of society requires that the engagements entered into by a nation under duress should be binding; for, if they were not so, wars would terminate only by the utter subjugation and ruin of the weaker party."

In other words, exactly as they terminated in the 20th century. If they terminated.

> When either belligerent believes the object of the war to have been attained, or is convinced that it is impossible of attainment; or when the military operations of either power have been so successful as to determine the fortune of war decisively in its favor,

---

22 "As you possess, so shall you possess."
23 As a matter of international law, the principle is used to determine the boundaries of newly-formed states.

a general truce is agreed upon, and negotiations are entered into with a view to the restoration of peace.

You see the flavor of these rules. They are designed for a world of genuinely independent states—as opposed to British or American protectorates. Under the rule of uti possidetis, statehood is an objective description. No one asks: should Hamas have a state? One asks: is Gaza a state? Under classical international law, the answer is clearly "yes."

Let's take a brief look at how this plan would create peace in the Middle East. First, the borders between Israel and its neighbors are permanently fixed. They are simply the present lines of demarcation, as set at the end of the 1967 war. In the West Bank there is an area of fuzzy jurisdiction—Israel maintains what might be called an imperfect occupation. Gaza is its own state. I suspect Israel would find it prudent to evacuate most of the West Bank and put it in the same status as Gaza. Call it Ramallah.

The US is completely neutral in these disputes. It gives Israel no aid. It gives the Palestinians no aid. It gives no one any aid. It does not need protectorates, "friends," etc. It has the H-bomb and Angelina Jolie. Others can love it for the latter or fear it for the former. Or possibly the reverse. It's up to them.

The Middle East, and specifically the area around Israel, is actually an area of great natural stability. The area is stable because the state which **does not want war**,[24] Israel, is much stronger than its aggressive, **irredentist** and **revanchist** neighbors, Gaza and Ramallah. Therefore, there are two possibilities.

One, Gaza and Ramallah recognize that they live next to the 800-pound gorilla. They watch their steps. They do not shoot rockets over the border, and they prevent their citizens from doing so. And there is no war.

Two, Gaza and Ramallah persist in attacking Israel. Under classical international law, Israel exercises its **right of redress** and does whatever it takes to stop the attacks. If "whatever it takes" means that Israel has to convert the human population of Gaza into biofuel, so be it. The basic principle of classical international law is that **every citizen of an enemy state is an enemy**.

Of course, the law of war is intended to make combat humane, and the **basic principle of humanitarian war** is that

> No forcible measures against an enemy which involve the loss of human life are justifiable which do not bear directly upon the object of which the war is undertaken, and which do not materially contribute to bring it to an end.

In other words, if Gazans are really so crazed with lust for Jewish blood that they will never stop blowing themselves up in cafes until the last Gazan is processed

---

[24] Reference to the strategy of Havlagah, or "Restraint," used by Zionists to avoid conflict with Arab belligerents during the period of the British Mandate.

AN OPEN LETTER TO OPEN-MINDED PROGRESSIVES

into a tankful of biodiesel, biodiesel it is. Otherwise, of course, these actions would be quite unjustifiable.

Of course, Gazans are not really this crazy. They are normal people. They would take option 1 in a heartbeat, and the only reason they haven't already is that they are just doing their jobs. Hating Israel is the national industry of Palestine. That is, via American and European aid, it generates more or less the entire Palestinian GDP. If Palestinians stop attacking Israel, if they just settle down and live their lives like the normal people they are, there will be no reason for anyone to give them money. And the money will stop.

Ah, you cry, but justice! The Palestinians cry for justice! Well, perhaps it is just for Israel to give the Palestinians money, or land, or cheezburgers, or something. I would like to think that this money should come from Israel, not from Washington. But if the Palestinians want money, or land, or cheezburgers, they will have to find some way of extracting these goods from Israel, or whoever else, on their own. Because the world of classical international law is not the world that is ruled by Uncle Sam, dispenser of justice to all.

This is the genius of classical international law. It is based on the concept of actual sovereignty. When you establish your Quaker "league for enforcing peace," or even your British "balance of power," you establish an international super-sovereign. Which is a world government. Which is not, in the hands of the Quakers, a workable design. It might be a workable design in the hands of the Nazis—but would you want it to be?

The Palestinian problem is the reductio ad absurdum of Quakerism. Quakers believe that peace can be created by redressing grievances. When this principle is pointed toward the left, it becomes no justice, no peace. When it is pointed toward the right, it becomes appeasement. For example, **New Zealand activist John Minto**, who has Quaker written all over him, has produced a brilliant reinvention of *Lebensraum*:

> An artificial state for four million displaced Palestinians to govern themselves over several disconnected pieces of poor quality land not wanted by Israel is not viable in any meaningful sense of the word.

Even if all the initial grievances are absolutely just by some objective standard, the cycle of grievance and reward will quickly attract gangsters and create a mafia grievance factory.

The tragedy is that Mr. Minto and his ilk are so close to seeing the true principle of peace: peace is learning to live with the world as it is, not as you want it to be. You'd think a Quaker would be able to see this in a flash. But I'm afraid power has corrupted them.

Do the Palestinians find themselves with "poor quality land?" Then agriculture is probably not their métier. Dubai has some pretty crappy land, as well.

Its residents spend far less time brooding over the subject of Jews. Perhaps a simple solution would be for Dubai to annex Gaza—contiguous borders, while preferable, are hardly essential in the 21st century. Forget about the past. Live in the future.

It is almost impossible to overestimate how politically dependent the world's nations are on the US. I suspect that if we embraced the principles of classical international law overnight, next week would see military coups in almost every country in the world. In the present world, a military government in, say, Brazil, would be ostracized and isolated into oblivion with remarkable speed. In the world of classical international law, the US does not care what form of government is practiced in Brazil. It only cares that Brazil does not invade it, harass its shipping, welsh on its debts, etc. There is a lot of order to restore in Brazil, and a lot of prestige to be won by restoring it. At least in Brazil. And why should it matter what Washington thinks of Brazil? Answer: it shouldn't.

The world of 2008 has one major sovereign state, the US. There are two smaller ones, Russia and China, which have passed through Communism to a system of government that might almost be described as neoreactionary. By avoiding dependency on American aid, the oil kingdoms of the Gulf also retained a certain level of sovereignty. Iran and its satellites are trying to achieve stable sovereignty by building nuclear weapons, and being insanely aggressive toward America. Hopefully their aggression will stop after they succeed, but who knows?

The salient financial feature of the present world is the gigantic trade deficit between the democratic world and the neoreactionary world—in favor of the latter. This is not a coincidence. The Gulf states are neoreactionary because they have oil, which has enabled them to preserve something vaguely like their traditional forms of government, rather than becoming just more Third World protectorates of the State Department. Russia too has oil, which after Communism had the same effect. And China has that real rara avis, a healthy capitalist industrial base, a consequence of its bold resistance to democracy.

This financial imbalance is oddly reminiscent of the situation between the Communist and Western worlds before the collapse of the former. Of course, it could just be a coincidence. Don't get your hopes up. This one will take a while.

There was a funny article the other day in the Times. It seems Kuwaitis have noticed[25] that they have democracy, that Dubai doesn't, and that the latter seems to be rather better off for it. (Don't miss the pictures of Kuwait's "financial district"—sidesplitting.) Not that Kuwait has much democracy. It's a constitutional monarchy. But Dubai is an absolute monarchy, and the difference is, um, remarkable. Especially since Kuwait has way more oil than Dubai.

25

AN OPEN LETTER TO OPEN-MINDED PROGRESSIVES

The great wave of Whiggery has washed to the end of the world and the top of the beach. Its source is not moral righteousness, but mere power. That power is waning. It still looks like the future, but not as much as it used to. Patches of sand are starting to show through the water. Will another wave come? Or will the water just wash back? And if so, will it wash back slowly, or will it all just disappear one day, the way Communism did?

105 Charles Stross Link to Stross's blog, Charlie's Diary, at antipope.org. Stross is the author of several sci-fi novels and short story collections, including *Accelerando* (2005), and *Glasshouse* (2006).

 105 Rimbaud

 105 Christmas wish list Charlie Stross. "What I want for Christmas." *Charlie's Diary*, 24 Dec. 2007.

 106 Nazi bomb Letters from Neils Bohr that surfaced in 2002 allege that despite Werner Heisenberg's assertions that he resisted efforts to produce a nuclear weapon on behalf of the Nazis, he in fact was committed to doing just that. James Glanz. "New Twist on Physicist's Role in Nazi Bomb." *New York Times*, 7 Feb. 2002.

 106 Neutral Point of View policy

107 Medicine Robert N. Proctor. *The Nazi War on Cancer.* (Princeton University Press, 2000).

 107 Deutsche Physik

 107 Jew

 107 Kevin McDonald

 108 black propaganda

 108 Swiftian satire

 108 Daniel Defoe

 108 The Shortest-Way with the Dissenters Daniel Defoe. *The Shortest-Way with the Dissenters: or, Proposals for the Establishment of the Church, with its Author's Brief Explication Consider'd, His Name Expos'd, His Practices Detected, and his Hellish Designs set in a True Light.* London, 1703.

AN OPEN LETTER TO OPEN-MINDED PROGRESSIVES

 108 Dissenters English protestants who sought to reform or split from the Church of England in the 17th and 18th centuries, and who played an active role in the English civil wars. The Dissenters also figure prominently in later in this volume in *How Dawkins Got Pwned*.

 108 Puritan

 108 Rowan Williams

 108 Brussels "European Commission"

 109 William of Orange

 109 machtlos

 109 Praise-God Barebone

 109 True History of the American Revolution Sydney George Fisher. *The True History of the American Revolution*. (J.B. Lippincott, 1902).

 109 New York Times review "'TRUE HISTORY.'; Sydney George Fisher's Theories About the American Revolution." *New York Times*, 3 Jan. 1903, p. BR6.

 110 Boer War

 115 History of England Link to Chapter 1 of Macaulay's book, preserved at yarchive.net.

 116 pro-American stance A month before the battle of Lexington and Concord, Burke attempted to convince Parliament to offer the American colonies certain concessions to reconcile their differences and avoid a war. His resolution was defeated in the House of Commons 270 to 78. Edmund Burke. *Speech to Parliament on Conciliation with America*. Great Britain, 22 Mar. 1775.

 116 Edmund Burke

LINKS & NOTES

 116 Reflections Burke's famous critique of the French Revolution. Edmund Burke. *Reflections on the Revolution in France.* (James Dodsley, Pall Mall, 1790).

 117 William Howe

 117 Charles Cornwallis

118 I, II Sydney George Fisher. *The Struggle for American Independence: Vo.1 & 2.* (J.B. Lippincott Company, 1908)

 118 A National Change of Heart Charles Francis Adams. "A National Change of Heart." *Lee at Appomattox: And Other Papers.* (Houghton Mifflin, 1902).

 119 put it Excerpt from Thompson's *The Great Shark Hunt: Strange Tales from a Strange Time.* (Simon & Schuster, 2011) p.39.

 120 Transvaal

 120 Spanish war

 120 Venezuela arbitration Originally linked to a NYT query for "Venezuela Arbitration," leading to an archived and paywalled article from October 3, 1899. In context, the reader will be better served with the Wikipedia entry on the event in question provided here.

 120 Suez crisis

 120 more equestrian terms Transcript of Osama bin Laden videotape released by the Pentagon in December of 2001.

 121 Howard Zinn

 121 Memoirs of Service Afloat Admiral Raphael Semmes. *Memoirs of Service Afloat, During the War Between the States.* (Kelly, Piet, & Co., 1869).

 121 Raphael Semmes

AN OPEN LETTER TO OPEN-MINDED PROGRESSIVES 147

 121 Lord's Resistance Army

 122 Joseph Tumulty

 122 Colonel Edward M. House

 122 Woodrow Wilson As I Know Him Joseph Patrick Tumulty. *Woodrow Wilson as I know Him*. (Doubleday, Page & Company, 1921).

 126 page 397 Ibid.

 126 concentration camps "Second Boer War concentration camps"

 126 Timothy McVeigh

 126 Eric Rudolph

 126 Byron de la Beckwith

 127 Peninsular War

 127 good friends Link to a blog post from Tom Maguire detailing Obama's friendship with Bill Ayers. Tom Maguire. "Let's Accept Michelle's Invitation." *JustOneMinute*, 1 May 2008.

 127 attributed Link to a translation of an article written by Shaykh Ayman al-Zawahiri for Al-Qaeda's official media organ, Al-Sahab. (trans. Laura Mansfield) Shaykh Ayman al-Zawahiri. "Realities of the Conflict Between Islam and Unbelief." *As-Sahab Media*, Dec. 2006.

 128 French Algeria

 128 personal narrative LT G. "Rules of Engagement." *Kaboom: A Soldier's War Journal: Embrace the Suck*, 23 Mar. 2008.

129 barbaric tortures Link to an article containing lurid details of torture devices and drawings recovered at an al-Qaeda safehouse in an April 2007 raid by U.S. military officials. ed. William Bastone. "Torture, Al Qaeda Style." *the smoking gun*, 24 May 2007.

 129 Viet Cong "Massacre at Hue"

 129 National Liberation Front

 129 People's Army of Vietnam (NVA)

 129 cold-blooded killers

 130 ecumenical movement

 130 mainline

 130 evangelical

 130 Unitarian Universalists

 130 here "American Malvern." *Time Magazine*, Religion, Vol. XXXIX No.11, p. 16 Mar. 1942, now permanently archived at Unqualified-Reservations.org.

 133 Malvern Conference 1941, chaired by William Temple, the Archbishop of Canterbury, with a focus on "the church's concern for the 'common good.'" New World Encyclopedia entry for "William Temple."

134 The Puritan Origins of American Patriotism George Mckenna. *The Puritan Origins of American Patriotism*. (Yale University Press, 2007).

 135 Quakers "William Penn"

AN OPEN LETTER TO OPEN-MINDED PROGRESSIVES 149

 135 fascinating 1917 discussion "Quakers and the War." Reprinted in *The War From This Side: Editorials From the North American, Vol. IV.* (J.B. Lippincott, 1919).

 137 Empsonian See Chapter 3.

 137 Locksley Hall Alfred Lord Tennyson. "Locksley Hall Sixty Years After." *Ballads and Other Poems, Vol. VI of The Works of Tennyson*, ed. Hallam Lord Tennyson. (Macmillan, 1908).

 137 Elements of International Law George B. Davis. *The Elements of International Law: With an Account of its Origins and Historical Development.* 3rd ed. (Harper & Brothers, 1908).

 139 uti possidetis

 139 uti possidetis juris

 140 does not want war "Havlagah"

 140 irredentist

 140 revanchist

 140 right of redress See, *Elements of International Law* p.271.

 140 every citizen of an enemy state is an enemy Ibid. p.282.

 140 basic principle of humanitarian war Ibid. p.295.

 141 New Zealand activist John Minto John Minto. "Apartheid and Palestine." *Christchurch Press*, 24 Dec. 2007. Posted at johnminto.org.nz.

 141 Lebensraum

142 lot of order Reference to the Brazilian crime film *Elite Squad* (Universal Pictures, 2007), directed by José Padilha, depicting the Special Operations police unit in Rio de Jainero.
 142 Kuwaitis have noticed Robert F. Worth. "In Democracy Kuwait Trusts, but Not Much." *New York Times*, 6 May 2008.

CHAPTER 6:
THE LOST THEORY OF GOVERNMENT
MAY 22, 2008

The best way to understand government is to assume everything you know about it is nonsense. Or so at least I claimed in Chapter 5. Let's demonstrate it by solving the problem from scratch.

Growing up in the modern Western world, you learned that in all pre-modern, non-Western societies, everyone—even the smartest and most knowledgeable—put their faith in theories of government now known to be nonsensical. The divine right of kings. The apostolic succession of the Pope. The Marxist evolution of history. Etc.

Why did such nonsense prosper? It outcompeted its non-nonsensical competitors. When can nonsense outcompete truth? When political power is on its side. Call it *power distortion*.

And why, dear open-minded progressive, do you think your theory of government, which you did not invent yourself but received in the usual way, is anything but yet another artifact of power distortion, adapted to retain your rulers in their comfortable seats?

Probably because there is a categorical difference between modern liberal democracy and the assorted monarchies, empires, dictatorships, theocracies, etc., which practiced the black art of official mind control. The priests of Amun tolerated no dissent. They flayed the heretic, the back-talker, the smartmouth, and stretched his still-living flesh to crack and writhe in the hot African wind, till the hyena or the crocodile came along to finish him. But now they are all **pushing up the asphodels**,[1] and Google hasn't even thought about deleting my blog.

You think of freedom of thought as a universal antibiotic, a sure cure for power distortion. It certainly allows me to post my seditious blasphemies—for now.

But as a progressive, your beliefs are the beliefs of the great, the good and the fashionable. And as we've seen over the past few chapters, power can corrupt the mind in two ways: by coercion, or by seduction. The Whig, the liberal, the radical, the dissenter, the progressive, protests the former with great umbrage—especially when his ox is being gored. Over the past four centuries, he has ridden the latter to power. He is Boromir. He has worn the Ring and worked it. And it, of course, has worked him.

Today's late Whiggery, gray and huge and soft, lounges louche on its throne, fastened tight to the great plinth of public opinion that it hacked from the rock of history with its own forked and twisted tongue. The mass mind, educated to perfection, is sure. It has two alternatives: the Boromir-thing, or Hitler. And who wants Hitler? Resistance is more than useless. It is ridiculous. The Whig cackles, and knocks back another magnum of Mumm's.

And a few small rats wear out our incisors on the stone. In this chapter we'll learn the real principles of government, which have spent the last four centuries sunk under a **Serbonian bog** of meretricious liberalism. ("The funk... of forty thousand years."[2]) We'll have to wait until Chapter 7 to see what government is today.

The two, of course, have nothing to do with each other. Nor is this likely to change soon. Nor can you do anything about it. So why bother? Why think about government?

The only defense I can offer is Václav Havel's idea of "**living in truth.**" As a fellow cog in the global public supermind, you are bombarded constantly and from every direction with the progressive theory of government, with which all humans who are not ignorant, evil or both must agree by definition, and which makes about as much sense as the Holy Trinity. If you are ready to be the nail that sticks up and is hammered down, you can be a "conservative," which ties up a few of the loose ends, and unties others. It also makes you a social pariah, unless most of your neighbors are named "Earl."

This shit is stressful. Most of us already have stressful lives. Do we need it? We don't. The nice thing about understanding government is that it gives you an off button for the endless political yammering. While it may replace this with a bit of despair as regards the future, the future is a long way off. And not entirely without hope, but that's another post.

In any case: government.

---

1 Reference to Asphodel Meadows, the resting place of ordinary souls in the Ancient Greek underworld.
2 Lyrics from Michael Jackson's *Thriller*.

AN OPEN LETTER TO OPEN-MINDED PROGRESSIVES

First, let's establish what a government is. A government is a *sovereign corporation*. It is **sovereign** because its control over its territory is not subject to any higher authority. It is a **corporation** because it has a single institutional identity. All governments in history fit this definition, unless their sovereignty is compromised by some stronger power. In this case, that power is the true sovereign, and your analysis should be aimed at it.

Second, what makes a government good or bad? The easiest way to think about this problem is to think *subjectively*. Assuming you have no power over the government's decisions, under what kind of government would you prefer to live? Given two governments A and B, what would make you move or want to move from A to B, or vice versa?

The key is that we are evaluating a government based on *what it does*, not *what it is*. As Deng Xiaoping—probably the greatest statesman of the 20th century—put it: "Who cares if the cat is black or white, so long as it catches mice?"

The subjective approach asks whether the government catches mice. It does not ask who the government's personnel are, or how they are selected, or how they are managed. Perhaps they are all Dinka warriors from the middle of nowhere, Sudan, chosen for their impassive visages as they execute the brutal Dinka ritual of auto-hemicastration with no implement but their own fire-hardened fingernails. If they govern well, so much the better.

Your subjective desires for government may be different from mine. They probably are. In a world of good governments, subjective preferences would reduce to the trivial and cosmetic. If I am in the market for fast food and I see a Burger King next to a McDonalds, I will go with the King. Why? Does it matter?

Fast food is a fine metaphor for government. You'd think managing a sovereign corporation is probably more complicated and difficult than operating a fast-food chain. Heck, operating a nonsovereign US state is probably harder than flipping burgers. And if B is harder than A, you'd think anyone who can pull off B would ace A.

But if I saw a McDonalds next to a Calmeat, Mickey would be my man. Of course, there is no Calmeat. We do not live in a world where the State of California sees fit to operate restaurants, fast or otherwise. There is no state burger. Even as an open-minded progressive, however, I'm afraid you will have to concede that if there was a Calmeat, it would either be either horrible or horribly overpriced, and probably both.

Why? It will become obvious, if it isn't already. But what it tells us—if this isn't already obvious—is that we don't live in a world of good government. California is better-governed than nine-tenths of the Earth's surface. And there is no way its government could flip a decent burger. As Mark Twain **put it:**

> Omar Khayam, the poet-prophet of Persia, writing more than eight hundred years ago, has said:

> "In the four parts of the earth are many that are able to write learned books, many that are able to lead armies, and many also that are able to govern kingdoms and empires; but few there be that can keep a hotel."

Twain's quote does not strike me as authentic—but I quail at the notion of Calstay. In any case: not only do we not live in a world of good government, we live in a world of *disastrously bad* government. If the 20th century does not go down in history as the golden age of awful government, it is only because the future holds some fresher hell for us.

So we are not concerned with the subtleties of good government. We are not interested in *excellent* government. It would be nice, but we would be satisfied with mere competence—perhaps with whatever enables McDonald's to survive in a world that contains not only BK but also In-N-Out, even though its burgers taste like boiled cardboard. Our goal is the mere *basics*.

Here are the basics: a government should be *secure*, *effective*, and *responsible*. None of this is rocket science. The only secret is that there is no secret.

Let's define and analyze these qualities individually, assuming the others in each. When we explain how to make a government responsible, we'll assume it is secure and effective. When we explain how to make it secure, we'll assume it is effective and responsible. Etc.

Let's start with effectiveness. Effectiveness is the ability to accomplish what you're trying to do. Under what design is a government most effective?

We can think of effectiveness as a measure of good management. A well-managed enterprise hires the right people, spends the right amount of money on them, and makes sure they do the right things. How do we achieve effective management?

We know one simple way: find the right person, and put him or her in charge. This single, frail being, our *administrator*, holds final decision-making authority—the Roman *imperium*—over budget, policy, and personnel.

In the military world, this is called *unity of command*. In the (nonsovereign) corporate world—and in the nonprofit world that opposes it—this individual is the *CEO*. Even that most anarchic of human endeavors, the **open-source project**,[3] tends to follow the administrator design.

Why does individual administration work? When said individual is a douche, it doesn't. There is no reliable formula for good management. But there are many reliable formulas for bad management. A better question is: why does management by committee *not* work?

Divided control of any human enterprise tends to fail because of a phenomenon generally known, around the office, as *politics*. Politics always emerges when management breaks down. An individual manager, with undivided control of some enterprise, can only succeed by making the enterprise succeed. Replace one

---

[3] Reference to *Benevolent Dictator for Life*, a title for a small number of open-source software development leaders who have final say within the community.

manager with two—the unorthodox administrative design known as "two-in-a-box," a disaster I personally have experienced—and either has a new way to succeed: making the other fail. The more cooks, the worse the broth.

In every human endeavor outside government itself, undivided administration is well-known to produce optimal results. If Peet's could beat Starbucks, Southwest JetBlue, or In-N-Out Mickey D's, by adopting a "separation of powers" or a "constitution" or some other architecture of leadership by consensus, one of them would certainly have tried it.

Contemplate, dear friends, the great heap of rococo procedural ornamentations that have replaced the simple principle of personal decision in the modern Western government. Montesquieuean separation of powers is the least of it. Outside the military, in which the principle of command still functions to some extent, it is simply impossible to find anyone with unified responsibility for getting anything done. And even military officers, while they have some vestiges of *imperium*—rapidly being sucked away by the judicial system—seldom control anything like their own budgets, and have zero power over personnel.

So: the modern aversion to individual management cannot be motivated by effectiveness. Undivided administration is more effective, period. We can only explain the penchant for collective decision-making as a function of responsibility or security. It is hard to see how it has anything to do with security. It must be a matter of responsibility.

But, in a system where no individual can be connected reliably with any success or failure, where is the responsibility? As none other than Woodrow Wilson put it, in 1885:

> It is quite safe to say that were it possible to call together again the members of that wonderful Convention [of 1787] to view the work of their hands in the light of the century that has tested it, they would be the first to admit that the only fruit of dividing power had been to make it irresponsible.

Wilson himself, of course, had a great deal of undivided power. Nor did he use it responsibly. When we think of sovereign executives, we tend to think of bad examples. We think of Hitler, not of Frederick the Great. We don't think of Sultan Qaboos or Lee Kuan Yew or Hans-Adam II. If you think this is a coincidence, think again. But perhaps a thought-experiment will help.

Washington, especially since it governs not only the United States but also most of the world, is just too huge to serve as a good thought-experiment for government. It's easier and more fun to think in terms of California, if California could somehow be a sovereign state. Assuming security and responsibility, how could we produce effective government in California?

The answer: find the world's best CEO, and give him undivided control over budget, policy and personnel. I don't think there is any debate about it. The world's best CEO is **Steve Jobs**.

Which would you rather live in: California as it is today, or Applefornia? Which would you rather carry: the iPhone, or the Calphone? I rest my case.

So let's segue into responsibility. Assuming a government is responsible and secure, we know how to make it effective: hire Steve. But how do we make it responsible?

Steve, after all, is a turbulent fellow. He is moody at best. He could easily go around the bend. And he is already a notorious megalomaniac, a tendency that total *imperium* over the Golden State—including its new military forces, whose heads are shaved, whose garb is white linen, and whose skill in synchronized martial-arts demonstrations is unmatched even on the Korean peninsula—can hardly ameliorate.

A responsible, effective government has three basic parts. One is the front-end: all the people who report to Steve. Two is the middle: Steve himself. Three is the back-end: the people Steve is responsible to.

Apple itself, like all public corporations in the modern system, has a two-level back-end: a board of directors, elected (in theory) by a body of shareholders. There is no reason to copy the details of this system. Corporate governance in the US today is nothing to write home about. It is the principles that matter.

Call the back-end the *controllers*. The controllers have one job: deciding whether or not Steve is managing responsibly. If not, they need to fire Steve and hire a new Steve. (Marc Andreessen, perhaps.)

This design requires a substantial number of reasonably cogent controllers, whose collective opinion is likely to be trustworthy, and who *share a single concept of responsibility*.

What happens if the controllers disagree on what "responsible" government means? We are back to politics. Factions and interest groups form. Each has a different idea of how Steve should run California. A coalition of a majority can organize and threaten him: do this, do that, or it's out with Steve and in with Marc. Logrolling[4] allows the coalition to micromanage: more funding for the threatened Mojave alligator mouse! And so on. That classic failure mode, parliamentary government, reappears.

Call a controller model with a single shared concept of responsibility *coherent*. How, with an impossibly fuzzy word like "responsibility," can we round up a large number of intelligent individuals who share a common definition? The task seems impossible. And our whole design relies on this coherent back-end.

Actually, there's one way to do it. We can define responsibility in *financial* terms. If we think of California as a *profitable* corporation, a capital asset whose purpose is to maximize its production of cash, we have a definition of responsibility which is not only precise and unambiguous, but indeed quantitative.

---

4 The trading of votes and favors.

AN OPEN LETTER TO OPEN-MINDED PROGRESSIVES

Moreover, this definition solves a second problem: how do we select the controllers? If our controllers are the parties to whom the profits are actually paid, and their voting power is proportional to the fractions they receive, they have not only a shared definition of responsibility, but an incentive to apply that definition in practice.

We have, of course, reinvented the **joint-stock company**. There is no need to argue over whether this design works. It does. The relevant question is: in the context of government, does this financial definition of responsibility actually match the goal we started out with?

In other words: will an effectively managed government (remember, we are assuming security and effectiveness), which is responsible only in the sense that it tries to maximize its profits in the infinite term, actually provide the good customer service that is our goal? Will it catch mice for us? Or will it flay us, and hang us out to dry, etc.?

As a progressive, you consider undivided government ("dictatorship") the root of all evil. It is impossible to enumerate the full list of reasons behind this belief. It's like asking you why you prefer a romantic candlelight dinner for two at a simple, yet elegant, French restaurant, to being dragged alive behind an 18-wheeler at highway speed until there is nothing on the rope but a flap of bloody skin. When we add the abominable and astonishing suggestion that said government should actually *turn a profit*, we reach maximum horror. But if we are not willing to question even our deepest beliefs, our minds are hardly open.

First, it helps to remember that profitability is hardly antithetical to good customer service. Again, try the restaurant analogy. If all restaurants were nonprofits, do you think we would have better food, or worse? How does a nonprofit restaurant differ from Calmeat, which has no institutional incentive to keep its diners coming back? Perhaps if the restaurant is a small cooperative run by people who really love food, it will continue to shine. California is not a small anything, and my own interactions with its employees have revealed no such passion.

Second, I suspect that your deepest fear about undivided government is that it will in some way prove *sadistic*. It will torment and abuse its residents for no reason at all. Perhaps, for example, Steve will decide to massacre the Jews. Why not? It's been done before!

Think about this for a minute. Steve is responsible to his controllers, who evaluate his performance based on his stewardship of one asset: California. The value of California is the sum of the value of its shares. If one goes up or down, so does the other.

Which is worth more? California, or California infested by Jew-eating crocodiles? Which can be made to produce more revenue? The former, clearly. Jews pay taxes. Crocodile dung doesn't. And from the perspective of either Steve or the Jews, what is the difference between crocodiles and stormtroopers? At least the former will work for free.

Perhaps this is skipping ahead slightly, but one way to understand why Stevifornia will not be sadistic and aggressive is to explain why the Third Reich and the Soviet Union were. Sadism was not profitable for Hitler or Stalin—not that they cared, all that much. But they cared a little. Money meant power, and Hitler and Stalin certainly cared for power.

The sadistic side of these states is best understood as part of their security model. Hitler and Stalin were not gods. They could not shoot lightning bolts or resist bullets. They rose to and stayed in power by ruthless intimidation, up to and certainly including murder. Stalin didn't kill all those Old Bolsheviks because they had bad breath or had made passes at his wife. In the 20th century's "totalitarian" states, murder foreign and domestic was an essential strut in the Leader's security design. We will not be reproducing this element. But I digress.

Third, as a progressive, you think of government as a *charitable* institution. You think of its purpose as *doing good works*. And indeed, today's governments do many good works. They also do many things that are not good works but purport to be, but that is beside the point. Let's assume that all its good works are good indeed.

Clearly, good works are not compatible with turning a profit. It is easy to see how California improves its bottom line by refraining from the massacre of Jews. It is hard to see how it improves its bottom line by feeding the poor, healing the lame, and teaching the blind to see. And indeed, it doesn't.

So we can separate California's expenses into two classes: those essential or profitable for California as a business; and those that are unnecessary and wasteful, such as feeding the poor, etc., etc. Let them starve! Who likes poor people, anyway? And as for the blind, bumping into lampposts will help them build character. Everyone needs character.

I am not Steve Jobs (I would be very ill-suited to the management of California), and I have not done the math. But my suspicion is that eliminating these pointless expenses alone—without any other management improvements—would turn California, now drowning in the red, into a *hellacious, gold-spewing cash machine*. We're talking dividends up the wazoo. Stevifornia will make **Gazprom** look like a pump-n-dump penny stock.

And suddenly, a solution suggests itself.

What we've done, with our separation of expenses, is to divide California's spending into two classes: essential and discretionary. There is another name for a discretionary payment: a dividend. By spending money to heal the lame, California is in effect paying its profits to the lame. It is just doing it in a very fiscally funky manner.

Thus, we can think of California's spending on good works as profits which are disbursed to an entity responsible for good works. Call it Calgood. If, instead of spending $30 billion per year on good works, California shifts all its good works and good-workers to Calgood, issues Calgood shares that pay dividends of $30 billion per year, and says goodbye, we have the best of both worlds. California is

AN OPEN LETTER TO OPEN-MINDED PROGRESSIVES

now a lean, mean, cash-printing machine, and the blind can see, the lame can walk, etc., etc.

Furthermore, Calgood's shares are, like any shares, **negotiable**. They are just financial instruments. If Calgood's investment managers decide it makes financial sense to sell California and buy Google or Gazprom or GE, they can go right ahead.

So without harming the poor, the lame, or the blind at all, we have completely separated California from its charitable activities. The whole idea of government as a doer of good works is thoroughly phony. Charity is good and government is necessary, but there is no essential connection between them.

Of course, in real life, the idea of Calgood is slightly creepy. You'd probably want a few hundred special-purpose charities, which would be much more nimble than big, lumbering Calgood. Of course they would be much, much more nimble than California. Which is kind of the point.

We could go even farther than this. We could issue these charitable shares not to organizations that produce services, but to the actual individuals who consume these services. Why buy canes for the blind? Give the blind money. They can buy their own freakin' canes. If there is anyone who would rather have $100 worth of free services than $100, he's a retard.

Some people are, of course, retards. Excuse me. They suffer from mental disabilities. And one of the many, many things that California, State of Love, does, is to hover over them with its soft, downy wings. Needless to say, Stevifornia will not have soft, downy wings. It will be hard and shiny, with a lot of brushed aluminum. So what will it do with its retards?

My suspicion is that Stevifornia will do something like this. It will classify all humans on its land surface into three categories: guests, residents, and dependents. Guests are just visiting, and will be sent home if they cause any trouble. Residents are ordinary, grownup people who live in California, pay taxes, are responsible for their own behavior, etc. And dependents are persons large or small, young or old, who are not responsible but need to be cared for anyway.

The basic principle of dependency is that a dependent is a **ward**. He or she surrenders his or her personal independence to some guardian authority. The guardian holds *imperium* over the dependent, i.e., controls the dependent's behavior. In turn the guardian is responsible for the care and feeding of the dependent, and is liable for any torts the dependent commits. As you can see, this design is not my invention.

At present, a large number of Californians are wards of the state itself. Some of them are incompetent, some are dangerous, some are both. Under the same principle as Calgood, these dependents can be spun off into external organizations, along with revenue streams that cover their costs.

Criminals are a special case of dependent. Most criminals are mentally competent, but no more an asset to California than Jew-eating crocodiles. A sensible way to house criminals is to attach them as wards to their revenue streams, but let the criminal himself choose a guardian and switch if he is dissatisfied. I suspect that most criminals would prefer a very different kind of facility than those in which they are housed at present. I also suspect that there are much more efficient ways to make criminal labor pay its own keep.

And I suspect that in Stevifornia, there would be very little crime. In fact, if I were Steve—which of course I'm not—I might well shoot for the goal of providing *free crime insurance* to my residents. Imagine if you could live in a city where crime was so rare that the government could guarantee restitution for all victims. Imagine what real estate would cost in this city. Imagine how much money its owners would make. Then imagine that Calgood has a third of the shares. It won't just heal the lame, it will give them bionic wings. But I digress.

So we move on to our third essential: security. (Note that this is **Arnold Kling**'s objection[5] to the above design, which I've given the cute name of **neocameralism**.[6])

Security is the art of ensuring that your decision process cannot be compromised by any force, domestic or foreign. Steve, for instance, is entirely indifferent to the opinions of Stevifornians, except inasmuch as those opinions affect his quarterly numbers. This is the ideal "type 3" state: you think what you want, and Steve does what he wants. The government neither controls public opinion, nor is controlled by it.

If nothing quite like a neocameralist government has ever existed in history, the reason is not hard to figure out. How do you secure an intricate decision mechanism like the above? What happens if the controllers decide to fire Steve, and Steve doesn't want to go? How does Steve remain in power if a million Stevifornians storm the presidential palace, and the guards side with the crowd and turn their guns around?

Fortunately, we do not have to design a solution that will protect **Charles X** (no relation to Malcolm) from the machinations of the treacherous **Marmont**. The neocameralist state never existed before the 21st century. It never could have existed. The technology wasn't there.

Secure neocameralism depends on a *cryptographic decision and command chain* (CDCC). Once the world has cryptographically secure government, it will wonder how it ever lived without it.

In the world of today, the security of all governments is dependent on *mere personal loyalty*. The US Army could take over Washington tomorrow, if it wanted to. It certainly cannot be compelled to obey the President, the Supreme Court, the Congress, or anyone else. It so happens that the US military has a strong tradition of loyalty—a tradition that was tested, for example, in the case of the **Bonus Ar-**

---

5 [QR code]

6 "The idea that a sovereign state or primary corporation is not organizationally distinct from a secondary or private corporation," originally coined in the UR post "Why I am not a libertarian."

my.⁷ Would today's Army fire on an American mob? Especially a mob that shared its political orientation? Hopefully we will not find out.

The only reason that we accept this appalling and dangerous state of affairs is that we don't know there's an alternative. But there is, actually—in the form of **permissive action links**.⁸ This is an old Cold War design that implements the command side of a CDCC, for nuclear weapons only. (The control codes are in the **President's pocket**.)

In a full CDCC government, the sovereign decision and command chain is secured from end to end by military-grade cryptography. All government weapons—not just nukes, but everything right down to small arms—are inoperable without code authorization. In any civil conflict, loyal units will find that their weapons work. Disloyal units will have to improvise. The result is predictable, as results should be.

Cryptographic command of the military has a critical effect on political dynamics: it makes public opinion irrelevant. Today, even the most militaristic of military despotisms has to invest considerable effort in persuading, cajoling or compelling the public to support it, because the army is inevitably drawn from that public. Witness Marmont, who decided his chances were better with Orléans than Artois.

This is the final blow in the elimination of politics. Men enter politics because they have a lust for power. Good men as well as bad men lust for power, and sometimes it does happen that good men lust for power, seize it, and use it to do good things. But it is more the exception than the rule. And the lust for power is an eminently practical one—if no power is available, no one will bother to scheme for it.

Take Apple, for example. Mac users, such as myself, are tied to its vagaries. For example, the battery for the MacBook Pro is shite. It's disposable. I believe it may actually be made of toilet paper, chewing gum, and old paper clips. I go through two a year, and I hardly use them.

How do I cope with this appalling injustice? I deal. Why do I deal? Because even if I went on to the right forums and whipped up a screaming mob and persuaded them to march around and around and around **1 Infinite Loop**, chanting slogans and burning old batteries, I know that it would have absolutely no impact on Steve's handling of the problem. (Which I suppose he doesn't think is a problem at all.) In fact, it would probably make him more stubborn.

There is simply no way for anyone outside Apple to influence Apple's decision process by the use of force. Apple is not sovereign. It does not have a white-robed black-belt army. It relies on the security forces of Uncle Sam, or at least Cupertino. But the problem is solved, anyway. And I consider this a good thing.

---

7 The name given to a demonstration of tens of thousands of World War I veterans and their supporters who gathered in Washington D.C. in 1932 to demand early redemption of their service bonuses, two of whom were shot at and killed by Washington police.

8 A special box that uses cryptographic mechanisms to prevent the unauthorized use of nuclear weapons.

Cryptography applies to the back-end as well: the decision side. If the controllers vote to refuse to renew Steve's key, and anoint Marc instead, Steve will no longer have command of the army. He won't even have command of his office door. He will have to call security to let him out of the building. (If you doubt that this is technically feasible, it is.[9])

Once we realize that 21st-century technology is needed to implement the neocameralist design, we understand why good old cameralism, Frederick the Great style, was the best that previous centuries could do. What Whigs call **absolute monarchy** (and non-Whigs just call monarchy) collapsed the controllers and the administrator into a single royal person, solving the decision problem quite neatly—and introducing a nasty biological variable into the responsibility mix. And on the command side it relied on loyalty, which was not always there.

Was royalism a perfect system? It was not. But if we imagine a world in which the revolutions and civil wars of the last four centuries had never happened, it is hard not to imagine that world as happier, wealthier, freer, more civilized, and more pleasant. At least if you're an unregenerate Jacobite like me.

---

9 Reference to *secret sharing*, a method for distributing information across a group so no one person's "share" is intelligible on its own.

AN OPEN LETTER TO OPEN-MINDED PROGRESSIVES 163

 152 pushing up the asphodels "Asphodel Meadows"

 152 Serbonian bog

 152 The funk... of forty thousand years.
The foulest stench is in the air
The funk of forty thousand years (Thriller night, thriller)
And grisly ghouls from every tomb
Are closing in to seal your doom
Rod Temperton, perf. Michael Jackson. "Thriller." *Thriller.* (Epic, 1983).

 152 living in truth Link to the Václav Havel Library Foundation website. *Living In Truth* was the title of his 1989 book containing the famous "green grocer" essay, "Power of the Powerless."

 153 put it-1 Mark Twain. *A Tramp Abroad.* (Chatto & Windus, 1906). Vol. 4, p.273.

 154 imperium

 154 unity of command

 154 open-source project "Benevolent Dictator for Life"

 155 put it Woodrow Wilson. Congressional *Government: A Study in American Politics.* (Houghton Mifflin, 1913) 15th Ed., p.285.

 155 Sultan Qaboos

 155 Lee Kuan Yew

 155 Hans-Adam II

156 Steve Jobs original link to the Jobs biography *Inside Steve's Brain* by Leander Kahney (Portfolio Hardcover, 2008).

156 Marc Andreessen

 156 Logrolling

 157 joint-stock company

 158 Gazprom

 159 negotiable "Negotiable instrument"

 159 ward

 160 Arnold Kling's objection Arnold Kling. "A Corporate State?" Econ-Log. *Econlib.org*, 15 Dec. 2007.

 160 neocameralism Mencius Moldbug. "Why I am not a libertarian." *Unqualified Reservations*, 13 Dec. 2007.

 160 Charles X

 160 Marmont

 160 Bonus Army The name given to a demonstration of tens of thousands of World War I veterans and their supporters who gathered in Washington D.C. in 1932 to demand early redemption of their service bonuses.

 161 permissive action links Steven M. Bellovin. *Permissive Action Links.* cs.columbia.edu.

 161 President's pocket "Gold codes"

 161 1 Infinite Loop "Apple campus"

AN OPEN LETTER TO OPEN-MINDED PROGRESSIVES 165

 162 it is "Secret sharing"

 162 cameralism

 162 absolute monarchy

CHAPTER 7: THE UGLY TRUTH ABOUT GOVERNMENT
MAY 29, 2008

In Chapter 6, dear open-minded progressive, we worked through a clean-room redesign of government. The result had no resemblance to present institutions—and little resemblance to past ones. Should this surprise you? Do you expect history's fruits to be sweet?

In this chapter we'll look at what those fruits actually are. Perhaps you didn't spend your eleventh-grade civics class hanging out behind the goalposts smoking cheeba. (If you are still in eleventh-grade civics class, it's much more exciting if you're stoned.) Perhaps you even read the Times on a regular basis. (The Times is even more awful when you're stoned.) Perhaps you assume, by default, that the vast parade of facts poured into your head by this and other such reliable sources must constitute at least a basic understanding.

You would be incorrect in this. And we have a Mr. Machiavelli, who is to government as Isaac Newton is to physics, Barry Bonds is to baseball, and Albert Hofmann is to LSD, to **tell us why:**

> He who desires or attempts to reform the government of a state, and wishes to have it accepted and capable of maintaining itself to the satisfaction of everybody, must at least retain the semblance of the old forms; so that it may seem to the people that there has been no change in the institutions, even though in fact they are entirely different from the old ones. For the great majority of mankind are satisfied with appearances, as though they were real-

ities, and are often even more influenced by the things that seem than by those that are.

So, for example, the Roman **Principate**, and even to some extent the **Dominate**, preserved the forms of the old Republic. If Rome under Augustus had had a New York Times, it would have been full of the doings of the Senate and the consuls. The Senators said this. The consuls did that. When in reality, everything that mattered went through Augustus. If the entire Senate had fallen through a manhole in the Forum, nothing would have changed—except, of course, that the illusion of the Republic could no longer be maintained.

(The Romans even had a word for a monarch—the good old Latin *Rex*. No Roman emperor, however dissolute, autocratic or hubristic, ever adopted the title of king. "Emperor" is simply an anglicization of *Imperator*, meaning "Commander"—i.e., a general.)

Often when the illusion ceases to delude anyone, it persists as a linguistic convention—especially on the tongues of officials. So in British official language one still may speak as if the Queen were the absolute personal ruler of the UK, when in fact she has no power at all. No one is confused by this. It is just a quaint turn of speech. Still, it has its effect.

Power is a shy beast. She flees the sound of her name. When we ask who rules the UK, we are not looking for the answer, "the Queen." The Queen may rock, but everyone knows she doesn't rule. Parting this thin outer peel, we come on the word "Parliament," with which most of us are satisfied. This is your official answer. The Queen holds nominal power. Parliament holds formal power. But does this tell us where the actual power is? Why should we expect it to? Since when has it ever?

Power has all the usual reasons to hide. Power is delicious, and everyone wants it. To bite into its crisp, sweet flesh, to lick its juices off your lips—this is more than pleasure. It is satisfaction. It is fulfillment. It is meaning. The love of a bird for a caterpillar is a tenuous and passing attachment next to the bond between a man and power. Of course power, like the caterpillar, may have other defenses—poison-filled spines, and the like—but why not start with camouflage? Why look like anything more than a stick or a leaf?

Of course, as a progressive, you have all sorts of ideas about where power is hiding. It is in the hands of the corporations, the crooked politicians, the bankers, the military, the television preachers, and so on. It would be unfair to denigrate all of these perspectives as "conspiracy theories," and it is also unfair to denigrate all conspiracy theories as false. Lenin, for instance, was a conspirator. So were Alger Hiss, Benedict Arnold, even **Machiavelli himself**.

Nonetheless, the best place to hide is usually **in plain sight**.[1] For example, Noam Chomsky once wrote a book called *Manufacturing Consent*, which argues that corporations exercise power by controlling the mass media. The phrase is bor-

---

1 Reference to the Edgar Allen Poe story *The Purloined Letter*.

rowed from Walter Lippmann's *Public Opinion*—a book which every progressive will do well to read. La Wik has a fine summary:

> When properly utilized, the manufacture of consent, Lippmann argues, is useful and necessary for modern society because "the common interests"—the general concerns of all people—are not obvious in many cases and only become clear upon careful data collection and analysis, which most of the people are either uninterested in or incapable of doing. Most people, therefore, must have the world summarized for them by those who are well-informed.
>
> Since Lippmann includes much of the political elite within the set of those incapable of properly understanding by themselves the complex "unseen environment" in which the affairs of the modern state take place, he proposes having professionals (a "specialized class") collect and analyze data and present the conclusions to the decision makers. The decision makers then take decisions and use the "art of persuasion" to inform the public about the decisions and the circumstances surrounding them.

Who is Lippmann's "specialized class?" Is it Chomsky's corporate CEOs? Rupert Murdoch, perhaps? Au contraire. It is folks like **Lippmann himself**—journalists. (Lippmann described his analysis and persuasion agency, somewhat infelicitously, as an "Intelligence Bureau.")

Thus we have two candidates for who is "manufacturing consent." It could be the corporate executives to whom the journalists report. Or it could be the journalists themselves, in plain sight. Or, of course, both—in the true **Agatha Christie** style.[2] As political detectives, we may ask: which of these parties has the means, motive, and opportunity?

But I am getting ahead of myself. Starting from the usual first principles, we are attempting to understand our system of government. What one word, dear progressives, best describes the modern Western system of government?

You probably said "democracy." If you got two words, you might say "representative democracy." So our progressive scratch-monkey, Mr. Stross, explains the success of democracy in terms of its supposed advantages, here.[3] (He actually comes surprisingly close to the truth—as we'll see in a little bit.)

Words mean whatever we want them to. But if we interpret the phrase representative democracy to mean a political system in which power is held by the representatives of the people as chosen in democratic elections, the United States

---

2 Reference to the plot of *Murder on the Orient Express*.

3

is a representative democracy in just the same sense that the Roman Empire was a republic, the United Kingdom is a kingdom, and the Chinese Communist Party is communist.

In fact, dear progressive, you fear and loathe democracy. Moreover, you are right to do so. Representative democracy is a thoroughly despicable system of government. It is dangerous and impractical at best, criminal at worst. And you hate it like the poison it is.

But you don't hate it under this name. You hate it under the name of politics. Think of the associations that the words political, partisan, politician, and so on, produce in your mind. You say: George W. Bush politicized the Justice Department. And this is a brutal indictment. If you hated black people the way you hate politics, you might say George W. Bush negroized the Justice Department, and the phrase would carry the same payload of contempt.

Similarly, when you hear antonyms such as apolitical, nonpartisan, bipartisan, or even the new and truly ludicrous *post-partisan*, your heart thrills with warmth and affection, just as it would if you were a racist and you heard the words Nordic, Anglo-Saxon, or amelanistic. And as it does when you hear the word democracy. You certainly would never say that George W. Bush democratized the Justice Department.

And yet, when you hear the phrase "apolitical democracy," it sounds slightly off. Can we have democracy without politics? Representative democracy without politics? What would that even mean? That there are no parties, perhaps? So let me get this straight—two parties is good, one party is bad (very bad), no parties at all is—even better? La Wik has a curious page for **non-partisan democracy**,[4] in which some of these issues are explored, in the typical disjointed and unenlightening manner.

This is simply one of these contradictions that we find in the modern, progressive mind. You have probably wondered, idly, about it yourself. Since, as we've seen, progressivism is an essentially religious movement, the mystery of politics, that necessary evil of democracy, slides neatly into the same lobe of your brain that was in less enlightened days reserved for the great questions of theology. How can God be three persons at once? A wondrous mystery indeed.

Two fresh yarns in the *Pravda*[5] illustrate the irony beautifully. In the first[6] (which we've linked to before), our brave reporter is positively amused to find a native tribe so benighted that they might imagine they'd be better off without democ-

---

4 [QR code]

5 The New York Times

6 [QR code] See also Chapter 5 endnote "Kuwaitis have noticed."

racy. In the second,[7] our fearless correspondent is shocked that, in darkest North America, the savages are so backward and credulous as to entertain the preposterous belief that counting heads amidst the mob is a sensible way to select responsible public officials.

Let's probe a little deeper into this mystery. If the actions of our democratic governments are not to be ascribed to the venal machinations of politicians, who is responsible for them? Who, in the ideal apolitical, nonpartisan, or post-partisan state, calls the shots? We are back to the basic question of power, which Lenin once summarized as "**Who? Whom?**" (This made more sense in English when we still used the word "whom." What Lenin meant was: who rules whom?)

So if politicians should not rule, who—dear progressive—should? If we continue our pattern of two-word answers, the answer is: public policy.

To the progressive—rather ironically, considering the history—Lenin's question is completely inappropriate. You reject the idea that government means that "who" must "rule" "whom." Rather, you believe that government, when conducted properly in the public interest, is an objective discipline—like physics, or geology, or mathematics.

It does not matter "who" the physicists, geologists, or mathematicians are. There is no German physics, liberal geology, or Catholic mathematics. There is only correct physics, correct geology, and correct mathematics. The process and criteria by which physicists separate correct from incorrect physics is quite different from that for geology or mathematics, and none of these processes is perfect or works instantaneously. But all have an obvious tendency to progress from error and ignorance to truth and knowledge.

Needless to say, if the United States were blessed with a Department of Mathematics—honestly I'm not sure why it isn't, but we can rest assured that if this wrong is ever righted, it will stay righted—it would be thoroughly inappropriate and irresponsible for George W. Bush to "politicize" the Department's deliberations on topology, computability, game theory, etc.

Public policy, of course, must not contradict physics, geology or mathematics. But these are not its main linchpins. When we look inside the magic box of public policy, we see fields such as law and economics and ethics and sociology and psychology and public health and foreign policy and journalism and education and...

And when we look at the history of these fields, we tend to see one of two things. Either (a) the field was more or less invented in the 20th century (sociology, psychology), or (b) its 20th-century principles bear very little relation to those of its 19th-century predecessor (law, economics). We saw this in Chapter 5, for example, with **international law**. But again, I am getting ahead of myself.

As a progressive, you regard the fields of public policy as more or less scientific. The 20th century is the century of scientific public policy. And just as there is

---

7

no German physics or Catholic mathematics, there is no German public policy or Catholic public policy. There is only public policy. There is no "who." There is no rule. There is no world domination. There is only global governance.

So we see why it's inappropriate for George W. Bush to "politicize" the Justice Department. It is because the Justice Department is staffed with legal scholars. Is George W. Bush a legal scholar? Is a boar hog an F-16? When politics intrudes on the realm of science, it's more than just a violation. It's a kind of rape. One is instantly reminded of the Nazi stormtroopers, dancing around their flaming piles of books. One, if one is an American, is also reminded of the mindless jockery that ruled one's high-school years. Do you, dear progressive, have any hesitation about picking a side in this dispute? Of course not.

Thus we see the fate of representative, political democracy, which survives as a sort of vestigial reptile brain or fetal gill-slit in the era of scientific government. In classic Machiavellian style, the form democracy has been redefined. It no longer means that the public's elected representatives control the government. It means that the government implements scientific public policy in the public interest. (Public policy is in the public interest by definition.)

We may summarize the whole in Lincoln's concise phrase: government of the people, by the people, for the people. All governments are of the people (they also provide animal control). The people being what they are, by the people turns out to be a bad idea. But we can still have government for the people, which gives us two out of three, which ain't bad. Since it is both of the people and for the people, and demos after all just means people, we can keep the good old word for our modern, scientific democracy.

You may already know all this, but perhaps it's worth a brief tour of how this system evolved.

The basically criminal nature of the old, political form of democracy has been discovered and rediscovered many times in American (and before that, of course, British) history. In his *American Creation*, the popular historian Joseph Ellis summarizes the Founders' judgment on democracy: "an alien, parasitic force." This of course would be their judgment as of the 1790s, not the 1770s, at which point they had had plenty of experience with said parasitic force. Any premodern history of the period—I recommend Albert Beveridge's four-volume *Life of John Marshall*—will show you why. There is a reason you didn't learn much about the First Republic in that eleventh-grade civics class.

The Second Republic, or Constitutional period, saw a return to government by enlightened aristocrats, first under the Federalists and later under the Jeffersonians, who rather cleverly rode a wave of mob agitation into office and then ruled in a distinctly Federalist style (a trick that would later be repeated). This era of good feelings lasted until the election of ur-politician Andrew Jackson, who among other works of genius invented the spoils system—the unabashed selection of political loyalists for government jobs.

The following period of political turmoil, while distinguished by occasional flashes of sanity (such as the best **system of government finance**[8] in history) and ameliorated by gridlock between North and South, which preserved a remarkably small and simple Washington, degenerated into the mass military insanity of the 1860s. Many Northern intellectuals, such as **Henry Adams**, had assumed that the defeat of the **Slave Power** would heal all the woes of the Federal City and transform it into the shining light it was meant to be. Au contraire.

Instead, in the Union period or Third Republic, what was by 20th-century standards a remarkably limited government, but by 18th-century standards an almost omnipotent one, fell into the hands of **ethnic machines, corrupt politicians, quasicriminal financiers, sinister wire-pullers, unscrupulous journalists, vested interests,**[9] and the like. History, which of course is always on the side of the winners, has written this down as the **Gilded Age**.

For all its faults, the Gilded Age system created perhaps the most responsible and effective government in US history. Architecture is always a good clue to the nature of power, and Gilded Age buildings, where they still stand, are invariably decorative. The country's prosperity and productivity was, of course, unmatched. Its laws were strict and strictly enforced—nothing like today's festering ulcers of crime were imaginable.

An English journalist of Tory bent, **G. W. Steevens**, wrote an excellent travelogue of Gilded Age America—*The Land of the Dollar*. (It's very readable, especially if you don't mind the N-word.) Steevens, in 1898, was unable to locate anything like a slum in New York City, and his intentions were not complimentary. It's an interesting exercise to compare the hyperventilations of a Gilded Age social reformer like Jacob Riis—the title *How The Other Half Lives* may ring a bell—to the world of **Sudhir Venkatesh**.[10] Riis's tenement dwellers are sometimes less than well-scrubbed. They can be "slovenly." They drink a lot of beer. Their apartments are small and have poor ventilation—ventilation, for some reason, seems to be a major concern. All these horrors still afflict the present-day residents of the Lower East Side, who are hardly in need of anyone's charity.

But the Gilded Age political system was, again, criminal. In other words, it was democratic. The old American system is probably best compared to the government of China today. While they evolved from very different origins, they have converged in that universal medium, corruption. Government serves as a profit center, but (unlike in neocameralism) the distribution of profits is informal. The dividends are fought over with a thousand nontransparent stratagems. Since China is not a democracy, vote-buying is not practiced there. It was certainly practiced here.

---

8 Reference to the creation of the Independent Treasury in 1846.
9 Tammany Hall, Richard Croker, Jay Gould, Mark Hanna, William Randolph Hearst, and "Gilded Age" respectively.
10 Reference to Venkatesh's 2008 pop-sociology book *Gang Leader for a Day: A Rogue Sociologist Takes to the Streets.*

And the bosses and plutocrats were not, by and large, cultured men. Sometimes I feel this is the main objection of their enemies. The American intellectual aristocracy simply could not tolerate a world in which their country was governed by these corrupt, boorish thugs. So, as aristocrats will, they plotted their revenge.

I mentioned "reform" earlier. And Machiavelli, if you scroll back to the top, uses the same word. Of course, he simply meant "change the form of." He implies no connotations. But notice, dear progressive, your associations with the word "reform." Like "nonpartisan" and all those other good words, it is connected with the happy part of your brain. La Wik's reform[11] page is not bad.

Politically, the deepest roots of the present regime are found in the Liberal Republicans and the Mugwumps of the early Union period. The cause they are most associated with is civil service reform, which removed the President's power to staff the civil service and replaced it with competitive examinations—which tended to select, of course, scions of said aristocracy.

La Wik has many other discussions of early progressivism: the settlement movement, the Fabians, the muckrakers. You were probably exposed to large doses of this in your 11th-grade civics class. (If you are still in 11th-grade civics class, take an extra hit for this material. You'll need it.)

It is interesting to go back and read, say, Lincoln Steffens, today. Unfortunately Google Books has failed us on his *The Shame of the Cities*, but here is a sample.[12] And Steffens' *Autobiography* (really a series of rants drawn loosely from his life) is easily obtainable. What comes through is, most of all, a tremendous sense of smugness and arrogance. Steffens, for example, will be talking to Teddy Roosevelt. A close personal friend. But the Pres doesn't always take Steffens' advice. He compromises, sometimes. That's because he's weak, or ignorant, or corrupt, or maybe all three.

Steffens' tone only works if you think of him as the underdog. But underdogs are infrequently found in the Oval Office, and hindsight indeed shows us that this underdog won. Which makes him the overdog. And while its long-departed ghost is easily recognizable in the rhetoric of, say, a Michael Moore, a brief glance at Steffens' work will show you that nothing like the political tradition he is attacking exists in the world today. (To the extent that there are ethnic political machines,[13] they are firmly in the hands of Steffens' successors.)

Whereas Steffens' tradition has flourished. He was the mentor, for example, of Walter Lippmann. If you traced the social network of modern journalism, all the

---

11

12

13 Kwame Kilpatrick, mayor of Detroit at the time of this post, prior to his 2013 conviction for federal fraud and racketeering charges.

AN OPEN LETTER TO OPEN-MINDED PROGRESSIVES 175

lines would go back to Steffens and his cronies. And the lines lead overseas, as well: Steffens went to Russia in 1919, and he loved it. As he wrote in 1930:

> Soviet Russia was a revolutionary government with an evolutionary plan. Their plan was not by direct action to resist such evils as poverty and riches, graft, privilege, tyranny and war, but to seek out and remove the causes of them. They were at present only laying a basis for these good things. They had to set up a dictatorship, supported by a small, trained minority, to make and maintain for a few generations a scientific rearrangement of economic forces which would result in economic democracy first and political democracy last.

"Economic democracy." Contemplate this concept, dear reader. Whatever "economic democracy" may be, it certainly has nothing at all to do with the practice of entrusting control of the state to elected representatives.

Steffens then allows Lenin, whom he is interviewing, to deliver a few paragraphs on the necessity of murdering the bourgeoisie, and finally delivers his famous line:

> "So you've been over into Russia?" asked **Bernard Baruch**, and I answered very literally, "I have been over into the future, and it works." This was in Jo Davidson's studio, where Mr. Baruch was sitting for a portrait bust. The sculptor asked if I wasn't glad to get back. I was. It was a mental change we had experienced, not physical. Bullitt asked in surprise why it was that, having been so elated by the prospect of Russia, we were so glad to be back in Paris. I thought it was because, though we had been in heaven, we were so accustomed to our own civilization that we preferred hell. We were ruined; we could recognize salvation, but could not be saved.

Indeed, what Steffens calls "applied Christianity," and UR readers will recognize as our good old friend, creeping Quakerism, is seldom far beneath the surface in his work. I think you get the drift, but let us summarize. (Note that "propaganda" is not yet a term of abuse in 1930.)

> In Russia the ultimate purpose of this conscious process of merging politics and business is to abolish the political state as soon as its sole uses are served: to make defensive war abroad and at home and to teach the people by propaganda and by enforced conditions to substitute new for old ideas and habits. The political establishment is a sort of protective scaffolding within which the temporary dictatorship is building all agriculture, all industries,

and all businesses into one huge centralized organization. They
will point out to you from over there that our businesses, too, are
and long have been coming together, merging trusts into combines, which in turn unite into greater and greater monopolies.
They think that when we western reformers and liberals resist this
tendency we are standing in the way of a natural, inevitable economic compulsion to form "one big union" of business. All that
they have changed is the ownership, which they (and Henry Ford)
think is about all that's wrong. Aren't they right to encourage the
process? Aren't we wrong to oppose it?

Note this recycling of ideas through Russia. There is nothing Russian at all about the dream Steffens is purveying. It is all in **Edward Bellamy**.[14] From day one, a substantial and influential section of the American intelligentsia were the patrons, intellectual and political, of the Soviet Union, which spent all eighty years of its life manfully trying to implement Bellamy's vision.

Imagine how, say, libertarians would react if Russia decided to turn itself into a libertarian utopia. Imagine how easily they might come to overlook the matter if achieving the libertarian utopia turned out to involve, oh, just a little bit of good old Russian-style killing. In self-defense, of course. Libertarians believe in self-defense. Don't they? And besides, we're just killing government officials... and so on.

Your understanding of the bond between the American aristocracy and the Soviets has been distorted by both right and left. The left has done everything possible to bury their complicity in the monstrous crimes of their Slavic epigones. The right has assisted them by misrepresenting the structure of this complicity, which was never—even in such clear-cut cases as **Alger Hiss**—a simple matter of treason. The American side was always the senior partner in the marriage. The prestige of their distinguished Western patrons was a key ingredient in the Soviet formula for legitimacy and internal control, and the growing staleness of the alliance contributed far more, I think, to the Soviet collapse than most today admit.

Anyway, let's briefly finish up our origin myth, which ends, of course, in 1933. An excellent history of the period is supplied by the historian (and Progressive) James Truslow Adams, who followed his four-volume *March of Democracy* with two volumes of yearbooks, written every year and not (so far as I can determine) edited afterward, covering each year to 1948. This provides a pleasant hindsightless feel found in few other treatments of the period. In his history of 1933, Adams reports:

> Nothing much was known about Roosevelt, except his smile. As **William Allen White** wrote at the time of his inauguration, "we are putting our hands in a grab-bag. Heaven only knows what we

---

14 Reference to Bellamy's 1888 utopian novel *Looking Backward*, and the socialist movement it inspired.

AN OPEN LETTER TO OPEN-MINDED PROGRESSIVES

shall pull out." With the disingenuousness apparently required of a Presidential candidate, his campaign speeches had not disclosed his real views...

Well, that's putting it mildly. In fact they had disclosed other views,[15] which were not his real views. (As Marriner Eccles put it, "given later developments, the campaign speeches often read like a giant misprint, in which Roosevelt and Hoover speak each other's lines.") Apparently White, for some reason, knew the story behind the script. Of course, if you don't believe in democracy, there is no reason not to treat it with contempt.

Adams, with only a mild glaze of sycophancy, reports the results:

> [FDR] was, in fact, with the help of what he considered the best expert advice, although always making final decision himself, trying experiments, and occasionally he frankly said so. In these experiments he has been motivated by two objects—one the overcoming of the depression, and the other the making over of the economic organization of the nation, the latter being what he called in his campaign speeches "the New Deal." It is this which appears—it is too soon to speak positively—his chief objective, and it is difficult as yet to judge what his conception of the new society may be. In his first year he has shown enormous courage but has, apparently, not seldom changed his point of view, as well as his advisers.
>
> As the latter loomed large in the administration, to a considerable extent displacing the regular Cabinet in public sight, the so-called "brain trust" requires some comment. Of recent years college professors have been more and more frequently called into consultation as "experts." Hoover made frequent application to them when President; Roosevelt did the same as Governor of New York; and foreign governments have done likewise. However, they have never been so in the forefront of affairs as since Roosevelt entered the White House, and this, together with the vagueness of what the "New Deal" might signify, helped to hinder the restoration of confidence. The lack of ability to foresee the future, to say nothing in too many cases of the absence of personal integrity, had indeed thrown the "big business men," the bankers and captains of industry, into the discard, but on the other hand the American has never had much belief in the practical ability of a

---

15 Democratic Party Platform, 1932

CHAPTER 7

professor, and the "experts" have disagreed among themselves as notably as doctors are said to do.

Moreover, Roosevelt chose many of his advisers from the distinct radical or left-wing group, the names of most of them being utterly new to the public. At first among the chief of these appear to have been Professor **Raymond Moley**, Doctor **R. G. Tugwell**, and **A. A. Berle, Jr.**, all of Columbia University, New York. In the summer of 1933 there were added to these and many others Professor G. F. Warren of Cornell, a leading advocate of the "commodity dollar," and Professor J. H. Rogers of Yale. At least twenty or thirty others could be mentioned. It is to the "brain trust" that we owe the carrying out of the vague "New Deal," or as a great admirer of the President prefers to call it, "the Roosevelt Revolution." What the final result may be, no one can yet say, but as we shall see at the end of the chapter, they have presented a staggering bill for the American citizen to pay.

Indeed. I doubt there is a more succinct history of the birth of "public policy." I date the Fourth Republic and the Progressive period to 1933.

We can read this story in two ways. We can read it as the coming of modern, scientific government in the United States. Or we can read it as the transfer of power from political democracy to the American university system—which, just for the sake of a catchy catchword, I like to call the Cathedral.

Albert Jay Nock had no doubts on the matter. Allow me to reproduce a section of his diary from 1933:

> 29 October—And so Brother Hitler decides he will no longer play with the League of Nations. This leaves the League in "ruther a shattered state," as **Artemus Ward** said of the Confederate army after Lee's surrender. "That army now consists of **Kirby Smith**, four mules, and a Bass drum, and is movin rapidly tords Texis."
>
> 30 October—Public doings in this country are beyond all comment. Roosevelt has assembled in Washington the most extraordinary aggregation of quacks, I imagine, that was ever seen herded together. His passage from the scene of political action will remove the most lively showman that has been seen in America since the death of P.T. Barnum. The absence of opposition is remarkable; Republicans seem to have forgotten that the function of an Opposition is to oppose. I say this in derision, of course, for our politics are always bi-partisan. I have talked with many people; no one has any confidence in Roosevelt's notions, but the "organs of public opinion" either praise him or are silent; and no one expects that Congress will call him on the carpet. The

only certain things are that his fireworks will cost a lot of money, and that they will enlarge our bureaucracy indefinitely. Most of the big Federal slush-fund that the taxpayers will create next year will go to local politicians, nominally for "improvements," unemployment or what not, but actually for an increase of jobs and jobbery. This ought to build up a very strong machine for the next campaign, as I am convinced it is meant to do—and all it is meant to do—and no doubt it will. I notice that the new move of **juggling with the price of gold** has been turned over to the [Reconstruction Finance Corporation] instead of to the Treasury; thus making the R.F.C. a personal agent of the President.

31 October—To my mind, there was never a better example of getting up a scare in order, as Mr. Jefferson said, to "waste the labours of the people under the pretence of taking care of them." Our improvement, such as it is, was under way in June, and there is no evidence whatever that Mr. Roosevelt's meddling has accelerated it. One is reminded of the headlong haste about framing the Federal Constitution, on the pretext that the country was going to the dogs under the Articles of Confederation; when in fact it was doing very well indeed, as recent researches have shown. All this is a despicable trick. The papers say that in this business of meddling with the gold market, Roosevelt is influenced by the theories of **Irving Fisher**. It reminds me that when I was in Europe I heard that one of Hitler's principal lieutenants is a chap that I used to know pretty well; the only name I can think of is Helfschlager, and that is not right. His family are the big art-dealers in Munich—**Hanfstängl**, that's it. I got well acquainted with him in New York, and saw him afterward in Munich, and came away with the considered belief that he is a fine fellow and uncommonly likable, but just as crazy as a loon. I have long had precisely that opinion of Fisher. Therefore if it is true that Irving Fisher is to the front in America and Helfschlager in Germany, I think the future for both countries looks pretty dark.

Don't miss La Wik on Irving Fisher.[16] The page demonstrates the dichotomy perfectly.

So, as so often here on UR, we have two ways to see reality. Either power has passed into the hands of the Cathedral, or it has disappeared and been replaced by mere science. "Public policy." Of course, you know what I think. But what do you think?

16

If we can conceive the Cathedral as an actual, non-divinely-inspired, political machine for a moment, suspending any resentment or reverence we may feel toward it, not assuming that the policies it produces are good or bad or true or false, we can just admire it from an engineering perspective and see how well it works.

First: if there is one pattern we see in the public policies the Cathedral produces, it's that they tend to be very good at creating dependency. We can observe the dependency system by imagining what would happen if Washington, DC, out to the radius of the Beltway, is suddenly teleported by aliens into a different dimension, where its residents will live out their lives in unimaginable wealth, comfort and personal fulfillment. We here on Earth, however, see the Federal City disappear in a flash of light. In its place is a crater of radioactive glass.

What would happen? Many, many checks would no longer arrive. Children would go hungry—not just in North America, but around the world. Old people would starve. Babies would die of easily preventable diseases. Hurricane victims would squat in squalor in the slums. Drug companies would sell poison, stockbrokers would sell worthless paper, Toys-R-Us would sell little plastic parts designed to stick in my daughter's throat and choke her. Etc., etc., etc.

Washington has made itself necessary. Not just to Americans, but to the entire world. Why does Washington want to help the survivors of **Cyclone Nargis**?[17] Because helping is what it does. It dispenses love to all. Its mission is quite simply to do good, on a planetary basis. And why does the government of Burma want to stop it? Why turn down free help, including plenty of free stuff, and possibly even some free money?

Because dependency is another name for power. The relationship between dependent and provider is the relationship between client and patron. Which is the relationship between parent and child. Which also happens to be the relationship between master and slave. There's a reason Aristotle devotes the first book of the *Politics* to this sort of kitchen government.

Modern Americans have enormous difficulty in grasping hierarchical social structures. We grew up steeped in "applied Christianity" pretty much the way the Hitler Youth grew up steeped in Hitler. Suggesting that slavery could ever be or have been, as Aristotle suggests, natural and healthy, is like suggesting to the Hitler Youth that it might be cool to make some Jewish friends. Their idea of Jews is straight out of *Jud Süß*.[18] Our idea of slavery is straight out of *Uncle Tom's Cabin*. If you want an accurate perspective of the past, a **propaganda novel**[19] is probably not the best place to start. (If you want an accurate perspective of American slavery, I recommend Eugene Genovese's *Roll, Jordan, Roll*, which is a little Marxist but only superficially so. No work like it could be written today.)

---

17 Major tropical storm that devastated Myanmar weeks prior to this post.
18 *Süss the Jew*, 1940 Nazi propaganda film.
19 Reference to *The Annotated Uncle Tom's Cabin* by Henry Louis Gates.

AN OPEN LETTER TO OPEN-MINDED PROGRESSIVES

Legally and socially, a slave is an adult child. (There's a reason the word **emancipation**[20] is used for the dissolution of both bonds.) We think of the master–slave relationship as usually sick and twisted, and invariably adversarial. Parent–child relationships can be all three. But they are not normally so. If history (not to mention evolutionary biology) proves anything, it proves that humans fit into dominance–submission structures almost as easily as they fit into the nuclear family.

Slavery is an extreme, but the general pattern is that the patron owes the client protection and subsistence, while the client owes the patron loyalty and service. The patron is liable to the public for the actions of the client—if they offend, he must make amends. In return, he has the right, indeed the obligation, to regulate and discipline his clients. He is a private provider of government. Thus Aristotle: slavery is government on the micro-scale. Heed the Greek dude.

So comparing the social paternalism of Washington to the classical relationship between master and slave is not at all farfetched, or even particularly pejorative. And if it is pejorative, it is because the 20th-century imitation often seems to resemble less a functional paternal bond than a dysfunctional one: less parent–child than parent–teenager. With many of Washington's clients, foreign and domestic, there is plenty of subsistence and even protection, but precious little loyalty, service, discipline or responsibility.

We are now in a position to understand the relationship between Washington and **Rangoon**. Rangoon (I refuse to call it "Yangon"—the idea that a government can change the name of a city or a country is a distinctly 20th-century one) refuses to accept the assistance of the "international community" because it does not want to become a client.

You'll find that any sentence can be improved by replacing the phrase "international community" with "State Department." State does not impose many obligations on its clients, but one of them is that you can't be a military government—at least not unless you're a left-wing military government with friends at Harvard. The roots of the present Burmese regime are basically **national-socialist**:[21] i.e., no friends at Harvard. Burma cannot go directly from being an enemy to being a rebellious teenager. It would have to go through the helpless-child stage first. And that means the end of the generals.

(One reason the **Jonah Goldbergs of the world** have such trouble telling their right from their left is that they expect some morphological feature of the State to answer the question for them. For anyone other than Goldberg, Stalin was on the left and Hitler was on the right. The difference is not a function of discrepancies in administrative procedure between the KZs and the Gulag. It's a function of social networks. Stalin was a real socialist, Hitler was a fake one. Stalin was part of the international socialist movement, and Hitler wasn't. But I digress.)

What, specifically, will happen if Burma admits an army of aid workers? What will happen is that they'll make friends in Burma. Their friends will not be the

---

20 As in, "emancipation of minors"
21 Reference to military dictator of socialist Burma from 1962-1988, Ne Win.

people in power—not quite. But they will probably be close to it. Thus the ties between the "international community" and all kinds of alternatives to the generals will be strengthened. Since the latter's position is already precarious at best, much better if a few of the victims have to eat mud for a month or two. They will fend for themselves in the end. People do.

And why is Washington playing this game? Just because it does. In that golden city are armies of desks, each occupied by a dedicated public servant whom the Cathedral has certified to practice public policy, whose job it is to care about Burma. And he or she does. That's what Washington does. As George H. W. Bush put it, "Message: I care."

When our patron's suffering clients are actually American citizens, this pattern—as Nock predicted, correctly—generates votes. Before the New Deal, vote-buying in America was generally local and informal. Retail, you might say. After 1933, it was wholesale.

But however much of a client it becomes (I really can't imagine the generals can hold out that much longer), Burma will never export electoral votes. Statehood is unimaginable. So why does Washington continue to molest the generals, in pursuit of the love and fealty of the Burmese people? Just because it does. There is adaptive value in "applied Christianity." That adaptive value derives from its domestic application. There is little or no adaptive value in restricting the principle to domestic clients, and it involves a level of conscious cynicism which is not compatible with the reality of progressivism. So the restriction does not evolve.

Thus the neo-Quakerism which supplies the ethical core of progressivism, and is evangelized with increasingly relentless zeal by the Cathedral's robeless monks, is completely compatible with the acquisition and maintenance of political power. Not only does the design work—I find it hard to imagine how it could work any better. Which does not mean that "applied Christianity" is evil, that the Burmese generals are good, or that their suffering subjects would not be better off under Washington's friendly umbrella.

Second, let's observe the relationship between the Cathedral and our old friend, "democracy." Since 1933, elected politicians have exercised minimal actual control over government policy. Formally, however, they have absolute control. The Cathedral is not mentioned in the Constitution. Power is a juicy caterpillar. Maybe it looks like a twig to most of us birds, but Washington has no shortage of sharp eyes, sharp beaks, and growling bellies.

We can see the answer when we look at the fate of politicians who have attacked the Cathedral. Here are some names: **Joseph McCarthy. Enoch Powell. George Wallace. Spiro Agnew.** Here are some others: **Ronald Reagan. Richard Nixon. Margaret Thatcher.**

The first set are politicians whose break with the Cathedral was complete and unconditional. The second are politicians who attempted to compromise and coexist with it, while pulling it in directions it didn't want to go. The first were destroyed. The second appeared to succeed, for a while, but little trace of their efforts

AN OPEN LETTER TO OPEN-MINDED PROGRESSIVES

(at least in domestic politics) is visible today. Their era ends in the 1980s, and it is impossible to imagine similar figures today.

What we see, especially in the cases of McCarthy and Powell (the recent BBC documentary[22] on Powell is quite good) is a tremendous initial burst of popularity, trailing off into obloquy and disrepute. At first, these politicians were able to capture large bases of support. At least 70% of the British electorate was on Powell's side. This figure may even be low.

But Powell—Radio Enoch[23] aside—never had the tools to preserve these numbers and convert them into power. Similar majorities[24] of American voters today will tell pollsters that they support Powellian policies: ending immigration, deporting illegals, terminating the racial spoils system.[25] These majorities are stable. No respectable politician will touch them. Why? Because they cannot afford to antagonize the Cathedral, whose policies are the opposite.

Recall La Wik's simple summary of the Lippmann system:

> The decision makers then take decisions and use the "art of persuasion" to inform the public about the decisions and the circumstances surrounding them.

Of course, all politicians in all Western countries depend on the official press to promote and legitimize their campaigns. Powell and McCarthy had no direct channel of communication with the Powellists and McCarthyists. They had to rely on the BBC and on ABC, NBC and CBS respectively. It's rather as if the US attempted to invade the Third Reich by booking passage for its soldiers on the Imperial Japanese Navy.

The OP (known to most bloggers as the "MSM") is part of the civil-service complex around the Cathedral—call it the Polygon. An institution is in the Polygon if it defers to the Cathedral on all disputable questions. Because to a devotee of the Cathedral, its perspectives are beyond question, no two devotees can disagree on any serious matter—unless, of course, both sides of the disagreement are represented in the Cathedral itself. And the Cathedral is not exactly noted for disagreeing with itself. At least, not from an external perspective.

You will not see the Times attacking Harvard, for example, or the State Department. They all have the same ant smell, as it were. The Times is not formally a government institution, as the BBC is, but it might as well be. If American journalism were coordinated into a Department of Information—as it was in World War

---

22 *Rivers of Blood* (2008)
23 Pirate radio station broadcasting right-wing content during the late 70's.
24
25 Reference to Affirmative Action.

I and World War II[26]—and journalists were granted **GS ranks**, very little in their lives would change. As civil servants, they would be exactly as immune to political pressure as they are at present, and they would have exactly the same access to government secrets that they have at present.

The Cathedral's response to these dissident politicians thus took two forms, one fast and one slow. Both would have been effective; together, they were devastating. First, the "art of persuasion"—more dramatically known as **psychological warfare**—convinced their supporters that the politicians themselves were sick, awful, and weird, and so by extension was anyone who followed them. Second, the Cathedral itself adapted to the doctrines of Powell and McCarthy by making opposition to them an explicit tenet of the faith.

Since the Cathedral educates the world's most fashionable people, and since it holds power and power is always fashionable, Cathedralism is fashionable more or less by definition. Of course, if you were fashionable, you knew instantly that Powell and McCarthy were on the slow boat to nowhere. But the unfashionable are always the majority, and they are not unfashionable because they choose to be. They are unfashionable because they can't pull off fashionable.

As it became clear to all that Powell and McCarthy were "not done," their fans disappeared. Their bases of support had been a mile wide and an inch deep. Their attacks on the Cathedral were pathetic and doomed, like taking on the Death Star with a laser pointer. Personally, both men were mercurial and unstable—Powell was a genius,1 the last real statesman in British politics, while McCarthy was an old-school hard-drinking politician with **Roy Cohn** on his team—and it is no surprise that none of their colleagues emulated their suicidal bravado.

As for the second class, the Thatchers and Nixons and Reagans, in terms of their own personal outcomes they were smarter. They attacked the Cathedral not across the board, but on single issues on which their support was overwhelming. Sometimes they actually prevailed, for a while, on these points—Reagan got his military buildup, Thatcher got deregulation, Nixon **defeated North Vietnam**.[27]

Of course, the Nixon administration also created EPA, initiated the **racial spoils system**,[28] and imposed **wage and price controls**. Thatcher got Britain **inextricably**[29] into the EU. And so on. These semi-outsider politicians provide a valuable service to the Cathedral: while opposing a few of its policies, they validate all the others as a bipartisan consensus, which everyone decent is obligated to support. They thus do the heavy lifting of persuading their supporters, who probably wouldn't read the Times even if they did trust it, to change with the changing

---

26 "Committee on Public Information" and "United States Office of War Information," respectively.
27 Reference to the 1972 Easter Offensive.
28 Supra
29 Richard North's blog *EU Referendum*, referenced here, and the larger story of Great Britain and its relation to the EU, is explored in greater detail in Chapter 8.

times. And the times are always changing. And we just can't not change with them, can we?

To the extent that democratic politics still exists in the Western world, it exists in the form of the two-party system. The parties have various names, which they have inherited from history. But there are only two parties: the Inner Party, and the Outer Party. It is never hard to tell which is which.

The function of the Inner Party is to delegate all policies and decisions to the Cathedral. The function of the Outer Party is to pretend to oppose the Inner Party, while in fact posing no danger at all to it. Sometimes Outer Party functionaries are even elected, and they may even succeed in pursuing a few of their deviant policies. The entire Polygon will unite in ensuring that these policies either fail, or are perceived by the public to fail. Since the official press is part of the Polygon and has a more or less direct line into everyone's brain, this is not difficult.

The Outer Party has never even come close to damaging any part of the Polygon or Cathedral. Even McCarthy was not a real threat. He got a few people fired, most temporarily. Most of them were actually Soviet agents of one sort or another. They became martyrs and have been celebrated ever since. His goal was a purge of the State Department. He didn't even come close. If he had somehow managed to fire every Soviet agent or sympathizer in the US government, he would not even have done any damage. As **Carroll Quigley** pointed out, McCarthy (and his supporters) thought he was attacking a nest of Communist spies, whereas in fact he was attacking the American Establishment. Don't bring a toothpick to a gunfight.

McCarthy never even considered trying to abolish the State Department—let alone State, Harvard, the CFR, the Rockefeller Foundation, and every other institution in the same class. By my count, if you lump all his efforts together with the entire phenomenon of McCarthyism, you get about 10 milli-Hitlers. (And not even Hitler, of course, succeeded in the end.)

An essential element in the "art of persuasion" is the systematic propagation of the exact opposite of this situation. Devotees of the Inner Party and the Cathedral are deeply convinced that the Outer Party is about to fall on them and destroy them in a new fascist upheaval. They often believe that the Outer Party itself is the party of power. They can be easily terrified by poll results of the type that Powell, etc., demonstrated. There are all kinds of scary polls that can be conducted which, if they actually translated into actual election results in which the winners of the election held actual power, would seriously suck. That's democracy for you.

But power in our society is not held by democratic politicians. Nor should it be. Indeed the intelligentsia are in a minority, indeed they live in a country that is a democracy, indeed in theory their entire way of life hangs by a thread. But if you step back and look at history over any significant period, you only see them becoming stronger. It is their beliefs that spread to the rest of the world, not the other direction. When Outer Party supporters embrace stupid ideas, no one has any reason to worry, because the Outer Party will never win. When the Inner Party goes mad, it is time to fear. Madness and power are not a fresh cocktail.

And thus we see the role of "democracy" in the Progressive period. Stross says:

> Democracy provides a pressure release valve for dissent. As long as the party in power are up for re-election in a period of months to (single digit) years, opponents can grit their teeth and remind themselves that this, too, shall pass... and wait for an opportunity to vote the bums out. Democracies don't usually spawn violent opposition parties because opposition parties can hope to gain power through non-violent means.

This is the theory. But since elected politicians in the Cathedral system have, as we've seen, no real power, what we're looking at here is not a pressure release valve, but a fake pressure release valve. The regular exchange of parties in "power" reassures you, dear voter, that if the State starts to become seriously insane, the valve will trip, the bums will be thrown out, and everything will return to normal.

In fact, we know exactly what Washington's policies twenty years from now will be. They will certainly have nothing to do with "politics." They will be implementations of the ideas now taught at Harvard, Yale and Berkeley. There is a little lag as the memes work their way through the system, as older and wiser civil servants retire and younger, more fanatical ones take their place. But this lag is getting shorter all the time. And by the standards of the average voter forty years ago, let alone eighty, Washington already is seriously insane. What is the probability that by your standards—as progressive as they may be—Washington forty years from now will not seem just as crazed? Fairly low, I'm afraid.

And this brings us to the third point about the public policy apparatus: while appearing unconscious of its audience, it adapts to it. This is the most incriminating point, because there is no good explanation for it, and the trend is quite ominous if projected outward.

Take the recent decision of the California Supreme Court, who have just discovered that the state's Constitution allows people of the same sex to marry. As a matter of policy, I have no objection at all to this. Quite the contrary. I think it's an excellent and sensible policy. I do, however, have an interest in where this policy came from.

This is what, in the 20th-century progressive public-policy world, we call "law." The craft of the lawyer used to be the craft of discovering how the words of a law were intended, by the officials who ratified the law, to imply that one's client was in the right. I think it's fairly safe to assume that the drafters and ratifiers of the California Constitution and its various amendments had no such understanding of their work. (Try reading the actual decision.[30] It's a fascinating hunk of boilerplate.)

30

AN OPEN LETTER TO OPEN-MINDED PROGRESSIVES

Nonetheless, the drafters wrought better than they knew. The practice of drafting laws which are vague to the point of meaninglessness, then empowering "judges" to "interpret" them, is simply another way of abolishing politics. Congress legislates this way all the time. All they are doing is transferring the power of legislation to a more private body, which is not subject to public scrutiny and the other painful woes of politics. The great thing about the gay marriage decision is that no one in California has any idea who made it. I think there are nine people on the California Supreme Court. Who are they? How did they get their jobs? Who the heck knows? No one seems to care at all.

The US Constitution was the first and greatest offender in this department. Its drafters did not even agree on such basic matters as whether a state could leave the Union. In practice, it made the Supreme Court the supreme legislative assembly, which over the last 200 years (mostly over the last 50) has created a body of decisions, perfectly comparable to Britain's **unwritten constitution**, that we call **constitutional law**. The idea that this legislative corpus can be derived in some mystical, yet automatic, way from the text of the Constitution is preposterous, and no one holds it.

Instead we have the **Living Constitution**, which always seems to live to the left. I've never heard anyone, not even the most deranged fundamentalist, propose reinterpreting the Constitution to provide rights to fetuses, an obvious corollary of this approach—if the Inner Party and the Outer Party were symmetric opposites, and the "life" of the Constitution was powered by political democracy.

Of course it is not. It does not rest in formal interpretation of texts. It rests in ethical judgments. It is the job of the legislator to make ethical judgments, and the California Supreme Court is doing its job. It's a pity it has to carpool with such a large bodyguard of lies, but that's the modern world for ya.

And we know where these ethical judgments come from. They are Inner Party judgments, and the Inner Party's ethics are Christian, Protestant, and Quaker in their origins. Fine. We all need ethics, and "applied Christianity" will do as well as anything else. What interests me is when these ethical judgments come about.

Imagine, for instance, that the California Supreme Court had decided in, say, 1978, that it was unethical—I mean, unconstitutional—for California to prohibit its male citizens from marrying each other. Is this a thinkable event? I think not. And yet the court's writ ran just as far and was just as powerful in 1978 as in 2008. And ethics, surely, have not changed.

The Living Constitution does not adapt with changes in ethics. It adapts with changes in public opinion—as long as that public opinion is shifting in the direction of "applied Christianity." Public opinion was ready for abortion in 1973—barely. It was ready for gay marriage in 2008—barely. It was not ready for gay marriage in 1973. What will it be ready for in 2033? One can see this as a noble concession to the great principle of democracy. One can also see it as the Cathedral getting away with whatever it can get away with, and nothing else.

Larry Auster, probably the most imaginative and interesting right-wing writer on the planet, who also happens to be a converted fundamentalist Christian with all the theopolitical baggage that you, dear open-minded progressive, would expect from such a person, has a good term for this: the *unprincipled exception*.[31] Briefly, an unprincipled exception is a policy that violates some absolute principle of ethics held by the policymaker, but is not openly acknowledged as such a violation.

For example, dear progressive, why is racism wrong? Racism is wrong because all humans are born simply as humans, having done nothing right or wrong, and it is incompatible with our deeply-held ethical principles to mark these newborn babies with indelible labels which assign them either privileges or penalties which they have not earned. Such as the privilege of being able to drink at sparkling-clean water fountains marked "Whites Only," or the penalty of having to go out back to the horse trough.

We hit that one out of the park, didn't we? Okay. So why is it ethical to label newborn babies as "American" or "Mexican," due to nothing but the descent and geographical position at birth of their parents, and give the former a cornucopia of benefits from which the latter is barred—such as the right to live, work, and drink from drinking fountains in the continental United States? What makes Washington think it is somehow ethical to establish two classes of human, "Americans" and "Mexicans," based only on coincidences of birth that are just as arbitrary as "black" versus "white," and treat the two completely differently? How does this differ from racism, Southern style?

You think this is ugly? Oh, we can get worse. Let's suppose the US, in its eagerness to treat these second-class humans, if not quite as well as possible, at least better than we treat them now, establishes a new guest-worker program which is open only to Nigerians. Any number of Nigerians may come to the US and work.

There are certain restrictions, however. They have to live in special guest-worker housing. They have to go to their workplace in the morning, and return before the sun sets. They may not wander around the streets at night. They must carry special guest-worker passes. Obviously, they can't vote. And they are strictly prohibited from using all public amenities, including, of course, drinking fountains.

Is it a more ethical policy to have this program, or not to have it? If you think no Nigerians could be found to take advantage of it, you're quite wrong. If you have the program, should you cancel it, and send the Nigerians home, to a life of continued poverty back in Nigeria? How is this helping them? On the other hand, our program has all the major features of **apartheid**. And surely no-apartheid is better than apartheid.

There is a very easy resolution to this problem: adopt the principle that **no person is illegal**. This rule is perfectly consistent with "applied Christianity." It is taught at all our great universities. It is implied every time a journalist deploys the

---

[31] "The unprincipled exception is a non-liberal value or assertion, not explicitly identified as non-liberal, that liberals use to escape the inconvenient, personally harmful, or suicidal consequences of their own liberalism without questioning liberalism itself."

euphemism "undocumented." And I'm sure there are dozens of ways in which it could be incorporated into our great Living Constitution. There is only one problem: the people are not quite ready for it.

But perhaps in thirty years they will be. Perhaps? I would bet money on it. And I would also bet that, by the time this principle is established, denying it will be the equivalent of racism. Us old fogeys who were born in the 1970s will be convulsed with guilt and shame at the thought that the US actually considered it ethically acceptable to turn away, deport, and otherwise penalize our fellow human beings, on the ridiculous and irrelevant grounds that they were born somewhere else.

So the Cathedral wins coming and going. Today, it does not suffer the political backlash that would be sure to ensue if the Inner Party endorsed opening the borders to... everyone. Still less if it actually did so. (Unless it let the new Americans vote as soon as they set foot on our sacred soil, which of course would be the most Christian approach.) And in 2038, having increased North America's population to approximately two billion persons, none of them illegal, and all living in the same Third World conditions which it has already inflicted on most of the planet, our blessed Cathedral will have the privilege of berating the past with its guilt for not having recognized the obvious truth that no person is illegal. Ain't it beautiful?

It is. But I have been talking about this Cathedral thing for long enough that I'm not sure you believe it really exists. Well. Do I have a treat for you.

It's not news that I believe the Cathedral is evil. And since it's 2008, you'd expect evil to have not only a name, but a blog. And sure enough it does. Evil's name is **Timothy Burke**, he is a professor of history (specializing in southern Africa) at Swarthmore, and his blog is **Easily Distracted**.[32]

The great thing about Professor Burke is that he appears to have a conscience. Almost every post in his blog can be understood as a kind of rhetorical struggle to repress some inner pang of doubt. He is the Good German par excellence. When people of this mindset found themselves in the Third Reich, they were "moderate Nazis." In Czechoslovakia or Poland they "worked within the system." Professor Burke is nowhere near being a dissident, but there is a dissident inside him. He doesn't like it, not at all. He stabs it with his steely knives. He can check out any time. But he can never leave. His position is a high one, and not easy to get.

The entire blog is characterized—indeed it could serve as a type specimen for—the quality that Nabokov called **poshlost**. Simply an embarrassment of riches. I am saddened by the fact that, as a new parent, I cannot devour the whole thing. But as a case study, I have selected this.[33] The whole post is a treat, but I am especially tickled by the line:

32

33

> I am drawn to procedural liberalism because I live in worlds that are highly procedural and my skills and training are adapted to manipulating procedural outcomes.

"Manipulating procedural outcomes." My entire post—maybe even my entire blog—reduced to three words. If you want to know how you are governed, this is it: you are governed by manipulating procedural outcomes. It's perfect. It belongs on someone's tomb.

But don't even click on link if you are not prepared to work up a little steam. Barack Obama's handling of his grandmother was brutal, perhaps, but it really has nothing on the job Professor Burke does on his mother-in-law:

> When I talk to my mother-in-law, I often get a clear view of its workings, and the role that mass culture (including the mainstream media) play in providing fresh narrative hooks and telling incidentals to its churnings. In the last two years, for example, every time I talk to her, she wants to return to the story of Ward Churchill. Or she wants to talk about how terrible crime is. Or about the problem of illegal immigrants. And so on. These are immobile, self-reproducing, stories. Their truth in her mind is guaranteed by something far outside the actualities and realities that compose any given incident or issue.

"These are immobile, self-reproducing, stories." I desperately, desperately, want his mother-in-law to find this post, read it, and slap Professor Burke very hard across his overgrown thirteen-year-old face. But I doubt it'll happen.

"Their truth in her mind is guaranteed by something far outside the actualities and realities that compose any given incident or issue." Can even this awful sentence do justice to the twisted mind of Timothy Burke? To the Cathedral as a whole, on which he is just one small gargoyle on a minor, far-flung flying buttress? Dear open-minded progressive, I invite you to read this post—or anything else on Professor Burke's remarkably revealing blog, if you remain undecided—and ask yourself again:

Do I trust the Cathedral? Do I consider it a source of responsible, effective public policy? And, in the long term, is it secure?

In Chapter 8, we try and figure out what to do if the answer turns out to be "no."

167 tell us why Niccolo Machiavelli, trans. Christian E. Detmold. *The Historical, Political, and Diplomatic Writings of Niccolo Machiavelli: Volume 2.* (James R. Osgood & Co., 1882), p. 154.

 168 Principate

 168 Dominate

 168 Machiavelli himself In 1513, the Medici accused Machiavelli of conspiracy against them and had him imprisoned. He denied the charges and was later released.

 168 in plain sight Edgar Allen Poe. "The Purloined Letter." *The Gift for 1845 (per.).* (Carey and Hart, 1845).

 168 Manufacturing Consent Noam Chomsky, Edward S. Herman. *Manufacturing Consent: The Political Economy of the Mass Media.* (Pantheon Books, 1988).

 169 Public Opinion Walter Lippmann. *Public Opinion.* (Harcourt, Brace & Co., 1922).

 169 Lippmann himself

 169 Agatha Christie style Agatha Christie. *Murder on the Orient Express.* (Collins Crime Club, 1934).

 169 here Charlie Stross. "Politics." *Charlie's Diary*, 26 Feb. 2008.

 170 post-partisan Jonathan Weisman. "GOP Doubts, Fears 'Post-Partisan' Obama." *Washington Post*, 7 Jan. 2008.

 170 non-partisan democracy

 170 the first Robert F. Worth. "In Democracy Kuwait Trusts, but Not Much." *New York Times*, 6 May 2008.

 171 the second Adam Liptak. "Rendering Justice, With One Eye on Re-election." *New York Times*, 25 May 2008.

LINKS & NOTES

 171 Who? Whom?

 171 international law George B. Davis. *The Elements of International Law: With an Account of its Origins and Historical Development.* 3rd ed. (Harper & Brothers, 1908).

172 American Creation: Triumphs and Tragedies at the Founding of the Republic. Joseph J. Ellis. (Knopf, 2007).

 172 Life of John Marshall Link to the Google books scan of Vol.1 is provided here. The other volumes can also be found on Google books. Albert J. Beveridge. *The Life of John Marshall, Vol.1-4.* (Houghton Mifflin Company, 1916-1919).

 172 First Republic

 172 Federalists

 172 Jeffersonians "Democratic-Republican Party"

 172 era of good feelings

 172 Andrew Jackson

 172 spoils system

 173 system of government finance

 173 Henry Adams

 173 Slave Power

 173 ethnic machines "Tammany Hall"

AN OPEN LETTER TO OPEN-MINDED PROGRESSIVES 193

 173 corrupt politicians "Richard Croker"

 173 quasicriminal financiers "Jay Gould"

 173 sinister wire-pullers "Mark Hanna"

 173 unscrupulous journalists "William Randolph Hearst"

 173 vested interests "Gilded Age"

 173 G. W. Steevens

 173 The Land of the Dollar G.W. Steevens. (Dodd, Mead and Company, 1898).

 173 Jacob Riis

 173 How The Other Half Lives: Studies Among the Tenements of New York. Jacob Riis. (Charles Scribner's Sons, 1890).

173 Sudhir Venkatesh Gang Leader for a Day: A Rogue Sociologist Takes to the Streets. (Penguin Press, 2008).

 174 reform "Reform movement"

 174 Liberal Republicans

 174 Mugwumps

 174 civil service reform "Pendleton Civil Service Reform Act"

174 progressivism

 174 settlement movement

 174 Fabians

 174 muckrakers

 174 Lincoln Steffens

 174 Shame of the Cities Lincoln Steffens. (McClure, Phillips & Co., 1904).

 174 here is a sample Link to the Introduction (pp. 1-18) of the above book provided by *History Matters,* hosted at the George Mason University.

 174 ethnic political machines "Kwame Kilpatrick"

 175 Bernard Baruch

 176 Edward Bellamy

 176 James Truslow Adams

176 March of Democracy: A History of the United States, Vol.1-6. James Truslow Adams. (Scribner's Sons, 1932-33).

 176 William Allen White

 177 other views Democratic Party Platforms: "Democratic Party Platform of 1932," June 27, 1932. Online by Gerhard Peters and John T. Woolley, *The American Presidency Project.* archived link.

AN OPEN LETTER TO OPEN-MINDED PROGRESSIVES 195

 177 Marriner Eccles

 177 brain trust

 178 Raymond Moley

 178 R. G. Tugwell

 178 A. A. Berle, Jr.

 178 Albert Jay Nock

178 diary Albert Jay Nock. *A Journal of These Days, June 1932-December 1933.* (W. Morrow, 1934).

 178 Artemus Ward

 178 Kirby Smith

 179 juggling with the price of gold According to Arthur Schlesinger's *The Coming of the New Deal*, FDR and Treasury Secretary Henry Morgenthau arbitrarily set the price of gold to deter speculators, with Morgenthau at one point quipping that prices were set through a "selection of lucky numbers." Arthur Meier Schlesinger. *The Age of Roosevelt, Volume II: The Coming of the New Deal, 1933-1935.* (Houghton Mifflin, 1958). p. 241.

 179 Reconstruction Finance Corporation

 179 Irving Fisher

 179 Hanfstängl

180 Cyclone Nargis

 180 first book of the Politics Link to Book 1 of Aristotle's *Politics*, hosted at the MIT Classics website.

 180 Jud Süß

 180 Uncle Tom's Cabin

180 propaganda novel Reference to Henry Louis Gates and Hollis Robbins' *The Annotated Uncle Tom's Cabin*. (W.W. Norton, 2006). Original link appeared to be an nonextant review of the book at *The Nation*.
180 Roll, Jordan, Roll: The World the Slaves Made. Eugene D. Genovese. (Vintage Books, 1976).

 181 emancipation

 181 Rangoon

 181 national-socialist "Ne Win"

 181 Jonah Goldbergs of the world Wikipedia for Goldberg's *Liberal Fascism* (2008). See Chapter 2.

 182 Joseph McCarthy

 182 Enoch Powell

 182 George Wallace

 182 Spiro Agnew

AN OPEN LETTER TO OPEN-MINDED PROGRESSIVES   197

 182 Ronald Reagan

 182 Richard Nixon

 182 Margaret Thatcher

183 recent BBC documentary dir. Ashley Gething. *Rivers of Blood*. (BBC Television, 2008). The video has since been removed from the BBC website.

 183 Radio Enoch

 183 majorities Steven A. Camarota, Roy Beck. "Elite Vs. Public Opinion: An Examination of Divergent Views on Immigration." *Center for Immigration Studies*, 1 Dec. 2002.

 184 racial spoils system

 183 MSM

 183 World War I "Committee on Public Information"

 184 World War II "United States Office of War Information"

 184 GS ranks "General Schedule (US Civil service pay scale)"

 184 psychological warfare

 184 Roy Cohn

 184 defeated North Vietnam The failed attack by the North Vietnamese, eventually resulted in territorial gains for the American-led South and a dramatically improved negiotating position.

LINKS & NOTES

 184 wage and price controls "Nixon shock"

 184 inextricably Richard North. "Retreat to Victory." *EU Referendum*, 27 May 2008.

 185 Carroll Quigley

 186 California Constitution

 186 decision In re Marriage Cases. S147999. (CA. Sup. Ct. 2008).

 187 unwritten constitution "Constitution of the United Kingdom"

 187 constitutional law Link to the entry for "Constitutional Law" at the *Legal Information Institute*, on the Cornell Law School website.

 187 Living Constitution

 188 Larry Auster Original link to Lawrence Auster's homepage at *View From the Right*.

 188 unprincipled exception Lawrence Auster. "The Unprincipled Exception Defined." *View From the Right*, 14 Jun. 2006.

 188 apartheid

 188 no person is illegal Link to a Google search for the term.

 189 Timothy Burke

 189 Easily Distracted As of 2022, Burke writes at his substack *Eight by Seven*.

AN OPEN LETTER TO OPEN-MINDED PROGRESSIVES

 189 poshlost

 189 this The article from where the phrase "manipulating procedural outcomes" was first borrowed. Timothy Burke. "Competency as a Cultural Value." *Easily Distracted*, 4 Jan. 2008.

CHAPTER 8:
A RESET IS NOT A REVOLUTION
JUNE 5, 2008

So, dear open-minded progressive, in Chapter 7 we established who runs the world: you do. Or rather, people who agree with you do. Or hopefully, people you used to agree with do.

I can hope, right? In this chapter, we'll do a little more than hope. We'll also look at change.

But first, let's nail down our terms. The great power center of 2008 is the *Cathedral*. The Cathedral has two parts: the accredited universities and the established press. The universities formulate public policy. The press guides public opinion. In other words, the universities make decisions, for which the press manufactures consent. It's as simple as a punch in the mouth.

The Cathedral operates as the brain of a broader power structure, the *Polygon* or *Apparat*—the permanent civil service. The Apparat is the civil service proper (all nonmilitary officials whose positions are immune to partisan politics, also known as "democracy"), plus all those formally outside government whose goal is to influence or implement public policy—i.e., NGOs. (There's a reason NGOs have to remind themselves that they're "non-governmental.")

(If we did not have an existing category for the press and universities, we could easily think of them as NGOs—in particular, the system wherein journalists are nominally supervised by for-profit media corporations is purely historical. If the Times and its pseudo-competitors ever fail, as they may well, the responsibility of funding and organizing journalism will fall to the great foundations,[1] who will certainly be happy to pick up the relatively small expense.)

I have blown a lot of pixels on the historical roots of the Cathedral. But this one-minute clip might tell you just as much: **Hollywood Supports New Deal and NIRA**.[2]

That, my dear open-minded progressive, is what we call a personality cult. No, that's not George W. Bush on the flag. If you don't recognize the eagle, he is this friendly fellow,[3] a symbol of the **National Recovery Administration**. And if you think there is anything ironic about its placement in the film, you're dead wrong.

And in what **secret speech**[4] was this cult denounced? It never has been. All mainstream thought in the United States, Democrat and Republican alike, descends in unbroken apostolic succession from the gigantic political machine of "That Man."[5] (The last of the FDR-haters were purged by **William Buckley** in the '50s.) The Cathedral connection, of course, is the academic **brain trust** mentioned in Chapter 7.

Today's Cathedral is not a personality cult. It is not a political party. It is something far more elegant and evolved. It is not even an organization in the conventional, hierarchical sense of the word—it has no Leader, no Central Committee, no nothing. It is a true peer-to-peer network, which makes it extraordinarily resilient. To even understand why it is so unanimous, why Harvard always agrees with Yale which is always on the same page as Berkeley which never picks any sort of a fight with the New York Times, except of course to argue that it is not progressive enough, takes quite a bit of thinking.

Yet as the video shows us, the Cathedral was born in the brutal hardball politics of the 20th century, and it is still best understood in 20th-century terms. Most historians would agree that the 20th century started in 1914—much as "the Sixties" denotes the period from 1965 to 1974—and I don't think it can be declared dead until this last great steel machine finally gums up and keels over. I'd be surprised if this happens before 2020—or after 2050.

The 20th century prudently and definitively rejected the 19th-century idea that government policies should be formulated by democratically elected representatives (whom you know and loathe as "partisan politicians"). Unfortunately, at least in the United States and the Soviet Union, it replaced the fallacy of representative government with the far more insidious fallacy of scientific government.

---

1 Ford, Gates, Mellon, etc.

2 [QR code]

3 [QR code]

4 Reference to Kruschev's 1956 "Secret Speech" criticizing Stalin's methods.

5 A pejorative nickname for FDR used by his political opponents.

AN OPEN LETTER TO OPEN-MINDED PROGRESSIVES 203

Government is not a science because it is impractical to construct controlled experiments in government. Uncontrolled or "natural" experiments are not science.[6] Any process which is not science, but claims to be science, or claims that its results exhibit the same objective robustness we ascribe to the scientific process, has surely earned the name of *pseudoscience*. Thus it is not at all excessive to describe 20th-century "public policy" as a pseudoscience. A good sanity check is the disparity between its **predictions**[7] and its **achievements**.[8]

Moreover, *all* the major 20th-century regimes maintained, and generally intensified, the underlying mystery of Whig government: the principle of *popular sovereignty*.

Even the Nazis acknowledged popular sovereignty. If the NSDAP had defined its leadership of Germany as a self-explaining proposition, it could have laid off Goebbels in 1933. Instead it went to extraordinary lengths to capture and retain the support of the German masses, and most historians agree that (at least before the war) it succeeded. If you don't consider this an adequate refutation of the principle of *vox populi, vox dei*,[9] perhaps you are a Nazi yourself.

This is the terrible contradiction in the **political formula**[10] of the modern regime. Public opinion is always right, except when it's not. It is infallible, but responsible educators must guide it toward the truth. Otherwise, it might fall prey to Nazism, racism, or other bad thoughts.

Hence the Cathedral. The basic assumption of the Cathedral is that when popular opinion and the Cathedral agree, their collective judgment is infallible. When the peasant mind stubbornly resists, as in the cases of **colonization**[11] or the **racial spoils system**,[12] more education is necessary. The result might be called *guided popular sovereignty*. It wins both coming and going.

In 1933, public opinion could still be positively impressed by group calisthenics displaying the face of the Leader, eagles shooting lightning bolts, etc., etc. By today's standards, the public of 1933 (both German and American) was a seven-year-old boy. Today's public is more of a thirteen-year-old girl (a smart, plucky, well-meaning girl), and guiding it demands a **very different tone**.[13]

6
7 Reference to Edward Bellamy's utopian novel *Looking Backward*. See Chapter 7.
8 Originally linked to the Wikipedia page for "Public Housing in the United States."
9 "The voice of the people, is the voice of God"
10 Reference to political theorist Gaetano Mosca's idea of "ruling elites" as the necessary central element of all political organization.
11 Reference to the popular disapproval of immigration reform. See endnote for "majorities" in Chapter 7.
12 Reference to a Michigan bill to overturn Affirmative Action, and to popular objections to Affirmative Action more broadly.
13 Original link to Barack Obama's White House page.

You are not a thirteen-year-old girl. So how did you fall for this bizarre circus? How can any mature, intelligent, and educated person put their faith in this gigantic festival of phoniness?

Think about it. You read the New York Times, or similar, on a regular basis. It tells you this, it tells you that, it reports that "scientists say" X or Y or Z. And there is always a name at the top of the article. It might be "Michael Luo" or "Celia Dugger" or "Heather Timmons" or "Marc Lacey" or... the list, is, of course, endless.

Do you know Michael or Celia or Heather or Marc? Are they your personal friends? How do you know that they aren't pulling your chain? How do you know that the impression you get from reading their stories is the same impression that you would have if you, personally, saw everything that Michael or Celia or Heather or Marc saw? Why in God's green earth do you see their "stories" as anything but an attempt to "manipulate procedural outcomes" by guiding you, dear citizen, to interpret the world in a certain way and deliver your vote accordingly?

The answer is that you do not trust them, personally. Bylines are not there for you. They are there for the journalists themselves. If the Times, like *The Economist*, lost its bylines and attributed all its stories to "a New York Times reporter," your faith would not change one iota. You trust Michael and Celia and Heather and Marc, in other words, because they are speaking (quite literally) *ex cathedra*.

So you trust the institution, not the people. Very well. Let's repeat the question: what is it about the New York Times that you find trustworthy? The old blackletter logo? The motto?[14] Suppose that instead of being "reporters" of "the New York Times," Michael and Celia and Heather and Marc were "cardinals" of "the One, Holy, Catholic and Apostolic Church?" Would this render them more credible, less credible, or about as credible? Suppose, instead, they were "professors" at "Stanford University?" Would this increase or decrease your trust?

For a hardened denialist such as myself, who has completely lost his faith in all these institutions, attempting to understand the world through the reports and analysis produced by the Cathedral is like trying to watch a circus through the camera on a cell phone duct-taped to the elephant's trunk. It can be done, but it helps to have plenty of external perspective.

And for anyone starting from a position of absolute faith in the Cathedral, there is simply no other source of information against which to test it. You are certainly not going to discredit the Times or Stanford by reading the Times or going to Stanford, any more than you will learn about the historical Jesus by attending a Latin Mass.

And as a progressive, you are no more interested in prying into these questions than the average Catholic is in explaining what makes the Church "One, Holy, and Apostolic." You do not see yourself as a believer in anything. You don't think of the Cathedral as a formal entity, which of course it is not. Its institutional infallibility is a matter of definition, not faith.

---

14 "All the news that's fit to print"

Rather, you focus your political energies on the *enemies* of the Cathedral. Perhaps the keystone of the progressive belief system is the theory that the Cathedral, far from being the boss hog, the obvious winner in all conflicts foreign or domestic, is in fact struggling desperately against the dark and overpowering forces of bigotry, religion, ignorance, corruption, militarism, etc. In a word—the Man.

We met the Man in Chapter 7 courtesy of Lincoln Steffens,[15] whose enemies—in the form of Gilded Age blowhards such as **Chauncey Depew**—at least really existed, and had real power. When **C. Wright Mills** wrote *The Power Elite*, their memory could at least be reasonably invoked. By the Chomsky era, the military-corporate-financial conspiracy was approaching the plausibility, if not the maliciousness, of its international Jewish counterpart. The 20th century's real power elite, of course, are Steffens, Mills and Chomsky themselves.

This is the classic propaganda trope in which resistance becomes oppression. Poland is always about to march into Germany. Every aggressive political or military operation in history has been painted, usually quite sincerely, by its supporters as an act of self-defense.

In reality, active resistance to the Cathedral is negligible. At most there is the Outer Party, which is completely ineffective if not counterproductive (more on this in a bit). The Outer Party can sometimes align itself with small acts of petty corruption, as in **Tom DeLay's K Street Project**.[16] This can hardly be described as a success. There are also phone-in operations, such as **NumbersUSA**,[17] which attempt to mobilize the last remnants of unreconstructed public opinion. The Cathedral, which fears the masses much more than it has to, is often demure in revealing its power to just steam right over them, and so it is possible to achieve small victories such as NumbersUSA's in maintaining the status quo. Finally, the initiative process, ironically a relic of early Progressivism itself, grants occasional laurels to a **Howard Jarvis** or **Ward Connerly**.[18]

But most resistance is of the passive, atomized, and inertial sort. People simply tune out. If they are especially determined and wily, they may practice the **Ketman**[19] of **Czesław Miłosz**. Or they believe, but they don't super-believe. They are the progressive version of Jack Mormons.[20] Naturally, even these small, private apathies enrage the fanatical.

Here is another inescapable contradiction. The average progressive, who is not open-minded (most people aren't) and is not reading this, cannot imagine even starting to perform the exercise of imagining a world in which his side is the over-

---

15 Author of *The Shame of the Cities* (1904).
16 GOP effort in the mid-90's to pressure lobbyists into hiring Republicans.
17 Grassroots anti-immigration organization.
18 California conservatives who led succesful statewide campigns on property taxes and anti-Affirmative Action respectively.
19 The practice of expressing false outward praise, while concealing opposition, described in Miłosz's *The Captive Mind* (1953).
20 Slang term for lapsed or unbaptized members of the LDS Church who nonetheless maintain good relationships with the community.

dog. Yet the very word "progress" implies that his cause in general tends to advance, not retreat, and history confirms this.

If you were advising a young, amoral, ambitious and talented person to choose a political persuasion solely on the probability of personal success, you would certainly advise her to become a progressive. She should probably be as radical as possible, hopefully without acquiring any sort of a criminal record. But as the case of Bill Ayers shows, even straight-out terrorism is not necessarily a bar to the circles of power (especially if, like Ayers, you started there in the first place).

The only reason to oppose progressivism is some sincere conviction. As **Edith Hamilton** said to **Freda Utley**: "Don't expect the material rewards of unrighteousness while engaged in the pursuit of truth." This has to be one of the finest sentences of the twentieth century.

Any such conviction may be misguided, of course. People being what they are, and progressivism being the creed of the most intelligent and successful people in the world, most opponents of progressivism are in some way ignorant, deluded or misinformed. Often the situation is simple: progressives are right, and they are wrong. This hardly assists the pathetic, doomed cause of antiprogressivism.

In the Post, the liberal historian Rick Perlstein stumbles on (and then, of course, past) the inconvenient reality of progressive dominance:

> Born myself in 1969 to pre-baby boomer parents, I'm a historian of America's divisions who spent the age of George W. Bush reading more newspapers written when Johnson and Richard Nixon were president than current ones. And I recently had a fascinating experience scouring archives for photos of the 1960s to illustrate the book I've just finished based on that research. It was frustrating—and telling.
>
> The pictures people take and save, as opposed to the ones they never take or the ones they discard, say a lot about how they understand their own times. And in our archives as much as in our mind's eye, we still record the '60s in hazy cliches—in the stereotype of the idealistic youngster who came through the counterculture and protest movements, then settled down to comfortable bourgeois domesticity.
>
> What's missing? The other side in that civil war. The right-wing populist rage of 1968 third-party presidential candidate George Wallace, who, referring to an idealistic protester who had lain down in front of Johnson's limousine, promised that if he were elected, "the first time they lie down in front of my limousine, it'll be the last one they'll ever lay down in front of because their day is over!" That kind of quip helped him rise to as much as 20 percent in the polls.

AN OPEN LETTER TO OPEN-MINDED PROGRESSIVES

It's easy to find hundreds of pictures of the national student strike that followed Nixon's announcement of the invasion of Cambodia in the spring of 1970. Plenty of pictures of the riots at Kent State that ended with four students shot dead by National Guardsmen. None I could find, however, of the counter-demonstrations by Kent, Ohio, townies—and even Kent State parents. Flashing four fingers and chanting "The score is four/And next time more," they argued that the kids had it coming.

The '60s were a trauma—two sets of contending Americans, each believing they were fighting for the future of civilization, but whose left- and right-wing visions of redemption were opposite and irreconcilable. They were a trauma the way the war of brother against brother between 1861 and 1865 was a trauma and the way the Great Depression was a trauma. Tens of millions of Americans hated tens of millions of other Americans, sometimes murderously so. The effects of such traumas linger in a society for generations.

Consider this example. The Library of Congress, which houses the photo archives of Look magazine and U.S. News & World Report, holds hundreds of images of the violent confrontation between cops and demonstrators in front of the Chicago Hilton at the 1968 Democratic National Convention, and, from the summer of 1969, of Woodstock. But I could find no visual record of the National Convention on the Crisis of Education. Held two weeks after Woodstock in that selfsame Chicago Hilton, it was convened by citizens fighting the spread of sex education in the schools as if civilization itself were at stake. The issue dominated newspapers in the autumn of 1969 and is seemingly forgotten today.

'68 wasn't a "trauma." It was a coup. It was a classic chimp throwdown in which, using tactics that were as violent as necessary, the New Left displaced the Old Left from the positions of power. "**Up against the wall, motherfucker, this is a stickup.**"[21] Truer words were never spoken. The victory of Obama, a Movement[22] man to the core, represents the final defeat of the Stalinist wing of the American left by its Maoist wing. (By "Stalinist" and "Maoist," all I mean is that the New Deal was allied with Stalin and the **Students for a Democratic Society** was aligned with Mao. These are not controversial assertions.)

But I digress. My point is that what we can infer, by our inability to recognize any serious successor in 2008 of George Wallace, the anti-sex-education movement,

---

21 Up Against the Wall Motherfucker was a Situationist Anarchist group that included would-be Warhol assassin Valerie Solanas.
22 Reference to The Weather Underground.

or the folks who thought that the National Guard's real mistake at Kent State was that they failed to follow up the victory by fixing bayonets and charging, is that these reactionaries *lost,* and their progressive enemies *won.* Generally in any conflict only one side can claim victory. And if after the battle we see that one side still flourishes and the other has been so thoroughly crushed that it is not only nonexistent, but actually forgotten, we sure know which is which.

The great myth of the '60s is that the Movement, somehow, failed. Actually, its foes—not Nixon's silent majority, who never had any real power in the first place, but the Establishment, the old Eleanor Roosevelt liberals, the **Grayson Kirks** and **S. I. Hayakawas** and **McGeorge Bundys**—lost almost every battle—including, of course, the Vietnam War itself. The SDSers and Alinskyites suffered hardly at all for their offenses, and moved smoothly and effectively into the positions of power they now hold, almost exactly as described in the **Port Huron Statement**.[23] (Which is unbelievably windy, even by my standards—scroll to the end for **Hayden**'s actual tactical battle plan.)

The case of the "silent majority" illustrates the system of guided popular sovereignty. A majority of American voters opposed the student movement. Just as a majority of Germans supported Hitler. The majority does not always win. The children of the "silent majority" are far, far less likely to express the views of a George Wallace, a **Spiro Agnew** or an **Anita Bryant** than their parents. The same can be said for the grandchildren of the Nazis. The Cathedral defeated both.

(Was this a good thing? I suppose it probably was. I am not a huge fan of George Wallace, or of Hitler. But they are both dead, you know. History is not a judicial proceeding. Quite frankly, I find it amateurish to take sides in the past. We study the past so that we can take sides in the present.)

The progressive is quite satisfied with the defeat of Hitler, which short of making pyramids of skulls, **Tamerlane**-style, was about as complete as it gets. But Wallace is another matter.

To a progressive, progressivism is right and its opposite is wrong. Thus any survival of the "silent majority," any sense in which the world has not yet been completely progressivized, any victory short of unconditional surrender, is a sign to progressives that the world remains dominated by their enemies. More energy is necessary, comrades.

The device of **unprincipled exceptions**[24] allows this bogus, self-congratulatory legend of defeat to persist indefinitely. As we've seen, the progressive story can be traced back centuries, and at every moment in its history it has existed in a society which has included reactionary power structures. For example, the concepts of property, corporations, national borders, marriage, armed forces, and so on, are

---

23 [QR code]

24 See Chapter 7.

AN OPEN LETTER TO OPEN-MINDED PROGRESSIVES

irredeemably unprogressive. Attacking on all these fronts simultaneously would result in nothing but defeat, real defeat.

So the continued existence of these reactionary phenomena provides evidence that progressives are struggling against **dark forces of titanic and unbounded strength**.[25] You have to be a bit of a reactionary yourself to see the truth: these institutions are simply a matter of reality. So it is reality itself that progressivism attacks. Reality is the perfect enemy: it always fights back, it can never be defeated, and infinite energy can be expended in unsuccessfully resisting it.

Thus Condoleeza Rice, for example, can claim that America is **only now**[26] becoming true to its principles. The Times **disagrees**[27]—it claims that America is not yet there. Rather, it is treating its illegal immigrants unjustly. Is it just for America to prevent any human being from setting foot on its noble soil? Or is "no person illegal?" The Times is silent on the question. But perhaps in a decade or two the answer will be revealed in our "living constitution." You see how cynical a response this great institution can expect, from a carping denialist such as myself, when it accuses some poor Outer Party shill of "breaking the law."

Anyway, I think I have gone far enough in describing the Cathedral. It is basically a theocratic form of government, minus the literal theology. Its doctrines are not beliefs about the spirit world. But they rest no less on faith. I certainly cannot see any reason to believe that these people have delivered, are delivering, or will deliver government that is secure, responsible, and effective. I can see plenty of reasons to expect that, as the unprincipled exceptions rise to the surface and are carved away, things will get worse.

In case you are still undecided on whether or not to support the Cathedral, dear open-minded progressive, I offer you a simple test. The test is a little episode in ancient history. The name of the episode is **Reconstruction**.

The question is: who is right about Reconstruction? Team A: Eric Foner, Stephen Budiansky, and John Hope Franklin?[28] Or Team B: Charles Nordhoff, Daniel Henry Chamberlain, and John Burgess?[29] For extra credit, throw William Saletan[30] in the mix. Team B has an advantage in that their books are available in one click. They have another advantage: they actually lived through the events

---

25 Reference to Jeff Sharlett's histrionic 2008 book *The Family: The Secret Fundamentalism at the Heart of American Power*.
26 Reference to comments Rice made in support of Obama's victory in the 2004 Democratic primary race.
27
28 Authors of *A Short History of Reconstruction* (1989), *The Bloody Shirt* (2008) and *Reconstruction After the Civil War* (1994).
29 Author of *The Cotton States* (1876), Governor of South Carolina from 1874-1877 and professor of constitutional law at Cornell, author of *Reconstruction and the Constitution* (1902).
30 Slate.com columnist

they describe. Team A has an advantage in an extra century or so of scholarship, and the vast marketing powers of the Cathedral. You don't actually need to buy their books—their ideas are everywhere. (Budiansky's breathless first chapter is, however, online.[31])

Note that there are no factual matters in dispute. The choice is merely one of interpretation. And all the authors linked above are, by any reasonable historical standard, liberals. Who do you find more credible, Team A or Team B? As you'll see, you can hardly agree with both.

If you get the same results from this experiment that I did, you may want to think about strategies for change. Change can be divided into two parts: capturing power, and using it.

My answer for how to use power will not change: I believe in secure, responsible, and effective government. This is not, in my humble opinion, a difficult problem. The difficult problem is how to get from here to there.

Let's start by looking at some ineffective strategies. In my opinion, the most common error made by antiprogressive movements is to mimic the strategies of progressivism itself. The error is in assuming that the relationship between left and right is symmetric. As we've seen, it is not.

The three main strategies for progressive success in the 20th century were violence, **Gramscian** or bureaucratic incrementalism, and **Fabian**[32] or democratic incrementalism. As antiprogressive strategies, I don't believe that any of these approaches has any chance of success. As (at the very least) distractions, they are counterproductive.

Revolutionary violence in the 20th century has such a strong track record that it's only natural for reactionaries to think of trying it. Furthermore, in Japan, Italy and Germany, the 20th century has three cases of reactionary movements (yes, I know Hitler did not claim to be a reactionary—but he was lying) which achieved success through violence. For a while.

Before their fascist movements rose to power, these countries all had one thing in common. They were monarchies. Is your country, dear reader, a monarchy? If not, I recommend—*strongly*—against any kind of reactionary violence, terrorism, "civil disobedience" (such as tax protesting), or any approach that even starts to smell of the above.

Fascism was a reaction to Communism. (Thus the word "reactionary.") It could exist because of one thing and one thing only: a political and especially *judicial* establishment that was fundamentally reactionary, and willing to turn a blind eye toward antirevolutionary thugs, who used Bolshevik techniques against the Bolshevists themselves. Is your country, dear reader, equipped with a reaction-

---

31 [QR code]

32 As in the Fabian Society.

ary judicial establishment? Are you sure? Are you really sure? Because if not, I recommend—*strongly*—against, etc.

In a world dominated by progressives, the fascist gate to power is closed, locked, welded shut, filled with a thousand tons of concrete, and surrounded by starving cave bears. Today's Apparat has entire departments[33] who do nothing but guard this door, which no one but a few pathetic dorks will even think of approaching. And this is even assuming that a regime which achieved power through fascist techniques would be superior in any way, shape, or form to the Cathedral, a proposition I consider extraordinarily dubious. Give it up, Nazis. Game over. You lose. Frankly, even the real Nazis were no prize, and few of them would regard their modern successors with anything but contempt. There is a reason for this.

We continue to Gramscian incrementalism. This is not without its merits. It even has its successes. I think the most effective arm of the modern "conservative" movement, far and away, has been the Federalist Society. The Federalists are absolutely decent and principled, they have separated themselves as far as possible from the Outer Party, and they have had a real intellectual impact. Frankly, you could do a heck of a lot worse.

On the other hand, it should not be necessary to join the Cathedral to have an intellectual impact on it, and one day it won't be. And as an institutional power play rather than a platform for intellectualizing, the idea of Gramscian reaction is just silly. At best, the Federalists, and their economic counterparts in the George Mason School, might make the Cathedral system work a little more efficiently. But the Cathedral tends to be much better at assimilating them than they are at subverting it—an intention which, you'll note, few of them will admit to.

Gramscian subversion works for a reason: the Gramscian progressive's real goal is power. In order to generate free energy which he can transmute into organizational power, he is ready to push his organization toward ineffective policies, which by virtue of their very ineffectiveness are a permanent source of work for him and his friends. A Gramscian reactionary, working in the same organization as these people and nominally collaborating with them, is forced into one of two options: attacking the progressives and trying to destroy their jobs, which will result in his certain destruction, or finding a way to betray his own principles, which will result in a comfortable and permanent sinecure. There is little suspense in the decision.

Ultimately, the Gramscian reactionary is in fact a Gramscian progressive. All he is doing is to create jobs for himself and his friends. The Cathedral is happy to employ as many tame libertarians or conservatives as it can find. As LBJ used to put it, better to have them inside the tent pissing out. Hence the infamous cosmotarians.[34] Perhaps if someone found a way to spread their dung on crops, they might have a reason to exist.

---

33 Reference to the Southern Poverty Law Center.
34 "Cosmopolitan libertarian," best exemplified by blogger Will Wilkinson.

We continue to Fabian incrementalism. You can see Glenn Reynolds endorse the Fabian strategy here.[35] I'm afraid I still have a soft spot for the **Instapundit**, who was perhaps my first introduction to the weird, scary world outside the Cathedral, and a gentle and pleasant introduction it was. But frankly, Reynolds doesn't pretend to be anything but a lightweight, and I see no reason to waste much time on him.

Fabian incrementalism means supporting either the Outer Party, or a minor party such as the Libertarians. By definition, if you are going to take power using the democratic process, you have to support some party or other.

There is an immediate problem with this: as we've seen, modern "democracies" do not allow politicians to formulate policy. It is a violation of their unwritten constitutions, and an unwritten constitution is just as hard to violate as a written one. Therefore, even when the Outer Party manages to win the election and gain "power," what they find in their hands is more or less the same sort of "power" that the Queen of England has.

My stepfather, a mid-level Washington insider who spent twenty years working as a staffer for Democratic senators, caviled vigorously at the idea that the Democrats are the "Inner Party" and Republicans are the "Outer Party." He pointed out that between 2000 and 2006, the Republicans held the Presidency and both houses of Congress.

I pointed out that he was actually underplaying his hand. During this period, Republican nominees also held a majority on the Supreme Court. By the eleventh-grade civics-class "separation of powers" theory, this would have given the Grand Old Party complete domination over North America. Without breaking a single law, they could have: liquidated the State Department and transferred sole foreign-policy responsibility to the Pentagon, packed the Supreme Court with televangelists, required that all universities receiving Federal funds balance their appointments between pro-choice and pro-life professors, terminated all research in the areas of global warming, evolution and sexual lubricants, etc., etc., etc.

Whereas in fact, in all the hundreds of thousands of things Washington does, there was exactly one major policy which the Bush administration and Congress pursued, but their Democratic equivalents would not have: the invasion of Iraq. Which you may support or oppose, but whose direct effect on the government of North America is hard to see as major. Moreover, this applies only to the first term of the Bush administration. We have no strong reason to believe that a Kerry administration would not have adopted the same policies in Iraq, including the "surge."

Why did the Republicans not use their formal control over the mechanisms of Washington to cement real control, as the Democrats did in 1933? There are many specific answers to this question, but the basic answer is that they never had

---

35

AN OPEN LETTER TO OPEN-MINDED PROGRESSIVES

real power. In theory, the Queen has just the same power[36] over the UK, and if she tried to use it all that would happen is that she would lose it. Exactly the same is true of our own dear Outer Party, on whatever occasion it should next get into office. It may get into office again. It will never get into power. (Although it retains the power to fill many juicy sinecures.)

There is a more subtle reason that the Outer Party is a rolling disaster: conservatives and reactionaries, whose political positions must be based on principle rather than opportunism (since if they were opportunists, they would always do better as progressives), find it difficult to agree. Progressives always find it easy to agree—as you might have noticed, their disputes are almost always over either tactics or personalities, almost never over principles. There is a reason for this.

Thus progressives have the advantage of spontaneous coordination, the glue that holds the Cathedral together in the first place. Their formula is *pas d'ennemis à gauche, pas d'amis à droite*,[37] and any unbiased observer must applaud at how smoothly they make it work. Their coalitions tend to hold, those of their enemies tend to fracture. Evil is stronger than good, because it is never worried or confused by scruples.

Third, Outer Party politicians who achieve any success are constantly tempted to succeed even more, by replacing their principles with progressive ones and allying with progressives. Since this alliance enables them to outcompete their principled competitors with ease, it takes a very determined figure to avoid it. In the ancient, grinning carapace of Senator McCain, this strategy has surely been pushed to its furthest possible extent—or so at least one would think. Then again, one would have thought the same of the original "compassionate conservative."

We can see a more extreme version of this in the pathetic gyrations of one of the Outer Party's outer parties, the Lew Rockwell libertarians, skewered with deadly aim at VDare[38] and roasted to a fine crisp at VFR.[39] I don't really agree with the details of Auster's analysis of libertarianism (here is mine[40]), but our conclusion is the same: the problem with libertarianism is that libertarianism is a form of Whiggery, and the first Whig was the Devil. (Furthermore, this idea of presenting Dr. Ron Paul, who so far as I can tell is nothing but a profoundly decent old man, as

---

36 The British monarch theoretically holds "reserve power" as a matter of *royal prerogative*.
37 See Chapter 1, "No enemies to the left, no friends to the right."
38
39
40

some kind of public intellectual, and putting his name on **blatantly ghostwritten books**,[41] reeks of 20th-century politics.)

Fourth, there is another way to succeed in the Outer Party. This might be called the Huckabee Plan. On the Huckabee Plan, you succeed by being *as stupid as possible*. Not only does this attract a surprising number of voters, who may be just as stupid or even stupider—the Outer Party's base is not exactly the cream of the crop—it also attracts the attention of the Cathedral, whose favorite sport is to promote the worst plausible Outer Party candidates. As usual with the Cathedral, this is a consequence of casual snobbery rather than malignant conspiracy, but it is effective nonetheless. It is always fun to write a human-interest story about a really wacky peasant, especially one who happens to be running for President.

And fifth, the very existence and activity of the Outer Party, this profoundly phony and thoroughly ineffective pseudo-alternative, is far and away the greatest motivator for Inner Party activists, who believe it is a monstrous danger to their entire world. Don't say they don't believe this. I believed in the right-wing menace, the *regs gevaar*[42] as it were, for the first quarter century of my life.

Without the Outer Party, the Cathedral system is instantly recognizable as exactly what it is: a one-party state. You'll note that when the Soviet Union collapsed, it wasn't because someone organized an opposition party and started winning in their fake elections. In fact, many of the later Communist states (such as Poland and China) maintained bogus opposition parties, for exactly the same reason we have an Outer Party: to make the "people's democracy" look like an actual, 19th-century political contest.

Without the Outer Party, the legions of Inner Party youth activists we see all over the place are exactly what they appear to be: **Komsomol members**.[43] They are young, ambitious people who serve the State to get ahead. In fact, often their goal is not to get ahead, but just to get laid. Once it is clear that the Inner Party is just the government, all the fun disappears from this enterprise. There are other ways to get laid, most of them less boring and bureaucratic.

If the Republicans could somehow dissolve themselves permanently and irrevocably, it would be the most brutal blow ever struck against the Democrats. It would make Obi-Wan Kenobi look like **Chad Vader**.[44] As I'll explain, passive resistance is not your only option, but it is a thousand million times better than Outer Party activism. *Do not support the Outer Party.*

Face it: political democracy in the United States is dead. It died on March 4, 1933, when the following words were uttered:

> But in the event that the Congress shall fail to take one of these two courses, and in the event that the national emergency is still

---

41 Reference to Paul's *The Revolution: A Manifesto* (2008).
42 Play on "*swart gevaar*," or the "black danger" from apartheid South Africa.
43 All-Union Leninist Young Communist League.
44 Hapless character from a 2000's-era Star Wars parody web sitcom.

AN OPEN LETTER TO OPEN-MINDED PROGRESSIVES 215

critical, I shall not evade the clear course of duty that will then confront me. I shall ask the Congress for the one remaining instrument to meet the crisis—broad Executive power to wage a war against the emergency, as great as the power that would be given to me if we were in fact invaded by a foreign foe.

FDR is often credited with "**preserving democracy.**" He "preserved democracy" in about the same way that the Russians **preserved Lenin**. More precisely, it was his opponents who preserved the pickled corpse of democracy, when again and again FDR made these kinds of crude threats and they failed to call his bluff. (**Justice Van Devanter** has a lot to answer for.)

Democracy sucks. It never worked in the first place. **Pobedonostsev** got it exactly right.[45] If you read British travelers' accounts of 19th-century American democracy, when we had the real original thing and theirs was still heavily diluted with aristocracy, the phenomenon sounds **terrifying and barbaric**.[46] It sounds, in fact, distinctly Nazi. And where do you think the Nazis got their mob-management technology? By listening to Beethoven, perhaps? By reading Goethe?

And since democracy is dead, the idea of restoring it is doubly quixotic. If you have to pick something dead to restore, at least find something that everyone understands is dead. It would actually be much easier, and certainly far more productive, to restore the Stuarts.

For example, the British writer Richard North, who is not a porn star but the proprietor of **EU Referendum**, perhaps the world's best blog on the reality of government today, has a fine **two-part**[47] essay on the failure of the eurosceptic movement—that is, the movement to rescue the UK from assimilation into the curiously Soviet-like and **thoroughly undemocratic EU**.

What astounds Dr. North so much is that no one seems to care. All the *Sturm und Drang* of the 19th century, all the democratic foofaraw and the jingoism and the socialism and all the rest, and the British people are letting it all just be sucked away into a **creepy-looking building** in Belgium, from which all important decisions are handed down by transnational bureaucrats who could sign on as extras in Brazil II[48] without the cost and inconvenience of a baby mask.

And it's not just the US. I mean, good lord, Ireland! All the ink that was shed over **Home Rule**. All the blood, too. The unquenchable Celtic passion of the fi-

---

45

46

47 Link to part II. Part I can be found there.

48 Reference to Terry Gilliam's sci-fi dystopia *Brazil* (1985).

ery, irrepressible Celt. And they can scarcely be bothered to give a tinker's damn whether they are governed from Dublin or from Brussels. What in the world can be going on?

What is going on is that the voters of both Britain and Ireland, though they may not know it consciously, are perfectly aware of the game. As anyone who has read the Crossman diaries[49] knows, their politicians handed off power to faceless bureaucrats a long, long time ago, just as ours did. The only real question is what city and office building their faceless bureaucrats work in, and what nationality they are. And why should it possibly matter?

So Dr. North concludes his entire well-reasoned discussion with this bathetic *cri de coeur*:

> To achieve that happy outcome, though, we have to answer the question that the élites have been evading ever since they decided to take refuge in the arms of "Europe": what is Britain's role in the world?
>
> On reflection, I have come to the view that it is the failure to address this question which has given rise to many of the ills in our society. As have our politicians internalised, so has the population. Lacking, if you like, a higher calling—the sense that there is something more to our nation than the pursuit of comfort, prosperity and a plasma television in the corner—we too have become self-obsessed, inwards-looking... and selfish.
>
> In effect, therefore, we are looking for the "vision thing"—a sense of purpose as a nation, a uniting ethos which will restore our sense of pride and reinforce our national identity which the EU has been so assiduously undermining.

What bland shite. Dr. North, here's a modest proposal for your "national identity."

I suggest a Stuart restoration in an independent England. Through some beautiful twist of fate, the Stuart succession has become entangled with the House of Liechtenstein, who just happen to be *the last working royal family in Europe*. The father-son team of Hans-Adam II and Hereditary Prince Alois are not decorative abstractions. They are effectively the CEOs of Liechtenstein, which is a small country but a real one nonetheless. As you'll see if you read the links, the last "reform" in Liechtenstein actually *increased* the royal executive power. Take that, 20th century!

And Prince Alois's son, 13-year-old Prince Joseph Wenzel, just happens to be the legitimate heir to the Stuart throne—illegally overthrown in a coup[50] based on

---

[49] Reference to Richard Crossman's controversial *Diaries of a Cabinet Minister*, posthumously published in 1975.
[50] The Glorious Revolution of 1688.

the notorious **warming-pan legend**.[51] Therefore, the structure of a restoration is obvious. The Hanoverians have failed. They have become decorative pseudo-monarchs. And as for the system of government that has grown up under them, it makes **Richard Cromwell** look like a smashing success. Restore the Stuarts under King Joseph I, with Prince Alois as regent, and the problem is solved.

Unrealistic? *Au contraire, mon frère.* What is unrealistic is "a sense of purpose as a nation, a uniting ethos which will restore our sense of pride..." Frankly, England does not deserve pride. It has gone to the dogs, and that may be an insult to dogs. If England is to restore its sense of pride, it needs to start with its sense of shame. And the first thing it should be ashamed of is the pathetic excuse for a government that afflicts it at present, and will afflict it for the indefinite future until something drastic is done.

For example, according to **official statistics**, between 1900 and 1992 the crime rate in Great Britain, indictable offenses per capita known to the police, increased by a factor of 46. That's not 46%. Oh, no. That's 4600%. Many of the offenders having been imported specially, to make England brighter and more colorful. This isn't a government. It's a crime syndicate.

Ideally a Stuart restoration would happen on much the same conditions as the **restoration of Charles II**, except perhaps with an extra caveat: a total **lustration** of the present administration. It has not partly, sort of, kind of, maybe, failed. It has failed utterly, irrevocably, disastrously and terminally.

Therefore, the entire present regime, politicians and civil servants and quangocrats and all, except for essential security and technical personnel, should be retired on full pay and barred from any future official employment. Why pick nits? The private sector is full of competent managers. You can import them from America if you need. Don't make the mistake of trying to sweep out the Augean stables. Just **apply the river**.[52] (If a concession must be made to modern mores, however, I think this time around there is no need to **hang any corpses**.[53])

In order to make a Stuart restoration happen, Dr. North, you have to accomplish one of the following two things. You either need to persuade a majority of the population of England (or Great Britain, if you prefer, but England as a historic jurisdiction without a present government is quite an appealing target) that it needs to happen, or you need to persuade the British Army that it needs to happen. The former is preferable. The latter is dangerous, but hardly unprecedented. Frankly, the present situation is dangerous as well.

---

51 The belief that James III was an illegitimate child of Mary of Modena, smuggled into her bed in a "warming pan" to replace her stillborn son and presumed end of the Stuart line.
52 According to myth, Hercules cleaned out the Augean stables by rerouting the Alpheus and Peneus rivers to wash away the filth.
53 After restoration, Charles II ordered the posthumous execution of several leaders of the regicide of Charles I, including Cromwell.

Neither of these options involves any of the following acts: starting a new political party, recruiting a paramilitary fascist skinhead stormtroop brigade, or engaging in eternal debates about the policies and procedures of the restored polity.

All of these are crucial, but the third especially. Note the difference between organizing a royal restoration and organizing a democratic revival. The latter, simply because of the open landscape of power it must create, offers an infinite plane across which an arbitrary oil slick of random crackpot ideas can spread out indefinitely, creating a movement with less cohesion than the average pubic hair. (See under: UKIP.) The former is a single decision. It is far less complicated than voting. Either you want to restore the rightful King of England, or you'd rather take your chances with the faceless bureaucrats. Either you're a neo-Jacobite, or you're not. There are no factions, parties, personality conflicts, etc., etc.

What will the new England look like? You don't even have to think about it. It is not your job to think about it. It is Prince Regent Alois's job—the miracle of absolute monarchy, Stuart-style. If he runs the place a quarter as well as he runs Vaduz, if he can get the crime rate per hundred thousand back down to 2.4 from 109.4, historians will be kissing his ass for the next four centuries. Perhaps he can get Lee Kuan Yew in as a consultant.

You have many difficulties in making a Stuart restoration happen, but perhaps the greatest is that most Englishmen simply have no idea what living in a competently governed country would be like. Liechtenstein, while quite well-run, is too small to serve as an illustration. Singapore is definitely a better bet.

Here is a speech[54] made last year by Lee Hsien Loong, who just, um, happens to be the son of Lee Kuan Yew. Read this speech, obviously composed by Prime Minister Lee himself (it certainly does not betray the speechwriter's art), and imagine living in a country in which the chief administrator talks to the residents in a normal voice as if speaking to grownups. Yes, men and women of England, this is what American-style democracy has deprived you of. We're sorry. We promise we won't do it again.

This sort of transition in government is what, here at UR, we call a *reset*. It's just like rebooting your computer, when for some reason it gets gunked up and seems to be running slowly. Are you interested in debugging it? Would you like to activate the kernel console, perhaps look at the thread table, check out some registers, see what virtual memory is doing? Is a bear Catholic? Does the Pope—anyway.

Or perhaps it's a little more like reinstalling Windows. The gunk could be a virus, after all. Rebooting will not remove a virus. Better yet, you could replace Windows with Linux. That way, you won't just get the same virus right away again. I think a Stuart restoration in England is about as close as it comes to replacing Windows with Linux.

There are three basic principles to any reset.

54

First, the existing government must be thoroughly lustrated. There is no point in trying to debug or reform it. There is certainly no need for individual purges, McCarthy-style, or for *Fragebogen*[55] and *Persilscheine*[56] à la 1945. Except for the security forces and essential technical personnel, all employees should be thanked for their service, asked to submit contact information so that they can be hired as temporary consultants if the new administration finds it necessary, and discharged with no hard feelings, an amnesty for any crimes they may have committed in government service, and a pension sufficient to retire.

Second, a reset is not a revolution. A revolution is a criminal conspiracy in which murderous, deranged adventurers capture a state for their arbitrary, and usually sinister, purposes. A reset is a restoration of secure, effective and responsible government. It's true that both involve regime change, but both sex and rape involve penetration.

Of course, a failed reset can degenerate into a revolution. No doubt many involved in the rise to power of Hitler and Mussolini thought of their project as a reset. They were quite mistaken. It is a cruel irony to free a nation of democracy, only to saddle it with gangsters.

There is a simple way to distinguish the two. Just as the new permanent government must not retain employees of the old government, it must not employ or reward anyone involved in bringing the reset about. A successful reset may involve an interim administration which does have personal continuity with the reset effort, but if so this regime must be discarded as thoroughly as the old regime. This policy eliminates all meretricious motivations.

Third, and most important, a reset must happen in a single step. It is not a gradual effort in which a new party builds support by incrementally moving into positions of responsibility, as the Labour Party did in the 20th century. As we've seen, this Fabian approach only works from right to left. The only way for a reactionary movement to acquire power incrementally is to soil itself by participating in political democracy, a form of government it despises as much as any sensible person. Besides, since there is no such thing as a partial reset, there are no meaningful incremental policies that resetters can support. You can restore the Stuarts or not restore the Stuarts, but you can't restore 36% of the Stuarts.

A reset is the result of a *single successful operation*. Ideally, the old regime simply concedes peacefully and of its own free will that it has lost the confidence of the people, and obeys all legal niceties in conveying full executive power to the new administration. This is more or less the way the Soviet satellites collapsed, for example. It can get more complicated than this, but not much more complicated. Whatever is done, there should be no security vacuum and certainly no actual fighting. Real reactionaries don't go off half-cocked.

---

55 "The Questionnaire," also the title to an Ernst von Solomon novel from 1954 based on the German denazification exam.
56 "Persil ticket," an idiom meaning "clean bill of health" to denote successful denazification.

There is a simple way to execute a reset without falling into the dead-end trap of politics, and without the assistance of the military. Conduct your own election. Enroll supporters directly over the Internet, verifying their identity as voters. Once you have a solid and unquestionable majority, form an interim administration and request the transfer of government.

And it will happen. You may not even need an absolute majority. The modern regime is quite immune to politics, but it is tremendously sensitive to public opinion. It cannot afford to be disliked. Like every bully, it is a great coward. Especially if it is given a comfortable way out—thus the amnesty and the pension. If you have your majority and still the regime does not concede, this, and only this, is the time to turn to the official elections.

The truth about the people who work for government is that, in general, they despise it. They are demoralized and disillusioned. They have slightly more excitement and energy than your average Stasi employee circa 1988, but not much. Working for the government in 1938 was incredible, unbelievable fun. Working for the government in 2008 is soul-destroying. If you gave the entire civil service an opportunity to retire tomorrow on full pay, nine out of ten would take it, and lick your hand like golden retrievers for the offer.

AN OPEN LETTER TO OPEN-MINDED PROGRESSIVES

 202 Hollywood Supports New Deal and NIRA Footage from a 1933 Busby Berkeley musical with pro New-Deal, pro National Industrial Recovery Act messaging. Dir. Lloyd Bacon, Busby Berkeley. *Footlight Parade.* (Warner Bros. Pictures, 1933).

 202 this friendly fellow Logo for the National Recovery Administration.

 202 secret speech "On the Cult of Personality and its Consequences"

 202 That Man John Q. Barrett. "'That One,' and 'That Man.'" *History News Network*, George Washington University, 2008.

 202 William Buckley

 202 brain trust

 203 not science Richard P. Feynman. "Cargo Cult Science." Commencement address. (Caltech, 1974).

 203 predictions Edward Bellamy. *Looking Backward: 2000-1887.* (Tickner & Co. 1888).

 203 achievements

 203 political formula "Gaetano Mosca - Political thought"

 203 colonization Scott Rasmussen. "Immigration Bill Failure Proves Rasmussen's First Law of Politics." *Rasmussen Reports*, 28 Jun. 2007.

 203 racial spoils system "Michigan Civil Rights Initiative"

 203 very different tone Homepage for BarackObama.com.

 204 ex cathedra

205 *Chauncey Depew*

 205 *C. Wright Mills*

 205 *The Power Elite* C. Wright Mills. (Oxford University Press, 1956).

 205 *Tom DeLay*

 205 *K Street Project*

 205 *NumbersUSA*

 205 *Howard Jarvis* A republican lobbyist who spearheaded California's Prop. 13 property tax law.

 205 *Ward Connerly* Led the University of California Board of Regents in abolishing Affirmative Action for admissions in 1995.

 205 *Ketman* Czesław Miłosz. *The Captive Mind*. (US: Knopf, 1953).

 205 *Czesław Miłosz*

 205 *Jack Mormons*

 206 *Edith Hamilton*

 206 *Freda Utley*

 206 *This* Freda Utley. *Odyssey of a Liberal: Memoirs*. (Washington National Press, 1970).

206 stumbles on Rick Perlstein. "Getting Past the 60's? It's Not Going to Happen." *Washington Post*, 3 Feb. 2008.

 207 Up against the wall, motherfucker, this is a stickup.

207 Movement Originally linked to a PBS documentary on the Weather Undeground. Dir. Sam Green and Bill Siegel. *The Weather Underground.* (Independent Lens, PBS, 2004).
 207 Students for a Democratic Society

 208 Grayson Kirks

 208 S. I. Hayakawas

 208 McGeorge Bundys

 208 Port Huron Statement The political manifesto written by the SDS, delivered in 1962 at Port Huron, Michigan, originally drafted by Tom Hayden, but officially credited to "Author" or "Viet Nam Generation." A link to the statement from the University of Virginia at Charlottesville is provided here.
 208 Hayden

 208 Spiro Agnew

 208 Anita Bryant

 208 Tamerlane

209 dark forces of titanic and unbounded strength Originally linked to Amazon page for Sharlett's book, an overwrought exposé of American "Christian fundamentalism" typical of progressive fear of "theocracy" that was so ubiquitous during the Bush era. Jeff Sharlett. *The Family: The Secret Fundamentalism at the Heart of American Power.* (Harper, 2008).

209 only now In praise of Obama's primary win, Rice said, "'We the people' is beginning to mean all of us." The original link was to a Larry Auster post about the statement "Rice's "Anti-Americanism, Again, and Inevitably" at *View From the Right* (4 Jun. 2008).

209 disagrees "The Great Immigration Panic." *The New York Times*, Opinion, 3 Jun. 2008.

209 Reconstruction

209 Eric Foner A Short History of Reconstruction, 1863-1877. (Perennial, 1989).

209 Stephen Budiansky The Bloody Shirt: Terror After Appomatox. (Viking, 2008).

209 John Hope Franklin Reconstruction After the Civil War. (University of Chicago Press, 1994).

209 Charles Nordhoff The Cotton States in the Spring and Summer of 1875. (D. Appleton & Company, 1876).

209 Daniel Henry Chamberlain Chamberlain was the author of numerous essays and articles on the Reconstruction period, including "Reconstruction in South Carolina" written for the April 1901 issue of *The Atlantic*, linked here.

209 John Burgess Reconstruction and the Constitution, 1866-1876. (Charles Scribner's Sons, 1902).

209 William Saletan "Not Black and White: Rethinking Race and Genes." *Slate*, 5 May 2008.

210 on line Stephen Budiansky. *The Bloody Shirt.* (reprinted New York Times, First Chapters, 30 Jan. 2008). Chapter 1.

210 Gramscian

210 Fabian

211 departments "Southern Poverty Law Center"

AN OPEN LETTER TO OPEN-MINDED PROGRESSIVES

 211 *Federalist Society*

 211 *George Mason School* Link to *Marginal Revolution*, the blog of GMU economics professors Tyler Cowen and Alex Tabarrok.

 211 *cosmotarians* Will Wilkinson. "I Only Sleep With Cosmotarians." *Will Wilkinson dot net*, 2 Dec. 2008.

 212 *here* Glenn Harlan Reynolds. "Reading the Ron Paul Revolution." *Pajamas Media*, 12 May 2008.

 212 *Instapundit* Glenn Reynolds' *nom de blog* and popular site.

 213 *the same power* "Reserve power."

 213 *sinecures* United States Government "Supporting Positions"

 213 *at VDare* Arthur Pendleton. "Lew Rockwell And The Strange Death (Or At Least Suspended Animation) Of Paleolibertarianism." *Vdare*, 14 May 2008.

 213 *at VFR* Lawrence Auster. "How the Paleolibertarians Went Left on Race and Nationhood." *View From the Right*, 25 May, 2008.

 213 *mine* "Why I Am Not a Libertarian." *UR*, 13 Dec. 2007.

 213 *the first Whig was the Devil* See Chapter 3.

  213 Dr. Ron Paul

214 *blatantly ghostwritten books* Ron Paul. *The Revolution: A Manifesto*. (Grand Central Publishing, 2008).

 214 *regs gevaar* "Swart gevaar"

214 *Komsomol members* All-Union Leninist Young Communist League

 214 *Chad Vader*

 215 *preserving democracy* Google search for "fdr 'preserve democracy.'"

 215 *preserved Lenin*

 215 *Justice Van Devanter*

 215 *Pobedonostsev*

 215 *exactly right* Konstantin Pobedonostsev, trans. Robert Crozier Long. *Reflections of a Russian Statesman*. (Grant Richards, 1898) p. 26

 215 *terrifying and barbaric* G.W. Steevens. *The Land of the Dollar*. (Dodd, Mead and Company, 1898) p. 185

 215 *EU Referendum* The paragraph links to the following posts by Richard North at his blog EU Referendum, in order:
"Retreat To Victory" (27 May, 2008)
"Retreat To Victory: Part II" (30 May, 2008)
"Myth of the Week: The European Union is democratically controlled, Part I – The Council of Ministers" (22 Jun. 2004)
"Myth of the Week: The European Union is democratically controlled, Part II – The European Parliament" (10 Aug. 2004)

 215 *creepy-looking building* Berlaymont building, EU headquarters in Brussels

 215 *Brazil II* Gilliam's 1985 film *Brazil* takes place in a techno-bureaucratic dystopia, where "Information Retrieval" technicians wear nightmarish baby masks vaguely resembling a modal European Commission employee. Link to a clip featuring the masks provided here.

 215 *Home Rule*

AN OPEN LETTER TO OPEN-MINDED PROGRESSIVES

  216 tinker's damn Gordon Rayner. "Irish Referendum could scupper EU treaty." *The Telegraph*, 31 May 2008.

  216 Crossman diaries Ben Fenton, "How Whitehall was beaten to the punch by the Crossman diaries." *The Telegraph*, 2 Jan. 2006.

  216 House of Liechtenstein

  216 the last working royal family in Europe "Politics of Liechtenstein"

  216 Hans-Adam II

  216 Hereditary Prince Alois

  216 Prince Joseph Wenzel

  216 coup "Glorious Revolution"

  217 warming-pan legend Samuel Hibbert Ware. *Lancashire Memorials of the Rebellion, MDCCXV.* (Printed for the Chetham Society, 1845). p.184.

  217 Richard Cromwell

  217 official statistics Joe Hicks and Grahame Allen. "A Century of Change: Trends in UK statistics since 1900." *House of Commons Library*, Research Paper 99/111, 21 Dec. 1999.

  217 restoration of Charles II "Stuart restoration"

  217 lustration

  217 apply the river

LINKS & NOTES

 217 hang any corpses "List of Regicides of Charles I"

 218 UKIP

 218 Lee Kuan Yew

 218 Lee Hsien Loong

 218 a speech Lee Hsien Loong. "National Day Rally English Speech." Nus University Cultural Center, 19 Aug. 2007.

 219 Fragebogen Ernst von Solomon. *Der Fragebogen*. (Rowohlt Verlag, 1951)

 219 Persilscheine

CHAPTER 9:
HOW TO UNINSTALL A CATHEDRAL
JUNE 12, 2008

I'm afraid, dear open-minded progressive, that we have wandered into deep and murky waters. You thought you were merely in for a bit of philosophical wrangling. Instead here we are, openly conspiring to restore the Stuarts.

The other day in an old book I found a cute little summary of the problem. The book is **Carlton Hayes'** *History of Modern Europe*, first published in 1916 and updated in 1924. Writing about modern Europe without mentioning America is a little like writing about the Lakers without mentioning Kobe Bryant, and in the 1924 addendum Professor Hayes simply gives up the ghost and tells us what's happened lately in the Western world. Of course I simply adore these kinds of contemporary digests. Here is the state of Protestant Christianity, circa 1924:

> Among Protestant Christian sects there were several significant movements toward cooperation and even toward formal union. Many barriers between them were broken down, at least in part, by the Young Men's Christian Association, which had been founded in the nineteenth century but which expanded very rapidly during and after the Great War. The Salvation Army, dating from about the year 1880, was another factor in the same process: it placed emphasis on spiritual earnestness, on evangelical work among the poor, and on charitable endeavors, rather than on sectarian controversies. There were also various "federations of churches," and in Canada, after the Great War, several Prot-

estant denominations were actually united. Such interdenominational and unifying movements were made easier by the fact that the original theological differences between the various sects were no longer regarded as very important by a large number of church members.

Some Protestants, reacting against the decline of dogma and the doubting of the miraculous and the supernatural, turned increasingly toward Christian Science or towards spiritualism or theosophy. In some countries, and especially in the United States, the current vogue of Darwinism and other theories of evolution caused a new outburst of opposition from stalwart groups of Protestants to the claims of "science," and a stubborn reaffirmation of their fundamental faith in the literal inspiration of the Bible. These "Fundamentalists," as they were called, were fairly numerous in several Protestant denominations, and they contested with their "Progressive" or "Modernist" brethren the control of Protestant churches, particularly the Presbyterian, Episcopalian, Baptist, and Methodist.

Now I ask you, dear open-minded progressive: is there anything familiar about this picture?

The YMCA and the Salvation Army are (sadly) no longer major players. But it seems obvious that Professor Hayes is describing our present "red-state" versus "blue-state" conflict. What's weird, however, is that he seems to be describing it as a *theological dispute*. Not exactly the present perception.

Your present-day "Progressive" or "Modernist" may retain some vestigial belief in God. Or not. But she certainly does not think of her faction as a *Christian supersect*. Meanwhile, her "Fundamentalist" adversaries have largely appropriated the label *Christian*. Neither side sees the red–blue conflict as that old staple of European history, the Christian sectarian war.

There are a couple of other interesting details in Professor Hayes' little narrative. One, he finds it noteworthy that the mainstream Protestant sects are for some odd reason *converging*. And indeed in 1924 it was a historical novelty to see Episcopalians and Presbyterians cooperating amicably on "charitable endeavors," forgetting all those nasty old "theological differences." **Dogs and cats, living together!**[1]

Two, it is clear at least from Professor Hayes' perspective that the "Progressive" or "Modernist" side of this conflict is the main stream of American Protestantism, and the "Fundamentalist" side is a weird, "stubborn" mutation.

To our modern "Fundamentalists" (the term has become so opprobrious that they will respond better, dear open-minded progressive, if you use the word "traditionalist"), the idea that "liberalism" is actually *mainstream Protestant Christiani-*

---

[1] *Ghostbusters* (1984)

AN OPEN LETTER TO OPEN-MINDED PROGRESSIVES

ty[2] is about as off-the-wall as it gets. And it must strike most "Progressives" as equally weird. But here it is in black and white, from a **legendary Columbia historian**. Obviously, someone is off the wall. Maybe it's me. Maybe it's you. Are you feeling paranoid yet, dear reader?

When dealing with historical movements it's often useful to ask: is this dead, or alive? If the former, what killed it, when, and how? If you cannot find any answers to these questions, it is a pretty good clue that you're looking at something which isn't dead.

And if it's not dead, it must be alive. And if it's alive, but you no longer identify it as a distinct movement, the only possible answer is that it has become *so pervasive that you do not distinguish between it and reality itself*. In other words, you do not feel you have *any serious alternative* to supporting the movement. And you are probably right.

Note that this is exactly how you, dear open-minded progressive, see the modern children of those stubborn "Fundamentalists." You read the conflict asymmetrically. You don't think of yourself as someone who believes in "Progressivism." You don't believe in anything. You are not a follower at all. You are a critical and independent thinker. Rather, it is your fundamentalist enemies, the tribe across the river, who are Jesus-besotted zombie bots.

The first step toward a historical perspective on the conflict is to acknowledge that *both* of these traditions are exactly that: traditions. You did not invent progressivism any more than Billy Joe invented fundamentalism. Thanks to Professor Hayes, we know this absolutely, because we know that both of these things existed 84 years ago, and you are not 84.

And what is the difference between a mere tradition and an honest-to-god religion? Theology. A many-god or a three-god or a one-god tradition is a religion. A no-god tradition is... well, there isn't really a word for it, is there? This is a good clue that someone has been tampering with the tools you use to think.

Because there must be as many ways to not believe in a god or gods as to believe in them. I am an atheist. You are an atheist. But you are a progressive, and I am not a progressive. If we can have multiple sects of Christianity, why can't we have multiple sects of atheism?

Let's rectify this linguistic sabotage by calling a no-god tradition an *areligion*. A one-god tradition is a *unireligion*. A two-god one is a *direligion*. A three-god one is a *trireligion*. One with more gods than you can shake a stick at is a *polyreligion*. And so on. We see instantly that while progressivism (2008-style) is *an* areligion, it does not at all follow that it is the *one true* areligion. Oops.

Question: in a political conflict between a direligion and a polyreligion, which side should you support? What about an areligion versus a trireligion? Let's assume that, like me, you believe in no gods at all.

---

2 See Chapter 5.

One easy answer is to say the fewer gods, the better. So we would automatically support the direligion over the polyreligion, etc. I think the stupidity of this is obvious.

We could also say that all traditions which promote gods are false, and therefore we should favor the areligion over the trireligion. Unfortunately, even if we assume that the areligion is right on the deity question and not even one of the three gods exists, the two could not engage in a political conflict if they did not disagree on many subjects in the temporal plane. Who is more likely to be right on these mundane matters, which actually do matter? We have no reason at all to think that just because the areligion is right about gods, it is right about anything else. And we have no reason at all to think that just because the trireligion is wrong about gods, it is wrong about anything else. So this is really just as stupid, and I do hope you haven't been taken in by it. (Lots of smart people believe stupid things.)

The second step is to acknowledge the possibility that, on any issue, *both* competing traditions could be peddling misperceptions. In fact, we've just seen it. Neither side wants you to know that progressivism is the historical mainstream of Protestant Christianity. Only in the pages of smelly old books, and of course here at UR, will you find this little tidbit of history. This is pretty standard for religions, which always have a habit of obscuring their own pasts.

Why do both sides agree on this misperception? The fundamentalist motivation is obvious. As a traditionalist Christian, you believe in God. It is obvious that anyone who doesn't believe in God cannot possibly be a Christian. The idea that there could be any kind of historical continuity between people who believe in God, and people who don't believe in God, is absurd. It's like saying that Jesus was "just some dude."

But as someone who doesn't believe in God, you have absolutely no reason to accept this argument. Do you care, dear open-minded progressive, what wacky stuff those wacky fundies believe in? Do you care whether they worship God in one person, God in three persons, God in forty-seven persons, or God in the person of a turtle? Um, no.

No: from the progressive side, there is a very different problem. The problem is that if Progressivism is indeed a Christian supersect, it is also a *criminal conspiracy*.

Assuming you're an American, dear open-minded progressive, you might have forgotten that it's quite literally *illegal* for the Federal Government to "make an establishment of religion." While its authors and ratifiers never meant the clause to mean what it means today, we do have a living Constitution, the law is what it is now, and over the last half-century our friends in high places have been quite enthusiastic about deploying it against their Fundamentalist foes.

Perhaps some perspective can be obtained by replacing the words "Modernist" and "Fundamentalist" in Professor Hayes' narrative with "Sunni" and "Shia." The First Amendment does not say, "Congress shall make no law respecting an establishment of Shiism." More to the point, it does not say "Congress shall make no law respecting an establishment of religion, until that religion manages to sneak God

AN OPEN LETTER TO OPEN-MINDED PROGRESSIVES 233

under the carpet, at which point go ahead, dudes." Rather, the obvious spirit of the law is that Congress shall be *neutral* with respect to the theological disputes of its citizens, such as that described by Professor Hayes. Um, has it been?

If you doubt this, maybe it's time to put on the Fundamentalens. This is a cute optical accessory that transforms all things Sunni into things Shia, and vice versa. When you're wearing the Fundamentalens, progressive institutions look fundamentalist and fundamentalist institutions look progressive.

In the Fundamentalens, Harvard and Stanford and Yale are fundamentalist seminaries. It may not be official, but there is no doubt about it at all. They emit Jesus-freak codewords, secret Mormon handshakes, and miscellaneous Bible baloney the way a baby emits fermented milk. Meanwhile, Bob Jones and Oral Roberts and Patrick Henry are diverse, progressive, socially and environmentally conscious centers of learning—their entire freshman class lines up to sing "Imagine" every morning.

Would it creep you out, dear open-minded progressive, to live in this country? It would certainly creep me out, and I'm not even a progressive—though I was raised as one.

An America where every progressive in any position of influence or authority was replaced by an equal and opposite fundamentalist, and vice versa, is one you would have no hesitation in describing as a *fundamentalist theocracy*. Which implies quite inexorably that the America we do live in, the real one, can be fairly described as a *progressive atheocracy*—that is, a system of government based on an official areligion, progressivism.

This areligion is maintained and propagated by the decentralized system of quasiofficial "educational" institutions which we, here at UR, have learned to call the *Cathedral*. In this chapter, we'll look, purely in a theoretical manner of course, at what it might take to get rid of this thing. If you find the exercise unpalatable, dear open-minded progressive, just snap the Fundamentalens back on and imagine you're trying to free your government from the icy, inexorable grip of Jesus. (Or the Pope. The resemblance between anti-fundamentalism and its older brother, anti-Catholicism, may be too obvious to mention—but I should mention it anyway.)

Obviously I don't object to the Cathedral on account of its atheism. If a theist can object to theocracy, an atheist can object to atheocracy. I object to the concept of official thought in general, to the details of progressivism in specific, but most of all to the insidious way in which the Cathedral has managed to mutate its way around the "separation of church and state" in which it so hypocritically indoctrinates its acolytes. The Cathedral is the apotheosis of chutzpah. It is always poisoning its parents, then pleading for clemency as an orphan.

I know, I know. We have been through all this stuff before. On the Internet it never hurts to repeat, however, and let's take a brief look at the Cathedral's operations in the case of one James Watson.

CHAPTER 9

Here is the transcript of an interview[3] between Dr. Watson and Henry Louis Gates. (If you care to go here[4] you can read Professor Gates' meandering, incoherent summary, and even watch some video.)

Bear in mind that this material, though only recently released, was produced shortly after the **struggle session** to which Dr. Watson was subjected early this year. The young firebrands over at *Gene Expression*[5] (many of whom themselves work inside the Cathedral, as of course all serious scientists must) had predictable responses:

> Painful to read.
>
> Is Watson one of these people who has balls only when he's dealing with people lower down the ladder, and none when he is dealing with people who can do him harm?
>
> Had to stop reading almost immediately. Presumably, his confession ended with his execution by a pack of trained dogs.
>
> What a simpering, mewling weakling he is in this interview. Terrified and cowed.

Okay. Obviously, as a bitter and negative person myself, I sympathize with these reactions. But, I mean, if we compare Dr. Watson to **Andrei Sakharov**—surely a fair comparison—did Dr. Sakharov go around shouting "Communism is a LIE! BETTER DEAD THAN RED!"? Somehow I doubt it. In fact, neither Watson nor Sakharov were executed by a pack of trained dogs. These guys aren't completely stupid. They know how far to push it.

And Dr. Watson even manages to get Professor Gates, whose career cannot be understood without reference to the color of his skin, to swallow the following harmless-looking red pill:

> JW: It was, we shouldn't expect that people in different parts of the world have equal intelligence, because we all know that. And people say that these should be the same. I think the answer is, we don't know.
>
> Q: We don't know. Not that they are.
>
> JW: No, no. I'm always trying to say is that some people... of left wing persuasion have said that there wasn't enough time for differences... we don't know. That's all.

3

4  The essay is here, though the video is no longer available at the archived link.

5 An erstwhile genetics-focused blog run by Razib Khan. See Chapter XIV.

Q: We don't know.

"We don't know." And we can tell that the pill has gotten deep down inside Professor Gates, it has been swallowed and digested and worked its way through the bloodstream and is starting to produce that awful wiry feeling in the glial cells, by a question he asks earlier:

> Q: But imagine if you were an African or an African American intellectual. And it's ten years from now. And you pick up *The New York Times*... (Hits Table) and some geneticist says, A, that intelligence is genetic, and B, the difference is measured on standardized tests. Between black people and white people, is traceable to a genetic basis. What would you, as a black intellectual, do, do you think?

Here is the problem: the message our beloved Cathedral has been implanting in all the young smart kids at Harvard and Yale and Stanford, the cream of the crop, the top 1%, not to mention the readers of the New York Times who are the top 10%, is not *"we don't know."*

Oh, no. The message is "we *do* know. And they *are* equal. In fact, we are so sure they're equal that if you even start to hint that you might disagree, we will do everything we can to destroy your life, and we will feel good about it. Because your opinions are evil and you are, too."

So it's not even a question of ten years from now. White-coated scientists, exercising their papal infallibility through the ordinary magisterium of Times Square, do not need to declare their final and inexorable proof of A and B, thus proving that the Cathedral has been broadcasting mendacity since 1924—and enforcing it since 1984. We need await nothing. Any intelligent person can already read the contradiction. Professor Gates has said it out loud.

If you accept Dr. Watson's fallback position, his intellectual Torres Vedras—as Professor Gates does—the Cathedral is already a goner. Its defeat is not a matter for further research. It is a matter of freshman philosophy. The Cathedral has chosen to fortify, not as a minor outpost but as its central keep, the position of not-A and not-B (actually, since not-A *or* not-B would suffice, the typical insistence on both is a classic sign of a weak position). Its belief in the statistical uniformity of the human brain across all subpopulations presently living is absolute. It has put all its chips on this one.

And the evidence for its position is really not much stronger than the evidence for the Holy Trinity. In fact, the Holy Trinity has a big advantage: there may be no evidence for it, but at least there is none against it. There is plenty of evidence against human neurological uniformity. The question is simply what standard of proof you apply. By the standards that most of us apply to most questions of fact, the answer is already obvious—and has been for at least thirty years. If not a hundred.

Moreover, there is a simple explanation for the reason that so many people believe in *human neurological uniformity* (HNU). It is a core doctrine of Christianity. Even more precisely, it is a core doctrine of the **neo-primitive Christianity** that we call Protestantism. And specifically, I believe it to be a mutated and metastasized version of the Quaker doctrine of the **Inner Light**. Basically, all humans must be neurologically uniform because we all have the same little piece of God inside us. (All the American Protestant sects, or at least all the Northern ones, became heavily Quakerized during the 19th century. But that's a different discussion.)

Thus what we call *hate speech* is merely a 20th-century name for the age-old crime of **blasphemy**. You might have noticed that it is not, and has never been, illegal to be an asshole. No government in history has ever come close to criminalizing rudeness, nastiness, meanness, or even harassment in general—not even in the workplace.

Denying the Inner Light, however, is another matter entirely. It's all too easy to put in the Fundamentalens, transport ourselves to **Margaret Atwood** world, and imagine the Commander processing an assembly-line of blasphemers with this handy neo-Quaker catchphrase. "Scorned the **Testimony of Equality**, violated **right ordering**, denied the Inner Light. Defendant, I think the case is clear. Five years of orientation."

So it is almost impossible for me to answer Professor Gates' question. Asking what a "black intellectual" should do after A and B are demonstrated is like asking what a professor of Marxist–Leninist studies should do after the fall of the Soviet Union. I don't know, dude. What else are you good at?

Professor Gates' entire department consists of the construction of increasingly elaborate persecution theories to explain facts which follow trivially from A and B. Agree on A and B, and the world has no need at all for Professor Gates, nor for any of his colleagues. He seems like a pretty sharp guy. Surely he can find something. If not, there's always pizza delivery.

The trouble is that—as we've just seen—A and B need not be shown to demonstrate the presence of official mendacity. It is sufficient to demonstrate that A and B are plausible. More strongly, it is sufficient to demonstrate that they are not implausible. Because we are constantly being "educated" to believe that they are implausible. The proposition is implied a thousand times for every time it is stated, but progressivism without HNU makes about as much sense as Islam without Allah.

So if refuting a proposition on which the Cathedral has staked its credibility is sufficient to defeat it, and that refutation is agreed on by all serious thinkers—why the heck is it still here?

Duh. If institutional mendacity is its stock in trade, why on earth should refutation bother it? You don't have to look far for other cases in which entire departments of the Cathedral have been devoted to the propagation of nonsense. What do you expect them to do, say "we're sorry, it's true, we are all a bunch of shills, we'll go work as taxi drivers now?"

If the Cathedral can lie now, it can lie then. It doesn't matter what Dr. Watson and his students produce, now or ten years from now. If it is impossible for the New York Times to produce a story saying that A and B are proven, no such story will appear. Rather, the standard of proof will simply be raised and raised again, as of course it has been already.

In other words: if the Cathedral were a trustworthy mechanism for producing and distributing information, we would expect it to correct any newly discovered error, and propagate the correction. But if it were a trustworthy mechanism, it would not *already be* in an obvious error state, have maintained that error state for decades, and show no signs at all of nudging Professor Gates out of the building and into his new career as a marketing executive. Therefore, to expect it to correct its own errors is naive—at best.

And therefore, you and I have two choices. We can accept that we live in a state of systematic mendacity, as people always have, note that it may well be getting worse rather than better, and figure out how to live with it. This would be the prudent choice. It demonstrates genuine wisdom, the wisdom of resignation and healthy personal motivation.

On the other hand, if you have enough time to read these essays, you have enough time to think about solutions. After all, you already live under a government which demands that you invest a substantial percentage of your neural tissue in the meaningless gabble of politics. This lobe should probably be devoted to dance, literature, or shopping. But we are, after all, human. In addition to our healthier and more positive cogitations, we sometimes express resentment. And what more pleasant riposte than to reprogram one's political control module, and turn it against its former botmasters?

So we can separate the problem into two categories. One is a *policy* question: how can the American political system be modified to free itself from the Cathedral? Two is a *military* question (considering war and politics as a **continuum**[6]): since the Cathedral does not wish to relinquish power, how can it best be induced to do so? The two are inseparable, of course, but it is convenient to consider them separately. In this chapter we'll look at the first.

There are two basic ways of executing this divorce. We'll call one a *soft reset* and the other a *hard reset*. Basically, a hard reset works and a soft reset doesn't. However, a soft reset is more attractive in many ways, and we need to work through it just to see why it can't work.

In a soft reset, we leave the current structure of government the same, except that we apply the 20th-century First Amendment to all forms of instruction, theistic or "secular." In other words, our policy is *separation of education and state*. In a free country, the government should not be programming its citizens. It should

---

6 Reference to Clausewitz's axiom "War as politics by other means."

not care at all what people think. It only needs to care what they do. The issue has nothing to do with theism. It is a basic matter of personal freedom.

You cannot have official education without official truth, i.e., *pravda*. Most—in fact, I'd say almost all—of our *pravda* is indeed true. Call it 99.9%. The remaining 0.1% is creepy enough. The Third Reich used the wonderful word *Aufklärung*, meaning enlightenment or literally "clearing-up." Every time I see a piece of public education designed to improve the world by improving my character, I think of *Aufklärung*. But of course, a good Nazi education imparted many true truths as well.

There are four major forms of education in a modern Western society: churches, schools, universities, and the press. Our open-minded progressives have done a fantastic job of separating church and state. I really don't think their work can be improved on. A soft reset is simply a matter of applying the precedent to the other three.

First, let's deal with (primary) schools. This is easy, because they are actually formal arms of the government. To separate school and state, liquidate the public school system, selling all its assets to the highest bidder. For every student in or eligible for public school, for every year of eligibility, compute what the school system was getting and send the check to the parents.

This is budget-neutral for state and family alike, and unlike "vouchers" it does not require Uncle Sam or any of his little brothers to decide what "education" is. If the worst parents in the world spend the money on XBoxes and PCP, it would still be a vast improvement on inner-city schools. The perfect is the enemy of the good.

This leaves us with the Cathedral proper: the press and the universities.

The great thing about our understanding of the "wall of separation" is that it works both ways. The distinction between a state-controlled church and a church-controlled state is nil. In the modern interpretation of the First Amendment, both are equally obnoxious. (Although I suspect most progressives would find the latter especially repugnant.)

The same Amendment prescribes the freedom of the press. But the freedom of the press and the separation of church and state are applied in very different ways. The suggestion of a state-controlled press evokes terrible fear and anger in the progressive mind. The suggestion of a press-controlled state evokes... nothing. Even the concept is unfamiliar. Unless they happen to be **Tony Blair**,[7] I don't think most progressives have even considered the idea that the press could control the state. No points for guessing why this might be.

And the same principle applies to our "independent" universities. Except briefly during the McCarthy period (about which more in a moment), no one in government has ever considered trying to tell the professors what to think, just as no one in government has ever considered telling the preachers what to preach. But

---

7

while professors and preachers are both free to offer policy suggestions, it would be a scandal if the latter's advice was regularly accepted.

Let's take a hat tip from the blogosphere's invaluable inside source in the Cathedral, Dr. "Evil" Timothy Burke,[8] who links with applause to an article by Patricia Limerick at the Chronicle of Higher Ed about how this works:

> In the early 21st century, there is no limit or constraint on the desire of public constituencies to profit from the perspective of a university-based historian.
>
> Even better, the usual lament of the humanities—"There is plenty of money to support work in science and engineering, but very little to support work in the humanities"—proves to be accurate only if you define "work in the humanities" in the narrowest and most conventional way. If, by that phrase, you mean only individualistic research, directed at arcane topics detached from real-world needs and written in inaccessible and insular jargon, there is indeed very limited money.
>
> But for a humanities professor willing to take up applied work, sources of money are unexpectedly abundant.

"Applied work." I love the phrase. It belongs right up there with "manipulating procedural outcomes." And what does the author, Professor Limerick, mean by "applied work?"

> Another nearly completed project, *The Nature of Justice: Racial Equity and Environmental Well-Being*, spotlights the involvement of ethnic minorities with environmental issues. The center works regularly with federal agencies ranging from the Environmental Protection Agency to the National Park Service.

"The involvement of ethnic minorities with environmental issues!" You can't make this stuff up. I suppose she doesn't mean that they leave used diapers on the beach, or engage in the ethnic cleansing of pelicans. (I don't think I've linked to Ms. Latte before. She appears to be a racist Jewish woman in her fifties. Her signature post is definitely this one.[9])

Why is it that Professor Limerick is not just regularly called upon to share her *Aufklärung* with the EPA[10] (don't miss the picture), but apparently quite well

---

8 See Chapter 7.
9 The paragraph originally linked to three posts from the now defunct blog Latte Island. No archived versions of the posts still exist.
10

compensated for it, whereas Ms. Latte has no such opportunity to contribute her insights on the Mexican–pelican interaction?

Well, a lot of reasons, really. But the main one is that EPA (to sound like an insider, drop the article) recognizes Professor Limerick as an *official authority*. Uncle Sam may not tell the University of Colorado what to do, but the converse is not the case. And if you are a bureaucrat fighting for some outcome or other, and you can bring Professor Limerick in on your side, you are more likely to win. Apparently she is compensated for the service. This is not surprising.

If we lived in a theocracy as opposed to an atheocracy, she might be Bishop Limerick, and her thoughts would carry just the same weight. They might be different thoughts, of course. They probably would be. (Frankly, I would much rather be governed by the Pope than by these people. At least it would be a change. And I do believe in "change.")

To separate university and state the way church and state are separated, we'd need to make some fairly drastic changes. Of course, all the rivers of state cash that flow to the universities need to be plugged. No grants to professors, no subsidies for students, no nothing. But this is the easy part.

The hard part is that to divorce itself completely, the state needs to stop recognizing the *authority* of the universities. For example, it is staffed largely with university graduates—many of whom are students of Professor Burke, Professor Limerick, and the like. Perhaps there is no way to avoid this, but there is a way to make it not matter: add university credentials to the list of official no-nos in HR decisions. Treat it like race, age, and marital status. Don't even let applicants put it on their resumes. Instead, use the good old system: competitive examination.[11]

Professor Limerick's little pep-talks aside, in some rare cases a government does need to conduct actual research. In that case, it needs to hire actual researchers. Want to hire a chemist? Give her a chemistry test. Nor need this be limited to new employees. Why not reexamine the present ones, to see if they know anything and have any brains?

Okay, that takes care of the universities. Moving on to the press.

There is a simple way for the state to separate itself from the press: adopt the same public communication policies used in private companies. Perhaps the leader in this area is that progressive favorite, Apple. This Google search[12] tells the story. Apple is unusual in that it actually has many deranged fans who want to extract nonpublic information, but of course the same can be said of governments.

All private companies in the known universe, however, have the same policy: any unauthorized communication with anyone outside the company, "journalist" or otherwise, is a firing offense. Often it will also expose you to litigation. Somehow, even Apple manages to be quite successful in enforcing this policy. In general, it simply doesn't happen. If you are familiar with the area of technology journalism,

---

11 Reference to the Civil Service Exam.
12 "Apple leak lawsuit," in reference to a 2006 story about a leak pertaining to the company's "Asteroid" music device.

you know that far from making for dull news, the rarity of leaks makes for extremely spicy and scurrilous trade rags—such as this one.[13] The day US foreign policy is reported à la Register is the day the Cathedral is no more.

When it comes to significant operational details that might affect a company's stock price, leaking information—whether authorized or not—is actually a *crime*. As well it should be. Managements used to be free to leak to the investment community, but this loophole was closed in one of the few positive changes in corporate law in recent years, **Reg FD**.[14]

The reasoning behind Reg FD is excellent. The problem with selective disclosure of financial information is that it creates a power loop between management and selected investors, allowing big fish to benefit from inside information that is more or less a payoff. It still happens, I'm sure—the edges of "material information" are fuzzy—but much less. Ideally, Reg FD would be extended to prohibit *any* informal communication with Wall Street. If a company has something to say, its Web site is the place to do it.

In government, selective disclosure creates a power network between the press and its sources. This network does not produce money, but just power. The power is shared between the sources and the journalists. The whole system is about as transparent as mud.

The case that created the modern American system of government by leak was the Pentagon Papers case, in which McNamara's policy shop at DoD (ironically, the ancestor of **Douglas Feith**'s much-maligned operation) wrote a study of Vietnam which revealed that the Viet Cong was not a North Vietnamese puppet, had the support of the Vietnamese people, and could never be defeated militarily, especially not by the corrupt and incompetent ARVN. The Joint Chiefs yawned. **Daniel Ellsberg** quite illegally leaked his own department's work to the Times, which used it quite effectively to amaze the public—which had no idea that Washington was a place in which the Defense Department might well employ whole nests of pro-VC intellectuals, and regarded the study as a **declaration against interest**. In the public's mind, the Pentagon was one thing. The fact that it was pursuing a war that its own experts had decided was unwinnable was permanently fatal to its credibility.

The Supreme Court **ruled**[15] that the Pentagon could not restrain publication of the study. They did not rule that the Times could not be prosecuted after the fact. But of course it never was. The coup had been accomplished. A new phase of the Fourth Republic was born. Later, the ARVN **defeated** the Viet Cong, whose "support" was based on **brutal terror**, and which was indeed no more than an **arm of the NVA**. No one cared. Doubtless Ellsberg's conscience was quite genuine,

---

13 [QR code]

14 Full Disclosure Rules
15 *New York Times Co. v. United States* (1971)

but facts matter. There's a fine line between speaking truth to power and speaking power to truth.

These hidden power networks (I am particularly enchanted by the word "whistleblower," which often simply means "informer") are one of the main tools that civil servants use to govern Washington from below. As a journalist, you maintain a complicated and delicate relationship with your sources, who are your bread and butter. Most of the power is probably on the side of the sources, but it goes in the other direction as well. In any case, no "investigative" journalist has to "investigate" anything—anyone in the government is perfectly happy to feed him not just information, but often what are essentially prewritten stories, under the table.

Eliminating selective disclosure terminates this whole nefarious network. When the US Government has something to say, it says it. And it says it to all Americans at the same time. There is no privileged network of court historians (a journalist is a historian of now) who get secret, special access. This is not a complicated proposition. (The system of officially favored journalists, like so many corruptions of American government, dates largely to FDR. Frankly, these swine have afflicted us too long.)

So that is the soft reset: the separation of education and state. It doesn't sound too hard, does it? Actually, I think it's impossible. Now that we've explained it, we can look at what's wrong with it.

Consider another attempt to deal with the Cathedral—McCarthyism. One could call it a *crude reset*. The idea was that, while all of these institutions were good and healthy and true, they had been infiltrated by Communists and their dupes. Purging these individuals and organizations—listed in publications such as *Red Channels*—would renew America's precious bodily fluids.[16]

Can purging work? One answer is provided by La Wik's page on McCarthyism, which could be rewritten as follows:

> During this time many thousands of Americans were accused of being racists or racist sympathizers and became the subject of aggressive investigations and questioning before government or private-industry panels, committees and agencies. Suspicions were often given credence despite inconclusive or questionable evidence, and the level of threat posed by a person's real or supposed racist associations or beliefs was often greatly exaggerated. Many people suffered loss of employment, destruction of their careers, and even imprisonment.

So, in place of *Red Channels*, we have the SPLC, and so on. The "Racist Scare" cannot be called a failure. It is socially unacceptable to express racist ideas in any context I can think of. There are certainly no racist movies, TV shows, etc. The McCarthyists no doubt would have been quite pleased if they could have made

---

16 *Dr. Strangelove* (1964).

socialism as politically incorrect as racism is today. They never had a millionth of the power they would have needed to do so.

The obvious inspiration for McCarthyism was the way in which the New Deal had succeeded in marginalizing and destroying its critics. If you're the Cathedral, this works. If you're an alcoholic senator scripted by a gay child prodigy,[17] it doesn't.

McCarthyism failed for many reasons, but the most succinct is what Machiavelli said: if you strike at a king, you need to kill him. The Cathedral is an institution rather than a person, and certainly no one needs killing. But if you just scratch it, you're just pissing it off. If McCarthy had said: look, we fought the war in the Pacific to save China from the Japanese, and then the State Department handed it to the Russians, this is a failed organization, let's just dissolve it and build a new foreign-policy bureaucracy—he might have succeeded. He was a very popular man for a while. He might well have been able to build enough public support to liquidate State. Or not. But if he'd succeeded, he would at least have one accomplishment to his name.

The soft reset I've described is, with all due respect to Roy Cohn, a much more sophisticated and comprehensive way to attack the Cathedral. It might work. But it probably won't.

First, the power structures that bind the Cathedral to the rest of the Apparat are not formal. They are mere social networks. If Professor Burke is right that he has real influence in the region he and his colleagues have devastated—southern Africa—it is probably because he has trained quite a few students who work at State or in NGOs in the area. (If he is wrong, all it means is that it's someone else who has the influence.) Short of firing all these people, there is nothing you can do about this structure. You can't prevent people from emailing each other.

Second, even if we could break down these social networks, we haven't touched the real problem. The real problem is that, as a political form, *democracy* is more or less a synonym for *theocracy*. (Or, in this case, atheocracy.) Under the theory of popular sovereignty, those who control public opinion control the government.

There is no nation of autodidact philosophers. Call them priests, preachers, professors, bishops, teachers, commissars or journalists—the botmasters will rule. The only way to escape the domination of canting, moralizing apparatchiks is to abandon the principle of *vox populi, vox dei*, and return to a system in which government is immune to the mental fluctuations of the masses. A secure, responsible and effective government may listen to its residents, but it has no reason to either obey or indoctrinate them. In turn, their minds are not jammed by the gaseous emanations of those who would seize power by mastering the mob.

So if you manage the Herculean task of separating Cathedral and state, but leave both intact, you have no reason to think that the same networks will not just form over again. In fact, you have every reason to believe that they will.

---

17 Roy Cohn

Third, and worst, the level of political power you would need to execute a soft reset is precisely the same level of power you would need to execute a hard reset. That is: full power, absolute sovereignty, total dictatorship, whatever you want to call it. Except inasmuch as it might be easier to construct a coalition to mandate a soft reset, softness has no advantage. The people who presently enjoy power will resist both with the same energy—all the energy they have. If you have the power to overcome them, why settle for half measures?

In a hard reset, we converge legality and reality not by adjusting reality to conform to the First Amendment, but by adjusting the law to recognize the reality of government power.

First, a hard reset only makes sense with the definition we gave in Chapter 8: unconditional replacement of all government employees. This will break up your social networks. A hard reset should also be part of a transition to some post-democratic form of government, or the same problems will reoccur. But this is a long-term issue.

Most important, however, in a hard reset we actually *expand* the definition of government. As we've seen, the nominally-independent educational organs, the press and the universities, are the heart of power in America today. They make decisions and manufacture the consent to ratify them. Fine. They want to be part of the government? Make them part of the government.

In a hard reset, all organizations dedicated to forming public opinion, making or implementing public policy, or working in the public interest, are *nationalized*. This includes not only the press and the universities, but also the foundations, NGOs, and other nonprofits. It is a bit rich, after all, for any of these outfits to appeal to the sanctity of property rights. They believe in the sanctity of property rights about as much as they believe in the goddess Kali.

Once they are nationalized, treat them as the public schools were treated in the soft reset. Retire their employees and liquidate their assets. Universities in particular have lovely campuses, many of which are centrally located and should be quite attractive to developers.

The trademarks, however, should be retained and sunk. The former employees of the New York Times can organize and start a newspaper. The former employees of Harvard can organize and start a college. But the former can't call it the New York Times nor the latter Harvard, any more than you or I could create a publication or a college with those names.

The goal of nationalization in a hard reset is not to create official information organs under central control. It is not even to prevent political opponents of a new regime from networking. It is simply to destroy the existing power structure, and in particular to liquidate the **reputation capital** that these institutions hold at present.

Harvard and the Times are authorities. Silly as it sounds, their prestige is simply associated with their names. If some former employees of the Times put up a website and call it, say, the *New York Journal*, no one knows anything about this

Journal. Is it telling the truth? Or is it a fountain of lies? It has to be evaluated on its actual track record.

If the old regime still exists, it could be restored at any moment. However you manage to construct the level of power you would need in order to reset Washington, or any other modern government, broad public opinion will be a significant component of your power base. In a reset, you want to construct this coalition once. You don't want to have to maintain it. Wresting public opinion away from the Cathedral is hard enough. It should not be an ongoing process, especially since the whole point is to ditch this black art of managing the mass mind.

In the Cathedral system, real power is held by the educational organs, the press and the universities, which are nominally outside the government proper. The minimum intervention required to disrupt this system is to withdraw official recognition from the press and the universities. However, any regime that has the power to do this also has the power to liquidate them, along with all other extra-governmental institutions. It is much safer to go this extra mile, rather than leaving the former Cathedral and its various satellites intact and angry.

Most of the historical precedents for this type of operation are pre-20th century. However, before the 20th century, systematic liquidation of information organs was quite common. Henry VIII's **dissolution of the monasteries** is an excellent example. Slightly farther afield, we have the **suppression of the Jesuits**. And in the 20th century, though less comparable, we have **denazification**.

Of course, these steps are all unbelievably extreme by modern American standards. All this means is that they will not happen unless those standards change. And this will not happen until Americans, "Progressive" and "Fundamentalist" alike, are convinced that their government is indisputably malignant and incapable of self-correction, and the only way to improve it is to replace it completely.

And how could this be accomplished? Obviously, it can't be.

229 *Carlton Hayes A Political and Social History of Modern Europe.* (Macmillan Company, 1924).

 230 *theosophy*

 230 *Dogs and cats, living together!* YouTube clip of Bill Murray in *Ghostbusters* (1984).

 231 *legendary Columbia historian* Link to a 1950 Time Magazine article about the beloved Professor Hayes' retirement from Columbia. "Education: Last Class." *Time*, 30 Jan 1950.

 232 *supersect* "Ant colony"

 233 *Imagine*

 233 *James Watson*

 234 *transcript of an interview* James Watson, inter. by Henry Louis Gates. "Color Controversy and DNA." *The Root*, 2 Jun. 2008.

 234 *Henry Louis Gates*

 234 *here* The original link is dead, and the video no longer seems to exist on the web. The article can still be read at the archived link provided here. Henry Louis Gates Jr. "The Science of Racism." *The Root*, 2 Jun. 2008.

 234 *struggle session*

 234 *predictable responses* Razib Khan. "Henry Louis Gates Jr. Interviews James Watson." *Gene Expression*, The Unz Review, 2 Jun. 2008.

 234 *Andrei Sakharov*

 235 *Torres Vedras*

AN OPEN LETTER TO OPEN-MINDED PROGRESSIVES 247

 235 plenty of evidence J. Philippe Rushton and Arthur Jensen. "Thirty Years of Research on Race Differences in Cognitive Ability." *Psychology, Public Policy, and Law*, 2005. Vol. 11, No. 2, p. 235-294.

 236 neo-primitive Christianity "History of Christianity"

 236 Inner Light

 236 hate speech Adam Liptak. "Unlike Others, U.S. Defends Freedom to Offend in Speech." *New York Times*, 12 Jun 2008.

 236 blasphemy

 236 Margaret Atwood

 236 Testimony of Equality

 236 right ordering "Quakers"

 237 continuum Carl von Clausewitz. *On War*. (Kegan Paul, Trench, Trübner & Co., 1908).

 238 Tony Blair "Blair on the media." Reuters speech on public life, 12 Jun. 2007.

 239 with applause Timothy Burke. "I Agree!" *Easily Distracted*, 14 May 2008.

 239 how this works Patricia Nelson Limerick. "Tales of Western Adventure." *The Chronicle of Higher Education*, 9 May 2008.

 239 Ms. Latte The oldest available archive of Latte Island is provided in the link here. None of the posts referenced in the chapter can be found, however.

239 with the EPA Patricia Limerick, author of the Chronicle of Higher Ed article supra, poses with Steven Johnson, Administrator of the EPA, on the occasion of a speech she delivered at the agency's annual meeting. Robert E. Roberts. "Patty Limerick Protects the Environment." *Center West newsletter*, University of Colorado Boulder.

240 competitive examination "Civil Service Entrance Exam"

240 Google search Link to Google search for "Apple leak bloggers lawsuit" which at the time of publication would have reliably returned results for the incident referenced in the footnote.

241 this one Link to the Register.com, an insider technology news site founded in 1998.

241 Reg FD "Full Disclosure Rules." *Invest FAQ*.

241 Douglas Feith

241 Daniel Ellsberg

241 declaration against interest

241 ruled "New York Times Co. v. United States"

241 defeated Link to a letter to the editor of the New York Times, from Charles Hill, assistant to Ambassador Ellsworth Bunker in Saigon, supporting the claim of Lewis Sorley in his book *A Better War* (1999) that our efforts to defeat the Viet Cong through "Vietnamization" had been successful.

241 brutal terror "Massacre at Hue," also appearing in Chapter 5.

241 arm of the NVA

242 McCarthyism

AN OPEN LETTER TO OPEN-MINDED PROGRESSIVES

 242 *Red Channels*

 242 *precious bodily fluids* Video clip from *Dr. Strangelove or: How I Learned to Stop Worrying and Love the Bomb* (1964).

 243 *gay child prodigy* "Roy Cohn"

 244 *reputation capital*

 245 *dissolution of the monasteries*

 245 *suppression of the Jesuits*

 245 *denazification*

CHAPTER X:
A SIMPLE SOVEREIGN BANKRUPTCY PROCEDURE
JUNE 19, 2008

Dear open-minded progressive, as we reach Chapter X it is time for some administrivia.

First, we are switching to Roman numerals. At least past 10, they are just classier. Also, if anyone wants to provide design suggestions, or what would be even more super-duper graphics, logos, templates, free hosting, free money, free beer, or even just free parenting advice, they may of course contact me at the usual address, linked to over on the right.[1]

I would note, however, that my email responsiveness of late has been unusually poor. In fact, it has been amazingly poor. For some reason I had entertained the idea that being chained to my daughter would enable me to actually *catch up* with the large number of extremely interesting and well-written epistles sitting unanswered, many a few months old, in my inbox. You see why UR is not a good source of financial advice.

However, my daughter is three months old today. (And her 8ra1n is growing like a prize melon—she pops out of the 0–6 month hats, she is firmly in the 6–9.) She may not scream less, but it seems like she screams less. So I will attempt to work into the pile, probably in reverse order.

Second, there is a second awful truth, which is that for my daughter's whole life, I haven't even been reading UR's comments section. This is a deed so shameful it is probably unknown in the Western world. In case you accept excuses, however, my excuse is that it is a sort of crude literary device. If it was written in response to

---

1 Moldbug originally had his home address displayed on his blogger site.

its weekly feedback—which, in the past, has often proved much more interesting than the post—UR would be very different. Chattier, more bloggy, and I suspect less interesting. Or so I claim. We'll never know, though, will we?

I will even be brazen enough to suspect that if I were reading them, the comments would not be quite as good. I do get the impression they haven't degenerated into mindless Web nonsense, puerile flamage, Jew-baiting and ads for spineless anal balloons. But if there is any such content I of course disclaim it. After I am done with this series I will edit out any and all stupid comments. If they are all stupid, there will be none left. Ha. As Terence Stamp put it: "Kneel before Zod! Kneel!"

I will, however, attempt a collective response to the non-stupid comments, unless they are so devastating as to leave me speechless. Please continue leaving them. You may not be enlightening me, at least not immediately, but you are enlightening others.

And speaking of **General Zod**: if you are finally resolved to consider yourself a pathetic dupe of the Mold, you are of course free to either describe or not describe yourself as a formalist, a reservationist, a restorationist, or even a Mencist. This last coinage sounds faintly ominous and evil, which of course is not true—Mencism is all happiness, smiles, and light. In turn, however, be prepared for the fact that anyone can accuse you, with perfect accuracy, of neo-Birchery, postfalangism, pseudo-Hobbesianism or even rampant moldbuggery. To paraphrase Barack Obama: if you don't have a knife, don't start a knifefight.

If I had to choose one word and stick with it, I'd pick "restorationist." If I have to concede one pejorative which fair writers can fairly apply, I'll go with "reactionary." I'll even answer to any compound of the latter—"neoreactionary," "postreactionary," "ultrareactionary," etc.

So when I call someone a "progressive," what I mean is that his or her creed is more or less the direct opposite of mine. Of course, we both believe that the sky is blue, apple pie is delicious, and Hitler was evil. And since we are both polite, mature, and open-minded people, we can converse despite our disagreements. But just as there is no such thing as a progressive reactionary, there is no such thing as a progressive restorationist. Or vice versa.

I am comfortable using the word "progressive" because, and only because, I know of no significant population of English speakers for whom it conveys negative connotations. Similarly, when speaking not of the ideas but of the set of people who hold these ideas (or, as they like to put it, "ideals"), the name **Brahmin** is time-honored and nonpejorative.

This is not a reference to the **Tam-Brams**. In fact, there is a fine practical definition of Brahmin in this video, which is long (15 minutes) but I feel worth watching: **Barack Speaks To HQ Staff & Volunteers**.[2]

2

AN OPEN LETTER TO OPEN-MINDED PROGRESSIVES

This is, of course, internal video from the Obama campaign. I don't think it was leaked. I think it was intentionally published, and so it has to be taken with a grain of salt. However, the people in it are all their real selves. For once, they are not acting. I recognize the meeting. It reminds me a lot of the first post-IPO meeting at the tech-bubble company I worked for.

There is one main difference: a few more blacks (and nowhere near so many Tamils). A few more. And the camera eye, hilariously, stalks and pounces on all the diversity it can find. But it cannot conceal the horrible truth: almost everyone inside the Good One's campaign is white. Maybe one in fifteen is black. Maybe one in twenty. Definitely not one in ten. And I suspect many of these hold positions for which melanin is a job requirement, i.e., working with the "community."

And weirdly, given this explanation, there are no, no, no Mexicans. Okay, maybe one or two. The video is grainy. It's hard to tell a Jeremiah Wright from a Cuauhtémoc Cárdenas. But I live in San Francisco, I am quite accustomed to encountering a progressive population with a strong Aztlanic contingent (SF State is, after all, the home of the notorious **Third World Strike**), and I ain't seeing it. (And isn't that **maneuver with Patti Solis Doyle**[3] charming? Doesn't that just show you the maturity level of the whole organization?)

Bell curves being what they are, you need one thing to achieve the Obama team's rarefied whiteness: an ultra-competitive, race-neutral employee filtering process. These people could be the audience at your average Google tech talk. Everyone in the room, whatever their skin color, is not just a Brahmin but a high Brahmin, a status held by anyone obviously smart enough to get a Ph.D., MD, etc., from a top school.

There is no mainstream American university whose general student body is anywhere near this segregated. Or anywhere near this *31337*,[4] I suspect. I wonder why that is. Isn't it curious, then, that so much of Obama's support should come from our wonderful universities, to which "diversity" is so important?

Surely, dear open-minded progressive, one can disagree honestly on whether employment decisions should be made on the basis of skin color. It is after all a **Humean ought**. Given how unusual the idea of racial preferences for colored people would have sounded to the Americans of, say, 1908, don't you find it a little unusual that there should be so little, um, variation, in all of these supposedly-independent decisions in Humean ought space, as produced by our glorious variety of supposedly-independent universities?

But I should be fair to pre-President Obama—whom I really like calling the Good One. I feel that if this locution could be persuaded to spread, it might be of some benefit to humanity. Needless to say, I don't mean it satirically.

Because after watching the clip above, my impression is that the Good One is exactly that: good. That is, he is good at his job, which is all you can ask of anyone.

---

3 Obama's selection of Doyle as his campaign chief-of-staff was seen as a direct insult to Hillary Clinton, with one Democratic operative calling it "The biggest 'Fuck you' ever."
4 "Elite"

More precisely, he talks like a competent manager. If I were working in at a startup and I had a boss who gave pep talks this good, I'd feel quite comfortable with the administration. Management is more than just talk, but can you call the Obama campaign anything but a successful operation? The graphic design alone is brilliant.

There is only one problem: this outfit is very good at winning presidential elections. We have no reason to think it is any good at anything else. The candidate is a great presidential candidate. He will probably be a good president, too. Of course, that is to say he will be good at reading his lines and pretending to be an 18th-century statesman, which is the job of a US President in 2008. Perhaps we should just write in Paul Giamatti, who I'm sure could act the Good One off the stage.

Moreover, the Nazis had an effective campaign team, too. Plus some pretty good graphic design to go with it. Most people don't know it, but the SS dress uniform was designed by **Hugo Boss**. If design is your criterion, the Third Reich was the best government of the century. In fact, even if *architecture* is your criterion, I will take Nazi architecture over progressive architecture, any day of the week and twice on Sundays.

And since the quality of architecture is indeed a good rule of thumb on which to judge the general quality of government, this is worrisome indeed. But all it means is that the case is an exception to the rule. Like anyone with any sense, I'd rather be governed by progressives than by Nazis.

(Nazis matter, because a Nazi-like outcome is the most catastrophic failure mode of any restoration effort. Restorationism is to fascism as a bridge is to a pile of rubble in the riverbed. Bridge collapses can be dangerous and unpleasant, but that doesn't make bridges a bad idea.)

But comparing one's enemies to Nazis is old hat. Progressivism has a much better match on the other pole of the totalitarian continuum. The meter lights up like a Christmas tree and the little arm goes all the way to the right. Or left, as it were.

Recently in a used bookstore I found five issues of *Soviet Life* from the midlate '80s. I had not previously been aware of this publication. I find it quite revealing. Unfortunately for me but fortunately for you, someone has already scanned **three whole issues** of *Soviet Life*. So I will not bore you with my endless, Gollum-like chortling over this bibliomanic coup.

But I thought it'd be fun to share one sweet little piece, from January 1986. Of course, this is a news story, not an ad. (No advertisements sully the pages of *Soviet Life*.)

> Georgian plastic surgeon Dr. Vakhtang Khutsidze helps people look younger. Just look at **Edith Markson**. Would you believe she is 72? Of course not. She is an attractive woman who looks many years younger than her actual age. That's what happens after treatment with **Dr. Khutsidze**, many of his satisfied patients maintain.

AN OPEN LETTER TO OPEN-MINDED PROGRESSIVES 255

Edith Markson, who has spent several years in the Soviet Union, heard about Dr. Khutsidze's skillful hands when she was in Tbilisi visiting a few of her theater friends. It was then she decided to have cosmetic surgery. Particularly since, as she told local reporters, a face lift would cost several thousand dollars back home in the States. In the USSR the operation costs from 30 to 100 rubles.

"I'm an ordinary American," Edith Markson said, "and I'm not responsible for official policymaking. Making friends with people from many countries is the best human politics. And now I've added Vakhtang Khutsidze, the Georgian doctor, to my list of friends."

Twenty-five years ago Dr. Khutsidze was one of the first plastic surgeons in the Soviet Union to use the so-called sparing method in nose operations. Ever since then he has performed approximately thousands of these operations. His work, which requires expert surgical skill, has a lot in common with sculpture, the surgeon maintains.

(Please don't skip the Edith Markson links—they really round out the episode.[5] The *Soviet Life* article comes with its own photograph, but I feared younger readers might find it disturbing. Although, frankly, the results are pretty good for "30 to 100 rubles.")

Then, for maximum disorienting effect, skip directly to this Times story[6]—which appeared on Tuesday. Do you notice any resemblance? Any at all? Obama, Prince Royal of the Blood, beloved by all God's children but especially the colored ones, from Bolivia to Clichy-sous-Bois?[7] What is he, the second coming of Comrade Brezhnev? Is the Times going to continue this kind of coverage after he's elected? That would really be turning the obvious up to 11.

I especially love how the Times' last piece describes Edith Markson as if she were an ordinary retiree, perhaps a cashier at Macy's or as a dental hygienist, who just happens to have moved to Manhattan in her late '70s "despite the fear of crime, grime, and hassles in the city that never sleeps":

> Edith Markson stumbled and crash-landed on the sidewalk in Greenwich Village shortly after her return to New York more than a year ago. The badly injured 80-year-old woman was spotted by

---

5 See Chapter endnotes, "Edith Markson."

6 [QR code]

7 Clichy-sous-Bois was the epicenter of the 2005 French riots, ignited by "alienation" and "lack of opportunity" of and for France's vibrant youth.

CHAPTER X

two homeless men, one of whom swooped her in his arms and majestically carried her one block to a nearby medical laboratory.

Even in old age, with a mending broken hip and a metal valve in her ailing heart, Mrs. Markson is surprised at how uplifting New York City can be. Coaxed back here from San Francisco by anxious relatives who wanted to keep an eye on her, she has found that the city has much to offer an "old lady" like herself.

"It's wonderful to know when you really get into trouble, somebody will come to help you," said Mrs. Markson, a widow who had left New York for what she thought was the last time four years ago. Instead, she now lives in a midtown Manhattan apartment where the management installed bars on her bathtub and security guards occasionally check on her.

Despite the fear of crime, grime and hassles in the city that never sleeps, experts say Mrs. Markson is one of a growing number of retirees who are bucking decades-old migration patterns by actually moving to New York for its quality of life.

Words fail me, dear open-minded progressive, they really do. As my wife, who happens to be a playwright in the city where Edith Markson's little theater company,[8] now essentially a permanent branch of the US Government, remains the *31337*, puts it: "does a theater promoter ever really retire?"

And the fact that the two "homeless men" "scooped her up" not just lovingly, not just respectfully, not just adoringly, but no less than "majestically," really takes the cake. Presumably they carry around spare Burger King crowns, to supply stumbling princesses of the arts with the requisite majesty.

I assert, dear open-minded progressive, that attempting to understand the world of today by reading the New York Times (and its fellow authorized channels) is a lot like trying to understand the Soviet Union by reading *Soviet Life*. Any such publication will be informative to a trained student of the period. But a proper appreciation of its real meaning requires significant independent understanding and a willingness to—dare I say it—deconstruct.

For example, the wonderful story of Edith Markson shows us that even still in 1986, the social networks in which a New York Times reporter might travel actually connected *into* the Soviet Union. At least, to her great new friend, Vakhtang Khutsidze—and to the hip young apparatchik who wrote them both up for *Soviet Life*.

Historically this Greenwich Village connection had always run straight from the Cathedral's high Brahmins to the Soviet *nomenklatura*—a word that explains Ms. Markson and Dr. Khutsidze with equal precision. By the '80s this, like everything else about the Warsaw Pact, was fraying—but what is Red October without

---

[8] The American Conservatory Theater in San Francisco, one of the biggest in the country.

John Reed?[9] Flash forward to Judge Guevara,[10] and it is all so perfectly clear. It looks like the same thing because it *is* the same thing.

Moreover, if you read the political essays in *Soviet Life*—about a third of the magazine seems to be political content—you realize that the Edith Marksons of the world followed, and did their level best to persuade everyone else to follow, the exact same party line on every political topic that appears in any of my *Soviet Life* issues, from the nuclear freeze to the Middle East to the abominable persecution of the black man.

Of course this last horror, our vast Caucasian conspiracy, has persisted to this day. It almost cost the Good One the nomination. Etc. Etc. Do I really need to mock this any further? But if you are still not convinced, there are always the O-Ba-Ma videos...

Dear open-minded progressive: frankly, progressivism is just creepy. Do you really want to associate yourself with it? And if the answer is yes, do you think you'll still want to be associated with it after the Good One's vigorous, musky buttocks have spent a year or two in George W. Bush's Aeron?

If the answer is still yes, I'm afraid you are just not spiritually prepared for the grueling mental ordeal that follows. Deep down inside, you are still a hippie. At the very least, do not continue reading this essay without at least one massive bong hit. Frankly, you'll need it.

Because finally, there are the lines for which the Good One will always, I feel, be known:

> I face this challenge with profound humility, and knowledge of my own limitations. But I also face it with limitless faith in the capacity of the American people. Because if we are willing to work for it, and fight for it, and believe in it, then I am absolutely certain that generations from now, we will be able to look back and tell our children that this was the moment when we began to provide care for the sick and good jobs to the jobless; this was the moment when the rise of the oceans began to slow and our planet began to heal; this was the moment when we ended a war and secured our nation and restored our image as the last, best hope on Earth.

Some people are inspired by this kind of emanation. If you are one, how can I fault you? You are probably a pretty nice guy, or gal. There is probably something else in your life besides the Good One—or, of course, his Good Causes. As your

---

9 Journalist, communist activist, and author of *Ten Days that Shook the World* (1919) about the 1917 Revolution.

10

attorney, I recommend a real effort to figure out what that thing might be. And maybe focus on it a little more.

For the rest of us, let me note merely that at present, the oceans' cold and inexorable rise, the salty revenge of Gaia's tears, the wave looming over Manhattan, is **three millimeters per year.** This puts us well within the new DSM-IV guidelines for **fulminating hydrophobia.** And I see no reason to tolerate such systematic servility to such a blatant case of contagious hypochondria.

This suggests a trivial test, a sort of *pons asinorum*, for any potential restoration. I suggest that as its initial act, any responsible and effective transitional government will set its tone and establish its good faith by assisting the Good One, along with his wife, his people, his wife's people, and frankly anyone who for whatever reason chooses to accompany him, to transfer their lives, pleasantly and with a minimum of personal disruption, to the Good One's scenic paternal homeland: the great African nation of Kenya.

It's entirely possible that Kenya will demand compensation for accepting this crowd. While hard to count in advance, it could easily number in the millions. If so, there is a simple solution: ask the Kenyans how much they want, and pay it. Think of it as a small but symbolic reparation for the vast tragedy of postcolonial Africa.

Of course, there would be no hard feelings on either side of this expatriation. In fact, the Kenyans might well make the Good One president-for-life. His people, the Luo, are riding high these days. And I actually think the Good One might prove a wonderful ruler of Kenya, which if **troubled** remains one of the **most beautiful countries on earth.**

For open-minded progressives who doubt that deporting political opponents has anything to do with responsible, effective government—the value of selective relocation as a security measure can hardly be doubted, of course—I have a question for you.

I'm going to play a magic trick. I'm going to pick a historical period in the recent past, in the memory of many of those now living. And I'm going to pick two sources of information. To you, source A will be a source of automatic, near-absolute reliability. To you, source B will be a blatant outlet of mendacious propaganda, produced by some of the nastiest people in history.

But on the major issue on which the two disagreed, hindsight has provided an answer. At least in my opinion, it is impossible to argue the proposition that source A was right and source B was wrong. And it is trivial to argue the converse. To even debate the issue is a sign of complete detachment from reality. Quite simply, B was right and A was wrong. Even Professor Burke admits it.[11]

11

AN OPEN LETTER TO OPEN-MINDED PROGRESSIVES

Our period is 1965 through 1980. Our source A is the *international press corps*.[12] Our source B is the *Rhodesian Ministry of Information*.[13] Our issue is the perspective of postcolonial African governments in general, the liberation movements in specific, and Robert Mugabe to be exact.

Dear open-minded progressive, if you can produce any explanation of this trust failure which is coherent, scholarly, realistic, and consistent with progressive ideals, I will admit defeat. Please do remember that extraordinary claims require extraordinary evidence. I don't like to hear hypotheses that involve UFOs, international Jewish conspiracies, Freemasons, or the like.

In fact, let's whale on UR's favorite crash-test dummy, Professor Burke, for a little while here. As I've said, this man (an assistant professor at Swarthmore) is my current case study for the fundamentally and irreparably evil character of the Cathedral. He comes across as a perfectly nice guy, of course, and I suspect that's exactly what he is. So was Albert Speer, who once wrote that you can't expect to recognize the Devil when he puts his hand on your shoulder.

You probably think it's excessive to compare Burke to Speer. Oh, no. Think again:

> The really major thing, I think, is that the Soweto uprising of 1976 and subsequent campaigns to make South Africa's townships "ungovernable" put the apartheid regime under what proved to be unbearable pressure, largely on the pure grounds of resource limitations. The apartheid state simply couldn't cope in the end with the demands that ungovernability put upon it, even when it put up a pretty good show of having everything under a tight authoritarian lid. Few of us saw this clearly in 1986–87 precisely because the state was putting on such a good performance, but underneath, the leadership was increasingly seeing collapse as inevitable.
>
> Let's review what led to ungovernability. The vast majority of the population without any vote or democratic outlet. An authoritarian state that legally defined almost all dissent as terrorism and gave itself entitlement to retaliate against dissent with imprisonment, torture, and murder. A state which routinely censored all media. A state which ignored property rights of most of its citizens. In short, a state which was in every respect the antithesis of

12

13

liberalism, in which there was literally no avenue for democratic or liberal protest for the vast majority of its citizens.

Let's review what ungovernability consisted of. Refusal to cooperate with any institution controlled directly or indirectly by the national government. So leaving school, refusing to pay any rents or fees assessed by governmental bodies, refusal to comply with orders from authorities no matter how routine those orders might be, and an embrace of violent resistance to the state and any perceived agents of the state. Making large areas of the country "no-go" areas for civil authorities unless they were accompanied by strong military forces. Murder or threat of murder of suspected collaborators.

As I said, I think it worked. I think it was justified not just because it worked but because there were no other alternatives. The apartheid state and the National Party spent twenty years steadily crushing all other avenues for political change and rewriting the laws and constitution of South Africa so as to define itself as the permanent and unchanging ruler of South Africa.

That's right. Our sweet, jocular D&D-playing history professor has just endorsed the practice of putting car tires full of gasoline around his fellow humans' necks, then **lighting them afire**.[14] I wonder how many d6 of damage that attack does?

(Professor Burke's historical analysis is also self-serving in the extreme. The proximate cause of the end of apartheid was the **1992 referendum** in which a majority of whites effectively voted to hand over their country to the ANC, a decision they would never have taken if they could have known the consequences. This was the victory of the *verligte* or "enlightened" Afrikaners over their *verkrampte* or "narrow" cousins. In other words, it is best seen as a triumph of psychological warfare. No points for telling us who was enlightening the "enlightened.")

As for the wonderful omelet cooked from these eggs, see this **BBC documentary**,[15] whose title is misleading (the BBC doesn't really mean that the "international community" should never again hand over a First World country to the well-spoken frontman of a **murderous**[16] gang), but whose **transcript** is glorious:

> KEANE: But you see here's what I can't understand, and I've known this country for a long time. It's just the ease with which people kill nowadays.

---

14 "Necklacing," a means of public execution in 80's South Africa, explicitly encouraged by Winnie Mandela, wife of Nelson.
15 *No More Mandelas* (2008), the 40-minute documentary is no longer available online.
16 Reference to the African National Congress, which was responsible for a number of terrorist attacks throughout the 80's.

AN OPEN LETTER TO OPEN-MINDED PROGRESSIVES

YOUTH: Yeah.

KEANE: How did that happen?

YOUTH: When I get up, I can go to town or I can took your car.

KEANE: Would it bother you to kill me to get the car?

YOUTH: If you don't want to give me your keys I'll kill you. It's nothing to kill you because of what.. I need the money to survive. You see I need more money. You see it feels like using a gun there's no feeling. There's no feeling. It's just yourself, you're the big boss. You got a gun, no one will tell you shit or f*** you. No one can tell you f*** you. If you said f*** me, I took out my firearm and I shoot you in your ears, then what will you say? You're dead! I will took all the things. If you don't get money, if you don't get a car you're nothing.

KEANE: Do you think that the life that you're living and the way that you're carrying on is what Mandela...

YOUTH: But...

KEANE: No, but hang on a second, is this what Mandela spent 27 years in jail for so you could go around killing people?

YOUTHS: No. No.

KEANE: So why do you still do it?

YOUTH: Because we want money. Listen, listen to me, because it's money. I have to rob this thing now.

KEANE: You want to rob the camera?

YOUTH: Yeah.

KEANE: You could do that, if you wanted, I know you could do that, but it wouldn't achieve any purpose. You might have money for a day and it's just brought trouble on you.

When they suggested stealing the camera we decided to leave. Crime is being fuelled by another legacy of apartheid, poverty. There is democracy, free speech and economic growth. But real wealth is in the hands of the few. Even though millions more now access electricity and water, two million new homes have been built and there are grants for the poorest of the poor, the growing economy hasn't delivered jobs. Official figures say 25% are out of work, though many economists estimate it could be as high as 40%. Millions of South Africans still live in squatter camps.

Sunday afternoon in Soweto:

How many of you live in this shed?

WOMAN: Four.

KEANE: What do you feel about the life you have here?

WOMAN: (translated) Life here isn't good. We've no electricity and so we have to use paraffin which makes the children sick.

KEANE: Do you ever think your life is going to get better, Joseph?

JOSEPH: Maybe my life would change if the Nationalist party came back, not the ANC.

KEANE: I don't believe you, come on, it was a white government that put you down, that treated you terribly. You can't really believe that.

JOSEPH: But in terms of work they didn't oppress us. We didn't struggle for work then.

KEANE: Now do I really think that he is serious about wanting a white government back? I don't think so. Not back to the days of forced removals and passbooks and all of that. But I'll tell you what it does do, when you listen to somebody expressing that kind of anger and frustration, you really get a sense of how the ANC, the people at the top, the elite, have drifted away from their core constituency, the people of the squatter camps, South Africa's dispossessed.

The ANC has indeed drifted away from its core constituency. But that constituency has nothing to do with "Joseph" or "Youth." It consists of Fergal Keane and Timothy Burke. And of course, a few others like them. (Unlike Albert Speer, all these individuals are replaceable.)

What we're seeing here is a power structure which has lost its connection to reality. Its rulers consider it the most ethical and responsible system of government in human history. In fact, it is morally and intellectually bankrupt.

There is no simple procedure for moral and intellectual restructuring. However, this system of government is not just morally and intellectually bankrupt. It is also *financially* bankrupt. This is a disaster, of course, but it gives us a concrete way to think about fixing all three of these problems at once.

A *restoration* is a regime-change procedure designed to safely and effectively reverse the damage which progressivism has inflicted on civilization, acting under the principles of good government that prevailed in theory, if not always in practice, in the late classical or Victorian period, and producing a new era in which secure, responsible and effective government is as easy to take for granted as tap-water you can drink, electricity that is always on, or a search engine that returns porn only if you searched for porn.

A good way to define a restoration is to model it as a *sovereign bankruptcy*. Since a government is just a corporation, albeit one whose rights are protected not by any higher authority but by its own military force, it is subject to the same inexorable laws of accounting.

More specifically, a restoration is a sovereign bankruptcy with *restructuring*. There are always three options in a bankruptcy: restructuring, liquidation, and acquisition. While it can be interesting to wonder what the People's Liberation

AN OPEN LETTER TO OPEN-MINDED PROGRESSIVES 263

Army would do with West Oakland, in general restructuring is the only practical option at the sovereign level.

In any restructuring, a restoration delivers temporary control to a bankruptcy receiver. The receiver's goal is to render the company both solvent and profitable. Solvency is achieved by converting debt to equity, diluting existing equity holders and treating equal commitments equitably. Profitability is achieved by optimizing corporate operations as the receiver sees fit.

In a sovereign bankruptcy, there is one extra quirk. At least in today's real world, the corporation which we are restructuring does not think of itself as a mere corporation. It doesn't even think of itself as a sovereign corporation. It thinks of itself as a mystical pact which echoes across the centuries from generation to generation, bonding human souls across time, space, language, gender and race. So we can expect its accounting to be a little funky. But accounting, still, is accounting. And not rocket science.

Let's start by taking a closer look at the general principles of restructuring.

First, restructuring starts with an enterprise which is in some way financially broken. Most commonly, it has defaulted on its debts. Sovereign corporations, however, have another failure mode, which is especially hairy and which we'll discuss in a moment.

Second, restructuring assumes an enterprise which is intrinsically profitable. In the sovereign case, this is almost automatic. An asset which cannot produce profits is worthless by definition, and no real country is worthless. Invite people to reside there; tax them; profit.

Third, restructuring produces an enterprise which is unlikely to renege on its commitments. In other words, it creates a new allocation of the future profits of the restructured enterprise. Typically these profits are inherently uncertain, so a common result of restructuring is a company with all equity and no debt.

An equity instrument is one that pays some percentage of a completely unpredictable profit. While we do not know the magnitude of the restructured corporation's future profits, we can still divide them into formal *shares*. These shares are distributed among *beneficiaries*, who receive their *dividends*. Shares are typically allocated according to the commitments made by the bankrupt enterprise.

Fourth, there is no requirement that the bankruptcy receiver preserve any policies, assets, divisions, brands, or employees of the old company. He or she has full operational authority, as of course is normal in the productive economy. Of course, the receiver must be responsible to some board, regulator, or other supervisory agent.

In a sovereign context, it is probably appropriate to capitalize the title: the Receiver. The goal of the Receiver is to convert the bankrupt government into one that produces maximum dividends for its beneficiaries, who may be internal or external. A restoration plan should give the Receiver a set of goals and a timeframe, and let her do the rest.

CHAPTER X

One way to imagine the Receiver's job is to imagine her endowed with a mythical symbol of power, the Wand of Fnargl. Within the country it controls, the Wand turns its holder into a sort of superhero. He can strike down anything or anyone with a bolt of fire, and he is invulnerable to all attacks. However, the Wand has a serious downside: it is disposable. After two years, it crumbles away to nothing.

Therefore, the Receiver has two years in which she holds full sovereign power. At the end of this period, she should leave a secure, responsible, and effective government which can sustain its sovereignty without recourse to magical instruments. While there is no Wand of Fnargl, its powers are clear, and can be reproduced albeit imperfectly by more mundane technologies. Sovereignty is a very well-defined concept. Thus it is a legitimate question to ask anyone what he or she would do, if appointed Receiver and handed the Wand.

For some distance, let's assume we are restructuring the country of **Elbonia**.[17] At present, Elbonia uses its own fiat currency, it has no formal distribution of benefits or clear ownership structure, its decision-making procedures are byzantine, opaque, and mutable, it is plagued by internal violence, it exercises significant power outside its own borders, and its decisions are often affected by external aggression.

After restructuring, Elbonia will be on a metallic standard. All its financial commitments will be formal. It will be, as America's first Chief Justice liked to put it, **governed by those who own it**. Its owners will establish precise and immutable decision-making structures. They will eliminate systematic internal violence, and they will neither tolerate external interference **nor interfere themselves**:[18]

> Our policy in regard to Europe, which was adopted at an early stage of the wars which have so long agitated that quarter of the globe, nevertheless remains the same, which is, not to interfere in the internal concerns of any of its powers; to consider the Government de facto as the legitimate Government for us; to cultivate friendly relations with it, and to preserve those relations by a frank, firm, and manly policy; meeting, in all instances, the just claims of every power, submitting to injuries from none.

Any restructuring must start with the currency. Elbonia's debts are denominated in its own fiat currency, so it cannot never default. Does that mean it's not bankrupt? No, that means it is sovereign. Bankruptcy is any state of indefensible accounting.

The Elbonian currency is, of course, the **grubnick**. What is a grubnick? It is certainly not a note certifying that the issuer holds, or will deliver on demand, a

---

17 "A fictional, non-specific, under-developed" country used in Scott Adams' *Dilbert* comic strip.
18 Reference to a "Frank, firm, and manly policy," an extension of the Monroe Doctrine, adopted by the United States in its dealings with warring European powers in the mid-19th century.

AN OPEN LETTER TO OPEN-MINDED PROGRESSIVES   265

specified quantity of anything. Once upon a time, believe it or not, this was considered **rather tacky**:

> The dollar, like so many of the world's greatest, inspires at first sight interest, but hardly affection. From a casual study of the monetary controversy now raging in this country, I had been led to expect that the dollar was a gold dollar, and that Mr Bryan wanted to turn it into silver. It cannot be too widely known that the dollar as he is spent is neither gold nor silver; he is a piece of paper. Not only so, but often a very worn and dirty piece of paper at that. It is astonishing how a dollar will age in three or four years. True, the paper reflects the greatest credit on its inventor; it never tears—though perhaps this is because no strong man ever really tries to tear it—still, it is but a piece of paper after all. It bears on its weather-beaten face an inscription to the effect that there has been deposited in the Treasury of the United States one silver dollar, which will be paid to the bearer on demand. Others of the breed merely assert that the United States of America will pay one dollar, without specifying its material. The mysterious philanthropist who deposited the silver dollar apparently prefers to remain anonymous; while where or how you cash it is left equally dark. It must certainly be somewhere in Washington, whence the United States of America date their promise, but the American Eagle is too old a bird to give any more precise address. The dollar, so far as my experience goes, is always illustrated, usually with a vignette photograph of some eminent citizen or other, occasionally also with scenes from the life of Columbus or some other appropriate subject. This gives an aesthetic as well as a commercial interest to the dollar, which cannot be too highly prized. Its nominal value is 4s. 2d.

What we see in **Mr. Steevens'** snarky reporting (from 1898) is a currency in the middle of the transition from old-fashioned **warehouse receipt** to our modern, up-to-date **Federal Reserve Note**—or grubnick.

From the accounting perspective, what is a grubnick? The answer is simple. It is not a *receipt*, because it does not denote title to some stored object. It is not *debt*, because it does not denote an obligation that is canceled by some delivery. Therefore, it can only be *equity*.

A grubnick, in other words, is a *share*. It is a *fraction* of some great total right. We do not know exactly what it is a share in, because we do not know what rights you would control if you had all the grubnicks in the world. If you manage to buy up all the Federal Reserve Notes in the world, do you own the Federal Reserve? If you get your hands on all the grubnicks, are you the sole and undisputed owner of Elbonia? These questions are without meaning.

In other words, we can define fiat currency as *dubious equity*. Owning a grubnick is like owning a share in **Yukos**.[19] If you own all the shares of Yukos, you own a lawsuit against the Russian government. What is this worth? It's up to the Russian government. At present the answer appears to be nothing, but Putin might always change his mind.

What we do know is that every dollar is equal to every other dollar. Every five-dollar bill has the same value, whether in dollars or gold or crude oil, as five one-dollar bills. Note that exactly the same is true for grubnicks, Yukos shares, etc., etc. Whatever they may be "worth" (more accurately, exchangeable for), they are amenable to mathematics.

Thus, if there are one trillion dollars in the world, and we accept the (dubious) assumption that if you own all the dollars you own the Federal Reserve, each dollar is a right to one trillionth of the Federal Reserve. Perhaps this is obvious, but it implies some corollaries.

One, creating new dollars does not affect the value of the Federal Reserve, however we choose to measure that value. Nor does it affect the value of Elbonia, Yukos, or any other right. It is common or garden-variety **stock dilution**. Dilution is often more convenient than transferring shares from old owners to new owners, but the principle is the same. If there exist one trillion dollars and we print ten billion new ones and give them to X, the effect is just as if we replaced each dollars held by anyone but X with 99 cents, added up the spare cents and gave them to X.

Now we can see just how screwy the accounting system of Elbonia is. Imagine a company which chooses to denominate its accounting *in its own stock*. Say Google valued its assets, such as its buildings, in Google shares. Its debt would be promises to pay Google shares. If it paid dividends, each share might spawn 0.05 new shares. This would be truly perverse accounting. But it would not be as perverse as a system in which Google ran its numbers in terms of shares in an internal tracking stock which represented a subsidiary whose assets and liabilities were not defined at all. That's fiat currency for you.

To restructure this bizarre financial teratoma, we need to (a) fix the number of grubnicks in the world, and (b) define the rights divided among all grubnick holders.

(b) is easy: we convert grubnicks into proper Elbonian equity. In a liquid market, ELBO shares can be converted to gold, crude oil, **Hummel figurines**, or any other commodity. The only question is: if you start with fraction X of all the grubnicks, what fraction of all the ELBO shares do you end up with? Let's say, quite arbitrarily, that a third of the equity in ELBO will go to present grubnick holders.

(a) is more interesting. Why don't we know how many grubnicks there are in the world? Isn't each one numbered? Indeed, each one is numbered. But the Elbo-

---

19 At the time of this writing, former owners of the Russian oil giant were embroiled in a protracted international court battle against the Russian government, seeking $100B in redress.

nian Reserve has the power to create more grubnicks, and it always uses this power when it has to.

Thus, when Elbonia promises you a grubnick, that promise is worth exactly as much as a grubnick, because there is no reason for Elbonia to break its promise. But there is also no constraint on Elbonia's ability to promise more grubnicks than it has actually created. Thus we have two kinds of grubnicks: actual grubnicks, and virtual grubnicks. If Elbonia is anything like America, the latter vastly outnumber the former.

For example, when you "deposit" a dollar in a bank, you do not own a dollar. You own a promise of a dollar from the bank. The bank is not the Federal Reserve, but via the FDIC the Federal Reserve "insures" your bank. The FDIC owns very few dollars, certainly not enough to protect all the banks in the world. But the Fed can print as many dollars as it likes. So your dollar "deposit," because it is backed by a chain that ends in a virtual promise from the Fed, is risk-free.

A Treasury bond is risk-free for the same reason—Uncle Sam is implicitly backed by Uncle Sam's own printing press. Thus, the bond is equivalent to a specialized kind of dollar bill, one that says "not valid until" a certain date—the date when the bond matures. In the world of equity, this is what we call **restricted stock**. Only a market can tell you how many grubnicks a restricted grubnick will trade for, but a restricted grubnick is still a grubnick.

Obviously, this is a financial Rube Goldberg machine. It can only be understood historically. Fortunately, there is a simple way to get the virtual grubnicks under control.

One: find all the assets (such as bank deposits) whose price in grubnicks is protected by Elbonia's power to print new grubnicks. Two: print the grubnicks, and buy the assets for their formal price. Three: fix the number of grubnicks outstanding. Four: convert grubnicks to ELBO shares, as desired. Five: sell the assets you nationalized, exchanging them for whatever monetary commodity your new accounting system uses. (Let's say it's gold.)

Doing this right will involve creating a *lot* of grubnicks. The best way to rationalize this is to understand that these grubnicks already exist. They just exist informally, and we need to formalize them. At present, for example, the US owes about $10 trillion in debt, in a world that contains less than 1 trillion actual dollars. Unless you are accustomed to the presence of virtual dollars, these numbers simply make no sense.

In the uneducated folk economics by which policymakers make their rule-of-thumb decisions today, this is held to be "inflationary." The general assumption, made more on the basis of sympathetic magic than anything else, is that more grubnicks means higher prices. But this is not true when we replace virtual grubnicks with real grubnicks, because the change is *portfolio-neutral*—your loan of 1000 grubnicks to the bank is replaced by 1000 actual grubnicks. Thus, you have no more or less money, thus your spending patterns do not change, and thus if everyone is affected in the same way there is no effect on market prices.

CHAPTER X

The Receiver has thus gained an important power. In order to make the transition as smooth as possible, she can declare *any obligation* of Elbonia, formal or informal, to be a debt which is denominated in grubnicks and guaranteed by virtual grubnicks. Elbonia will then acquire that debt, since it is after all guaranteed, paying out in freshly-printed grubnicks. Rampant equity dilution is a very, very normal practice in any restructuring.

Suppose, for example, Elbonia has guaranteed lifetime medical care to all its residents. To the Receiver, this is an obligation like any other, even if it is not a formal obligation in the same sense as paying off a bond. Elbonia, at least in her unrestructured state, is too ramshackle a barge to make any useful distinction between formal and informal debts.

Therefore, Elbonia can shed this politically complex and nasty obligation by calculating the cost of an equivalent insurance policy for each resident, assuming the resident has such a policy, and buying it back with fresh grubnicks. If the resident wants to use those grubnicks to buy medical insurance, by definition she can afford it. Or she can spend them on beer and heroin. It's up to her. The whole conversion is a **Pareto optimization**.

This flood of new cash has no chance of descending into a hyperinflationary spiral, because it is part of a one-time restructuring in which the semantics and quantity of shares become fixed. Hyperinflation is what happens when a government falls into a state in which it is continually funding operating losses by paying off its creditors with freshly diluted stock. In the financial markets the same effect is produced by a **toxic convertible**.[20] This is a device one might use in a desperate attempt to avoid bankruptcy, a fate to which we have already reconciled ourselves.

To prevent fluctuations in grubnick purchasing power, the Receiver can also create restricted grubnicks with a "not valid until" date. Thus, when buying out a medical insurance policy or other annual obligation, the compensated parties may receive restricted grubnicks that can pay each year's policy as it falls due, rather than getting a giant lump sum that can be spent on a yacht and will drive the yacht market haywire.

Thus armed not only with absolute political and military sovereignty, but also with the weird economic superpower of the fiat-currency printing press, our Receiver faces her next challenge: dealing with the horde of Elbonian government employees, most of whose occupations are not in any realistic sense productive.

The basic principle of a sovereign restructuring is to separate all outlays of the government into two classes: essential payments, and inessential payments. Obviously, wages paid to an inessential employee (such as a sociology professor—remember, we are nationalizing the universities) are inessential payments. Another word for "inessential payment" is *dividend*. From an accounting perspective, ines-

---

[20] Made popular in the late 90's, also known as a "death spiral convertible," like a convertible bond but fixed to a dollar price rather than a number of shares, so that shares increase as the stock price goes down.

sential employees are performing makework to hide the fact that they are actually receiving dividends, i.e., acting as bloodsucking parasites.

Of course, with the Wand of Fnargl, the Receiver could just fire them. Quite literally, in fact. But is this fair? Our sociology professor jumped through quite a few hoops, none of which he invented himself, in order to receive what is probably not a very large payment. His so-called career may be pointless, but that means he should be retired, not fired. And he should be retired on a pension that includes a significant fraction of his present pay, maybe even all of it. He has, in short, acquired a certain level of ownership in Elbonia, he has done so through means that were entirely fair and open to all, and it is not our place to decide whether or not he deserves these spoils. Since Elbonia is already paying him, it can obviously afford to continue doing so.

Moreover, as a sociology professor he is part of the ruling class, and the Wand of Fnargl does not last forever. Keep your friends close, as they say, and your enemies closer. He is already being paid to lie for money to support the old regime. If you continue to pay his salary, but let him say and do whatever he wants, will he turn around and bite you? Perhaps some will, but it is not human nature. A more likely response is permanent, doglike loyalty. This response can be accentuated, if need be, by requiring the professor to put his name on a list of prominent figures who support the new government. If he changes his mind, he can stop or restart his pension to match the fluctuations of his conscience.

This gets even better when we get to the few parts of the Cathedral that are relatively healthy. One example is biomedical research, which requires delicate and expensive toys, and so commands a considerable amount of funding over and above faculty salaries. To destroy the institutions while making the researchers very, very happy, simply make everyone's grant or stipend their own permanent property. Divide the funding among the whole team, right down to the grad students. Result: a class of financially independent researchers who can work on whatever they want, wherever they want, sans paperwork. Perhaps a few will decide they don't care about curing cancer and do care about living in the South of France, but they will not be the cream of the crop. Is there anyone who really believes that the grant review process adds value or improves the quality of science?

The Receiver has thus brought order to Elbonia's books. Essential expenses—spending on goods and services that are actually necessary to maximize the Elbonian revenue—turn out to be a small proportion of budgetary outlays. The rest is profit. Elbonia, as we always knew, is massively profitable.

The Receiver's goal is not to redirect this profit, although she can redirect it if need be, but simply to understand it. Who is profiting? How much are they profiting? We find these profiteers—who in many cases are not wealthy fat cats, but philanthropists who provide vital services to the needy—and exchange their informal commitments for formal securities, i.e., grubnicks. We eliminate any makework or other pointless camouflage that may have been used to disguise the profit relationship. And everyone is happy.

Elbonia does need revenue, of course. Since the new Elbonia will keep its books in gold, it should collect taxes in gold. The simplest way to tax, which is also one that affects all uses of Elbonian soil and cannot be evaded, is a self-assessed tax on all land and fixed structures. As a property owner, you assess your own property, which is offered for sale at the assessed price. If you don't want to sell, set your price above the market, and pay a little more tax.

Elbonia can also make a market for ELBO shares, in gold. Since grubnicks are to be converted to ELBO shares, this market will produce the critical grubnick-to-gold ratio. As people realize how weird it is to buy a cup of coffee with shares, the financial system will gradually return from equity to metallic currency.

The Receiver thus has the finances of Elbonia straight. She can then turn her powers toward repairing the sadly decayed framework of government. Her fiduciary responsibility is not just to preserve the value of the Elbonian franchise while the financial restructuring completes, but also to enhance it as much as possible. Given the low quality of government that Elbonia has suffered in the past, this is not hard.

The best target for the Receiver is to concentrate on restoring the **Belle Époque**. This implies that in two years, (a) all systematic criminal activity will terminate; (b) anyone of any skin color will be able to walk anywhere in any city, at any time of day or night; (c) no graffiti, litter, or other evidence of institutional lawlessness will be visible; and (d) all 20th-century buildings of a socialist, brutalist, or other antidecorative character will be demolished.

We can see how far the US at present is from this goal by **this awful, hilarious story**[21] in the LA Times. I simply cannot muster the mockery to do justice to this piece. Read it all. "Well, if I tell you who shot Ray Ray, I'll never work again in this community." Indeed. Meanwhile, elsewhere in the basin, "loose-knit bands of blacks and Latinos" **prowl the streets**, "looking for people of the other color to shoot." Visit **South Africa** before South Africa visits you.

This is just over. It doesn't work. It's done. Stick a fork in it.

First, the Receiver recognizes that this is a *military* problem. These "gangs" are *militias*. Not only that, they are militias with an ideology, and that ideology is violently hostile to the society that hosts them. You are not going to convert them into Quakers by giving them big hugs. Nor is there any rational reason to deal with them via judicial procedures designed to contain the sporadic deviancy, or even psychopathy, that appears in any healthy society.

The ideology of the gangs is an ideology of pure war and hatred. It is no more tolerable than neo-Nazism, and in fact the best way to deal with these subcultures is to think of them as Nazi. They are certainly adept at converting hate into violence.

On the other hand, the fact that these formations are essentially barbaric paramilitary units validates one of the main arguments of the loony left. America's brimming prisons are essentially POW camps. Their inhabitants do not recognize

---

21

AN OPEN LETTER TO OPEN-MINDED PROGRESSIVES

the laws they were convicted under, or accept the society that convicted them. In terms of cultural reality, they are aliens.

The Receiver's message is: the war is over. Your side lost. Reconcile yourself to this, demonstrate that you have done so, and you can return to society. We can use all the manual labor you can put out—for one, we have ugly buildings to tear down, graffiti to remove, and so on.

Modern technology makes it easy for Elbonia to destroy any Morlock subcultures the former management may have inflicted on it. A trivial database query can identify the set of humans in the country who are either (a) productively employed, (b) independently wealthy, or (c) a well-supervised dependent of (a) or (b). Everyone else, including all minors, gets the tag.[22] This inconspicuous device fits on your ankle and continuously reports your position to the authorities. If no crimes are committed near your location, you have nothing to worry about.

This is just the start. Elbonia is saddled with a large number of residents who are effectively dependents of the state—for example, those who receive housing subsidies. These people need to be reprocessed to determine whether they can become members of productive society, and during this time there is no reason to leave them where they are. Elbonia's revenue comes from its property values, and the presence of a Morlock population is not good for same.

Therefore, we can expect the Receiver to establish secure relocation centers, in which the 20th century's artificially decivilized subpopulations will receive social services in a controlled environment while they are reintroduced to civilized society. Mandatory apprenticeship in productive skills, language training to ensure all residents are fluent acrolect speakers, and in general a high degree of personal discipline will be hallmarks of these facilities.

There is no need to allow dysfunctional subcultures to persist in any context, not even in prison. The 20th-century prison is, like so many features of present society, a dead end. Modern technology can realize the ideal of many 19th-century penological reformers: universal solitary confinement.

In the 19th century, solitary confinement drove prisoners insane. In the 21st, adequate social interaction can be delivered electronically. Individual cells with virtual reality consoles are not a recipe for insanity. Virtualized prisoners are much easier to control, guide and evaluate. They are also easier and cheaper to guard and feed. In Third World conditions, entire slums can be surrounded, secured, and the residents moved into modular data hotels with sealed individual or family cells, in which they can live perfectly fulfilling second lives.[23] There is simply no reason for open squalor and barbarism to persist anywhere on the planet. Outdoor relief[24] is an idea whose time has come and gone.

---

22 Tracking device
23 Reference to *Second Life*, a metaverse-like online immersive "game" reaching peak popularity around the time of UR's original publication.
24 Elizabethan social welfare program

CHAPTER X

From the standpoint of a society from which all forms of modern barbarism have been eradicated, the old, unrestored Elbonia will look almost unimaginably brutal and unlivable. When you have lived all your life in a country in which there is no crime and the streets are safe, the idea of "no-go zones" or random muggings, rapes, etc., will terrify you much as if the same assaults were committed by uncontrolled wild animals.

For example, I simply can't imagine what it would be like to live in San Francisco if there were fifty or sixty leopards loose in the city. But I can see how people would get used to it. Leopards are nocturnal, so you stay in at night. They hide in trees, so you cut down the trees. They tend to hunt in certain areas, so you avoid those areas. And the situation could develop gradually—the first leopard is a huge news story, the second is a smaller story, and they build up over time. After a while, the experience of walking down the street while checking for leopards would strike you as completely normal and unremarkable. If one day the leopards were removed, however, you would definitely notice it.

AN OPEN LETTER TO OPEN-MINDED PROGRESSIVES

 252 *General Zod*

 252 *Brahmin* "Boston Brahmin"

 252 *Tam-Brams*

 252 *Barack Speaks To HQ Staff & Volunteers* Video clip from June of 2008 of then Senator Barack Obama speaking to his staff in a campaign office room as the presumptive Democratic nominee for president.

 253 *Third World Strike* Overview of the Third World Strike, at San Francisco State's Leonard Library *Strike Collection* database.

 253 *maneuver with Patti Solis Doyle* Jason Horowitz. "Clinton Bundler on Obama's Doyle Pick: The Biggest 'Fuck You' Ever." *The New York Observer*, 16 June 2008.

 253 *31337*

 253 *Humean ought*

 254 *Hugo Boss*

 254 *Soviet Life*

 254 *three whole issues* "On Marriage and Family | Roosevelt-Litvinov: Man to Man Talk." (Feb. 1969), "Tashkent Celebrates its 2000th Anniversary." (Aug. 1983), and "Free Health Care | Turkmenia and Uzbekistan Today | Poet Mikhail Lermontov." (Oct. 1984), hosted at *marxistfr.org*.

 255 *Edith Markson* "Edith Markson, 81, Promoter of Theater." *New York Times*, Obit., 16 Sep. 1994.

 254 *Dr. Khutsidze* CV and About page for Zurab Khutsidze, "Legendary doctor, and founder of the world famous Tsope rhinoplasty school." *TsopeClinic.com*.

 255 *Edith Markson-1-1* photo of Markson from the *Online Archive of California*

254 *Edith Markson-2* Lynda Richardson. "For Its Ease and Excitement, Retirees Return to New York." *New York Times*, 23 Aug. 1993.

 255 *this Times story* Michael Kimmelman. "For Blacks in France, Obama's Rise Is Reason to Rejoice, and to Hope." *New York Times*, 17 Jun. 2008.

 255 *Clichy-sous-Bois*

 255 *Times' last piece* Supra, Richardson.

 256 *little theater company* "American Conservatory Theater"

 256 *nomenklatura*

 257 *John Reed*

 257 *Judge Guevara* Blog post featuring a photo of Lorain County, Ohio judge, James Burge in his office with posters of Che Guevara and Barack Obama framed on his wall. In 2015 Burge was convicted on twelve counts of criminal conduct related to financial dealings, in addition to receiving sanctions for courtroom misconduct, and was subsequently suspended from practicing law (*Disciplinary Counsel v. Burge*, Slip Opinion No. 2019-Ohio-3205.) CDR Salamander. "Attracting them like flies." *cdr salamander*, 13 Jun. 2008.

 257 *O-Ba-Ma* See Chapter 4, will.i.am. "We Are the Ones." *Change is Now: Renewing America's Promise*. 2008.

 257 *videos* Ibid. "Yes We Can."

 258 *three millimeters per year* "Sea-level rise"

 258 *troubled* Tracy McVeigh. "Dozens die in Kenyan riots." *The Guardian*, 26 Jan. 2008.

AN OPEN LETTER TO OPEN-MINDED PROGRESSIVES

 258 most beautiful countries on earth The *Lonely Planet* online guide to Kenya.

 258 admits it A critique of Heidi Holland's 2008 New York Times op-ed "Make Peace With Mugabe," that includes a broader critique of modern African history. Timothy Burke. "Playing Reindeer Games," *Easily Distracted*, 8 Apr. 2008.

 259 international press corps "Africa: We Want Our Country." *Time Magazine*, 5 Nov. 1965.

 259 Rhodesian Ministry of Information "A Case for Rhodesia." *Rhodesian Ministry of Foreign Affairs*, 16 Mar. 1978.

 259 Albert Speer

 259 Think again Burke. "The End of Apartheid, Direct Action and Its Costs." *Easily Distracted*, 29, Aug. 2006.

 260 lighting them afire "Necklacing"

 260 d6 "Polyhedral dice"

 260 1992 referendum

 260 BBC documentary BBC no longer hosts the video on its website, but an article about the film by the director is available in the link provided here. A link to the transcript of the film can be found in the endnote "transcript" below. Fergal Keane. "No More Mandelas." *BBC One*, News, 11 Feb. 2008.

 260 murderous "1983: Car Bomb in South Africa kills 16." *BBC*, On This Day, 20 May.

 260 transcript Full transcript of *No More Mandelas*. Fergal Keane, Jeremy Vine, Desmond Tutu, Jacob Zuma, anonymous "Youth," et al. (2008).

 262 Fergal Keane

262 *People's Liberation Army*

 264 *Elbonia* "Dilbert"

 264 *governed by those who own it* William Jay. *The Life of John Jay.* (J. & J. Harper, 1833) p. 70.

 264 *nor interfere themselves* "The European War." *The New York Times Current History*, Vol. IX, 1916. p.157.

 264 *grubnick*

 265 *rather tacky* G.W. Steevens. *The Land of the Dollar.* (Dodd, Mead and Company, 1898).

 265 *Mr. Steevens*

 265 *warehouse receipt*

 265 *Federal Reserve Note*

 266 *Yukos* In 2014 The Hague arbitration court awarded Yukos' former owners $50B against the Russian government, the largest such award in history, later invalidated, then reinstated in 2020. The final outcome is unsettled as of this publication.

 266 *stock dilution*

 266 *Hummel figurines*

 267 *restricted stock*

 268 *Pareto optimization*

AN OPEN LETTER TO OPEN-MINDED PROGRESSIVES

 268 toxic convertible "Death spiral financing"

 270 Belle Époque

 270 this awful, hilarious story Joe Mozingo. ""L.A. fights back." *Los Angeles Times*, 1 May, 2008.

 270 prowl the streets Lee Baca. "In L.A., race kills." *Los Angeles Times*, 12 June, 2008.

 270 South Africa Boitumelo Magolego. "On malwerekwere..." *Mail & Guardian*, Thought Leader, 15 May 2008.

 271 Morlock

 271 the tag

 271 acrolect "Post-creolo continuum - Stratification"

 271 second lives "Second Life"

 271 Outdoor relief

CHAPTER XI:
THE TRUTH ABOUT LEFT AND RIGHT
JUNE 26, 2008

Dear open-minded progressive, perhaps you were horrified by Chapter X.
I mean, I did propose the liquidation of democracy, the Constitution and the rule of law, and the transfer of absolute power to a mysterious figure known only as the Receiver, who in the process of converting Washington into a heavily-armed, ultra-profitable corporation will abolish the press, smash the universities, sell the public schools, and transfer "decivilized populations" to "secure relocation facilities" where they will be assigned to "mandatory apprenticeships." If this doesn't horrify you, I'm not sure what would.

And do I even mean it seriously? Or am I just ripping off Daniel Defoe? Dear open-minded progressive, perhaps you have come to realize that your narrator is not always a reliable one. He has played tricks on you in the past. He will probably do it again. The game is deep, and not for the unwatchful.

The first thing to remember is that by even reading these horrible, horrible things, you have demonstrated exactly how open your mind is. You are in the 99.99th percentile of open-minded progressives. You are certainly one of the most open-minded people in the world. Your only conceivable worry is that your mind is so open that your brain has fallen out. Obviously this is a real danger. But life is dangerous.

The second thing to remember is that *no one else endorses this plan.* Or even anything close. In the political world of 2008, restorationism is completely off the map. It is off the table. It is outside the room. It is outside the building. It is running stark naked and crazy through the woods. In a word, it is pure moldbuggery.

And because at present we *do* live in a democracy, this means it is *not dangerous*. At least not at present. It could become dangerous, of course—perhaps if UR was as popular as **Stuff White People Like**. Which it ain't, and which it won't be. But what better reason to keep an eye on it?

The third thing to remember is that the whole plan of restoration through national bankruptcy is predicated on the assumption that the bankruptcy administrator—the nefarious Receiver—is responsible, effective, and not least *sane*. Clearly, if he or she turns out to be Hitler or Stalin, we have just recreated Nazism or Stalinism. Even if you agree with me that Washington is the malignant tumor of the ages, morally, intellectually and financially bankrupt, dead in the water and drifting toward **Niagara**,[1] you can't cure cancer with cyanide and LSD.

And the fourth thing to remember, dear open-minded progressive, is that if perhaps you can be convinced that some things you used to think were good are actually evil, you can be convinced that some things you used to think were evil are actually good. After all, you do have an open mind. No sensible mind is very open on this side of the skull, though, and for good reason. If there is a crack, it is a narrow one. What hopes to fit it must fit a postcard.

So let's swing straight at the ball: the problem of political alignment. Should you be leftist, a rightist, or a centrist? Perhaps we can answer the question from first principles.

Suppose a great wind whips us into space, and sets us down on an Earthlike planet, Urplat, which is completely foreign to us. We quickly discover that Urplat has a democratic political system just like ours. Moreover, Urplat's political thinkers are always squabbling, just like ours. And even better, an Urplatian position in this longstanding conflict can be described usefully by a single linear dimension, just like our "left" and "right."

However, the political axis of Urplat is transformed in some unknown way from ours. Its poles are not left and right, but M and Q. You have no way of knowing how M and Q might map to Earth terms. M–Q could be left–right, or right–left, or some other weird thing.

What you know is that M and Q are *contradictory principles*. Each is some fundamental understanding of human society which indisputably contradicts the other. Of course, it is possible for any person to maintain some combination of M beliefs and Q beliefs—most simply, by using the M-principle to understand one issue and the Q-principle for another. This creates the weird phenomenon of a continuous dimension between M and Q, when the question obviously has a fundamentally boolean quality.

Furthermore, M and Q can be easily misapplied. And either can be combined with any sort of venal or sadistic nastiness. Thus, evaluating the actions of individuals who claim to follow the M or Q principles is not a straightforward way to evaluate the choice between M and Q.

---

1 Reference to Thomas Carlyle's *Shooting Niagara: And After?* (1867) on the perils of embracing modernity.

We know there is a choice, because we know that at most one of M and Q can be good and true. We must therefore conclude that the other is evil and wrong. Of course, both could be evil and wrong. If we find that one is evil and wrong, we should do another checkup to ensure that the other is good and true. But if we find that one is good and true, the matter is settled—the other is the dark side of the Force.

Moreover, the choice matters—because on Urplat, humans have special Jedi powers. Only we can wield the weapon of the Urplatin Jedi, the *Iron Mouse*. And it takes both of us—you, dear open-minded progressive, and me the closed-minded reactionary. If we can agree, we can either end the conflict permanently in favor of M or Q, or any mixture of the two. Any dissent will be promptly silenced by the *Mouse*.

So what criteria can we use to decide between M and Q? The many followers of each great way, of course, are lobbying us with beluga and Porsches and blondes. Or at least the Urplatin equivalent of these fine goods. Nonetheless, we are stern, and will choose only the truth.

A simple test (a) might be to *take a vote*. If more Urplatins prefer M, their planet will be governed for the indefinite future on the M-principle. If they favor Q, likewise.

But, frankly, this is shite. If Q is evil and the Urplatins vote for Q, we have just condemned them and their children to a world of infinite suffering. Past Q-ist movements have perhaps been tempered by a modicum of M, mere personal decency, or mitigating venality. But if we enforce Q with the *Iron Mouse*, there will be no escape. If Q is wrong, wrong shall result. You may not have a problem with this, but I do, and it takes both of us to move the *Mouse*.

And is there any way in which we can guarantee that the headcount of Urplatin supporters corresponds to the absolute truth or falsity of M or Q? Answer: no. Many, perhaps even most, of the Urplatins are dumb as rocks. Therefore, this test is not useful.

A simple way to fix the test—(b)—is to restrict the vote to Urplatins who are at least as smart as whichever of the two of us is dumber. That way we cannot possibly agree to describe any voter as "dumb as a rock." The description is inherently insulting to one of us.

So we are only considering the view of smart Urplatins. Even better, if we see a difference between smart Urplatins and dumb Urplatins, we can penalize whichever principle, M or Q, is popular with the dumb ones. If we see that Q is generally believed by the smarter Urplatins and M is more popular with the dumb ones, we pretty much have the answer. Right?

Okay. Let's assume Q is the smart position and M is the dumb position. We know one fact about Urplat. Does this tell us that Q is good and true, and M is wrong and evil?

At the very least, this proposition depends on the intelligence of Urplatins. If a dumb Urplatin has an IQ of 80, in Earth terms, and a smart one has an IQ of

120, we can pretty easily see that on any question on which they might disagree, the latter is more likely to be right.

Or can we? How do we know this? And is our result the same if the IQs are, say, 120 and 160 respectively? What about 160 and 250? Surely it is neurologically possible for an Urplatian to have an arbitrarily high intelligence, at least as measured by any human scale.

And if the proposition is true for stupid = 160 and smart = 250, it means that an Urplatin with an IQ of 160 can be fooled by whichever of M or Q is evil and wrong. If so, one with an IQ of 120 can surely be fooled. Since one can never be so stupid that one can't discover the truth by throwing darts, it is therefore possible for the Urplatins of IQ 80 to be right and those of IQ 120 to be wrong, which violates the proposition. So we cannot learn that M or Q is right or wrong, just because the smart Urplatins follow Q and the stupid ones cling to M.

However, this fact does tell us something: Q is *more competitive* than M.

Think of Q and M as two populations of parasites, competing for a one population of hosts. Ignoring the fact that Urplatins can harbor a mixture of Q and M perspectives on different subjects, or simply not care, simplify the problem by imagining that each Urplatin has a boolean flag: Q or M.

Although neither Q nor M may have any central organizing body responsible for the propagation of Q-ism or M-ness, if there was such an intellectual central planner, it would choose the smart hosts over the less-smart ones. If you're a sexually transmitted virus, you want to be in a promiscuous gay host, preferably an airline steward. If you're an intellectually transmitted principle, you want to be in a smart and loquacious host, preferably a university professor.

We expect to see some corollaries of this Q–M asymmetry, and we do. If smart people are more likely to host Q, we'd expect Q to be more fashionable than M. If you want to get ahead in life, acting smart is always a good start—whether you're smart or not. If smart people tend to host Q, hosting Q is a great way to look smart.

Q becomes a kind of *social lubricant*. Anywhere, any time, the best way to meet and mate with other young, fashionable people is to broadcast one's Q-ness as loudly and proudly as possible.

Also, if Q is more competitive than M, we'd expect to see Q progressing against M over time. Again, this is exactly what we see. The M–Q conflict is at least a hundred years old, and when we exhume the frozen thoughts of century-old Q-ists from dusty old libraries, their specific beliefs would put them deep in the M range—often at extreme M levels—if they lived today.

But does any of this answer the question? It does not. At least one of Q or M is darkness. But we cannot tell which.

If Q is the dark side and M is mere sanity, we see immediately what Q is: a transmissible mental disease, which spreads by infecting education workers. If Q is mere sanity and M is the dark side, this same system is in the business of overcoming superstition and leading the people of Urplat, despite the ancient prejudices to which they stubbornly cling, toward the truth. And this is certainly how Q-ists see the matter.

And if they are both evil? But this is difficult to imagine. If both M and Q are dark, there must be some truth which contradicts them both. And it must be less successful than either M or Q.

To a Q-ist, the situation makes perfect sense. The progress toward Q is the slow and painful victory of good over evil. Evil has many advantages, because it can avail itself of evil strategies, whereas the good restrict themselves to achieving good ends by good means. However, the truth has a great advantage: it rings clear, like a bell. No lie can fake it.

There is just one small problem with this explanation. We would expect M to disappear much more quickly than it already has. If M is a lie and it is socially disadvantageous to express it, why, after 200 years, do we still have M? All the cards are stacked against it.

Whereas if Q is a lie and M is the truth, we have all the ingredients for an eternal soap opera. Q has the snaky suppleness of mendacity, its tasty apple flavor, its stylish and sinful delights. M has the rigid backbone of a truth that can be suppressed, but never quite crushed, that reappears spontaneously wherever men and women, often of the socially awkward subspecies, have the misfortune to think for themselves.

We've constructed what Professor Burke would call a "narrative." But, compared to the level of tough thinking that we'd need to actually demonstrate that Q is the dark side and M is the light, our narrative has the strength of tissue paper. It is enough for suspicion, and no more.

Therefore, we need to pull the veil aside and (c) look at what M and Q actually mean.

Note that we are still on Urplat—we are not claiming that M and Q correspond to right and left, or left and right, or anything of the sort. We are just devising abstract meanings for M and Q that could, on this imaginary planet we've made up, correspond to the facts we've stipulated: M and Q can coexist, M and Q are contradictory, and Q is consistently more fashionable than M.

Our definitions of M and Q revolve around the ancient Urplatin word *nomos*. If you are for M, you are for the *nomos*, which makes you a *pronomian*. If you are for Q, you are against the *nomos*, which makes you an *antinomian*. The contradiction is obvious.

Let's start by explaining the *nomos* and its supporters, the pronomians.

The *nomos* is the *natural structure of formal promises* around which Urplatins organize their lives. To a pronomian, any Urplatin should be free to make any promise. In return, he or she can expect to be held responsible for that promise: there is no freedom to break it. All promises are voluntary until they are made, and involuntary afterward. A pair of reciprocal promises, a common phenomenon on Urplat, is an *agreement*.

The details of individual promises and agreements are infinite, and constantly changing. But the high-level structure of the *nomos* is a consequence of reality, and it changes little. To demonstrate this point, let's derive the *nomos* from pure reality.

First, Urplatians are not robots. They breed in families, just as we do. An Urplatian family is based on two agreements: one between the parents of the little Urplatian tyke, and one between the child and its parents.

To a pronomian, the relationship between parents and children is simple. The agreement has only one side. Children promise their parents everything, including complete obedience for as long as the parents require. Parents need make no promise to a newborn infant, because an infant is helpless, and cannot compel any concession. If they choose they can emancipate the child when it comes of age, but if they choose they can require it to serve them all their lives. They even hold the power of life and death over it, again until they relinquish this power. (The pronomian supports both prenatal and post-natal abortion.)

Note that this regime—which does not exactly match the family law of, say, California, but is more or less an accurate description of the situation in early Rome—is optimal for the parents. In other words, parents can have no reason to prefer a legal system which gives them less power over their children. If they want to relinquish this power or even assign it to others, nothing is stopping them.

Note also the asymmetry of the agreement between parents and child. By recognizing the helplessness of the infant, we recognize that it has no choice but to accept any definition of the relationship that its parents may propose. The agreement is a promise in one direction because the child has no power to compel any reciprocal promise.

The pronomian sees these kinds of patterns everywhere in the *nomos*. There is only one *nomos*, because there is only one reality. The parameters of parenting do not change. The power dynamics are known. The answer is final.

If men and women, not to mention children, were in all cases honest and trustworthy, they could cooperate without a structure of formal promises. Since they are not, they benefit from formal promises and mechanisms for enforcing those promises. But—to the pronomian—this structure is no more than a recognition of reality.

One of the simplest patterns of agreement is *property*. Property is a system in which one Urplatin claims the sole power to dominate some good—play with a toy, drive a car, fence off a plot of land—and all other Urplatins promise to respect that right. As with the relationship between parents and infants, the origin of property is the balance of power. In a world which contains no property agreements whatsoever, Urplatins can construct a property system based on the reality of current possession.

Another key pattern is the *proprietorship*. The marriage we saw above is a simple case of partnership. In general, however, a proprietorship exists whenever multiple Urplatins decide to work collaboratively on a shared enterprise.

There are two ingredients to a proprietorship: *collective identity* and *fractional ownership*. Collective identity allows the proprietorship to act as a unit, to make and collect promises of its own. Fractional ownership divides the enterprise into precisely-defined *shares*, which in an *anonymous proprietorship* can be traded as property. (It's probably best not to define your marriage as an anonymous proprietorship.)

The natural structure of a proprietorship is that *ownership*, *benefit*, and *control* are synonymous. I.e., if you divide the enterprise into a hundred shares, each share owns a hundredth of the business, receives a hundredth of the profit, and exercises a hundredth of the decision-making power. Of course, it is possible to construct a system of agreements which does not follow this pattern, but in most cases there is no need to. Again, the *nomos* is not prescriptive; these structures emerge as natural patterns of agreement.

But the most important structure in the *nomos* is the *hierarchy of protection*. Protection is what makes all these promises work.

A protector is an enforcer of promises. For some promises in some contexts, protection is not necessary: the cost of breaking any promise may exceed the gain to the promisebreaker. For example, someone who has a reputation for breaking promises may have trouble forming new agreements. This is an unusual condition, however, and not to be relied on. In many contexts—e.g., "insider trading"—a broken promise can be worth all an individual's reputation and more.

By definition, above the top level of the hierarchy of protection there is no protector. That top level, therefore, consists of *unprotected authorities*—typically proprietorships, but sometimes persons. These *unauthorities* have no authority which can settle their disputes. They must resort to war, which in Urplatin is called the *ultima ratio regum*—i.e., the last resort of unauthorities.

Unauthorities do, however, make promises to each other. For example, an unauthority must possess an area of land to which it maintains exclusive control—an *undomain*—because its operations must be somewhere. (If it lacks an undomain, it is subject to the protection of some other unauthority, and thus cannot be an unauthority itself.) The undomain of the unauthority is its property because, as described above, all others have agreed to respect it. But it has no protector other than itself.

The key to success as an unauthority is to ensure that no other unauthority has a positive incentive to violate its promises to you. For example, disrespect of property rights—invasion—is the simplest form of unprotected promise violation. To prevent such assaults, an unauthority must maintain the military and political strength to make the assailant regret the decision to attack. Any less punishment is inadequate; any more is vindictive.

An unauthority makes a crucial mistake when it relinquishes the responsibility of protecting itself to another, stronger unauthority. If unauthorities cooperate against a common threat, they should cooperate for a limited time and a specific reason, and their league should be a league of equals. For an Earth example, Poland, Hungary, Czechoslovakia and Romania make a good defense league. Poland, Hungary, Czechoslovakia and England do not make a good defense league, because the best case of the relationship is that the first three have become protectorates of the last. I.e., they are already halfway to being its property.

Every Urplatin living within an unauthority's undomain is its *client*. To be the client of an undomain is to promise it absolute and unconditional obedience. No unauthority has any use for internal enemies. Moreover, an unauthority cannot be compelled to respect any promise it may make to its clients—there is no force that can compel it. Clients must rely on the desire of the unauthority to maintain its reputation for fair dealing.

Fortunately, an unauthority is a business by definition—its undomain is capital, on which it naturally desires a maximum return. Its return on the property defines the value of the business, and is defined by the value of the subrights to the same property that it concedes to its clients. If its actions decrease this valuation, the unauthority's own stock goes down. And property in a lawless and mercurial undomain is certainly worth less than property protected by an unauthority which is careful of its reputation.

On the same principle, because an unauthority maintains exclusive control within its undomain, it can and should enforce the promises that its clients make to each other. As we saw in the case of the parents, maximum promise enforcement is optimal customer service. Since the better the customer service, the higher the value of the property, and the higher the value of the property, the higher the value of the undomain, a prudent unauthority will do its best to uphold the *nomos*.

So, for example, A may promise to B that he will serve B faithfully for the rest of his life, and B may have him whipped if he disobeys. In fact, since parents own their children, A may consign his child C to this same relationship, and so on through the generations. B, of course, presumably makes some promise in return for this remarkable concession.

That's right: we have just reinvented hereditary slavery. We have also reinvented absolutist or "divine-right" monarchy, the *jus gentium*,[2] and in fact a whole menagerie of blasts from the past. We start to see why not everyone wants to be a pronomian.

(It is a separate discussion, really, but while we're talking about hereditary slavery I can't resist mentioning *A South-Side View of Slavery* by Rev. Nehemiah Adams. If your knowledge of the "peculiar institution" is derived entirely from *Uncle Tom's Cabin*, perhaps it's worth reminding you that *Uncle Tom's Cabin* was a propaganda novel. It's not quite like getting your views on Jews from *Jud Süß*, but... and if you prefer modern sources by respected academics, try this remarkably un-presentist presentation, whose agreement with the Rev. Adams is quite impressive.[3])

Now, let's look at the *antinomian* side of the ledger.

---

[2] "The law of nations"
[3] The links and references in the paragraph are treated in more depth in Chapter 7: "The Ugly Truth About Government."

As you may know, **antinomian**[4] is actually an English word. (And *nomos* is Greek. Okay, I lied. But I warned you.) It is usually applied in the archaic sense of religious law, but the derivation is sound, and the word is defensible in the present day.

An antinomian is anyone who seeks, consciously or unconsciously, to disrupt or destroy the *nomos*. He is a breaker of oaths, a burner of deeds, a mocker of laws—at least, from the pronomian perspective. From his own perspective he is a champion of freedom and justice.

I admit it: I am a pronomian. I endorse the *nomos* without condition. Fortunately, I do not have to endorse hereditary slavery, because any restoration of the *nomos* begins with the present state of possession, and at present there are no hereditary slaves. However, if you want to sell yourself and your children into slavery, I don't believe it is my business to object. Try and strike a hard bargain, at least. (A slightly weakened form of pronomianism, perhaps more palatable in this day and age, might include mandatory emancipation at twenty-one.)

So my idea of the antinomian perspective will be a little jaundiced. But I'll try to be fair.

Perhaps the most refined form of modern antinomianism is *libertarianism*. Libertarianism is a fine example of the antinomian form, because the elements of the *nomos* that it attacks are specified with the elegant design sense that one would expect from the founder of modern libertarianism—probably the 20th century's greatest political theorist, Murray Rothbard.

Rothbardian libertarianism rejects two aspects of the *nomos*. First, it rejects the entire concept of the unauthority—in Earth-speak, the principle of sovereignty. Rothbardians are called anarcho-capitalists for a reason: they deny the legitimacy of the state, unless operated according to strict Rothbardian principles. Note that they do not require, say, Disney to operate Disneyland according to libertarian principles. This is because, to a Rothbardian, Disney's title to Disneyland is legitimate, whereas (say) Iceland's title to Iceland is not.

Rothbard has an **intricate system**,[5] borrowed originally from Locke, for determining whether or not a title is legitimate. To say that this system is unamenable to objective interpretation is to put it mildly. But the titles of existing unauthorities all appear to be illegitimate. This makes libertarianism a revolutionary ideology. Since its antinomianism is so restricted and its lust for blood is minimal, however, it is not an especially dangerous (or effective) one.

Antinomians who reject sovereignty have two main alternatives. Either they support private, amorphous, and even territorially overlapping "protection agencies" (a design whose military plausibility is, to put it kindly, small), or they believe that government is legitimate if and only if it obeys a set of "natural laws." Again here we see the proximity to the pronomian. But the Rothbardian concept of nat-

---

4 "Against laws"
5 Reference to Chapter 7 of Rothbard's *The Ethics of Liberty*, "Interpersonal Relations: Voluntary Exchange."

ural law misses the Hobbesian fact that in the true *nomos*, there is no party that can enforce a state's promises to its clients.

This matters, because legalism without sovereignty has a simple result: the personal rule of judges. The error is to imagine the existence of a superhuman legal authority which can bind a state against itself, enforcing a "government of laws, not men." As the bizarre encrustations of precedent that history builds up around every written constitution demonstrate, this is simply a political perpetual-motion device. All governments are governments of men. If final decisions are taken by a council of nine, these nine are the nine who rule. Whether you call them a court, a junta or a politburo is irrelevant.

Since I am a bit of a geek, though, the Rothbardian interpretation that interests me most is his approach to **contract law**.[6] Note how Rothbard rejects the idea of binding promises, and is forced to construct impossibly elaborate structures of property rights. If I promise to paint your house, I have really sold you a title to a paint job, and if I do not then paint your house I am guilty of theft for having stolen said paint job. I think.

The Rothbardian design breaks down completely in a frequently-mentioned exception, the case of insider trading. Here is a randomly-Googled **example**[7] of the kind of Jesuitic Talmudry to which libertarians resort when confronted with this problem. To a pronomian, the answer is simple: if you are to be given material non-public information, you promise to go to jail if you disclose it. Note that this is exactly how it works now. (Note also that to anyone who has ever had a real job, the idea of legal insider trading is transparently ridiculous.)

The tactical error of the libertarian, Rothbardian or otherwise, is to believe that the state can be made smaller and simpler by making it weaker. Historically, the converse is the case: attempts to weaken an unauthority either destroy it, resulting in **chaos and death**,[8] or force it to compensate by enlarging, resulting in the familiar "**red-giant** state." The pronomian prefers a state that is small, simple, and very strong. It respects the rights of its clients not because it is forced to respect them, but because it has a financial incentive to respect them, and it obeys that financial incentive because it is managed responsibly and effectively.

All things considered, however, libertarianism is a mild, innocuous form of antinomianism. Let's skip immediately to the writer who may be the most popular philosopher on earth today, **Slavoj Žižek**. Here we see antinomianism in an almost pure, indiscriminate form, as in **this lovely passage**:

---

6 Reference to Chapter 19 of Rothbard's *The Ethics of Liberty*, "Property Rights and the Theory of Contracts."

7

8 Reference to the chaotic 12th c. English civil war commonly called "The Anarchy."

The Benjaminian "divine violence" should be thus conceived as divine in the precise sense of the old Latin motto vox populi, vox dei: NOT in the perverse sense of "we are doing it as mere instruments of the People's Will," but as the heroic assumption of the solitude of sovereign decision. It is a decision (to kill, to risk or lose one's own life) made in the absolute solitude, with no cover in the big Other. If it is extra-moral, it is not "immoral," it does not give the agent the license to just kill with some kind of angelic innocence. The motto of divine violence is fiat iustitia, pereat mundus: it is JUSTICE, the point of non-distinction between justice and vengeance, in which "people" (the anonymous part of no-part) imposes its terror and makes other parts pay the price—the Judgment Day for the long history of oppression, exploitation, suffering—...

The anonymous part of no-part. The big Other. Listen to this scoundrel, this charlatan, this truly evil man. Or buy his book, with its **lovely cover**.[9] You won't be the first. If I, dear open-minded progressive, ever become as popular on America's college campuses as Slavoj Žižek, you may feel free to expend as much concern over my "secure relocation facilities" as Professor Žižek's rusty old guillotine, which has lost not a drop of its eternal thirst.

Did I mention that I'm not an antinomian? From Rothbard to Robespierre is a long leap, no doubt, but we can observe some commonalities.

Antinomians believe that the present state of affairs is unsatisfactory. So, of course, do I. The *nomos* is horribly corroded and encrusted with all sorts of gunk. However, the pronomian's goal is to discern the real structure of order under this heap of garbage, scrape it down to the bare skeleton, replace any missing bones, and let the healthy tissue of reality grow around it.

To the pronomian, this structure is arbitrary. Weirdly-shaped borders? Leave them as they are. High taxes? All that tax revenue is paid to someone, who probably thinks of it as his property. Who am I to say it isn't? There are some property structures, notably patent rights, which I (like most libertarians) find very unproductive. If so, the government needs to print money and buy them back. Fortunately, it has a large, high-speed **intaglio press**.[10]

The pronomian seeks to restore the *nomos*, whose outlines are clear under the mountain of byzantine procedure, wholesale makework and vote-buying, criminal miseducation, and other horrors of the liberal-democratic state. The antinomian sees many of the same horrors. But he does not share the pronomian's goal: minimizing the reallocation of property and authority. Where the pronomian simply wants to replace the management, reorganize the staff, and discard the inscrutable

---

9 *In Defense of Lost Causes* (Verso, 2008), picturing a guillotine blade.
10 Reference to the "Bernanke Doctrine," which gave the Fed broad latitude to control the money supply.

volumes of precedent that have absconded with the name of *law*, the antinomian wants to destroy power structures that he conceives as illegitimate.

And, of course, he wants to rebuild them according to his ideals. Unless he is a complete nihilist, which of course some are. But it is the destructive tendency that makes antinomianism so successful. The utopia is never constructed, or if it is it is not a utopia. Success is a precondition to utopia, and success involves achieving the power to destroy.

The most common species of antinomian is, of course, the simple anarchist. The most bloodthirsty and intrusive states of the 20th century were based on a philosophy—Marxism—which saw itself as fundamentally opposed to government. People really did believe that the socialist paradise would be something other than a state.

Near where I live, on one of the most fashionable shopping streets in the world, is an **anarchist bookstore**.[11] On its side wall is a **mural**.[12] The mural contains two slogans:

> History remembers 2 kinds of people, those who kill and those who fight back.
>
> Anarchism strives toward a social organization which will establish well-being for all.

I am flabbergasted by how revealing these slogans are. History, at least when written by honest historians, remembers one kind of people: those who kill. It also notes that those who kill always conceive of themselves as "fighting back." As for "a social organization," it is simply our old friend, the State.

Thus, anarchism defines itself: it is an attempt to capture the state, and its juicy revenues, through extortion, robbery and murder. When it succeeds, it will distribute the loot among its accomplices, and "establish well-being for all." At least in theory.

As we've seen, the one thing an antinomian cannot abide is a formal and immutable distribution of the revenues of state. He must constantly redistribute, he must wash his hands on the stream of cash, giving to Peter and taking from Paul, or his supporters have no reason to support him. In other words, he is basically a criminal.

Why is antinomianism, this criminal ideology, so popular? Fashionable, even? Why is it such a good fit for Q? Because people love power, and any movement with the power to destroy anything, or even just "change" it, has just that: power.

---

11 Bound Together Books on Haight St., San Francisco.

12

Antinomianism allows young aristocrats to engage in the activity that has been the favorite sport of young aristocrats since **Alcibiades** was a little boy: scheming for power. According to **this article**,[13] for example, there are "over 7500 nonprofits" in the Bay Area, "3800 of which deal with sustainability issues." These appear to employ approximately half of our fair city's *jeunesse dorée*,[14] occupying the best years of their lives and paying them squat. Meanwhile, container ships full of empty boxes thunder out the Golden Gate, along with approximately two trillion dollars a year of little green pieces of paper. However, if you're 23 and all you care about is getting laid, interning at a nonprofit is definitely the way to go.

Amidst all this appalling nonsense, productive people keep their heads down and manage to engage in a few remaining productive pursuits. The *nomos* endures. Nor, not even if the Good One is elected, will the guillotine and the tumbrils reappear any time soon.

But antinomianism leaves its scars nonetheless. Almost literally.

The simplicity and flexibility of the *nomos* creates, or should create, an endless stream of "diversity" in the best sense of the word. It's almost impossible to imagine the variety of schools, for example, that would spring up if all parents could educate their children as they saw fit. Structures of voluntary agreement tend to rely heavily on mere personal decision, and the products and services they create tend to embody personal style. For example, one of the many reasons that Belle Époque buildings tend to be so much more attractive than postwar buildings is, I think, that signoff on the design was much more likely to be in the hands of an individual than a committee.

Antinomianism, with its love for reaching into these structures of private agreement and breaking them to serve some nominally noble purpose, has the general effect of replacing individual decisions with committee decisions, personal responsibility with process, and personal taste with official aesthetics. The final stage is the worst form of bureaucracy—litigation, an invisible tyrant whose arms wrap tighter and tighter around us every year. This is sclerosis, scar tissue, Dilbert, Brezhnev, boredom and incompetence for everyone everywhere.

Most observers interpret bureaucratic sclerosis as a sign of a government which is too powerful. In fact it is a sign of a government which is too weak. If seventeen officials need to provide signoff for you to repaint the fence in your front yard, this is not because George W. Bush, *El Jefe Máximo*, was so concerned about the toxicity of red paint that he wants to make seventeen-times-sure that no wandering fruit flies are spattered with the nefarious chemical. It is because a lot of people have succeeded in making work for themselves, and that work has been spread wide and well. They are thriving off tiny pinholes through which power leaks out of the State. A strong unauthority would plug the leaks, and retire the officials.

13

14 "gilded youth"

CHAPTER XI

Outside the Communist bloc proper, of course, the ultimate in power leakage and resulting bureaucracy was India's infamous **Permit Raj**, which still to some extent exists. Needless to say, if the subcontinent was run on a profit basis, the Permit Raj would not be good business. In fact, quite amusingly and with no apparent sense of irony, The New York Times recently printed **an article** in which the following lines appear:

> Vietnam's biggest selling point for many companies is its political stability. Like China, it has a nominally Communist one-party system that crushes dissent, keeps the military under tight control and changes government policies and leaders slowly.
>
> "Communism means more stability," Mr. Shu, the chief financial officer of Texhong, said, voicing a common view among Asian executives who make investment decisions. At least a few American executives agree, although they never say so on the record.
>
> Democracies like those in Thailand and the Philippines have proved more vulnerable to military coups and instability. A military coup in Thailand in September 2006 was briefly followed by an attempt, never completed, to impose nationalistic legislation penalizing foreign companies.
>
> "That sent the wrong signal that we would not welcome foreign investment—this has ruined the confidence of investors locally and internationally," the finance minister Surapong Suebwonglee said in an interview in Bangkok.

The ironies! Of course, perhaps it is not so ironic after all, as perhaps the main reason that the old **China Hands**, the men (such as **Owen Lattimore**) who by "manipulating procedural outcomes"[15] gave **China to Mao**, thought the Communists were the shizzle is that they were obviously so *strong*. America could really do great things in Asia with the ruthlessly indoctrinated divisions of the PLA on its side, as opposed to Chiang Kai-Shek, who looked like his main interests were opium and little boys.

After fifty million deaths and the annihilation of traditional Chinese culture, what still remains is that strength. There is not much antinomianism in China, which has reduced its totalitarian pretensions to one simple and easily-obeyed rule: do not challenge the Party for power. The result, though profoundly flawed, is the most successful capitalist country in the world. All things considered, it is certainly one of the best to do business in—as the article describes.

---

15 See Chapter 7.

AN OPEN LETTER TO OPEN-MINDED PROGRESSIVES

And there is another effect of antinomianism: **this**.[16]

"That's how we do it out here, man!" In my primitive search of the Pravda, I find no evidence that this happened. Therefore, I must conclude that it did not, and the video is faked.

Because imagine the breach of the **limes** between barbarism and civilization that this would represent! If you could show this video to an American of 1908, he would simply conclude that civilization has collapsed. It has not. It lives. 580 is safe, mostly. I think. This sort of thing simply can't happen.

But it can, and it can go on for quite a while without (probably) affecting my life (too much). Nonetheless, it is not getting better. It is getting worse. And nobody is proposing anything like anything that would fix it—except, of course, for me. And I'm crazy.

So Q, of course, is left, and M is right. That is, M—pronomianism—is the *essential principle* of the political right wing. We very rarely see this principle in anything like its undiluted form. But still: why dilute it? Why look around for partial fixes? Why not cure the problem in one step?

Pure Toryism of this sort has a hidden advantage: it is a **Schelling point**. True, it is very difficult to persuade people to abandon all of the different strains of antinomianism that have nested in their brain, each of which assures them that a simple restoration of the *nomos*, with sovereign bankruptcy and a plenary Receiver, is unthinkably "fascist."

However, the eternal problem in organizing any kind of reactionary movement is that if you can get two "conservatives" together in a room, you can generally persuade them to form three political parties. Dissidents by definition are people who think for themselves. They do not have the advantage of the Q-virus, which pulls them all together around the Good One. And like normal people, they tend to disagree.

This is why the search for the essential principle, the *nomos*, the philosopher's stone of the right wing, matters. If you can persuade those who distrust the system as it is to discard everything, liberal or conservative—not just "diversity," and the Good One, and police who hug criminals, but even the Constitution and the Flag and the World Wars and Democracy and the Pledge and the Bill of Rights and all the rest of that stale mythology—if you can talk your audience down to the bare metal, convince them that their political system is scrap, that it is not even remotely recoverable, and then present them with a single principle of government that is at or near this level of simplicity, you'll have a group of people who are all on *exactly the same page*.

This, in a word, is organization. And organization is what gets things done.

16

280 *Stuff White People Like* See Chapter 1.

 280 *Niagara* Thomas Carlyle. *Shooting Niagara: And After?* (Chapman & Hall, 1867).

 286 *jus gentium*

 286 *A South-Side View of Slavery* Rev. Nehemia Adams. (T.R. Marvin, 1855).

 286 *Uncle Tom's Cabin*

 286 *propaganda novel* See also Chapter 7, Reference to Henry Louis Gates and Hollis Robbins' *The Annotated Uncle Tom's Cabin*. (W.W. Norton, 2006). Original link appeared to be a review of the book at *The Nation*.

 286 *Jud Süß* See Chapter 7.

286 *presentation* See Chapter 7, *Roll, Jordan, Roll*.

 287 *antinomian*

 287 *nomos*

 287 *intricate system* audio of Chapter 7, "Interpersonal Relations: Voluntary Exchange" from Rothbard's *The Ethics of Liberty* (New York University Press, 1998), hosted at the Ludwig von Mises Institute website.

 287 *Locke* Link to the entry for "Locke's Political Philosophy" at the Stanford Encyclopedia of Philosophy website.

 288 *contract law Supra*, Rothbard. Link is to a PDF of the entire book, hosted at the Mises Institute website. "Contract Law" pertains to Chapter 19, found on page 133 of this version.

 288 *example* Darren. "Insider Trading in a Stateless Society." *No Coercion*, 23 Jan. 2008.

AN OPEN LETTER TO OPEN-MINDED PROGRESSIVES

 288 chaos and death "The Anarchy"

 288 red-giant

 288 Slavoj Žižek

 288 this lovely passage Slavoj Žižek. "Robespierre or the 'Divine Violence' of Terror." *lacan.com*, 2006.

 289 intaglio press "Bernanke Doctrine"

 290 anarchist bookstore Bound Together Anarchist Collective Bookstore, 1369 Haight St., San Francisco, CA, 94117.

 290 mural

 291 Alcibiades

 291 this article Janna Brancolini. "Environmental shake up." *48hills*, Green City, 17. Jun. 2008.

 291 jeunesse dorée

 292 Permit Raj

 292 an article Keith Bradsher. "Investors Seek Asian Options to Costly China." *New York Times*, 18 Jun. 2008.

 292 China Hands

 292 Owen Lattimore

LINKS & NOTES

 292 gave China to Mao Freda Utley. *The China Story.* (Henry Regnery, 1951).

 293 this Youtube video of the 580 freeway in Richmond, CA being completely overtaken by a "sideshow." Description from the user who originally uploaded the video: "north richmond 510 bay area. Fuck all you hater ya mad cause ya cant be like us."

 293 limes "Limes (Roman Empire)"

 293 Schelling point

CHAPTER XII: WHAT IS TO BE DONE?

JULY 2, 2008

Dear open-minded progressive, every true conversation is a whole life long. (Isn't that the sort of thing a progressive would say? I can almost imagine it on a Starbucks cup.) Also, every journey starts with a single step, and all good things come to an end. And no meeting may adjourn without action items.

So, in the famous words of **Lenin**, what is to be done? As briefly as possible without jeopardizing UR's reputation for pompous prolixity, let's review the problem.

The leading cause of violent death and misery galore in the modern era is *bad government*. Most of us grew up thinking we live in a time and place in which Science and Democracy, which put a man on the moon and brought him back with Tang, have either cured this ill or reduced it to a manageable and improving condition. That is, most of us grew up believing—and most Americans, whatever their party registration, still believe—in *progress*.

Both these statements are facts. But there are two ways to interpret the second. Either (a), blue pill, the belief in *progress* is an accurate assessment of reality, or (b), red pill,[1] it isn't. Our pills correspond to visions of the future, and neither is my invention. The blue pill is marked *millennium*. The red pill is marked *anakyklosis*.[2]

---

[1] The concept of blue pills vs. red pills was first raised in UR's second blog post "The case against democracy: ten red pills" (24 Apr. 2007).
[2] "Millennialism," the belief there will be a future Golden Age, v. the belief that history is "cyclical."

To choose (b), we have to believe that hundreds of millions of people living in a more or less free society, many of whom are literate and even reasonably knowledgeable, completely misunderstand reality—and more specifically, history. A hard pill to swallow? Not at all, because the blue pill tastes just as big going down. To believe in *progress*, you have to believe that similar numbers of our ancestors were just as misguided—enthralled by racism, classism, and other nefarious "ideologies," from which humanity is in the progress of cleansing itself.

Both pills, in other words, claim to be red. But when we note that progressive ideas flow freely through the most influential circles in our society, whereas reactionary ideas are scorned, marginalized and often even criminalized, we can tell the difference.

This week I tried a small experiment: I went over to Professor Burke's, having previously emailed a chivalrous warning that I was talking trash about him on my blog, and on no real provocation at all viciously attacked the man. After all, presumably if you're a full professor specializing in the history of Southern Africa, it should be no problem for you to brush away any catcalls from the peanut gallery on this matter—perhaps even brutally humiliating the catcaller if his persistence exceeds your patience, and you're feeling sadistic this morning. Rank hath its duties, and its pleasures too.

Obviously I'm a biased observer, but this is not my impression of the interaction. Feel free to draw your own conclusions. Threads are (opening, and a little awkwardly on my part) here, (mainly) here, and (closing) here.[3]

At the very least, don't miss the Professor's own post on the last (**Big Wonkery**[4]): the inspiration is unclear, but this is more or less his restatement of the Cathedral hypothesis—from within the nave, as it were. Everything he says is 100% true, and I do like the phrase "Big Wonkery." Didn't I tell you the man had a conscience?

The reason Professor Burke and his henchmen have such difficulty in handling the reactionary onslaught is not that I am smarter than him. It is *certainly* not that I know more about Rhodesia. (He is a professional historian—I am an armchair historiographer.) The reason is that, since his narrative is hegemonic and mine is marginalized, I have heard all his arguments and he has heard few of mine. (Also, the facts of the case could hardly be more glaring.)

The Professor is a sort of professional moderate, a one-eyed man in the kingdom of the blind. Put him next to your stock postcolonial theorist, and the man looks positively level-headed. His "thunderbolt of rage" is pure reactionary righteousness. (Through **La Wik**, I discovered this **wonderful evocation**[5] of the mod-

---

3 Reference to three of Burke's posts, "When Wertham Comes A-Calling," "The People Are the Enemy," and "Big Pharma, Big Wonkery" respectively. Links in the endnotes.

4

5  Norvelle DeAtkine's account of the Jordanian crisis in 1970, and the renaming of "Thawra" Airport to "Reactionary Airfield."

AN OPEN LETTER TO OPEN-MINDED PROGRESSIVES 299

ern reactionary experience. "Reactionary Airfield!" "Thawra" means "revolution," of course.) But something—inertia, ambition, tradition, or mere medical incapacity—keeps the Professor from opening his other eye, and maybe always will. There were many such figures in the late Soviet Union. Indeed Gorbachev himself was one.

It's also fascinating to observe how what we might call, kindly, a "policy-oriented historian," thinks and operates. For comparison, here is the blog of a history-oriented historian.[6] The blog's author, **Christopher Knowles**, has taken the motto of Leopold von Ranke, *wie es eigentlich gewesen*,[7] as his blog title, and his personal affection for the world he studies is obvious. Indeed some study the past because they love it, others because they hate it. Not to be too inflammatory, but Professor Burke studies Rhodesia much as the scholars of *Rassenkunde*[8] once studied Jews: if Rhodesia or Rhodesians ever did anything stupid, evil, or both, the Professor is sure to be an expert on the matter. And again, he is far, far superior to your average postcolonial theorist. (I wonder if he knows that **Rhodesian MRAP designs** are saving American lives as we speak. Or if he cares. Or if he even approves.)

Anyway. Enough of this dinner theater. I've tried a good many arguments for the red pill, or "declinist narrative" as Professor Burke would put it. The audience being inherently irregular, I try to throw in one a week, and I don't think I've trotted out the following for a while.

Imagine that there had been no scientific or technical progress at all during the 20th century. That the government of 2008 had to function with the technical base of 1908. Surely, if the quality of government has increased or even just remained constant, its performance with the same tools should be just as good. And with better technology, it should do even better.

But without computers, cell phones or even motor vehicles, 19th-century America could **rebuild destroyed cities instantly**[9]—at least, instantly by today's standards. Imagine what this vanished society, which if we could see it with our own eyes would strike us as no less foreign than any country in the world today, could accomplish if it got its hands on 21st-century gadgets—without any of the intervening social and political *progress*.

When we think of *progress* we tend to think of two curves summed. X, the change in our understanding and control of nature, slopes upward except in the most dire circumstances—the fall of Rome, for example. But X is a confounding variable. Y, the change in our quality of government, is the matter at hand. Extracting Y from X+Y is not a trivial exercise.

---

6 *How It Really Was*

7 "how it really was"
8 Reference to Hans Günther's influential *Racial Science of the German People* published in 1922.
9 Reference to the rebuilding of San Francisco after the 1906 earthquake.

But broad thought-experiments—like imagining what would become of 1908 America, if said continent magically popped up in the mid-Atlantic in 2008, and had to modernize and compete in the global economy—tell a different story. I am very confident that Old America would be the world's leading industrial power within the decade, and I suspect it would attract a lot of immigration from New America. The seeds of decay were there, certainly, but they had hardly begun to sprout. At least by today's standards.

Surely a healthy, stable society should be able to thrive in a steady state without any technical improvements at all. But if we imagine the 20th century without technical progress, we see an almost pure century of disaster. Even when we restrict our imagination to the second half of the twentieth century, to imagine the America of 2008 reduced to the technology of 1950 is a bleak, bleak thought. If you are still taking the blue pills, to what force do you ascribe this anomalous decay?

Whereas the red pill gives us an easy explanation: a decaying system of government has been camouflaged and ameliorated by the advance of technology. Of course, X may overcome Y and lead us to the **Singularity**, in which misgovernment is no more troublesome than acne. Or Y may overcome X, and produce the **Antisingularity**[10]—a new fall of Rome. It's a little difficult to invent self-inventing AI when you're eating cold beans behind the perimeter of a refugee camp in Redwood Shores, and Palo Alto is RPG squeals, mortar whumps and puffs of black smoke on the horizon, as the Norteños and the Zetas finally have it out over the charred remains of your old office park. Unlikely, sure, but do you understand the X–Y interaction well enough to preclude this outcome? Because I don't.

Swallowing the red pill leads us, like **Neo**, into a completely different reality. In reality (b), bad government has not been defeated at all. History is not over. Oh, no. We are still living it. Perhaps we are in the positions of the French of 1780 or the Russians of 1914, who had no idea that the worlds they lived in could degenerate so rapidly into misery and terror.

Is the abyss this close? I don't think so, but surely the **materials**[11] are present.[12] The spark is a long way from the gasoline—Ayers and his ilk strike most of Americans as more clownish than anything, and our **modern revolutionaries**[13] have never been so out of touch with the urban underclass (for whom John Derbyshire proposes the wonderful Shakespearian word **bezonian**[14]). Nonetheless, the first political entrepreneur who finds a way to deploy gangstas as stormtroopers, a trick the **SDS** often threatened but never quite mastered, will have pure dynamite on his hands.

---

10 "The Antisingularity," a UR post from May 2007 presenting the hypothesis that "technical progress and social progress are uncorrelated, and may even run in opposite directions."
11 Reference to the video of the Richmond, California "sideshow" from Chapter XI.
12 Reference to Bill Ayers.
13 Reference to "Stop Huntingdon Animal Cruelty," an international animal rights organization.
14 "Worthless person, a beggar" from *Henry VI, Part II*.

More probable in my opinion is a slow decline into a Brezhnevian future, in which nothing good or new or exciting or beautiful is legal. X peters to a crawl. Y continues. And only after many, many decades—probably not in our lifetimes—does the real dystopian experience start. Or the system could fail catastrophically, and produce not the rarefied algorithmic authoritarianism of UR, but some kind of awful **Stormfront** neofascism. (Why is it that the more Nazi you are, the uglier your website is? Never mind, I think I know.) Or it could all just work out fine.

But can we count on this? We cannot. So, as thoughtful and concerned people, we have three reasons to think about solutions. One is that we are thoughtful and concerned people. Two is that thinking about government in a post-democratic context is an excellent way to clear our minds of the antinomian cant with which our educators so thoroughly larded us. And three is that once the cant is cleared, it's actually kind of fun and refreshing to think about government. The problem is not new, but it has been lying fallow for a while.

First: the problem. Our goal is to convert a 20th-century government, such as USG or "Washcorp," into a sovereign organization which is stable, responsible and effective. For simplicity, I'll assume you're an American. If you are not an American, you almost certainly live under an American-style, post-1945 government. Substitute as necessary.

Our logic is that secured real estate is the oldest and most important form of capital. I.e.: it is a productive asset. There is only one responsible and effective way to manage a productive asset: make it turn a profit. To maximize the profit is to maximize the price of the asset. To maximize the price of a sovereign jurisdiction is to maximize the price of the properties within it. To maximize real-estate prices is to maximize the desirability of the neighborhood. To maximize the desirability of the neighborhood is to maximize the quality of life therein. To maximize the quality of life is the goal of good government. Ergo: responsible and effective government is best achieved by sovereign capitalism, i.e., neocameralism.

Watch the Austrian economist **Hans-Hermann Hoppe**—since Rothbard's premature demise, probably the superstar of the school today—**struggle with this problem**.[15] Professor Hoppe is an antinomian of the libertarian species. He is a sound formalist at every layer up to the top, where he rejects the concept of sovereign property as a royalist plot. (Actually, in medieval Europe, sovereign fiefs could easily be **bought and sold**[16]—and note that no "natural rights" protected the **Quitzows from the Hohenzollerns**.[17]) Professor Hoppe writes:

15

16 Reference to Charles IV's purchase of Brandenburg for the House of Luxembourg in 1373.

17 The von Quitzows were a noble family of Brandenburg, subject to the control of the ruling Hohenzollerns.

Under these circumstances, a completely new option has become viable: the provision of law and order by freely competing private (profit-and-loss) insurance agencies.

Even though hampered by the state, insurance agencies protect private property owners upon payment of a premium against a multitude of natural and social disasters, from floods and hurricanes to theft and fraud. Thus, it would seem that the production of security and protection is the very purpose of insurance. Moreover, people would not turn to just anyone for a service as essential as that of protection.

There's one difference: an insurance agency exists under the protection of a government which enforces its contracts. Whereas English actually has a word for an unprotected protection agency. It's called a *gang*. (The Russian word *krysha*,[18] meaning "roof," is also quite evocative.)

In real life, for obvious military reasons, gangs tend to organize themselves around *territories*, or contiguous blocks of real estate. Historically, situations in which gang territories overlap are unusual. As formal rules develop for the internal organization of the gang, and its relations with other gangs, the gang becomes a country. Formalization maximizes the gang's profits and greatly improves its clients' quality of life.

We are starting from the other direction: a gigantic, mature if not senescent vegetable-marrow[19] of a government. Awful as it is, degenerate as its laws have become, it is still a government, and a government is still a good thing. It is considerably easier to liquidate and restructure USG than to turn **MS-13** and the **Black Guerrilla Family** into the Hapsburgs and Hohenzollerns.

When we left off this problem, we had liquidated USG and transferred full operating control of its assets to a mysterious bankruptcy administrator known only as the Receiver.[20] We had not described: (a) how the process is initiated, (b) how the Receiver is selected, or (c) what policies, beyond terminating "foreign policy," quelling the bezonians, and installing a sensible tax system, we can expect the Receiver to follow.

Frankly, (c) is not worth a lot of speculation. The democratic habit, in which ordinary people—or even UR readers, who are very unlikely to be ordinary people—conceive ourselves capable of understanding how a country is best administered, is one to be broken at all costs. I drive a car on a regular basis, but I have no idea what I would do if someone put me in charge of Ford. I am typing this message on a Mac, but my first act as CEO of Apple would be to resign. (Well, I might do something about the $**#!% batteries first.) I love film, but don't try to make me direct one. And so on.

---

18 Term for the Russian mafia.
19 Photo of a very large pumpkin from bigpumpkins.com.
20 See Chapter X "A Simple Sovereign Bankruptcy Procedure."

Moreover, the fact that we have assigned the Receiver full administrative authority means, by definition, that he or she is not constrained by the whims and fancies of whatever movement produced the office. A restoration has one goal: responsible and effective government. The details are out of its planners' hands.

However, we can think about some things. For example: there are very few decisions that need to be taken on a continental level. USG provides continental defense, hardly hard in North America, but whose absence would eventually be felt. There are certainly some continent-scale environmental issues. I can't think of much else. In a country with responsible and effective government, even immigration can be a local issue: if you don't have permission to live and/or work somewhere, the technology required to prevent you is hardly Orwellian.

So I suspect the Receiver's restructuring plans might involve dividing North America into, say, its largest 100 or 200 or 500 metropolitan areas (USG's historical internal boundaries being of little importance), each of which gets its own little mini-Receiver, devoted as usual to maximizing asset value. To paraphrase Tom Hayden: one, two, three, many Monacos.

Eventually, there is no reason why these principalities could not be independently traded and even locally sovereign, perhaps owning the continental assets of USG, consortium-style, rather than the other way around. Initially, however, USG's financial liabilities are as vast as its assets—exactly as vast, since it needs to become solvent. Unless we want to make the dollar worthless, which we don't, the entire country must remain federal property.

Imagining restructuring at a local level helps in a couple of ways. First, redundancy counts: if Seattle, for some reason, winds up with Kim Jong Il as its Receiver, and he promises to be good but quickly resorts to his old habits, the residents can always flee to Portland. If Kim gets the whole continent, the continent is screwed. Second, it is simply easier to imagine how a city could be restored, especially if you happen to live in that city.

The San Francisco Bay Area, for example, is a jewel even in its present dilapidated state, its no-go areas, modernist crimes against architecture, froth of beggars and rim of tacky sprawl. I can scarcely imagine what a Steve Jobs, a Frederick the Great, a Mountstuart Elphinstone, or an administrator of similar caliber would make of it.

But how (b) do we select such an administrator? The crucial question is the back-end of this administrative structure. A Receiver is not a "benevolent dictator." If angels were available to meet our staffing needs, that would be one thing. They are not. There is no responsibility without accountability. The trick is in preventing accountability from degenerating into parliamentary government, i.e., politics—which is how we got where we are at present.

To prevent the emergence of politics, a stable, established neocameralist state relies on the fact that its shares are held by a widely distributed body of investors, each of whose management control is precisely proportional to the share of the profits the investor receives, and none of whom has any way to profit privately by causing the enterprise to be mismanaged. The result is a perfect alignment of interests among all shareholders, all of whom have exactly the same one-dimensional goal: maximizing the value of their shares. Experience in private corporate governance shows that such a body tends to be reasonably competent in selecting managers, and almost never succumbs to anything like politics.

When converting a democratic state into a neocameralist one, however, a great deal of care is needed. For example, since any bankruptcy procedure converts debt to equity, quite a few shares must end up in the hands of those who now hold dollars, bank or Treasury obligations, rights to entitlement payments, etc., etc. Will these individuals be (a) rationally motivated to maximize the value of their assets, and (b) effective in selecting competent management that will act according to (a)? Or won't they? There is no way to know.

I think I am on reasonably firm ground in asserting that once democratic politics can be made to go away, this design offers no avenues by which it can revive itself. However, keeping the thing dead is one thing. Killing it is quite another.

Today's administrative states are irresponsible because their actions tend to be the consequence of vast chains of procedure which separate individual decisions from results. The result is hopelessly dysfunctional and ineffective, often becomes seriously detached from reality, and demands an immense quantity of pointless busywork. However, it has the Burkean (Ed, not Tim) virtues of stability, consistency, and predictability. It works, sort of.

When you take all this process, policy and precedent, rip it up, and revert to responsible personal authority, you gain enormously in effectiveness and efficiency. But the design places a tremendous engineering load on the assumption of responsibility and the absence of politics. This simply can't be screwed up. If it is, the consequences can be disastrous. Hello, Hitler. Also, did I mention Hitler? Finally, there is the possibility of creating a new Hitler.

Obviously, it's time for us to have a serious discussion of Hitler. Anyone who proposes anything even remotely resembling an absolute personal dictatorship needs a Hitler position. Because, after all, I mean, Hitler.

Albert Jay Nock, who needs no introduction here at UR, and many of whose words will stand the test of time long after we are dead, wrote the following in his diary for July 23, 1933:

> The wretched state of things in Germany continues. It is a manifestation of a nation-wide sentiment that any honest-minded person must sympathize with, but its expression, under the direction of a lunatic adventurer,[21] takes shape in the most revolting enormities.

This is simply the best summary of National Socialism I have ever seen. And it was written only six months after the swine came to power.

---

21 Hitler

AN OPEN LETTER TO OPEN-MINDED PROGRESSIVES

Fascist-style approaches to terminating democracy in the 21th century face two unsolvable problems. One is that the democracies have, in their usual style, overdone the job of arming themselves against anything like fascism—they are absurdly terrified of it. Fascism is a salmon trying to jump over Boulder Dam. Two is that even if your salmon could jump over Boulder Dam, the result would be... fascism. Which would certainly be an improvement in some regards. But not in others.

The Boulder Dam analogy is well-demonstrated by La Wik's page for **direct action**.[22] Note that every example on the page is in the revolutionary or progressive category. The term does not seem to apply to reactionary or fascist "direct action," although tactics have no alignment. Of course, the gangster methods that Hitler and Mussolini used in coming to power were direct action in a nutshell—as were the actions of the **Southern Redeemers**.[23]

The answer is that "direct action" depends on the tolerance and/or connivance of the police, military, and/or judicial system. In Weimar Germany, nationalists had all three—mostly relics of the Wilhelmine government—on their side. Denazification reversed this. Today in Europe, antifas can beat up their opponents with a wink and a nod from the authorities, whereas neo-Nazis get the book thrown at them. The answer: duh. Don't be a neo-Nazi.

Anyone interested in overthrowing democracy desperately needs to read the great memoir of **Ernst von Salomon**, *Der Fragebogen*, published in English as *The Answers* but better translated as *The Questionnaire*. (The title is a reference to the **denazification questionnaires** which all Germans seeking any responsible postwar position had to complete.)

Salomon, who despite his name was not Jewish (though his wife was), was never a Nazi. He was, however, a hardcore nationalist, and not just any hardcore nationalist: he was a member of the notorious post-**Freikorps** death squad, **Organisation Consul**,[24] and personally involved in the assassination of **Rathenau**, for which he served time. (If it's any defense, he was 19, and his role was limited to procuring the getaway car.) He was also a brilliant writer who made a living turning out movie scripts—before, during, and after the Third Reich. A good comparison is **Ernst Jünger**, also wonderfully readable if a little more abstruse.

Der Fragebogen is a gloriously-fresh introduction to the world of Weimar, which most of us have encountered only from the liberal side. If you have trouble understanding how Nock could sympathize with the destruction of Weimar while abhorring Hitlerism, von Salomon is your man. The opening alone is a work of genius:

22

23 Southern wing of the Democratic party who made efforts to reverse the tide of Reconstruction.

24 Nationalist, anti-communist terror organization active during Weimar.

CHAPTER XII

MILITARY GOVERNMENT OF
GERMANY: FRAGEBOGEN

WARNING: Read the entire Fragebogen carefully before you start to fill it out. The English language will prevail if discrepancies exist between it and the German translation. Answers must be typewritten or printed clearly in block letters. Every question must be answered precisely and no space is to be left blank. If a question is to be answered by either 'yes' or 'no,' print the word 'yes' or 'no' in the appropriate space. If the question is inapplicable, so indicate by some appropriate word or phrase such as 'none' or 'not applicable.' Add supplementary sheets if there is not enough space in the questionnaire. Omissions or false or incomplete statements are offences against Military Government and will result in prosecution and punishment.

I have now read the entire Fragebogen or questionnaire carefully. Although not specifically told to do so, I have even read it through more than once, word for word, question for question. This is not by any means the first questionnaire with which I have grappled. I have already filled in many identical Fragebogens, and a great number of similar ones, at a time and in circumstances concerning which I shall have a certain amount to say under the heading *Remarks*. Apart from that group of Fragebogens there were others: during the period January 30th, 1933, to May 6th, 1945, which is usually called the 'Third Reich,' or with cheap wit 'the Thousand-Year Reich,' or briefly 'the Nazi Regime,' or correctly the period of the National-Socialist government in Germany—during those years, too, I was frequently confronted with Fragebogens. I can confidently assert that I invariably read them through with care.

In order to satisfy any doubts on the matter let me say at once that the perusal of all these questionnaires has always produced the same effect on me: a tumult of sensations is let loose within my breast in which the first and the strongest is that of acute discomfort. When I try to identify this sensation of discomfort more exactly, it seems to me to be very close to that experienced by a schoolboy caught at some mischief—a very young person, on the threshold of experience, suddenly face to face with an enormous and ominous power which claims for itself all the force of law, custom, order and morality. He cannot yet judge the world's pretension that whatever is right; at present his conscience is good when he is in harmony with that world, bad when he is not. He cannot yet guess that a happy moment will one day come when he

AN OPEN LETTER TO OPEN-MINDED PROGRESSIVES

will weigh the world and its institutions in the scales of that still dormant conscience of his, will weigh it and will find it wanting and in need of rebuilding from the foundations up.

Now in view of the matters which I have had to discuss in my answer to Question 19, I am clearly nowise entitled to express my opinions on matters of conscience. Nor is it I who wish to do so. Yet how am I to account for the tone and arrangement of this questionnaire if its general intention is not a new incitement to me to examine this conscience of mine?

The institution which, in all the world, seems to me most worthy of admiration, the Catholic Church, has its system of confession and absolution. The Church recognizes that men may be sinners but does not brand them as criminals; furthermore, there is only one unforgivable sin, that against the Holy Ghost. The Catholic Church seeks to convert and save the heathen, who is striving to be happy according to his lights; but for the heretic, who has once heard the call and has yet refused to follow it, there can be no forgiveness. This attitude is straightforward and consistent and entails certain sublime consequences. It leads directly to the secrecy of the confessional. It also means that each man, in his search for grace, is very largely dependent on his own, innermost determination. A fine attitude, and one that I might myself embrace did not I fear that the very quintessence of the Church's teaching—yes, the Ten Commandments themselves—were in painful contradiction to a whole series of laws that I have recently been compelled to observe.

For it is not the Catholic Church that has approached me and requested that I examine my conscience, but another and far less admirable institution, Allied Military Government in Germany. Sublimity here is at a discount. Unlike the priest with the poor sinner remote from the world in the secrecy of the quiet confessional, A.M.G. sends its questionnaire into my home and, like an examining judge with a criminal, barks its one hundred and thirty-one questions at me: it demands, coldly and flatly, nothing less than the truth; it even threatens twice—once at the beginning and once at the end—to punish me; and the nature and scope of the punishment envisaged I can only too vividly imagine. (See *Remarks*, at the end of this questionnaire.) [Salomon was badly beaten, and his wife was raped, by American soldiers in a postwar detention camp. —MM]

It was representatives of A.M.G., men in well-creased uniforms with many brightly coloured decorations, who made it unambiguously clear to me that every man worthy to be called a man should study his conscience before deciding whether or not to act in any specific way. They sat in front of me, one after the other, those agreeable and well-groomed young people, and spoke with glibness and self-assurance about so great a matter as a man's conscience. I admired them for their apodictic certainty; I envied them their closed and narrow view of the world.

Salomon's book was a bestseller in postwar Germany. It is now anathema, of course, in that thoroughly occupied country—in which only the faintest trace of any pre-American culture can still be detected.

Here (to get back to Hitler) are some of Salomon's observations on the Nazis:

> At that time—it was high summer of 1922 and the Oberammergau Passion Play was being acted—Munich was filled with foreigners. Even the natives had not the time to attend big political rallies. Thus I did not even have a chance to hear Hitler—and now I shall go to my grave without ever having once attended a meeting where I could hear this most remarkable figure of the first half of the twentieth century speak in person.
>
> "What does he actually say?" I asked the Kapitän's[25] adjutant.
>
> "He says more or less this," the adjutant began, and it was significant that he could not help mimicking the throaty voice with the vengeful undertones, "he says, quite calmly: 'My enemies have sneered at me, saying that you can't attack a tank with a walking stick...' Then his voice gets louder and he says: 'But I tell you...' And then he shouts with the utmost intensity: '... that a man who hasn't the guts to attack a tank with a walking stick will achieve nothing!' And then there's tremendous, senseless applause."
>
> The Kapitän said: "Tanks I know nothing about. But I do know that a man who tries to ram an iron-clad with a fishing smack isn't a hero. He's an idiot."
>
> I know not whether the Kapitän, lacking in powers of oratory as he was, found Hitler's methods of influencing the masses as repugnant as I did, but I assumed this to be the case. I also obscurely felt that for the Kapitän, deeply involved in his political concept, to be carried forward on the tide of a mass movement must seem unclean. Policy could only be laid down from 'above,' not from 'below.' The state must always think for the people, never through the people. Again I obscurely felt that there could be no compromise here, that all compromise would mean falsification.
>
> But it was precisely his effect on the masses that led to Hitler's success in Munich. He employed new methods of propaganda,

---

25 Hermann Ehrhardt, Freikorps commander and leader of the Organization Consul.

AN OPEN LETTER TO OPEN-MINDED PROGRESSIVES

> hitherto unthought of. The banners of his party were everywhere to be seen, as was the gesture of recognition, the raised right arm, used by his supporters; the deliberate effort involved in this gesture was in itself indicative of faith. And everywhere was to be heard the greeting, the slogan *Heil Hitler!* Never before had a man dared to include his essentially private name in an essentially public phrase. It implied among his followers a degree of self-alienation that was perhaps significant; no longer could the individual establish direct contact with his neighbour—this third party was needed as intermediary.

And, ten pages later:

> The word 'democracy' is one that I have only very rarely, and with great reluctance, employed. I do not know what it is and I have never yet met anyone who could explain its meaning to me in terms that I am capable of understanding. But I fear that Hitler's assertion—that his ideological concept was the democratic concept—will prove a hard one to refute. The enlightenment of the world from a single, central position, the winning of mass support through convincing arguments, the legitimate road to power by way of the ballot-box, the legitimisation by the people itself of power achieved—I fear it is hard to deny that these are democratic stigmata, revelatory perhaps of democracy in a decadent and feverish form, but democratic none the less. I further fear that the contrary assertion—that the totalitarian system as set up by Hitler was not democratic—will prove a hard one to justify. The totalitarian state is the exact opposite of the authoritarian state, which latter, of course, bears no democratic stigmata but hierarchical ones instead. Some people seem to believe that forms of government are estimable in accordance with their progressive development; since totalitarianism is certainly more modern than the authoritarian state system, they must logically give Hitler the advantage in the political field.

And I fear, dear open-minded progressive, that this is the first time in your life you've seen the word *authoritarian* in a positive context. The weird crawlies that crawl in when we leave our minds ajar! Perhaps yours is too open, after all. Better stop reading now.

In case Salomon isn't quite clear, let me paraphrase his theory of Hitler and the State. Salomon, and his hero Kapitän Ehrhardt, were essentially militarists and monarchists, believers in the old Prussian system of government. In 1849 when Friedrich Wilhelm IV refused to "accept a crown from the gutter" (in other words, to become constitutional monarch of Germany under an English-style liberal system created by the **Revolutions of 1848**), he was expressing much the same philosophy.

While there is more mysticism to it, and anyone raised in a democratic society must cringe instinctively at the militaristic tone, Salomon's philosophy is more or less the same as neocameralism. (Understandably, since after all it was Frederick the Great who gave us **cameralism**.) Salomon's view of public opinion is mine: that it simply has nothing to do with the difficult craft of state administration, any more than the passengers' views on aerodynamics are relevant to the pilot of a 747. In particular, most Americans today know next to nothing about the reality of Washington, and frankly I don't see why they should have to learn.

In the totalitarian system as practiced by Hitler and the Bolsheviks, public opinion is not irrelevant at all. Oh, no. It is the cement that holds the regime together. Most people do not know, for example, of the frequent plebiscites by which the Nazis validated their power. But they do have a sense that Nazism was broadly popular, at least until the war, and they are right. Moreover, even a totalitarian regime that does not elicit genuine popularity can, like the Bolsheviks, elicit the pretense of popularity, and this has much the same power.

When describing any political design, a good principle to follow is that the weak are never the masters of the strong. If the design presents itself as one in which the weak control the strong, try erasing the arrowhead on the strong end and redrawing it on the weak end. Odds are you will end up with a more realistic picture. Popular sovereignty was a basic precept of both the Nazi and Bolshevik designs, and in both the official story was that the Party expressed the views of the masses. In reality, of course, the Party controlled those views. Thus the link which Salomon draws between democracy and the Orwellian mind-control state, two tropes which we children of progress were raised to imagine as the ultimate opposites.

Salomon is obviously not a libertarian, or at least not as much of a libertarian as me, and I suspect that what disturbs him is less the corruption of public opinion by the German state, than the corruption of the German state by public opinion. Regardless of the direction, the phenomenon was a feedback loop that, in the case of Nazism, led straight to perdition.

Here is another description of democracy. Try to guess where it was written, and when:

The New Democracy

> What is this freedom by which so many minds are agitated, which inspires so many insensate actions, so many wild speeches, which leads the people so often to misfortune? In the democratic sense of the word, freedom is the right of political power, or, to express it otherwise, the right to participate in the government of the State. This universal aspiration for a share in government has

no constant limitations, and seeks no definite issue, but incessantly extends, so that we might apply to it the words of the ancient poet about dropsy: *crescit indulgens sibi*.²⁶ For ever extending its base, the new Democracy aspires to universal suffrage—a fatal error, and one of the most remarkable in the history of mankind. By this means, the political power so passionately demanded by Democracy would be shattered into a number of infinitesimal bits, of which each citizen acquires a single one. What will he do with it, then? how will he employ it? In the result it has undoubtedly been shown that in the attainment of this aim Democracy violates its sacred formula of "Freedom indissolubly joined with Equality." It is shown that this apparently equal distribution of "freedom" among all involves the total destruction of equality. Each vote, representing an inconsiderable fragment of power, by itself signifies nothing; an aggregation of votes alone has a relative value. The result may be likened to the general meetings of shareholders in public companies. By themselves individuals are ineffective, but he who controls a number of these fragmentary forces is master of all power, and directs all decisions and dispositions. We may well ask in what consists the superiority of Democracy. Everywhere the strongest man becomes master of the State; sometimes a fortunate and resolute general, sometimes a monarch or administrator with knowledge, dexterity, a clear plan of action, and a determined will. In a Democracy, the real rulers are the dexterous manipulators of votes, with their placemen, the mechanics who so skilfully operate the hidden springs which move the puppets in the arena of democratic elections. Men of this kind are ever ready with loud speeches lauding equality; in reality, they rule the people as any despot or military dictator might rule it. The extension of the right to participate in elections is regarded as progress and as the conquest of freedom by democratic theorists, who hold that the more numerous the participants in political rights, the greater is the probability that all will employ this right in the interests of the public welfare, and for the increase of the freedom of the people. Experience proves a very different thing. The history of mankind bears witness that the most necessary and fruitful reforms—the most durable measures—emanated from the supreme will of statesmen, or from a minority enlightened by lofty ideas and deep knowledge, and that, on the contrary, the extension of the representative principle is accompanied by an abasement of political ideas and the vulgarisation of opinions in the mass of the electors. It shows also that this extension—in

---

26 "The direful dropsy increases by self-indulgence," from the *Odes of Horace*.

great States—was inspired by secret aims to the centralisation of power, or led directly to dictatorship. In France, universal suffrage was suppressed with the end of the Terror, and was re-established twice merely to affirm the autocracy of the two Napoleons. In Germany, the establishment of universal suffrage served merely to strengthen the high authority of a famous statesman who had acquired popularity by the success of his policy. What its ultimate consequences will be, Heaven only knows!

The manipulation of votes in the game of Democracy is of the commonest occurrence in most European states, and its falsehood, it would seem, has been exposed to all; yet few dare openly to rebel against it. The unhappy people must bear the burden, while the Press, herald of a supposititious public opinion, stifles the cry of the people with its shibboleth, "Great is Diana of the Ephesians." But to an impartial mind, all this is nothing better than a struggle of parties, and a shuffling with numbers and names. The voters, by themselves inconsiderable unities, acquire a value in the hands of dexterous agents. This value is realised by many means—mainly, by bribery in innumerable forms, from gifts of money and trifling articles, to the distribution of places in the services, the financial departments, and the administration. Little by little a class of electors has been formed which lives by the sale of votes to one or another of the political organisations. So far has this gone in France, for instance, that serious, intelligent, and industrious citizens in immense numbers abstain from voting, through the difficulty of contending with the cliques of political agents. With bribery go violence and threats, and reigns of terror are organised at elections, by the help of which the respective cliques advance their candidates; hence the stormy scenes at electoral demonstrations, in which arms have been used, and the field of battle strewn with the bodies of the killed and wounded.

Organisation and bribery—these are the two mighty instruments which are employed with such success for the manipulation of the mass of electors. Such methods are in no way new. Thucydides depicts in vivid colours their employment in the ancient republics of Greece. The history of the Roman Republic presents monstrous examples of corruption as the chief instrument of factions at elections. But in our times a new means has been found of working the masses for political aims, and joining them in adventitious alliances by provoking a fictitious community of views. This is the art of rapid and dexterous generalisation of ideas, the composition of phrase and formulas, disseminated with the confidence of burning conviction as the last word of science, as dogmas of politicology, as infallible appreciations of events, of men, and of institutions. At one time it was believed that the faculty of analysing facts, and deducing general principles was the privilege of a few enlightened minds and deep thinkers; now it is considered an universal attainment, and, under the name of convictions, the generalities of political science have become a sort of current money, coined by newspapers and rhetoricians.

The faculty of seizing and assimilating on faith these abstract ideas has spread among the mass, and become infectious, more especially to men insufficiently or superficially educated, who constitute the great majority everywhere. This tendency of the people is exploited with success by politicians who seek power; the art of creating generalities serves for them as a most convenient instrument. All deduction proceeds by the path of abstraction; from a number of facts the immaterial are eliminated, the essential elements collated, classified, and general formulas deduced. It is plain that the justice and value of these formulas depend upon how many of the premises are essential, and how many of those eliminated are irrelevant. The speed and ease with which abstract conclusions are arrived at are explained by the unceremonious methods observed in this process of selection of relevant facts and in their treatment. Hence the great success of orators, and the extraordinary effect of the abstractions which they cast to the people. The crowd is easily attracted by commonplaces and generalities invested in sonorous phrases; it cares nothing for proof which is inaccessible to it; thus is formed unanimity of thought, an unanimity fictitious and visionary, but in its consequences actual enough. This is called the "voice of the people," with the pendant, the "voice of God." The ease with which men are drawn by commonplaces leads everywhere to extreme demoralisation of public thought, and to the weakening of the political sense of the people. Of this, France to-day presents a striking example, and England also has not escaped the infection.

The author is the great Russian statesman and reactionary **Konstantin Pobedonostsev**. The book is *Reflections of a Russian Statesman*. (A fascinating mix of cogent observations of the West, and impenetrable Orthodox mysticism—I recommend it highly.) The date is 1869. Is there anything in Pobedonostsev's description of democracy that does not apply to the contest of Obama and McCain? Not that I can see. So much for the inevitable triumph of truth.

There is not a single significant American writer—even if you count Confederates as American, which is a big if—as right-wing as Pobedonostsev. He is to the right of everyone. He may even be to the right of **Carlyle**, even the old Carlyle who (two years earlier) produced the terrifying vision of *Shooting Niagara*. Well, we shot Niagara, all right, and Russia got her Parliament. For a few months. And as for Germany, the consequences are no longer Heaven's secret.

We have moved no closer to answering Lenin's question. But we have a better idea of what is *not* to be done.

A restoration can't be produced by fascist violence and intimidation, because fascism today has no sympathizers in high places. It can't be produced by democratic demagoguery, both because the concept itself would be corrupted by filtration through the mass mind, and because said mind is simply not smart enough to evaluate the proposition logically—and logic is its only strength. (It's certainly not emotionally appealing.) Moreover, when democratic techniques are used to seize absolute power, the result is Hitler.

Yet at the same time, we can't expect the truth to triumph on its own, because said truth has been floating around since the 1860s—at least—and it has gotten nowhere at all. And worst of all, the design is reliable only in the steady state. Even if the political energy to make it happen, without either thug intimidation or democratic hypnotism, can somehow be produced, there is no magical reason to expect the initial shareholders, who know nothing more about managing a country than you or I, to be free from politics, to choose a Receiver who knows his ass from his elbow, or even to let one who does know his ass from his elbow do his job.

So perhaps nothing can be done. We should just bend over and enjoy it. Do you, dear open-minded progressive (or other UR reader), have any suggestions?

AN OPEN LETTER TO OPEN-MINDED PROGRESSIVES 315

 297 *Lenin* Vladimir Lenin's famous treatise "What Is To Be Done" was first published in the journal of the Russian Social Democratic Labor Party *Iskra*, No. 4 in May 1901, hosted at marxist.org.

 297 *Tang*

 297 *millennium* "Millenialism"

 297 *anakyklosis* "Kyklos"

 298 *here* Timothy Burke. "When Wertham Comes A-Calling." *Easily Distracted*.

 298 *here-1* "The People Are the Enemy."

 298 *here-2* "Big Pharma, Big Wonkery."

 298 *La Wik* "Reactionary"

 298 *wonderful evocation* Norvell B. DeAtkine. "Ambassador Dean Brown and the Jordanian Crisis of 1970." *American Diplomacy*, University of North Carolina, Oct. 2001.

 299 *history-oriented historian*

 299 *Christopher Knowles* Research Fellow at Kings College London.

 299 *Leopold von Ranke*

 299 *Rassenkunde*

 299 *Rhodesian MRAP designs* Dr. J.R.T Wood. "The Pookie: A History of the World's first succeful Landmine Detector Carrier." *jrtwood.com*, 2005.

299 rebuild destroyed cities instantly Carl Nolte. "The Great Quake: 1906-2006 | Rising from the Ashes." *SF Gate*, 18 Apr. 2006.

 300 Singularity

 300 Antisingularity Moldbug. "The Antisingularity." *UR*, 11 May 2007.

 300 materials See Chapter XI endnote "this."

 300 present "Bill Ayers"

 300 modern revolutionaries "Stop Huntingdon Animal Cruelty"

 300 bezonian from *Henry VI Part II*:
Great men oft die by vile bezonians.
A Roman sworder and banditto slave
Murdered sweet Tully; Brutus' bastard hand
Stabbed Julius Caesar; savage islanders
Pompey the Great; and Suffolk dies by pirates.
John Derbyshire. "Vile bezonians." *National Review Online Diary*, Jun. 2008.

 300 SDS "Students for a Democratic Society." See Chapter 8.

 301 Stormfront Link to the *Stormfront* forum, "White Pride Worldwide."

 301 Hans-Hermann Hoppe

 301 struggle with this problem Hans-Hermann Hoppe. "On the Impossibility of Limited Government and the Prospects for a Second American Revolution." *Mises Institute*, 28 Jun. 2008.

 301 bought and sold "Margraviate of Brandenburg"

 301 Quitzows

AN OPEN LETTER TO OPEN-MINDED PROGRESSIVES

 301 *Hohenzollerns*

 302 *krysha* "Russian mafia"

 302 *vegetable-marrow* Illustrative photographic sample from bigpumpkins.com.

 302 *MS-13*

 302 *Black Guerrilla Family*

 302 *Receiver* Definition for "Receivership" by Carla Tardi at *Investopedia*, "a court-appointed tool that can assist creditors to recover funds in default and can help troubled companies avoid bankruptcy."

 303 *Monacos* Google image result for "Monaco."

 303 *Steve Jobs*

 303 *Frederick the Great*

 303 *Mountstuart Elphinstone*

304 *Ed* "Edmund Burke"

304 *Tim* "Timothy Burke" of *Easily Distracted*.

 304 *Albert Jay Nock* See Chapter 7.

304 *diary* Albert Jay Nock. *A Journal of These Days, June 1932-December 1933*. (W. Morrow, 1934).

305 direct action

 305 Southern Redeemers

 305 Ernst von Salomon

 305 The Answers See Chapter 8. Ernst von Solomon. *Der Fragebogen.* (Rowohlt Verlag, 1951).

 305 denazification questionnaires Link to the entry for "Fragebogen" at the *UK National Archives* Wiki.

 305 Freikorps

 305 Organisation Consul

 305 Rathenau

 305 Ernst Jünger

 308 Kapitän's "Hermann Ehrhardt"

 309 Friedrich Wilhelm IV

 310 Revolutions of 1848

 310 cameralism

 311 crescit indulgens sibi

312 *Great is Diana of the Ephesians* Acts 19:28

 313 *Konstantin Pobedonostsev*

 313 *Reflections of a Russian Statesman* See Chapter 8. Konstantin Pobedonostsev, trans. Robert Crozier Long. *Reflections of a Russian Statesman*. (Grant Richards, 1898).

 313 *Carlyle* A more in-depth examination of this claim can be found in the Unqualified Reservation series *Moldbug On Carlyle*.

 314 *Shooting Niagara* See Chapter XI.

CHAPTER XIII:
TACTICS AND STRUCTURES OF ANY PROSPECTIVE RESTORATION

JULY 10, 2008

Dear open-minded progressive, I've been holding out on this one way too long. What is to be done? Let's try and actually answer the question this time.

To be precise: by what procedures might a 20th-century liberal democracy be converted, safely, permanently and with reasonable continuity of administration, into a sovereign corporation that can be trusted to deliver secure, reliable and effective government? If you, dear open-minded progressive, chose to agree with me that this is actually a good idea, how might we go about trying to make it happen?

As I've mentioned a couple of times, my father's parents were CPUSA activists,[1] so I do have a personal heritage of quasi-religious conspiratorial revolutionary thinking. But revolutionary tactics and structures are not, in general, useful to reactionaries. A restoration is the opposite of a revolution. Both imply regime change, but both **apoptosis** and **necrosis** involve cell death. There is no continuum between the two.

The signature performance of the modern revolution is the irregular military parade. I.e.: cars or pickup trucks full of well-armed youths in their colorful native attire, driving up and down your street while (a) honking, (b) waving hand-lettered banners, (c) chanting **catchy slogans**,[2] and (d) discharging their firearms in a vaguely vertical direction. Occasionally one of the vehicles will pull up in front of a house and discharge its occupants, who enter the building and emerge with an infidel,

---

1 See Chapter 4.
2 Reference to "Umshini wami," translated to "Bring my machine [gun]," used as a struggle song by Mandela's ANC.

racist, Jew, spy, polluter, Nazi or other criminal. The offender is either restrained for transportation to an educational facility, or enlightened on the spot as an act of radical social justice. Yes, we can!

Whereas in the ideal restoration, the transfer of power from old to new regime is as predictable and seamless as any electoral transition. With all rites, procedures and rituals correct down to the fringe on the Grand Lama's robe, the Armani suits on his Uzi-toting bodyguards, and the scrimshaw on the yak-butter skull-candle he lights and blows out three times while chanting "Obama! Obama! Llama Alpaca Obama!" The Heavenly Grand Council releases itself from the harsh bonds of existence, identifies its successor, asks all employees to remove their personal belongings from their offices, and instructs senior eunuchs to report for temporary detention.

Obviously, we live in America and we have no Grand Lama. However, our government has a clear procedure for 100% legal closure: it can pass a constitutional amendment which terminates the Constitution. While it would be foolish to insist on this level of legal purity, it would be crass not to aspire to it.

But let's acquire a little neutral distance by saying that we live in *Plainland*, we are presently ruled by *Plaingov*, and we wish to replace it with *Plaincorp*. The transition should be a total reset: the policies, personnel and procedures of Plaincorp have nothing in common, except by coincidence, with the operations of Plaingov. Of course, Plaincorp inherits Plaingov's assets, but with a completely new decision framework. Arbitrary restructuring can be expected.

For obvious reasons, I prefer the word *reset*. But English does have a word (borrowed from French) for a discontinuous transition in sovereignty: *coup*. Not every coup is a reset, but every reset is a coup. The French meaning, a *blow* or *strike*, is a perfect shorthand for a discontinuous transition of sovereignty. If this transition involves a complete replacement of the sovereign decision structure, it is a reset. For example, if Plaingov's military initiates a reset, as obviously it will always have the power to, we would be looking at a *military reset*.

I am not a high-ranking military officer and I doubt you are either, and if the military reset is the only possible transition structure neither of us has much to contribute. While in my opinion just about every country on earth today would benefit from a transition to military government, the whole point of a military coup is that unless you are actually a member of the General Staff, your opinion doesn't matter. So why should we care? It is hard to be interested in the matter.

(I should note, however, that according to **Gallup** America's most trusted institution is—you guessed it. Followed directly by "small business" and "the police." The military is almost three times as popular as the Press. It is six times as popular as Congress. You do the math, kids! When the tanks finally roll, there will be no shortage of cheering. (And oddly enough, the other half of the Cathedral did not make the poll. Perhaps it fell off the bottom, and was discarded.))

The only alternative to a military coup is a political coup, or to be catchy a *democoup*. In a democoup, the government is overthrown by organizing a critical mass of political opposition to which it surrenders, ideally just as the result of overwhelming peer pressure. Certainly the most salient example is the fall of the Soviet Union, including its puppet states and the wonderfully if inaccurately named Velvet Revolution. (Again, a reaction is not a revolution.) Other examples include the Southern Redemption, the Meiji Restoration, and of course the English Restoration.

In each of these events, a broad political coalition deployed more or less nonviolent, if seldom perfectly legal, tactics to replace a failed administration with a new regime which was dedicated to the restoration of responsible and effective government. Note that all of these are real historical events, which actually happened in the real world. I did not just make them up and edit them into Wikipedia. Yes, dear open-minded progressive, change can happen.

If there is one fact to remember about a restoration via democoup, it's that this program has *nothing* to do with the traditional 11th-grade civics-class notion of democratic participation. Obviously, we are not trying to replace one or two officials whose role is primarily symbolic. We are trying to replace not the current occupants of the temporary and largely-ceremonial "political" offices of Plaingov, but Plaingov itself—lock, stock and barrel. Indeed, we are using democratic tactics to abolish democracy itself. (There is nothing at all ironic in this. Is it ironic when an absolute monarch decrees a democratic constitution?)

By definition, a reset is a *nonincremental* transition. To the extent that there is some gradual algorithm which slowly weakens Plaingov and pulls it inexorably toward the brink of implosion, gradualist tactics may be of use. But the tactics are useful only as they promote the goal, and the goal is not gradual.

We are all familiar with gradual revolutions, on the Fabian or Gramscian plan.[3] And tactics are tactics, for good or evil: in the war between the hosts of Heaven and the armies of Satan, both the demons and the angels drive tanks and fly jet fighters. So why is it that history affords many examples of sudden revolution, many examples of gradual revolution, some examples of sudden reaction, and almost no examples of gradual reaction?

Even if we had no explanation for this observation, it is always imprudent to mess with Clio.[4] But we do have an explanation: revolution, being fundamentally antinomian (opposed to law and order), is entropic. Revolution is the destruction of order, degradation into complexity. Slow destruction is decay, cancer and corrosion. Rapid destruction is annihilation, fire and gangrene. Both are possible. Sometimes they form a delightful cocktail.

But reaction, being pronomian (favoring law and order), is the replacement of complex disorder with simple geometric forms. If we assume that disorder snowballs and creates further disorder, a common entropic phenomenon (think of the cascade of events that turns a normal cell into a cancerous cell), any attempt at a gradual reaction is fighting uphill. You treat cancer cells by killing them, not by turning them back into healthy, normal tissue.

---

3 See Chapter 8 for more on Fabian and Gramscian progressivism.
4 The Greek muse of history.

Of course, this is just a metaphor. We are not killing people. We are liquidating institutions. Let's try and keep this in mind, kids.

But not too much in mind, because the metaphor of termination is critical. Metaphorically, here is how we're going to liquidate Plaingov: we're going to hit it **extremely hard in the head**[5] with a sharp, heavy object which traverses a short throw at very high speed. Then we'll crush its body under an enormous roller, dry the pancake in a high-temperature oven, and grind it into a fine powder which is mixed with molten glass and cast as ingots for storage in a deep geological cavity, such as a salt mine. The shaft is filled with concrete and enclosed by a dog-patrolled double fence with the razor-wire facing *inward*. This still may not work, but at least it's a shot.

Less metaphorically, the starting point for a democoup is a *program*. Call it X. Success involves (a) convincing a large number of people to support the proposition that *X should be done*, and (b) organizing them to act collectively so as to *make X happen*.

To define the democoup we have to explain what it's not: civics-class democracy. Let's try a farcical experiment in civics-class democracy, just to see how pointless it is.

We start, obviously, by forming the Mencist Party. A new product in the marketplace of ideas. Of course, we have new ideas, so we need a new brand. In the classic democratic spirit, our new party must organize itself around either (a) a shared vision of government policy ("racist corporate fascism," let's say), (b) a flamboyant personality (me, obviously), or (c) both.

The Mencist Party faces obstacles so huge as to be comical. First: what is racist corporate fascism? Since Mencism is out beyond the fringes of the fringes, it will only attract supporters who are genuinely passionate about our vision of racist corporate fascism. Of course this label is designed to attract only the most independent-minded of independent thinkers—to put it gently. Therefore, racist corporate fascism must become a "big tent" which, for the sake of enlarging itself and appearing important, embraces all supporters whose views can be vaguely described as racist corporate-fascist.

In fact I have no idea what "racist corporate fascism" might be. I just like the name. But this is reckless, and it causes problems. For example, is RCF anti-Semitic, or not? Of course, I, Mencius, am not anti-Semitic, but do I strain every muscle to purge Mencists who express what may be **very mild** anti-Semitic views? If so, the Mencist Party will become an **Avakianesque**[6] exercise in cult leadership. If not, it will become a blurry, lager-soaked exercise in vulgar plebeian puerility, à la **Stormfront**. Of course, all Mencists must support the political candidacy of Mencius (who will no doubt decline into referring to himself in the third person). But will anyone else? Ha.

---

5 Reference to a "cattle gun."
6 Bob Avakian, founder of the Revolutionary Communist Party, USA.

More generally, it's easy to see the organizational difficulty of constructing a movement around a vision of government, whether a detailed policy vision (Sailer's plan for school reform[7] comes to mind), or a general theory of government such as libertarianism. If our supporters are required to think in the democratic tense, to imagine themselves or at least their ideas in power, we have taken on an extraordinary boat-anchor of unproductive internal infighting. What is libertarianism? Dear God. There's a fine line between herding cats and being herded by them.

And if supporters are required to elect a public personality whom they conceive as a personal friend, much as the readers of *People* imagine that they know Brad Pitt, it (a) only takes one tiff to estrange this fragile bond, and (b) does not ensure that the Leader will have any actual power when he does get into office. Like today's Presidents, all of whom have been actors (that is, their job is to read from scripts written by others) for the last 75 years, he will spend most of his time trying to retain the fickle sycophants who put him where he is.

Our modern democratic elections are an extremely poor substitute for actual regime change. As we've seen, democracy is to government as gray, slimy cancer is to pink and healthy living tissue. It is a degenerate neoplastic form. The only reason America has lasted as long as she has, and even still has more than a few years left, is that this malignancy is at present encysted in a thick husk of sclerotic scar tissue— our permanent civil service. Democracy implies politics, and "political" is a dirty word to the civil-service state. As well it should be. Its job is to resist democracy, and it does it very well.

Therefore, any attempt to defeat the sclerotic Cathedral state by a restoration of representative democracy in the classic sense of the word, in which public policy is actually formulated by elected officials (such as the Leader, Mencius), is a bayonet charge at the Maginot Line. The Mencist Party could go all the way and elect President Mencius, and it would still be shredded into gobbets of meat by presighted bureaucratic machine guns. In short: a total waste of time. Much better to bend over and pretend to enjoy it.

When we think of a democoup instead of a democratic party, all of these problems disappear. (They are replaced by other problems, but we'll deal with those in their turn.)

Supporters of a democoup propose a program of action, not a policy vision or a personality. The demonstrators who chanted "*Wir sind das Volk*"[8] were not seeking election to the East German Parliament. They were seeking the termination of state socialism. Everyone in the crowd had *exactly* the same goal. The movement was *coherent*—a laser, not a flashlight.

"Racist corporate fascism" is a flashlight. "Elect President Mencius" is a flashlight. Even "secure, responsible and effective government" is something of a flash-

---

7

8 "We are the people"

light, although the beam starts to be reasonably tight—compare, for example, to *sonnō jōi*.⁹ "Restore the Stuarts" is a laser. It may not be the best possible laser (we'll look at others), but it is definitely a laser.

One common democratic assumption is that a movement cannot succeed in wielding power without accumulating a proper majority of support. In fact, none of the movements involved in the fall of Communism mobilized anywhere near a majority. The demonstrations did not have half the country in the streets. They were pure exercises of brutal democratic power, and they succeeded, but they had nothing to do with elections or majorities.

And of course our Western version of socialism, largely because it has not entirely pulled the fangs of democratic politics, is much more responsive to public opinion than any Communist state. Last year the immigration-restriction lobby **NumbersUSA** almost singlehandedly deprived the Inner Party of the pleasure of importing what would have certainly been millions of loyal voters. How many people contacted Congress at their behest? I'd be amazed if it was a hundred thousand.

When we look beyond elections and consider direct influence on government, we see the tremendous power of cohesion, commitment and organization. It is pretty clear, for example, that a minority of Americans supported the American Revolution. But the Patriots were far more motivated and energetic than the Tories. We may deplore the result, but it certainly can't hurt to look into the tactics.

A curious example of reactionary cohesion has emerged recently, in—of all places—my hometown of San Francisco. SF's awful local Pravda, the Chronicle,¹⁰ recently introduced a comments section. Unlike its more careful large competitors, the Chron (a) supports comments on every article, and (b) allows commenters to vote each other *both up and down*.¹¹ Note that this allows the casual reader to *compare the respective political strength of two opposing currents of opinion*—because up and down votes do not cancel each other.

And the result, in the progressive capital of the world? Threads like **this one**,¹² in which comments like

> This makes me embarrassed to live in San Francisco. This scenario is absolutely absurd. Why not just invite all escaped convicts, paroled sex offenders, child molesters, and drug dealers to SF and give them free housing and free food. Simply ridiculous.

---

9 "Revere the emperor, expel the barbarians," political slogan from 19th-century Japan in support of overthrowing the Tokugawa Shogunate and restoring the Emperor.
10 Online as SFGate.com.
11 Predictably, reader comments at SFGate have since been disabled. Records of the comments quoted in this Chapter are therefore lost to history.
12

AN OPEN LETTER TO OPEN-MINDED PROGRESSIVES

> LOL, "Hello!" innocent or not, Deport ALL Illegal Immigrants. As long as it's illegal it's NOT innocent. Fair is Fair. Our Government is insane on this issue.
>
> Far left-liberalism is not a political philosophy, it is a form of mental illness.
>
> OK (expletive deleted), that does it, that's it. I've never had even a traffic ticket in this mid-lifetime of mine, but that's it, give me a six-shooter, some ammo, some places to rob and pilfer, who's gonna join me in one long party of criminal behavior? Look, face it, we're SUCKERS, SUCKERS. There's no incentive in God's Earth to obey the law anymore, why? I've been doing it wrong all this time, there's no sanction for crime anymore. I could use $5,000 for a vacation, I'm just gonna borrow it by force. Why obey laws anymore?

can be "elected" by scores of, respectively, 426 to 4, 371 to 17, 346 to 55, and 484 to 15.

(The best one of these threads ever, though, was one I saw about the "homeless." There was one page in which about a third of the comments were "deleted by SFGate," and the remaining two thirds were peppered with ones like—and I remember this specifically, I am not making it up—"I used to really care about the homeless, but these days I could care less. As far as I'm concerned, we might as well roll 'em up in carpets and throw them in the Bay." To wild virtual applause, of course. Congratulations, San Francisco! The city of **Herb Caen**, the hungry i and the **Barbary Coast** has delivered a new treat—the Bürgerbräukeller[13] @ SFGate.)

Even more interestingly, after the Honduran crack-dealer articles and these reactions appeared (the latest thread, which promises to be glorious, is here[14]), our **notoriously spineless mayor**,[15] or rather his producers, chose to pseudo-reverse[16] his earlier pseudo-non-decision. Where did he get his pox vopuli from? Where do you think? The Chronicle has spawned a monster.

This humble corporate **BBS**,[17] intended as anything but a weapon for reactionary information warfare, is on the way to becoming a real thorn in the side of its Pravda masters. Indeed, the tone of all minor newspapers in America is increasingly reminiscent of *Soviet Life*. The cheery self-adulation, the sock-suck-

---

13 Location of Hitler's 1923 "Beer Hall Putsch."

14

15 Gavin Newsom

16

17 "Bulletin Board System"

ing worship of venal petty bureaucrats, and everywhere the icy plastic chill of Occam's Butterknife:[18]

> On many occasions I had the opportunity to discuss the service industries with Western colleagues. They invariably noted differences with the services that are available in the USSR and what they are accustomed to at home. They told me that, compared to Western standards, this sector is poorly developed in the USSR, but they didn't hesitate to add how fabulously inexpensive most of our services are. For instance, the cost of laundering a man's shirt is about 10 kopecks (20 cents). However, this second point is not widely known.
> [...]
> People are now buying more. A separate apartment for every family, a rarity in the mid-fifties, has now become the rule. Today eight out of 10 urban families live in their own apartments. And many more refrigerators, TV sets, vacuum cleaners and shoes are being produced in the country. The demand for laundries, dry cleaners, repair shops and car-care centers has risen accordingly.
> [...]
> To speed up progress in all areas of the service industries and to more efficiently employ the advantages of a planned economy, the USSR State Planning Committee (Gosplan) has developed a comprehensive program for the expansion of consumer-goods production and the sphere of everyday services for the period 1986 to 2000.
> [...]
> From 1986 to 1990 the number of telephones will increase by from 1.6 to 1.7 times as compared to the current five-year period, and five times by the year 2000. By then it is projected that all residents of small towns will have their own telephones installed in their homes.

Etc., etc., etc. No wonder the most successful new newspaper in America[19] can make a steady living by parodying our version of this material. The form is deathless. It speaks from beyond the grave of socialism. (We're not filling the shafts on those salt mines for nothin'.) Imagine if the actual *Pravda*, in 1986, had set up some little comment board—using paper and cork, probably. The threads would have filled up with exactly the same flavor of reckless petty dissidence.

---

18 Steve Sailer coinage, an inversion of "Occam's razor," indicating a needlessly complex explanation for a given observation.
19 *The Onion*

AN OPEN LETTER TO OPEN-MINDED PROGRESSIVES

This little board has become what might be called a *focus* of political energy. A couple of crucial points about the SFGate *Sturmabteilung*[20]—who might also be described as the Ku Klux Chron, or more historically as the Third Vigilance Committee[21] (I can just picture a hip 3VC logo).

One, the denizens of these boards are a *tiny minority* of San Francisco voters. A thousand votes is not a hill of beans in a city of 750,000. Many of them probably live in the suburbs, not SF proper. The idea that they are representative of SF public opinion proper is ludicrous.

Two, these lopsided percentages are not even representative of the opinions of Chronicle readers. There are certainly plenty of articles on which progressive commenters and comment upvoters congregate, though the ratios are never this glaring. I suspect that there is a small hooligan community which skims SFGate for a certain type of article, and flocks as naturally as any specialized moth to its rare orchid in the dankest, fleshiest navels of the urban underbelly. It is simply obvious that these are not good and healthy people. Why should their opinions count?

They count because the power of a democratic signal is proportional to five variables: the size of the antenna, the material of the antenna, the coherence of the message, the broadcast wattage, and the clarity of reception. In other words: the number of people who agree, the social status of those people, the extent to which they actually agree on any one thing, how much they actually care, and the extent to which the decision-maker (the signal's recipient) can trust the poll.

If you have 10% of the American population who answers 'yes' to a cold-call telemarketer pitching some stupid survey which asks a dumb question whose answer no one knows anything about, like "should the US bomb Iran?", you have a pathetically weak signal. People of average social status are being asked an obvious question that they can be expected to have a casual opinion on, and no more. They have about two neurons devoted to Iran policy. One of these cells may know where Iran is, and the other may know that they wear turbans there. No one will be tempted to bomb Iran, or even consider it, on the strength of this signal.

If you have 10% of the American population, each one a homeowner whose identity has been validated and whose preferences are regularly refreshed in the database, who are on record in favor of abolishing Washington and restoring the Stuarts, and have agreed to vote as a bloc toward this objective, you have a very different phenomenon. Is this enough to abolish Washington, etc.? Probably not, but it might be enough to get a Stuart prince in the Cabinet. While it is not clear that this would be of any value, the principle should be clear.

I suspect the SFGate signal is getting through because it is extremely clear, the people expressing their opinions are extremely vehement, and it is clear that no one is vehement enough in opposition to them to descend into the muck of the

---

20 Hitler's "Brownshirts"
21 The San Francisco Vigilance Committee was established on two separate occasions during the Gold Rush period as an extralegal intervention on the city's rampant crime problem.

dank-orchid articles and vote the Nazi comments down. So the **hooked cross**[22] rises again, in the cradle of the United Nations. How ironic.

(Of course, in reality I'm sure the commenters are all good people, and I regret being tempted to refer to them as the Ku Klux Chron. In fact they are constantly saying things like "I'm not a Republican, but..." **Conquest's law**[23] is always at work.)

In any case: back to the program. We have already described X (Chapter X), but our program is incomplete. We have the formula for a responsible and effective government: a financial structure designed to maximize tax receipts by maximizing property values. We have a program for converting Plaingov into Plaincorp: deliver the former, bag and baggage, to a bankruptcy administrator or Receiver, who restructures the operation and converts its many financial obligations to well-structured securities. We have even suggested some restructuring options—although these matters cannot, of course, be predecided, as the Receiver's sovereignty is undivided.

We do not know whom this Receiver guy or gal is (other than Steve Jobs). (Let's say it's a gal. If Steve wants the job, I'm afraid he'll have to have himself cut.) We do not know who selects the Receiver, and/or reviews her performance. In other words, we have the second half of program X, but not the first.

Frankly, I presented it this way in order to make it sound as shocking and unappealing as possible. Dear open-minded progressive, you have already read through the dramatic climax. Your mind is as open as an oyster on the half-shell. You have seriously considered the idea that your country might be a better place if democracy is terminated, the Constitution is cancelled, and the government is handed over to an absolute dictator whose first act is to impose martial law, and whose long-term plan is to convert your country into a for-profit corporation. Now we can try to translate these shocking suggestions into a more palatable form.

First, it is a mistake to focus on the Receiver. She is not a dictator in the classic sense. A dictator, or even an absolute monarch, has both power and authority: his person is the source of all decisions, his decisions are final, his position is not subject to any external review.

The Receiver—or her long-term replacement, the Director (you might say I subscribe to the **auteur** theory of management; the Receiver's job is to convert Plaingov into Plaincorp, the Director is the chief executive of Plaincorp going forward)—is in a different position. Her decisions are final, so she has absolute authority. But she is an employee, so she has no power. She is just there to do a job, and if she is doing it badly she will be removed.

In the long term, power in Plaincorp belongs to the proprietors—the shareholders, the owners of Plaincorp's equity instruments. But as we discussed in Chapter XII, the right people to hold initial equity in Plaincorp, probably for the most part

---

22 Swastika
23 Law 1: everyone is conservative about what he knows best.

holders of Plaingov's old paper currency and equivalent obligations, may not be the best people to manage Plaincorp. Especially during the critical transition period.

Rather, any plan in which Plaingov relinquishes its sovereign power must involve a transfer of that power to an agency which is *intrinsically trustworthy*. Let's call this the *Trust*. The Receiver is an employee of the Trust, which selects her, reviews her performance regularly, and replaces her if there is any doubt as to her excellence. Sovereignty is an attribute of the Trust, not of the Receiver.

Once Plaincorp is on its feet and running, it will provide a *test* of the proposition that good government equals sound stewardship of sovereign capital. However, the Trust must start off by *assuming* this proposition—that is, its mission is to provide good government, on the assumption that good government maximizes the value of Plainland to Plaincorp. If this assumption appears mistaken, the Trust should not complete the transition to neocameralism. Rather, it should find something else to do, and do it instead. All responsibility is in its hands.

Of course, a degenerate form of the Trust–Receiver design is the old royalist model—the Trust is the royal family. There may even be just one Trustee, the Receiver herself. This is the result we'd obtain by restoring the Stuarts through the House of Liechtenstein. It succeeds, if it succeeds, by putting all the eggs in one very sound basket. The Princes of Liechtenstein are experienced rulers and blatantly responsible, the royalist design is tried and tested (if hardly perfect), and the option can be described without too much genealogical contortion as a restoration of legal authority in any country which traces its sovereignty to the British Empire.

Still, the saleability of the proposition has to be considered. Most people living today have been heavily catechized in the virtues of democracy, the magical wisdom of crowds, and the evils of personal government. There is no getting around it: we have to change their minds on the **first point**. Rearing a fresh crop of Jacobites, however, may exceed even the Internet's vast untapped potential as an information-warfare medium.

So there is a more palatable design for the Trust: a good, old-fashioned parliament, updated of course for the 21st century. This is not democracy, however. Its members each have one vote, but they are not chosen by any sort of election.

Voters raised in the democratic tradition will only be willing to trust sovereignty in the hands of a collective governing body, which operates internally on the basis of one man, one vote. Internally, the Trust is an extremely simple and elegant democracy of trustees. Presumably, following the classic corporate-governance model, the trustees elect a Board, who select the Receiver and review her performance. Just as the Board can fire the Receiver at any time, the trustees can fire the Board. All true power is held by the trustees.

Ideally there are at least thousands, preferably tens or even hundreds of thousands, of trustees. In a pinch, sovereignty can be handed to the Trust simply by running Plaingov's present-day electoral system, but restricting suffrage to trustees—an ugly, but functional, transition plan. The only question is: who are these people? Or more precisely, who should they be?

Think about it, dear open-minded progressive. Presumably you believe in democracy. Presumably your belief is not motivated by the opinion that the average voter has any particular insight into or understanding of the difficult problem of government. Therefore, you believe that there is some sort of amplification effect which somehow transforms the averageness of hominids into the famed "**wisdom of crowds.**" (Actually, as Tocqueville noted, at least when it comes to government by crowd, we are generally looking at an **information cascade** at best, and a particularly wicked feedback loop at worst. But never mind.)

However, whether or not you believe in the wisdom of crowds, you surely believe that any wisdom they may express is derived from the wisdom of their component individuals. There is certainly no **hundredth-monkey effect** in which simply collecting a large number of bipeds and collating their multiple-choice tests can somehow draw truth out of the vastly deep.

Therefore, you will always be able to improve the quality of representatives generated by any democratic system, by improving the quality of the voters. This is the point of the Trust: to dramatically improve the quality of government by replacing universal suffrage with highly qualified suffrage. Our Trustees should be just that—extremely trustworthy.

Okay, this is good. Let's say our goal is to select the 100,000 most trustworthy and responsible adults in Plainland. They will serve as the trustees who oversee the complicated and dangerous transition from Plaingov to Plaincorp. By definition, each of these individuals is in the 99.95th percentile of trustworthiness and responsibility. (I am certainly not in this group.)

Is it not obvious that these people would select competent management? I think it's obvious. But the plan is unworkable, so there is no reason to debate it.

By what process will we select these individuals? Who shall recruit the recruiters? It is difficult and expensive to find just one individual with these executive qualifications. Moreover, in a sovereign context, the filtering process itself will serve as a political football—many progressives might decide, for example, that only progressives can be trusted. It is impossible to end a fight by starting a new fight.

This insane recruiting process cannot occur either under Plaingov or under Plaincorp. It cannot occur under Plaingov, because it will be subject to Plaingov politics and will carry those politics, which are uniformly poisonous, forward into Plaincorp. At this point the reset is not a reset. But it cannot occur under Plaincorp, because the trustees are needed to select the Receiver. And there can be no intervening period of anarchy.

But there is a hack which can work around this obstacle. You might think it's a cute hack, or you might think it's an ugly hack. It probably depends on your taste. I think it's pretty cute.

The hack is a *precise heuristic test* to select trustees. The result of the test is one bit for every citizen of Plainland: he or she either is or is not a trustee. The test is *precise* because its result is not a matter of debate—it can be verified trivially. And it is *heuristic* because it should produce a good result on average, with only occasional horrifying exceptions.

My favorite PHT defines the trustees as the set of all active, certified, nonstudent **pilots** who accept the responsibility of trusteeship, as of the termination date of Plaingov. The set does not expand—you cannot become a trustee by taking flying lessons, and any rejection or resignation of the responsibility is irreversible. In other words, to paraphrase Lenin: all power to the pilots. (There are about 500,000 of them.)

Let's look at the advantages of this PHT. I am not myself a pilot—I am neither wealthy enough, nor responsible enough. But everyone I've ever met who was a pilot, whether private, military or commercial, has struck me as not only responsible, but also independent-minded, often even adventurous. This is a particularly rare combination. To be precise, it is an *aristocratic* combination, and the word *aristocracy* is after all just Greek for *good government*. Pilots are a fraternity of intelligent, practical, and careful people who are already trusted on a regular basis with the lives of others. What's not to like?

If we care to broaden this set, we can extend it by adding *all practicing medical doctors*, or *all active and retired police and military officers*, or better yet both. Believe it or not, doctors were once one of America's most reactionary professions, in the forefront of the struggle against FDR. They also made housecalls. Now they are a bunch of Communist bureaucrats. But the boys in blue can keep them in line. Our fighting men know what to do with a Communist, if they have a free hand. More to the point, each of these professions is a technically demanding task in which the professional is trusted with the lives of others.

So we have a nice, clear, laser-like program. Washington has failed. The Constitution has failed. Democracy has failed. It is time for restoration, for national salvation, for a full reboot. We need a new government, a clean slate, a fresh hand which is smart, strong and fair. All power to the pilots!

321 apoptosis

 321 necrosis

 321 catchy slogans "Umshini wami"

 322 Gallup Jeffrey M. Jones. "Confidence in Congress: Lowest Ever for Any U.S. Institution." *Gallup*, 20 Jun. 2008.

 323 the fall of the Soviet Union

 323 Velvet Revolution

 323 Southern Redemption

 323 Meiji Restoration

 323 English Restoration

 323 Fabian In Chapter 8 Fabian and Gramscian progressivism are defined as democratic and bureaucratic types respectively.

 323 Gramscian Ibid.

 323 Clio

 324 extremely hard in the head "Captive bolt pistol"

 324 very mild Link to Steve Sailer's "very mild anti-semitic" article, "The Cuban Compromise." *Vdare*, cross-posted at iSteve, 6 Jul. 2008.

AN OPEN LETTER TO OPEN-MINDED PROGRESSIVES

 324 Stormfront

 325 plan for school reform Sailer. "Sailer's Four-Point Plan for Improving Schools." *Vdare*, cross-posted at iSteve, 29 Jun. 2008.

 325 Wir sind das Volk

 326 sonnō jōi

 326 NumbersUSA

 326 this one Jaxon Van Derbeken. "8 crack dealers shielded by S.F. walk away" *SFGate*, 1 Jul. 2008.

 327 Herb Caen

 327 hungry i

 327 Barbary Coast

 327 Bürgerbräukeller

 327 here Jaxon Van Derbeken. "S.F. working on protocol for teen illegals" *SFGate*, 10 Jul. 2008.

 327 pseudo-reverse Jaxon Van Derbeken. "S.F. mayor shifts policy on illegal offenders" *SFGate*, 10 Jul. 2008.

 327 BBS "Bulletin Board System"

 328 Occam's Butterknife Steve Sailer. "Mapping the Unmentionable: Race and Crime." *Vdare*, 13 Feb. 2005.

328 most successful new newspaper in America Link to the homepage for The Onion.

 328 Pravda

 329 Sturmabteilung

 329 Third Vigilance Committee

 330 hooked cross "Swastika"

330 Conquest's law Robert Conquest apparently only ever articulated his "laws" in conversation, so there is no single book or article to which they can be attributed, leading to some disagreement over their precise language. They are generally formulated as:
1. Everybody is a conservative about what he knows best.
2. Any organization not explicitly right-wing becomes left-wing over time.
3. The simplest way to explain the behavior of any bureaucratic organization is to assume that it is controlled by a cabal of its enemies.

 330 auteur

 331 Stuarts "Prince Joseph Wenzel of Liechtenstein"

 331 House of Liechtenstein

331 first point "In *A Gentle Introduction to Unqualified Reservations*, Moldbug proposes a refinement to neocameralism called a *joint-stock republic*, which avoids this issue by replacing ordinary votes with negotiable shares. A joint-stock republic is still arguably a 'universal-suffrage democracy,' only with voting according to shares instead of a simple counting of heads. The principle that needs to be abandoned then is not democracy itself—a rather hard sell in this day and age—but the much more weakly held principle of 'one person, one vote.'" (UR ed.).

AN OPEN LETTER TO OPEN-MINDED PROGRESSIVES

332 wisdom of crowds. James Surowiecki. *The Wisdom of Crowds: Why the Many Are Smarter Than the Few and How Collective Wisdom Shapes Business, Economies, Societies and Nations.* (Doubleday; Anchor 2004).

332 information cascade

332 hundredth-monkey effect

333 pilots "Pilot certification in the United States"

CHAPTER XIV:
RULES FOR REACTIONARIES
JULY 17, 2008

Dear open-minded progressive, I hope you've enjoyed this weird excursion.

We all like to think we have open minds, but only a few of us are tough enough to snort any strange powder that's shoved under our noses. You have joined that elite crew. Thirteen chapters ago you may have been a mere space cadet. Now you are at least a space lieutenant, perhaps even a captain or a major. And what fresh galaxies remain to explore!

But first: the solution.

Well, first the problem. This is a blog, after all. We can't really expect everyone to have read all the back issues. Repetition is a necessity, and a virtue as well. A true space lieutenant, surprised by the Slime Beast of Vega, has his acid blaster on full-auto and is pumping a massive drug bolus into its sticky green hide before he even knows what's happening. His reaction is not thought, but drill—the apotheosis of practice.

Our problem is *democracy*. Democracy is a dangerous, malignant form of government which tends to degenerate, sometimes slowly and sometimes with shocking, gut-wrenching speed, into tyranny and chaos. You've been taught to worship democracy. This is because you are ruled by democracy. If you were ruled by the Slime Beast of Vega, you would worship the Slime Beast of Vega. (A more earthly comparison is Communism or "people's democracy," whose claim to be a more advanced form of its Western cousin was perfectly accurate—if we mean "advanced" in the sense of, say, "advanced leukemia.")

There are two problems with democracy: the first-order and the second-order.

CHAPTER XIII

The first-order problem: since a governed territory is capital, i.e., a valuable asset, it generates revenue. Participation in government is also the definition of power, which all men and quite a few women crave. At its best, democracy is a permanent, gunless civil war for this gigantic pot of money and power. (At its worst, the guns come out.) Any democratic faction has an incentive to mismanage the whole to enlarge its share.

Without quite understanding this problem, **Noah Webster**, in his **1794 pamphlet on the French Revolution**, described its symptoms perfectly. Webster was writing during the quasi-monarchist Federalist restoration, when Americans had convinced themselves that it was possible to create a republic without political parties. The Federalists held "faction" to be the root of all democratic evils—much as their progressive successors are constantly yearning for a "post-partisan" democracy. Both are right. But complaining that democracy is too political is like complaining that the Slime Beast of Vega is too slimy.

Webster wrote:

> As the tendency of such associations is probably not fully understood by most of the persons composing them in this country, and many of them are doubtless well-meaning citizens; it may be useful to trace the progress of party spirit to faction first, and then of course to tyranny.
>
> [...]
>
> My second remark is, that contention between parties is usually violent in proportion to the trifling nature of the point in question; or to the uncertainty of its tendency to promote public happiness. When an object of great magnitude is in question, and its utility obvious, a *great* majority is usually found in its favor, and *vice versa*; and a large majority usually quiets all opposition. But when a point is of less magnitude or less visible utility, the parties may be and often are *nearly equal*. Then it becomes a trial of strength—each party acquires confidence from the very circumstance of *equality*—both become assured they are *right*—confidence inspires boldness and expectation of success—pride comes in aid of argument—the passions are inflamed—the *merits* of the cause become a subordinate consideration—victory is the object and not public good; at length the question is decided by a small majority—success inspires one party with pride, and they assume the airs of conquerors; disappointment sours the minds of the other—and thus the contest ends in creating violent passions, which are always ready to enlist into every other cause. Such is the progress of party spirit; and a single question will often give rise to a party, that will continue for generations; and the same men or their adherents will continue to divide on other ques-

tions, that have not the remotest connection with the first point of contention.

This observation gives rise to my third remark; that nothing is more dangerous to the cause of *truth* and *liberty* than a party spirit. When men are once united, in whatever form, or upon whatever occasion, the union creates a partiality or friendship for each member of the party or society. A coalition for any purpose creates an attachment, and inspires a confidence in the individuals of the party, which does not die with the cause which united them; but continues, and extends to every other object of social intercourse.

Thus we see men first united in some system of religious faith, generally agree in their *political* opinions. Natives of the same country, even in a foreign country, unite and form a separate private society. The Masons feel attached to each other, though in distant parts of the world.

The same may be said of Episcopalians, Quakers, Presbyterians, Roman Catholics, Federalists, and Antifederalists, mechanic societies, chambers of commerce, Jacobin and Democratic societies. It is altogether immaterial what circumstance first unites a number of men into a society; whether they first rally round the church, a square and compass, a cross, or a cap; the general effect is always the same; while the union continues, the members of the association feel a particular confidence in each other, which leads them to believe each other's opinions, to catch each other's passions, and to act in concert on every question in which they are interested.

Hence arises what is called *bigotry* or *illiberality*. Persons who are united on any occasion, are more apt to believe the prevailing opinions of their society, than the prevailing opinions of another society. They examine their own creeds more fully, (and perhaps with a mind predisposed to believe them), than they do the creeds of other societies. Hence the full persuasion in every society that theirs is *right*; and if I am right, others of course are *wrong*. Perhaps therefore I am warranted in saying, there is a *species of bigotry* in every society on earth—and indeed in every man's own particular faith. While each man and each society is freely indulged in his own opinion, and that opinion is mere *speculation*, there is peace, harmony, and good understanding. But the moment a man or a society attempts to oppose the prevailing opinions of another man or society, even his arguments rouse passion; it being difficult for two men of opposite creeds to dispute for any time, without becoming angry. And when one party attempts in practice to interfere with the opinions of another party, violence most generally succeeds.

Note that Webster (a) assumes that the problem of factions is solvable; (b) assumes that voters start with a generally accurate understanding of the problem of government, which will generate the right answer on all important questions; (c) assumes that voters will not form coalitions for the mere sordid purpose of looting the state, i.e., "achieving social justice"; and (d), of course, demonstrates the correct or dictionary definition of the word *bigotry*.

All these assumptions, which in 1794 were at least plausible, are now anything but. (And our modern bigots are as diverse as can be.) Yet the juggernaut of democracy rolls on. New excuses are needed, new excuses are found.

This leads us to the second-order problem. While democracy may start with a population of voters who understand the art of government, as America indeed did (the extent to which 18th-century Americans understood the basic principles of practical government, while hardly perfect, was mindboggling by today's standards), it seldom stays that way. Its fans believe that participation in the democratic process actually improves the mental qualities of the citizen. I suppose this is true—for certain values of the words "improves."

The real problem with democracies is that, in the long run, a democratic government *elects its own people*. I refer here to **Bertolt Brecht**'s verse:

> After the uprising of the 17th June
> The Secretary of the Writers Union
> Had leaflets distributed in the Stalinallee
> Stating that the people
> Had forfeited the confidence of the government
> And could win it back only
> By redoubled efforts. Would it not be easier
> In that case for the government
> To dissolve the people
> And elect another?

One way to elect a new people is to import them, of course. For example, to put it bluntly, the Democratic Party has **captured California**, once a **Republican stronghold**, by importing arbitrary numbers of Mexicans. Indeed the Third World is stocked with literally billions of potential Democrats, just waiting to come to America so that Washington can buy their votes. Inner Party functionaries **cackle gleefully**[1] over this achievement:

1

AN OPEN LETTER TO OPEN-MINDED PROGRESSIVES

For all this [2008] primary season's obsession with the single (and declining) demographic of white working-class men in Rust Belt states, America is changing rapidly across all racial, generational and ethnic lines. The Census Bureau announced last week that half the country's population growth since 2000 is due to Hispanics, another group [in addition to blacks] understandably alienated from the G.O.P.

Anyone who does the math knows that America is on track to become a white-minority nation in three to four decades. Yet if there's any coherent message to be gleaned from the hypocrisy whipped up by Hurricane Jeremiah, it's that this nation's perennially promised candid conversation on race has yet to begin.

(BTW, isn't that photo of Frank Rich[2] amazing? Doesn't it just radiate pure power and contempt? Henry VIII would probably have asked the painter to make him look less like Xerxes, King of Kings.)

But this act of brutal Machiavellian thug politics, larded as usual with the most gushing of sentimental platitudes,[3] is picayune next to the ordinary practice of democratic governments: to elect a new people by re-educating the children of the old. In the long run, power in a democracy belongs to its information organs: the press, the schools, and most of all the universities, who mint the thoughts the others disburse. For simplicity, we have dubbed this complex the *Cathedral*.

The Cathedral is a feedback loop. It has no center, no master planners. Everyone, even the Sulzbergers, is replaceable. In a democracy, mass opinion creates power. Power diverts funds to the manufacturers of opinion, who manufacture more, etc. Not a terribly complicated cycle.

This feedback loop generates a playing field on which the most competitive ideas are not those which best correspond to reality, but those which produce the strongest feedback. The Cathedral is constantly electing a new people who (a) support the Cathedral more and more, and (b) support a political system which makes the Cathedral stronger and stronger.

For example, libertarian policies are not competitive in the Cathedral, because libertarianism minimizes employment for public-policy experts. Thus we would expect libertarians to come in two flavors: the intellectually marginalized, and the intellectually compromised.[4]

Many of the LvMI types feel quite free to be skeptical of democracy. But they are skipping quite a few steps between problem and solution. They are still thinking in the democratic tense. Their plan for achieving libertarianism, if it can be

---

2

3 "No person is illegal." See Chapter 8.
4 Reference to the Ludwig von Mises Institute (LvMI) and the Cato Institute, respectively.

described as a plan, is to convince as many people as possible that libertarian policies are good ones. These will then elect libertarian politicians, etc., etc.

When you say, *I am a libertarian*, what you mean is: *I, as a customer of government, prefer to live in a state which does not apply non-libertarian policies.* The best results in this line will be achieved by capturing a state yourself, and becoming its Supreme Ruler. Then no bureaucrats will bother you! Given that most of us are not capable of this feat, and given that the absence of government is a military impossibility, the libertarian should search for a structure of government in which the state has *no incentive* to apply non-libertarian policies. Obviously, democracy is not such a structure.

Thus a libertarian democracy is simply an engineering contradiction, like a flying whale or a water-powered car. Water is a lot cheaper than gas, and I think a flying whale would make a wonderful pet—I could tether it to my deck, perhaps. Does it matter? Defeating democracy is difficult; making democracy libertarian is impossible. The difference is subtle, but...

Worse, the most competitive ideas in the democratic feedback loop tend to be policies which are in fact *counterproductive*—that is, they actually cause the problem they pretend to be curing. They are quack medicines. They keep the patient coming back.

For example, Britain today is suffering from an "epidemic" of "knife crime." To wit: every day in Great Britain, **60 people**[5] are stabbed or mugged with a knife. (Admire, for a moment, the passive voice. Presumably the knives are floating disembodied in the air, directing themselves with Jedi powers.) The solution:

> On Tuesday, Jacqui Smith, the Home Secretary, will publish her Youth Crime Action Plan. It includes a proposal to make young offenders visit casualty wards to examine knife wounds in an attempt to shock them into mending their ways.

I swear I am not making this up. Meanwhile, experts agree, prison terms **should be abolished**[6] for minor crimes, such as burglary:

> The Independent Sentencing Advisory Panel also said that there should be a presumption that thieves, burglars and anyone convicted of dishonesty should not receive a jail term.

I'm sure that'll help. **Scientists around the world**[7] conclude:

---

5 Linked headline reads: "Knife crime claims 60 victims a day." Full text linked in the endnotes.
6 "Tens of thousands of criminals to be spared short jail terms." Ibid.
7 "Tackling knife crime: different approaches." Ibid.

AN OPEN LETTER TO OPEN-MINDED PROGRESSIVES 345

> It takes a multi-level approach to prevention. If you want to approach violence protection with juveniles, you need to engage in prevention early on—with social skills and anger coping lessons in schools from a young age.

The real experts, of course, are the yoofs themselves:[8]

> However, the government should be praised for not taking an automatically authoritarian approach. Their policy of getting young people to talk to stabbing victims rests on the belief that kids respond to education and are capable of empathy, something that the Conservative policy of locking anyone up caught carrying a knife doesn't seem to appreciate.

To say the least. It wouldn't be the first time the narrow-minded have defied scientific research:[9]

> But researchers at Manchester University's school of law found evidence which directly contradicts core assumptions of government policy.

Having spoken to and won the trust of more than 100 gang members, associates and informers, they concluded that in general gangs are not tightly organised; they do not specialise in dealing drugs; and their violence is not provoked primarily by turf wars. They also found no basis for the popular belief that most street gangs are black.

> Robert Ralphs, the project's lead fieldworker, said: "Police and other statutory agencies respond to gangs as clearly identifiable groups of criminally-involved young people, where membership is undisputed."
>
> "In reality, gangs are loose, messy, changing friendship networks—less organised and less criminally active than widely believed—with unclear, shifting and unstable leadership."
>
> By failing to understand this basic structure, the researchers say, police mistakenly target and sometimes harass individuals who, though gang members, are not breaking any law; the police also repeatedly follow, stop and search the gang members' family, friends and classmates. This alienated both the gang members and their associates who might otherwise have helped police.
> […]

---

8 "How can our politicians understand blade culture?" Ibid.
9 "Youth violence: Tactics against gangs fatally flawed - report." ibid.

Judith Aldridge, who led the research, said: "They are mainly victims. So, there is a desperate need to appropriately assess the needs of these young people and their families—and not blame them."

Etc. I'm sure none of this is new to you. Britain makes such a wonderful example, however, because its descent into Quaker-thug hell is so fresh, and proceeded from such a height. Witness, for example, this lovely story[10] from the Times archive, which is barely 50 years old—"in the lives of those now living," unless of course they have since been stabbed:

JUDGE ON RACE GANG WARFARE: 7-YEAR SENTENCES

Two men were each sentenced at Central Criminal Court yesterday to seven years' imprisonment for their part in an attack on John Frederick Carter, fruit trader of Sydney Square, Glengall Road, Peckham, who received injuries to his face and head which required 60 stitches.

They were Raymond David Rosa, aged 31, bookmaker's clerk, of Northborough Road, Norbury, S.W., and Richard Frett, aged 34, dealer, of Wickstead House, Falmouth Road, S.E. The jury had found them both guilty of wounding Carter with intent to cause him grievous bodily harm.

Passing sentence, Mr. Justice Donovan said: "I have not the least doubt that there are other and very wicked persons behind you, but the tools of those persons must realize that if discovery follows punishment will be condign."

"MORE LIKE CHICAGO"

Summing up yesterday, his Lordship said that the facts of this case sounded more like Chicago and the worst days of prohibition than London in 1956.

Putting two and two together, the jury might think this was another case of race gang warfare. If that were so, then it raised the question of whether the reluctance of Mr. and Mrs. Carter to swear that the two men they had previously picked out were concerned in the attack was due to fear. It was that possibility which put this case into quite a different category. It put it into a category where gross violence had been perpetrated upon a man but after identifying his assailants he and his wife had expressed doubts in the witness-box. The jury were not concerned with the merits

---

10 Original archived article is unaccessible. The events described are from an incident in May of 1956.

or de-merits of Carter. The issue was much wider than Carter's skin: it was simply one of the maintenance of law and order without which none could go about with safety.

Etc., etc. Notice that both of these miscreants are in possession of at least nominal *occupations*. Mr. Justice Donovan, honey, with all due respect, you don't know nothin' 'bout no "race gang warfare."

And finally, completing our tour of the British criminal justice system, we learn that:[11]

> Two South Africans who overstayed their British visas were jailed for life on Friday for the murders of two men strangled during a series of violent muggings.
>
> Gabriel Bhengu, 27, and Jabu Mbowane, 26, will be deported after serving life sentences.

No, that's not a misprint:

A life sentence normally lasts around 15 years.

Orwell could not be more satisfied. "A life sentence normally lasts around 15 years." With not a hint of irony in the building.

Something is normal here, and it is either 1956 or 2008. It can't be both. If Mr. Justice Donovan, or the Times reporter who considered a mere 60 stitches somehow newsworthy, were to reappear in modern London, their perspective on the art of government in a democratic society unchanged, they would be far to the right not only of Professor Aldridge, but also of the Tories, the **BNP**, and perhaps even **Spearhead**.[12] They would not be normal people. But in 1956, their reactions were completely unremarkable.

What's happened is that Britain, which before WWII was still in many respects an aristocracy, became Americanized and democratized after the war. As a democracy, it elected its own people, who now tolerate what their grandparents would have found unimaginable. Of course, many British voters, probably even most, still do believe that burglars should go to prison, etc., etc., but these views are on the way out, and the politics of love is on the way in. Politicians, who are uniformly devoid of character or personality, have the good sense to side with the future electorate rather than with the past electorate.

11

12 Website run by right-wing political activist Simon Sheppard, imprisoned four times (as of this publication) for political speech crimes.

And why are the studies of Professor Aldridge and her ilk so successful, despite their obvious effects? One: they result in a tremendous level of crime, which generates a tremendous level of funding for "criminologists." Two: they are counterintuitive, i.e., obviously wrong. No one would pay a "social scientist" to admit the obvious. Three: as per Noah Webster, they appeal to the ruling class simply because they are so abhorrent to the ruled class.

And four: they are not disprovable, because if pure, undiluted Quaker love ever becomes the only way for British civilization to deal with its ferals, they won't leave much of Professor Aldridge. She might, like **Judith Todd**,[13] regard her suffering as a Christlike badge of distinction. She would certainly, like Ms. Todd, express no guilt over her actions. But it won't happen, because Britain will retain the unprincipled exceptions and the few rough men it needs to keep it from the abyss for the indefinite future. And for that same future, Professor Aldridge and her like will be able to explain the debacle in terms of the "cycle of violence." As Chesterton put it:

> We have actually contrived to invent a new kind of hypocrite. The old hypocrite, Tartuffe or Pecksniff, was a man whose aims were really worldly and practical, while he pretended that they were religious. The new hypocrite is one whose aims are really religious, while he pretends that they are worldly and practical.

From the perspective of the customer of government, however, it is irrelevant *why* these events happen. What matters is that they *do happen*, and that they do not *have to happen*. If statistics did not confirm that stabbings in London were not, in the lives of those now living, a routine event, that Times article should be sufficient. (In fact, I'll take one good primary source over all the statistics in the world.)

And this, in my reactionary judgment, makes NuLabour *responsible* for these events. As surely as if Gordon Brown and Professor Aldridge themselves had gone on a stabbing spree.

Consider the following fact: in April 2007, an American Special Forces captain, Robert Williams, forced his way into the home of a young Iraqi journalist, whom he raped, tortured, and attempted to murder. Williams ordered the woman to stab out her own eyes. When she tried and failed, he sliced up her face with a butcher knife. After asking her if she "liked Americans," he forced her to swallow handfuls of pills, which destroyed her liver, and when leaving the building after an 18-hour ordeal he tied her to a sofa and set a fire under it. She escaped only by using the fire to burn away the ropes around her hands.

And why haven't you heard of this event? Obviously you don't read the papers. Williams, it turns out, was linked to a fundamentalist Christian cell inside the US military, one of whose leaders, **General William Boykin**, was a mentor to none other than John McCain...

---

13 Daughter of Garfield Todd, former prime minister of Southern Rhodesia, who participated in the "liberation struggle" to free the country of white-minority rule.

Okay. At this point, I am obviously just making stuff up. If this event had happened, you wouldn't need to read the papers. Or watch television. The only way you would not know of the event is if you were a hermit in the deep bush in Alaska, and it was the middle of winter. It would be the defining event of the American occupation of Iraq, and as soon as the snow thawed and the caribou came back, a dog-team would arrive at your cabin and bark out the news.

Unless the Pentagon covered it up. And given that this search[14] produces almost 2 million hits, doesn't that seem a likely possibility?

It did happen, however. Not in Baghdad, but in Manhattan. The real Robert Williams[15] is not a white supremacist, but a black one. The anonymous victim is a journalism student at Columbia. And how many stories in the local newspaper of record, many of whose employees must be Facebook friends of the victim, did these events generate? I found six. All of them buried deep in the "New York Region" section, whose crime reporters I'm sure are on the fast track to superstar status at the NYT. Not.

Note that this is exactly how the Pentagon, in our imaginary Baghdad rape, would have wanted the situation handled. A coverup is always a possibility, but risky. It can leak. Whereas if the journalists themselves agree that the event is *not important*, that it is fundamentally *random*, that it certainly does not deserve the crime-of-the-century treatment that the Times of London, in 1956, would have given the real Robert Williams.

It is very unfortunate, of course, that a Special Forces officer abused a young Iraqi woman. But it is the exception, not the rule. It has nothing to do with the Special Forces as a whole, or with General Boykin, or certainly with John McCain. A few stories in the back of the paper, and the whole sad event is documented for the record. And our troops continue their honorable work in Iraq, saving babies from gangrene and bringing happiness to orphaned goats.

Would I accept this whitewash? Probably not. But I would be more likely to accept it than the New York Times. Clearly, the real Robert Williams and his ilk have no enemies at the Times. But they have an enemy in Larry Auster, who wrote:

> So here's a question that ought to be asked of Obama at a presidential debate:
> Sen. Obama, you said in your speech on race last March 18 that as long as whites have not ended racial inequality in America, whites have to expect the sort of hatred and rage that comes from Jeremiah Wright, who identifies the source of evil in the world as "white man's greed."

---

14 "Pentagon coverup"
15 Grisly account from The New York Times of a torture and rape from June of 2008.

CHAPTER XIII

> In this country today, black on white violence is a fact of life, and in addition to the steady stream of black on white rapes and murders there have been racially motivated black on white crimes of shocking brutality and horror, including not only rape and sodomy, but torture, disfigurement, burning. Cases in point are the Wichita Massacre in December 2000 in which five young white people were captured and tortured, and four of them murdered, the torture-murder of Channon Christian and Christopher Newsom in Knoxville in January 2007, and the torture and disfigurement of a young women in New York City in April 2007.
>
> Senator, is it your position that until whites have ended racial inequality in America, whites have to expect to be targeted by white-hating black thugs? In fact, aren't such criminals only acting out in physical terms the same seething anti-white anger, hatred, and vengefulness which has been enacted verbally by the pastor, and through whoops, yells, and cries from the congregration [*sic*], every week in your church for the last 30 years, and which you have justified as an understandable and inevitable response to racial inequality?

If Sen. Obama has replied, I'm not aware of it. Perhaps he's not a *View From the Right* reader.

The crucial point is that your democratic mind handles these two identical crimes, one real and one imaginary, in very different ways. In the imaginary crime, your reflex is to extend a chain of collective responsibility to all the ideologies, institutions, and individuals who remind you even remotely of the criminal, or can be connected with him in some general way. (Capt. Williams was certainly not *ordered* to rape an Iraqi journalist.) In the real crime, responsibility extends only to the perpetrator, and perhaps not even to him—after all, he had a difficult childhood.

Dear open-minded progressive, this is how elegantly democracy has infected your brain. To the anonymous London reporter of 1956, the fact that this horrific crime could happen in Manhattan in 2008, and no one, not even the fellow Columbia-trained journalists a hundred blocks downtown, would find it especially important, would suggest some kind of *anesthesia*, some disconnection of the natural chimpanzee response of fear and rage. But this response has not been disabled in general—because we see it displayed in all its glory when an American soldier puts a pair of underpants on someone's head, somewhere in Mesopotamia.

Thus we are looking at *selective anesthesia*—by historical standards, our reaction to one offense is unusually sedated, and our reaction to the other is unusually inflamed. Of course, this does not exclude the possibility that in both cases, the old reaction was wrong and the new reaction was right. But it is difficult for me—perhaps only because I am insufficiently versed in progressive doxology—to construct

AN OPEN LETTER TO OPEN-MINDED PROGRESSIVES

an ethical explanation of the change. On the other hand, I find it very easy to construct a *political* explanation of the change.

Here's another way to look at the same issue. Suppose, dear open-minded progressive, that the San Francisco Police Department embarked on a **reign of lawless terror**,[16] killing a hundred people or so a year, at least half of whom were innocent, and beating, raping, etc., many more. Would the good progressives of San Francisco stand for it? I think not. Because we don't believe that the police should be above the law. We believe that when they commit crimes, they should be tried and sent to jail just like everyone else.

So we believe that, ethically, a policeman's crimes are no different from a street thug's. Or do we? Not as far as I can tell. I think San Franciscans are much *more* likely to express fear and anger at the idea of a policeman committing lawless violence. Don't you find this slightly odd? Which would you rather be hit over the head by: a policeman, or a mugger? I would rather not be hit over the head at all, thank you.

If the SFPD were as high-handed and above the law as the paramilitary gangs it (in theory) opposes, you, dear open-minded progressive, would agree that the only solution is a higher power: the National Guard. They have **bigger guns**, after all. But if you prefer martial law to the SFPD's reign of terror, why don't you prefer martial law to MS-13's reign of terror?

And this is exactly the problem. The reality is that *almost every country in the world today*—and certainly every major American city—could use a solid dose of **martial law**.

Because all are beset by criminal paramilitary organizations which (a) are too powerful to be suppressed by the security forces under the legal system as it presently stands, (b) if judged by the same standards as the security forces constitute a gigantic, ongoing human-rights violation, and (c) if associated with the civilian and nongovernmental organizations which protect them from the security forces, *implicate the former* as major human-rights violators.

So when a **liberal surgeon in South Africa**,[17] whose trustworthiness strikes me as complete, **writes**:

> I recently watched the movie capote. i enjoyed it. but, being south african, i was interested in the reaction the movie portrayed of the american community to the murders that the movie is indirectly about. their reaction was shock and dismay. their reaction was right.
>
> but in south africa there is a similar incident every day. i don't read the newspaper because it depresses me too much. you might

---

16 Reference to "Fajitagate," a 2002 incident in San Francisco that began with a streetfight among off-duty cops and eventually culminated in the resignation of the SFPD Chief of Police.

17 Author Bongi, at the blog *other things amanzi*.

CHAPTER XIII

> wonder why i, a surgeon, am posting on this. one reason may be because i often deal with the survivors (two previous posts found here and here). at the moment i have three patients who are victims of violent crime. one is the victim of a farm attack. an old man who had his head caved in with a spade. why? just for fun, it seems. but maybe the reason i'm writing this post is because i'm south african. this is my country and i'm gatvol.[18]
>
> just three recent stories. some guys broke into a house. they gagged the man. it seemed that whatever they shoved into his mouth was shoved in too deep, because as they lay on the bed violating his wife, he fought for breath and finally died of asphyxiation.
>
> then there is a woman alone at home. some thugs broke in and asked where the safe was. they were looking for guns. she told them she had no safe and no guns. they then took a poker, heated it to red hot and proceeded to torture her with it so that she would tell them what they wanted to hear. because she could not, the torture went on for a number of hours.
>
> then there is the story of a group of thugs that broke in to a house. they shot the man and cut the fingers of the woman off with a pair of garden shears. while the man lay on the floor dying, the criminals took some time off to lounge on the bed eating some snacks they had found in the fridge and watch a bit of television.
>
> [...]
>
> there is crime everywhere but the most brutal and the violent crimes without clear motives are almost exclusively black on white. this is one more thing the government denies and even labels you as racist if you say it. it may not be put too strongly to say it is very nearly government sanctioned.

We start to smell a small, ugly smell of the future. After all, if all the people in the world could vote, or if they all moved to America, the electorate would look a lot like the New South Africa—the "Rainbow Nation," the great hope for **human oneness**.[19] Oops.

Unfortunately, our surgeon's database is a little out of date. America is no longer shocked by "**In Cold Blood**" events. There are simply too many of them. But there are nowhere near as many as in South Africa. (And even if I were not convinced by the surgeon's uncapitalized demeanor, **other sources confirm the result**.[20])

---

18 South African slang, "fed up, irritated."
19 Reference to "Ubuntu" philosophy of pan-African human "oneness."
20 Reference to 2006 statements from Charles Nqakula, SA Minister of Safety and Security, who told citizens to leave the country if they were concerned about crime, despite SA having the second highest murder rate in the world at the time.

AN OPEN LETTER TO OPEN-MINDED PROGRESSIVES

In fact the simplest way to evaluate a government for human-rights violations is to think of *all* violence as the responsibility of the state, whether it is committed by men in uniforms or not. Otherwise, employing **paramilitary criminals**[21] to do your dirty deeds, for a measure of plausible deniability, is far too easy. And **quite popular these days**.[22] There is no sharp line between an army and a militia, between a militia and a gang, and between a gang and a bunch of criminals. As the **laws of King Ine of Wessex** famously put it:

> We use the term "thieves" if the number of men does not exceed seven, and "brigands" for a number between seven and thirty-five. Anything beyond this is an "army."

(A short course in actual Saxon history, such as that linked above, cannot come too soon for **many libertarians**, who throughout the history of English legal theory have been overfond of construing the medieval world as a paradise of ordered liberty. Indeed we inherit many elegant constructs from medieval law. And one reason they are so elegant is that they had to operate in such a brutal environment of pervasive violence.)

There is no reason at all that a libertarian, **such as myself**, cannot favor martial law. I am free when my rights are defined and secured against all comers, regardless of official pretensions. Freedom implies law; law implies order; order implies peace; peace implies victory. As a libertarian, the greatest threat to my property is not Uncle Sam, but thieves and brigands. If Uncle Sam wakes up from his present sclerotic slumber and shows the brigands a **strong hand**, my liberty has been increased.

You see what happens when you open your mind and snort the mystery powder. You wind up on YouTube, listening to an effeminate, deceased **dictator**[23] scream *"¡Tendré la mano más dura que se imaginen!"*[24] I don't think that one needs much translation.

And how about **this one**:

> Frankly, I begin to think that the U.S. is about ready for an Il Duce right now...

Except that when you follow the link, it's not at all what you think. At least, it has nothing to do with the "Pinochet Youth." The original post was actually on a site for **insider political gossip** in New York State, which was linked from the NYT. And the **author**[25] strikes me as, *rara avis*, a completely honest and dedicat-

---

21 Arkan, infamous Serbian paramilitary commander during the Yugoslav Wars.
22 Reference to the paramilitary organizations, the Janjaweed, Interahamwe, Hezbollah, and Sons of Iraq.
23 Pinochet
24 "I will have the strongest hand you can imagine!"
25 Larry Littlefield

ed career public servant, certainly an Obama voter, and certainly not a follower of Mussolini or any similar figure.

And yet the quote is not out of context at all. **Read the essay.**[26] If I'm worth your time, Littlefield is too:

> Letting go of one's illusions is a difficult process that takes a long, long time, but I am just about there. From a young age I have been a believer in public services and benefits as a way of providing some measure of assurance for other people, people I rely on every time I purchase a good or service, of a decent life regardless of one's personal income or standing. After all, I initially chose public service as a career. And I have been a defender of the public institutions when compared with those who were only concerned with their own situation and preference put in less, or get out more, as if the community was a greedy adversary to be beaten in life rather than something one is a part of. Now, however, I see that it is probably hopeless.

Admittedly, Albany is one of the worst Augean stables of bureaucracy in America. If Hercules had to clean it out, he wouldn't find the Hudson sufficient. He'd have to find a way to get the St. Lawrence involved. But is Albany that different from Sacramento, or from Washington itself? Of course not.

Of course, neither Albany nor Washington needs a Duce. It needs a CEO. Like any gigantic, ancient and broken institution, it has no problem that can't be fixed by installing new management with **plenary authority**. (It might help to move the capital, as well. Put it in Kansas City, or better yet San Francisco, so that progressives can see the future up close.)

But the reality is: this thing is *done*. It is *over*. It is *not fixable* by *any form* of conventional politics. Either you want to keep it, or you want to throw it out. Any other political opinions you may have are irrelevant next to this choice.

On that note, let's review our rules for reactionaries.

Rule #1 is the one we just stated. Reaction is a *boolean decision*. Either you want to discard our present political system, including democracy, the Constitution, the entire legal code and body of precedent, the UN, etc., etc., or you think it's safer to muddle along with what we have now. Either is a perfectly legitimate opinion which a perfectly reasonable person may hold.

Of course, it is impossible to replace something with nothing. I've presented some designs for a restoration of secure, responsible and effective government. What I like about these designs is that they're simple, clear and easy to understand,

---

26

and they rely on straightforward engineering principles without any mystical element. In particular, they do not require anyone to be a saint.

But here is another simple design: military government. Hand plenary power to the Joint Chiefs. Let them go from there. This won't do permanently, but for a few years it'd be fine. That should be plenty of time to figure out what comes next.

Here is yet another: restrict voting to homeowners. Note that this was widely practised in Anglo-American history, and for very good reason. As John Jay put it: those who own the country ought to govern it. Mere freehold suffrage is a poor substitute for military government, and it too is not stable in the long run. But it would be opposed by all the same people, and it would constitute a very hard shake-up in exactly the right direction.

Here is a third: dissolve Washington and return sovereignty to the states. Here is a fourth: vest plenary executive authority in the Chief Justice, John Roberts. Here is a fifth: vest plenary executive authority in the publisher of the New York Times, "Pinch" Sulzberger. Here is a sixth: vest plenary executive authority in the Good One, Barack Obama. I am not altogether fond of the jobs that the latter two are doing with the limited authority they have now, but they are at least prepared for power, and real authority tends to create real responsibility in a hurry.

At present, any of these things is such a long way from happening that *the choice does not matter at all*. What matters, dear open-minded reactionary, is that you have had enough of our present government, you are done, finished, gatvol, and you want to replace it with something else that is secure, responsible, and effective.

In other words, rule #1: the reactionary's opposition to the present regime is *purely negative*. Positive proposals for what to replace it with are out of scope, now and for the foreseeable future. Once again, think in terms of the fall of Communism: the only thing that all those who lived under Communism could agree on was that they were *done with Communism*.

The advantage of rule #1 is that, applied correctly, it ensures a complete absence of internal conflict. There is nothing to argue over. Either you oppose the government, or you support it.

One exception to rule #1 is that the same coherent pure negativity, and resulting absence of bickering, can be achieved by opposing *components* of the government.

For example, I believe that both America and the rest of the planet would achieve enormous benefits by a total shutdown of international relations, including security guarantees, foreign aid, and mass immigration, and a return to the 19th-century policy of neutrality—an approach easily summarized by the phrase *no foreign policy*. I believe that government should take no notice whatsoever of race—*no racial policy*. I believe it should separate itself completely from the question of what its citizens should or should not think—*separation of education and state*.

These are all purely negative proposals. They all imply lopping off an arm of the octopus, and replacing it with nothing at all. If any of them, or anything similar, is practical and a full reset is not, then all the better. However, any practical outcome in this direction is at present so distant that it is hard to assess plausibility.

Rule #2 is that a restoration cannot succeed by either of the following methods: the Democrats defeating the Republicans, or the Republicans defeating the Democrats. More precisely, it cannot involve imposing progressivism on traditionalists/"fundamentalists," or traditionalism on progressives.

Traditionalism and progressivism are the two major divisions of Christianity in our time. Not all traditionalists are Catholics, and many progressives are, but "fundamentalism" today occupies the basic political niche of Catholicism in the European tradition, and progressivism is clearly the **Protestant mainstream** (historically Unitarian, Congregationalist, Methodist, etc.; doctrinally, almost pure Quaker).

If secure, responsible, effective government has to wait until this religious war is over, it will wait *forever*. Or there will be a new **Bartholomew's Day**.[27] Neither of these options is acceptable to me. Are they acceptable to you? Then you may not be a restorationist.

Of course, each of these Christian sects is intimately connected, exactly as Noah Webster describes, with a political party and a set of politically constructed opinions about what government is and how it should be run. Since progressivism is politically dominant, one would expect it to have the most political content and the least religious content, and indeed this is so. And as we've seen, in a democracy there is no reason to expect anyone's political opinions to have any relationship to the actual art of responsible, effective government.

Nonetheless, it is entirely possible to be an apolitical progressive. Progressivism is a culture, not a party. Charity, for example, is a vast part of this culture, and no reasonable person can have anything against charity, as long as it remains a purely personal endeavor and does not develop aspects of political violence, as it did in the late 20th century. Environmentalism is a part of this culture, and who doesn't live in the environment? Etc., etc., etc.

The fangs can be pulled without much harm to the snake. In fact, the snake has never really needed fangs, and will find itself much more comfortable without them.

Rule #3: in case this is not a corollary of rule #1, a reset implies a *total breach* with the Anglo-American political tradition.

The fact that an institution is old, and has carried the respect of large populations for decades or centuries, is always a reason to honor and respect it. That you oppose Washington, the real organization that exists in the real world, does not mean that you oppose America, the abstract symbol. (Nor does it mean you oppose America, the continent in the Northern Hemisphere, whose destruction would be quite the engineering feat.) It does not mean that you want to burn or abolish the flag, etc., etc., etc. Similarly, the fact that I'm not a Catholic doesn't mean that if I met the Pope, I'd say, "Fuck you, Pope!" As a matter of fact I would probably want to kiss his ring, or whatever is the appropriate gesture.

On the other hand, we have no reason to think that the political designs we have inherited from this tradition are useful in any way, shape or form. All we know

---

27 A string of targeted assassinations and mob violence by Catholics against the Huegonots during the French Wars of Religion.

is that they were more militarily successful than their competitors, which may well have been flawed in arbitrary other ways. If the Axis had defeated the Allies, a feat which was quite plausible in hindsight, we would face a completely different set of reengineering challenges, and it would be the Prussian tradition rather than the Whig that had to be discarded.

Historical validation is a good thing. But history provides an extraordinary range of examples. And there is no strong reason to think the governments recent and domestic are any better than the governments ancient and foreign. The American Republic is over two hundred years old. Great. The **Serene Republic of Venice** lasted eleven hundred. If you're designing from the ground up, why start from the first rather than the second?

A total breach does not imply that everything American (or everything Portuguese, if you are trying to reboot Portugal; but not much in the government of modern Portugal is in any sense Portuguese) must be discarded. It means everything American needs to be justified, just as it would be if it was Venetian. If you believe in democracy: why? If you favor a bicameral legislature, a supreme court, a department of agriculture: why?

Rule #4: the only possible weapon is the truth.

I hope it's unnecessary to say, but it's worth saying anyway, that the only force which can terminate USG by military means is the military itself. There is no reason to talk about this possibility. If it happens, it will happen. It certainly won't happen any time soon.

This means that democracy can only be terminated by political means, i.e., democracy itself. Which means convincing a large number of people. Of course, people can be convinced with lies as well as with the truth, but the former is naturally the specialty of the present authorities. Better not to confuse anyone.

What is the truth, anyway? The truth is reality. The truth is what exists. The truth is what rings like a bell when you whack it with the back of a knife. It is very difficult to recognize the truth, but it is much easier to recognize it when it's right next to an equal and opposite lie. A certain device called the Internet is very good at providing this service.

Here is an example. The wonderful kids at Google, who are all diehard progressives and whom I'm sure would be horrified by the uses I'm making of their services, have done something that I can only compare to Lenin's old saying about the capitalists: that they would sell the rope that was used to hang them. Likewise, progressives seem determined to publish the books that will discredit them. As in the case of the capitalists, this is because they are good, not because they are evil. But unlike Lenin, we are good as well, and we welcome these accidental unforced errors.

I refer, of course, not to any new books. It is very difficult to get reactionary writing published anywhere, even (in fact, especially, because they are so sensitive on the subject) by the conservative presses. However, as UR readers know, the majority of work published before 1922 is online at Google. It is often hard to read, missing for bizarre reasons that make no sense (why scan a book from 1881 and then not put the scans online?), badly scanned, etc., etc. But it is there, and as we've seen it is quite usable.

And there are two things about the pre-1922 corpus. One, it is far, *far* to the right of the consensus reality that we now know and love. Just the fact that people in 1922 believed X, while today we believe Y, has to shake your faith in democracy. Was the world of 1922 massively deluded? Or is it ours? It could be both, but it can't be neither. Indeed, even the progressives of the Belle Époque often turn out to be far to the right of our conservatives. WTF?

Two, you can use this corpus to conduct a very interesting exercise: you can *triangulate*. This is an essential skill in defensive historiography. (If you like UR, you like defensive historiography.)

Historiographic triangulation is the art of taking two or more opposing positions from the past, and using hindsight to decide who was right and who was wrong. The simplest way to play the game is to imagine that the opponents in the debate were reanimated in 2008, informed of present conditions, and reunited for a friendly panel discussion. I'm afraid often the only conceivable result is that one side simply surrenders to the other.

For example, one fun exercise, which you can perform safely for no cost in the privacy of your own home, is to read the following early 20th-century books on the "Negro Question": *The Negro: The Southerner's Problem*, by Thomas Nelson Page (racist, 1904); *Following the Color Line*, by Ray Stannard Baker (progressive, 1908); and *Race Adjustment: Essays on the Negro in America*, by Kelly Miller (Negro, 1909).[28] Each of these books is (a) by a forgotten author, (b) far more interesting and well-written than the pseudoscientific schlock that comes off the presses these days, and (c) a picture of a vanished world. Imagine assembling Page, Baker and Miller in a hotel room in 2008, with a videocamera and little glasses of water in front of them. What would they agree on? Disagree on? Dear open-minded progressive, if you fail to profit from this exercise, you simply have no interest in the past.

However, an even more fun one is the now thoroughly forgotten Gladstone–Tennyson debate. I forget how I stumbled on this contretemps, which really does deserve to be among the most famous intellectual confrontations in history. Sadly, dear open-minded progressive, it appears to have been forgotten for a reason. And the reason is not a good one.

You may know that Tennyson, in his romantic youth (1835), wrote a poem called *Locksley Hall*. Due to its nature as 19th-century dramatic verse, *Locksley Hall* is unreadable today. But its basic content can be described as romantic juvenile liberalism. Here is some of the pith, if pith there is:

> Men, my brothers, men the workers, ever reaping something new:
> That which they have done but earnest of the things that they shall do:

---

28 Links to each book are provided in the endnotes.

AN OPEN LETTER TO OPEN-MINDED PROGRESSIVES   359

> For I dipt into the future, far as human eye could see,
> Saw the Vision of the world, and all the wonder that would be;
> Saw the heavens fill with commerce, argosies of magic sails,
> Pilots of the purple twilight dropping down with costly bales;
> Heard the heavens fill with shouting, and there rain'd a ghastly dew
> From the nations' airy navies grappling in the central blue;
> Far along the world-wide whisper of the south-wind rushing warm,
> With the standards of the peoples plunging thro' the thunder-storm;
> Till the war-drum throbb'd no longer, and the battle-flags were furl'd
> In the Parliament of man, the Federation of the world.
> There the common sense of most shall hold a fretful realm in awe,
> And the kindly earth shall slumber, lapt in universal law.

I'm not sure whether this is supposed to remind us more of the UN, the British Empire, or *Star Trek*. Perhaps all three. But you get the idea. The "Parliament of man" couplet, in particular, is rather often quoted.

Well. So, Tennyson was a romantic young liberal when he wrote this. In 1835. In 1885, when he wrote (adding ten years for some dramatic reason) *Locksley Hall, Sixty Years After*, he was neither romantic, nor young, nor—um—liberal. While the sequel is also unreadable today, for more or less the same reasons, here are some couplets from it:

> I myself have often babbled doubtless of a foolish past;
> Babble, babble; our old England may go down in babble at last.
> Truth for truth, and good for good! The Good, the True, the Pure, the Just;
> Take the charm 'For ever' from them, and they crumble into dust.
> Gone the cry of 'Forward, Forward,' lost within a growing gloom;
> Lost, or only heard in silence from the silence of a tomb.
> Half the marvels of my morning, triumphs over time and space,
> Staled by frequence, shrunk by usage into commonest commonplace!
> 'Forward' rang the voices then, and of the many mine was one.
> Let us hush this cry of 'Forward' till ten thousand years have gone.
> France had shown a light to all men, preached a Gospel, all men's good;
> Celtic Demos rose a Demon, shrieked and slaked the light with blood.
> Aye, if dynamite and revolver leave you courage to be wise:
> When was age so crammed with menace? Madness? Written, spoken lies?
> Envy wears the mask of Love, and, laughing sober fact to scorn,
> Cries to Weakest as to Strongest, 'Ye are equals, equal-born.'
> Equal-born? O yes, if yonder hill be level with the flat.
> Charm us, Orator, till the Lion look no larger than the Cat.
> Till the Cat through that mirage of overheated language loom
> Larger than the Lion,—Demos end in working its own doom.

> Those three hundred millions under one Imperial sceptre now,
> Shall we hold them? Shall we loose them? Take the suffrage of the plow.
> Nay, but these would feel and follow Truth if only you and you,
> Rivals of realm-ruining party, when you speak were wholly true.
> Trustful, trustful, looking upward to the practised hustings-liar;
> So the Higher wields the Lower, while the Lower is the Higher.
> Step by step we gained a freedom known to Europe, known to all;
> Step by step we rose to greatness,—through tonguesters we may fall.
> You that woo the Voices—tell them 'old experience is a fool,'
> Teach your flattered kings that only those who cannot read can rule.
> Tumble Nature heel o'er head, and, yelling with the yelling street,
> Set the feet above the brain and swear the brain is in the feet.
> Bring the old dark ages back without the faith, without the hope,
> Break the State, the Church, the Throne, and roll their ruins down the slope.
> Do your best to charm the worst, to lower the rising race of men;
> Have we risen from out the beast, then back into the beast again?

Etc. Obviously, either someone has been reading **Pobedonostsev**, or great minds just happen to think alike. I don't think you have to be a Victorian liberal to see that this is highly seditious material. Inflammatory, even. Not bad for an old fart.

Well, **William Gladstone**, who was both a Victorian liberal and an old fart himself, reads this, and of course he shits a brick. The poem might as well have been a personal attack on Gladstone himself—especially that bit about "Celtic Demos," which is not a terribly well-concealed reference to Irish **Home Rule**.

And what does he do? He's not just a statesman, but a real aristocrat. Does he challenge Tennyson to a duel? A bit late in the day for that. No, he takes time out, from his busy duties as Prime Minister, to write a **response**.[29] Not in verse, since taking on Tennyson in trochaic couplets is like challenging Chuck Norris in Fight Club. But Gladstone was a master of prose—listen to this wicked little intro:

> The nation will observe with warm satisfaction that, although the new Locksley Hall is, as told by the Calendar, a work of Lord Tennyson's old age, yet is his poetic "eye not dim, nor his natural force abated."

Take note, kids. This is how you start out if you're really going to crucify someone. Gladstone continues by flattering the person for a few paragraphs. Then he flatters the poem for a page or so. Then he changes his angle slightly:

29

Perhaps the tone may even, at times, be thought to have grown a little hoarse with his years. Not that we are to regard it as the voice of the author.

Oh, no. Not at all. Then (page 319) Gladstone spends another page agreeing with Tennyson. Yes, the French Revolution was terrible. And the riots of **Captain Swing**.[30] Etc., etc. But it all worked out in the end, didn't it? What bliss was it to be young, after the **First Reform Bill**?[31] Etc., etc.

And then finally (page 320) Gladstone launches into full-on shark-attack mode:

> During the intervening half century, or near it, the temper of hope and thankfulness, which both Mr. Tennyson and the young Prophet of Locksley Hall so largely contributed to form, has been tested by experience. Authorities and people have been hard at work in dealing with the laws, the policy, and the manners of the country. Their performances may be said to form the Play, intervening between the old Prologue, and the new Epilogue which has just issued from the press. This Epilogue, powerful as it is, will not quite harmonize with the evergreens of Christmas. The young Prophet, now grown old, is not, indeed (though perhaps, on his own showing, he ought to be), in despair. For he still stoutly teaches manly duty and personal effort, and longs for progress more, he trows, than its professing and blatant votaries. But in his present survey of the age as his field, he seems to find that a sadder color has invested all the scene. The evil has eclipsed the good, and the scale, which before rested solidly on the ground, now kicks the beam. For the framing of our estimate, however, prose, and very prosaic prose, may be called in not less than poetry. The question demands an answer, whether it is needful to open so dark a prospect for the Future; whether it is just to pronounce what seems to be a very decided censure on the immediate Past.

What follows is a rather amazing document—a compact and thorough defense of Victorian liberalism and democracy, and its prospects for the future:

> In the words of the **Prince Consort**, "Our institutions are on their trial," as institutions of self-government; and if condemnation is to be pronounced, on the nation it must mainly fall, and must sweep away with it a large part of such hopes as have been either fanatically or reflectively entertained that, by this provision of self-government, the Future might effect some moderate improvement upon the Past, and mitigate in some perceptible de-

---

30 Anonymous signatory of threatening letters, and mythical figurehead of the 1830 so-named Swing Riots.
31 A major restructuring of the English electoral system in 1832.

gree the social sorrows and burdens of mankind. I will now, with a view to a fair trial of this question, try to render, rudely and slightly though it be, some account of the deeds and the movement of this last half century.

I should not attempt to abuse Gladstone by excerpting him. But one morsel—especially considering the above—stands out as particularly choice:

One reference to figures may however be permitted. It is that which exhibits the recent movement of crime in this country. For the sake of brevity I use round numbers in stating it. Happily the facts are too broad to be seriously mistaken. In 1870, the United Kingdom with a population of about 31,700,000 had about 13,000 criminals, or one in 1,760. In 1884, with a population of 36,000,000, it had 14,000 criminals, or one in 2,500. And as there are some among us who conceive Ireland to be a sort of pandemonium, it may be well to mention (and I have the hope that Wales might, on the whole, show as clean a record) that with a population of (say) 5,100,000 Ireland (in 1884) had 1,573 criminals, or less than one in 3,200.

Words fail me, dear open-minded progressive, they really do.

But try the experiment: read the rest of Gladstone's essay, and ask yourself what he and Tennyson would make of the last century of British history, and her condition today. Suffice it to say that I think someone owes someone else an apology. Of course, they're both dead, so none will be forthcoming.

In general what I find when I perform this exercise, is that—as far to the right of us as 1922 was—the winner of the triangulation tends to be its rightmost vertex. Not on every issue, certainly, but most. (I'm sure that if I were to try the same trick with, say, **Torquemada** and **Spinoza**, the results would be different, but I am out of my historical depth much past the late 18C.)

What's wonderful is that if you doubt these results, you can play the game yourself. Bored in your high-school class? Read about the **Civil War** and **Reconstruction** and **slavery**. Unless you're a professional historian, you certainly won't be assigned the primary sources I just linked to. But no one can stop you, either. (At least not until Google adds a "Flag This Book" button.)

I am certainly not claiming that everything you find in Google Books, or even everything I just linked to, is true. It is not. It is a product of its time. What's true, however, is that each book is the book it says it is. Google has not edited it. And if it says it was published in 1881, nothing that happened after 1881 can have affected it.

Here is another exercise in defensive historiography: skim this facile 2008 treatment[32] of Francis Lieber, then read the actual document[33] that Lieber wrote. The primary source is not only better-written, but shorter and more informative as well. (One page is mis-scanned, but one can make out the wonderful words "the utmost rigor of the military law"...)

You'll see immediately that the main service Professor Bosco, the modern historian, provides, is to deflect you from the brutal reality that Lieber feeds you straight. Lieber says: do Y, because if you do X, Z will happen. The Union Army did Y, and Z did not happen. The US in Iraq, and modern counterinsurgency forces more generally, did X, and Z happened.

The modern law of warfare, which Lieber more or less founded, has been twisted into an instrument which negates everything he believed. The results have been the results he predicted. I know it's a cliche—but history is too important to be left to the historians.

Rule #5: *quality is better than quantity*. At least when it comes to supporters.

Any political conspiracy, reactionary or revolutionary, is in the end a social network. And we observe an interesting property of social networks: their quality tends to decline over time. It does not increase. Facebook, for example, succeeded where Friendster and Orkut failed, by restricting its initial subscriber base to college students, which for all their faults really are the right side of the bell curve.

In order to make an impact on the political process, you need quantity. You need moronic, chanting hordes. There is no way around this. Communism was not overthrown by Andrei Sakharov, Joseph Brodsky and Václav Havel. It was overthrown by moronic, chanting hordes. I suppose I shouldn't be rude about it, but it's a fact that there is no such thing as a crowd of philosophers.

Yet Communism *was* overthrown by Sakharov, Brodsky and Havel. The philosophers *did* matter. What was needed was the combination of philosopher and crowd—a rare and volatile mixture, highly potent and highly unnatural.

My view is that up until the very last stage of the reset, quality is everything and quantity is, if anything, undesirable. On the Internet, ideas spread like crazy. And they are much more likely to spread from the smart to the dumb than the other way around.

One person and one blog is nowhere near sufficient, of course. What we need is a sort of counter-Cathedral: an institution which is actually more trustworthy than the university system. The universities are the brain of USG, and the best way to kill anything is to shoot it in the head.

32

33

To be right when the Cathedral is wrong is to demonstrate that we live under a system of government which is bound together by the same glue that held up Communism: lies. You do not need a triple-digit IQ to know that a regime held up by lies is doomed. You also do not need a triple-digit IQ to help bring down a doomed regime. Everyone will volunteer for that job. It's as much fun as anything in the world.

Solely for the purpose of discussion, let's call this counter-Cathedral *Resartus*—from Carlyle's great novel, *Sartor Resartus* (*The Tailor Reclothed*).

The thesis of *Resartus* is that the marketplace of ideas, free and blossoming as it may seem, is or at least may be infected with lies. These lies all have one thing in common: they are related to the policies of modern democratic governments. Misinformation justifies misgovernment; misgovernment subsidizes misinformation. This is our feedback loop.

On the other hand, it's clear that modern democratic governments are doing many things right. Perhaps in all circumstances they are doing the best they can. Perhaps there is no misinformation at all. The hypothesis that such feedback loops can form is not a demonstration that they exist.

Therefore, the mission of *Resartus* is to establish, using that crowdsourced wiki-power we are all familiar with, the truth on every dubious subject. Perhaps the truth will turn out to be the official story, in which case we can be happy.

The two sites today which are most like *Resartus* are **Climate Audit** and **Gene Expression**.[34] Both of these are, in my humble opinion, scientific milestones. CA's subject is climatology; GNXP's subject is human biodiversity. There are also some general-purpose truth verifiers, such as **Snopes**, but Snopes is hopelessly lightweight next to a CA or a GNXP.

CA and GNXP are unique because their mission is to be authorities in and of themselves. They do not consider any source reliable on the grounds of mere institutional identity. Nor do they assume any institutional credibility themselves. They simply try to be right, and as far as I can tell (lacking expertise in either of their fields, especially the statistical background to really work through their work) they are.

CA—created and edited by one man, **Steve McIntyre**, who as far as I'm concerned is one of the most important scientists of our generation—is especially significant, because unlike GNXP (which is publicizing mainstream research that many would rather see unpublicized), McIntyre, starting with no credentials or academic career at all is actually attacking and attempting to destroy a major flying buttress of the Cathedral. And one with major political importance, not to mention economic. Imagine a cross between Piltdown Man, the Dreyfus Affair, and Enron, and you might get the picture.

If the fields behind anthropogenic global warming (AGW), paleoclimatology and climate modeling, are indeed pseudosciences and go down in history as such, I find it almost impossible to imagine what will happen to their promoters. Their

---

34 Blogs run by Stephen McIntyre and Razib Khan, respectively.

promoters being, basically, everyone who matters. McIntyre is best known for his exposure of the hockey stick, but what's amazing is that CA seems to find a similar abuse of mathematics, data, or both—typically less prominent—about every other week or two.

The scientific achievement of GNXP is less stunning, but its implications are, if anything, larger. I've discussed human neurological uniformity and its absence already (Chapter 9). But let's just say that a substantial component of our political, economic, and academic system has completely committed its credibility to a proposition that might be called the *International White Conspiracy*. Statistical population variations in human neurology do not strike me as terribly exciting per se—a responsible, effective government should be able to deal with anything down to your high-end *Homo erectus*. Lies, however, are always big news. If there is a much, much simpler explanation of reality which does not require an International White Conspiracy, that is a problem for quite a few people—the vast majority of whom are, in fact, white.

At the same time, CA and GNXP and relatives (LvMI, though it's not just a website, has many of the same fine qualities) were not designed as general-purpose information-warfare devices. There is some crossover, but I suspect most CA posters are unaware of or uninterested in GNXP, and often the reverse. Many people are natural specialists, of course, and this is normal.

The idea of *Resartus*—which, as usual, anyone can build in their own backyard (contact me if you are interested in resartus.org) is to build a general-purpose site for answering a variety of large, controversial questions. A smart person should be able to visit *Resartus* and decide, with a minimum of effort, who is right about AGW or human biodiversity or peak oil or the Kennedy assassination or evolution or string theory or 9/11 or the Civil War or...

To build a credible truth machine, it's important to generate true negatives as well as true positives. For example, I favor the conventional wisdom on evolution and 9/11. On peak oil and the Kennedys, I simply don't know enough to decide. (Actually, I live in terror of the idea that someone will convince me that Oswald didn't act alone. So I try to avoid the matter.) Therefore, I would hope that any attempt to audit Darwin, as McIntyre audited Mann, would result in a true negative.

The easiest way to describe the problem of *Resartus* is to describe it as a crowd-sourced trial. Indeed, any process that can determine the truth or falsity of AGW, etc., should be a process powerful enough to determine criminal guilt or innocence. Certainly many of these issues are well into that category of importance—in fact, I would not be surprised if one day we see legal proceedings in the global-warming department. There have already been some suspicious signs of "lawyering up."

A trial is not a blog, nor is it a discussion board. One of the main flaws of Climate Audit is that it does not provide a way for AGW skeptics and believers to place each others' arguments and evidence side by side, making it as easy as possible for neutral third parties to evaluate who is right. I am confident that CA is on the money, but much of this confidence is gut feeling.

In the evolution world, the TalkOrigins Index to Creationist Claims has probably come the closest to setting out a structured argument for evolution, in which every possible creationist argument is listed and refuted. However, a real trial is adversarial. The prosecutor does not get to make the defense lawyer's arguments.

On *Resartus*, the way this would work is that the *creationist community* itself would be asked to list its claims, and edit them collectively, producing the best possible statement of the creationist case. Not showing up should not provide an advantage, so evolutionists should be able to add and refute their own creationist claims. Creationists should in turn be able to respond to their responses, and so ad infinitum, until both sides feel they have said their piece.

As an evolutionist, I feel that this process, which could continue indefinitely as the argument tree is refined, evidence exhibits were added, etc., etc., would demonstrate very clearly that evolutionists are right and creationists are blowing smoke. As a matter of fact, as someone who's served on a jury, I feel that such an argument tree would be far more useful than verbal lectures from the competing attorneys.

And if these structures were available *on one site* for a wide variety of controversial issues, it would be very, very easy for any smart young person with a few hours to spare to see what the pattern of truth and error, and its inevitable political associations, started to look like. It certainly will not be easy to construct a nexus of more reliable judgments than the university system itself, but at some point someone will do it. And I think the results will be devastating.

When I look at the thinking of people who disagree with me, and especially when I look at the thinking of the educated public at large (New York Times comments, on the few articles which they are enabled for, are an invaluable vox populi for the Obamabot crowd) I am often struck by the fact that their perspective differs from mine as a result of small, seemingly irrelevant details in the interpretation of reality.

If you believe that John Kerry was telling the truth about his voyages into Cambodia, for example, you will hear the word "Swiftboating" in a very different way. On a larger subject, if James Watson is right, our historical interpretation of the 1860s will simply have to change. Details matter. Facts matter.

Our democratic institutions today, though far more distributed and open than the systems of Goebbels or Vyshinsky, are basically designed to run on an information system that funnels truth down from the top of the mountain. This is a brittle design. If it breaks—if it starts distributing sewage along with the rosewater—it loses its credibility. If it loses its credibility, the government loses its legitimacy. When a government loses its legitimacy, you don't want to be standing under it.

The Cathedral is called the Cathedral for another reason: it's not the Bazaar.[35] Coding, frankly, is pretty easy. Reinterpreting reality is hard. Nonetheless, I think this thing will come down one of these days. And I would rather be outside it than under it.

35

AN OPEN LETTER TO OPEN-MINDED PROGRESSIVES 367

 340 Noah Webster

 340 1794 pamphlet on the French Revolution Noah Webster. *A Collection of Papers on Political, Literary, and Moral Subjects.* (Webster & Clark, 1843) p. 24.

 342 Bertolt Brecht's verse Referenced in a Vdare column by James Fulford "Swept Away - North of the Border" (2003) about Canadian immigrants voting en bloc in opposition to the Quebec referendum.

 342 captured California Carla Marinucci. "Obama well ahead in California, poll shows." *SFGate*, 16 Jul. 2008.

 342 Republican stronghold Nate Silver. "Electoral History Charts." *FiveThirtyEight*, 29 Apr. 2008.

 342 cackle gleefully Frank Rich. "The All-White Elephant in the Room." *New York Times*, 4 May 2008.

 343 announced Conor Dougherty and Miriam Jordan. "Surge in U.S. Hispanic Population Driven by Births, Not Immigration." *Wall Street Journal*, 1 May 2008.

 343 Sulzbergers Link to the New York Times homepage.

 343 intellectually marginalized Mises Institute homepage.

 343 intellectually compromised Cato Institute homepage.

 344 60 people Ben Leach. "Knife crime claims 60 victims a day." *Telegraph*, 13 Jul. 2008.

 344 should be abolished Christopher Hope. "Tens of thousands of criminals to be spared short jail terms." *Telegraph*, 8 Jul. 2008.

 344 Scientists around the world Angela Balakishnan. "Tackling knife crime: different approaches." *Guardian*, 14 Jul. 2008.

 345 yoofs themselves Rowenna Davis. "How can our politicians understand blade culture?" *Guardian*, 14 Jul. 2008.

345 scientific research Nick Davies. "Youth violence: Tactics against gangs fatally flawed - report." *Guardian*, 14 Jul. 2008.

346 this lovely story Originally linked to an article that ran in May of 1956, archived at the theTimes.co.uk website, but which is no longer available. No alternative links to the article–or related articles–could be found.

347 we learn that "South Africans jailed for murders in UK." *Mail & Guardian*, 9 May 2008.

347 BNP "British National Party"

348 Judith Todd RW Johnson. "Mugabe was rotten from the start." *TimesOnline*, 23 Sep. 2007.

355 put it G.K. Chesterton. *What's Wrong With the World*. (Dodd, Mead and Co., 1912).

348 General William Boykin

349 this search Google search for "Pentagon coverup."

349 six New York Times search query for "columbia rape\ 'robert williams' \"

349 Larry Auster See Chapter 7.

349 wrote Lawrence Auster. "The Morningside Heights Atrocity, and a Question for Obama." *View From the Right*, 7 Jun. 2008.

349 said ibid. "The Real Meaning of Obama's Race Speech," 27 Mar. 2008.

350 Wichita Massacre Stephen Webster. "The Wichita Massacre." *American Renaissance*, Vol. 13, No. 8, Aug. 2002.

350 someone's head See Chapter 1 endnote "stand on a box."

AN OPEN LETTER TO OPEN-MINDED PROGRESSIVES

 351 reign of lawless terror "Fajitagate"

 351 bigger guns YouTube clip and famous quote from the 1992 film *Split Second*.

 351 martial law The Lieber code of 1863, setting out rules of conduct for Union soldiers during the Civil War.

 351 liberal surgeon in South Africa other things amanzi homepage.

 351 writes Bongi. "south african crime." *other things amanzi*, 15 Jun. 2008.

 352 here Ibid. "it is difficult to cut a head off with a panga." 20 Nov. 2007.

 352 here-1 Ibid. "stories of guns." 17 May. 2007.

 352 gatvol UrbanDictionary.com result for "gatvol."

 352 human oneness

 352 In Cold Blood Truman Capote. (Random House, 1966).

 352 other sources confirm the result "Charles Nqakula - Crime rate controversy."

 353 paramilitary criminals "Arkan"

 353 quite "Janjaweed"

 353 popular "Interahamwe"

LINKS & NOTES

 353 these "Hezbollah"

 353 days "Sons of Iraq"

 353 laws of King Ine of Wessex Ben Levick. "The Anglo-Saxon Fyrd c.400-878 AD" *Regia Anglorum*, 2005.

 353 many libertarians Nick Szabo. "State vs. Anarchy – the false dichotomy." *Unenumerated*, 23 Jun. 2008.

353 such as myself "Moldbug refers here to the general philosophy of valuing individual liberty and minimal government, not libertarianism as a political movement. See *Moldbug on Carlyle* and 'Why I am not a libertarian' for more." (UR ed.).

 353 strong hand Originally linked to a since removed Youtube video of Pinochet, famous for his "strong hand," a term he used often to describe his governing style. The linked video here is a tribute song to the General, "Mano Dura Pinochet," which the editors have deemed an adequate substitute for the original.

 *353 dictator* "Pinochet"

 353 this one Larry Littlefield. "Preparing for Institutional Collapse." *Saying the Unsaid in New York*, larrylittlefield.wordpress, reposted 17 Aug. 2014.

 353 insider political gossip Link to the "About" page for the now defunct website Room Eight.

 353 author Saying the Unsaid in New York, About page. Littlefield describes himself as a nonpartisan "policy wonk."

354 *Read the essay.* See "this one" supra.

 354 plenary authority

 355 widely practised "Forty-shilling freeholders," shorthand for those who had the franchise through possession of freehold property.

AN OPEN LETTER TO OPEN-MINDED PROGRESSIVES

 355 *put it* William Jay. Life of John Jay. (J. & J. Harper, 1833) p.70. See Chapter X.

 356 *Protestant mainstream*

 356 *Bartholomew's Day*

 357 *Serene Republic of Venice*

 358 *The Negro: The Southerner's Problem* Thomas Nelson Page. (Charles Scribner's Sons, 1904).

 358 *Following the Color Line* Ray Stannard Baker. (Doubleday, Page & Company, 1908).

 358 *Race Adjustment: Essays on the Negro in America* Kelly Miller. (Neale Publishing Company, 1909).

 358 *Tennyson*

 358 *Locksley Hall* See Chapter 5.

 359 *Locksley Hall, Sixty Years After* Alfred Lord Tennyson. (Macmillan and Co., 1886).

 360 *Pobedonostsev* See Chapters 8 and XII *Reflections of a Russian Statesman*.

 360 *William Gladstone*

 360 *Home Rule*

 360 *response* W.E. Gladstone. "'Locksley Hall' and the Jubilee." *The Eclectic Magazine of Foreign LIterature, Science, and Art*, Vo. 45., Leavitt, Trow, & Company, 1877.

361 First Reform Bill

 361 Prince Consort

 362 Torquemada

 362 Spinoza

 362 Civil War George Lunt. *The Origin of the Late War: Traced From the Beginning of the Constitution to the Revolt of the Southern States.* (D. Appleton and Company, 1866).

362 Reconstruction Charles Nordhoff. *The Cotton States in the Spring and Summer of 1875.* (D. Appleton and Company, 1876). See Chapter 8.

362 slavery Rev. Nehemia Adams. *A South-side View of Slavery, Or, Three Months at the South, in 1854.* (T.R. Marvin, 1855). See Chapter XI.

 363 facile 2008 treatment David Bosco. "Moral Principle vs. Military Necessity." *The American Scholar*, 1 Dec. 2007.

 363 Francis Lieber

 363 actual document Francis Lieber. *Guerilla Parties: Considered with Reference to the Laws and Usages of War.* (D. Van Nostrand, 1862).

 364 Sartor Resartus See Chapter 2. Thomas Carlyle. (Fraser's Magazine, 1831).

 364 Climate Audit Archived link to the homepage of climateaudit.org.

 364 Gene Expression Archived link to the homepage of unz.com/gnxp/.

AN OPEN LETTER TO OPEN-MINDED PROGRESSIVES 373

 364 Steve McIntyre A year after this post, McIntyre became the central antagonizing figure at the heart of the Climatic Research Unit email scandal in 2009, also referred to as "Climategate." Much of the leaked emails were concerned with how to combat McIntyre's skepticism of the prevailing climate change consensus.

 365 hockey stick David Strumfels. "The rise and fall of the Hockey Stick." *A Medley of Potpourri*, 27 Dec. 2013 (reprinted from *A Sceptical Mind*).

 365 white Stuff White People Like. See Chapter 1.

 366 TalkOrigins Index to Creationist Claims Edited by Mark Isaak, 2006.

 366 Goebbels

 366 Vyshinsky

 366 Bazaar Eric S. Raymond. "The cathedral and the bazaar." *First Monday*, Vol. 3, No. 3, 2 Mar. 1998.

HOW DAWKINS GOT PWND

CHAPTER 1:
A REALLY UGLY BUG
SEPTEMBER 26, 2007

Richard Dawkins recently wrote a book called *The God Delusion*. You've probably heard of it.

Professor Dawkins is a great scientist and one of my favorite writers. And I have no quarrel at all with his argument. I was raised as a scientific atheist, and I've never seen the slightest reason to think otherwise. These days I prefer the word "nontheist"—for reasons which will shortly be clear—but there's no substantive difference at all. Except in the context of role-playing games, I have no interest whatsoever in gods, goddesses, angels, devils, dryads, water elementals, or any such presumed metaphysical being.

Nonetheless, it's my sad duty to inform the world that Professor Dawkins has been *pwned*. Perhaps you're over 30 and you're unfamiliar with this curious new word. As La Wik puts it:

> The word "pwn" remains in use as Internet social-culture slang meaning: *to take unauthorized control of someone else or something belonging to someone else by exploiting a vulnerability.*

(At least here at Unqualified Reservations, *pwned* alliterates with *posse* and rhymes with *loaned*.) How could such a learned and wise mind exhibit such an exploitable vulnerability? And who—or what—has taken unauthorized control over Professor Dawkins? The aliens? The CIA? The Jews? The mind boggles. As well it should. Patience, dear reader. All will become clear.

Professor Dawkins' explanation of religion, with which I agree completely, is that religion is a memeplex built around a central delusion, the God meme—an entirely unsubstantiated proposition. Religion exists because this memeplex is adaptive. This explanation is both necessary and sufficient. It is also parsimonious, à la Occam's razor. It may not be simple, but it's a heck of a lot simpler than "God."

(I dislike the word "meme" and the complex of terminology that's grown up around it, mainly because (a) the word has a dorky sound, and (b) it means the same thing as "idea." However, in deference to Professor Dawkins and his numerous acolytes, I'll use it for this discussion.)

In Darwinian terms, Professor Dawkins' main point is that the adaptive interests of religion—or of any other memeplex—are not necessarily the same as the adaptive interests of its host. As a celibate priest, for example, you are helping Christianity to be fruitful and multiply. It's performing no such service for you.

Biologists have a word for this: parasitism. Probably because he wants to be nice, Professor Dawkins tries not to use the p-word. But he's clearly thinking it.

The God delusion is a parasitic meme because, being alien to reason, it does not serve the interests of the host. Furthermore, some of the memeplexes—or "religions"—which include it include far more pernicious memes, such as suicide bombing, which are lethal both to the host and anyone within its blast radius. The case would seem to be closed.

But immunology is tricky. After all, if Professor Dawkins is right, anyone who believes in God is most certainly pwned—that is, infected by a parasitic religious memeplex. This category includes some of the smartest people in the world today. Intelligence is certainly no barrier to memetic infection. Worse, there have clearly been periods of civilized history in which *everyone* was infected by this parasite. The things are dangerous, there is no doubt.

Therefore, without disputing Professor Dawkins' Darwinian conclusion, I think it's prudent to step back a little, and attack the problem with a slightly broader and more careful approach.

The God Delusion is what immunologists might call a *specific* immune response. Professor Dawkins notes that religion is alien to the reasoning mind. He notes that it reproduces and evolves. He sees that similar phenomena have caused many problems in the past and continue to do so in the present. He identifies a common feature of these problems, the God meme, and churns out antibodies to it.

This process is not infallible. Suppose, for example, you note that a patient is ill and can't eat. You take a biopsy of his guts and find that they're full of—bacteria! Bacteria are clearly not human. They're a well-known cause of disease. So the obvious problem is that the patient has a bacterial infection, and you prescribe broad-spectrum antibiotics. Meanwhile, the poor fellow is dying of colon cancer, and you're trying to eradicate his intestinal flora.

Biological immune systems make all kinds of mistakes. Presumably the same is true of memetic immunology. After all, what was the Inquisition thinking? They thought of heresy exactly the same way Professor Dawkins thinks of religion: as a sort of mental virus, whose eradication, while unavoidably painful, would bring peace and sanity.

In memetic immunology, it's often very difficult to distinguish parasite from counterparasite. When we see two populations of memes in conflict, we know both cannot be healthy, because a healthy meme is true by definition and the truth cannot conflict with itself. However, we might very well be watching two parasites competing with each other. They will certainly both claim to represent truth, justice and the American way.

So I think it might be worthwhile to attack the question from another angle, using the analogy of a *generalized* immune response. Rather than asking ourselves whether specific traditions, such as Christianity, Judaism, Islam, etc., are parasitic, we can focus on the problem of parasitic memeplexes as a whole.

If Christianity, Judaism, Islam, etc., turn up on this screen, perhaps we'll want to point some T-cells at them. But a generalized approach will also detect any *other* parasitic memeplexes we may be infected with. After all, the God delusion isn't the only delusion in the world.

One way to approach generalized memetic immunology is to design a *generic parasitic memeplex*. Avoiding specific details which may confuse us, and focusing on the combination of adaptive success and parasitic morbidity, we can construct design rules for an optimal memetic parasite. We can evaluate potential threats by looking at how well they fit this template, which should be as nasty as possible.

When dealing with actual biological agents, of course, we can work in biosafety labs. The most dangerous viruses, such as smallpox, Ebola, and the 1918 flu, cannot be safely handled without elaborate, multiply redundant containment systems. Some would argue that they cannot be safely handled at all.

With memes and memeplexes, there's none of this. By designing the memeplex, we effectively release it into the wild. Fortunately, UR has a small and discreet audience, which strikes me as very wise and conscientious. I'm sure none of you will be tempted to abuse this dangerous memetic technology, which in the hands of less scrupulous thinkers could easily become a formula for total world domination. Remember, this is only a test.

So our generic parasitic memeplex will be as virulent as possible. It will be highly contagious, highly morbid, and highly persistent. A really ugly bug. Let's focus on these design aspects separately: contagion, morbidity, and persistence.

A contagious memeplex is one that spreads easily. The template may not have to infect everyone in the world—although that's certainly one option. However, for any really significant morbidity, we'll want massive, lemminglike misdirected collective action. This requires mass infection.

There are three general ways to transmit a memetic parasite: parental transmission, educational transmission, and social transmission. Needless to say, our template should be a champ at all of them.

If your parasite can't be transmitted *parentally*, it's really not much of a parasite. Children learn the basic principles of reality and morality before they are six, and—as the Jesuit proverb goes—anything that can slip in at this age is likely to stick. "Give me the child and I will give you the man." Fortunately, any simple idea, even if it is nonsense, can be transmitted at this age. Unless the template is fundamentally dependent on some meme which children are unlikely to grasp, such as partial differential equations, parental transmission is no problem.

But *educational transmission*—infection of children and young adults by institutions whose ostensible purpose is to instill universal knowledge and ethics—is the mainstay of any successful memetic parasite. Since these same institutions educate future educators, replication can continue indefinitely.

Over multiple generations, educational transmission outcompetes parental transmission. Changes of religion by executive fiat, for example, are common in European history. In the more recent past, the Allied victors eradicated militarist traditions in Germany and Japan through their control of the educational system. Furthermore, by treating the press as an educational institution, we can create a system of continuing, lifelong reinfection in which parasitic memes are omnipresent. (Of course, it's important to remember that exactly the same techniques can also cure a memetic infection.)

But neither parental nor educational transmission can bootstrap itself from a small initial infection. While most parasitic memes probably originate as mutations of preexisting memes, they can certainly be invented from scratch (unlike genes). And even a mutation has to spread somehow.

Therefore, no memetic parasite is complete without a system for *social transmission*: informal transmission among adults, following existing social networks.

The first step in designing for social transmission is minimizing preexisting immunity. Nazism, for example, would not be an adaptive meme for a 21st-century parasitic memeplex, because so many prospective hosts have strong negative reactions to Nazism, Nazis, swastikas, etc. Any meme which conflicts with its prospective hosts' present perception of reality or morality is socially maladaptive.

The second step in designing for social transmission is to look at the *status structure* of social networks, and construct memes that will flow naturally along the usual network direction: from high status to low status.

That is, our parasite should be *intellectually fashionable*. All the cool people in town should want to get infected. And infection will make them even cooler. They will be the hosts with the most. For example, one common trope in various religious traditions is asceticism: the voluntary renunciation of material comforts. Since this tends to be much easier for those who start out wealthy and comfortable, it's an effective status marker. Any memes that can associate themselves with asceticism gain a clear adaptive advantage.

Our parasite is now optimized for contagion. But is it bad? Is it truly evil and destructive? The most contagious parasitic meme in the world, if all it brings to its hosts and those around them is happiness and prosperity, isn't worth worrying about.

So we need to move on to *morbidity*, which is a fancy medical word meaning "badness." The key to memetic morbidity is that, for a really nasty parasite, morbidity must be essential to its reproductive cycle. Otherwise, because morbidity is after all nasty, it will probably be maladaptive. Our parasite will be outcompeted by a benign mutation of itself—totally defeating the purpose. D'oh.

Most forms of morbidity involve a *political* step in the replication process. In other words, they allow the parasite to obtain informal *power*, which it can use to take over educational institutions, suppress counterparasites and competing parasites, etc., etc. There is no period in the history of any human civilization in which political (including military) power has not been a critical factor in the struggle of ideas. This is not to say that such a level playing field or "marketplace" of memes cannot be created—only that it has not yet been done.

First, a parasitic meme is not even parasitic if it is not *delusional*. It must contain some assertion which is alien to reason, which no sensible person would independently invent. The "God delusion"—a metaphysical construct, like Russell's teapot, with no basis in reality—is a perfect example.

How can a delusion be, on its own, adaptive? Very easily. A delusion is a perfect organizing principle for any kind of political movement. By accepting some body of nonsensical doxology, you demonstrate your loyalty to the group. The result is cohesive collective action. As we'll see, most forms of parasitic morbidity involve a political step in the replication cycle.

A frequent strategy, for example, is to present the delusion as recondite and counterintuitive, and the truth as simplistic and wrong. This "emperor's new clothes" strategy is a proven recipe for defeating Occam's razor. Who, for example, really understands the Trinity? But if you don't understand the Trinity, aren't you just stupid? Through internal competition, this counterintuitive delusion generates a revolutionary elite deeply steeped in Trinitology. The harder it is to understand the delusion, the more dedicated your cadre will be.

Another good general strategy for high morbidity is *antinomianism*, the opposition to law. Since the rule of law can be defined in terms of property rights—property is any right that you can own—any meme that opposes property opposes law. It therefore declares continuous and informal transfers of resources to be morally justified. Antinomianism builds political power by providing an easy avenue for punishing enemies and rewarding supporters, all in the service of whatever bogus concept of "justice" our parasite concocts as a replacement for law.

Finally, our parasite will employ a strategy of *politicization*, insisting that everyone in a society be involved in the contest for political power. Since our memetic parasite is already bound to one or more political factions, politicization leaves no one with the option to ignore it, and simply live their lives. Neutrality is not acceptable. All those who are not actively infected, and who do not openly endorse the parasite, are by definition its enemies. And they will be crushed. The safest thing is to play along, and raise your children in the faith—even if you don't really believe, they will.

CHAPTER 1

High contagion and adaptive morbidity will allow our parasite to spread widely and rise to power, where it can continuously propagate itself through educational institutions. But there is still another problem: *persistence*. If our parasite does not resist competitors, or succumbs easily to healthy counterparasites, it won't last long and it won't be much of a threat. It should be as hard as possible for hosts to reject the parasite, whether they are replacing it with a competitor or simply returning to reason.

Our first defense against rejection is mere *euphoria*. It should feel good to be infected. It should improve the host's self-esteem, making them feel like a better, happier person. If they need to make sacrifices for their faith, if they suffer for it, fine. They are doing what's right.

At a certain level, euphoria graduates into full-on *anesthesia*. Anesthetized hosts can endure horrific suffering, or the moral pain of inflicting suffering on others, in the name of the faith. Did a wolf come into your house and eat your baby? You have been blessed. The wolf is the sacred animal of Rome. Your baby now dwells with the gods of the city. If the wolf comes again, pet him and speak to him sweetly, and at least give him a hamburger or something.

Indiscriminate and total anesthesia constitutes *ovinization*. An ovinized individual never imagines responding to any kind of threat with any kind of defensive action, certainly not violence. To the ovinized, anything bad that happens is either (a) an accident, or (b) the result of some sin or other moral error. The concept of an "enemy" does not exist.

Needless to say, euphoria, anesthesia and ovinization all greatly inhibit the ability of our hosts to react against their parasite and eject it—and its followers—from their lives. But sometimes this is not enough. Humans, after all, are bipedal apes. They evolved from some very truculent ancestors. Even if they are specialized for civilization—a certain degree of genetic ovinization is almost certainly present in populations which have lived in governed societies for many generations—occasional throwbacks are to be expected.

Therefore, diversionary *hysteria* is another essential tactic in our parasite's bag of tricks. Hosts who would otherwise be tempted to notice the morbidities of infection, and attribute them to the parasite itself, must be diverted. Either their defensive energies will be directed toward other symptoms which are in fact not serious, or they will attribute the real problems to other causes which are not in fact significant.

We can kill two birds with one stone by directing our hysteria toward those who reject the parasite, and identifying their efforts to cure it as the cause of the morbidity. This strategy of *counterimmunity*, in which the infected treat disinfection as if it were contagious—which, of course, it is—has been a staple of memetic parasites throughout the ages.

The goal of a counterimmune strategy—such as the Inquisition—is to eradicate heresy. But this is actually only the simplest approach to counterimmunity. We can get much fancier.

Suppose, for example, our parasite does not try to eradicate counterimmune responses, but in fact tolerates them. However, we make sure the heretical memes are contained and cannot engage in any serious attack on our replicative cycle. That way, we have them where we can see them—under control. How might we accomplish this?

One approach is to maintain a *neutered false opposition*. This gang of tolerated heretics, against whom our wise philosophers speak out at every opportunity, must be unable to establish a replicative cycle of their own.

For example, the tame heretical memeplex may include a meme which is delusional, and which anyone intelligent is obviously resistant to—thus binding to, and disabling, the dangerous countermemes which would attack our parasite, by blocking the "early adopters" who would otherwise be tempted to consider the heresy. Similarly, it may include unfashionable memes which impair its power of social transmission. And it may be administratively excluded from educational transmission. It is hard to prevent parental transmission, but as we've seen, over time parents will tend to lose the battle against educational institutions, especially if social transmission is also blocked.

An especially effective approach is to treat the heretical memeplex as if it were, in fact, the dominant parasitic meme. Thus, siding with the parasite will be seen as an act of resistance and defiance, a pose which tends to be fashionable. Furthermore, if the delusional strategy is employed, our friendly hosts will be able to identify obvious delusions among the heretics, who will be unfashionable and educationally isolated.

Since parasites mutate, evolve and improve over time, a good choice for a tame heresy may in fact be an old edition of our parasite itself. Normally this would simply be discarded, and not tolerated at all. By definition it is less competitive. However, if we do tolerate it, we can modify it to attract heretics, doubters, and unbelievers of all kinds, keeping them safely neutered. Hosts infected with the latest version of the parasite will treat these sticks-in-the-mud as deluded fools who have not yet liberated themselves from these ancient doctrines, and seen the new, brighter light—who, even worse, are working actively to prevent the truth from being born. Clearly, they must be stopped. And so on.

I think at this point we have a pretty good design for a successful memetic parasite. Don't you agree? If not, how do you think the parasite could be improved? (Of course, this sort of "intelligent design" by no means implies that any such beastie was designed by some purposive plan. We are just trying to reverse-engineer the effects of Darwinian selection.)

Now let's compare Professor Dawkins' target, the God delusion, to this ideal parasite.

Forgetting other religions for a moment, Christianity clearly fits the profile. Every one of the strategies observed above has been employed by some Christian sect, some set of believers in the "God delusion," at some point in time.

However, if I may project a little, Professor Dawkins' readers are not concerned about the Anabaptists, the Arians, the Monophysites, the Nestorians, or any such obsolete sect. They are concerned with vintage-2007 American Christian "fundamentalism." If your goal is to solve a problem, the problem must exist in the present tense.

Fundamentalist Christianity—I prefer the term "salvationism," because the belief that only those who are born again in Christ will be saved is essential to almost all "fundamentalist" sects—certainly matches some of the above descriptions.

For example, it is clearly political, and it is clearly using doctrine as an organizing tool. Antinomianism is a little harder to find—salvationists for the most part are, if anything, big believers in law and order. But depriving women of the right to control their bodies counts to some extent, although this right cannot be transferred and thus only attacks enemies, without benefiting supporters. If this isn't morbidity, I don't know what is.

In the contagion department, however, salvationism is curiously lacking. Compared to other successful memetic parasites of the past—for example, Catholicism before the Reformation—its presence in educational institutions is negligible. In fact, under present law, salvationism is entirely barred from the entire mainstream educational system. At present its great ambition seems to be to sabotage the teaching of Darwinian evolution in American public schools, a goal which it has been generally unsuccessful in. And even if they were to succeed in this, I find it almost entirely impossible to see how it could be of any adaptive value to the salvationist memeplex.

Nor is social transmission of any help, because salvationism is incredibly unfashionable. Quick—how many salvationist celebrities can you name? At the average chic dinner party in Manhattan, how many of the guests are likely to be salvationists? How many salvationists are employed by *Vanity Fair*, *The New Yorker*, Random House, Viking or Knopf? And so on.

So, one might argue, the salvationist meme is a threat, it is just a small threat. It needs to be kept in its place, that's all. Sure, the influence of the God delusion has been steadily decreasing for the last four hundred years. But if we take our eye off it, it might come back! I'm certainly not prepared to dismiss this as absolutely inconceivable.

However, there's another candidate we have to consider.

In the first chapter of *The God Delusion*, Professor Dawkins describes himself as "a deeply religious non-believer." He calls his belief system "Einsteinian religion," and waxes poetical as follows:

> Let me sum up Einsteinian religion in one more quotation from Einstein himself: "To sense that behind anything that can be experienced there is a something that our mind cannot grasp and whose beauty and sublimity reaches us only indirectly and as a feeble reflection, this is religiousness. In this sense I am religious."

It's easy to see that this statement is not exactly the general theory of relativity. In fact, it appears to have no factual content at all. Hm.

What, exactly, is this "Einsteinian religion"? Did Professor Dawkins invent it? Did Einstein? What else do Einsteinians believe in, besides "beauty and sublimity"? Are there other Einsteinians, or need only distinguished scientists apply? If an Einsteinian were to stoop to anything so mundane as voting, who would he or she vote for?

And how does "Einsteinian religion" stack up against our parasite test? We'll consider these fascinating issues in Chapter 2.

377 The God Delusion (Bantam Books, 2006). Dawkins' bestseller, based on his television documentary for Channel 4 called *The Root of All Evil*, placed him alongside Sam Harris, Christopher Hitchens, and Daniel Dennett as one of the "Four Horsemen" of the "New Atheism."

377 La Wik "Leet - Owned and Pwned"

378 memeplex

378 numerous acolytes An archived link to RichardDawkins.net, a Dawkins fan site, dated from around the time of this post. The images and overall aesthetics really capture the spirit of the era.

378 parasitism

381 Russell's teapot

CHAPTER 2:
M.41 AND M.42
OCTOBER 4, 2007

After a brief period of vagrancy and reflection, mostly in a disconnected state, I got back the other day and actually hesitated for a couple of days to look at the comment thread on Chapter 1, which I had dispatched, with more than my usual rambling and carelessness, from Powell's in Portland. (Mrs. Moldbug and I got on the R1100R and took a motorcycle pilgrimage to Chris McCandless's bus, where we stayed up three nights in a row, just thinking, then did a bunch of acid and emptied our pistols maniacally into the woods. "Smoke dat moose!", we were chanting. "Git dem maggots! Smoke dat moose!")

Anyway. I didn't expect many comments on Chapter 1. It's really only the first part of the argument, and it would be charitable to call it a first draft. (Fortunately the practice known, in what calls itself the real world, as "editing," is considered unethical on a blog—and rightly so.) So I was delighted to see the conversation that ensued. It strikes me as one of the best UR threads so far, and hopefully I don't need to repeat my appreciation for the quality of discussion here.

The commenters have certainly done a fine job of figuring out where I'm going with this. If I started with any suspense, it is gone. But please indulge me when I restate the argument in my own words—if only for clarity of further discussion.

My hypothesis is that Professor Dawkins is not just an atheist. He is a *Christian atheist*. Or as I prefer to put it, a *nontheistic Christian*. His "Einsteinian religion" is no more or less than the dominant present-day current of *Christianity itself*—"M.42," as commenter Faré so concisely put it:

> There's a good reason why the current dominant version of the Minotaur (to use the term by Bertrand de Jouvenel) shall use a previous version as its sparring partner: so as to win power, the previous version is precisely what it had to fight and win against, to begin with.
>
> [Let us call the current Minotaur "M.42" and call its immediate predecessor "M.41."] So that M.42 [could] win over M.41, it had to take on M.41, discredit it, win over it. And thus, for a while, M.41 is still dominant while M.42 is actually subversive; then M.42 gains dominance but still has M.41 as a serious rival against which to vie for power. When the victory is complete and irreversible, M.41 is a favorite sacrificial goat; it's so much fun to hit a helpless victim, when your technique is perfected. Of course, by the time you're there, the version of M.41 you're kicking in the head has devolved a lot; it is no more the arrogant M.41b of your youth, sure of its power—it is the pitiful M.41y of today, near the end of the line.

If we accept this hypothesis, the conclusion that Professor Dawkins has been pwned strikes me as quite incontrovertible. He thinks he is attacking superstition on behalf of the armies of reason. In fact he is attacking M.41 on behalf of the armies of M.42. D'oh!

Of course, I'm sure Professor Dawkins is quite sincere in his beliefs. Hosts always are. However, he has devoted a remarkable level of ratiocinative attention to one phenotypically insignificant meme—the God delusion—in which M.42 conflicts with M.41. My view is that this behavior is best explained by memetic infection, i.e., pwnage.

I share Professor Dawkins' preference for the derived M.42 meme, at least at this one spot on the chromosome. But I can't help observing that (a) M.42 and M.41 are both large and intricate memeplexes; (b) it strikes me as by no means obvious that when M.42 and M.41 are compared *in toto*, M.42 is more reasonable or less morbid than M.41; (c) M.42 (like M.41) includes many other memes which replicate via the same arational indoctrination paths as the God delusion; and (d) while some of the M.42 (and M.41) memes are quite reasonable, others strike me as inadequately examined at best, transparently preposterous at worst.

Ergo, pwning Professor Dawkins is quite adaptive for M.42. It focuses potential hosts on the question of whether M.42 is superior to M.41 on this particular point—as it clearly is. This distracts them from considering the more general and interesting question of whether or not M.42, considered by itself, is stark raving bonkers, and if so constructing a reasonable perspective which is reassembled from scratch and which can correct both M.42 and M.41.

I would love to see Professor Dawkins rotate his impressive intellectual artillery to this angle. But if I'm right that his neocortex has been devoured and replaced by a foam of M.42 cysts, I wouldn't exactly hold my breath. *Megaloponera foetens*[1] to the white courtesy phone.

My interpretation makes sense if and only if the following claims are sensible:

1. The concept of "nontheistic Christianity" is coherent.
2. "Einsteinian religion" is best classified as a sect of nontheistic Christianity.
3. This sect is the most successful version of Christianity today.
4. It includes propositions which are inconsistent with reason.
5. These propositions are associated with significant morbidity.

(This chapter examines claims 1–3; we'll take a look at claims 4 and 5 starting in Chapter 3.)

Before considering these claims, let's adjust our terms a little. Precise thinking requires clear, emotionally neutral, and aesthetically elegant terminology. While in general I buy the Dawkinsian model of "memetics," I think it falls short on all these counts.

Let's call a memeplex stable enough to propagate across generations a *tradition*. Not only is this an actual word in the actual English language, it also has the virtue of being nonjudgmental. Surely anyone who is not a complete, foaming-at-the-mouth fanatic, of whatever persuasion, can admit that the world contains both good traditions and bad traditions.

An individual infected by such a memeplex is a *host* who *subscribes* to the tradition. If the subject and object must be reversed, the tradition *directs* the host. An institution which propagates some tradition is a *repeater* of that tradition. The name of a tradition is its *label*.

Specific features of traditions can be called *themes*. For example, the *God theme* is a trait of many traditions. The *Trinity theme* is a trait of many Christian traditions. Traditions can be taxonomically grouped and classified, along the lines of Professor Dawkins' biological analogy, and we can follow the analogy in calling a group of related traditions a *clade*.

Different versions of a single related theme are *variants*. A set of themes transmitted as a unit can be called a *haplotheme* (in analogy with a genetic **haplotype**). Any two themes which cannot simultaneously direct one individual *conflict*. We can also follow biology in referring to *ancestral* and *derived* variants, and borrow other terminology from **cladistics**. And the set of themes an individual subscribes to is that individual's *kernel*.

Like many simple bacteria, traditions have no reproductive barriers. They can exchange themes across clade lines, or *introgress*. Thus their taxonomy is strictly speaking not a tree, but a lattice, **DAG**,[2] bush, etc. As in biology, however, intro-

---

[1] The "stink ant," most well known for the parasitic fungus of the Tomentella genus that infects its brain, leading the ant on a death march up to the rain forest canopy.
[2] Directed acyclic graph, a type of directed graph that describes the relationships in a family tree.

gression is often insignificant at the 30,000-foot level, and we can usually get away with ignoring it.

If a theme makes a substantive claim about reality (Hume's "is"), we can call it *factual* or *mundane*. If it makes a moral statement about right and wrong (Hume's "ought"), we can call it *ethical*. If it makes neither, we can call it *metaphysical*.

If a theme is not justified by reason, we can call it *arational*. Metaphysical themes are arational by definition. Mundane themes are arational if they depend on logical fallacies or violate Occam's razor. No single ethical theme can be arational, but a set of ethical themes is arational if it ascribes mutually inconsistent ethical values to a single action. While any action can be either right or wrong, no action can be both right and wrong.

If a tradition causes its hosts to make miscalculations that compromise their personal goals, it exhibits *Misesian morbidity*. If it causes its hosts to act in ways that compromise their genes' reproductive interests, it exhibits *Darwinian morbidity*. If subscribing to the tradition is individually advantageous or neutral (defectors are rewarded, or at least unpunished) but collectively harmful, the tradition is *parasitic*. If subscribing is individually disadvantageous but collectively beneficial, the tradition is *altruistic*. If it is both individually and collectively benign, it is *symbiotic*. If it is both individually and collectively harmful, it is *malignant*. Each of these labels can be applied to either Misesian or Darwinian morbidity. A theme that is arational, but does not exhibit either Misesian or Darwinian morbidity, is *trivially morbid*.

Thus, one might translate the part of Professor Dawkins' argument I agree with as the claim that the God theme is arational, because the variant in which "God" interacts with earthly affairs is mundane and fallacious (being unsubstantiated and unfalsifiable), and the variant in which "God" does not interact with earthly affairs is metaphysical. At least in the latter form, I see the God theme as trivially morbid. Professor Dawkins disagrees—he associates various Misesian and Darwinian morbidities, parasitic and malignant, with various historical variants of the God theme. I see this as the result of confusing theme and haplotheme.

My counterargument is that Professor Dawkins' "Einsteinian religion" is the most successful modern-day tradition in the Christian clade, that it includes many arational themes, and that this tradition, evaluated as a whole, exhibits Misesian parasitic morbidity and Darwinian malignant morbidity. Therefore I believe it needs to be terminated with extreme prejudice. I am relatively unconcerned about other Christian traditions, as I consider them of negligible present-day political power and therefore negligible collective morbidity—though, of course, this situation could always change.

Fortified by this doxology, let's get back to demonstrating pwnage.

Our first essential claim is that the concept of *nontheistic Christianity* is not, as most readers would probably assume at first glance, self-contradictory or meaningless.

This is very easy to see. In the biological analogy, *nontheistic Christianity* is a phrase in the same class as *flightless bird* or *bipedal tetrapod*. The adjective in this phrase is morphological, the noun is taxonomic. There is no contradiction at all.

Professor Dawkins is hoist by his own petard here. Since the biological analogy is his own invention, he cannot possibly object to the application of the modern cladistic method. If we classify traditions according to a single morphological feature, the God theme, we might as well classify both birds and bats as "flying, warm-blooded animals." Perhaps this was good enough for Aristotle, but it's certainly not good enough for Professor Dawkins.

We can watch Eliezer Yudkowsky, who for all his faults is certainly an intelligent young man, falling into this trap here.[3] He implicitly classifies a wide variety of historical traditions as either theistic or nontheistic, just as a naive taxonomist might classify animals as flying or non-flying, bipedal or quadrupedal, etc. In Yudkowsky's defense, this confusion—which is inherent in the usual modern usage of the word *religion*—is so common as to be conventional. But that doesn't make it cogent. Overcome that bias, Eliezer![4] You can do it!

In my opinion, the only sensible way to classify traditions—as with species—is by ancestral structure. While the existence of introgression and the absence of reproductive isolation makes it technically impossible to construct a precise cladogram of human traditional history, we can certainly produce sensible approximations. Note that perhaps an even better analogy is to languages and linguistic history, in which cladistic classification is commonplace.

So: Professor Dawkins is an atheist. But—as his writing makes plain—atheism is not the only theme in his personal kernel. Professor Dawkins believes in many other things. He labels the tradition to which he subscribes as *Einsteinian religion*. Since no one else has used this label, he is entitled to define *Einsteinian religion*—perhaps we can just call it *Einsteinism*—as whatever he wants. And he has.

My observation is that Einsteinism exhibits many synapomorphies with Christianity. For example, it appears that Professor Dawkins believes in the *fair distribution of goods*, the *futility of violence*, the *universal brotherhood of man*, and the *reification of community*. These might be labeled as the themes of *Rawlsianism, pacifism,*[5] *fraternism* and *communalism*.

Following the first two links above will take you to UR discussions of these themes, in which I outline their evolutionary history in the Christian clade and make a case for their morbidity. I have not yet discussed fraternism and communal-

3

4 This is a reference to Overcoming Bias, a group blog that included Yudkowsky and George Mason University economics professor Robin Hanson. Yudkowsky's articles at Overcoming Bias were later moved to Less Wrong.

5  Moldbug elaborates on his particular usage of the terms Rawlsianism and pacificism here and here.

ism, but I'll say a little about them later. If nothing else, they are certainly very easy to find in the Bible.

If Professor Dawkins were not a Christian atheist, but rather a Confucian or Buddhist atheist, or even an Islamic atheist (some clades of Sufism come daringly close to this *rara avis*), we would not expect to see these obvious synapomorphies with Christianity. Instead, we would expect to see synapomorphies with Confucianism, Buddhism or Islam, and we would have to construct a historical explanation of how these faiths made it to Cambridge. Fortunately we are spared this onerous task.

Nontheistic Christianity, therefore, can describe any tradition in the Christian clade in which the ancestral God theme has been replaced by the derived theme of atheism or agnosticism.

This is no more surprising than the replacement of the ancestral **Trinitarian** theme, which was part of all significant Christian traditions for a thousand years, with the derived **Unitarian** theme. Every variant of Christianity, by definition, considers itself orthodox. And as such it must question the legitimacy of any other Christian tradition which contains conflicting themes. To a good Trinitarian circa 1807, a Unitarian was simply not a Christian. Today, while most Christian traditions still officially conform to Trinitarianism, few spend a huge amount of time worrying about the Holy Ghost. If more examples are needed, denying the divinity of Jesus is another obvious intermediate form between Christian theism and Christian atheism.

We can also ignore the fact that Professor Dawkins does not classify Einsteinism as a form of Christianity, and nor do any non-Einsteinian Christian traditions. Clearly, accepting a tradition's classification of itself, or of its competitors, is foolish in the extreme. These minor thematic features are best explained adaptively.

For example, it would be maladaptive for Einsteinism to self-classify as Christian. One of the most adaptive features of M.42 is that nontheistic or secular Christianity can be propagated by American official institutions, which are constitutionally prohibited from endorsing its ancestor and competitor, M.41 or theistic Christianity. Considering as this set includes the most influential repeater network in the world, the US educational system, it's hard to see what could justify abandoning such a replicative advantage.

It would also be maladaptive for theistic Christianity to classify nontheistic Christianity as Christian. M.41 deploys the unchristian nature of its enemy, the dreaded "secular humanism," as a rallying point for its dwindling band of followers. If Einsteinian religion were Christian, M.41 would have to define its (increasingly ineffective) counterattack not as a defense of faith, but as a mere theological spat. Once this may have had some resonance, but in a world where God Himself is under fire, it's hard to excite anyone over such sectarian minutiae.

Therefore, I conclude that claim 1 is satisfied: nontheistic Christianity is a sensible concept.

As for claim 2, I've already described some of the links between Einsteinism and Christianity. Let's sharpen this claim, however, by proposing a hypothetical chain of events that outlines the exact historical connection.

My belief is that Professor Dawkins is not just a Christian atheist. He is a *Protestant atheist*. And he is not just a Protestant atheist. He is a *Calvinist atheist*. And he is not just a Calvinist atheist. He is an *Anglo-Calvinist atheist*. In other words, he can be also be described as a *Puritan atheist*, a *Dissenter atheist*, a *Nonconformist atheist*, an *Evangelical atheist*, etc., etc.

This cladistic taxonomy traces Professor Dawkins' intellectual ancestry back about 400 years, to the era of the English Civil War. Except of course for the atheism theme, Professor Dawkins' kernel is a remarkable match for the **Ranter, Leveller, Digger, Quaker, Fifth Monarchist**, or any of the more extreme **English Dissenter**[6] traditions that flourished during the **Cromwellian interregnum**.

Frankly, these dudes were freaks. Maniacal fanatics. Any mainstream English thinker of the 17th, 18th or 19th century, informed that this tradition (or its modern descendant) is now the planet's dominant Christian denomination, would regard this as a sign of imminent apocalypse. If you're sure they're wrong, you're more sure than me.

Fortunately, Cromwell himself was comparatively moderate. The extreme ultra-Puritan sects never got a solid lock on power under the Protectorate. Even more fortunately, Cromwell got old and died, and Cromwellism died with him. Lawful government was restored to Great Britain, as was the Church of England, and Dissenters became a marginal fringe again. And frankly, a damned good riddance it was.

However, you can't keep a good parasite down. A community of Puritans fled to America and founded the theocratic colonies of New England. After its military victories in the **American Rebellion** and the **War of Secession**, American Puritanism was well on the way to world domination. Its victories in World War I, World War II, and the Cold War confirmed its global hegemony. All legitimate mainstream thought on Earth today is descended from the American Puritans, and through them the English Dissenters.

Of course, the tradition evolved over time. Its theology took significant steps toward modern secularism in the form of **Unitarianism**, which deleted the Trinity and other points of Calvinist doctrine, and especially under **Transcendentalism**, which elided the nasty idea of hell and declared that God loves everyone. Many of Professor Dawkins' reveries about Einsteinian pantheistic natural grandeur are reminiscent of **Emerson**, who was trained as a Unitarian minister. During and after the War of Secession, New England Christianity established a cozy relationship with the Federal government, which it has continued to the present day, under labels such as *liberalism* and *progressivism*.

Two new histories of this process, though they are written by "conservatives" and thus become hopelessly confused after World War II, are David Gelernter's

---

6 For a more detailed treatment of the Dissenters, see Chapter 5 of *Open Letter*.

Americanism and George McKenna's *The Puritan Origins of American Patriotism*. (I've only just started the latter, but so far I find it far superior, and I say this though I love Gelernter to death.) The same phenomenon was ably defined by Murray Rothbard as **postmillennial pietism**.[7] For a snapshot of this terrifying militarist theocracy in action around WWI, try Richard Gamble's *The War for Righteousness*. (Most people probably don't know that the original noun which adjoined the adjective *progressive* was "Christianity.") For an especially unusual M.41-flavored look at American Puritanism replicating in its favorite niche—government schools—check out R. J. Rushdoony's *Messianic Character of American Education*. And for a primary-source view of this tradition at the last point in history at which it had the humility to classify itself as mere religion, rather than absolute righteousness and truth, see one of my favorite examples, the Time Magazine article "American Malvern"[8] from 1942—written in the lifetime, as they used to say, of those now living. What's so interesting about "American Malvern" is that it describes a recognizably progressive *political* program in *religious* terms, i.e., as "super-protestant." Professor Dawkins would certainly qualify as a "super-protestant" by its definition.

Of course, Professor Dawkins is not American, but English. Sharing a language and culture, however, American Puritanism (and the broader clade of American **mainline Protestantism**) and the English Dissenters evolved largely as a single community. For example, in the War of Secession, Britain's Anglican aristocracy tended to support the Confederates, and its Evangelical churchmen the Union. As American Puritanism won military victories and grew in political power, its British counterparts advanced as well. Everyone loves a **strong horse**.

After World War II, American influence ensured that the entire country was more or less surrendered to the Labour Party—the **political organ of the Nonconformist tradition**. The result is well described in Peter Hitchens' über-reactionary, but quite cogent, *Abolition of Britain*, or somewhat more apolitically in Theodore Dalrymple's *Life at the Bottom*. New Labour is more or less a Cromwellian restoration, and one can only hope that its long-awaited comeuppance will be enlivened by the hanging of a **corpse or two**.[9]

Professor Dawkins himself was raised as a **high-church Anglican**, an animal now essentially extinct on Planet Three. The **present Archbishop of Canterbury**[10] is so **low-church**, it's surprising he can preach anywhere but an underground parking garage. If he were any lower-church, he'd be in either Hell or China. And as of late, the so-called Tories have undergone the same **degrading humiliation**.[11] In the UK, any significant resistance to "super-protestantism" is now a footnote of histo-

---

7 Reference to Rothbard's essay "Origins of the Welfare State in America" (1996).
8 See Chapter 5 of *Open Letter*.
9 Reference to the posthumous executions ordered by Charles II after the Stuart Restoration, including the hanging of Cromwell's freshly excavated carcass.
10 Rowan Williams, who held the position from 2002-2012.
11 Reference to then Conservative Party leader David Cameron. He would become Prime Minister in 2010.

ry. The country's descent into sheer ecstatic barbarism, as long foretold by critics of the Nonconformist ascendancy, is now at hand.[12]

(It's worth noting that before 1945, anti-Americanism in Europe was essentially a right-wing tradition, primarily opposed to Yankee millennialist democratism. As I have written,[13] postwar anti-Americanism is an entirely different animal, which might be more accurately described as "ultra-Americanism." It is a consequence of the projection of American power, specifically of the New Deal, which represented the culminating triumph of the American progressive tradition, into a conquered Europe. These days, Europe has almost the same relationship to the US as the US, in the days when it was the refuge of Dissenter mania, bore to the UK.)

Moving briefly to the Continent, we encounter the strange phenomenon of the so-called "Enlightenment." Of course, everyone is enlightened by their own lights, so this word tells us nothing. In my view, the "Enlightenment" and the similarly self-congratulatory "Reformation" are best understood as a continuum. But the former is notable because it may constitute the basal synapomorphy of nontheistic Christianity. Briefly, the revocation of the Edict of Nantes[14] created a niche in France where it was more adaptive to be an unbeliever than a Protestant. The result was the rise of the philosophes, and eventually the terrifying Rousseauvian cult of Reason, which should have been enough to make everyone swear off atheism forever.

Surprisingly, it wasn't. And there is no better demonstration of the ties between the English Dissenters and the French Jacobins, and thus of the connection between Puritanism and atheism, than figures such as Rev. Richard Price, whose pro-Jacobin sermon, *Discourse on the Love of our Country*, was so memorably ass-raped by Edmund Burke in his *Reflections*.

If we compare Rev. Price's sentiments with those of the Rev. Harvey Cox, a modern exponent of secular theology—see *The Secular City 25 Years Later*,[15] written exactly two centuries after the *Discourse*—the family resemblance is unmistakable. I can't think of a single point on which either of these reverends could raise his voice to the other. Puritanism and secularism are simply the same thing. The existence of such modern sects as Unitarian Universalism demonstrates that there are zero thematic conflicts between the two. In UUism, the God theme is reduced to such irrelevance that congregants in the same church can simply agree to disagree

---

12

13

14 Edict of Fontainebleau

15

on it. But you certainly won't find them disagreeing on the proposition that, say, all men are brothers.

Of course, I've discussed this phenomenon before on UR. The label I prefer for the modern version of the Puritan tradition—Professor Dawkins' Einsteinism—is Universalism.[16] I hope I'm not boring people by continually harping on the subject, but I'd like to take a few paragraphs to once again justify this terminology.

One criticism of "Universalism" is that this label is not used by any present-day Christian denomination to identify itself. I regard this as a virtue, not a vice. First, one of the main themes of Universalism is that it does not self-classify as a Christian sect. Second, one notes that most Christian sects in the past have wound up attached to labels which were originally composed by their enemies. This stands to reason. After all, if these traditions are parasitic, one can expect them to be a little bit deceptive.

Another criticism of the label "Universalism" is that the word is derived from—and easily confused with—the simple English word *universalism*. Earlier, I tested some artificial labels which did not have this limitation, but after a while they struck me as dorky. (However, they mean the same thing and you can use them if you like—if you don't mind sounding dorky.) Suffice it to say that although Methodists are indeed often methodical, the Jurassic strata are indeed exposed in the Jura, etc., etc., the fact that most Universalists can indeed be described as universalist does not render these labels in any way, shape, or form equivalent or synonymous.

As a term of technical theology, *universalism* also has a specific, although now much-disused, meaning: the belief that everyone is saved, and no one will go to Hell. Fortunately, Universalists in my sense of the word are certainly *universalists* in this sense—i.e., they don't believe in Hell, and they do believe that every human is essentially good. Michael S. wrote very eloquently about this correspondence here.[17]

Of course, if what you really mean is *universalist* in either English sense above, rather than Universalist as in a believer in Universalism the post-Puritan tradition, I can't ask you to mean something else. But here at UR the former is a confusing term, and if you feel the need to use it, please at least consider searching for a synonym. Above all, if you mean Universalism with a capital U, please say Universalism with a capital U. You can deploy inverted commas, as in "Universalism," if you have any residual skepticism.

How do we relate Einsteinism to Universalism? One easy approach is to look at Einstein himself. Einstein was an assimilated, non-observant Jew with a Reform background, **Reform Judaism** being essentially a Jewish version of Protestantism. (In Israel, Reform is not really considered Jewish at all.) A good summary

---

16  Link to the UR post "Universalism: postwar progressivism as a Christian sect."

17 Link to UR guest post "Universalism and original sin" by commenter Michael S.

of Einstein's beliefs is here.[18] Note his affection for Quakerism, the Cromwellian über-Puritan sect *par excellence*. I have no qualms at all about describing Einstein as a Universalist.

It's also amusing to read Einstein's 1939 time-capsule message to 6939, whose entire text is:

> Our time is rich in inventive minds, the inventions of which could facilitate our lives considerably. We are crossing the seas by power and utilize power also in order to relieve humanity from all tiring muscular work. We have learned to fly and we are able to send messages and news without any difficulty over the entire world through electric waves.
>
> However, the production and distribution of commodities is entirely unorganized so that everybody must live in fear of being eliminated from the economic cycle, in this way suffering for the want of everything.
>
> Furthermore, people living in different countries kill each other at irregular time intervals, so that also for this reason anyone who thinks about the future must live in fear and terror. This is due to the fact that the intelligence and character of the masses are incomparably lower than the intelligence and character of the few who produce something valuable for the community.
>
> I trust that posterity will read these statements with a feeling of proud and justified superiority.

Note the confession of faith in economic central planning, a common Progressive Era belief. I feel quite confident that the residents of 6939, whomever they may be, will read that one with a feeling of proud and justified superiority. If not quite in the way Einstein intended.

If you are a Universalist (I was certainly raised as a Universalist, so I sympathize), and you are having trouble believing in the existence of this tradition, its Christian heritage, or its involvement with the American political system, please allow me to recommend some books. Try George Packer's *Blood of the Liberals*, Anthony Lukas's *Common Ground*, Richard Ellis's *Dark Side of the Left*, Arthur Lipow's *Authoritarian Socialism in America*, Steven Pinker's *The Blank Slate*, and Gordon Wood's *Radicalism of the American Revolution*. What all these works have in common is that they were written by orthodox Universalists, not "conservatives," and as such they will not set off the massively hypertrophied M.41 alarm that comes with your M.42 infection. The result will be a rather weird

18

and eclectic picture of American Universalist history, with many gigantic lacunae, but it ought to at least get you started.

Let me step back and take one last look at this entire phenomenon. Again, I am arguing that the Enlightenment is not orthogonal to the Reformation, that secularism is best considered as a form of Protestantism. Moreover—though this is a separate discussion—the modern battle between "left" and "right" displays clear continuity with the Protestant–Catholic conflict. As an extremely rough approximation, when we factor out the God theme, what we see is that leftism is Protestantism and rightism is Catholicism.

One of the reasons this generalization is so rough—it's easy to find counter-examples, such as modern Northern Ireland, in which Catholics are clearly "left" and Protestants are "right"—is that Catholicism and Protestantism are themselves extremely vague terms. **Ultramontanism and liberation theology** are both nominally Catholic, although I would certainly describe the latter as a Protestantizing "low-church" intrusion. **Jansenism** is another historical example of Protestantized Catholicism, which competed with the *philosophes* for the niche left open by the expulsion of the Huguenots. And the **adaptive radiation of the Protestant clade** needs no comment. **Homoplasies and introgressions** are legion in this gigantic bag of worms.

One way to produce a better generalization is to see this same conflict as not a competition between two clades, but between two adaptive niches. We can describe these niches very abstractly as *pietist* and *liturgist*. Pietist traditions in Christianity are abstract, ascetic, monastic, philosophical, and democratic. Liturgist traditions are ritualist, charismatic, materialistic, doctrinal, and hierarchical. Strains of Christianity going back well before the Reformation can be described as occupying the pietist or liturgist niche, often shifting between them.

With this adaptive taxonomy, atheism, secularism, laicism,[19] etc., appear as extreme variants of pietism. The urge to tear down all ritual, to worship Reason and Man rather than Church and God, to whitewash the frescoes and melt down the candlesticks, is everpresent in pietism. Professor Dawkins' entire shtick is perfectly consistent with the pietist niche. No wonder it's so successful.

Whereas the "fundamentalist" American born-again Christians, whom Professor Dawkins so loathes and so longs to outlaw—as if they weren't already quite thoroughly expelled from the official educational system, not to mention utterly eradicated in Europe—have developed a faith that, though its cladistic origins are thoroughly Protestant, is clearly settling in to the liturgist niche.

Indeed, Professor Dawkins seems to feel exactly the same way about these awful people that his Dissenter forebears felt about those scheming Papists. For literally centuries, fear of the Romish menace animated Protestant faithful on both sides of the pond. The fact that any serious possibility of an Anglo-Catholic resto-

---

19 A political system free of any ecclesiastical authority or influence.

ration ended in 1746[20] was hardly a check on this rich, ever-flowing wellspring of demagogic paranoia.

The **Kulturkampf** in Germany and the **Dreyfus affair** in France (note that just because the anti-Dreyfusards were wrong about Dreyfus, doesn't mean they were wrong about everything) are other, more recent outbreaks of the liturgist–pietist war—which Professor Dawkins seems so eager to resurrect. Essentially, Professor Dawkins and his fellow **New Atheists** have planted the seed of a political movement which might well be described as neo-**anticlericalism**. I'd like to think that if they took a closer look at the **past fruits of this particular vegetable**,[21] they might think twice and decide to backpedal with a quick dose of Roundup.

I believe that at this point I have adequately demonstrated claim 2. If you are not convinced, I really have no idea what I could say to convince you further.

As for claim 3—the claim that Universalism is the most successful Christian tradition today—this strikes me as simply obvious.

Some confusion may be afforded by the definition of *success*, by which I mean of course Darwinian, that is, *reproductive* success. The fact that the most influential repeaters of the Western world—the universities, state schools and the official press—are by any standards Universalist organs, is quite sufficient to demonstrate claim 3. It's also worth nothing that Universalism is far, far more fashionable—that is, simply *cooler*—than any of its competitors. To find social situations in which it's a faux pas to express Universalist sentiments, you have to dig very deep on the fashion scale, certainly well into Wal-Mart or **yobbo**[22] territory (in the US and Britain respectively). The converse is not exactly the case.

Explaining that George W. Bush, who is at least nominally a salvationist (though the veneer is pretty thin and pretty transparent, I have to say), is president of the most powerful country on Earth, is not going to convince me that your anti-salvationist fears are justified. First, you might want to take a look at the actual power of the US President, and the achievements of a far more dedicated, powerful and popular salvationist—Ronald Reagan—in rolling back Universalism or promoting salvationism. Does the word "nada" mean anything to you?

Second, the reason the US has a president who is at least nominally salvationist is simply that the number of diehard salvationists and the number of fanatical Universalists in the US is roughly equal. Considering the fact that the latter control essentially all institutions by which traditions are installed in the young—not to mention the fact that Universalists are **importing new voters** like it was going out of style—we can expect the balance of power to shift toward Universalism. Which is pretty much what it's been doing for about the last 150 years.

Where, for instance, is **Anita Bryant** today? What mainstream Republican even dares to oppose "affirmative action"? Where are even the pro-lifers, for God's

---

20 Reference to "Jacobitism."
21 Reference to the Spanish "Red Terror."
22 British and Australian slang for an uncultured person.

sake? You couldn't get 5% of the vote in the US now for the bedrock shibboleths of the 1970s' salvationist reaction.

I am certainly not a salvationist. *Au contraire*—I am a hardcore, deep-fried atheist. And my connection with Middle-American culture is not much stronger than that of **Pauline Kael**, who famously didn't know anyone who voted for Nixon. I would certainly not enjoy living in an America which was dominated by salvationists, if we define dominance as the sort of power Universalism enjoys today.

But this possibility strikes me as remote to the point of absurdity. And quite frankly, I refuse to let myself be led around by the nose by kneejerk reactions of fear and hate. **Selah.**[23] If you are not convinced on claim 3, again, there is little more I can say. Perhaps you should try washing your eyes out with a little soapy water.

---

23 A contemplative pause

387 R1100R Model of a BMW motorcycle.

 387 Chris McCandless's bus Subject of the Jon Krakauer book, and subsequent film *Into the Wild* (1996, 2007).

 387 Faré UR commenter and owner of the blog *Cybernethics*.

 388 Minotaur de Jouvenel first coined this term in his 1945 book *On Power: Its Nature and the History of Its Growth* (Les Editions du Cheval Ailé). The Minotaur was a stand-in for the immense power of the modern centralized state to mobilize all aspects of a society toward a single aim.

 388 Bertrand de Jouvenel

 388 reassembled from scratch Moldbug undertakes the project of assembling an ideology "from scratch" in his August, 2007 post "A reservationist epistemology."

 389 Megaloponera foetens

 389 Trinity theme This idea is further explored in David Stove's "What is Wrong With Our Thoughts? A Neo-Positivist Credo," from Chapter 7 of Stove's *The Plato Cult and Other Philosophical Follies*, hosted at UR and briefly referenced in Chapter 1 of *An Open Letter to an Open-Minded Progressive.*

 389 clade

 389 haplotype

 389 cladistics

 389 DAG "Directed acyclic graph"

 390 Misesian Link to an introduction to von Mises' *Human Action* (1948), at the Ludwig von Mises Institute website, 1 Nov. 1998.

390 Darwinian Link to Darwin's *The Origin of Species*.

 391 Eliezer Yudkowsky

 397 here Eliezier Yudkowsky. "Religion's Claim to be Non-Disprovable." *LessWrong*, 4 Aug. 2007.

 391 cladogram

 391 synapomorphies

 391 Rawlsianism "The Rawlsian God: Cryptocalvinism in Action." *UR*, 28 Jun. 2007.

 391 pacifism "The mystery of pacifism." *UR*, 1 Jul. 2007.

 392 Trinitarian

 392 Unitarian

 393 Ranter

 393 Leveller

 393 Digger

 393 Quaker

 393 Fifth Monarchist

393 English Dissenter

 393 Cromwellian interregnum

 393 American Rebellion "American Revolution"

 393 War of Secession "American Civil War"

 393 Unitarianism "Unitarian Universalism"

 393 Transcendentalism

 393 Emerson

394 Americanism David Galernter. *Americanism: The Fourth Great Western Religion.* (Doubleday, 2007).

394 The Puritan Origins of American Patriotism See Chapter 5 of *Open Letter.* George Mckenna. *The Puritan Origins of American Patriotism.* (Yale University Press, 2007).

 394 postmillennial pietism Rothbard, Murray N. "Origins of the Welfare State in America." *Journal of Libertarian Studies* 12, No. 2 (1996): pp.193–232., hosted at the Mises Institute online.

394 The War for Righteousness Richard M. Gamble. *The War for Righteousness: Progressive Christianity, the Great War, and the Rise of the Messianic Nation.* (ISI Books, 2003).

 394 R. J. Rushdoony

394 Messianic Character of American Education Rousas John Rushdoony. *The Messianic Character of American Education: Studies in the History of the Philosophy of Education.* (Ross House Books, reprinted 1995).

 394 American Malvern Chapter 5 of *Open Letter* quotes the article at length. "American Malvern." *Time Magazine,* Religion, Vol. XXXIX No.11, p. 16 Mar. 1942, now permanently archived at Unqualified-Reservations.org.

LINKS & NOTES

 394 mainline Protestantism

 394 strong horse "When people see a strong horse and a weak horse, by nature, they will like the strong horse," Osama bin Laden to a room full of supporters in Qandahar, Afghanistan, shortly after 9/11. The famous video recording was released by the Pentagon on Dec. 13 of 2001. A transcript is linked here.

394 political organ of the Nonconformist tradition Tristram Hunt. "Labour goes back to its roots." *The Guardian*, 5 Feb. 2006.

394 Abolition of Britain Peter Hitchens. *The Abolition of Britain: From Winston Churchill to Princess Diana*. (Encounter Books, 2000).

394 Life at the Bottom Theodore Dalrymple. *Life at the Bottom: The Worldview That Makes the Underclass*. (Ivan R. Dee, 2003).

 394 corpse or two Link to the diary entry of Samuel Pepys from 30 Jan. 1661, hosted at pepysdiary.com.

 394 high-church Anglican "High Church"

 394 present Archbishop of Canterbury "Rowan Williams"

 394 low-church

 394 degrading humiliation "David Cameron"

 395 long foretold Thomas Carlyle. *Shooting Niagara: And After?* (Chapman & Hall, 1867) p. 46.

 395 at hand John Upton. "In the Streets of Londonistan." *London Review of Books*, Vol. 26, No. 2, 22 Jan. 2004.

 395 I have written "The secret of anti-Americanism." *UR*, 8 Aug. 2007.

 395 basal synapomorphy

395 revocation of the Edict of Nantes "Edict of Fontainebleau"

 395 philosophes

 395 cult of Reason

 395 Rev. Richard Price

 395 Discourse on the Love of our Country Richard Price. "A Discourse on the Love of our Country" delivered on Nov. 4, 1789, at the Meeting-House in the Old Jewry, to the Society for Commemorating the Revolution in Great Britain, 1789.

 395 Reflections See Chapter 5 of *Open Letter*. Edmund Burke. *Reflections on the Revolution in France*. (James Dodsley, Pall Mall, 1790).

 395 Rev. Harvey Cox

 395 secular theology

 395 The Secular City 25 Years Later Harvey Cox. "The Secular City." *The Christian Century*, 7 Nov. 1990, hosted at Religion Online.

 396 Universalism "Universalism: postwar progressivism as a Christian sect," *UR*, 17 Jul. 2007.

 396 universalism

 397 here UR guest post "Universalism and original sin" by commenter Michael S., 31 Jul. 2007.

 396 Reform Judaism

 396 here-1 "The Religious Background and Religious Beliefs of Albert Einstein." *Adherents.com*, 20 April 2007.

LINKS & NOTES

 397 time-capsule "Westinghouse time capsule"

 397 Blood of the Liberals George Packer. (Farrar, Straus and Giroux, 2000).

 397 Common Ground A Turbulent Decade in the Lives of Three American Families. J. Anthony Lukas. (Vintage, 1986).

 397 Dark Side of the Left: Illiberal Egalitarianism in America. Richard J. Ellis. (University Press of Kansas, 1998).

 397 Authoritarian Socialism in America: *Edward Bellamy and the Nationalist Movement.* Arthur Lipow. (University of California Press, 1991).

 397 Radicalism of the American Revolution Gordon S. Wood. (Vintage, 1991).

 398 Ultramontanism

 398 liberation theology

 398 Jansenism

 398 adaptive radiation

 398 Homoplasies

 398 introgressions

 398 pietist

 398 liturgist

399 ended in 1746 "Jacobitism"

 399 Kulturkampf

 399 Dreyfus affair

 399 New Atheists Gary Wolf. "The Church of the Non-Believers." *Wired*, 1 Nov. 2006.

 399 anticlericalism

 399 past fruits of this particular vegetable "Red Terror (Spain)"

 399 yobbo "Yob"

 399 importing new voters Peter Brimelow. "Electing a New People." *Vdare*, 30 May 2000.

 399 Anita Bryant

 400 Pauline Kael

 400 Selah.

CHAPTER 3:
MANITOU AND THE *ZEITGEIST*
OCTOBER 11, 2007

Having made a case that there is such a thing as Universalism, that it is a nontheistic Christian tradition, and that the distinction between theistic and nontheistic traditions is not terribly significant (see also **Eric Hoffer**, who said much the same thing in *The True Believer*), it seems reasonable to take a fresh look at the effect of Universalism on present-day society, and to decide in which ways its effects can be described as positive or negative.

We should certainly expect to find positive effects of Universalism. If nothing else, any decent memetic parasite has the trivial positive effect of interfering with, undercutting, and generally destroying any potential competitors. For example, one cannot simultaneously be an Aztec and a Catholic. (Or at least not a good Aztec and a good Catholic.)

G. K. Chesterton had a handle on the trivial positive effect when he noted that when people try to believe in nothing, they often wind up **believing in anything**. Universalists think they believe in nothing. In reality they believe in Universalism. And this has the trivial positive effect of keeping them from worshiping anything else, such as Baal, Hitler, or Manchester United. Like clean water, fresh air, or a good selection of ethnic restaurants, the trivial positive effect is easy to forget until you find yourself without it.

There are probably other positive effects of Universalism. And we should probably note them when we stumble over them. If only to be fair. However, hiding its light under a bushel is not exactly Universalism's style. Why would it be? So let's accentuate the negative.

In describing the negative effects of Universalism, we're looking for three basic criteria. First, we want to show that the theme is *arational*, that is, alien to reason. Second, we want to show that it is *adaptive*, i.e., that it helps Universalism (and itself) propagate. Third, we want to show that it is *morbid*, i.e., that it makes bad stuff happen.

"Morbidity" just means "badness." Badness is always in the eye of the beholder. However, an easy way to escape this problem of Hume's ought is to use the standards of Universalism itself. This gets a little tricky when Universalism contradicts itself, but we'll deal. Recall also that, by the standards of Universalism itself, any arationality is trivially morbid. But I'm afraid we may turn up some less trivial morbidities.

If we find no arational, adaptive morbid themes, we can conclude that Universalism is not a parasitic tradition at all. It is actually a symbiotic tradition. I don't think there are any historical examples of a perfectly symbiotic tradition, but perhaps Universalism is simply the first. (It certainly claims to be the first.)

We'd also like to understand the *ancestry* of these themes. As several commenters pointed out, explaining (for example) that some theme originated in 17th-century England, among some group of people now generally acknowledged as major wackjobs,[1] does not show that it's arational or morbid. But it may help us understand why the theme is so successful. And it often helps to start with ancestry, because it creates a nice narrative flow.

Let's start with what might well be Universalism's central belief, the principle of *fraternism*. *Fraternism* is the belief that all men and women are created equal.

As my jocular overstrikes indicate, the ancestry of fraternism ain't exactly no Voynich manuscript. Universalism is a generally pietist strain of Protestant Christianity. Pietism deemphasizes ritual, authority, and God, in favor of devotion, equality, and Man. Universalism could be summarized easily as the worship of humanity, and indeed the New Testament is positively strewn with fraternist doxology. I'll go with Occam on this one.

From a theological perspective, there's an easy way to see why all men and women are born equal. It's because they all have souls, and a soul is a soul. There is no such thing as a big soul, a little soul, a yellow soul, a green soul, or a white soul. In fact, to a modern Universalist, there is not even such a thing as a bad soul. All dogs go to Heaven, and all souls are good. (If there's anyone we have to thank for this one, it's Emerson.) If a person does bad things, it is not that his or her soul is bad, but that it is in some way wounded, untaught or misguided.

Of course Universalism does not use the word *soul*. Instead it deploys the word *human*.

This word *human*, in Universalism, is what I call a *cult word*. Its emotional associations are so strong that it's simply impossible to reason around. *God* is of

---

1 Reference to the "Fifth Monarchists," 17th-century English Puritan sect named for a prophecy from the Book of Daniel.

course a cult word to a theist (and, in its own way, to an atheist—which is why I prefer "nontheist").

If I were writing Professor Dawkins' book, and I actually wanted to convince believers rather than just whipping the choir into a mouth-foaming orgy of hate, I might start by changing the word. One might say: assuming that *God* is the same thing as *Manitou*,[2] does *Manitou* exist? If your reader is unwilling to accept a mere change of labels, he or she is beyond reason. Otherwise, the discussion has freed itself from unproductive emotional reflexes.

Similarly, we can avoid the word *human* by deploying the precise Linnean term *hominid*. Or it should be precise, anyway. The paleontologists seem to change its meaning every five minutes. As per La Wik, the current proper term for "bipedal ape" is *hominan*—which at the time of this writing gets less than 1000 Google hits. People! Are you *trying* to confuse us? Until you get your story straight, I'll stick with *hominid* as anything in genus *Homo*.

If the fossil record is to be believed (who knows—maybe all those bones date to 4004 BC, when *Manitou* instantiated the universe), the past contained quite a few types of hominid whose like is no longer to be found. Which I have to say is a pity. Perhaps they would have made good pets. However, we can refer to the set of hominids now living on Planet Three as *neohominids*.

A *human* is a neohominid with a soul. But since all neohominids have souls, the qualification is redundant. So we can restate Universalist fraternism: *all neohominids are born equal*.

Now, let's evaluate this proposition. First, per the doxology from Chapter 2, we need to describe whether it is factual, ethical, or metaphysical. Is it a description of reality? Does it ascribe moral valence to some action? Or is it just a sticky lump of linguistic ambergris?

I think most Universalists consider fraternism factual. Some might say it's also ethical, but I think it's more accurate to say that Universalists consider it unethical to act on or propagate afraternism (disbelief in fraternism). If fraternism is true, afraternism is false, and since it is unethical to act on or propagate a lie, the factual case covers this.

So fraternism is a factual claim. Next we need to consider what this sentence is actually saying. We get *neohominids*, we get *born*, but what about this word *equal*?

An alien might well assume it meant *identical*. So for example, all black 2007 Honda Civic DXes are created equal. There may be some minor assembly differences, but we would not expect these differences to matter, at least to whoever is buying the vehicle, and we would not expect to see any detectable patterns of difference, except of course for option package, etc. And neohominids don't have option packages—though it would certainly be cool if they did.

However, we notice various differences between newborn neohominids, such as the shape of the nose, the texture of the hair, the color of the poop, etc., etc. So

---

2 "A god or spirit as the object of religious awe or ritual among some American Indians."

identical is not an option. We are left with the conclusion that congenital differences between neohominids are in some sense *unimportant*.

For example, perhaps these differences do not affect the neohominid's ability to succeed at various tasks of economic significance. While this was not true in the past, in the world of 2007 most of a neohominid's economic productivity is the result of its central nervous system. Of course, the CNS of a newborn neohominid is not only unproductive, but downright annoying. What we mean is obviously its potential for development. And we can also disregard diseased or otherwise malformed individuals.

So, without I think much loss of information, we can state fraternism as the proposition that *all healthy neohominids are born with equal potential for neurological development.* Is this proposition rational, or arational?

Whichever it is, Professor Dawkins certainly buys it. He writes (p. 266, *TGD*):

> Thomas Henry Huxley, by the standards of his times, was an enlightened and liberal progressive. But his times were not ours, and in 1871 he wrote the following:
>
>> No rational man, cognizant of the facts, believes that the average negro is the equal, still less the superior, of the white man. And if this be true, it is simply incredible that, when all his disabilities are removed, and our prognathous relative has a fair field and no favor, as well as no oppressor, he will be able to compete successfully with his bigger-brained and smaller-jawed rival, in a contest which is to be carried out by thoughts and not by bites. The highest places in the hierarchy of civilization will assuredly not be within the reach of our dusky cousins.
>
> It is a commonplace that good historians don't judge statements from past times by the standards of their own... Had Huxley... been born and educated in our time, he would have been the first to cringe with us at his Victorian sentiments and unctuous tone. I quote them only to illustrate how the Zeitgeist moves on.

What, exactly, is this *Zeitgeist* thing? Is it anything like *Manitou*? We'll return to this fascinating question.

In any case, had Professor Huxley been born and educated in North Korea, he would have been the first to praise the Dear Leader. Had he been born and educated in 4th-century Byzantium, he would have been the first to perform the **proskynesis**[3] before the Emperor Constantine. Had my aunt had balls, she'd be my uncle.

And had Professor Huxley *himself* been extracted from 1871—perhaps the *Zeitgeist* has some kind of supplemental time-travel feature—he might want to

---

3 "The act of bowing down before a lord or ruler, especially in ancient Persia."

know *why* Professor Dawkins disagrees so confidently—so, dare I say, *unctuously*—with him. This arrogant, bewhiskered troglodyte, still damp with the ichor of the twelfth dimension, might even dare to demand some actual *evidence*.

Obviously, it would be easy for us to satisfy Professor Huxley. Once he saw that one out of five Americans drives a Haitian car, that the last two winners of the Nobel Prize for Chemistry hailed from Papua New Guinea, and that Japan has trouble exporting anything it can trade for Mozambican semiconductors, I'm sure he'd sing a different tune. As Thomas Friedman once put it, back when he had something to say, "a Swiss soldier stole my Syrian watch."

In all seriousness, what is the evidence for fraternism? Why, exactly, does Professor Dawkins believe that all neohominids are born with identical potential for neurological development? He doesn't say. Perhaps he thinks it's obvious.

Perhaps, if he's anything like **Cosma Shalizi** (and Professor Shalizi is, if anything, even smarter than Professor Dawkins), he believes that there is no convincing evidence[4] that all neohominids are *not* born with identical potential for neurological development. Similarly, another very smart person, **Aaron Swartz**, sees no convincing evidence[5] that neohominid males and females are *not* neurologically identical.

Of course, Professor Dawkins has no convincing evidence that *Manitou* does *not* exist. Now isn't this fascinating? Don't you just love these double negatives?

What we have here is a factual proposition which has swept to dominance not through the presentation of any evidence, but by the simple trick of *reassigning the burden of proof* to rest solely on those who doubt it. It is not the fraternists who have to demonstrate that fraternism is true. It is the afraternists who have to demonstrate that it's false. D'oh!

If I were to claim that the neohominid male liver is functionally indistinguishable from the neohominid female liver—that there is no sexual dimorphism in the neohominid liver—I'd expect someone to ask me why I was justified in making this claim. I would not expect them to accept the response that I see no convincing evidence that my claim is untrue. And this is despite the fact that the liver is not directly involved in the neohominid reproductive cycle. When we replace *liver* with *brain*, we have a considerably longer row to hoe. Yet somehow, the *Zeitgeist* shows up and hoes it overnight. If only it would do the same for my laundry.

If you're actually interested in a positive empirical case for afraternism, let me recommend **Thompson & Gray 2004**.[6]

4

5

6

And it's worth noting that afraternism is **Steven Pinker's dangerous idea**.[7] Michael Hart's *Understanding Human History* has to be the worst job of book design in human history, and my general reaction is that Hart understands neohominids a heck of a lot better than he understands history. However, all the cool kids are reading it.

But my concern is not empirical. It is philosophical and historical. What I'm interested in is how and why it came to be the case that fraternism is assumed true until proven false, and afraternism is assumed false until proven true.

One simple answer is that, since we are assuming Universalist ethics, fraternism is the ideal state of the world. My ethics are basically Universalist, and if I had a blue button I could push to institute fraternism—regardless of the actual present state of reality—I'd push it, and I'd feel good about pushing it. If I had an opposite red button, I wouldn't push it, and if I accidentally pushed it anyway I would feel *really, really bad*.

Thus we can say that fraternism is *optimistic* and afraternism is *pessimistic*. But is it rational to assert that optimistic propositions should be assumed true until proven false, and pessimistic propositions should be assumed false until proven true? Not in the slightest. We are back at square one.

One could also suggest a technical explanation, which might go like this: since there is no reproductive isolation between any two neohominid populations, we should expect these populations to be genetically homogeneous. Anyone who wants to make a case for any kind of genetic inhomogeneity, therefore, should have to make it. Perhaps **Lewontin's fallacy** could be drug into the picture as well, just for color.

However, as we can see by outwardly visible traits such as nose shape, hair texture, etc., the antecedent is false. It's possible that the disparities in visible traits are the result of **genetic drift**. It's also possible that they're the result of **natural selection**. But it doesn't matter which, because any evolutionary process that can vary a visible feature can vary an invisible one. (We've recently learned that neohominid populations show substantial evidence of **recent selection**—much more recent than the divergence of continental gene pools. But even before we knew this, we had no biological reason to assign fraternism the benefit of the doubt.)

Clearly, fraternism did not get the benefit of the doubt in 1871. So at some point it must have changed, *n'est-ce pas*? How, when, and why?

Perhaps **Charles Francis Adams, Jr.**, can enlighten us on the subject. As the great-grandson and grandson of Federalist and Whig Presidents, son of and aide to one of the North's **leading abolitionist statesmen**, and a Union general himself, one might expect he had some opinions on the matter. And one would be right. From a **1913 speech**:

7

Beyond all this, and coming still under the head of individual theories, was the doctrine enunciated by Thomas Jefferson in the Declaration of Independence—the doctrine that all men were created equal—meaning, of course, equal before the law. But the theorist and humanitarian of the North, accepting the fundamental principle laid down in the Declaration, gave to it a far wider application than had been intended by its authors—a breadth of application it would not bear. Such science as he had being of scriptural origin, he interpreted the word "equal" as signifying equal in the possibilities of their attributes—physical, moral, intellectual; and in so doing, he of course ignored the first principles of ethnology. It was, I now realize, a somewhat wild-eyed school of philosophy, that of which I myself was a youthful disciple.

[...]

So far, then, as the institution of slavery is concerned, in its relations to ownership and property in those of the human species—I have seen no reason whatever to revise or in any way to alter the theories and principles I entertained in 1853, and in the maintenance of which I subsequently bore arms between 1861 and 1865. Economically, socially, and from the point of view of abstract political justice, I hold that the institution of slavery, as it existed in this country prior to the year 1865, was in no respect either desirable or justifiable. That it had its good and even its elevating side, so far at least as the African is concerned, I am not here to deny. On the contrary, I see and recognize those features of the institution far more clearly now than I should have said would have been possible in 1853. That the institution in itself, under conditions then existing, tended to the elevation of the less advanced race, I frankly admit I did not then think. On the other hand, that it exercised a most pernicious influence upon those of the more advanced race, and especially upon that large majority of the more advanced race who were not themselves owners of slaves—of that I have become with time ever more and more satisfied. The noticeable feature, however, so far as I individually am concerned, has been the entire change of view as respects certain of the fundamental propositions at the base of our whole American political and social edifice brought about by a more careful and intelligent ethnological study. I refer to the political equality of man, and to that race absorption to which I have alluded—that belief that any foreign element introduced into the American social system and body politic would speedily be absorbed therein, and in a brief space thoroughly assimilated. In this all-important respect I do not hesitate to say we theorists and abstractionists of the North, throughout that long anti-slavery discussion which ended with the 1861 clash of arms, were thoroughly wrong. In utter disregard of fundamental, scientific facts, we theoretically believed that all men—no matter what might be the color of their skin, or the texture of their hair—were, if placed under exactly similar conditions, in essentials the same. In other words, we indulged in the curious and, as is now admitted, utterly erroneous theory that the African was, so to speak, an Anglo-Saxon, or, if you will, a Yankee "who had never had a chance,"—a fellow-man who was guilty, as we chose to express it, of a skin not colored like our own. In other words, though carved in ebony, he also was in the image of God.

Apparently the *Zeitgeist* doesn't just work in one direction. What is this *Zeitgeist*, anyway? Here is Professor Dawkins' definition:

In any society there exists a somewhat mysterious consensus, which changes over the decades, and for which it is not pretentious to use the German loan-word *Zeitgeist* (spirit of the times).

If we adopt a slightly more literal translation, we could call our mysterious phenomenon the *Spirit of Time*. And if we ignore the even more mysterious backward lurch from 1871 to 1913, and simply accept Professor Dawkins' interpretation of our *Spirit*'s actions, we see that the *Zeitgeist* is a basically optimistic force. Its goal appears to be that history turns out for the better (again, defining *better* in terms of Universalist ethics). Pretty nice to have around the house, wouldn't you say?

In fact, Professor Dawkins' *Zeitgeist* is so nice that it's indistinguishable from a concept that would have been quite familiar to any member of the Adams family[8]—the old Anglo-Calvinist or Puritan concept of Providence. Perhaps this is a false match. But it's quite a close one.

Another word for *Zeitgeist* is *Progress*. It's unsurprising that Universalists tend to believe in *Progress*—in fact, in a political context, they often call themselves *progressives*. Universalism has indeed made quite a bit of progress since 1913. But this hardly refutes the proposition that Universalism is a parasitic tradition. Progress for the tick is not progress for the dog.

Whether we call it *Providence*, *Zeitgeist* or *Progress*, the idea of a mysterious force that causes history to flow in some direction—which generally happens to be the right one—is called historicism. Karl Popper is your man on this one.[9]

Needless to say, historicism is profoundly arational. It is also rampant in the West today. You can't open a newspaper without reading some sentence that makes no sense at all unless the *Zeitgeist* is behind the curtain. Historicism also informs

---

[8] As in John and John Quincy et al.
[9] Reference to Popper's *The Poverty of Historicism* (1957).

the consensus understanding of the recent past among even the best-educated Westerners today. You have to go back about 250 years—i.e., to the predemocratic era—before ahistoricist explanations start to predominate.

(Recently I ran into the most astounding little book, this **ahistoricist history of the French Revolution**,[10] written by an obscure Canadian historian who appears to be a specialist. Very calm and highly recommended. Imagine that all your life you'd been drinking what you thought was water but was in fact corn syrup, and then someone gave you a glass of actual water. The taste of a good revisionist history is simply unmistakable.)

In any case, I digress. The point is that we've found two thoroughly arational themes in the Universalism complex: *fraternism* and *historicism*. Moreover, these are arational in exactly the same sense as the *Manitou* delusion. They are not demonstrably false. They are just (a) believed by billions of people, and (b) essentially unsubstantiated.

We can extend this list with the two arational Universalist themes I've discussed before, **Rawlsianism** (also discussed here[11]) and **pacifism**.[12] And there is a fifth which I haven't yet given its due, *communalism* (the error of ascribing individual identity to neohominid groups).

I think I've done a fair job of demonstrating arationality for at least the first four. Arationality implies at least trivial morbidity. I think I'll leave the task of showing nontrivial morbidity for fraternism and historicism to the reader's imagination, on which I don't think it makes any particularly onerous demands.

However, I haven't really discussed adaptiveness. And, if we want to demonstrate pwnage, we have to show adaptiveness, because arational themes could be in some way accidental or transient, a result of thematic drift, as it were. If these arationalities do not contribute to the reproductive success of Universalism, they will probably go away on their own, and they are much less worrisome. Thus, describing Professor Dawkins as pwned may be a stretch. I'll start tying some of these ends together in **Chapter 4**.

---

10 J.F. Bosher's *The French Revolution* (1989).
11

12 For Rawlsianism and pacificism see Chapter 2.

409 Eric Hoffer

 409 The True Believer: Thoughts on the Nature of Mass Movements. (Harper & Brothers, 1951).

 409 believing in anything This is usually quoted as something like, "When a man stops believing in God, he doesn't then believe in nothing, he believes in anything." Although frequently ascribed to Chesterton, in fact there is no credible evidence that he ever wrote or said anything to this effect. (Nevertheless, the point remains.)

 410 Hume's ought

 410 major wackjobs "Fifth Monarchists"

410 men and women This detail has mutated even further as of the Current Year. Because phrases like "men and women" reinforce the gender binary, orthodox Universalists would now regard such terminology as insufficiently inclusive, and would be more likely to say something like "people of all genders."

 410 Voynich manuscript

 410 pietist

 410 All dogs go to Heaven Reference to the 1998 children's film.

 410 Emerson Richard Higgins. "Emerson's mirror." *UUWorld*, 28 Feb. 2003.

 411 Manitou

 411 hominid

 411 every five minutes "Ape - History of hominoid taxonomy"

411 Homo

 411 ambergris

 412 Thomas Henry Huxley

 412 proskynesis

413 something to say Reference to Freidman's *From Beirut to Jerusalem* (Anchor, 1995).

 413 Cosma Shalizi Personal webpage for professor of statistics, Cosma Rohilla Shalizi.

 413 no convincing evidence Shalizi. "Yet More on the Heritability and Malleability of IQ." *Three-Toed Sloth*, 27 Sep. 2007, at bactra.org.

 413 Aaron Swartz This was written well before Swartz became a major public figure over his arrest and federal prosecution for downloading JSTOR pdfs while in grad school at MIT, and his subsequent suicide in 2013. At the time, Swartz was best known for his involvement with Wikipedia.

 413 no convincing evidence-1 Swarz. "The Case Against Lawrence Summers." *aaronsw.com*, 9 Mar. 2005.

 413 Thompson & Gray 2004 Jason Malloy. "ScienceWeek Idiots." *Gene Expression*, 7. Nov. 2005.

 414 Steven Pinker's dangerous idea Pinker. "Preface to Dangerous Ideas." *Edge*, 31 Dec. 2006.

 414 Understanding Human History: An analysis including the effects of geography and differential evolution. Michael Hart. (Washington Summit Publishers, 2007), link to a pdf at lesacreduprintemps19.files.wordpress.

 414 Lewontin's fallacy

414 genetic drift

 414 natural selection

 414 recent selection Carl Zimmer. "This Week in Human Evolution." *National Geographic*, The Loom, 8 Mar. 2006.

 414 Charles Francis Adams, Jr.

 414 leading abolitionist statesmen "Charles Francis Adams Sr."

 414 1913 speech Chalres Francis Admas, Jr. "Tis Sixty Years Since." Founder's Day, University of South Carolina, 16 Jan. 1913 (reprinted by MacMillan Company, 1913).

 416 Adams family "Adams political family"

 416 Providence

 416 historicism

 416 this one Popper's book, *The Poverty of Historicisim* (Routledge, 1957) dismantles the central tenets of historicism, regarding it as a fundamentally flawed approach to explaining social and cultural phenomenon.

417 ahistoricist history of the French Revolution J.F. Bosher. *The French Revolution.* (W.W. Norton, 1989).

 417 Rawlsianism "The Rawlsian god: cryptocalvinism in action." *UR*, 28 Jun. 2007.

 417 here-2 "What if there's no such thing as chaotic good?" *UR*, 1 May 2007.

 417 pacifism "The mystery of pacifism." *UR*, 1 Jul. 2007.

CHAPTER 3:
A MYSTERY CULT OF POWER
OCTOBER 18, 2007

In the previous three chapters, I've argued that Professor Dawkins is pwned because he's chosen quite unthinkingly to lend his literary talents to a received tradition I call *Universalism*, which is a nontheistic Christian sect. Some other current labels for this same tradition, more or less synonymous, are *progressivism, multiculturalism, liberalism, humanism, leftism, political correctness*, and the like. My only excuse for minting my own term is that these other labels, since they are in common use, imply various associations which may confuse the reader.

In my humble but convinced opinion, Universalism is far more important, far more dangerous, and far more antirational than its theistic Christian competitors, which Professor Dawkins attacks with such fury. He thinks he's a **Galileo**, **Vavilov** or **Darwin**. But if my perspective is accurate, Professor Dawkins is more a **Caccini**, **Lysenko** or **Wilberforce**. He is pwned in every sense of the word, and history will treat him in its usual harsh manner. A few librarians may remember him as a curiosity of the era.

Of course, I am just a humble blogger and I have no control at all over history. Sometimes I write out my screeds in tiny, cramped longhand, and staple them to telephone poles. You, dear reader, should treat them as if you found them that way. After all, anyone can start a blog.

In my opinion, however, Universalism is the dominant modern branch of Christianity on the Calvinist line, evolving from the English Dissenter or Puritan tradition through the Unitarian, Transcendentalist, and Progressive movements. Its ancestral briar patch also includes a few sideways sprigs that are important enough to name but whose Christian ancestry is slightly better concealed, such as Rousseauvian laicism, Benthamite utilitarianism, Reform Judaism, Comtean positivism, German Idealism, Marxist scientific socialism, Sartrean existentialism, Heideggerian postmodernism, etc., etc., etc. All but the first can be traced back to the first, and Rousseau himself was a Genevan and acknowledged his political debt to Calvin's republic. So Universalism traces almost all of its memetic DNA to this hateful little phony, this pissant, heretic-roasting tyrant on the lake, Jehan Cauvin—so well-sketched by Stefan Zweig.

Which is no reason to automatically condemn it. After all, Scarlett Johansson traces all of her actual DNA to chimps. Evolution can change anything. Universalism as we know it today, à la Port Huron Statement, would be quite unrecognizable to any of its 16th-century or 17th-century ancestors. It would shock the living daylights out of most of its 18th-century or 19th-century ones. It is what it is. It is not something else.

Most of my previous discussions of Universalism have been devoted simply to the task of demonstrating that the label is apt, that the tradition is real, and that its pedigree is accurate. I don't regard this as audacious at all, since most religions and other traditions in history have been named by their enemies. Labels such as *Unitarian*, *Methodist*, *Whig*, *Tory*, and many others originated as hostile slurs and were subsequently accepted as accurate.

[Start Here]But again, the thing can only be judged as itself. I've described a few ways in which I think Universalism should be considered harmful—for example, in Chapter 3. But I don't think I've really presented a high-level overview of the thing as it is today, abjuring any and all snide references to the Jukes and Kallikaks in its stud book.[1]

Universalism, in my opinion, is best described as a *mystery cult of power*.

It's a *cult of power* because one critical stage in its replicative lifecycle is a little critter called the *State*. When we look at the big U's surface proteins, we notice that most of them can be explained by its need to capture, retain, and maintain the State, and direct its powers toward the creation of conditions that favor the continued replication of Universalism. It's as hard to imagine Universalism without the State as malaria without the mosquito.

It's a *mystery cult* because it displaces theistic traditions by replacing metaphysical superstitions with philosophical *mysteries*, such as *humanity*, *progress*, *equality*, *democracy*, *justice*, *environment*, *community*, *peace*, etc.

None of these concepts, as defined in orthodox Universalist doctrine, is even slightly coherent. All can absorb arbitrary mental energy without producing any rational thought. In this they are best compared to Plotinian, Talmudic, or Scholas-

---

[1] The Jukes and Kallikaks families were titular subjects in a series of books on the heritability of pathological behaviors, and oft-cited case-studies in support of the eugenics movement at the end of the 19th century.

tic nonsense. (I link to this **David Stove piece**[2] often, and I encourage anyone who hasn't read it to do so. No, this does not constitute an endorsement of everything that Professor Stove ever wrote.)

The Universalist mysteries are best regarded as *mechanisms*. When we apply our neohominid intuitions to a successful adaptive system such as Universalism, we should think of its goal as replicative success. Of course, a tradition is not a person, just as a meme is not a gene, and it no more has goals than a meme has Mendelian inheritance. It's especially important not to confuse the personal goals of Universalists with the adaptive goals of Universalism. But with these caveats, we can use this analogy to deploy our **mirror neurons** in our own defense.

For Universalism, as for any other tradition, the adaptive purpose of a mystery is to *confuse* its host. Lacking a clear perception of reality, the infected host behaves in ways that an uninfected host would not. We can call this confusion *camouflage*.

As compared to the behavior of the uninfected, sometimes these actions are beneficial to the host, or to a group which includes the host, but their actual effect is contrary to the host's ethical standards. We can call this *positive camouflage*. Sometimes these actions are harmful to the host or a group which includes the host. We can call this *negative camouflage*.

If we can deploy the e-word, positive camouflage contributes to *evil* by convincing those who do evil that they are actually doing good. For example, if we believe Himmler's **Posen speech**, those who perpetrated the Holocaust believed that they were carrying out a difficult but necessary duty. Negative camouflage contributes to evil by preventing its victims from resisting it. While we're on Nazis, the great example is the **Oxford Union peace resolution**.[3]

Of course, if we are to deploy the e-word, we have to tackle the thorny problem of defining good and evil. We have two approaches to this.

One, we can define our moral axis with respect to Universalism itself. For example, if we apply this test to Nazism, we see that Nazism was evil even with respect to itself. Nazi ethics defined good as the power and prosperity of the *Deutsche Volk* and its guide Adolf Hitler. The result of Nazi policies was the physical destruction of Germany, the conversion of the German people to Universalism, the total suppression of *Volkisch* thought, and the death of Adolf Hitler—not exactly as advertised. This approach gives us *reflexive evil* or *reflexive good*.

Two, we can define our moral axis with respect to the personal or reproductive interests of you yourself, dear reader. If this criterion makes sense only with respect to a group, we can speak of the group of UR readers—which includes me, because I sometimes do try to slog through my own long posts. If Universalism harms or

advances your or our personal interests, we say it exhibits Misesian *evil or good*. If it harms or advances your or our reproductive interests, it exhibits *Darwinian evil or good*.[4]

Darwinian morality is an especially good reality check, because the neohominid brain is of course designed to advance its own Darwinian interests. Any tradition that can persuade it to do otherwise has to be some pretty heavy crack. As we'll see, Universalism more than fits the bill. However, to generate a really strong moral conclusion, we'd like to see agreement among all three criteria: reflexive, Misesian and Darwinian.

One easy way to do this is to examine some scenarios in which Universalism could lead to either the *extinction of the neohominid species*, or the *destruction of Western civilization*. Clearly, any such result represents the triumph of reflexive, Misesian and Darwinian evil. And if such results are plausible, worrying about anything smaller is a waste of time.

Let's unravel this problem by starting with the Universalist mystery of *progress*, which, as we saw in Chapter 3, Professor Dawkins calls the *Zeitgeist* or *Spirit of Time*.

First, it's worth noting that Chapter 7 of *The God Delusion*, in which Professor Dawkins introduces this concept, opens with a quote by one **Sean O'Casey**:

> Politics has slain its thousands, but religion
> *has slain its tens of thousands*.

La Wik describes O'Casey as a "nationalist and socialist." Frankly, he sounds like an **evil little fucker**.[5] This evil little fucker was born in 1880, and presumably he uttered his little ort of shite at some point before nationalist, socialist politics—not to mention National Socialism proper—managed to slay its **tens of millions**. The fact that Professor Dawkins could, in 2007, quote this Stalinist flack and his fatuous, thoroughly-obsolete line—and his legion of acolytes swallow it without a hiccup—may be a sufficient demonstration of Universalist pwnage.

But if it's worth continuing, it's worth repeating Professor Dawkins' definition of the *Zeitgeist*: *a mysterious consensus, which changes over the decades*. For some reason, these changes over the decades almost always favor Universalism itself. This is of course *progress*, and our *Spirit of Time* bears a suspicious resemblance to the M.O. of Divine Providence, minus of course the Divine bit.

Since Professor Dawkins does not have Providence to lean on, he is forced to find a rational explanation for this historical curiosity. His struggles are wonderful reading:

---

4 See Chapter 2 for more on the *Misesian* v. *Darwinian* dichotomy.

5

> Where, then, have these concerted and steady changes in social consciousness come from? The onus is not on me to answer. For my purposes it is sufficient that they certainly have not come from religion.

Exeter Hall[6] would beg to differ. So would Henry Ward Beecher, Walter Rauschenbusch, William Sloane Coffin,[7] etc., etc.

> We need to explain why the changing moral *Zeitgeist* is so widely synchronized across large numbers of people and we need to explain its relatively consistent direction.

Indeed.

> First, how is it synchronized across so many people? It spreads itself from mind to mind through conversations in bars and at dinner parties, through books and book reviews, through newspapers and broadcasting, and nowadays through the Internet.

Not to mention the State and its entire educational system, from kindergarten to grad school. Obviously this is less important than "bars and dinner parties." But I'm just saying.

> Changes in the moral climate are signalled in editorials, on radio talk shows, in political speeches, in the pattern of stand-up comedians and the scripts of soap operas, in the votes of parliaments making laws and the decisions of judges interpreting them.

That's an interesting word—"signalled."

> One way to put it would be in terms of changing meme frequencies in the meme pool, but I shall not pursue that.

Fortunately, Professor Dawkins, you don't have to.

> What impels it in its consistent direction? We mustn't neglect the driving role of individual leaders who, ahead of their time, stand up and persuade the rest of us to move on with them.

---

6 A meeting place located on the Strand in London, center of the British anti-slave movement, especially its religious aspects, and referenced in Thomas Carlyle's 1849 essay "An Occassional Discourse on the Negro Question."
7 These men were all religious figureheads at the center of various progressive movements spanning the 19th and 20th centuries.

Curiously enough, leaders come in **all kinds of flavors**.[8] We mustn't neglect the fascinating question of why the Universalist ones always win, and the others always lose. Oh, wait, we must neglect it. Obviously these aren't the droids we're looking for.

> In America, the ideals of racial equality were fostered by political leaders of the calibre of Martin Luther King,

I know it's cheap, but I simply can't resist the temptation to attach a little innuendo to the word "calibre." As Dr. King himself **put it**, "I'm not a Negro tonight!"

> and entertainers, sportsmen and other public figures such as Paul Robeson, Sidney Poitier, Jesse Owens and Jackie Robinson.

Isn't it interesting how the *Zeitgeist* seems to correlate with dermal pigmentation?

> The emancipations of slaves and of women owed much to charismatic leaders. Some of these leaders were religious; some were not. Some who were religious did their good deeds because they were religious. In other cases their religion was incidental.

Presumably if Professor Dawkins discovered a fossil which looked a little like a chimpanzee and a little like a neohominid, he might regard it as an indication of a link between the two. Sadly, in the memetic department, this lobe of his brain seems to be in the off position.

> Although Martin Luther King was a Christian, he derived his philosophy of non-violent civil disobedience directly from Gandhi, who was not.

The number of historical solecisms in this sentence is astounding. The modern idea of **civil disobedience**—that is, breaking the actual legal law, in favor of some mysterious higher law, an obvious case of positive camouflage—dates to neither King nor Gandhi, but to **Thoreau** and the Transcendentalists, who were of course direct ancestors of Universalism.

As for Gandhi, this **Richard Grenier** essay[9] is simply essential. But what it fails to point out is that Gandhi's weird communist pseudo-Hinduism was an invention, a sort of **Ossianism** or **Kwanzaa**, an Indian equivalent of the phony Gaelic revival associated with the **Fenian** movement. Like Nehru, Gandhi was a British

---

8 Reference to Kim Jong-il, Francisco Franco, Engelbert Dollfuss, and Idi Amin.
9

lawyer with brown skin. Their movement—like its Irish counterpart—succeeded entirely through its alliance with British political forces, and in specific the Nonconformist and proto-Universalist Labour Party. For example, in Paul Scott's *Jewel in the Crown*, one character is a Nonconformist missionary nun, and it's taken for granted that she has a picture of Gandhi on her wall and despises the Raj.

Anyway, to finish with this sport:

> It is beyond my amateur psychology and sociology to go any further in explaining why the moral *Zeitgeist* moves in its broadly concerted way.

Professor Dawkins, if you were to go any less further, you'd need a rear-view mirror.

> For my purposes it is enough that, as a matter of observed fact, it *does* move, and it is not driven by religion—and certainly not by scripture.

Which obviously makes it a product of pure reason.

> It is probably not a single force like gravity, but a complex interplay of disparate forces like the one that propels Moore's Law, describing the exponential increase in computer power.

Boys and girls, can you say "epicycle"?

The epicycle in Professor Dawkins' theory of history is needed to explain why, when we look at history, good always prevails over evil. Or almost always:

> Even when he was railing against Christianity, Hitler never ceased using the language of Providence: a mysterious agency which, he believed, had singled him out for a divine mission to lead Germany.

This second "mysterious agency" appears just six pages from Professor Dawkins' own *Zeitgeist*. One really wonders whether this man has read his own book.

Of course, a theism-independent perspective of memetic evolution eliminates our need for the epicycle. What Professor Dawkins is observing is simply the selective success of Universalism. Universalism succeeded because it was better-adapted than its competitors. Since Professor Dawkins is a Universalist, of course he views this as the triumph of good over evil. But his *Zeitgeist* is no more than the well-known fallacy of **survivor bias**. And Hitler's Providence, which doubtless made itself scarce around 1942, is exactly the same animal.

So the question remains: why does good so consistently triumph over evil?

If we exclude supernatural forces which cause the good side to win elections, battles and wars, we are left with no explanation at all of this strange phenomenon, so reminiscent of Tom Stoppard's *Rosencrantz & Guildenstern Are Dead*. "Heads. Heads. Heads. Heads. Heads..."[10]

It's true that people want to be good. Perhaps we should expect them to flock to the good side, outnumbering the evil. On the other hand, when we remember the phenomenon of positive camouflage, and see that most who do evil think of themselves as doing good, it's hard to take this seriously. And moreover, actual good has to be actually good, whereas evil by definition is capable of anything. If the military advantage is anywhere, it would seem to lie with the latter.

Essentially, what we've found behind this particular Universalist mystery is the assertion that Universalism has triumphed because Universalism is good and good triumphs. Good triumphs because Universalism is successful and Universalism is good. Spot the unsubstantiated assertion!

Just as we have no reason at all to assume that neohominid populations are geographically uniform, we have no reason at all to assume that Universalism is good—in either the reflexive, Darwinian, or Misesian sense. Of course we learned in school that Universalism is good, in at least the first and third senses. But who did we learn this from? Universalist teachers. Again, all we know is that Universalism is successful. And we can say the same of Universalism's ancestors. The winners write history. If Nazism had won its war, citizens of the Nazi 2007 would see history as an inevitable progress toward the National Socialist present.

Thus, Universalist historicism is effective camouflage both negative and positive. The circular reasoning behind the mystery of *progress*, *Zeitgeist* or *Providence* dissuades those who might be harmed by Universalism from considering the possibility that Universalism is not, in fact, good, and needs to be fought against. And it persuades those whose interests Universalism advances that they are serving good, not evil.

We are now in a position to strip off this camouflage and have a look at what's behind it.

If *progress* is simply the victory of Universalism, and Universalism need not be entirely good, we need to construct an interpretation of history which recognizes both *progress* and *decay*. Where Universalism is good, its victory is by definition *progress*. Where Universalism is bad, its victory must be *decay*. Without mysterious or supernatural pro-good forces, we would expect to see some mix of the former and the latter.

Let's cap this exercise at about 250 years, i.e., at 1757. Some Universalist distortions may go back farther, but they dwindle rapidly. Before this period it is usually hard, when reading a typical Universalist history, to tell which side is supposed to be righteous and which wrongtious. Once we get to the American and French Revolutions, we are left in no doubt.

---

10 YouTube clip of Gary Oldman's Rosencrantz and Tim Roth's Guildenstern improbably flipping a coin "heads" 78 times in a row.

It is very difficult for a modern American to construct the history of the last 250 years as a history of decay. Decay is especially concealed by the obvious history of technical and scientific progress. While this has no reason at all to correlate with political or cultural progress, the two are certainly not hard to confuse.

However, one way to look at the question is to look at the traditional opposite of the word *progressive*: that is, *reactionary*.

Howard Zinn, for example, has given us a progressive interpretation of history.[11] What is a comparable reactionary narrative? Professor Zinn, of course, would like us to believe that any narrative less progressive than his is reactionary. But perhaps it is only reactionary compared to Professor Zinn.

What we really need is an interpretation of history so reactionary that it contains no Universalism or proto-Universalism at all. Instead, it should start with the mainstream perspective of 1757, and interpret all evidence of impending Universalism as the story of decline, disaster and decay.

Then, we can compare the progressive and reactionary narratives on a level playing field, evaluating the relative credibility of both, and decide on what points to accept—thus allocating Universalist history, and implicitly Universalism itself, between progress and decay.

For this we need our pure reactionary theory of history. Needless to say, this is a very specialized product. It is not sold in any stores. It is not even found in a single volume. Nonetheless, the Internet is of great assistance in assembling the product.

If I had to pick ten books from which to construct a reactionary theory of modern history, I would pick the following (in order of composition, which makes a good reading order):

- Edmund Burke—*Reflections on the Revolution in France*
- Henry Maine—*Popular Government*
- W. E. H. Lecky—*Democracy and Liberty*
- Walter Lippmann—*Public Opinion*
- Edgar Lee Masters—*Lincoln the Man*
- Albert Jay Nock—*Memoirs of a Superfluous Man*
- John T. Flynn—*As We Go Marching*
- Bertrand de Jouvenel—*On Power*
- Erik von Kuehnelt-Leddihn—*Liberty or Equality*
- James Burnham—*Suicide of the West*

I've included links to online editions where available. All of these are, in my opinion, absolute classics and should be read by anyone even remotely interested in history.

(A question for readers: can anyone recommend a good reactionary history of the American Revolution? Or should I say, Rebellion? For some reason, I haven't bumped into any Tory treatments which live up to the above standard.)

Let me also mention James Stephen's *Liberty, Equality, Fraternity*, a wonderful book which is a little too close to the Maine to make this list, and also suffers

---

11 *A People's History of the United States* (1980)

from the disability that I have not yet read all of it. However, just to show that there is nothing new under the sun, here is how Stephen's classic opens:

> The object of this work is to examine the doctrines which are rather hinted at than expressed by the phrase 'Liberty, Equality, Fraternity.' This phrase has been the motto of more than one Republic. It is indeed something more than a motto. It is the creed of a religion, less definite than any one of the forms of Christianity, which are in part its rivals, in part its antagonists, and in part its associates, but not on that account the less powerful. It is, on the contrary, one of the most penetrating influences of the day. It shows itself now and then in definite forms, of which Positivism is the one best known to our generation, but its special manifestations give no adequate measure of its depth or width. It penetrates other creeds. It has often transformed Christianity into a system of optimism, which has in some cases retained and in others rejected Christian phraseology. It deeply influences politics and legislation. It has its solemn festivals, its sober adherents, its enthusiasts, its Anabaptists and Antinomians. The Religion of Humanity is perhaps as good a name as could be found for it, if the expression is used in a wider sense than the narrow and technical one associated with it by Comte. It is one of the commonest beliefs of the day that the human race collectively has before it splendid destinies of various kinds, and that the road to them is to be found in the removal of all restraints on human conduct, in the recognition of a substantial equality between all human creatures, and in fraternity or general love. These doctrines are in very many cases held as a religious faith. They are regarded not merely as truths, but as truths for which those who believe in them are ready to do battle, and for the establishment of which they are prepared to sacrifice all merely personal ends.
>
> Such, stated of course in the most general terms, is the religion of which I take 'Liberty, Equality, Fraternity' to be the creed. I do not believe it.
>
> I am not the advocate of Slavery, Caste, and Hatred, nor do I deny that a sense may be given to the words, Liberty, Equality, and Fraternity, in which they may be regarded as good. I wish to assert with respect to them two propositions.
>
> First, that in the present day even those who use those words most rationally—that is to say, as the names of elements of social life which, like others, have their advantages and disadvantages according to time, place, and circumstance—have a great dispo-

sition to exaggerate their advantages and to deny the existence, or at any rate to underrate the importance, of their disadvantages.

Next, that whatever signification be attached to them, these words are ill-adapted to be the creed of a religion, that the things which they denote are not ends in themselves, and that when used collectively the words do not typify, however vaguely, any state of society which a reasonable man ought to regard with enthusiasm or self-devotion.

Compare to Maine's brilliant reactionary blast:

It has always been my desire and hope to apply the Historical Method to the political institutions of men. But, here again, the inquiry into the history of these institutions, and the attempt to estimate their true value by the results of such an inquiry, are seriously embarrassed by a mass of ideas and beliefs which have grown up in our day on the subject of one particular form of government, that extreme form of popular government which is called Democracy. A portion of the notions which prevail in Europe concerning Popular Government are derived (and these are worthy of all respect) from observation of its practical working; a larger portion merely reproduce technical rules of the British or American constitutions in an altered or disguised form; but a multitude of ideas on this subject, ideas which are steadily absorbing or displacing all others, appear to me, like the theories of jurisprudence of which I have spoken, to have been conceived a priori. They are, in fact, another set of deductions from the assumption of a State of Nature. Their true source has never been forgotten on the Continent of Europe, where they are well known to have sprung from the teaching of Jean-Jacques Rousseau, who believed that men emerged from the primitive natural condition by a process which made every form of government, except Democracy, illegitimate. In this country they are not often explicitly, or even consciously, referred to their real origin, which is, nevertheless, constantly betrayed by the language in which they are expressed. Democracy is commonly described as having an inherent superiority over every other form of government. It is supposed to advance with an irresistible and preordained movement. It is thought to be full of the promise of blessings to mankind; yet if it fails to bring with it these blessings, or even proves to be prolific of the heaviest calamities, it is not held to deserve condemnation. These are the familiar marks of a theory which claims to be independent of experience and observation on the plea that it bears the credentials of a golden age, non-historical and unverifiable.

Let me quickly explain my reactionary theory of history, which comes from reading weird old forgotten books such as the above. Note that this theory is quite simple. Depending on your inclinations, you may regard this as a good thing or a bad thing.

In order to get to the reactionary theory of history, we need a reactionary theory of government. History, again, is interpretation, and interpretation requires theory. I've described this theory before under the name of **neocameralism**,[12] but on a blog it never hurts to be a little repetitive.

First: government is not a mystical or mysterious institution. A government is simply a group of people working together for a common aim, i.e., a corporation. Whether a government is good or bad is not determined by who its employees are or how they are selected. It is determined by whether the actions of the government are good or bad.

Second: the only fundamental difference between a government and a "private corporation" is that the former is *sovereign*: it has no higher authority to which it can appeal to protect its property. A sovereign corporation owns its territory, and maintains that ownership by demonstrating unchallenged control. It is stable if no other party, internal or external, has any incentive to attack it. Especially in the nuclear age, it is not difficult to deter prospective attackers.

Third: a good government is a well-managed sovereign corporation. Good government is efficient management. Efficient management is profitable management. A profitable government has no incentive to break its promises, abuse its citizens (who are its capital), or attack its neighbors.

Fourth: efficient management can be implemented by the same techniques in sovereign corporations as in nonsovereign ones. The company's profit is distributed equally to holders of negotiable shares. The shareholders elect a board, which selects a CEO.

Fifth: although the full neocameralist approach has never been tried, its closest historical equivalents to this approach are the 18th-century tradition of enlightened absolutism as represented by Frederick the Great, and the 21st-century non-democratic tradition as seen in lost fragments of the British Empire such as Hong Kong, Singapore and Dubai. These states appear to provide a very high quality of service to their citizens, with no meaningful democracy at all. They have minimal crime and high levels of personal and economic freedom. They tend to be quite prosperous. They are weak only in political freedom, and political freedom is unimportant by definition when government is stable and effective.

12

Sixth: the comparative success of the American and European postwar systems appears to be due to their abandonment of democratic politics as a practical mechanism of government, in favor of a civil-service *Beamtenstaat* in which democratic politicians are increasingly symbolic. The post-communist civil-service states, China and Russia, appear to be converging on the same system, although their stability is ensured primarily by direct military authority, rather than by a system of managed public opinion.

Seventh: the post-democratic civil-service state, while not utterly disastrous, is not the end of history. It has two problems. One, the size and complexity of its regulatory system tends to increase without bound, resulting in economic stagnation and general apathy. Two, more critically, it can neither abolish democratic politics formally, nor defend itself against changes in information flow that may destabilize public opinion. Notably, the rise of the Internet disrupts the feedback loop between public education and political power, allowing noncanonical ideas to flourish. If these ideas are both rationally compelling and politically delegitimating, the state is threatened.

Eighth: therefore, productive political efforts should focus on peacefully terminating, restructuring and decentralizing the 20th-century civil-service state along neocameralist lines. The ideal result is a planet of thousands, even tens of thousands, of independent city-states, each managed for profit by its shareholders.

Note that this perspective has nothing at all in common with the Universalist theory of government. Note also the simplicity of the transition that it suggests *should* have happened, from monarchy as a family business to a modern corporate structure with separate board and CEO, eliminating the vagaries of the hereditary principle.

Now let's look—from this reactionary perspective—at what actually *did* happen.

First, in America and Europe from the late 18th through the middle of the 19th century, we see a series of violent changes in power, in which states were overthrown and territories captured by disorganized mobs of their own residents, sometimes in cahoots with the army. These were called *revolutions*. They were almost entirely destructive phenomena, with no major point to recommend them. There is no revolution in this period which had benign results. The French revolutions of 1789 and 1830, for example, can be blamed entirely on irresolute monarchs without the courage, dexterity or both to use the military against the mob.

Moreover, even when states did not capitulate totally to revolutionary mobs, they often surrendered partially, as for example in the **Reform Bill** of 1832. This led to a progressive acceleration of democracy, and its inevitable accomplice, paramilitary violence. The US, for example, in the height of its democratic period from 1828 to 1932, was almost never without violent elections or political gangs. Democratic government before the civil-service era was also corrupt on an almost indescribable scale.

Democracy, and democratic ideologies and religions, had become power cults which attracted and selected for the ambitious and unscrupulous. Numerous corrupt systems which could command voting blocs sprung up, from urban ward-heeler machines to yellow-journalist newspapers. Deceiving the voting population was job one for these political engineers, and public opinion on all political subjects—government, law, economics, and war—began to diverge significantly from reality.

This situation culminated in the first great total war of the democratic era, the War of Secession between Union and Confederacy. The proximate cause of the War of Secession was the anti-slavery campaign, a political-religious nationalist movement in the North that harangued the South with apocalyptic rhetoric, supported paramilitary terrorist attacks on it, extracted vast quantities of tax through an almost punitive tariff, unilaterally and informally rewrote the Constitution to strengthen its own power and hold the South captive, and in general did everything it could to stoke Southern paranoia. But the latter was hardly lacking, as the South had developed its own bizarre nationalist movement, a romantic cult which glorified a hereditary caste system and threatened to invade the entire Western hemisphere, Yankeeland excluded—and only because it was bad land for sugarcane, tobacco or cotton. Neither of these competing nationalisms was conceivable in the 18th century, and both are most parsimoniously ascribed to the effect of 80 years of democracy on the mass mind.

The War of Secession was a war of mass destruction in which all previously known laws of war were violated, generally by the North with its revived Puritan cult of righteousness. It killed half a million men and brought happiness to none but the killers—not even the slaves, whose liberation was a sham but whose destitution was certainly not. As such it prefigured the even more destructive wars of the following century. It also destroyed the American tradition of limited government, setting the scene for the megastate to come.

Probably the most destructive result of the 19th-century democratic movement was the rise of militant nationalism, which beleaguered aristocratic elites found all too effective in deflecting the sympathies of the increasingly violent mob. Contrary to the promises of democrats, the first tastes of socialist plunder only whetted the mob's appetite for more. Democratic factions divided according to their preferred food for this great beast: money or blood.

This jingoist tendency, also inconceivable in the 18th century, eventually culminated in the war which destroyed European civilization, the Great War. The first outbreak of the Great War, which lasted from 1914 to 1918, killed millions of young men and left Russia in the hands of a barbaric neo-Jacobin military death cult. The same cult later devastated Spain, where order was fortunately restored under a nationalist movement that was at least neither socialist nor expansionist. Finally, the ultimate synthesis of nationalism and socialism, fascism, restarted the Great War, which became a worldwide conflict between the militarist and socialist traditions. At the end of the Great War in 1945, memory of the *Belle Époque* had dwindled to near extinction, and there was no significant political force which supported the restoration of the classical liberal era.

The US had succumbed to a socialist revolution under false electoral premises in 1932.[13] This was primarily the result of a financial panic, which was caused by unscrupulous dilution of the currency in the boom of the 1920s, through the new Federal Reserve System. After the first phase of the Great War, the gold standard, which was never entirely stable under the Anglo-American fractional-reserve system, had been restored in a broken form (the "gold-exchange standard") which was more tolerant of dilution through state-guaranteed maturity-mismatched lending, but not tolerant enough. The collapse of this system allowed inflationist economists to claim that capitalism itself had failed, not unlike the famous orphan who requested clemency for the murder of his parents. This brought on a socialist revolution, the New Deal, in which the Federal government and the Progressive civil-service machine claimed unlimited legislative power to deal with the emergency it had created for itself.

It has never relinquished this power, nor can it ever be expected to. It has never restored a metallic currency, nor can it ever be expected to. Its civil service and judiciary are entirely insulated from democracy. Its legislative body, which remains bicameral for reasons now only historical, has an incumbent reelection rate in the high 90s. Its two political parties, which are no longer meaningful organizations and are now mere labels, are identical on virtually all substantive domestic policy issues. Most of their efforts are put into fighting proxy wars against each other, often involving American soldiers, on distant parts of the globe which have no relevance at all to domestic security. The Federal government consumes 30% of GDP, and the US borrows 6% of GDP from abroad every year just to stay afloat. Crime is rampant, with many parts of many major cities effectively uninhabitable by any civilized person, and a substantial criminal class. Some cities, such as Detroit, have been entirely cleansed of their white population and in some places are even reverting to prairie (but very dangerous prairie). Former residents of the cities, whose old Irish, Italian and Jewish quarters no longer exist, have fled to more defensible quarters in hideous strip-mall suburbs. Encouraged by both parties, which jockey for their votes, uneducated peasants from Latin America are flooding in unknown numbers across its uncontrolled borders. Fortunately, so far this new generation of immigrants has seen little of the joys of the criminal lifestyle, but this seems to change quickly for their children. In short, the US is rapidly becoming a Third World country, not unlike present-day Brazil. The only mercy is that its respite from democracy has lasted.

After the Great War, the socialist powers fell out, as gangs often do. The first split was the US–Soviet split, in which the latter turned out to be more interested in territory and power than in a position as a US satellite. In the resulting Cold War, these two powers dismembered the remnants of European law and order in

---

13 Reference to the Democratic Party Platform published after FDR's nomination for president. See Chapter 7 of *Open Letter* for more on this episode.

the Third World, in the worst scramble for colonial supremacy the world had yet seen. Any pretext of bringing good government to uncivilized peoples was forgotten, and any nationalist thug, preferably as socialist as possible, was a satisfactory client for either side. Most of the non-European world, including even formerly civilized countries such as China, reverted to the rule of national-socialist warlords who competed for American and Soviet favor. Some, such as Yugoslavia and China, split from both factions and courted the aid of both. Perhaps a hundred million people around the world were murdered in this "liberation," which is still revered as such worldwide. The supposedly "independent" countries of the Third World are still dependent on aid from the US and its European satellites. There is only one independent Third World country in the world—Somaliland.

Meanwhile, competing branches of the US government still engage in Third World proxy wars, in which the Defense Department and its political allies and satellites (the Republican Party, the arms and energy industry, Israel) face off against the State Department and its allies and satellites (the Democratic Party, the NGOs and universities, Europe, Palestine). The true nature of these conflicts, which would end instantly if the US was under unitary leadership, or even if both American factions could agree to cut off all "aid" to all their foreign satellites, is admitted by no one. It is considered entirely normal that the US often arms, and always talks with, both sides of these bizarre, incurable pseudo-wars.

Lately, the old Third World national-socialist movement has managed to refit itself with an Islamic façade, and destroyed a couple of very large buildings in New York, killing thousands of people. No effective effort against the perpetrators has been mounted, probably because any successful American military effort brings political prestige to the American right and threatens to reignite the old era of nationalist jingoism, a threat which terrifies the American left—and for good reason. So many individuals involved with the attack live and continue their efforts in a country which is not at war with the US, nor vice versa. Most Americans consider this entirely normal. The concept of war itself has been under attack for the last fifty years, in favor of an entirely new legal model which is derived from domestic criminal justice, and which seems designed to make it as difficult as possible for civilized forces to defeat uncivilized ones, a theory which certainly fits the short-term political needs of its proponents. The resulting concept of "asymmetric warfare" is also generally accepted, with only a little grumbling, as a necessary burden that must be shouldered by our great and moral nation.

Other than this, everything is fine. Technology is moving along pretty well. Moore's Law continues to zoom along. We have fast computers and fancy mobile phones and other things that no one in the 18th century could dream of. If they could see our political system, however, I'm afraid they'd understand it all too well.

Frankly, any system of thought that can convincingly present this history as a case of *progress* is capable of anything. Readers may, of course, differ with my interpretation of events. But hopefully at this point they at least understand why I see Universalism as a parasitic tradition.

421 *Galileo*

 421 *Vavilov*

 421 *Darwin*

 421 *Caccini*

 421 *Lysenko*

 421 *Wilberforce*

422 *Stefan Zweig* The Right to Heresy: Castellio against Calvin. (Beacon Press, 1951).

 422 *Port Huron Statement* See also Chapter 8 of *Open Letter*.

 422 *considered harmful*

 422 *Jukes*

 422 *Kallikaks*

 422 *stud book* "Breed registry"

 423 *David Stove piece* "What is Wrong With Our Thoughts..." See Chapter 2 of *Dawkins*, and Chapter 1 of *Open Letter*.

 423 *mirror neurons*

423 Posen speech

 423 Oxford Union peace resolution Link to the New York Times obituary for David Graham, lead author of the Oxford Union's statement on its vote against fighting for "King and Country" in 1933. The statement was said to have encouraged Hitler that the British would not resist Nazi military efforts, but this interpretation has been cast into significant doubt. Eric Pace. "David Graham, 87, Is Dead; Antiwar Debater at Oxford." *New York Times*, 27 Aug. 1999.

 424 Misesian Link to *Human Action* (1998)

 424 Darwinian Origin of Species

 424 Sean O'Casey

 424 evil little fucker "Sean O'Casey, Irish Playwright, Is Dead at 84." *New York Times*, 19 Sep. 1964.

 424 tens of millions "Democide"

 425 Exeter Hall This is the same essay in which Carlyle coins the phrase "dismal science" to describe the field of economics. He makes the case that the marriage of the "dismal science" and "Exeter Hall Philanthropy"–i.e., political economists and Christian evangelicals–led by the "sacred cause of Black Emancipation...will give birth to progenies and prodigies; dark extensive moon-calves, unnameable abortions, wide-coiled monstrosities, such as the world has not seen hitherto!" Carlyle. "An Occasional discourse on the Negro Question." Reference in David M. Levy's and Sandra J. Peart's article "The Secret History of the Dismal Science: Part I, Economics, Religion and Race in the 19th Century." *Econlib*, 22 Jan. 2001.

 425 Henry Ward Beecher

 425 Walter Rauschenbusch

425 *William Sloane Coffin*

 426 *all* "King Jong-il"

 426 *kinds* "Francisco Franco"

 426 *of* "Engelbert Dollfuss"

 426 *flavors* "Idi Amin"

 426 *put it* This quote comes from Taylor Branch's King biography *Pillar of Fire: America in the King Years, 1963-64.* (Simon & Schuster, 1998). Link to Slate review of the book by David Greenberg, "All King's Men" (4 Feb. 1998).

 426 *civil disobedience*

 426 *Thoreau*

 426 *Richard Grenier essay* "The Ghandi Nobody Knows." *Commentary Magazine*, March 1983.

 426 *Ossianism*

 426 *Kwanzaa*

 426 *Fenian*

 427 *Jewel in the Crown* Scott. (Heineman, 1966).

 427 *epicycle* "Deferent and epicycle"

427 survivor bias

 428 Rosencrantz & Guildenstern Are Dead Dir. Tom Stoppard. (Cinecom Pictures, 1990).

 428 Heads. Heads. Heads. Heads. Heads… "Rosencrantz & Guildenstern Are Dead (Heads)." uploaded 10 Nov. 2007.

 428 no reason at all Cahal Milmo. "Fury at DNA pioneer's theory: Africans are less intelligent than Westerners." Independent, 17 Oct. 2007.

 428 The winners write history. "Whig history"

 429 progressive interpretation of history Howard Zinn. *A People's History of the United States: 1492-Present.* (Harper & Row, 1980).

 429 Edmund Burke

 429 Reflections on the Revolution in France (James Dodsley, Pall Mall, 1790). Archived link to full text at constitution.org. See Chapter 5 of *Open Letter* for a link to the Google Books version.

 429 Henry Maine

 429 Popular Government with an Introduction by George W. Carey (Liberty Fund, 1976). PDF available at the Liberty Fund website.

 429 W. E. H. Lecky

 429 Democracy and Liberty edited and with an Introduction by William Murchison, 2 vols. Liberty Fund, 1981). Ibid.

 429 Walter Lippmann

 429 Public Opinion (Harcourt, Brace, & Co. 1922). Hypertext version available at the University of Virginia American Studies department website.

429 *Edgar Lee Masters*

429 *Lincoln the Man* (Dodd, Mead, & Company, 1931).

 429 *Albert Jay Nock*

 429 *Memoirs of a Superfluous Man* (Harper Brothers, 1943). PDF available at Mises Institute website.

 429 *John T. Flynn*

 429 *As We Go Marching* (Doubleday, 1944). Ibid.

 429 *Bertrand de Jouvenel*

 429 *On Power* (Les Editions du Cheval Ailé, 1945). Link to Viking Press English translation by J.F. Huntington, 1949, at archive.org. See also Chapter 2.

 429 *Erik von Kuehnelt-Leddihn*

 429 *Liberty or Equality* (Caxton Printers, 1952). Available at Mises.

 429 *James Burnham*

429 *Suicide of the West: An Essay on the Meaning and Destiny of Liberalism* (The John Day Company, 1964).

 429 *James Stephen*

 429 *Liberty, Equality, Fraternity* (Liberty Fund, 1874). Available at Liberty Fund.

432 neocameralism "Against political freedom" *UR*, 16 Aug. 2007. Also discussed in the 13 Dec. 2007 post "Why I am not a libertarian." Briefly stated: "The idea that a sovereign state or primary corporation is not organizationally distinct from a secondary or private corporation."

 433 Reform Bill See Chapter 14 of *Open Letter*.

 434 Belle Époque

 435 false electoral premises Democratic Party Platforms: "Democratic Party Platform of 1932," June 27, 1932. Online by Gerhard Peters and John T. Woolley, *The American Presidency Project*.

CHAPTER 5: PLANET 3.01
OCTOBER 25, 2007

So, in the course of the previous chapters, we've established that Professor Dawkins is pwned.

He is pwned because he is serving the interests of a tradition called Universalism, a nontheistic sect of Christianity which is currently the planet's dominant religion. And Professor Dawkins has not done his homework on Universalism. As we've seen, he's accepted orthodox Universalist interpretations of major aspects of reality—if anthropology and history count as "major"—in exactly the same way that his favorite strawmen accept theistic metaphysics: by declaring it true until proven false. He appears to be quite unaware of how creepy this is.

Or at least he was unaware. If he is reading these messages, Professor Dawkins is now sunk, I'm sure, in misery and despair. He is questioning his own sanity. Is there any path back to reality? Is anything left but sickness, confusion, lies? Can anything now be real and good and true? Or has the worm but lunched too long?

The answer, actually, is yes. The worm *has* lunched too long. There is no escape. Not for Professor Dawkins, not for me, not for you, not for anyone. We'll simply have to deal.

If the infection were fresh, we could escape just by asking and answering two simple questions. One: is Universalism good, or evil? Two: if the latter, what should I, personally, do about it?

If Universalism were Scientology—or the cult of Kim Jong Il—or even Communism—this might be an effective initial state from which to consider its merits or demerits. But Universalism is to these pissant little knockoffs as the Holy Roman Catholic and Apostolic Church is to **Robert Schuller's Hour of Power**. As Detective Durkin **put it** in *Split Second*, "We need bigger guns... We've got to get bigger guns!"

In fact, if you just *translate* the word "Catholicism" into 21st-century English, it comes out... **you guessed it**.[1] I was recently disappointed to learn that, contrary to the assertion of my 10th-grade English teacher, "Darth Vader" does not actually mean "Dark Father" in Dutch. That would be *Donker Vader*, which somehow doesn't have the same *je ne sais quoi*. But you get the idea. The point is that this thing, whatever you care to call it, is at least two hundred years old and probably more like five. It's basically the *Reformation itself*. It's certainly the most up-to-date revision of Jouvenel's Minotaur. And just walking up to it and denouncing it as evil is about as likely to work as suing **Shub-Niggurath** in small-claims court.

So, if there's any way to even contemplate this history-devouring horror, it can only be by thinking *around* Universalism. We cannot hope to assault the Elder Ones. We cannot even offend them. Our only hope is to amuse them for a little while.

In other words: it may be a fun parlor game to answer every political question by asking how the **Duke of Wellington**[2] would handle it. But we lack anything like the shared cultural capital we'd need to simply evaluate the proposition that Universalism is just evil, and needs to be terminated with extreme prejudice. We can't even imagine how to think these thoughts. And Universalism at every turn would be telling us we were evil for even starting to think them.

On the bright side, however, by accepting the possibility that Universalism exists, that it is not simply "ethics" or "justice" or "science" or "history," you have already taken the first step toward thinking around it. Let's take a few more steps and see where we end up.

First, remember that Universalism is a *mystery cult of political power*. As John Gray **puts it**, "Modern politics is a chapter in the history of religion." This is not to excuse Professor Gray, whose incredible legerdemain in skipping directly from the French Revolution to George W. Bush does much more to conceal than to explain. But, as Hunter S. Thompson used to **put it**, even a blind pig finds an acorn every once in a while.

To engage the neohominid instinct for worship, you need a *grand mystery*: some question of transcendental importance to which no meaningful answer can be constructed. It is even better if inside the mystery is some *high agency*, some power which works in mysterious ways. **Christopher Moltisanti** decided that the **higher power** for his 12-step program was his Mafia oath. Sometimes I suspect that if you go to an AA meeting in Berkeley, their higher power is the United Nations, or maybe the State Department, or even just NPR.

---

1 Universal; all-encompassing
2 Arthur Wellesley, one of the commanders chiefly responsible for defeating Napoleon at Waterloo.

In this chapter, we're going to try to raise the tone, and avoid taking these cheap little digs at Universalism or Universalists. The point is: the spiritual antennae of the Universalist are aimed almost exclusively in the direction of the State. When a Universalist thinks about good or evil, she thinks about the good State and the evil State.

Our goal, in learning to think around Universalism, is to construct a way to think about the State that is morally neutral, and that does not depend at all on Universalist concepts. The end product should be a complete, drop-in replacement for Universalism which does not challenge or threaten it in any way.

Our first step is a full linguistic reconstruction of politics and history. I'll outline this reconstruction for the State I live in, which I think is reasonable, because this particular polity happens to more or less dominate the world. (As **Thom Yorke** put it, "**Radiohead** works like the United Nations. I'm the US.") If you live in Greenland or Poland or Uzbekistan or wherever, the transformation should not be too difficult.

Just as we saw in the Universalist concept of *humanity*, there is an enormous inherent confusion in Universalist political linguistics. When I talk about *America* or *the US*, I may mean one of the following concepts: a political organization, a geographical region, or a population of neohominids. For the first or the third, I may mean this concept solely in the present, or I may be referring to some period of historical continuity. A more preposterous hodgepodge could scarcely be contemplated.

Frankly, this is ridiculous. It has to go. The **Empsonian ambiguity**—a programmer might call it **overloading**—may be poetically touching, that is, if you're a political shill-poet like **Lowell, Whitman, MacLeish** or **Dove**. Finish your ode to Stalin and get outta here. The rest of us would like a way to clearly refer to clear, specific concepts.

One way to do this is to imagine we're thinking about an alternate reality. In Reality #2, there is a clone of Planet 3, Planet 3.01, which is exactly identical and follows the same orbit around the Sun, 180 degrees out of phase so that neither can see the other.

On Planet 3.01, the temperate and subtropical latitudes of the northern continent in the western hemisphere are a region called *Plainland*. (An English translation of **Vinland**.) The inhabitants of Plainland are the *Plainlanders*.

Culturally, our Plainlanders fall into five major castes:[3] the *Brahmins, Dalits, Helots, Optimates* and *Vaisyas*. They can also be divided by descent: *European, African, Asian* or *Beringian*. And their political conflicts identify them as either *Coaster* (blue) or *Middler* (red). Of course, none of these categories is precise or complete. All sorts of overlaps and subcategories exist. Nonetheless, these very rough high-level abstractions are quite useful.

---

3 See Moldbug's "Castes of the United States."

Plainland is owned by a sovereign corporation, or *sovcorp*. Its name is *Washcorp*: the Washington Corporation. (I like this slightly better than one I tried earlier, *Fedco*. It sounds even more neutral and enormous. Of course, Planet 3.0 has plenty of actual companies named both Washcorp and Fedco,[4] but none is particularly significant.)

A *corporation* is just a set of people working together with a common purpose—basically, any organization. I should probably replace this word as well, but it is such an effective offensive weapon that it would be a pity to just throw it out, and the English meaning is extremely clear.

A corporation is *sovereign*—and thus a sovcorp—if there is no controlling legal authority to which it can appeal, and it is responsible for enforcing and defending its own law. Again, the English meaning of this word is extremely clear and historically accurate.

Aside from the fact that it is sovereign, Washcorp owns Plainland in the same sense that any person or organization owns any piece of property. It exercises absolute and total domination and control. Plainlanders exist at Washcorp's sufferance. It can expel them, kill them, or order them to obey arbitrary commands. There is no other power to which they can appeal, and no Plainlander or combination of Plainlanders has, or could conceivably have, even a thousandth of the military force needed to defeat Washcorp. Nor does any such force exist anywhere else on the planet.

Note that Planet 3.01 remains identical to Planet 3.0 in all substantive details. Let me add, however, the stipulation that on Planet 3.01, and within the boundaries of Plainland, Washcorp is absolutely invincible. It is not even worth thinking about thinking about a military strategy which could wrest Plainland from the eternal iron grip of Washcorp. Also, the flag of Washcorp is a red W inscribed in a white circle on a black field, and this sigil is honored with the Roman salute. Everything else is the same, though.

I should also describe the history of Washcorp. It was founded by an aristocrat and military leader, General Washington (hence the name), a prominent sympathizer of a paramilitary gang called the Sons of Liberty. The Sons evolved into the first identifiable ancestor of Washcorp as we know it today, the Continental Congress, with its Continental Army under Washington, who swiftly established himself as princeps.

This version of Washcorp is the *First Corporation* or the *Continental Corporation*. The period of its formal existence, 1776 to 1789, is the *Continental Period*. The First Corporation's goal was to use violent force to seize Plainland from its original European owner, the sovcorp British Crown. Assisted by political divisions within British Crown, it succeeded in this task and assumed ownership of Plainland through adverse possession, winning the *War of Atlantic Separation*.[5]

---

[4] Washington Companies and an ersatz department store chain based in Southern California, respectively.
[5] The American Revolution, or "American Rebellion" as it's called in Chapter 2.

The original First Corporation was very weak and had limited power over its subsidiaries, the **provinces of Plainland**,[6] which retained much of their original sovereignty as recognized in both its primary contract, the Articles of Confederation, and its deed of cession as conceded by British Crown, the **Treaty of Paris**. In 1789, a group of prominent managers wrested power from the First Corporation and replaced it with the *Second* or *Constitutional Corporation* (1789–1861), which left the relationship between Washcorp and its provinces informal.

The primary contract of the Second Corporation, the Constitution, was designed by its primary architect Alexander Hamilton, one of Washington's cronies, to shift sovereign power gradually, subtly and irreversibly away from the provinces and toward Washcorp itself. (Compare to the similar approach of present-day Eurocorp.) Interprovincial tensions always undermined this strategy, and in 1861 a group of provinces joined forces and attempted to seize the southern half of Plainland in the *War of Southern Separation*.[7]

Under the messianic dictator Abraham Lincoln, Washcorp won this war and subjugated the rebellious provinces. No more was heard about provincial sovereignty. The War of Southern Separation effectively revoked the Constitution, and converted Washcorp's management process to an informal system with no strict textual basis, opening the *Third* or *Nationalist Period* (1861–1933). It is also notable for its introduction of military slavery—i.e., the draft—to Washcorp's playbook. All major Washcorp wars through the 1970s were fought with Plainlander slave soldiers.

The Third Corporation retained many elements of the old Constitutional system, notably the theory that Washcorp's sovereign discretion was constrained by a list of enumerated powers. However, it also developed a state religion of transcendental power worship, or Nationalism. The quintessential Nationalist tract was the science-fiction novel *Looking Backward* by the **Social Gospel** fanatic **Edward Bellamy**, which predicted with remarkable prescience that by the year 2000, Washcorp would exercise complete and detailed control over the lives and occupations of all Plainlanders.

The essential idea of Nationalism was that Washcorp was deeply and fundamentally good, and could bring this spirit of righteousness to everything it touched or did. If this seems hard to understand, it is best explained as a continuation of the Protestant **postmillennial** tradition, with its emphasis on achieving the New Jerusalem, the kingdom of Christ on earth.

Nationalism can only be understood with respect to the system known as democracy, in which Plainlanders reconsecrate their obeisance to Washcorp regularly and indirectly, pledging their submission to one of several (typically two, but rarely one or three) political gangs, or parties. The parties alternate in power according to headcount of registered supporters. In the late Constitutional and early Nationalist periods, Washcorp operated under the **spoils** system, in which the parties distrib-

---

6 The United States
7 American Civil War

uted Washcorp's revenue to their supporters by disguising these dividends as the salaries for so-called jobs.

Democracy, which had deep roots in the **English Dissenter**[8] sects to which early Euro-Plainlanders subscribed, is best seen in terms of the system of ritual legitimacy it replaced, **divine-right monarchy**. The older divine-right sovcorps legitimized their ownership—that is, persuaded their subjects not to rebel—by attributing it to divine intervention. Democracy arrived with the advent of new religious systems which stressed the divine nature of humanity. This **Inner Light**, of which all adult males (and later females) had exactly one, could be counted and summed. If Washcorp was directed by this arithmetic, its actions could not fail to be righteous.

As the 20th century opened, Nationalism evolved into its more sophisticated successor Progressivism, a label still used today. Progressivism, which is essentially the political projection of Universalism, was a check to the abuses of democracy, reducing the power of corrupt elected officials in favor of permanent Washcorp employees, or civil servants. (Perhaps the word "master" would be more apropos.) Progressives consider these employees "professional," "nonpartisan," "objective," etc., but they still operate under the moral umbrella of democracy, whose righteousness is undiminished however symbolic or passive its elected officials may become. Note that this is not unlike the modern fate of constitutional monarchy.

In extreme progressivism, as practiced today by **Eurocorp**,[9] meaningful politics can be eliminated entirely, but the sovcorp still considers itself perfectly democratic. Needless to say, so do its subjects. The defunct "people's democracies" of Russia and Central Europe, though dominated by security forces rather than educational organs, followed a similar pattern.

Washcorp was also a leader in developing a comprehensive official education system. Like many techniques of 20th-century sovcorps, official education—which includes official primary, secondary and tertiary instruction, official scientific research, official journalism and broadcasting, etc.—is essential to prevent democracy from degenerating into civil war or rebellion. Otherwise, political conflicts are simply too real, and parties become attracted by the creative opportunities of escalating violence. Either the sovcorp's security organs become its first line of defense, or it succumbs to the mayhem. There are no modern examples of a stable democratic sovcorp without an effective system of official education.

Needless to say, coordinating the opinions of the population is one way to make them loyal workers and soldiers in wartime, and reliable taxpayers in peacetime. 20th-century sovcorps can be classed broadly by their choice between two models of domestic security: *educracy*, in which the sovcorp manages the opinions of its subjects with an official education system and confirms that this system

---

8 See Chapter 2.
9 Reference to the concept of a "democratic deficit," wherein an ostensibly democratic body fails to operate according to democratic principles, first used to describe the European Economic Community, the predecessor to the EU.

is working by subjecting itself to democratic elections, and *securocracy*, in which the sovcorp forgets democracy and simply trusts its security forces as the ultimate guardians of order.

This is a continuous spectrum: all securocratic sovcorps also maintain official education systems, and all educratic sovcorps have effective, trustworthy security forces. But there is generally a consistent pattern of dominance in conflicts between educational and security agencies—for example, between journalists and policemen—which favors one or the other.

Official education was an essential step in Washcorp's new goal for the 20th century, the conquest of Europe. By intervening in the **First Great War**, Europe's first total civil war since 1815, at a point when the Central and **Entente** Powers had nearly defeated each other, Washcorp smashed the remnants of the **Concert of Europe**, destroyed the **House of Romanov** and conveyed its possessions to the new, ultraprogressive and ultraviolent sovcorp *Sovetskiy Soyuz*,[10] and began the process of remodeling Europe as a cluster of Washcorp client states. By forming an alliance with Sovetskiy Soyuz, the notorious **Popular Front**, and by using **diplomatic ultimatums** to intimidate the Japanese sovcorp **Dai Nippon**[11] into a hopeless preemptive attack, Washcorp inserted itself into the Second Great War, completed the destruction of Europe and Japan with merciless, indiscriminate **bombing campaigns** that killed more than a million civilians, and graduated to the task of dividing global power between itself and Sovetskiy Soyuz. When you're feelin' it, as they say, you're feelin' it.

Meanwhile, the Nationalist Period ended in 1933 with the rise of the Voldemort system, or **New Deal**. Washcorp had destroyed its financial system by adopting the British model of **central banking**, in which Washcorp itself guaranteed the value of private loans. During the 1920s this created a pyramid of debt substantially exceeding the quantity of gold available to pay it, and when the pyramid collapsed Plainland—along with most other countries—was devastated. This set the stage for the rise of an unscrupulous aristocrat, Lord Franklin Voldemort, often known simply as *That Man*, whose rule inaugurated the current *Fourth* or *Universalist Corporation*.

Lord Voldemort, elected on a **platform** of scaling back Washcorp, instead seized absolute power, eliminating the last formal limits to Washcorp's domestic power. His staff of extreme Progressives dedicated themselves to implementing Bellamy's vision of an **Industrial Army**,[12] an ideal planned society in which Washcorp employees coordinated all productive activity in Plainland. (Voldemort even put his name on a book called *Looking Forward*.) Nationalist holdouts prevented this vision from being realized before Washcorp's intervention in the Second Great War, but after 1941 the last anti-Voldemort forces were politically isolated and destroyed. The postwar period saw an enormous expansion of official education in the Pro-

---

10 Soviet Union
11 Empire of Japan
12 Reference to the National Recovery Administration. See Chapter 8 of *Open Letter*.

gressive tradition, completing and cementing the Fourth Corporation, which rules Plainland to this day.

All official education in Plainland today instructs Plainlanders to revere Lord Voldemort and his movement. All orthodox political factions claim pure Voldemortian descent. And all private businesses operate as quasiautonomous subsidiaries of Washcorp, which has settled on the elegant design of allowing their managers full entrepreneurial freedom, while maintaining total regulatory control over their operational policies and procedures.

However, all is not utterly copacetic in Plainland. The 1920s saw the first outbreaks of genuine anti-Washcorp murmuring since the War of Southern Separation, as some Plainlanders started to realize that their interests and Washcorp's were not always identical. After the proto-Voldemortian era of Progressive fanatic **Woodrow Wilson**, the Return to Normalcy—i.e., sanity—of **Warren Harding** and **Calvin Coolidge** actually reduced the size and importance of Washcorp. The same feat was achieved by **Ronald Reagan**, and attempted unsuccessfully by a variety of failed political rebellions, such as those of **Strom Thurmond, Joseph McCarthy, Barry Goldwater,** and **George Wallace**. While none of these movements actually aimed at the destruction of Washcorp, and none had any chance of permanently checking its expansion, they can only be described as worrisome.

One fascinating response to the development of discontent is the rise of pro-Washcorp ultraloyal pseudo-opposition movements, comparable to Catholic **ultramontanism**.[13] After the Second Great War, the size, efficiency and ideological consistency of Washcorp's system of official education considerably increased. The 1960s saw the harvest of this program, with the rise of extremist ultra movements such as the **SDS**. The SDS's manifesto, the **Port Huron Statement**, is worth reading in full[14]—as a Universalist confession, as an expression of faith in the absolute righteousness of Washcorp (if led, of course, by the enlightened), and an action plan for seizing the universities and redoubling the ideological intensity of official education. Needless to say, the plan succeeded, and the ideas of the SDS are now mainstream.

With Washcorp becoming the default employer and financial guardian of all Plainlanders, political conflict in Plainland increasingly transitioned to a highly stable phase in which all significant conflict was not between pro-Washcorp and anti-Washcorp Plainlanders, but between different factions within Washcorp itself.

These battles tended to play out in Washcorp's so-called "foreign policy." In the 1940s, the high Voldemortian plan of creating a single global sovcorp, by converting the victorious alliance of the Second Great War, the **United Nations**, into a permanent sovcorp cartel which could cohere gradually in the usual manner, suffered a major setback when a schism appeared between Washcorp and its primary

---

13 Position within the Catholic Church emphasizing the authority of the Pope.
14 See Chapter 8 of *Open Letter*.

progressive client, Sovetskiy Soyuz. This **Anglo–Soviet split**[15] was due to the paranoid, militaristic management style of the securocratic progressive "people's democracies," as was demonstrated by further mafia-style catfights, such as the Titoist and Maoist splits with Moscow.

However, the Anglo–Soviet split also divided Washcorpers into one faction whose primary goal was opposing Soviet power, and another faction whose primary goal was healing the split and restoring unity in the global progressive movement. These factions faced off in three Asian proxy wars, two of which actually involved Plainlander slave soldiers: the Chinese, Korean, and Vietnamese civil wars.

In the Chinese civil war, different departments of Washcorp backed opposing armies, with the State Department supporting Mao and the Pentagon Chiang Kai-shek. State succeeded with the aid of the New Deal political general **George Marshall**, imposing an arms embargo on Chiang, who was reactionary and corrupt, and ensuring his defeat at the hands of Mao, who was a murderous megalomaniac. Not only did Mao murder 30 million Chinese, but only three years later his slave armies were fighting directly against the Pentagon's own.

It was slightly difficult to explain to Plainlanders that, while Hitler's Nazi myrmidons were so evil that it was necessary to level Germany and accept no terms but unconditional surrender, Mao's progressive volunteers could not even be frowned at until they had actually crossed the Korean border—and preferably not even the **38th parallel**.[16] Progress, however, can explain anything, and by the 1950s Washcorp had had a lot of practice.

The even more bizarre gladiatorial bloodbath of Vietnam, in which it was almost impossible to recognize anything resembling a military strategy or objective, was so hard for Plainlanders to understand that it actually wound up as a political victory for the ultra-loyalist radicals, now recognizable as our modern-day "bluestate" Coasters. Vietnam was so confusing that after the Pentagon had won a complete military victory over the South Vietnamese insurgents, State prevailed by simply capturing Congress and imposing a surprise arms embargo on the corrupt, reactionary leaders of South Vietnam, treating them much as it had treated Chiang. The resulting North Vietnamese invasion surely reminded a few diplomatic silverbacks of the good old Popular Front days, when the Red Army rode into Poland on Plainland-made Jeeps.

The pattern repeated itself across most of the planet. Any ally was a good ally for State, so long as it was not reactionary and corrupt, i.e., an ally of the Pentagon. The more nationalist, socialist, and violent, however, the better. For some reason it was important for Washcorp to have more allies in more places than Sovetskiy Soyuz, and these three factions—Pentagon, State, and Soviet—competed for the privilege of funneling money and weapons to the murderous and criminally mismanaged Third World sovcorps that emerged from the postwar destruction of European law and order in most of Africa and Asia. Tens of millions of people

---

15 Reference to the Cold War.
16 Dividing line between North and South Korea.

were killed and billions left destitute in this new imperial scramble, which is still described today as the "liberation" and "independence" of the Third World. Apparently "liberation" requires the rule of sovcorps whose managers have the right skin color, and "independence" involves receiving billions of dollars a year in "aid."

The so-called "conservative" strategy, in which confused, half-brainwashed Middlers attempted to revolt against the Coaster departments of Washcorp through aggressive military provocations overseas, which if victorious would strengthen Middler politicians and the Middler-dominated armed forces (now mercifully relieved of slave troops), after a few minor successes in the 1980s and 1990s found its tragic, yet blackly comical, Waterloo in Iraq.

After a spectacular attack by national-socialist neo-Islamic terrorists on New York, Plainlanders became vehemently, if temporarily, done with the systematic adoration of any Third World thug whose only saving grace was to be an enemy of the Pentagon. Coasters found it impossible to prevent the Pentagon's invasion of Iraq, whose ruling sovcorp, **Baathco**,[17] had done an exceptionally poor job of maintaining its membership as a State Department client. Instead Baathco had cultivated the Europeans, leaving two degrees of separation between itself and State. Two turned out to be one too many.

The invasion of Iraq was a smashing military success. But it was a tactical success and a strategic defeat, because the tremendous political power of 21st-century progressivism left the Pentagon with no viable options. It could not rule Iraq as a possession, as **Arthur MacArthur** had in the Philippines. It could not govern Iraq as a subjugated enemy, like his son[18] in Japan. It could not restore a monarchy, as **Kermit Roosevelt** had in Iran. It could not even install one of its patented reactionary, corrupt dictators, like Chiang or **Diem** or **Syngman Rhee**.

No, the same military force that subjugated the South of Plainland itself and ruled it under the **Lieber Code**, which let it shoot any uniformless combatant, without a trial—that, under the same code, invaded the Philippines and turned it into one of the most famously pro-Washcorp regions outside Plainland itself— that obliterated Germany and Japan from the air, killing a million civilians, and reconstructed them as pacifist communes under the notorious JCS 1067[19]—could only execute a politically and militarily absurd plan which installed a democratic sovcorp, using proportional representation of all systems, promised to leave as soon as the ballots were dry, and bound itself to obey rules of engagement probably insufficient to impose order in Newark, New Jersey.

It might as well have issued every Iraqi with an AK-47, an RPG and three IEDs, and ordered everyone to join a paramilitary gang as soon as possible, winners to be selected by whatever prowess they could demonstrate in killing Plainlanders.

---

17 The Ba'ath Party
18 Douglas MacArthur, who oversaw the occupation of Japan from 1945 to 1951.
19 A draconian revision to the "Morgenthau plan" insisted upon by FDR, that the German people were to have their living standards dramatically reduced as punishment for the war.

While this strategy was certainly well-designed for Coaster factions to prevent a military and hence Middler victory, it was not exactly designed to make Washcorp popular among Middlers. As if it they didn't love it already! And with its security forces essentially in the hands of its enemies, Washcorp faces a difficult political struggle. As its educational system becomes increasingly stagnant and moribund, inculcating at least as much apathy as loyalty, its natural evolution would be to transition from educracy to securocracy. But its own military caste despises it profoundly.

The only way to keep them in check is more democracy. Which means extending the franchise. Which, since the entire framework of nationalism depends on the identity between geography, sovcorp and population, and the ideal solution of letting actual Europeans vote in Washcorp elections is simply beyond reach, means importing more and more Beringian voters from Mexico, while reducing the power of the White House (no Democrat has won the Euro-Plainlander presidential vote since Lyndon Johnson), in favor of that of Congress, which through seniority and gerrymandering has achieved the ideal Universalist combination of democratic legitimacy and civil-service stability. As demonstrated by its approval ratings, which seem to hover barely in the double digits without any degradation of power. Whereas if a President has an 11% rating, not even his hairdresser will do his combover the way he asks.

Now that the last strategy which seemed to offer some hope to Middlers, invading the world and restoring Western civilization to places from which it has spent the last hundred years evaporating, is off the table, the evolutionary path of Washcorp seems obvious. Until such time as its creditors tire of loaning it another trillion dollars every year, it will join Eurocorp in its gradual progress toward becoming a bureaucratic, Brezhnevian *Beamtenstaat*. As in Europe, the distinction between working as a direct employee of Washcorp and working for a "private" company will become increasingly irrelevant, as companies become branded, financially independent arms of the State in which the entire process of production is dictated by regulation, à la **ISO 9000 or Sarbox**.[20]

So: this is Washcorp. I hope I have covered the major points. Hopefully for any missing details, it should be reasonably easy to translate the official story to fit with the above. The official story is almost never wrong as a matter of fact. It is usually just interpretation.

Of course, even if this jaundiced and decidedly unofficial biography of Washcorp is an accurate perspective, *Hume's ought* does not entitle us to claim that Washcorp is evil. Still less are we left with any idea of what to do about it, if it is.

However, there are still some interesting observations we can make.

The first observation is that the employees of Washcorp are overwhelmingly Universalist—except for the disgruntled military.

---

20 Sarbanes-Oxley and ISO 9000 refer to a set of standards and practices adopted by businesses and organizations to meet the statutory and accounting requirements of the U.S. government.

The second is that Washcorpers think of their employer as a fundamentally charitable—i.e., eleemosynary[21]—institution. It's not just that Washcorp has Google's motto, "Don't be evil." The point is so obvious that to state it is to sully it. The meaning of Washcorp is that Washcorp does good.

Not just for Plainland, of course, but for the whole world. Because Universalists do not, of course, value Plainlanders over any other neohominids. And Washcorpers are Universalists, so good to Washcorp is Universalist good. The archaic legacy policies and procedures that force Washcorp to discriminate in favor of Plainlanders are distasteful and detestable, and should be discarded as fast as possible. Ideally, Washcorp itself would become only an unimportant unit of a single global sovcorp.

The third is that, even though the source of Washcorp's fundamental goodness is its connection to public opinion, which can never be misguided or evil, there is still a way to evaluate Washcorp without reference to the cult of democracy. Democracy, like the principle of divine right, legitimizes Washcorp's ownership of Plainland. To a good Universalist, the only way in which Washcorp can become evil is if it abandons democracy, in which case it is no longer legitimate and should be treated as a tyrannical dictatorship. Until then, it is good. Etc.

A formalist, however, can duck this entire trap. A formalist has no interest at all in Washcorp's **political formula**.[22] She does not care whether Washcorp's democracy is good democracy, bad democracy, or no democracy at all. To her, Washcorp simply owns Plainland. There is no why. Ownership is demonstrated by unchallenged control. Washcorp has it. Perhaps some debate is possible over what other parts of the world Washcorp owns. As far as Plainland goes, it's a no-brainer.

The formalist, therefore, judges Washcorp only by its actions. She can say: why does Washcorp do X or Y? Why do the people involved with Washcorp act in ways that lead it to do X or Y? Would it be better, in her opinion, if it did Z instead? And—granted that Washcorp is invincible and cannot be destroyed—how, if at all, can she act to help change it into something whose actions are more desirable?

We'll cover this in Chapter 6. But essentially, my view is that people who oppose Washcorp are simply barking up the wrong tree. It's not just that Washcorp can't be defeated. It's that even trying to weaken it is a mistake. Weaken a sovcorp, make it less efficient, and it compensates by getting larger and more complex.

Rather, I think only the way to fix Washcorp is to *improve it out of existence*. It needs to become so much more powerful and so much more efficient that it no longer exists as such. And this effort must not contradict Universalism in any way, shape or form. If this doesn't make any sense or strike you as possible, please be patient and stay tuned.

---

21 "Eleemosynary" organizations are charitable, in contrast with "lucrative" organizations.
22 The UR post "Democracy as adaptive fiction" offers an explanation of what "political formula," a phrase borrowed from Gaetano Mosca (see Chapter 8 of *Open Letter*), means in this context and its particular manifestation in modern democracies.

444 Robert Schuller

 444 Hour of Power

 444 put it Youtube clip from *Split Second* (1992), also linked in Chapter 14 of *Open Letter*.

 444 you guessed it Wiktionary entry on "catholic"

 444 Shub-Niggurath

 444 Duke of Wellington

444 puts it Gray. *Black Mass: Apocalyptic Religion and Death of Utopia.* (Farrar, Straus and Giroux, 2007).

 444 put it-1 A line from p. 246 of Thompson's *The Great Shark Hunt* (Simon & Schuster 1979).

 444 Christopher Moltisanti Mob boss Tony Soprano's cousin and protégé in *The Sopranos*, whose drug habits and failed rehabilitation attempts are a central theme in the show.

 444 higher power

 445 Thom Yorke

 445 Radiohead

 445 Empsonian ambiguity Reference to Empson's *Seven Types of Ambiguity*. Also referenced in Chapter 3 and Chapter 5 of *Open Letter*.

 445 overloading "Operator overloading"

445 Lowell

 445 Whitman

 445 MacLeish

 445 Dove

 445 Vinland

 445 castes "Castes of the United States." *UR*, 6 May, 2007.

 445 Beringian "Here Moldbug uses Beringian to refer to all indigenous Americans, i.e., all peoples in the Americas descended from those who crossed the Bering land bridge into North America during the Last Glacial Maximum. In particular, Beringian refers both to "American Indians" and to the electorally much more important Latin American mestizos." (ed. UR)

 446 Fedco From "Why, when, and how to abolish the United States." *UR*, 3 Jul. 2007.

 446 Washcorp

 446 Fedco

 446 Roman salute

 446 Sons of Liberty

 446 Continental Congress

446 Continental Army

 446 princeps

 446 British Crown

 446 adverse possession

 447 Treaty of Paris

448 *Eurocorp* Reference to Christopher Booker's *Great Deception: Can the European Union Survive?* (Continuum, 2005).

 447 *Looking Backward* See Chapter 7 of *Open Letter,* and how Bellamy's 1888 book prefigured the aspirations of the Communist movement.

 447 Social Gospel

 447 Edward Bellamy

 447 postmillennial

 447 spoils system

 448 English Dissenter

 448 divine-right monarchy

 449 First Great War "World War I"

449 Entente "Allies of World War 1"

 449 Concert of Europe

 449 House of Romanov

 449 Popular Front

 449 diplomatic ultimatums Reference to the thesis put forward in Charles Tansill's *Back Door to War: Roosevelt Foreign Policy 1933-1941* that Roosevelt sought to further embroil the U.S. in the European conflict and provoked the Japanese to attack American territory in order to do so. (Greenwood Press Publishers, 1952). PDF available at Mises.

 449 Dai Nippon

 449 bombing campaigns "US bombing campaigns during World War II"

 449 New Deal

 449 central banking

 449 platform "Democratic Party Platform of 1932." See Chapter 4 and Chapter 7 of *Open Letter*.

 449 Industrial Army "National Recovery Administration"

 450 Woodrow Wilson

 450 Warren Harding

 450 Calvin Coolidge

HOW DAWKINS GOT PWNED 459

 450 Ronald Reagan

 450 Strom Thurmond

 450 Joseph McCarthy

 450 Barry Goldwater

 450 George Wallace

 450 ultramontanism

 450 SDS

 450 Port Huron Statement Chapter 8 of *Open Letter* goes into much greater detail about the significance of the SDS and the Port Huron Statement and where it fits within the larger matrix of progressive activism animating the 60's.

 450 United Nations

 451 Anglo–Soviet split "Cold War"

 451 George Marshall

 451 myrmidons

 451 38th parallel "Division of Korea"

 452 Baathco "Ba'ath Party"

452 *Arthur MacArthur*

 452 *his son* "Douglas MacArthur"

 452 *Kermit Roosevelt*

 452 *Diem*

 452 *Syngman Rhee*

 452 *Lieber Code* See Chapter 14 of *Open Letter*.

 452 *JCS 1067*

 453 *ISO 9000*

 454 *eleemosynary* The dichotomy between eleemosynary and lucrative organizations is elaborated on in the UR post "The state is not a stable eleemosynary institution." *UR*, 30 Aug. 2007.

 454 *political formula* "Democracy as adaptive fiction." *UR*, 25 Jul. 2007.

CHAPTER 6:
THE LOGIC OF LAW AND POWER
NOVEMBER 1, 2007

At this point we've established, at least to my satisfaction, that (a) there is such a thing as Universalism; (b) Universalism is an educationally-transmitted tradition that works just like any theistic religion, and is best understood as a descendant of Christianity; (c) Professor Dawkins is (despite his **occasional twinges of conscience**[1]) operating as a vector of Universalism; and (d) orthodox Universalism insists on some rather unsupported conclusions about biology, and some theories of history and politics which seem less than parsimonious.

This is all very well and good. But it hasn't brought us that much closer to constructing a way of thinking which is thoroughly non-Universalist, from which we can look back at Universalism and evaluate it aesthetically as a whole. Is Universalism basically normal and healthy, with a few historical quirks? Or is it basically weird and creepy, with a few redeeming graces?

This is obviously a subjective judgment. It's obvious what I think. But I cannot change anyone else's opinion by just repeating my own.

Rather, I think the only way to evaluate Universalism is to construct a reference ideology so foreign to Universalism that the Universalist immune system does not attack it, because it does not recognize it as comparable to any past or present enemy. By imagining the perspective of someone raised to believe in this ideology—

which I've called neocameralism or formalism[2]—you can start to assemble your own picture of what Universalism might look like from the outside.

In the last two chapters I synthesized a bit of neocameralist history. In this chapter, we'll do a little "political science"—a singularly inapt name for the logic of law and power.

Universalism, again, is a mystery cult of power. Its supreme being is the State. And all of the Universalist mysteries—*humanity*, *democracy*, *equality*, and so on—cluster around the philosophy of collective action. Christianity has been a state religion since Constantine, of course, but it always also included magical and metaphysical mysteries, which the advance of science has rendered superfluous at best, embarrassing at worst. So Universalism, unlike its ancestors, is not concerned with *the Trinity* or *transubstantiation* or *predestination*. But its political mysteries remain chewy enough to delight the most hypertrophied of mental mandibles.

We want to avoid all this. Therefore, we have to build a new language which describes the logic of collective action in a way that does not remind us of Universalism. We'll retain the Universalist legal or political terminology only in cases where the old word is (a) precisely defined, and (b) has no positive connotations.

Essentially, formalism is a system of collective action in which the only sin is to break your own promise. Neocameralism is formalism on a political scale.

Formalism starts with the idea of an *agreement*. When you are party to an agreement, you promise others that your future actions will follow some pattern. For example, you may promise to paint Joe's house, as long as Joe promises to pay you for the job. You and Joe may also agree on how unexpected events, disputes, and so forth, will be handled.

The concept of *property* emerges naturally from formalism. You and Joe agree to be neighbors, rather than enemies. You construct an agreement which draws an imaginary line on the ground, and keep your respective cattle on your respective sides of the line.

Another concept that will emerge in any system of agreements is the *corporation*. A corporation is just a named pattern of agreement. If you and Joe construct a shared sheep-dip, it may be easiest to describe this virtual entity as a corporation, and describe its agreements with Fred's Pesticide Supply as agreements between two parties—rather than between you, Joe, and all the owners and employees of Fred's. Without this level of indirection, agreements would balloon to incredible size through cascading inclusion.

This model of labeling and indirection can be applied to even the most trivial cases. Instead of dealing with Joe, you can deal with JoeCorp, whose sole owner is Joe. There is really no use in constructing a system of agreements which does not recognize virtual entities.

Neocameralism deals with the special case of *sovereign corporations*, or *sovcorps* (Chapter 5). A sovcorp is a corporation which is not dependent on any other power. To make agreements with other sovcorps, it must ensure that it is not in the

---

2 See "A formalist manifesto."

other sovcorp's interest to break those agreements—otherwise, it will probably do so. How it achieves this is the problem of *security*.

Universalism, of course, has its own word meaning "sovcorp." In fact, if you discard every doctrine or mystery of Universalism except for those which determine what a legitimate sovcorp is and whether or not it's righteous, you'll find that you still have most of it left. As **Hume noted**, righteousness is not susceptible to logic. We cannot disprove Universalism by describing its political doxology as weird. We can only attempt to construct an alternative system from which Universalism may strike us as, in retrospect, weird.

First, you and I are not sovcorps. We are people. We may be employees of sovcorps. We may be customers of sovcorps. We may even be slaves of sovcorps. Depending on the exact details of the relationship, some or all of these words may apply. However, if you make your home on a patch of land owned by some sovcorp S, it is certainly fair to describe you as a *tenant* of S. And anyone reading this today is certainly a tenant of some sovcorp—in my case, Washcorp.

Therefore, from the perspective of a tenant, we can ask: what makes a sovcorp good or bad?

This question is too abstract to be useful. To sharpen it slightly, we should place it in terms that are both relative and personal. We can do this by saying: given two sovcorps S and T, identical except in feature F, would you, dear reader, rather be a tenant of S or of T? For example, would you consider moving from T to S to take advantage of F, or from S to T to escape from F?

This approach leads us to two orthogonal criteria for judging sovcorps. A sovcorp should be judged by its *stability*, and by its *actions*.

We cannot assess a sovcorp without assessing its stability. If it fails to maintain security, the consequences are likely to be appalling. Transitions of power at the sovereign level, while they certainly may replace a worse sovcorp with a better one, can result in an arbitrary level of collateral damage. While it is always in the winner's interest to seize the territory and its occupants intact, as both constitute capital, tactical considerations may demand devastation.

There are certainly cases in which a tenant may favor war or revolution. However, there is no reason to support a violent transition in power unless (a) that transition is likely to succeed, and (b) its destination is preferable to its origin, counting all tactical devastation. Neither of these tests is anywhere near positive in the West today, so I don't find these cases interesting. And unless the tests are met, a tenant should always prefer a stable sovcorp (longevity can be easily assessed with a prediction market) to an unstable one.

Note that stability replaces the Universalist mystery of *legitimacy*. Legitimacy is an outlier in Universalist political doxology: it dates back to a pre-Universalist era which had far more in common with neocameralism. Universalists have no moral explanation of why any ruthless armed gang which seizes control of a historically-significant territory should be termed a *government*, develop the mysterious grandeur associated with this word, and be entitled to its seat in the United Nations. Apparently that's just the way it is. Can you say "epicycle," boys and girls?

Given stability, we arrive at a second criterion, which that a sovcorp should be judged by its *actions*. As tenants, we can have no possible reason to care who is running the sovcorp or why, except inasmuch as this contributes to its stability.

For example, if I live in Plainland, do I have any good reason to care about the identity of the administrators or the owners of the sovcorp that owns Plainland? They could be Plainlanders. They also could be from Deutschland, Thailand, or Somaliland. As a tenant, what matters to me is not who they are, but what they do. It will probably be cheapest for the sovcorp to employ Plainlanders as its low-level functionaries, but for executives and owners this is quite irrelevant. And using foreigners as executives has its own advantage for the sovcorp—they are far less likely to become involved in conflicts of interest.

When we consider other elements of sovcorp design, therefore, we will consider them only inasmuch as they affect the actions and the stability of the sovcorp. For example, is the **rotary system**[3] a desirable feature in a sovcorp? Perhaps, but only if it makes the sovcorp more stable or its actions more desirable.

In my opinion as a tenant, there are four characteristics which describe the actions of the kind of sovcorp I prefer. Bear in mind that, since the first function of a sovcorp is security, its most desirable attribute is stability, and there is no stability without security, authentic security motivations justify exceptions to any of these principles.

One, the sovcorp respects all agreements between itself and its tenants. A good sovcorp employs an external arbitrator which resolves all disputes that may result from conflicting, confusing or poorly-drafted agreements. It accepts the arbitrator's judgment as final.

Two, the sovcorp can enforce any agreement between its tenants. Since the sovcorp needs a security force to protect itself against other sovcorps, it must maintain unchallenged military control of its territory. It can—and should—allow tenants to invoke this power in their own agreements. For example, I can agree with Joe that if he pays me to paint his house, but I don't paint his house, Washcorp will descend upon me and give Joe his money back. As a tenant, I have no reason to prefer a sovcorp which does not provide this service.

Three, the sovcorp does not artificially restrict its tenants. In other words, it maintains **Pareto optimality**. For example, I have no reason to prefer a sovcorp which does not allow me to wear red clothing, because my garish garb cannot harm Joe or anyone else. (Point two can be seen as a special case of point three—a sovcorp that does not enforce tenant agreements cannot be Pareto optimal, because any sovcorp has this capability.)

---

3 Discussed in the UR post "A landscape of bewildering contradictions."

Four, the sovcorp does not tax its tenants, except as needed to secure its territory. And this is not a tax, but a security fee. A sovcorp should not be profitable. It should exist to protect and serve, not to harvest and render. Obviously, one reason to move from S to T may be that T has lower taxes—as long as these are not so low that security is jeopardized.

Now: which of these things is not like the other?

Obviously, as a tenant, I prefer all four of these features. But if I have to give up any one, I will give up the fourth. Giving up any of the other three involves at best major weirdness, and at worst a bullet in the head. Giving up profitable taxation involves, essentially, a rent increase.

A profitable sovcorp will attempt to maximize revenue. In other words, it will try to hit the top of the Laffer curve. Given that all sovcorps in the world today, and almost all in history, operate as revenue maximizers, this should not be too frightening or controversial.

There are three major reasons why profitability is a desirable feature in a sovcorp, despite its obvious disadvantage from the perspective of the tenant.

The first is that a profitable sovcorp is a more stable sovcorp. A sovcorp that is not maximizing revenue is leaving money on the table. Attackers can use the prospect of capturing this revenue stream to capitalize their attempts to defeat the sovcorp. The promise of loot has been an essential motivator in many invasions and revolutions. The miracle of capitalism allows the attacker to deploy this resource before it is even captured. If the defender cannot do likewise—because it is in some way bound to not maximize revenue—the advantage shifts to the attacker.

The second is that the nonprofit sovcorp is actually a general case of the profitable sovcorp. This is easy to see. If the nonprofit sovcorp were to go profitable and maximize its revenue, it would increase every payment P made by its tenants from P_n, the nonprofit fee, to P_p, the profitable tax. It can easily duplicate the effect by going profitable anyway, and treating $(P_p - P_n)$ as a dividend payment or rebate. This is Pareto-optimizing, because the recipient of this dividend can treat the right to receive it as a share, and sell the share.

The third is an argument I made in this post:[4] that the advantage of profitability, from the tenant's perspective, is that it creates a coherent management objective. Profitable corporations tend to provide better customer service, because coherently managed organizations tend to be more efficient. This is why you never see the National Hamburger Society on the list of restaurants at the next exit.

Of course, a sovcorp is not a restaurant. We can reasonably ask whether it *should* be efficient. As tenants, would we prefer to live in a territory managed by a sovcorp which has coherent corporate goals, and achieves them at minimum expense? Or one whose owner is slow, bumbling, and harmless?

---

4 "The state is not a stable eleemosynary institution." See also Chapter 5.

In my view, once you get to the point where it is preferable for a sovcorp to be inefficient, you are already into war-or-revolution territory. A sovcorp should be inefficient only in doing evil. If it's in the evil business, it has already violated one of the major criteria, and it's hardly worth debating its efficiency.

Once we've decided that our sovcorp should be both profitable and efficient, we are into very familiar territory. We know a lot about how to design profitable, efficient corporations.

A profitable, efficient sovcorp has two forms of capital. The first is the territory it owns. The second is its reputation. It protects these not out of the goodness of its heart, but for financial reasons—which, unlike the hearts of corporate managers, are extremely reliable.

So, for example, the sovcorp does not renege on its agreements with its tenants, because the capital value of a territory in which the rule of law holds is much greater than one in which it doesn't. Prosperity flees uncertainty, and sovcorps profit by taxing prosperity. And it is quite unheard of for corporate executives to intentionally drive their own stock price down.

Thus, a profitable, efficient sovcorp should obey the first three rules above (and not, of course, the fourth). The problem would seem to be solved.

We would expect a profitable and efficient—and hence desirable—sovcorp to look very much like today's private, non-sovereign corporations. That is, we would expect them to distribute their revenues as dividends to a set of voting shareholders, who choose a board in voting by shares, which chooses a CEO, who has complete management authority.

And yet today's sovcorps look nothing like private corporations at all.

They are not in any way profitable. They are renowned not for their efficiency, but for their inefficiency. They are managed by byzantine networks of conflicting committees and books of procedure. Their managers do not have hire-and-fire power. Their customers are part of their executive selection process. They do not come even close to Pareto optimization. There is really no resemblance at all. The only thing today's "governments" have in common with the sovcorp design above is that a "government" is, without question, a sovereign corporation.

So this analysis leaves us with three interesting questions.

First, why did this simple design process produce a sovcorp architecture so different from the one that history has bequeathed to us?

Second, how do shareholders maintain control of a sovcorp, when there is no higher sovereign authority to enforce the corporate charter? Why won't the managers just perform an **autogolpe**?[5] And who decides whether a security exception is "authentic?"

Third, how does understanding Universalism help us answer the first and second questions?

---

5 Self-coup

461 occasional twinges of conscience "Professor Dawkins, Dr. Watson, and the Flying Spaghetti Monster." *UR*, 30 Oct. 2007.

462 Constantine "Although Constantine had laid the foundation, Christianity didn't officially become the state religion of the Roman Empire until 380 A.D., when Emperor Theodosius I issued the Edict of Thessalonica. In any case, Christianity had actually been a state religion since 301 A.D., the year it became the official religion of Armenia." (ed. UR).

 463 Hume noted "Is-ought problem"

464 rotary system "A landscape of bewildering contradictions." *UR*, 20 Aug. 2007.

 464 Pareto optimality

465 Laffer curve

 465 this post "The state is not a stable eleemosynary institution." *UR*, 30 Aug. 2007.

466 autogolpe "Self-coup"

CHAPTER 7:
THE AGE OF DEMOCIDE
NOVEMBER 8, 2007

At the risk of sounding like Maya Angelou, the only way to end is to return to the beginning. Our beginning is of course Professor Dawkins, and that little blind spot in the back of his head which we've learned to call Universalism.

Let's not forget what makes Professor Dawkins so pwned. The great exploit is that the good professor genuinely believes that he subscribes to *no belief system at all*. As Sam Harris puts it:

> We should not call ourselves "atheists." We should not call ourselves "secularists." We should not call ourselves "humanists," or "secular humanists," or "naturalists," or "skeptics," or "anti-theists," or "rationalists," or "freethinkers," or "brights." We should not call ourselves anything.

In other words: the only pattern that describes our beliefs is reason, reality, or truth. Thus no additional label is necessary. There is no word for people who believe that a dropped stone accelerates at 9.8 meters per second squared. Why should there be?

If you're right, of course, you're right. However, it is not difficult to see the potential for arrogance and intolerance in any such reluctance to self-label. No 13th-century Frenchman would have labeled himself as "a Catholic." He did not call himself anything, any more than Sam Harris. His beliefs were universal—that's what *catholic* means.[1] But were they true? Certainly not by Sam Harris's light.

Admittedly, this "No Logo" approach—which I suspect Professor Dawkins is a little too sharp to fall for—is preferable to the appalling coinage *bright*, which suggests that anyone who disagrees is not only ignorant but also stupid. 21st-century fanaticism really knows no shame.

But even the term *atheist* defines a belief system as an absence of creed—and thus of credulity. (If you're an atheist, as I am.) Thus it is essentially the same sort of evasion. The *atheist* label serves as a token of agreement between Professor Dawkins and his burgeoning legion of followers that the only pattern which describes their collective beliefs is that they have escaped from—or at least failed to succumb to—one particular barbaric, medieval superstition. While this may be correct, it's hardly modest.

Let's say there are two kinds of belief systems. A *class A* belief system propagates nothing but an accurate perception of reality. A *class B* belief system propagates fictions, distortions, contradictions, and/or other general nonsense. Since no one has any conscious desire to believe in nonsense, it's hard to see how any class B belief system can survive unless it can disguise itself as a class A belief system. (I see no reason to think there has ever been any such beast in the wild as a class A belief system.)

The hack that has exploited Professor Dawkins is almost too simple to work. It's truly elegant. When I was 17, I found a `setgid` violation on a SunOS kernel profiler and used it to find the address of my U area, which I could zero from the console debugger, giving my shell process root. I found this terribly cool. Then I showed it to an older hacker, who must have been all of 21 (Tom Lawrence? Is Tom Lawrence in the building? I think he worked at SGI for a while...) and he showed me how he'd used a link editor on the kernel objects to construct a version of SunOS (bootable from the console debugger) with a disabled `setuid()` function, on which *all processes* were unavoidably root. Trust me—this was much, much cooler. But it wasn't as cool as "atheism."

By sacrificing a single metaphysical construct—"God"—this new release of Christianity, Universalism, has constructed a convincing case (at least it seems to convince Professor Dawkins) that it has transitioned from a class B system to a class A system. And how has it done this? Simply by pointing to its predecessor, and noting that the former is class B. Well, duh.

Everyone knows that Western thought today, even in its most fashionable incarnations, has Christian roots. But somehow, most of us think it's possible to escape the implications of this connection by simply denying the Christian label, and adopting a metaphysical doctrine—atheism—which is repugnant to the unwashed who have not made this great leap. The result is that we land in "No Logo" nirvana. We are the enlightened ones. Hail us!

---

1 See Chapter 5.

Imagine if I tried the same with Nazism. I could march around in a brown leather uniform all day, waving a swastika banner and condemning the filthy Zionist–Bolshevik hordes. When questioned by the **usual voices of decency**, I could respond that:

- I don't support Nazism. In fact, I oppose it. So I'm not a Nazi.
- I'm half-Jewish. The Nazis would never have me. So I'm not a Nazi.
- Nazis believe in the leadership of Adolf Hitler. I don't. So I'm not a Nazi.
- My inverted swastika is actually a Hindu fertility symbol. So I'm not a Nazi.

Etc., etc., etc. How much ice do you think this would cut with the diversity committee? But somehow, when the creed is Christianity rather than Nazism, it can be ditched as easily as a Muslim's wife. Just say: "I'm an atheist, I'm an atheist, I'm an atheist." And no one will ever be able to accuse you of being a religious fanatic, at least not without substantial preparatory explanation. What more perfect cover story for an actual religious fanatic?

Anyway. I apologize if I'm getting a little repetitive here. I don't think this trick can be analyzed too many times. I grew up as a Universalist myself, and there's nothing like finding one of those **Brawndo moments** in one's own head, especially after 30-plus years of believing any such mental baggage was reserved for one's lessers. "**But Brawndo has electrolytes.**"[2] And so it does.

This poor little blog cannot possibly hope to topple or even shake the great Gibraltar that is the Universalist church. But what I love about exploring Universalism, what makes it so fun for me, is that there's a genuine sense of newness to it. The anaesthetic that the Universalist brainworm secretes, euphoric though it is—who can deny the believer's genuine joy?—conceals all kinds of fascinating adaptive structures. With the **magic sunglasses**,[3] these pop right out in living color, and you can see them every day on the front page of the Times. It's like going on a galactic mission to Planet Earth. America the home of the free and the brave, and Plainland the home of the Universalist corporate theocracy, are the same physical place. But you can be excused for wishing you hadn't left your spacesuit back on the ship.

To continue the discussion from Chapter 6, we were talking about governments. Or as we say when we use the magic sunglasses, sovcorps.

The fundamental problem of modern history is to understand the great massacres of the 20th century. To at least the first approximation, any general theory of modern history must be a theory of **democide**.

I've expressed this before, but let me state it more bluntly: the cause of democide is democracy. The democides of the 20th century—plus one important adumbration, the War of Secession, the first modern total war—can only be understood as a consequence of the victory of democracy. And therefore of the defeat of the Concert of Europe and the **Holy Alliance**.

Needless to say, this belief is the polar opposite of Universalist doctrine. Of all Universalist cult words, there is perhaps none more holy than *democracy*. And

---

2 Reference to the film *Idiocracy* (2006).
3 Reference to the sunglasses worn in the 1988 horror classic *They Live*.

these days the especially daring may be so bold as to praise Enoch Powell, but no significant political intellectual (at least in my lifetime) has tipped much hat to Wellington, Metternich or Castlereagh. I always liked Shelley's verse:

> I met Murder on the way—
> He had a mask like Castlereagh—
> Very smooth he looked, yet grim;
> Seven blood-hounds followed him;
> All were fat; and well they might
> Be in admirable plight,
> For one by one, and two by two,
> He tossed them human hearts to chew
> Which from his wide cloak he drew.

The latter stanza is doggerel, but the former with its cute anti-sightrhyme is really memorable. Which is a shame in a way. Because if anyone's philosophy came flanked by murderous hounds, it was Shelley's revolutionary democratic nationalism. Whereas all Castlereagh's reactionary monarchism produced was European peace and prosperity for most of a century. But why should history be sane?

Of course, Universalists have their own theory of democide. In the Universalist narrative, the cause of democide is dictatorship, or more precisely *autocracy*.

I have been unable to determine the exact meaning of this word. However, it seems to be the case that a sovcorp is either a *democracy*, or an *autocracy*. I've certainly never heard of any regime that was both democratic and autocratic, or any that was neither. So presumably they are antonyms. However, a common synonym for the former is *self-government*. Since this is also the literal meaning of the latter, we can see that we're on some tricky linguistic ground.

So we have two theories of democide to compare: the reservationist[4] theory (mine), and the Universalist theory (everyone else's). If popularity is your ruler, the answer is obvious. But in that case, surely there are other blogs you could be reading.

In questions of this appalling magnitude, I find the best way to "overcome bias"[5] is often to find perspectives which seem to make each answer obvious. Once we recognize that both A and B are obviously true, and A is inconsistent with B, we are in the right mindset for actual thought.

From the reservationist perspective, democracy is obviously the cause of democide—because the Age of Democracy is also the Age of Democide. The last major outbreak of indiscriminate mass murder in Europe was the massacre of Béziers in

---

4

5 Reference to the blog Overcoming Bias, run by Elezier Yudkowsky and Robin Hanson, which would eventually split into Less Wrong.

the **Albigensian Crusade**, which is easy to explain as a breakdown in military discipline, and whose memory also has suspicious links to the anticlerical **Black Legend**.

This was in 1209. (Possibly some nasty things also happened in the **Thirty Years' War**. But defenestration is not democide. Nor is famine or the pest. And even if we admit that the **Sack of Magdeburg** was no picnic, it was again a *failure* of discipline—the opposite of **Eichmann**.)

Then, 580 years later, the association between popular government and democide opens with the French Revolution (if not with **Cromwell's plantation of Ireland**), and continues to pop up everywhere. Every sovcorp which has ever committed democide has claimed to be the one true representative of the People. Black Legend notwithstanding, significant cases of monarchist mass murder are hard to find. (For example, most of what you know about the so-called "Inquisition" isn't true.)

Furthermore, before our great Age of Democracy, it was widely assumed that progress would simply continue and civilization would only get more civilized. The famous example is **Gibbon**, from his *General Observations*:

> It is the duty of a patriot to prefer and promote the exclusive interest and glory of his native country; but a philosopher may be permitted to enlarge his views, and to consider Europe as one great republic, whose various inhabitants have attained almost the same level of politeness and cultivation. The balance of power will continue to fluctuate, and the prosperity of our own or the neighbouring kingdoms may be alternately exalted or depressed; but these partial events cannot essentially injure our general state of happiness, the system of arts, and laws, and manners, which so advantageously distinguish, above the rest of mankind, the Europeans and their colonies. The savage nations of the globe are the common enemies of civilized society; and we may inquire with anxious curiosity, whether Europe is still threatened with a repetition of those calamities which formerly oppressed the arms and institutions of Rome. Perhaps the same reflections will illustrate the fall of that mighty empire, and explain the probable causes of our actual security.
>
> The Romans were ignorant of the extent of their danger, and the number of their enemies. Beyond the Rhine and Danube, the northern countries of Europe and Asia were filled with innumerable tribes of hunters and shepherds, poor, voracious, and turbulent; bold in arms, and impatient to ravish the fruits of industry. The Barbarian world was agitated by the rapid impulse of war; and the peace of Gaul or Italy was shaken by the distant revolutions of China. The Huns, who fled before a victorious enemy, directed their march towards the West; and the torrent

was swelled by the gradual accession of captives and allies. The flying tribes who yielded to the Huns assumed in their turn the spirit of conquest; the endless column of Barbarians pressed on the Roman empire with accumulated weight; and, if the foremost were destroyed, the vacant space was instantly replenished by new assailants. Such formidable emigrations can no longer issue from the North; and the long repose, which has been imputed to the decrease of population, is the happy consequence of the progress of arts and agriculture. Instead of some rude villages, thinly scattered among its woods and morasses, Germany now produces a list of two thousand three hundred walled towns; the Christian kingdoms of Denmark, Sweden, and Poland, have been successively established; and the Hanse merchants, with the Teutonic knights, have extended their colonies along the coast of the Baltic, as far as the Gulf of Finland. From the Gulf of Finland to the Eastern Ocean, Russia now assumes the form of a powerful and civilized empire. The plough, the loom, and the forge, are introduced on the banks of the Volga, the Oby, and the Lena; and the fiercest of the Tartar hordes have been taught to tremble and obey. The reign of independent Barbarism is now contracted to a narrow span; and the remnant of Calmucks or Uzbecks, whose forces may be almost numbered, cannot seriously excite the apprehensions of the great republic of Europe. Yet this apparent security should not tempt us to forget that new enemies, and unknown dangers, may possibly arise from some obscure people, scarcely visible in the map of the world. The Arabs or Saracens, who spread their conquests from India to Spain, had languished in poverty and contempt, till Mahomet breathed into those savage bodies the soul of enthusiasm.

[...]

Europe is now divided into twelve powerful, though unequal, kingdoms, three respectable commonwealths, and a variety of smaller, though independent, states; the chances of royal and ministerial talents are multiplied, at least with the number of its rulers; and a Julian, or Semiramis, may reign in the North, while Arcadius and Honorius again slumber on the thrones of the South. The abuses of tyranny are restrained by the mutual influence of fear and shame; republics have acquired order and stability; monarchies have imbibed the principles of freedom, or, at least, of moderation; and some sense of honour and justice is introduced into the most defective constitutions by the general manners of the times. In peace, the progress of knowledge and industry is accelerated by the emulation of so many active rivals:

> in war, the European forces are exercised by temperate and undecisive contests. If a savage conqueror should issue from the deserts of Tartary, he must repeatedly vanquish the robust peasants of Russia, the numerous armies of Germany, the gallant nobles of France, and the intrepid freemen of Britain; who, perhaps, might confederate for their common defence. Should the victorious Barbarians carry slavery and desolation as far as the Atlantic Ocean, ten thousand vessels would transport beyond their pursuit the remains of civilized society; and Europe would revive and flourish in the American world which is already filled with her colonies and institutions.

Only a few years after Gibbon wrote these words, barbarism erupted in the heart of Europe—not among the Uzbecks and Calmucks, but in Paris herself. The City of Light became the City of Terror. Naturally, the tragedy is celebrated to this day.

Of course, Gibbon agreed with Burke about this. (He also famously wrote that "if a man were called to fix the period in the history of the world, during which the condition of the human race was most happy and prosperous, he would, without hesitation, name that which elapsed from the death of Domitian to the accession of Commodus [i.e., the Antonine period].") Basically, everyone sensible agreed. However we may perceive it today, in its own wake the French Revolution was no more considered defensible than the Third Reich is today.

From the 1790s through the 1820s, the word *revolution* actually had negative connotations in the King's English. If you had invented some new steam gizmo, you would be no more likely to describe it as *revolutionary* than a modern inventor would be to describe her work as *fascist*. ("My new fascist programming language—with *really strong* typechecking.") Even if all you meant was that your gizmo went around in circles, you'd probably find some different word.

For example, note how Shelley denounces the Liverpool[6] regime in *Masque of Anarchy*[7]—he accuses it of being anarchy under a mask of law. Actually suggesting that law was bad and anarchy was good would have been too much even for Shelley. (Anything that was too much for Shelley was too much for anyone.)

I don't find the links from Robespierre to Stalin and Mao particularly debatable. As for Hitler, the Jacobins and Nazis were both violent, charismatic street-gang movements with aggressive utopian ideals and a penchant for paranoid conspiracy theories, whose popular base was concentrated in the lower middle class. I.e.: Hitler was practically Robespierre 2.0.

---

6 Reference to Robert Jenkinson, 2nd Earl of Liverpool and Prime Minister from 1812-1827.
7 Title of the Shelley poem quoted above. See endnote "verse" for more.

The great **Carroll Quigley**'s observations about democracy and the Great War are also quite pertinent. From *Tragedy and Hope*, Quigley's criminally underread history of the century:

> The influence of democracy served to increase the tension of a crisis because elected politicians felt it necessary to pander to the most irrational and crass motivations of the electorate in order to ensure future election, and did this by playing on hatred and fear of powerful neighbors or on such appealing issues as territorial expansion, nationalistic price, "a place in the sun," "outlets to the sea," and other real or imagined benefits. At the same time, the popular newspaper press, in order to sell papers, played on the same motives and issues, arousing their peoples, driving their own politicians to extremes, and alarming neighboring states to the point where they hurried to adopt similar kinds of action in the name of self-defense. Moreover, democracy made it impossible to examine international disputes on their merits, but instead transformed every petty argument into an affair of honor and national prestige so that no dispute could be examined on its merits or settled as a simple compromise because such a sensible approach would at once be hailed by one's democratic opposition as a loss of face and an unseemly compromise of exalted moral principles.

Quigley is of course describing the phenomenon known as **jingoism**. Compared to its 1914 incarnation, jingoism is a pretty minor problem these days. My guess is that we have the decline of political democracy, and the rise of bureaucratic democracy, to thank for this.

One thing most people don't know about the Great War is that all sides were democracies. There were no "absolute" governments in Europe in 1914. Recognizable democratic politics existed in every country. Calling **Wilhelmine Germany** in some way *autocratic* because Germans did not elect the Kaiser makes no more sense than calling the US *autocratic* because Americans do not elect the Supreme Court, or Europeans the European Commission.

(Which is not to say it makes no sense at all. But it makes the notion of a *war for democracy* risible. Much as 25 years later, the next *war for democracy* resulted in the enslavement of half of Europe and most of Asia. Could I make this stuff up?)

In jingoism we see the Concert of Europe's last gasp for political oxygen. Reactionary aristocrats toward the end of the *Belle Époque* found that jingoist nationalism was their only way to compete for public favor with the socialists, whose program of plunder had obvious democratic appeal. The three classical traditions of Continental reaction—**Legitimism**, **Orléanism**, and **Bonapartism**—wound up congealing into a single shrunken and unattractive mass, in the shape of the **anti-Dreyfusards**, which combined the worst features of Bonapartism and

Orléanism. It's hardly surprising that the defenders of Esterhazy[8] have drifted out of historical respectability.

If we are looking for an objective definition of *democracy* rather than a moralistic one, there's no way we can stick with the Western distinction between *representative democracy* and the more malignant 20th-century forms, *people's democracy* and *folkish democracy*.

The idea of representation is implicit in the symbolic doxology of all these regimes, even to some extent in divine-right (as opposed to propertarian) monarchy—which is perhaps best seen as a sort of proto-democracy. Symbolically, the democratic State represents the *General Will*, the aspirations and needs of the entire community. The link between State and *People* is axiomatic in all democracies.

Like sausage-making, the rituals by which this submission is established and renewed rarely reward excessive inspection. Hitler loved his plebiscites, the Americans demand a two-party circus, the Europeans have parliaments and proportional representation, the Soviets got along fine with just one party, the East Germans had various toy oppositions, etc., etc., etc. Frankly, if there is a major categorical distinction here, I just ain't seeing it.

The distinction between political and apolitical democracy does not strike me as terribly significant. In fact, the latter is probably preferable. Certainly all modern democracies have delegated most important tasks to apolitical bureaucrats. As **James Burnham** pointed out 65 years ago in *The Machiavellians*, the administrative relevance of elected officials in the Western democracies is steadily decreasing. The insane orgiastic elections of the American 19th century are gone.

The difference between **liberal democracy** and **totalitarian democracy** is much more relevant. But it is a matter of the State's actions, not its management structure. I certainly favor liberal if not libertarian government, and I despise the tyrannical megastate. But I see no reason at all why the electoral structure of a democratic state should have much bearing on whether it is liberal or tyrannical.

The EU, for example, has little more in the way of electoral politics than the Soviet Union, but it is a much nicer place to live. I suspect the main difference is just that the former is in Western Europe and the latter was brought to us by Russia—a great and beautiful country, but never one noted for its appreciation of personal independence.

From a practical political perspective, the problem faced by all democracies is the same. The regime's survival is dependent on its popularity. Its military is only a backup, and probably will not be willing to resist any serious popular protest. Therefore, to establish any stability, the democratic State must manage public opinion. This is also known as *manufacturing consent*, and it typically involves a substantial system of official or quasiofficial education and/or journalism.

So a good way to see which faction holds real power in a democratic state is to look at which can get its people into influential roles in education and/or journalism. For example, if anyone reading this still retains any doubt in the matter, this

---

8 The actual perpetrator of the treason for which Dreyfus was convicted.

algorithm shows us that the Republicans are the real party of power in the US, and the Democrats are a toy or decoy opposition. Statistics show that the vast majority of political contributions from educators and journalists in the US go to Republicans. Obviously this is why political opinions in the US are constantly shifting to the right. An amoral young political entrepreneur will "lead" this shifting moral *Zeitgeist*, and adjust his positions to be mainstream at such time as he expects to contend for office. This may be why so many young American intellectuals support torturing terrorists who refuse to accept Jesus as their personal savior.

Once we understand jingoism as a symptom of democracy, and once we realize that the structure or even existence of a democratic political system is not terribly important, the inference from democracy to democide starts to approach the obvious level. It is the Eastern totalitarian democracies of the 20th century that seem more the rule, and the Western liberal democracies more the exception. And we begin to suspect that the West is liberal despite democracy, whereas the East was totalitarian because of it.

You will find people who don't smoke and get lung cancer. And you may find non-democratic states which go off the rails and engage in mass murder. But generally, wherever you find the effect, it's not hard to guess the cause. Smoking obviously causes lung cancer, and democracy obviously causes democide. Duh.

But then we look at the Universalist theory of democide—and we see an equally obvious answer, which strikes us as much simpler. It certainly demands no long essay to explain.

We all know this theory. It tells us that democide is the result of evil dictatorships. When we look at the Age of Democide—discounting occasional moments of military exuberance, such as the strategic bombing of Japan and Germany—what we see is very clear. We see that mass murder is practiced by dictators, such as Hitler, Stalin, Mao, Saddam, Pol Pot, etc., etc., etc. Meanwhile, under representative democracy, we see peace and prosperity. Ergo, democracy is the cure for democide, and absence of democracy is the cause. Duh.

Of course, my reservationist opinion is that this argument seems simple and obvious only because we know it so well. ("But Brawndo has electrolytes!") But at least we have the contradiction, and it puts us in the right mood for actual analytic thought.

Our goal in this last part of the Dawkins essay is to *understand* Universalism, and to see it *adaptively*—to explain why it has outcompeted all the other crazy things people could believe, but don't.

Explaining Universalism's historical roots and sectarian pedigree is always interesting, but it always carries a slight hint of *eau de McCarthy*.[9] The history of the thing (once again, I recommend McKenna's *Puritan Origins of American Patriotism*) helps us sort up from down and get some idea of what questions to ask. But fundamentally—as some commenters have observed—the history of Universalism tells us no more than we learn by knowing that political party X is descended from

---

9 As in Joseph.

Nazis, or Communists, or whatever. Like its biological counterpart, memetic evolution can cover an impressive distance in a short time. (Consider the Socreds.[10])

So the question is: why is Universalism so successful? Why are so many Americans and Europeans these days Universalists? Especially so many smart, well-informed, talented Americans and Europeans? And why does the intensity of Universalism seem to be growing?

(If you doubt the latter point, I have two words for you: Operation Wetback. If you need three, try Louise Day Hicks. Professor Dawkins' *shifting moral Zeitgeist* may deserve some more prosaic name than the Spirit of Time, and its morality is arguable as morality is. But it's pretty hard to say it ain't shifting. And yes, that bit about torturing terrorists for Jesus was satire.)

The critical issue, I think, is the relationship between Universalism and the State.

As I noted in Chapter 4, this is at least as close as the connection between malaria and the mosquito. You can imagine something like Universalism whose transmission vector was not the State. You can also imagine something like malaria whose transmission vector was, say, the tick. But it's hard to imagine anyone calling it "malaria."

Even closer is the relationship between Universalism and democracy. These phenomena have quite clearly evolved together. At this point we are talking about multiple features of the same organism—more like the relationship between malaria schizonts and trophozoites.[11] (Okay, yuck. But remember, folks, this is just an analogy.)

Whatever the details of the lifecycle, it seems pretty clear that one of these beasties is the chicken and the other one is the egg. Thus, picking one at random, let's start with democracy and explain why Universalism is so successful in a democratically managed sovcorp. (A fun exercise would be to take the opposite path, and explain why democracy is so successful in a sovcorp whose tenants are Universalists.)

Our goal is to understand Universalism from a historical perspective which is completely non-Universalist. While it was certainly not utterly free from democratic cant, the Burkean Europe that the Congress of Vienna tried to create, and did to some extent and for some time create, is certainly as close as we can come to such a perspective. It certainly beats the next competitor, the Antonine Rome of Marcus Aurelius.

(The nice thing about both these periods is that they were both relatively non-Universalist, yet relatively acceptable to Universalist taste. You simply can't argue that Castlereagh had anything in common with Hitler. He would have had Hitler horsewhipped. The thought of Stalin in the presence of Aurelius is similarly comical and depressing.)

---

10 British Columbia Social Credit Party
11 Stages of the malaria-causing parasite plasmodium as it moves from mosquitoes to human blood cells.

We can construct a complete non-Universalist narrative of the State, therefore, by pulling out the good old what-ifs, and imagining that instead of decaying into nationalist democracy the Concert of Europe had advanced into neocameralism.

Let's review the neocameralist theory of the sovcorp for a moment.

A sovcorp is a corporation that owns a populated territory, and is not dependent on any other power to enforce its claim of property. A planet whose surface area is divided among multiple sovcorps is a stable property system if and only if no sovcorp can profit by attacking another. This can be assured by a variety of means—military deterrence or compellence, collective security, etc., etc. Tall fences make good neighbors, but a nuke or two doesn't hurt neither. Rationally managed sovcorps are especially good at deterrence, because the game theory is much simpler if you assume rational actors.

(The basic difference between neocameralism and **anarcho-capitalism** is that I don't think this sort of self-enforcing property model scales militarily, at least not anywhere near to the level where individuals are sovereign. I mean, someone is crazy here, and I don't think it's me. But then I wouldn't, would I?)

Assuming military stability, the essential property of a stable neocameralist sovcorp is that its revenues are formalized and distributed equally among its shareholders, who own and manage it in proportion to their holdings. An immutable corporate charter sets the sovcorp's rights and responsibilities, and prevents a majority of shareholders from abusing a minority, e.g., by confiscating their shares.

And who ensures that the corporate definition is immutable? Again, there is no such thing as a self-enforcing law. The ultimate decision algorithm in every dispute is always military. Fortunately, obeying simple rules is what military men do best. If the **Schelling point** of simple, precise formal law fails, there's always my favorite gimcrack technical solution—**cryptographic weapon locks**. In the 21st century, there's no reason every rifle—even every bullet—can't have one.

My belief is that, except for the minor matter of taxation, which will go to the **Laffer maximum** and stay there, a neocameralist sovcorp's interests are perfectly aligned with the interests of its tenants. Specifically, a profitable, efficiently-run sovcorp—even in the degenerate and undesirable case of a single global monopoly—will operate a libertarian government which maintains **Pareto optimality**. My reasoning is that any Pareto inefficiency represents an uncaptured tax, which affects the Laffer curve but generates zero revenue. Basically, the territory and residents of a sovcorp are its capital, and a well-run corporation, sovereign or otherwise, treats its capital the way the way Mother Teresa holds a baby bird.

So we can imagine a coherent alternate history in which the States of the Concert of Europe converted themselves into neocameralist sovcorps, by formalizing their revenues, dividing them into shares, and ceding management to the shareholders. Essentially, from the perspective of a monarch, this is like converting a family business into a public corporation. History shows that it's possible to run a sovcorp as a family business, but it doesn't really demonstrate that it's a good idea.

If I'm right that a shareholder-controlled sovcorp is stable, this would almost certainly have averted the democides of the 20th century. So why didn't it happen?

The answer, unfortunately, is that I don't think it was a realistic possibility.

The problem is that it's one thing to suggest that an informal business be formalized, and another to do it. And it's even harder in a sovcorp. Even if the idea is obvious and available, which in 1815 it clearly was not, there are many cases where it may be simply impossible.

No European monarchy was ever anything like "absolute." The so-called *Age of Absolutism*[12] is misnamed—as the book behind the link demonstrates elegantly.

First, "absolute" is in any case a pejorative slur. A better word would be *coherent*. A coherent enterprise can coordinate all of its actions through a single central decision process. (This does not mean that a coherent sovcorp needs to engage in economic central planning.)

Second, coherence was not a quality but an aspiration of the old European monarchies, and a distant aspiration at that. Probably the most coherent 18th-century sovcorp was the Prussia of Frederick the Great, but to call even Prussia absolutely coherent would be stretching the term. The weakness of the French monarchy is adequately demonstrated by the circumstances of its collapse. The same goes, although much later, for the Russians. And so on.

So the monarchies of old Europe were both informal (with no clear equity structure) and incoherent (with no clear management structure). Imagine the task of formalizing an informal, incoherent monarchy. Being a minister at the Bourbon court was not an easy job—especially when you realize that at the time, there was actually no such thing as bourbon. I think if I had Necker's[13] job, I'd want to come home to a nice tall mint julep every night.

In the neocameralist scheme, we can distinguish four clear aspects of sovereign corporate governance. One is *revenue*: how is the sovcorp's cash flow handled? Another is *law*: what promises has the sovcorp made to its tenants? A third is *power*: who controls the administrative apparatus of the sovcorp? A fourth is *operations*: who works for the sovcorp?

A well-managed sovcorp is a single accounting entity which collects and distributes all revenue centrally, and which treats all payments as formal obligations.

A well-managed sovcorp obeys all its own laws, and binds itself with new laws only when it is satisfied that it will not have to break them. It keeps a public list of these laws, and it does not bind itself to obey any unwritten rules that are not laws.

A well-managed sovcorp is managed by the holders of the equity tranche of its securities, like any normal corporation. These shareholders make the management decisions because they have the highest exposure to risk and reward. (Although it is not utterly ridiculous to give votes to debtholders as well.) The shareholders are precisely defined and publicly listed, their shares are fungible, and voting is by blocks of shares.

---

12 Written by Max Bellof (HarperCollins, 1962).
13 Jacque Necker, finance minister to Louis XVI.

A well-managed sovcorp distinguishes between its shareholders and its employees. The latter work at the sovcorp's administrative pleasure and can be dismissed at any time upon notice from the board. Any overlap between employees and creditors is coincidental and irrelevant. The same goes for any overlap between employees and customers.

Needless to say, no sovcorp in history has fit this profile. And France in 1788 was very, very far from it. In fact, it was a morass of venal offices, scheming factions, diverted revenues, etc., etc., etc. The Bourbon regime of 1788 may not have been doomed by the *Zeitgeist* to destruction, and it may not have been a nightmare of proto-Nazi tyranny. In fact, it wasn't either. But to call it well-managed would be going way, way too far.

When a sovcorp has an informal creditor structure and an incoherent power base, the two tend to overlap and interact in a very ugly way. Factions are constantly scheming for money and power. Some may have more money than power, some more power than money. Historically, telling people to stop scheming is not an effective way to stop them from scheming.

The natural path of development for a malstructured corporation is to become more malstructured. The informal structures of money and power are no less real for their informality. Their complexity tends to increase over time.

The typical mechanism of complexity collapse for a sovcorp is for an incoherent power base to break down into incoherent management, which works at cross purposes to itself. Incoherently managed organizations tend to operate by process rather than initiative, using procedural orders instead of *Aufragstaktik* or "mission orders." The resulting codes of procedure snowball into a giant mass of red tape, and the organization becomes paralyzed.

If the sovcorp does not have a central balance sheet, its revenues will be diverted not only by its power base, but also by its employees. The result is that employees effectively become creditors. Exactly the same can happen with customers, who will always take anything they are given. The result is that the whole elegant structure of the owner-controlled corporation devolves into a homogeneous, disorganized mass of so-called "stakeholders."

So, even if my contention that the neocameralist sovcorp is stable is correct, it is not the sort of stability that acts as a strong attractor. A slightly malstructured sovcorp will not tend to fix itself. It will tend to become even more malstructured.

This perspective lets us see democracy from a neocameralist perspective.

A modern democracy is nothing more and nothing less than a *very* malstructured sovcorp. Its basic problems are that its power base—its voters, who are at least in theory the owners of this collective enterprise—is completely deformalized. Voters cannot sell their shares, nor does a share guarantee an equal percentage of government revenue. New shares are constantly being issued to children of citizens and immigrants, a process with no relationship to any sound governance practice. The confusion of customers and shareholders is complete.

As a consequence, the sovcorp develops an incoherent management structure marked by constant factional tensions, overgrowth of process, etc., etc. It also develops an overgrowth of employees, who are thinly disguised shareholders—a.k.a., "jobs for the boys."

Worst of all, this management structure often has very little local incentive to treat the sovcorp's capital properly. Decisions that damage overall capital may generate revenue for a certain subset of shareholders, and not for anyone else.

The danger is especially acute when some shareholders are insecure. Violent conflict over the direction of sovcorp revenues is not at all impossible. Here we start to see the roots of democide. When management is incoherent, sovereignty itself becomes nebulous. Which parts of Washcorp wanted to invade Iraq, and which parts didn't? The question is easy to answer: look at the changes in revenue flow as a result of the decision. While the decision to invade Iraq was a rare example of coherent (if not intelligent) management in Washcorp, it is not difficult to see which agencies supported it and which didn't. They match the prediction.

In other words, we have left the simple world of corporate governance and entered into the hairy world of **public choice theory**. Neocameralist corporate governance has grave difficulty in explaining why a sovcorp would want to massacre its tenants. Public choice theory is only too glad to oblige.

Finally, when we see a democratic sovcorp as a profoundly mismanaged sovcorp, we start to be able to understand why Universalism is so darned successful.

Once again, Universalism is a *mystery cult of power*. And when we look at Universalism's mysteries—*equality, social justice, peace*, and so on—we see something I find very interesting.

We note that all of these mysteries serve as excellent excuses for why an individual should (a) break the law, (b) revise the law, (c) revise the distribution of property, or (d) organize with others to achieve (a), (b), or (c).

In a formalist society, there is one rule of social good behavior: obey the law. In a Universalist society, there is an enormous panoply of political mysteries, all of which can be deployed in the service of power. Since gaining power is always advantageous to the individual who gains it, it is advantageous to just about anyone in a Universalist society to be as Universalist as possible.

The result is that, as in decadent cultures throughout history, the principal occupation of talented and energetic young people is not productive effort. It is scheming for power.

For example, consider all the ambitious young people working at various "non-governmental organizations." I'm sure hardly any of them think of themselves as scheming for power. However, they are all so eager to work for NGOs that they have driven salaries down to the bare minimum required to purchase Ramen noodles and happy-hour cocktails.

NGOs have the N in their acronym for one reason: because their general mission is to affect government policy, the beast being too paralyzed in process to make its own decisions. The term "paragovernmental" might be more appropriate. Essentially, these young people are all drones working for the State. They are certainly not producing goods or services.

Why are they so interested in this so-called work? Perhaps it's because their country's productive industries have been paralyzed in red tape to the point of complete Dilbert-Brezhnev Office-Space syndrome. But it may also be because they are paid not just in money but in power—the power to influence policy, to "change the world"—and this power translates to social status. Which, not to be too blunt, gets you laid.

Needless to say, a well-managed sovcorp has a minimal capacity to compensate its employees by paying them with power, not money. This is because it has a coherent decision process, which cannot indefinitely expand the supply of decisions. It also maintains Pareto optimality, so it does not intrude on its customers' private decisions. Someone always has to be CEO, and his or her balls or ovaries will no doubt sink and become plump. But in the neocameralist world, there is a bounded supply of policy, and the bound is small.

The natural endpoint of compensation in power is pure camp-guard sadism. However, before this point is reached, an infinite number of regulations can be written. No doubt they will be.

It gets worse. Because the obvious question is: in a democracy, why do voters put up with this?

After all, at least until the democracy reaches its degenerate terminal state, there are always far more tenants who are not employees of the sovcorp than those who are. Surely the mere tenants can react, and use their democratic rights to keep their sovcorp from metastasizing endlessly in the fashion described above? But for some reason, they don't. Even when they live in a country with a long tradition and an ironclad legal guarantee of "limited government."

A simple answer is that this small problem can be solved with the easy approach of vote-buying. In other words, the democratic masses can be converted not into employees, but into creditors of the sovcorp. Of course, this creditor relationship should be kept informal—otherwise, the creditor may just sell her formal negotiable asset, and her vote will not stay bought. Ideally, the sovcorp should provide the creditor not even with money, but with services, which can be very easily withdrawn if votes are not forthcoming. This makes a mockery of Pareto optimality, but it's great for maintaining continuity of government.

However, the question remains unanswered. Men vote not for bread alone. They also vote with their hearts. And the system of democratic government, as described above, is so utterly loathsome that I can't imagine anyone being persuaded to vote for it.

Also, neohominids have collective social instincts that override their personal interests. Everyone in a modern democracy, while doing his or her little bit to go to the box and support the State, is confident that their fractional management decision is leading the sovcorp in a direction that will enhance peace, freedom and prosperity.

But if you can convince people that democracy is the cure for democide, rather than its cause, you can convince anyone of anything. Historically, democratic voters have made many decisions that they thought would lead to peace, freedom and prosperity, and instead led to war, slavery and poverty. Why should it be otherwise? I don't have a magic oracle of truth in my head. Do you? Does anyone else?

The trouble is that, while war, slavery and poverty are in general bad things, they may well be profitable for some. Especially in small doses. And if you can create a feedback loop by which Universalism causes war, slavery or poverty, but does so in such a way as to reward those who practice and promote Universalism, you have a loop that can continue indefinitely.

Take, for example, the "peace process" in Israel and Palestine. Now 60 years old and counting. How confident are you that this "peace process" is not, in fact, the cause of this similarly unending conflict? It certainly generates a very comfortable living, full of meaning and importance and not a few frequent-flier miles, for all those involved. Why shut it down?

And this, in my opinion, is why we have Universalism. We have Universalism because it is adaptive in a democratic sovcorp. Similarly, Universalism (and its ancestors) create democracy, in much the same way that they create "peace processes." The whole thing is an artifact of sovereign corporate governance gone horribly awry.

In short, the *adaptive* function of Universalism is to glorify and expand the modern democratic sovcorp. Of course, it has no purpose in any moral or metaphysical sense. It just exists.

Universalism is the latest, greatest incarnation of Bertrand de Jouvenel's Minotaur. It can also be seen as a perfectly distributed conspiracy, à la H. G. Wells,[14] with no central structure at all. And finally, it provides a complete explanation of Robert Conquest's three laws of politics:

1. Everyone is conservative about what he knows best.
2. Any organization not explicitly right-wing sooner or later becomes left-wing.
3. The simplest way to explain the behavior of any bureaucratic organization is to assume that it is controlled by a cabal of its enemies.

In short, the thing is a menace. It's probably too late for Professor Dawkins. But perhaps it's not too late for the rest of us.

---

14 Reference to his 1928 book, *The Open Conspiracy: Blue Prints for a World Revolution*.

469 *puts it* Sam Harris. "The Problem with Atheism." *SamHarris.org*, 2 Oct. 2007.

 470 *No Logo*

 470 *bright* "Brights movement"

 471 *usual voices of decency* The link is to an article from Charles Johnson's blog (the *other* Charles Johnson) *Little Green Footballs*, a "conservative," pro-Iraq war outlet at the time UR was written, but which has since departed from its conservative slant. The article in question deals with Johnson's assertions that the Flemish Vlaams Belang is a "far-right...neo-nazi" party. Johnson. "A White Power Rat in the Vlaams Belang Youth Magazine." *little green footballs*, 6 Nov. 2007.

471 *Brawndo moments* No longer available YouTube clip from the film *Idiocracy* (2006). See below.

 "471 *But Brawndo has electrolytes.*" YouTube clip where Luke Wilson's character attempts to explain why Brawndo, an "electrolyte" based sports beverage, is not ideally suited for agriculture. These clips are often removed from YouTube but can be easily found by searching for the quoted phrase.

 471 *magic sunglasses* John Carpenter. *They Live*. (Universal, 1988).

 471 *democide*

 471 *Holy Alliance*

 472 *praise Enoch Powell* Simon Heffer. "When will Tories admit that Enoch was right?" *The Telegraph*, 7 Nov. 2007.

 472 *Wellington* "Arthur Wellesley"

472 *Metternich*

472 *Castlereagh* "Robert Stewart"

 472 *verse* From *The Masque of Anarchy*, written in 1819 in the aftermath of the Peterloo Massacre. Archived here at historyhome, created by Dr. Marjorie Bloy.

 472 *reservationist* "A reservationist epistemology." *UR*, 28 Aug 2007. See also Chapter 2.

 473 *Albigensian Crusade*

 473 *Black Legend*

 473 *Thirty Years' War*

 473 *Sack of Magdeburg* Of all the atrocities of the Thirty Years' War, the sacking of the Protestant German city of Magdeburg, was perhaps the most gruesome of all.

 473 *Eichmann*

 473 *Cromwell's plantation of Ireland*

 473 *isn't true* Link to Wikipedia's article on Revisionist accounts of the inquisition.

 473 *Gibbon*

 473 *General Observations* From *The Decline and Fall of the Roman Empire*, reproduced at the Christian Classic Ethereal Library linked here.

 475 *Antonine*

 475 *Liverpool* "Robert Jenkinson"

475 *too much for Shelley* "Percy Bysshe Shelley - Politics"

 476 *Carroll Quigley*

 476 *Tragedy and Hope* (The Macmillan Company, 1966). Available in full at archive.org.

 476 *jingoism*

 476 *Wilhelmine Germany*

 476 *Legitimism* See Chapter 3 of *Open Letter*.

 476 *Orléanism*

 476 *Bonapartism*

 476 *anti-Dreyfusards* "Dreyfus Affair"

 477 *Esterhazy*

 477 *General Will*

 477 *James Burnham*

 477 *The Machiavellians* (John Day, 1943).

 477 *liberal democracy*

477 *totalitarian democracy*

 477 *manufacturing consent*

 478 *Puritan Origins of American Patriotism* (Yale University Press, 2007). See Chapter 2.

 479 *Socreds*

 479 *Operation Wetback*

 479 *Louise Day Hicks*

 479 *schizonts and trophozoites "Plasmodium falciparum"*

 479 *Marcus Aurelius*

 480 *anarcho-capitalism*

 480 *Schelling point*

 480 *cryptographic weapon locks* "Permissive action links." See Chapter 6 of *Open Letter*.

 480 *Laffer maximum*

 480 *Pareto optimality*

481 *Age of Absolutism* Max Belloff (HarperCollins, 1962). The original link was for an Amazon page for the book. No additional relevant information was provided.

481 Frederick the Great

 481 Necker

 482 Aufragstaktik "Mission-type tactics"

 482 stakeholders

 483 jobs for the boys Derivation of "old boys network."

 483 public choice theory

 485 H. G. Wells The Open Conspiracy: Blue Prints for a World Revolution. (Golancz, 1928).

 485 Robert Conquest

INDEX

A

Adams, Charles Francis 118, 414
Adams, James Truslow 176
Alinsky, Saul 80
American Civil War 447
American Malvern 130, 394
American Revolution 109, 446
Anarchism 290
Anti-anti-communism 91
Antimilitarism 128
Antinomians 286
Apparat. See Polygon
Auster, Larry 188, 349

B

Baker, Nicholson
  Human Smoke 32
Bellamy, Edward
  Looking Backward 176, 447
Brahmins
America's ruling class 25
Brecht, Bertolt 342
Burke, Timothy 189, 239, 259, 298

C

Cathedral
  creating dependencies 180
  Definition 96
  educational transmission 380, 448
  Spontaneous Coordination 97
  Two parts of 201
Charles I 69
China 78
Cold War 450
Concert of Europe
  Great War 476
Conquest, Robert 485
Conservatism
  failed project of 76
  Iraq War 452
  opposition to Cathedral 182

Corner Man 42, 68
Counter-Cathedral
  Resartus 364
Currency as a Share 265

D

Dabney, Robert Lewis 76
Darnton, John 66
Darwinian morbidity 390
Davis, George B. 137
Dawkins, Richard
  The God Delusion 412, 424
Defoe, Daniel 108
de Jouvenel, Bertrand
  Minotaur 388
Democracy
  accumulating majority support 326
  civics-class futility 324
  counterproductive ideas 344
  democide 471
  elects its own people 342
  insurgency as theater 127
  manufacturing consent 477
  objective definition of 477
Dissenters. See Quakers

E

Ecumenical Movement 130
Einstein, Albert 397
Einsteinian (religion)
  as most successful tradition 390
  definition 384
  Einsteinism 391
Eleemosynary Institution 158, 454
Enlightenment 395
Epsom, William 65, 181

F

Fascism
  perception of 54
  reaction to Communism 210
Fisher, Sydney George 109
Formalism
  basic idea of 5
  Formalist Manifesto 9
  idea of agreements 462

G

Gavin, Michelle 28
Gibbon, Edward 473
Gladstone, William 360
Goldberg, Jonah
  crappy little country 42
  Liberal Fascism 52
Grey, Edward 55

H

Harris, Sam 469
Hayes, Carlton 229
Hoppe, Hans-Herman 301
Human Neurological Uniformity 236
Huxley, Thomas Henry 412

I

Independence
  test for 44
Inner Party 185
Insurgency 127
International Community
  as predatory force 43
  euphemism for State Department 181
International Law
  classical 137
  The Monroe Doctrine 264
Italy
  unification 51

J

Johnson, Samuel 89

INDEX 495

K

Khan, Razib 234, 365

L

Libertarianism
  Classical Liberalism 99
  Libertarian Democracy 343
Lippmann, Walter
  Public Opinion 169, 183
Littlefield, Larry 353
Living Constitution 187
Lizza, Ryan 80

M

Macaulay, Thomas
  History of England 72, 115
Machiavelli, Niccolo 167
Maine, Henry 431
Mamet, David 20
Manipulating procedural outcomes 190
Markson, Edith 254
Martial Law 351
McCarthyism 242
McCarthy, Joseph 183
McIntyre, Steve 364
Memetic Immunology 379
Militarism 54
Minto, John 141
Misesian morbidity 390
Moderation 4
Monarchism
  Absolute 481
  as a Trust 331
Muppet State 45

N

Nationalism
  as power worship 447
  definition 30

National Recovery Administration 202
  as industrial army 449
Nazism
  as reactionary movement 79
  synoptic official story 95
Neocameralism
  aspects of governance 481
  definition 432
  prevention of politics 303
New Deal
  as end of Nationalist era 449
  Brain Trust 177
  vote buying 182
Nitti, Francesco 53
Nock, Albert Jay 178, 304
Nonpartisan 170
Nontheistic Christianity
  definition 392
  not self-contradictory 390
No person is illegal 131, 188
North, Richard 215

O

Obama, Barack 80, 253
Outer Party 185, 213

P

Pacifism 6
Patron-Client Relationship 180
Pentagon Papers 241
Perlstein, Rick 206
Plainland
  a non-Universalist model 445
  Plainland, Plaingov, Plaincorp 322
  Trusts 331
Pobedonostsev, Konstantin 310
Political Alignment 280
Polygon 183
Popper, Karl
  Open Society 92
Powell, Enoch 183

Progress. See Whig History
Progressivism
  20th century strategies 210
  as entropy 82
  as theocracy 233
  built on self-interest 81
  opposite of reactionary 70
  Super Protestant 134
  synoptic official story 96
  unprincipled exceptions 208
Pronomians 283
Public Policy 171
Puritanism. See Quakers

Q

Quakers
  from Dissenters 135
  intellectual lineage 393
  peace by redress of greivances 141
  world government 141
Quigley, Carroll 476

R

Reactionary
  as Legitimists 69
  comments section 326
  definition 68
  rules for reactionaries 354
  theory of history 429
Receiver 263, 330
Red Pill 297
Reset
  definition 218
  every reset is a coup 322
  Hard Reset 244
  nonincremental transition 323
  Soft Reset 237
Restructuring 262
Rhodesia
  independence 29
Rolling Stones

  Sympathy for the Devil 89
Roosevelt, Franklin Delano 214
Rothbard, Murray 287

S

Seward, Desmond 49
Shelley, Percy Bysshe 472
Social Justice 7
Somaliland 30
South Africa 259
Sovcorp
  criteria for judging 463
  definition of government 153
  preferred characteristics 464
  sovereign corporation 446
  Washington corporation 446
Steevens, George Warrington 265
Steffens, Lincoln 174
Stephens, James 429
Stross, Charles 105
Stuart Restoration 216
Students for a Democratic Society
  myth that movement failed 207
  Port Huron Statement 208, 450
Synopsis 96

T

Temperley, Harold 75
Tennyson, Alfred 137, 358
Townies 25
Tumulty, Joseph 122

U

Ultra-Americanism 120
Universalism
  definition 134
  Fraternism 410
  legitimacy 463
  mystery cult of power 422, 462, 483
  negative effects 410

relationship to the state 479
  Unitarian 393

V

Vietnam War 451
Violence as responsibility of state 353
von Salomon, Ernst 305

W

Washcorp. See Sovcorp
Watson, James 233
Webster, Noah 340
Whig History
  definition 70
  mysterious force 71
  shift in Synopsis 99
  theory of rebellion 126
Whigs
  alliance with Patriots 117
  as political faction 111
  concessions to America 115
World Peace. See International Law

Y

Yudkowsky, Eliezer 391

Z

Zeitgeist
  Definition 416
Zimbabwe. See Rhodesia
Žižek, Slavoj 288

RECOMMENDED BOOKS

Reactionary Theory of Modern History

Reflections on the Revolution in France by Edmund Burke (James Dodsley, Pall Mall, 1790)

Popular Government by Henry Maine (London, 1885)

Democracy and Liberty by W.E.H. Lecky (London; New York: Longmans, Green, 1896)

Public Opinion by Walter Lipmann (Harcourt, Brace, & Co. 1922)

Lincoln the Man by Edgar Lee Masters (Dodd, Mead, & Company, 1931)

Memoirs of a Superfluous Man by Albert Jay Nock (Harper Brothers, 1943)

As We Go Marching by John T. Flynn (Doubleday, 1944)

On Power by Bertrand de Jouvenel (Les Editions du Cheval Ailé, 1945)

Liberty or Equality by Erik von Kuehnelt-Leddihn (Caxton Printers, 1952)

Suicide of the West: An Essay on the Meaning and Destiny of Liberalism by James Burnham (The John Day Company, 1964)

American History

True History of the American Revolution by Sydney George Fisher (J.B. Lippincott, 1902)

The Puritan Origins of American Patriotism by George Mckenna (Yale University Press, 2007)

The Life of John Marshall, Vol.1-4. by Albert J. Beveridge (Houghton Mifflin Company, 1916-1919)

A South-Side View of Slavery by Rev. Nehemia Adams (T.R. Marvin, 1855)

Roll, Jordan, Roll: The World the Slaves Made by Eugene D. Genovese (Vintage Books, 1976)

Memoirs of Service Afloat, During the War Between the States by Admiral Raphael Semmes (Kelly, Piet, & Co., 1869)

The Land of the Dollar by G.W. Steevens (Dodd, Mead and Company, 1898)

Human Smoke: the Beginnings of World War II, the End of Civilization by Nicholson Baker (Simon & Schuster, 2008)

World History

The Shortest-Way with the Dissenters: or, Proposals for the Establishment of the Church, with its Author's Brief Explication Consider'd, His Name Expos'd, His Practices Detected, and his Hellish Designs set in a True Light by Daniel Defoe (London, 1703)

Reflections of a Russian Statesman Konstantin Pobedonostsev, trans. Robert Crozier Long (Grant Richards, 1898)

The Elements of International Law: With an Account of its Origins and Historical Development. 3rd ed. by George B. Davis (Harper & Brothers, 1908)

Der Fragebogen by Ernst von Solomon (Rowohlt Verlag, 1951)

Tragedy and Hope by Carroll Quigley (The Macmillan Company, 1966)

The Abolition of Britain: From Winston Churchill to Princess Diana by Peter Hitchens (Encounter Books, 2000)

Progressivism

Messianic Character of American Education: Studies in the History of the Philosophy of Education by Rousas John Rushdoony (P & R Press, 1963)

The War for Righteousness: Progressive Christianity, the Great War, and the Rise of the Messianic Nation by Richard M. Gamble (ISI Books, 2003)

Radical Chic & Mau Mauing the Flak Catchers by Tom Wolfe (Farrar, Straus & Giroux, 1970)

Life at the Bottom: The Worldview That Makes the Underclass by Theodore Dalrymple (Ivan R. Dee, 2003).

Universalist History

Blood of the Liberals by George Packer (Farrar, Straus and Giroux, 2000)

Common Ground: A Turbulent Decade in the Lives of Three American Families by J. Anthony Lukas (Vintage, 1986)

Dark Side of the Left: Illiberal Egalitarianism in America by Richard J. Ellis (University Press of Kansas, 1998)

Authoritarian Socialism in America: *Edward Bellamy and the Nationalist Movement* by Arthur Lipow (University of California Press, 1982)

Radicalism of the American Revolution by Gordon S. Wood (Vintage, 1991)